What's for dinner?

Romilla Arber

What's for dinner?

Romilla Arber

buy well cook well eat well

I love the clever way in which Romilla has organised recipes into weekly menus along with shopping lists. This book is just packed with practical and healthy ideas – perfect for busy cooks who want healthy, delicious and simple meals.

Monisha Bharadwaj

To my mother Patricia Dorothy Turner Wickremeratne who inspired and encouraged with this endeavour and many other things besides

First published in Great Britain in 2008
by St Christopher's Publishing Ltd

ISBN: 978-0-9547931-4-2

Printed by Butler, Tanner & Dennis Ltd, Frome

Contents

What's for dinner?

One book for all seasons

I decided to write this book one Monday morning when confronted with the weekly problem of what I could muster from the kitchen to feed my family. I would go to the supermarket, buy various items, then go home and search through cookbooks to decide what to cook with these ingredients. I would then discover I was missing a certain ingredient and would have to go back to the supermarket. I found myself shopping at least three times a week. Of course, I tried it the other way round, going through the cookbooks first and compiling a menu, but this took far too long; and either way I threw away unused food at the end of the week.

I realized that morning that planning a week's food and shopping for it was a time consuming headache and a problem I resented. I should add that I live in a rural area, without a wide choice of local producers. I do purchase most of my meat from a local farm and grow as many vegetables as I can in my garden. I buy organic produce whenever I can, not because I believe it has magic qualities but because I think it tastes better and I know that more care has gone into its production. And I try to buy seasonal produce and am conscious of food miles when purchasing fruit and vegetables.

However, like most people, I also use supermarkets, both for convenience and because of the range of food available. In the depths of winter I am happy to buy fresh pineapple for my son, because it's a fruit he loves and it's good for him. In my opinion, life without supermarkets is a step too far. Denying yourself access to this convenience under the pressures of modern day living is unrealistic, making us slaves to a way of life that is impossible to sustain.

The purpose of this book is to help you plan, shop and prepare delicious, home-cooked meals without difficulty, increasing the chances of a healthy existence for you and your children. I think it is vitally important that people cook at home and in doing so teach their children to enjoy food. I hope that the advice and recipes I have included here will give confidence to those who need it, inspiration to those who lack it and the realization that by being a little more organized you can produce good tasty meals with the minimum of fuss.

I have a family of six. My four children range from 2 to 10 years. One of the legacies I want to leave them is a love for and appreciation of good food. I was brought up in a family of six. Until I was 7 years old my mother stayed at home and my father worked as a teacher. Consequently, we did not have a lot of money to spend on food. We certainly did not go out to eat and I was nearly 18 years old before I first went to a restaurant. Nevertheless, eating was a pleasure as we always ate good healthy fare.

So exactly what is good healthy food? For me a good diet is a balanced diet, one that comprises a daily consumption of fresh fruit and vegetables, a limited consumption of meat and regular amounts of fish, pulses and cereals. The most important principle for me, however, is that meals should be home-cooked with as little reliance on processed food as possible. By processed food I mean food that has been adulterated by chemicals to last longer, add artificial taste or appear delectable. Food like this generally has a higher salt, sugar and fat content than naturally produced food and has become the mainstay of so many unhealthy, fast-food diets. For some reason people seem to have lost the ability, the knowledge and the confidence to get into the kitchen and produce home-cooked food. The consequences of this for our nation and the next generation are severe.

My interest in food and love of cooking came from my mother. She realized, all those years ago, what a beneficial effect eating well had on our behaviour, our concentration levels and our physical development. She saw how being cooked for by her gave us a sense of security as a family. But it was not until I had children of my own that I fully realized the importance of a home-cooked diet and that it was my responsibility as a parent to ensure that my children grew up to be healthy adults. I can ask their schools to provide better lunch menus or hope that the government puts pressure on manufacturers to put less salt and sugar in their food but, ultimately, it is my responsibility to ensure that my family eats well and learns to appreciate the importance of a good diet.

This book is a planning manual, intended to assist you to plan the meals you cook and the food you need to buy. Over the years I have used recipes from many different cookbooks and have come to know which ones work well and which ones don't. I have found that no one cookery book, whatever its approach, can provide the basis of a weekly diet, and not many of us have the skill or the confidence to make up our own recipes, especially when hungry people are waiting to be fed. A collection of cookbooks might do the trick, but you'd need a lot of time to sift through them to find suitable recipes for everyone in the family, and they don't come cheap. This book, I hope, is the answer. It contains a year's supply of recipes, many of which were inspired by other cookbooks, and some of which I have discovered through self exploration. The weekly menus are largely seasonal and contain the correct levels of nutrition essential in a healthy diet. I have tried to make sure that the meals will appeal to children without pandering to the notion that children should be fed different food from adults.

I hope this book will take the pain out of producing good home-cooked food. Cooking should not be an inconvenience. A meal's evolution from shop to table should be a pleasure that your whole family enjoys.

NOTES

- *Every recipe feeds 6 people: 2 adults and 4 children.*
- *All salt measurements relate to sea salt so if you are using ordinary salt you may want to use a little less.*
- *I have tried to be accurate with cooking times as I think that exact cooking times help the less experienced cook but cooking is not an exact science so do check your food as it cooks.*
- *Bring meat and eggs to room temperature before cooking them as this effects their cooking time.*
- *Don't use expensive extra virgin olive oil to cook with. Save it for drizzling and dressing.*
- *When using the shopping lists remember that you will have store cupboard items left over from previous weeks.*
- *All references to butter are to unsalted butter.*
- *All shopping lists are available at www.whatsfordinner.org.uk*

JANUARY

Week 1

Shopping list

MEAT

- ☐ 400g sausage meat (if you can't get sausage meat then just squeeze out the pork from some good quality pork sausages)
- ☐ 150g calves' liver
- ☐ 500g minced beef
- ☐ 500g minced pork
- ☐ 3 loins lamb
- ☐ 1.9kg chicken

FISH

- ☐ 6 fillets trout

VEGETABLES

- ☐ 2 Romaine lettuces
- ☐ 1½ cucumbers
- ☐ 6 spring onions
- ☐ 500g parsnips
- ☐ 9 onions
- ☐ 1 garlic bulb
- ☐ 2 carrots
- ☐ 1 bunch celery
- ☐ 1.25kg potatoes
- ☐ 400g broccoli
- ☐ 100g swede
- ☐ 1 bunch watercress

FRUIT

- ☐ 1 sharp eating apple
- ☐ 3 lemons
- ☐ 150g blueberries
- ☐ 150g blackberries
- ☐ 200g raspberries

FRESH HERBS

- ☐ sage
- ☐ flat-leaf parsley
- ☐ mint
- ☐ rosemary

FRIDGE ITEMS

- ☐ 5 eggs
- ☐ 300g pot houmous
- ☐ 3 packs butter
- ☐ 200g crème fraîche
- ☐ 150ml single cream
- ☐ 150ml double cream
- ☐ 600ml full fat milk
- ☐ 1 small pot natural yoghurt
- ☐ 125g Parmesan cheese
- ☐ 200g feta cheese
- ☐ 100g frankfurters
- ☐ 1 pack puff pastry
- ☐ vanilla ice cream
- ☐ 1.5 litres chicken stock

KITCHEN CUPBOARD ITEMS

- ☐ salt
- ☐ white loaf for breadcrumbs
- ☐ 1 or 2 packs pitta bread
- ☐ olive oil
- ☐ extra virgin olive oil
- ☐ balsamic vinegar
- ☐ dried yeast
- ☐ 1kg strong white bread flour
- ☐ 140g plain flour
- ☐ 450ml white wine
- ☐ 2 x 400g tins chopped tomatoes
- ☐ tomato purée
- ☐ Dijon mustard
- ☐ brandy
- ☐ 30g creamed coconut
- ☐ 1 vanilla pod
- ☐ 125g caster sugar
- ☐ 250g basmati rice
- ☐ 1 panettone
- ☐ baking powder
- ☐ maple syrup
- ☐ chicken stock cubes

SPICES

- ☐ coriander seeds
- ☐ cumin seeds
- ☐ fennel seeds
- ☐ fenugreek
- ☐ black pepper
- ☐ cinnamon stick

Liver and sausage burgers
+ white rolls + salad

This is a great way of getting children to eat liver, which is not something mine will do otherwise. I found this recipe in Margaret Costa's *Four Seasons* and I have adapted it slightly. If you decide to buy your bread instead of using the recipe, use muffins, as they don't go soggy when the hot burgers are placed in them. If you are making the rolls then you will need 2 hours 30 minutes before you eat, in which to prepare the bread. Prepare the bread first and then get on with the burgers. I think this is the perfect white roll recipe for burgers.

Liver and sausage burgers

30g butter

250g onion, finely chopped

400g sausage meat (if you can't get sausage meat then just squeeze out the pork from some good quality pork sausages)

1 sharp eating apple, cored and finely chopped

3 tablespoons white breadcrumbs

150g calves' liver, well chopped

1 dessertspoon sage leaves, finely chopped

salt and pepper

2 eggs, beaten

a little flour

2 tablespoons olive oil

- Warm the butter in a saucepan and gently cook the onions for 10 minutes until softened.
- Place the sausage meat, apple, breadcrumbs and liver in a mixing bowl and add the cooked onion.
- Add the sage and season well.
- Bind together with the egg. On a floured surface, shape the mixture into six burgers.
- Chill the burgers until you are ready to cook them.
- Heat the olive oil in a frying pan and then cook three burgers at a time. To prevent the burgers from falling apart cook each one for 5 minutes on each side, on a medium heat, without moving them around.
- Serve each burger in a roll with the salad below.

White rolls

300ml warm milk
2 teaspoons dried yeast
1 teaspoon sugar
500g strong white bread flour
1½ teaspoons salt

- Warm the milk and place a little in a small bowl with the yeast and sugar.
- Stir once and then leave for 1 minute.
- Place the flour and salt in the bowl of a food mixer or, if you are making them by hand, in a large mixing bowl.
- Make a well in the centre and pour in the yeast mixture and the rest of the milk.
- Mix until the mixture forms a dough.
- On a floured surface knead the dough for 10 minutes, or 5 minutes' kneading with a dough hook in a food mixer.
- Place the dough back in the bowl, cover with a clean tea towel and leave to rise for 45 minutes.
- Knock back the dough by punching the air out of it and leave for another 45 minutes.
- Preheat the oven to 200°C/400°F/gas 6.
- Shape the dough into six buns.
- Place the rolls on a greased baking tin, cover and leave them to rise for 30 minutes.
- Just before placing the rolls in the oven, brush them with olive oil, using a pastry brush.
- Place them in the oven and bake for 20 minutes.

Salad

1 Romaine lettuce, shredded
½ cucumber, chopped into 2cm chunks
3 spring onions, roughly chopped
For the dressing
2 tablespoons extra virgin olive oil
½ tablespoon balsamic vinegar
salt and pepper

- Place the lettuce, cucumber and spring onions in a serving dish.
- Mix the dressing ingredients together and then drizzle them over the salad just before serving.
- Toss the salad.

Curried parsnip soup + focaccia

Focaccia is a wonderful bread and a favourite with my children. This is a foolproof recipe that produces near-perfect results. Get on with the bread first and then tackle the soup while the bread dough is rising.

Curried parsnip soup

45g butter
500g parsnips, peeled and sliced into large chunks
150g chopped onions
100g potatoes, peeled and chopped
1 clove garlic, peeled and crushed
1 tablespoon flour
1 dessertspoon curry powder*
1.5 litres chicken stock
150ml single cream
2 tablespoons flat-leaf parsley, chopped

- Heat the butter in a large saucepan.
- Add the parsnips, onions, potatoes and garlic and cook on a low heat, covered for 10 minutes.
- Add the flour and curry powder and stir.
- Add the stock and bring to a simmer.
- Cover and simmer gently for 40 minutes.
- Remove from the heat and process the soup either in a food processor or with a hand-held blender and season to taste.
- Warm through when ready to serve and add the cream and parsley.

Focaccia

1 sachet dried yeast
280ml water, warmed
3 tablespoons olive oil
1 heaped teaspoon salt
2 tablespoons fresh rosemary, chopped
500g white bread flour
rosemary sprigs
extra virgin olive oil for drizzling
sea salt

- Mix the yeast with a little water in a large mixing bowl and leave to stand for 5 minutes.
- Add the oil, the remaining water, salt, chopped rosemary and 250g of the flour.
- Combine to a sticky dough and turn out onto a floured surface.
- Keep adding flour from the remaining 250g as you knead the dough until it is smooth and silky. You may not need all of the flour.
- Place the dough back in the mixing bowl. Drizzle a teaspoon of olive oil over it to coat it.
- Cover with a tea towel and leave to rise for 1 hour.
- Knock back the dough by punching the air out of it and roll into a rectangle.
- Press into a greased roasting or baking tin measuring approximately 27cm x 42cm. Cover and let rise for another hour.
- Preheat the oven to 220°C/425°F/gas 7.
- Press your fingertips into the dough to make dimpled impressions at intervals on the top.
- Place rosemary sprigs into the dimples in the bread dough and drizzle with olive oil.
- Sprinkle with sea salt and bake for 20–25 minutes.

**** To make your own curry powder***
1 tablespoon coriander seeds
1 dessertspoon cumin seeds
1 teaspoon fennel seeds
½ teaspoon fenugreek

- *Place the coriander seeds into a small, heavy-bottomed pan and heat through for 30 seconds.*
- *Add the other ingredients and toast until you smell the lovely aroma of the spices.*
- *Transfer the spices to a coffee grinder, a small processor or grind them in a pestle and mortar.*

Spaghetti ragù

In England we call this spaghetti bolognaise. I am sure that most people reading this will have cooked spaghetti bolognaise before. I have, however, tasted good versions and terrible versions of the dish. The method described by Marcella Hazan, the Italian cookery writer, is the one that I have used over the years and I think it produces the best results. The most common mistake made when cooking a ragù sauce is not to cook it for long enough. A good ragù needs to be cooked slowly for two hours.

2 tablespoons olive oil
1 medium onion, finely diced
1 carrot, finely diced
1 stick celery, finely chopped
1 clove garlic, finely chopped
500g minced beef
500g minced pork
150ml full fat milk
150ml white/red wine
salt and pepper
2 x 400g tins chopped tomatoes
1 tablespoon tomato purée
Parmesan cheese for serving

- Heat the olive oil in a heavy-bottomed saucepan.
- Add the onion, carrot, celery and garlic.
- Reduce the heat to medium and cook the vegetables for 10 minutes. Try not to brown them.
- Add the minced beef and pork, and turn up the heat so that the meat browns quickly.
- Next, pour in the milk. The milk helps to tenderize the meat. Cook on a high heat until the milk has all but bubbled away.
- Then add the wine, cooking until the wine has reduced and lost its alcoholic smell.
- Season the sauce with salt and pepper.
- Reduce the heat to medium again and add the tomatoes and the tomato purée.
- Bring the sauce to a simmer and then reduce the heat so that there is the slightest simmer.
- Cover and leave for 1 hour.
- Taste and adjust seasoning.
- Remove the lid of the saucepan and continue to cook on a slight simmer for another hour.
- Serve with spaghetti, tagliatelle or penne.

TIP

Cooking the pasta: *Make sure that you don't undersalt the cooking water. Mary Contini, an Italian cookery writer, says that pasta water should be as salty as the Mediterranean Sea.*

Fried river trout
+ boiled potatoes + broccoli

> Trout is a must at any English dinner table. It is plentiful and cheap and has not flown halfway across the world to get to you.

Fried river trout

75g butter
6 fillets trout
salt and pepper
2 tablespoons brandy
150ml double cream
2 tablespoons flat-leaf parsley, finely chopped
1 lemon

- Melt the butter in a frying pan.
- When the butter begins to foam add the trout fillets. It is probably best to cook three fillets at a time as they only take a couple of minutes.
- Cook the fish for 1 minute on each side, seasoning with salt and pepper as it cooks.
- Remove the skin from the fish as it cooks. It should come away easily.
- Remove the fillets from the pan.
- Keeping the pan on the heat add the brandy, cream and parsley and stir well with a wooden spoon.
- Squeeze the lemon juice over the fish fillets and serve with the sauce and vegetables.

Boiled potatoes

750g potatoes, peeled and quartered
salt
butter
black pepper

- Place the potatoes in a saucepan of salted water.
- Bring to the boil and reduce the heat to a simmer for 12–15 minutes, depending on the size of the potatoes.
- Serve with a dab of butter and a some freshly ground black pepper.

Broccoli

300g broccoli
salt and pepper

- Prepare the broccoli by cutting it into smallish florets. Don't cut the florets into single stemmed pieces, as they are more likely to taste soggy once cooked.
- Bring a pan of salted water to the boil and cook the broccoli for 3 minutes.

Spicy sliced lamb with houmous and warm pittas + green salad

This meal has a slight Greek theme to it. The houmous goes well with the lamb and it is a winner with children as they love pitta bread.

Spicy sliced lamb

2 tablespoons olive oil
3 loins lamb
salt and pepper
3 teaspoons curry powder*
200g feta cheese
1 sprig fresh mint leaves torn into rough pieces
1 tablespoon extra virgin olive oil
juice ½ lemon
1 or 2 packs pitta bread
300g pot houmous

- Preheat the oven to 200°C/400°F/gas 6 and place a baking tray inside to heat through.
- Heat the olive oil in a frying pan.
- When the oil is hot, brown the loin joints all over in the frying pan.
- Season each loin with salt and pepper and roll each one in some of the curry powder.
- Place the seasoned fillets on the hot baking tray and cook in the oven for 6 minutes.
- When they are cooked remove them from the oven and set aside for 5 minutes.
- Carve each one into thinnish slices and lay on a plate.
- Crumble over the feta cheese and garnish with the mint leaves.
- Drizzle the lamb slices with the olive oil.
- Finish off with a squeeze of lemon juice and a grinding of salt and pepper.
- Warm the pittas on a tray in the oven for 5 minutes.
- Halve the pittas and serve with the sliced lamb, houmous and green salad.

Green salad

1 Romaine lettuce, shredded
½ cucumber, chopped into 2cm chunks
3 spring onions, roughly chopped
For the dressing
2 tablespoons extra virgin olive oil
salt and pepper
1 dessertspoon natural yoghurt
1 lemon

- Place the lettuce, cucumber and spring onions in a serving dish.
- Place the olive oil in a small bowl with some salt and pepper.
- Add the yoghurt a little at a time as the dressing will curdle if you add it too quickly.
- Squeeze in the lemon juice and season with salt and pepper.

**** To make your own curry powder***
1 tablespoon coriander seeds
1 dessertspoon cumin seeds
1 teaspoon fennel seeds
½ teaspoon fenugreek

- *Place the coriander seeds into a small, heavy-bottomed pan and heat through for 30 seconds.*
- *Add the other ingredients and toast until you smell the lovely aroma of the spices.*
- *Transfer the spices to a coffee grinder, a small processor or grind them in a pestle and mortar.*

Cheese and vegetable pie

This is a good recipe for using up all that leftover cheese from Christmas.

2 tablespoons olive oil
1 medium onion, finely diced
1 stick celery, finely chopped
1 carrot, finely diced
100g swede, peeled and diced into 1cm cubes
400g potatoes, peeled, quartered and boiled until almost tender
50g butter
salt and pepper
100ml chicken stock, (a stock cube will do)
100g broccoli florets
200g crème fraîche
1 teaspoon Dijon mustard
100g hard cheese, grated. (You can use any cheese you have in the fridge that has a strongish flavour. I used Parmesan, a hard goat's cheese and some Cheddar).
100g frankfurter, sliced
1 pack puff pastry
1 beaten egg to glaze

- Preheat the oven to 200°C/400°F/gas 6.
- Heat the olive oil in a medium frying pan.
- Add the onion, celery, carrot and swede and cook on a low heat for 5 minutes.
- Add the cooked potatoes and the butter and season with salt and pepper.
- Pour in the stock and add the broccoli.
- Bring to a simmer, cover and simmer gently for 8 minutes.
- If the vegetables are not quite cooked, give them a little longer.
- Stir in the crème fraîche, the mustard, the cheese and the frankfurter.
- Check the seasoning.
- If the puff pastry is not ready-rolled, roll it out to a rectangle measuring approximately 35cm x 23cm.
- Place the pastry on a baking sheet and then pile the filling onto the middle.
- Pull the long sides of the pastry rectangle up and join in the middle with a little fold over. Then fold over the ends.
- It doesn't really matter if the pie opens slightly at the top during cooking, but make sure the ends are sealed securely.
- If you can't fit all the filling in, then put some by to use when you serve the pie.
- Using a pastry brush, glaze the pie with a beaten egg, and bake for 30 minutes.

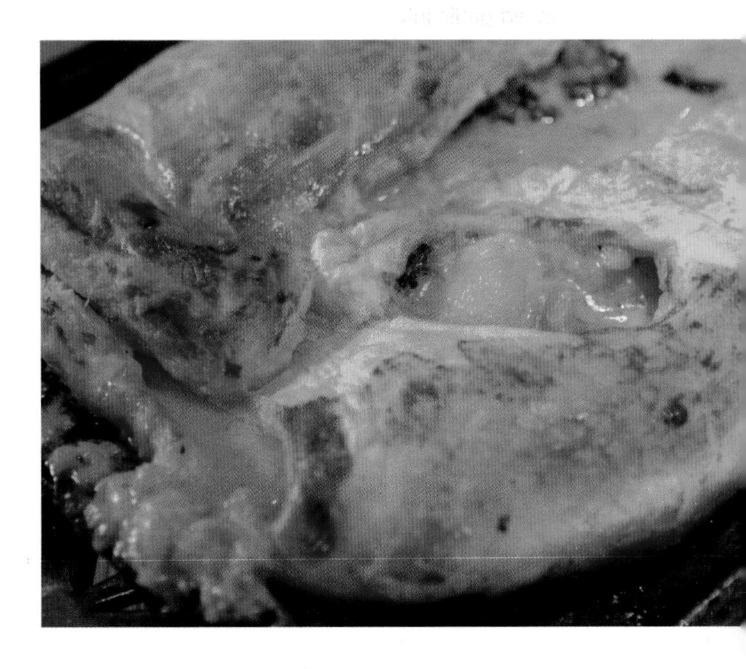

Pot-roasted chicken
+ curried pilaf rice + watercress salad

The chicken recipe with some modification comes from a book by Frances Bissell called *A Cook's Calendar,* which was published in the 1980s but is no longer in print.

Pot-roasted chicken

1.9kg chicken
1 clove garlic, peeled and sliced thinly into slivers
½ lemon
salt and pepper
1 tablespoon olive oil
1 onion, thinly sliced
2 tablespoons brandy

- Preheat the oven to 200°C/400°F/gas 6.
- Take the chicken and cut little incisions in the breast with a sharp knife.
- Insert garlic into these incisions and then rub the chicken with the lemon.
- Insert the lemon into the neck cavity and season the bird with salt and pepper.
- Heat the oil in a large, flameproof casserole dish and slowly cook the onion on a medium heat for 5 minutes.
- Turn the heat up and place the chicken, breast side down, on top of the onions to brown. Try not to burn the onions.
- Once the breast is browned, turn the chicken over and add the brandy.
- Cook for 2 minutes.
- Remove the casserole dish from the heat and place it in the oven for 1 hour and 20 minutes until the juices from the chicken run clear.

Curried pilaf rice

2 tablespoons olive oil
1 onion, finely chopped
1 clove garlic, peeled and crushed
250g basmati rice
1 teaspoon curry powder*
30g creamed coconut
600ml hot chicken stock (a stock cube is fine)
salt and pepper

- Heat the oil in a saucepan, and add the onion and garlic.
- Fry for 5 minutes until the onion is soft.
- Add the rice and fry for another minute.
- Sprinkle in the curry powder and add the creamed coconut, stirring while it dissolves.
- Add the stock and season with a little salt and pepper.
- Bring the rice to the boil and then reduce the heat, cover the saucepan, and cook on a gentle simmer for 15 minutes.

Watercress salad

1 bunch watercress
½ cucumber, sliced
For the dressing
1 dessertspoon extra virgin olive oil
1 teaspoon balsamic vinegar
salt and pepper

- Place the watercress and cucumber in a serving dish and dress with the oil and vinegar.
- Season with salt and pepper.

**** To make your own curry powder***
1 tablespoon coriander seeds
1 dessertspoon cumin seeds
1 teaspoon fennel seeds
½ teaspoon fenugreek

- *Place the coriander seeds into a small, heavy-bottomed pan and heat through for 30 seconds.*
- *Add the other ingredients and toast until you smell the lovely aroma of the spices.*
- *Transfer the spices to a coffee grinder, a small processor or grind them in a pestle and mortar.*

Baked berries on panettone with ice cream

Although I make my own ice cream, I am not suggesting that everyone has the time to do so. You can just as well buy vanilla ice cream for this recipe. It's a good source of calcium, which is especially important for children. The fruit is not very seasonal but I occasionally crave these berries as winter releases its grip.

300ml dry white wine
2.5cm piece cinnamon stick
1 vanilla pod, split lengthways
100g caster sugar
150g blueberries
150g blackberries
200g raspberries
15g butter
3 x 1.5cm slices panettone, cut in half
vanilla ice cream

- Preheat the oven to 200°C/400°F/gas 6.
- Pour the wine into a small saucepan along with the cinnamon stick, vanilla pod and sugar.
- Bring to the boil and cook on a gentle simmer for 1 minute.
- Place the fruit in a small ovenproof dish and pour the wine solution over the fruit.
- Bake for 15 minutes.
- When ready to serve, melt the butter in a large frying pan.
- Add the panettone slices in two batches.
- Fry the panettone slices gently in the butter for 30 seconds until each side has become brown.
- Place a piece of panettone on each dessert plate.
- Pile a few spoons of the baked berries on top of each piece, along with a scoop of ice cream.

Fluffy dessert pancakes

These pancakes are lighter than the more usual drop scones or pancakes. They are absolutely delicious with maple syrup and maybe some chopped banana.

115g plain flour
¼ teaspoon salt
2 level teaspoons baking powder
1 tablespoon caster sugar
2 eggs
150ml milk
50g butter, melted
maple syrup for serving

- Weigh the flour and put it in a mixing bowl with the salt, baking powder and sugar.
- Separate the eggs into two bowls.
  A good tip is to make sure you put the whites into a small bowl as they will get lost in a large one and prove very hard to whisk stiffly.
- Gently beat the egg yolks and add the milk and the melted butter.
- Add the egg yolks, milk and butter to the flour and stir gently into a loose mixture. Do not beat or over mix.
- Whisk the egg whites until they form stiff peaks and then fold them into the flour mixture using a metal spoon.
- Heat a frying or pancake pan and when hot brush it with melted butter.
- Drop the batter in tablespoons onto the pan, two at a time.
- When they puff up and bubble, flip the pancakes over and cook on the other side.
- Keep the cooked pancakes warm by wrapping them in a clean tea towel in a low oven until ready to eat.
- Serve them with maple syrup.

JANUARY

Week 2

Monday p22	Beef curry + rice + dry potato curry
Tuesday p23	Mushroom risotto
Wednesday p24	Winter vegetable soup
Thursday p25	Smoked haddock + sautéed potatoes + buttered spinach + poached eggs
Friday p26	Chicken pie + broccoli
Saturday p28	Pasta in a tuna fish sauce
Sunday p29	Loin of pork + braised white cabbage + sautéed potatoes with pancetta and sage
Sunday pudding p30	Microwave-steamed chocolate pudding
Extra tasty treat p31	Chocolate chip cookies

Shopping list

MEAT

- ☐ 1kg stewing steak
- ☐ 4 chicken breasts, boneless
- ☐ 1.5kg rolled loin pork

FISH

- ☐ 750g smoked haddock fillets

VEGETABLES

- ☐ 1 red chilli
- ☐ 3 red onions
- ☐ 2 shallots
- ☐ 4 onions
- ☐ 1 garlic bulb
- ☐ 3.75kg potatoes
- ☐ 300g mixed mushrooms e.g. shitake, oyster, chestnut
- ☐ 1 bunch celery
- ☐ 1 carrot
- ☐ 1 parsnip
- ☐ 1 leek
- ☐ ½ swede
- ☐ 250g spinach leaves
- ☐ 1 head broccoli
- ☐ 500g plum tomatoes
- ☐ 1 medium white cabbage

FRUIT

- ☐ 1 lemon

FRESH HERBS

- ☐ flat-leaf parsley
- ☐ thyme
- ☐ sage

FRIDGE ITEMS

- ☐ 3 packs butter
- ☐ 170g sliced pancetta
- ☐ 13 eggs
- ☐ 50g Parmesan cheese
- ☐ 125ml double cream
- ☐ 3 litres of home-made chicken stock

KITCHEN CUPBOARD ITEMS

- ☐ salt
- ☐ vegetable oil
- ☐ olive oil
- ☐ 300ml coconut milk
- ☐ 500g basmati rice
- ☐ 45g dried porcini mushrooms
- ☐ 500g Arborio risotto rice
- ☐ 500g pasta
- ☐ 540g plain flour
- ☐ white wine vinegar
- ☐ chicken stock cubes
- ☐ dark soy sauce
- ☐ 1 small tin anchovies
- ☐ 100g tinned tuna fish
- ☐ 250ml white wine
- ☐ 50g walnuts
- ☐ vanilla essence
- ☐ baking powder
- ☐ 140g white chocolate
- ☐ 265g good quality milk chocolate
- ☐ 125g good quality plain chocolate
- ☐ 80g caster sugar
- ☐ 80g muscovado sugar
- ☐ 100g soft brown sugar

SPICES

- ☐ 2–3 strands saffron
- ☐ fresh ginger
- ☐ 7 curry leaves
- ☐ cinnamon sticks
- ☐ fenugreek
- ☐ 6 cardamom pods
- ☐ 4 cloves
- ☐ ground ginger
- ☐ ground cumin
- ☐ cumin seeds
- ☐ black mustard seeds
- ☐ whole nutmeg
- ☐ 4 juniper berries
- ☐ black pepper
- ☐ dried oregano

Beef curry
+ rice + dry potato curry

Curry is a great meal to cook in advance and then heat up when you are ready to eat. The flavour actually benefits from sitting for a while between cooking and eating.

Beef curry

1kg stewing steak cut into 2.5cm chunks
1 red chilli
2–3 strands saffron
2 small red onions, 1 finely diced and 1 finely sliced
2 cloves garlic, peeled and finely chopped
3 slices fresh ginger, peeled and finely chopped
7 curry leaves
3cm piece cinnamon stick
600ml water
salt
1 tablespoon vegetable oil
¼ teaspoon fenugreek
300ml coconut milk
6 cardamom pods, pods discarded and seeds ground in a pestle and mortar
4 cloves, ground in a pestle and mortar
¼ teaspoon ground ginger
1 dessertspoon ground cumin
juice ½ lemon

- Place the meat in a large saucepan.
- Add the chilli, saffron, the diced red onion, the garlic, ginger, curry leaves and cinnamon stick.
- Pour on the water and season well with salt.
- Bring to the boil and simmer gently, uncovered, for 1 hour 30 minutes so that most of the liquid disappears. Add a little more water as it cooks, if it seems a bit dry.
- Once the meat is cooked, heat the oil in a small frying pan.
- Fry the sliced onion and the fenugreek until the onion turns brown.
- Add this to the meat, along with the coconut milk, ground cardamom seeds, ground cloves, ginger, cumin and lemon juice.
- Let it simmer for 15 minutes and then serve with the rice and potatoes.

Rice

400ml basmati rice
600ml water
½ teaspoon salt

- Place the rice and water in a saucepan with the salt and bring to the boil.
- Turn the heat down low, cover the saucepan, and cook for 15 minutes.
- Remove from the heat and leave covered for 10 minutes.

Dry potato curry

750g potatoes, peeled, halved and boiled
2 tablespoons vegetable oil
1 red onion, finely sliced
½ teaspoon cumin seeds
½ teaspoon black mustard seeds
2.5cm fresh ginger, peeled and finely chopped

- Thickly slice the cooked potatoes.
- Heat the oil in a large frying pan and add the onion, cumin, mustard seeds and ginger.
- Fry until the mustard seeds start to pop.
- Add the cooked potatoes.
- Sauté the potatoes until golden brown.

Mushroom risotto

One of the keys to cooking a good risotto is to cook it for the correct amount of time. Generally, risotto rice takes about 20 minutes to cook, but this is not exact. Italians will tell you that the right time to stop cooking a risotto is when the rice is *al dente*, but if you are not used to eating risotto you may think that *al dente* rice is too hard. The best advice I can give you is to keep a teaspoon by the saucepan while you cook the risotto, start tasting the rice after 20 minutes and then stop cooking it when you think it tastes right.

1.5 litres home-made chicken stock
45g dried porcini mushrooms, soaked in a little warm water from the kettle for 5 minutes, and then roughly chopped
30g butter (for the mushrooms)
3 tablespoons olive oil
300g mixed mushrooms e.g. shitake, oyster, chestnut, sliced not too thinly
1 clove garlic, peeled and finely chopped
100g sliced pancetta, chopped
45g butter (for the rice)
1 large shallot, very finely chopped
500g Arborio risotto rice
Parmesan cheese for serving

- Pour the chicken stock into a large saucepan and bring it to a gentle simmer.
- Drain the dried mushrooms, adding the mushroom water to the simmering stock.
- Heat the butter for the mushrooms and one tablespoon of the olive oil in a frying pan.
- Add all the mushrooms and the garlic and cook for 5 minutes on a medium heat, stirring occasionally.
- Increase the heat and add the pancetta, stirring round to brown the pancetta and the mushrooms. Set aside.
- In another large saucepan, heat the butter for the rice and the remaining olive oil.
- Add the shallot and sauté for 5 minutes until soft and translucent.
- Add the rice and stir quickly and thoroughly for 1 minute to get the grains well coated with the oil and melted butter.
- Add a ladle of the hot stock and stir.
- Keeping the rice quite wet, add another ladle of stock just before the rice starts to stick to the pan.
- Keep adding the stock in this way, a ladle at a time.
- After 20 minutes test the rice and if it is ready add the mushrooms and pancetta.
- Add a few knobs of butter to the cooked risotto and serve with freshly-grated Parmesan cheese.

Winter vegetable soup

This is a great soup for cold winter evenings, making use of the best of the winter vegetables. Serve with rounds of cheese sandwiches.

50g butter
1 tablespoon olive oil
1 onion, sliced
1 celery stick, chopped into chunks
1 carrot, peeled and chopped into chunks
1 parsnip, peeled and chopped into chunks
1 leek, chopped into chunks
4 medium potatoes, peeled and cut into chunks
½ swede, peeled and chopped into chunks
1 sprig fresh thyme
1.5 litres home-made chicken stock
salt and pepper

- Melt the butter with the olive oil in a large saucepan.
- Add the vegetables and the thyme, and stir them around to coat them in the butter and oil.
- Cook gently for 5 minutes.
- Add the stock, cover and cook on a gentle simmer for 20 minutes.
- Season with salt and pepper and serve with cheese sandwiches.

Smoked haddock + sautéed potatoes + buttered spinach + poached eggs

One marriage made in heaven is smoked haddock and poached egg. Prepare the vegetables first and then turn your attention to the fish and eggs.

Smoked haddock

750g smoked haddock fillets, skinned
milk
pepper
1 sprig fresh thyme

- Preheat the oven to 200°C/400°F/gas 6.
- Place the haddock fillets in a baking tray, cover them with milk and season with pepper. Place the sprig of thyme in the milk with the fish.
- Bake for 5 minutes.
- Remove from the oven and cut the fish into six portions.

Sautéed potatoes

1kg potatoes, peeled and quartered
2 tablespoons olive oil
salt and pepper

- Boil the potatoes in salted water until tender.
- Drain them and cut into 3cm chunks.
- Heat the oil in a large sauté pan, add the potatoes and sauté them on a medium heat for 20 minutes until golden brown.
- Season just before serving.

Buttered spinach

250g spinach leaves
salt
knob of butter
nutmeg
black pepper

- Place the spinach in a large saucepan with a tablespoon of water and a sprinkling of sea salt.
- Cover and place the saucepan on a low heat.
- Gradually wilt the spinach for 10 minutes, until all the leaves are a glossy dark green.
- Then remove the lid and stir round for a few seconds to get rid of any excess water. Drain any extra water off if there is too much.
- Add a knob of butter, a tiny grating of nutmeg, and a good grinding of pepper.

Poached eggs

6 eggs
1 teaspoon white wine vinegar

- Take a large sauté pan and pour into it 2–3cm of water.
- Add the vinegar and get the water simmering. A simmer is all that is necessary to poach eggs and will stop the egg white breaking up too much.
- Crack the eggs one at a time into a ramekin, without breaking the yolk, and then pour the egg into the water. You can poach two eggs at a time.
- Poach for 1 minute and then, if you are not serving the meal straight away, place in a bowl of cold water. You can pop them back into the warm water just before you are ready to serve.
- Put the fish on top of some spinach on each plate and top with a poached egg.
- Serve with the potatoes.

Chicken pie
+ broccoli

The thought of a home-made chicken pie gets me salivating, but I have made chicken pies in the past that have been a huge disappointment, partly because they were time-consuming and also because they were dry and bland. This recipe produces a pie that lives up to my expectations.

Chicken pie

For the pastry

300g plain flour
180g butter
salt
2 egg yolks
2 tablespoons cold tap water

For the filling

400ml chicken stock (a stock cube will do)
4 chicken breasts, skinless and cut into 2cm cubes
1 tablespoon olive oil
30g butter
1 onion, diced
2 tablespoons plain flour
3 tablespoons dark soy sauce
400g potatoes, peeled, cooked and cut into 3cm chunks
2 tablespoons flat-leaf parsley, chopped
salt and pepper
1 egg yolk mixed with 1 tablespoon water to glaze the pie

To make the pastry

- Put the flour and butter in a food processor, or in a bowl if you are combining by hand, and incorporate them so that the resulting mixture looks like fine breadcrumbs.
- Add a pinch of salt.
- Mix the egg yolk with the cold water in a small bowl and then add them to the flour mixture.
- Whizz the pastry in the food processor, or mix by hand, and then turn out onto a work surface and combine thoroughly until you have firm dough.
- Wrap the dough in cling-film and place it in the fridge for 30 minutes to chill.

To make the pie

- Preheat the oven to 180°C/350°F/gas 4.
- Place a baking sheet in the oven.
- Heat the chicken stock in a medium-sized saucepan and bring to a gentle simmer.
- Place the chicken pieces in the stock.
- Cover and simmer for 1 minute.
- Remove the chicken pieces from the stock and set both the stock and the chicken aside.
- In a medium frying pan heat the olive oil and the butter and gently sauté the onion for 5 minutes until soft.
- Add a tablespoon of flour and stir around to mix into the fat.
- Remove from the heat and gently add the soy sauce, a tablespoon at a time, stirring to incorporate before adding another.
- Once the soy sauce is mixed in, add the chicken stock and bring to a simmer.
- Then add the chicken, cooked potatoes, and parsley and check the seasoning.
- Set aside to cool while you prepare the pastry case.
- This is a top and bottom pie, so grease a pie dish, tin or plate with a diameter of anything between 28 and 30cm or make two smaller pies.
- Divide the pastry into two pieces bearing in mind that you need slightly more pastry for the bottom of the pie than you do for the top.
- Roll out the bottom of the pie and line the tin or plate.
- Spoon in the chicken and potatoes and then pour in as much gravy as you can without it overflowing.
- Reserve the rest of the gravy to serve when the pie is ready or pour it into the slits in the top of the pie when it comes out of the oven.
- Roll out the pastry lid, place it on the top and pinch the edges to seal.

- Make two slits in the top of the pie and brush the pastry with the egg glaze.
- Place on the baking sheet in the oven and cook for 30 minutes.

Broccoli

1 head broccoli, trimmed and cut into florets
salt
black pepper

- Bring a pan of salted water to the boil.
- Add the broccoli and simmer for 3 minutes.
- Drain and serve with black pepper.

Pasta in a tuna fish sauce

This a real store cupboard dish that uses items that one often has lying around in the kitchen cupboards.

500g plum tomatoes
3 tablespoons olive oil
1 onion, finely chopped
2 cloves garlic, peeled and finely chopped
3 salted anchovies
2 teaspoons dried oregano
100g tinned tuna fish, drained and flaked
salt and pepper
500g pasta, cooked, follow the packet instructions
Parmesan cheese, grated for serving

- First, prepare the tomatoes by placing them in a bowl and pouring boiling water over them.
- Leave them in the hot water for a few minutes before draining them. Once they are cool enough to handle you will be able to peel them easily.
- Roughly chop the tomatoes and leave them to one side.
- Heat the olive oil in a sauté pan.
- On a low heat, gently cook the onion and garlic for 10 minutes until soft.
- Add the anchovies and mix them in with the back of a wooden spoon, mashing them as you stir.
- Add the tomatoes and oregano and cook on a gentle heat for 20 minutes.
- Add the tuna and cook on a low heat for another 10 minutes.
- Season with salt and pepper.
- Meanwhile, cook the pasta.
- Once ready, serve with the grated Parmesan.

Loin of pork + braised white cabbage + sautéed potatoes with pancetta and sage

Try to buy the pork for this recipe on the bone. If you can't then adjust the weight of the joint to around 1kg (2.2lb). The braised white cabbage is the perfect accompaniment for the pork.

Loin of pork

1.5kg rolled loin pork
olive oil
salt

- Preheat the oven to 230°C/450°F/gas 8.
- Place the joint of pork in a roasting tin.
- Rub the rind with the olive oil and the salt.
- Place the joint in the oven and roast for 25 minutes.
- Reduce the heat to 160°C/320°F/gas 2 and roast for 1 hour 15 minutes.
- Remove from the oven to rest for 20 minutes.
- Meanwhile, prepare the vegetables as the meat is cooking.

Braised white cabbage

1 medium white cabbage, any discoloured outer leaves removed
50g butter
1 shallot, finely chopped
1 clove garlic, peeled and finely chopped
4 juniper berries, bruised in a mortar and pestle
250ml white wine
1 sprig fresh thyme
salt and pepper

- Halve the cabbage and remove the thick core in the middle, then slice it fairly thinly.
- Heat the butter in a large saucepan.
- Add the shallot and garlic and fry on a medium heat for 5 minutes until soft.
- Add the cabbage and reduce the heat to low.
- Cover and cook for 15 minutes.
- Add the juniper berries, stir and cook, covered, for another 10 minutes.
- Turn up the heat and add the wine. After 1 minute reduce the heat again and stew, uncovered, for 10 minutes.
- Stir in the thyme leaves, season and serve.

Sautéed potatoes with pancetta and sage

3 tablespoons olive oil
750g potatoes, peeled, quartered, and boiled until tender in salted water
70g pancetta, sliced and roughly chopped
6 sage leaves
pepper and salt

- Heat the olive oil in a frying pan.
- Add the potatoes, sage and pancetta, and fry until the potatoes are nicely browned.
- Season with salt and pepper.

Microwave-steamed chocolate pudding

This is the best steamed chocolate pudding recipe I have ever come across. It appears in Barbara Kafka's *Microwave Gourmet*. It is so simple to make, which I think always adds to the satisfaction when making something that also tastes wonderful. I change it slightly when I am making it for children, using a mix of milk and plain chocolate, as I think it would be too rich for them otherwise.

125g good quality milk chocolate
125g good quality plain chocolate
120g unsalted butter, softened
100g soft brown sugar
1 teaspoon vanilla essence
125ml double cream
40g plain flour
½ teaspoon baking powder
3 eggs

- Grease a 1 litre pudding basin.
- Chop the chocolate in a food processor until reasonably fine.
- Add the butter and sugar to the chocolate, and process until combined.
- Add the remaining ingredients and process to a smooth mixture.
- Pour into the pudding basin and cover tightly with microwave film.
- Cook in the microwave on its highest setting for 5 minutes. To avoid burning your fingers pierce the film with the tip of a sharp knife, and then remove the film and cover the top of the basin with a heavy plate. This keeps the pudding hot while it stands for 10 minutes.
- Unmould the pudding onto a plate and serve with cream.
- When you unmould the pudding it doesn't look very grand, but the taste more than makes up for it.

Chocolate chip cookies

Chocolate chip cookies must be one of the West's favourite sweet treats. After I left home I would occasionally think about the chocolate chip cookies my mother used to make and the smell of them baking in the oven. It's quite surprising how long lasting food memories can be.

140g good quality milk chocolate
100g butter, softened
80g caster sugar
80g muscavado sugar
1 egg, beaten
½ teaspoon vanilla essence
150g plain flour
pinch of salt
½ teaspoon baking powder
140g white chocolate, cut into chunks
50g walnuts, chopped

- Preheat the oven to 180°C/350°F/gas 4.
- Grease two baking sheets, as this recipe makes 16 large cookies or several more smaller ones.
- Place the milk chocolate in a glass bowl over a saucepan of simmering water. (Make sure the water doesn't touch the glass bowl).
- When melted set aside to cool.
- Beat the butter and sugars with an electric mixer until smooth and light.
- Beat in the egg, vanilla essence and melted chocolate.
- Sift in the flour, salt, baking powder, white chocolate chunks and chopped nuts.
- If your kitchen is particularly warm and the mixture seems less than firm, place it in the fridge for 20 minutes or so, as otherwise the cookies will spread too much in the oven and lose a bit of their thickness.
- Heap tablespoons of the mixture onto the baking sheets, spacing them well apart.
- Bake them for 12–15 minutes.
- Let them cool for a couple of minutes and then place them on a rack to cool.

Week 3

Shopping list

MEAT

- ☐ 10–12 lamb cutlets
- ☐ 1 kg chicken thighs and drumsticks
- ☐ 8–10 sausages
- ☐ 1.5kg unsmoked gammon joint

FISH

- ☐ 500g cooked prawns

VEGETABLES

- ☐ 250g cauliflower
- ☐ 800g fennel bulbs
- ☐ 2 little gem lettuces
- ☐ ½ cucumber
- ☐ 3 spring onions
- ☐ 2 onions
- ☐ 1 bunch celery
- ☐ 1 carrot
- ☐ 200g baby leaf spinach
- ☐ 2 bags watercress
- ☐ 2.75kg potatoes
- ☐ 1 savoy cabbage
- ☐ 1 shallot
- ☐ 1 garlic bulb
- ☐ 1 whole green chilli
- ☐ fresh ginger

FRUIT

- ☐ 1 lemon
- ☐ 500g plums

FRESH HERBS

- ☐ coriander
- ☐ sage
- ☐ rosemary
- ☐ bay leaf

FRIDGE ITEMS

- ☐ 150g Parmesan cheese
- ☐ 150g salami
- ☐ 200g buffalo mozzarella
- ☐ 50g Taleggio cheese
- ☐ 150g frozen peas
- ☐ 200g Gruyère cheese
- ☐ 350g cooked ham
- ☐ 10 eggs
- ☐ 1.1 litres milk
- ☐ 700ml double cream
- ☐ 3 packs butter

KITCHEN CUPBOARD ITEMS

- ☐ 400ml unsweetened coconut milk
- ☐ 500g basmati rice
- ☐ 400g penne
- ☐ 800ml passata
- ☐ 1 white loaf for breadcrumbs
- ☐ extra virgin olive oil
- ☐ vegetable oil
- ☐ olive oil
- ☐ balsamic vinegar
- ☐ 1 bouillon or Kallo chicken stock cube
- ☐ goose fat
- ☐ maple syrup
- ☐ Dijon mustard
- ☐ 500g dried haricot beans
- ☐ 400g tin chopped tomatoes
- ☐ 190g caster sugar
- ☐ 50g soft brown sugar
- ☐ icing sugar for dusting
- ☐ 150g ground almonds
- ☐ a vanilla pod
- ☐ vanilla essence
- ☐ 725g plain flour
- ☐ raspberry jam
- ☐ salt
- ☐ Worcestershire sauce
- ☐ soy sauce
- ☐ 1 loaf crusty bread

SPICES

- ☐ coriander seeds
- ☐ fenugreek
- ☐ black peppercorns
- ☐ dried curry leaves
- ☐ black mustard seeds
- ☐ paprika
- ☐ cayenne
- ☐ turmeric
- ☐ 1 tablespoon tamarind paste
- ☐ dried oregano
- ☐ whole nutmeg
- ☐ ground ginger
- ☐ ground cinnamon

Prawn curry with coconut milk
+ rice + pea, potato and cauliflower curry

I think a version of this prawn curry originally came from a Madhur Jaffrey book. The list of ingredients is quite long but do not let this put you off; it is actually quite straightforward to make.

Prawn curry with coconut milk

2 tablespoons whole coriander seeds
¼ teaspoon fenugreek seeds
1 teaspoon whole black peppercorns
10 dried curry leaves
2 tablespoons vegetable oil
1 teaspoon black mustard seeds
1 medium sized onion, diced
3 cloves garlic, cut into fine slivers
1 teaspoon fresh ginger, peeled and grated
450ml water
1 tablespoon paprika
a pinch cayenne
¼ teaspoon turmeric
¾ teaspoon salt
1 whole green chilli, deseeded
1 tablespoon tamarind paste
400ml unsweetened coconut milk
500g cooked prawns

- Heat a heavy-bottomed frying pan.
- When the pan is hot add the coriander seeds, the fenugreek and the peppercorns.
- Stir them for 1 minute until they are lightly toasted.
- Once the spices are ready, remove them from the heat and grind them with the curry leaves in a pestle and mortar, as finely as possible.
- Next heat the oil in a medium-sized saucepan over a medium flame.
- When hot add the mustard seeds. As soon as these start to pop turn the heat down and add the onion.
- Fry the onion for 10 minutes, stirring occasionally.
- Add the garlic and cook for 30 seconds.
- Add the ginger, stir and cook for a few more seconds.
- Add the water, paprika, cayenne pepper, turmeric, salt, green chilli, ground spice mixture and the tamarind paste.
- Pour in the coconut milk and bring to a simmer. Cook for 5 minutes.
- Add the prawns and warm them through.

Boiled rice

500ml basmati rice
750ml water
salt

- Put the rice in a saucepan, with the water and a pinch of salt.
- Place the rice on a high heat and as soon as it comes to the boil, cover the saucepan with a lid and turn the heat right down to very low. Leave it like this for 15 minutes, stirring only once during the cooking time.
- Remove from the heat and leave it covered for another 10 minutes before you remove the lid.

Pea, potato and cauliflower curry

500g mixture potatoes, cauliflower and frozen peas
250ml water
1 tablespoon vegetable oil
½ teaspoon salt
1 teaspoon sugar
2 tablespoons fresh coriander, chopped
1 tablespoon fresh ginger, peeled and grated

- Peel the potatoes and cut them into 2cm cubes.
- Prepare the cauliflower by trimming it and cutting it into florets.
- Pour the water, oil, and salt into a large frying pan and bring to the boil.
- Add the potatoes, cover the pan and simmer for 5 minutes.

- Add the cauliflower and cook covered for another 5 minutes.
- Add the peas and cook for another 3 minutes.
- At the end of this time check that all the vegetables are tender. If not, cook for a little longer.
- Add the sugar, coriander and ginger to the vegetables.
- Simmer for another minute.
- Serve immediately with the prawns and rice.

Grilled lamb cutlets + fennel with cream and cheese + roast potatoes

Fennel has a strong flavour and so may not be popular with many children. But give this a go anyway as the cheese and cream will make it more appealing. You can prepare another vegetable as a fallback, just in case. Prepare the vegetables first and then cook the lamb.

Grilled lamb cutlets

10–12 lamb cutlets
salt and pepper

- Preheat the grill to hot.
- Put the lamb on top of the grill rack and place it under the grill.
- Turn the cutlets once they are brown and crispy on one side and cook on the other side.
- Season well with salt and pepper.

Fennel with cream and cheese

800g fennel bulbs, tough outer leaves removed and quartered
salt and pepper
300ml double cream
4 tablespoons Parmesan cheese, grated

- Preheat the oven to 200°C/400°F/gas 6.
- Bring a saucepan of salted water to the boil.
- Put the fennel into the water and simmer for 7 minutes, until tender to the tip of a sharp knife.
- Place the fennel in a single layer in an ovenproof dish.
- Season with salt and pepper.
- Pour over the cream and sprinkle with the Parmesan cheese.
- Place in the oven for 25 minutes, until the cheese is turning brown.

Roast potatoes

1kg potatoes, peeled and quartered
2 tablespoons olive oil
salt

- Preheat the oven to 220°C/425°F/gas 7.
- Parboil the potatoes in boiling salted water for 5 minutes.
- Drain and place them in a roasting tray with 2 tablespoons olive oil.
- Place the potatoes in the oven for 45 minutes, turning them occasionally, until golden brown.

Pasta pie
+ green salad

This recipe is adapted from the 'Sicilian Pasta Pie' recipe in Tamasin Day-Lewis's *Good Tempered Food*, which really is such a motivational cookbook. Just when I get fed up with producing food for the hungry masses I open one of her books and get inspired all over again.

Pasta pie

400g penne
800ml passata
50g Parmesan, freshly grated
good sprinkling dried oregano
salt and pepper
2 hard boiled eggs, sliced
150g salami, cut into strips
200g buffalo mozzarella, cut into small cubes
50g Taleggio cheese, cut into small cubes – if you can't get Taleggio then use Camembert
2 tablespoons brown or white breadcrumbs
2 tablespoons olive oil

- Preheat the oven to 190°C/375°F/gas 5.
- Lightly grease an ovenproof gratin dish.
- Cook the pasta until it is *al dente*, following the packet instructions.
- Drain the pasta, pour on the passata and mix the two together in the saucepan.
- Add the Parmesan and the dried oregano. Mix well and season with salt and pepper.
- Assemble the pie by putting a layer of tomato pasta on the bottom of the ovenproof dish and then layer half of the sliced eggs on top of the pasta.
- Next comes the salami, half of the mozzarella, and then the Taleggio.
- Repeat the layering, ending with a layer of pasta.
- Sprinkle with the breadcrumbs and drizzle with the olive oil.
- If you are not ready to eat at this stage then the dish can sit and wait. Otherwise, place in the oven for 30 minutes.
- Serve as soon as it comes out of the oven.

Green salad

2 little gem lettuces, roughly shredded
½ cucumber, sliced
3 spring onions, sliced
handful young spinach leaves
handful watercress
3 dessertspoons extra virgin olive oil
1 dessertspoon balsamic vinegar
salt and pepper

- Place the salad ingredients in a serving bowl.
- Mix the olive oil and balsamic vinegar together with the salt and pepper and pour this over the salad.

TIP

When you have a dish that includes tomatoes, such as this pasta pie, avoid using tomatoes in the salad. A green salad is far more appropriate.

Chicken stew

I am not snobbish about using stock cubes instead of fresh stock, especially now that you can buy the cubes that don't contain MSG, although I do resist using them in risottos as I think the flavour of the stock cube tends to dominate when it should not. A stock cube works perfectly well here and makes for a wholesome and tasty meal.

2 tablespoons olive oil
1kg chicken thighs and drumsticks, skin removed
1 onion, finely diced
1 stick celery, chopped into 1cm cubes
1 carrot, peeled and cut into 1cm cubes
3 medium potatoes, peeled and chopped into 2cm pieces
1 bouillon or Kallo chicken stock cube or 600ml fresh chicken stock
3 handfuls frozen peas
3 handfuls baby leaf spinach
salt and pepper

- Heat the oil in a large heavy-bottomed saucepan.
- Brown the chicken pieces all over.
- Remove them from the pan and set aside.
- Keeping the saucepan on a medium heat add the onion, celery, carrot and potato and stir to coat. Keep stirring the vegetables occasionally.
- Let the vegetables cook for about 5 minutes then add the browned chicken pieces and the stock.
- Cover the saucepan and cook for 15 minutes on a low heat.
- Add the peas and bring the pot to a simmer again.
- Cook for another 15 minutes.
- Test the seasoning and add pepper and more salt if needed. If you've used a stock cube remember to go easy on the salt.
- You can now put the stew aside until you are ready to eat. When you reheat the stew, add the spinach. It will wilt nicely into the stew and its beautiful green colour will add a jewel-like quality to the dish.
- Serve with crusty bread.

Ham and Gruyère crêpes
+ watercress salad

This is a good meal to prepare in advance. Assemble the crêpes and then put them under the grill just before serving to warm through. The recipe makes about 12 crêpes.

Ham and Gruyère crêpes

For the crêpe batter

200ml cold water

200ml milk

4 eggs

½ teaspoon salt

300g flour

100g butter, melted

For the Béchamel sauce

75g butter

50g flour

550ml milk, warmed

100ml double cream

nutmeg

150g Gruyère cheese, grated

salt and pepper

For the filling

350g cooked ham, sliced

2–3 handfuls Gruyère cheese, grated

To make the crêpe batter

- Place the liquids, eggs and salt into a food processor.
- Add the flour and butter, and whizz until smooth and creamy.
- Set aside for at least an hour.
- In the meantime prepare the Béchamel sauce.

To make the Béchamel sauce

- Melt the butter in a small saucepan.
- Add the flour and stir over the heat for few seconds.
- Remove the saucepan from the heat and gradually add the warm milk, stirring all the time to avoid lumps.
- Return the saucepan to the heat and bring the sauce to the boil, stirring continuously.
- Reduce the heat and simmer on a very low heat for 5 minutes.
- Add the cream, a good grinding of nutmeg, the cheese and seasoning and set aside.

To make the crêpes

- Take a pancake skillet or a heavy frying pan.
- Lightly rub with a little butter and place the pan on the heat.
- When the fat starts to smoke, pour half a ladle or 2 tablespoons of batter into the pan.
- Remove the pan from the heat and quickly tilt it in all directions so that the batter spreads over the pan in a thin layer.
- Give the pan a shake, and as soon as the crêpe starts to move it is ready to turn.
- If you are confident, flip the crêpe in the air or turn it over with a spatula.
- Cook until brown on the other side, which will only take a few seconds.
- Pile the cooked crêpes onto a plate by the hob.
- Fill them by placing a piece of ham in one quarter of the crêpe. Then fold it in half so that it looks like a semi-circle and then fold over again so you have a quarter circle.
- Place the filled crêpes in an ovenproof dish in overlapping layers.
- Pour over the sauce and sprinkle with a good handful or two of Gruyère cheese.
- Place under a hot grill until bubbling and brown.
- Serve with watercress salad.

Watercress salad

1 bag watercress

salt and pepper

1 tablespoon olive oil

- Place the watercress in a serving bowl and dress with the salt, pepper and olive oil.

Sausages + sautéed potatoes + savoy cabbage

To make a nutritious meal out of sausages you really have to make sure they are of good quality. They will be more expensive but worth the extra cost as they are much better for you.

Sausages

8–10 sausages
olive oil

- Fry the sausages in a little olive oil in a large frying pan. Brown them on a reasonably high heat and then reduce the heat until they are cooked through, which should take about 20 minutes.

Sautéed potatoes

750g potatoes
salt
1 dessertspoon goose fat or 2 tablespoons olive oil
black pepper
dried herbs (optional)
paprika (optional)

- Peel the potatoes and bring them to the boil in a saucepan of salted water.
- Let them simmer for 10–15 minutes until cooked.
- Drain them and bash them about in the saucepan by shaking it back and forth.
- Melt a dessertspoon of goose fat, or use 2 tablespoons of olive oil, in a frying pan and when it is hot, add the potatoes.
- Turn the heat down slightly and move the potatoes around frequently, making sure you turn them over, until they are nicely browned all over.
- Turn the heat down low and leave them, only stirring occasionally, until you are ready to serve.
- At this stage you can adjust the seasoning by adding more salt and pepper, or if you like to be a bit more creative, a sprinkling of dried herbs and paprika.

Savoy cabbage

1 savoy cabbage, shredded finely
small knob of butter
salt and pepper
squeeze of lemon juice

- Place the cabbage in a large saucepan with a dessertspoon of water and the butter.
- Cover the cabbage and cook on a low heat, stirring occasionally, for 5 minutes.
- Season to taste with salt, freshly-ground black pepper and a squeeze of lemon juice.

Roasted ham
+ haricot beans in barbecue sauce

I usually buy a 1.5kg unsmoked gammon joint for six of us. This will mean a bit left over for sandwiches or to accompany a salad on another day. The children like it fried on a piece of toast with a fried egg on top.

Roasted ham

1.5kg unsmoked gammon joint

For the glaze

1 tablespoon maple syrup

1 dessertspoon soft brown sugar

1 dessertspoon Dijon mustard

1 dessertspoon any chutney in the cupboard

- Preheat the oven to 200°C/400°F/gas 6.
- A 1.5kg gammon joint will take 1 hour 30 minutes to cook, so adjust your timings accordingly if you have a smaller or larger joint.
- Place the joint in a large saucepan and cover it with water. Bring the water to the boil and then reduce the heat, cover and cook for 1 hour.
- Take the glaze ingredients and mix them together in a small bowl.
- Remove the gammon from the water, place it in a meat tin and cut off the rind.
- Using a pastry brush or a wooden spoon, cover it with the glaze.
- Place the joint in the oven and bake for 30 minutes.
- Leave it to rest for 20–30 minutes before attempting to carve it.

Haricot beans in barbecue sauce

350g dried haricot beans, soaked overnight

1 sage leaf, 1 sprig rosemary and 1 bay leaf, tied together with kitchen string

1 tablespoon olive oil

1 shallot, peeled and finely chopped

1 clove garlic, peeled and finely chopped

400g tin chopped tomatoes

2 teaspoons brown sugar

2 or 3 medium potatoes, peeled and chopped into 2cm cubes

1 tablespoon soy sauce

1 tablespoon maple syrup

1 tablespoon Worcestershire sauce

salt and pepper

- Rinse the beans and place in fresh water so that they are adequately covered. Add the herbs.
- Bring to the boil and then reduce the heat to a steady simmer and cook, partially covered, for an hour or until the beans are soft.
- Warm the olive oil in another saucepan.
- Add the shallot and cook until soft.
- Add the garlic and cook for 1 minute. Do not let the garlic brown as this makes the flavour bitter.
- Add the tomatoes, sugar, potatoes, soy sauce, maple syrup and Worcestershire sauce and season with salt and pepper.
- Cook on a good simmer, uncovered, stirring occasionally until the potato is soft for approximately 30 minutes.
- Add the cooked beans and cook for a further 10 minutes before serving with the ham.

TIP

The main thing to note when cooking dried pulses is to remember to put them into a saucepan or bowl of cold water and soak them overnight. There is nothing magical about this process; it just reduces the cooking time. Do not salt the beans until they are cooked as salt stops the beans from softening.

Plum and almond crumble + custard

Plum crumble is one of those heavenly dishes; when you taste it you wonder why you don't cook it more often.

Plum and almond crumble

500g plums halved and stoned
125g plain flour
90g caster sugar
150g ground almonds
½ teaspoon ground ginger
½ teaspoon ground cinnamon
140g butter, cold from the fridge and cubed

- Preheat the oven to 180°C/350°F/gas 4.
- Place the prepared plums in a gratin dish.
- To prepare the crumble topping place the flour in the bowl of a food processor, or a mixing bowl.
- Add the sugar, almonds, spices and butter.
- Whizz the butter and the dry ingredients together until they are like breadcrumbs. Don't worry too much about how fine they are.
- Sprinkle the mixture over the plums and bake for 35 minutes.

Custard

2 whole eggs
2 egg yolks
2 tablespoons caster sugar
600ml milk and double cream mixed
1 vanilla pod or a drop or two of vanilla extract

- Place the eggs, egg yolks and the sugar in a glass bowl and whisk with a hand whisk for 2 minutes.
- Pour the milk and cream into a measuring jug.
- Add the vanilla pod or extract.
- Heat the milk and cream in a microwave on high for 2 minutes. You want the milk and cream to be almost at boiling point.
- Place the glass bowl with the eggs and sugar over a saucepan of simmering water. Make sure the water does not touch the bottom of the bowl.
- Add the milk and cream to the egg mixture, stirring all the time with a wooden spoon to avoid lumps. If you are using a vanilla pod then split it open at this stage and scrape the seeds into the custard.
- Keep stirring for 10 minutes by which time you should have a good consistency. An indication of when the custard is thick enough is that it will coat the back of the wooden spoon. It will not be as thick as shop-bought custard.
- Avoid reheating home-made custard, as it may curdle.

Swiss tarts

My mother used to make these cakes for my brothers and me when we were children and we never tired of them. They have a crumbly, melting texture. I wouldn't recommend adults eating too many, however, as they have a high butter content. The recipe originally came from an old cookbook of my mothers.

250g butter, softened
50g caster sugar
½ teaspoon vanilla essence
250g plain flour, sifted
salt
To finish
raspberry jam and icing sugar

- Preheat the oven to 200°C/400°F/gas 6.
- Line a cake tray with paper cases.
- Cream the butter and sugar until light and fluffy, using an electric mixer or a hand-held blender.
- Add the vanilla essence and half the flour.
- Blend for 3 minutes.
- Add the rest of the flour and a good pinch of salt and beat for 3 minutes.
- Spoon the mixture into the paper cases.
- Bake for 15 minutes.
- When the cakes have cooled sprinkle them with sifted icing sugar and spoon a blob of jam into the centre of each one.

TIP

The key to making these cakes is to make sure you have beaten the mixture thoroughly.

Week 4

Monday p46	Fried garlic chicken sandwiches with mustard mayonnaise
Tuesday p48	Pasta and potato soup + cheese on toast
Wednesday p49	Easy beef kebabs + egg fried rice
Thursday p50	Salade Niçoise + baked potatoes
Friday p51	Baked cod with tomatoes, potatoes and parsley
Saturday p52	Chicken with rosemary + mashed potato + green peas
Sunday p53	Beef fillet steaks with horseradish sauce + gratin dauphinois + peas and carrots
Sunday pudding p54	American apple pie
Extra tasty treat p55	Almond gingerbread + caramel custard

Shopping list

MEAT
- ☐ 3 chicken breasts, boneless
- ☐ 450g tender beef fillet or sirloin
- ☐ 6 beef fillet steaks
- ☐ 1 kg chicken thighs and drumsticks

FISH
- ☐ 700g cod fillets

VEGETABLES
- ☐ 2 Romaine lettuces
- ☐ 3 spring onions
- ☐ 8 tomatoes
- ☐ 1 cucumber
- ☐ 300g fresh peas
- ☐ 325g carrots
- ☐ 3.5kg potatoes
- ☐ 3 onions
- ☐ 1 red onion
- ☐ 1 shallot
- ☐ 1 bunch celery
- ☐ 1 garlic bulb
- ☐ 6 baking potatoes
- ☐ 250g green beans
- ☐ 1 bag mixed salad leaves
- ☐ fresh root ginger

FRUIT
- ☐ 4 lemons
- ☐ 6 eating apples

FRESH HERBS
- ☐ mint
- ☐ rosemary
- ☐ flat-leaf parsley

FRIDGE ITEMS
- ☐ 250ml double cream
- ☐ 850ml milk
- ☐ 200g crème fraîche
- ☐ 75g Parmesan cheese
- ☐ 6 slices pancetta
- ☐ 3 packs butter
- ☐ 100g Gruyère cheese
- ☐ 330g frozen petits pois
- ☐ 12 eggs
- ☐ vanilla ice cream

KITCHEN CUPBOARD ITEMS
- ☐ 6 mini baguettes or rolls (if not making you own)
- ☐ 3 x 400g tins chopped tomatoes
- ☐ 25g ground almonds
- ☐ 50g blanched almonds
- ☐ 85g golden syrup
- ☐ bicarbonate of soda
- ☐ 1 jar cornichons
- ☐ 250g self-raising flour
- ☐ 200g plain flour
- ☐ cornflour
- ☐ dried yeast
- ☐ 500g strong white flour
- ☐ vanilla extract
- ☐ penne
- ☐ 1 bottle dry white wine
- ☐ 1 bottle red wine
- ☐ salt
- ☐ 500g basmati rice
- ☐ dark soy sauce
- ☐ sesame oil
- ☐ groundnut oil
- ☐ light olive oil
- ☐ balsamic vinegar
- ☐ 1 small tin anchovy fillets
- ☐ olive oil
- ☐ 2 x 125g tins tuna fish
- ☐ handful black and green olives
- ☐ Dijon mustard
- ☐ creamed horseradish
- ☐ 230g soft brown sugar
- ☐ 50g caster sugar

SPICES
- ☐ ground ginger
- ☐ cinammon
- ☐ whole nutmeg
- ☐ coriander seeds
- ☐ cumin seeds
- ☐ fennel seeds
- ☐ fenugreek
- ☐ black pepper
- ☐ dried chillies

Fried garlic chicken sandwiches with mustard mayonnaise

This is a great light supper, which the children really enjoy. You can either make the baguettes and mayonnaise or buy them, but, needless to say, the sandwiches are much nicer with home-made bread and mayonnaise.

3 chicken breasts, skinless
6 medium baguettes (see recipe below)
1 portion mayonnaise (see recipe below)
¼ cucumber, sliced
1 Romaine lettuce, shredded
6 cornichons, split down the middle
3 spring onions, sliced
1 tablespoon olive oil
1 clove garlic, peeled and bashed
salt and pepper
1 lemon
6 slices pancetta

For the baguettes
375ml hand-hot water
2½ teaspoons dried yeast
500g strong white flour
1½ teaspoons salt

For the mayonnaise
2 egg yolks
2 teaspoons Dijon mustard
150ml groundnut oil
150ml light olive oil
1 tablespoon cold water
salt

To make the baguettes

- Measure 300ml of warm water into a small bowl and sprinkle on the yeast.
- Leave for 2 minutes.
- Place the flour and salt in a large mixing bowl.
- Make a well in the centre of the flour and pour the water and yeast mixture into it.
- Draw in some flour to make a thick mixture in the middle, leaving most of the flour dry at the edge of the bowl.
- Cover the bowl with a clean tea towel and leave in a draught-free place for 20 minutes.
- Mix in the remaining water and turn out the mixture onto a lightly floured surface.
- Work together to form a dough and then knead by hand for 10 minutes or in a mixer for 5 minutes.
- You will find that the dough is quite sticky and it should be. Resist adding more flour if you can, unless you find it too difficult to knead.
- Return the dough to the bowl, cover and leave to rise for at least an hour.
- Next, knock back the dough by punching the air out of it and leave it to rise for 30 minutes more.
- Knock back again and leave for a further 30 minutes.
- Preheat the oven to 240°C/475°F/gas 9.
- Cut the dough into six pieces, roll each one out into a sausage shape and place on a greased baking sheet. Cover with the clean tea towel and leave to rise for 30 minutes.
- Cut diagonal slashes in the top of the bread and place in the oven for 20 minutes.

To make the mayonnaise

- Place the egg yolks in a bowl with the mustard and mix until combined.
- Combine the groundnut oil and olive oil in a measuring jug.
- Start adding the oil to the egg yolks and mustard, quite literally a drop at a time, making sure that each addition is fully incorporated before adding the next. If you add the oil too quickly it will curdle.
- The mayonnaise will become thick. It may seem too thick, but once it gets to this stage add a tablespoon of cold water, which instantly creates the right consistency by emulsifying the mixture.
- Add salt to taste.

- If you are using shop-bought mayonnaise then just add the mustard to that.

To make the sandwiches

- Thinly slice the breast fillets lengthways so each breast becomes four thin slices. Set aside.
- Split each cooked baguette lengthways and spread one side lightly with the mustard mayonnaise.
- Place some cucumber, some lettuce, one cornichon, and some spring onion on one half and set about cooking the chicken and pancetta.
- Heat the olive oil in a frying pan.
- Add the garlic clove and stir round while the oil becomes hot.
- Remove the garlic clove as it browns and then add the thin slices of chicken, which will only take 1 minute to cook.
- Season them with salt and pepper and a squeeze of lemon juice, and set aside.
- Quickly fry the pancetta, and then add some chicken and pancetta to each of the remaining sides of the baguettes.
- Press the sandwiches together and serve.

Pasta and potato soup
+ cheese on toast

I make this soup regularly as all my children like it. It is also quick and nutritious, which covers all the bases as far as I am concerned.

Pasta and potato soup

3 tablespoons olive oil
2 cloves garlic, peeled and kept whole
1 small dried chilli
2 medium onions, peeled and very finely chopped
2 x 400g tins chopped tomatoes
4 medium potatoes, peeled and diced
2.5 litres hot water
salt
2 good handfuls dried, chunky pasta i.e. shells or penne
Parmesan cheese, freshly grated

- Warm the olive oil in a large saucepan and add the garlic and chilli. Remember not to let the oil get too hot before you add the garlic as you don't want to brown it, you just want to flavour the oil.
- Almost immediately add the chopped onion and stir to coat the onion in the oil.
- Cover the saucepan and cook the onion on a low heat until it is soft and translucent.
- Next add the tomatoes, the potatoes, half the water and a good teaspoon of salt.
- Cover the soup and cook slowly at a gentle simmer, for about 30 minutes until the potatoes are soft.
- Remove the garlic.
- Add the remaining water and the pasta and cook for 1 minute less than the time indicated on the packet so that the pasta is *al dente*.
- Check the seasoning and put the cheese on the table so that people can add it as they desire.

Cheese on toast

I am not going to patronize anyone by explaining how to make cheese on toast. You can use brown or white bread and don't think you should just stick to Cheddar cheese. Experiment with other cheese you may have in your fridge. Remember to leave the cheese under the grill until it starts to go brown, as I think this makes the difference between a good cheese on toast and a wonderful cheese on toast.

Easy beef kebabs + egg fried rice

Get the rice ready first for this meal as the beef cooks in a jiffy.

Beef kebabs

450g tender beef fillet or sirloin
2 teaspoons fresh root ginger, very finely grated
1 teaspoon garlic, peeled and finely crushed
½ teaspoon ground cumin
½ teaspoon curry powder*
¾ teaspoon salt
freshly-ground black pepper
1 dessertspoon olive oil

- Cut the meat into very thin strips, about 7cm long and about 1cm wide.
- Put the slices into a bowl and add the ginger, garlic, cumin, curry powder, salt and a good grinding of black pepper.
- Cover with cling-film and put in the fridge for 1 hour if you can but don't worry if you haven't got time for this.
- Brush a heavy frying pan with the oil and put it on a high heat.
- When hot, put in as many slices as you can, laying them flat.
- Once the meat has browned, which should only take a few seconds, turn the strips over and brown them on the other side.
- Transfer to a warm serving plate and serve with the rice.

Egg fried rice

500ml basmati rice
750ml water
2 eggs, made into an omelette and chopped up
80g frozen peas, cooked
1 shallot, finely chopped
1 raw carrot, chopped and finely diced
1 tablespoon dark soy sauce
2 teaspoons sesame oil
1 dessertspoon groundnut oil

- Place the rice in a saucepan with the water and a small pinch of salt.
- Put the saucepan on a high heat and as soon as it comes to the boil, cover the saucepan with a lid and turn the heat right down.
- Leave it on a low heat for 15 minutes.
- Remove from the heat but leave the pan covered for a further 10 minutes and allow to cool.
- Heat a wok or frying pan and add the groundnut oil and the chopped carrot and stir-fry for 1 minute.
- Remove the carrot and set aside.
- Add the shallot and again stir-fry until soft. This will take about 2 minutes.
- Now add the rice, keeping the wok temperature high, and add the other ingredients, including the carrot, stirring between each addition.

***To make your own curry powder**

1 tablespoon coriander seeds
1 dessertspoon cumin seeds
1 teaspoon fennel seeds
½ teaspoon fenugreek

- *Place the coriander seeds into a small, heavy-bottomed pan and heat through for 30 seconds.*
- *Add the other ingredients and toast until you smell the lovely aroma of the spices.*
- *Transfer the spices to a coffee grinder, a small processor or grind them in a pestle and mortar.*

Salade Niçoise
+ baked potatoes

This is my own, child-friendly version of Salade Niçoise, so it may not please true *aficionados*. I serve it on a large platter as I find that it is more attractive to children, especially the fussy ones. I set it out in sections so that the fish is separate from the lettuce and the tomatoes separate from the cucumber, and so on. This sounds mad, but if it gets the children to eat it then we can't complain. It also looks very attractive.

Salade Niçoise

1 red onion, thinly sliced and soaked in chilled water for 30 minutes
4 tomatoes, thinly sliced
anchovy fillets (2/3 per person)
½ cucumber, sliced
2 x 125g tins tuna fish, drained and broken up
handful black and green olives
250g green beans, cooked
1 crispy lettuce, shredded
2 handfuls mixed salad leaves

For the salad dressing

3 dessertspoons olive oil
1 dessertspoon balsamic/red wine vinegar
1 teaspoon Dijon mustard
salt and pepper

- Lay each ingredient out together on a large serving dish.
- Mix the ingredients for the dressing in a small bowl and drizzle over the salad.

Baked potatoes

6 baking potatoes
butter for serving
salt and pepper

- Preheat the oven to 220°C/425°F/gas 7.
- Pierce the potato skins with a sharp knife and bake for 1 hour 30 minutes.
- Split each one and serve with butter, salt and pepper.

Baked cod with tomatoes, potatoes and parsley

I know we should not be eating cod at the moment until the stocks have increased but my supermarket does not stock gurnard or pollack and there is no fishmonger near me. I buy line-caught cod, which is supposed to be better.

Baked cod

1kg potatoes, peeled and cut lengthways into quarters
1 medium onion, finely diced
2 sticks celery, finely chopped
2 cloves garlic, peeled and smashed
400g tin chopped tomatoes
3 tablespoons olive oil
juice 1 lemon
1 teaspoon sugar
salt and pepper
700g cod fillets
2 tablespoons flat-leaf parsley, chopped
1 tablespoon Parmesan, grated

- Preheat the oven to 200°C/400°F/gas 6.
- Lay the potatoes in a roasting tin along with the onion, celery, garlic and tomatoes.
- Add the olive oil, lemon juice, sugar, salt and pepper and gently mix together.
- Bake for 25 minutes.
- Turn the potatoes and return to the oven for 30 minutes.
- At the end of this time lay the fish in among the potatoes and season.
- Drizzle over another tablespoon of olive oil and cook for 10 minutes.
- Sprinkle with the parsley and the Parmesan and serve.

Chicken with rosemary + mashed potato + green peas

This is based on a recipe from Claudia Roden's *Mediterranean Cookery* and is a quick, wholesome, child-friendly meal.

Chicken with rosemary

50g butter

1 tablespoon olive oil

3 large cloves garlic, peeled and chopped in half

3 sprigs rosemary

1kg chicken thighs and drumsticks, skin removed

salt and pepper

200ml dry white wine

- Heat the butter and oil in a heavy-bottomed frying pan with the garlic and rosemary.
- When this starts to sizzle, put in half the chicken pieces and cook over a medium heat.
- To get the chicken pieces brown all over will take about 5 minutes. Resist moving the chicken too often as it won't brown.
- Cook the next batch of chicken in the same way.
- Once the chicken pieces are golden brown all over return them to the frying pan, season and add the wine.
- Once the wine has been bubbling for 1 minute turn the heat down, cover and simmer for 30 minutes.
- Serve warm with the mashed potato and green peas.

Mashed potato

1kg potatoes, peeled and quartered

salt

200ml warmed milk

40g butter

black pepper

- Place the potatoes in cold, salted water and bring to the boil. Turn the heat down to a robust simmer on a medium heat. Once the potatoes are soft but not mushy, drain them thoroughly and put them through a ricer or mash with a masher.
- Return the mashed potato to the saucepan and place over a low heat.
- Add the milk and butter and gently stir in. Check for seasoning.
- Remove from the heat.
- You can flavour the mashed potato with a little grated Parmesan cheese if you like, as this will go nicely with the chicken.

Green peas

250g frozen petits pois

fresh mint and butter for serving

- Place the peas in boiling water and drain them once cooked.
- Serve with a little butter and chopped mint.

TIP

I use a potato ricer to make mashed potato, as I have found it is the only way of removing all the lumps and it is much quicker than a masher. I also resist the temptation of cutting the potatoes into small cubes prior to cooking them, as while the potatoes may cook more quickly, I do not think they taste as good. If you don't have a ricer then use a normal masher.

Beef fillet steaks with horseradish sauce + gratin dauphinois + peas and carrots

Prepare the potatoes first as they take the longest to cook. The sauce can be done next, then the peas and carrots. The fillets can be cooked at the last moment.

Beef fillet steaks

60g butter
6 beef fillet steaks
250ml red wine
salt and pepper
For the horseradish sauce
200g crème fraîche
1 tablespoon creamed horseradish
1 dessertspoon Dijon mustard

To cook the steaks

- Warm a serving dish at an oven temperature of 110°C/225°F/gas ¼.
- Melt half the butter in a sauté or frying pan.
- Fry the fillet steaks three at a time in the butter for 2 minutes on each side for medium rare. Adjust the time accordingly if you prefer your meat rare or well done.
- Place the three steaks in the warm serving dish while you cook the rest.
- Once you have cooked all the steaks keep them warm and return the sauté pan to a high heat.
- Pour in the wine and let this sizzle away for 1 minute.
- Now add the rest of the butter and stir this in over the heat.
- Pour the sauce over the steaks and serve with a dollop of horseradish sauce on the top of each steak.

To make the horseradish sauce

- In a small bowl mix together the horseradish sauce ingredients.

Gratin dauphinois

1kg waxy potatoes, peeled and sliced to the thickness of a pound coin
1 clove garlic, peeled and left whole
salt and pepper
100g Gruyère cheese, grated
75g butter
200ml milk
nutmeg

- Preheat the oven to 170°C/325°F/gas 3.
- Rinse the potatoes in cold water and pat them dry with kitchen paper.
- Butter an ovenproof gratin dish.
- Rub the garlic clove over the buttered dish.
- Layer half the potatoes on the bottom of the dish.
- Season them with salt and pepper. Sprinkle over half the cheese and half the butter cut into small pieces.
- Arrange the remaining potatoes on top and season with salt and pepper.
- Sprinkle on the remaining cheese and the rest of the butter, again in little pieces.
- Pour on the milk and sprinkle on a grating of nutmeg.
- Bake for 1 hour 30 minutes.

Peas and carrots

300g fresh peas
300g carrots, peeled and thinly sliced
30g butter
salt and pepper

- Place the vegetables in a small saucepan along with the butter.
- As the butter melts reduce the heat to low. Cover and cook for 5 minutes until tender, stirring them occasionally without letting them brown.
- Season with salt and pepper and serve.

American apple pie

American apple pie is quite different from the English variety. I really enjoyed this when we had it one Sunday.

American apple pie

For the pastry

250g self-raising flour

salt

170g butter, chilled and cubed

1 tablespoon lemon juice

2–3 tablespoons water

For the filling

6 eating apples, peeled, cored and quartered

1 tablespoon caster sugar

1 tablespoon cornflour

1 teaspoon cinnamon

juice 1 lemon

20g butter, cubed

1 beaten egg to glaze

To make the pastry

- Place the flour and a pinch of salt together in a food processor bowl.
- Add the butter and process to a breadcrumb consistency.
- Add the lemon juice and the water gradually, blending as you go, as you may not need all the water.
- Turn the mixture out onto a work surface and form it into a ball.
- Wrap the pastry in cling-film and place it in the fridge to chill for 20 minutes.

To make the pie

- Preheat the oven to 220°C/425°F/gas 7.
- Grease a pie dish or tin.
- Place the apples in a bowl with the sugar, cornflour, cinnamon, lemon juice and butter and mix around with your hands so that the apples are coated all over.
- Roll out half the pastry and line the pie tin with it.
- Pile the apples onto the base of the pie and cover with the other piece of rolled out pastry.
- Cut a couple of slits in the pie and glaze the pastry with a beaten egg.
- Place the pie on a baking tray and bake for 30 minutes.
- Serve with ice cream.

Almond gingerbread
+ caramel custard

This cake is dazzlingly easy to make and tastes delicious. The custard perks it up a bit as it becomes a little dry if it is not eaten straightaway.

Almond gingerbread

200g plain flour
1 teaspoon bicarbonate of soda
1 teaspoon ground ginger
25g ground almonds
50g blanched almonds, roughly chopped
85g butter
85g brown sugar
85g golden syrup
1 egg
6 tablespoons milk

- Grease and line an 18cm square cake tin.
- Preheat the oven to 160°C/320°F/gas 2½.
- Sift the flour, bicarbonate of soda and ground ginger into a mixing bowl.
- Add the ground almonds and the chopped almonds to the flour and other ingredients in the mixing bowl.
- Place the butter, sugar and syrup in a saucepan and heat until the butter has melted.
- Pour this liquid mixture into the flour mixture and beat well.
- Add the egg and the milk and pour into the cake tin.
- Bake for 55 minutes.
- Test with a skewer, if it comes out clean the cake is done. Turn out once cooled.

Caramel custard

6 egg yolks
60g soft brown sugar
250ml full fat milk
250ml double cream
1 teaspoon vanilla extract

- Place the egg yolks and the sugar in a glass bowl.
- Whisk the eggs and sugar with a hand whisk for 2 minutes.
- Pour the milk and cream into a measuring jug.
- Add the vanilla.
- Heat the milk and cream in a microwave on high for 2 minutes. You want the milk and cream to be almost at boiling point.
- Place the glass bowl over a saucepan of simmering water. Make sure the water does not touch the bottom of the bowl.
- Add the milk and cream to the egg yolks, stirring all the time with a wooden spoon to avoid lumps.
- Keep stirring for 10 minutes by which time you should have a good consistency. An indication of when the custard is thick enough is that it will coat the back of the wooden spoon. It will not be as thick as shop-bought custard.
- Avoid reheating home-made custard, as it may curdle.

Week 5

Shopping list

MEAT

- ☐ 1kg chicken thighs and drumsticks
- ☐ 1.7kg leg lamb
- ☐ 500g minced beef
- ☐ 1kg diced leg lamb

FISH

- ☐ 6 mackerel fillets

VEGETABLES

- ☐ 650g carrots
- ☐ 200g broccoli
- ☐ 250g purple sprouting broccoli
- ☐ 200g Brussels sprouts
- ☐ 1 red pepper
- ☐ 5 onions
- ☐ 1 red onion
- ☐ 1 bunch celery
- ☐ 220g watercress
- ☐ 1 seasonal cabbage or curly kale
- ☐ 4.5kg potatoes
- ☐ 1 garlic bulb
- ☐ ½ cucumber
- ☐ 4 tomatoes
- ☐ 1 parsnip
- ☐ 1 leek

FRUIT

- ☐ 4 lemons

FRESH HERBS

- ☐ thyme
- ☐ flat-leaf parsley
- ☐ bay leaves
- ☐ coriander

FRIDGE ITEMS

- ☐ 3 packs butter
- ☐ 12 eggs
- ☐ 1.5 litres chicken stock
- ☐ 100g soft goat's cheese
- ☐ 100g Gruyère cheese
- ☐ 100g Cheddar cheese
- ☐ 1 standard pack feta cheese
- ☐ 300g frozen petits pois
- ☐ 200g crème fraîche
- ☐ 950ml milk
- ☐ 1 pack puff pastry
- ☐ 100g sliced pancetta

KITCHEN CUPBOARD ITEMS

- ☐ 12 pitted black olives
- ☐ 150ml red wine
- ☐ 1 bottle dry white wine
- ☐ 400g tin chopped tomatoes
- ☐ 400g tin chickpeas
- ☐ tomato purée
- ☐ 150g dried porcini mushrooms
- ☐ baking powder
- ☐ salt
- ☐ olive oil
- ☐ 475g plain flour
- ☐ balsamic vinegar
- ☐ 1 box beef stock cubes
- ☐ 1 box chicken stock cubes
- ☐ 150g icing sugar
- ☐ 435g caster sugar
- ☐ 100g white chocolate
- ☐ 100g good quality dark chocolate
- ☐ 1 jar instant coffee
- ☐ 40g cornflour
- ☐ vanilla essence
- ☐ Dijon mustard
- ☐ horseradish sauce
- ☐ 1 French loaf

SPICES

- ☐ pepper
- ☐ cumin seeds
- ☐ coriander seeds
- ☐ ground cinnamon
- ☐ whole nutmeg
- ☐ dried oregano
- ☐ cloves

Vegetable soup
+ goat's cheese and pancetta crostini

Unless I am making soup for a special occasion, such as a dinner party, I do not tend to follow a recipe but just use it as a means of finishing odds and ends in the fridge. It's a good way of getting the children to eat vegetables they would not normally eat, such as sprouts, red peppers and cabbage and of using up on a Monday the leftover vegetables from the Sunday roast.

Vegetable soup

100g Brussels sprouts, destalked, peeled and halved
1 red pepper, deseeded and roughly chopped
100g carrots, peeled and chopped
1 onion, peeled and roughly chopped
2 sticks celery, roughly chopped
50g watercress
a handful of cabbage or curly kale
any cold vegetables from the day before, or a large potato peeled and chopped
40g unsalted butter
1.5 litres chicken stock
salt and pepper
flat-leaf parsley, chopped

- Put all the vegetables in a large, heavy-bottomed saucepan with the butter.
- Cover the pan and on a low heat cook the vegetables for 10 minutes, taking care to stir them occasionally so they do not stick.
- Pour over enough of the stock to cover the vegetables. You may like the soup to be thicker or thinner, so experiment accordingly. Remember you can always add a little more stock at the end if you wish.
- Cover the soup and cook for 40 minutes until all the vegetables are soft.
- Remove the soup from the heat and blend it in a liquidiser or a food processor. Alternatively, use a hand-held blender, which will save you the bother of having to wash up the liquidiser or food processor afterwards.
- Once you have the soup as smooth as you like check the seasoning.
- When ready to serve, add the chopped parsley.

Goat's cheese and pancetta crostini

1 baguette
100g soft goat's cheese, such as Soignon
100g sliced pancetta

- Preheat the grill.
- Slice the baguette width-ways into 1cm thick discs.
- Place the bread on the rack of the grill pan and toast it gently on one side.
- Spread the untoasted side with the cheese.
- Meanwhile, fry the sliced pancetta and then cut it into little pieces and set aside.
- Place the goat's cheese toast under the grill for a few seconds until melted.
- Place a piece of pancetta on each one as they are finished.
- Serve with the warm soup.

Fried chicken pieces + feta and chickpea salad + gratin dauphinois

This is one of the first recipes I wrote for this book and it captures what I was trying to achieve when the book was conceived; simple, heart-warming food that makes you glad the day is coming to an end and you are home to enjoy time with your loved ones.

Fried chicken pieces

1–2 tablespoons olive oil
2 sprigs fresh thyme
1kg chicken thighs and drumsticks, skin removed
knob of butter
juice 1 lemon

- Heat the oil in a heavy-bottomed frying pan with the thyme until hot.
- Place as many chicken pieces into the saucepan as will fit. Keep the heat high and cover the pan.
- Fry the chicken for 2 minutes, without moving the pieces around, as you want each side to become beautifully brown and crispy.
- Turn the chicken pieces and fry for another 2 minutes without moving them.
- Remove the chicken pieces from the pan when they are brown. Carry on until all the chicken pieces are golden.
- Return all the chicken pieces to the pan.
- Turn the heat down to medium, cover and cook for approximately 30 minutes, turning occasionally.
- When you are ready to serve the chicken, remove the joints from the pan and turn the heat up high.
- Add the knob of butter to the pan and, when it is melting and beginning to bubble, scrape all the chicken bits and juices together.
- Add the lemon juice and stir.
- Pour the sauce over the chicken.

continues

Gratin dauphinois

1kg waxy potatoes, peeled and sliced to the thickness of a pound coin
1 clove of garlic, peeled and left whole
salt and pepper
100g Gruyère cheese, grated
75g butter
200ml milk
nutmeg

- Preheat the oven to 170°C/325°F/gas 3.
- Rinse the potatoes in cold water and pat them dry with kitchen paper.
- Butter an ovenproof gratin dish.
- Rub the garlic clove over the buttered dish.
- Layer half the potatoes on the bottom of the dish.
- Season them with salt and pepper. Sprinkle over half the cheese and half the butter cut into small pieces.
- Arrange the remaining potatoes on top and season with salt and pepper.
- Sprinkle on the remaining cheese and the rest of the butter, again in little pieces.
- Pour on the milk and sprinkle on a grating of nutmeg.
- Bake for 1 hour 30 minutes.

Feta and chickpea salad

1 standard pack feta cheese, cubed
½ cucumber, cubed
4 tomatoes, cubed
12 pitted black olives, halved
bunch fresh coriander, roughly chopped
400g tin chickpeas, drained
1 red onion, sliced thinly and soaked in cold water for 30 minutes
For the dressing
3 dessertspoons olive oil
1 dessertspoon balsamic vinegar
salt and pepper

- Place all the salad ingredients in a serving bowl.
- To dress, mix the oil and vinegar together in a small bowl and season with salt and pepper.
- Drizzle the dressing over the salad.

TIP

You can be creative with this salad and add more of one ingredient if you like or more herbs and green peppers.

Vegetable pie
+ watercress salad

It is important to give your body a rest from meat at least once a week. This is difficult to achieve when you have children, as 'no meat' generally means 'vegetables'. I think this vegetable pie goes some way to convincing children and meat-loving adults that vegetarian meals can be great.

Vegetable pie

1 tablespoon olive oil
1 onion, finely chopped
500g potatoes, peeled, quartered and cooked in salted water until tender
200g frozen petits pois, defrosted
100g Brussels sprouts, finely sliced
2 heaped tablespoons crème fraîche
1 heaped teaspoon Dijon mustard
1 tablespoon horseradish sauce
100g Cheddar cheese, grated
2 tablespoons flat-leaf parsley, chopped
salt and pepper
1 pack puff pastry
1 egg yolk for sealing and glazing

- Preheat the oven to 200°C/400°F/gas 6.
- Heat the oil in a large sauté pan.
- Add the onion and cook for 7 minutes until softened.
- Add the potatoes, peas and sprouts to the onion and cook for 5 minutes, stirring occasionally.
- Spoon on the crème fraîche, mustard and horseradish sauce.
- Remove from the heat, and sprinkle on the cheese and parsley.
- Check for seasoning and adjust if necessary.
- Roll out the pastry to a rectangle measuring approximately 30 x 40cm.
- Place the pastry on a large baking sheet.
- Pile the vegetable filling onto one half of the pastry, leaving a 2cm margin round the edge.
- Using a pastry brush, brush the edge of the pastry with the egg yolk.
- Fold the pastry over so that the pie is sealed.
- Glaze the top of the pie with the rest of the egg.
- Bake for 30 minutes.

Watercress salad

1 bag watercress
salt and pepper
1 tablespoon olive oil

- Place the watercress in a serving bowl and dress with the salt, pepper and olive oil.

Lamb and potato stew
+ buttered carrots

A lamb stew means a quick stew, so is ideal for a midweek meal.

Lamb and potato stew

150g dried porcini mushrooms
2 tablespoons olive oil
1kg diced leg of lamb
1 onion, finely chopped
2 tablespoons tomato purée
750g potatoes, peeled and quartered
1 bay leaf
400ml meat stock (a cube will do)
salt and pepper
2 tablespoons flat-leaf parsley, chopped

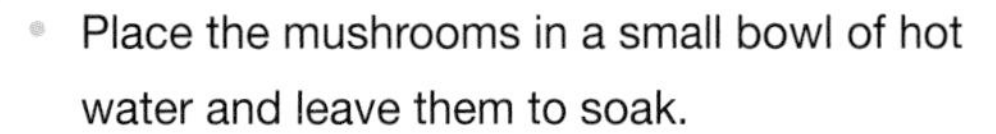

- Place the mushrooms in a small bowl of hot water and leave them to soak.
- Warm the olive oil in a large heavy-bottomed saucepan.
- Brown the meat in batches and set aside.
- Keep the pan on the heat and add the onion to the same oil, cooking them for 5 minutes.
- Drain the mushrooms, retaining the water, and add the mushrooms to the onions.
- Sauté the mushrooms and onions on a low heat for 5 minutes.
- Return the meat to the pan and add the tomato purée, potatoes and bay leaf.
- Add the mushroom water and the stock and bring to a simmer. Season.
- Cover and simmer on a low heat for 1 hour 30 minutes.
- Sprinkle with parsley to serve.

Buttered carrots

300g carrots, peeled and cut into 5mm slices
10g butter
salt and pepper

- Place the carrots in a saucepan with the butter on a low heat.
- Cover and cook the carrots, stirring occasionally for 10 minutes, until the carrots are soft.
- Season with salt and pepper.

Mackerel in mustard sauce + boiled potatoes + purple sprouting broccoli

Oily fish should be part of a family's weekly diet. Mackeral is perfect as it is readily available and reasonably priced. As it is so oily, it needs to be served with a sauce that counter-acts its flavour. This is a version of the recipe in Sophie Grigson's book *Fish*. I was too scared to attempt to cook fish dishes before I found this book. I took a gamble when I first cooked this meal for my children, thinking they could well rebel and refuse to eat it, but they surprised me and wolfed down the lot.

Mackerel in mustard sauce

6 mackerel fillets
salt and pepper
1 onion, chopped finely
2 sprigs thyme
1 sprig flat-leafed parsley
1 bay leaf
150ml dry white wine
2 tablespoons Dijon mustard
45g butter
fresh parsley or chervil, chopped

- Preheat oven to 240°C/475°F/gas 9.
- Season the mackerel fillets with salt and pepper.
- Lightly grease an ovenproof dish and make a bed of the onion, thyme, parsley and bay to lay the fish fillets upon, skin side up.
- Pour the wine over the fish and bake uncovered for 9 minutes.
- Remove the dish from the oven and keep the fish warm while you prepare the sauce.
- Strain the cooking juices from the fish into a small saucepan, discarding the onion and other bits.
- Boil the liquid on a high heat for 1 minute.
- Add the mustard and butter and whisk until the butter melts.
- Simmer for 2 minutes and then spoon the sauce over the fish and sprinkle with the herbs.

Boiled potatoes

800g potatoes, peeled and quartered
salt
butter for serving
black pepper

- Boil the potatoes in plenty of salted water until tender.
- Drain the potatoes and then return them to the saucepan, along with the butter.
- Season with a good grinding of black pepper.

Purple sprouting broccoli

250g purple sprouting broccoli
salt and pepper
a little butter

- Boil a saucepan of water.
- Add the broccoli and simmer for 3 minutes.
- Drain and season with salt, pepper and a little butter.

TIP

If you are using broccoli with all its leaf and not the pre-prepared supermarket stuff, then discard most of the foliage for the compost, as it does not become tender as quickly as the florets. Also, if the vegetables are nice and fresh they will not need any salt when cooking. You can season them when you serve them.

Meat and vegetable lasagne

Most people like lasagne as it is comfort food and is easy eating. I have changed the traditional recipe here by including more English seasonal vegetables in the quest for variety, but I hope I have not lost the essence of why people love lasagne.

For the filling

2 tablespoons olive oil
1 onion, finely chopped
1 stick celery, finely chopped
1 carrot, peeled and cubed
1 clove garlic, peeled and chopped
1 parsnip, peeled and cubed
3 medium potatoes, peeled and cut into 2cm cubes
1 leek, cut into 1cm slices
500g minced beef
150ml milk
150ml red wine
400g tin chopped tomatoes
100g frozen peas
½ teaspoon of dried oregano
salt and pepper

For the Béchamel sauce

600ml milk
1 onion, peeled and studded with 4 cloves
1 bay leaf
60g butter
1 tablespoon plain flour
salt and pepper
nutmeg

To make the filling

- Heat the olive oil in a large saucepan.
- Add the onion, celery, carrot, garlic, parsnip, potatoes and leek.
- Cover and sweat them over a low heat for 5 minutes, stirring occasionally.
- Add the minced beef and stir continuously until it is browned all over, breaking up the meat while it browns.
- Add the milk and simmer vigorously for 5 minutes.
- Add the wine and simmer vigorously for 5 minutes.
- Add the tomatoes and the peas and lower the heat to a very gentle simmer.
- Add the oregano, and season well with salt and pepper.
- Cover the meat and vegetables and let them simmer gently for an hour.
- You can prepare the Béchamel sauce in the meantime.

To make the Béchamel sauce

- Place the onion and bay leaf in a saucepan with the milk and bring to the boil.
- Remove from the heat and cover, letting the onion and bay leaf flavours infuse the milk for 15–20 minutes.
- Melt the butter in a separate saucepan and add the flour, stirring round for a few minutes.
- Add the milk a little at a time, stirring continuously.
- Season with salt, pepper and nutmeg.
- Bring to the boil and then turn the heat down to a minimum and cook for 20 minutes, stirring occasionally.

To assemble the lasagne

- Preheat the oven to 200°C/400°F/gas 6.
- Spread half the meat sauce on the bottom of an ovenproof dish.
- Follow with a layer of the lasagne sheets, half the Béchamel sauce and a sprinkling of Parmesan cheese.
- Repeat with the rest of the meat sauce, another layer of lasagne sheets, the rest of the Béchamel sauce, and finish with a sprinkling of Parmesan cheese.
- Bake for 30 minutes.

Roast spiced lamb + crispy potatoes + carrots and broccoli

For this recipe I bought a 1.7kg leg of New Zealand lamb. The potato recipe gives you beautifully crisp potatoes with little fuss and they go very well with the roast lamb. It's also a good chance to use all those small potatoes that get left because you usually grab the big ones to avoid fiddly peeling.

Roast spiced lamb

1.7kg leg of lamb
2 teaspoons cumin seeds
1 teaspoon coriander seeds
¼ teaspoon ground cinnamon
1 teaspoon salt
1 tablespoon olive oil

For the gravy

1 dessertspoon plain flour
200ml white wine
250ml meat or chicken stock (a stock cube will do)

To cook the lamb

- Preheat the oven to 230°C/450°F/gas 8.
- Place the joint of lamb into a roasting tin.
- Combine the cumin, coriander, cinnamon and salt using a pestle and mortar and grind to a rough powder. Don't worry about getting it too fine.
- Pour the olive oil onto the lamb and sprinkle over the spices, pressing them onto the lamb with your fingers.

continues

- Place the meat in the oven for 15 minutes and then reduce the temperature to 180°C/350°F/ gas 4 and cook for another 45 minutes.
- This should ensure you end up with the lamb cooked to medium.

To make the gravy

- Remove the meat from the roasting tin, placing the joint on a warm plate.
- Place the roasting tin on the stove on a medium heat. Sprinkle on the flour and stir round to loosen the bits from the pan and to soak up the fat from the meat.
- Add the white wine and simmer for 2 minutes.
- Add the meat or chicken stock.
- Bring to a simmer and cook for 10 minutes, stirring occasionally.

Crispy potatoes

1kg smallish potatoes
salt
2 tablespoons olive oil
pepper
some fresh thyme leaves

- Preheat the oven to 240°C/475°F/gas 9.
- Remove the eyes from the potatoes, but don't peel them. Place them in salted water and bring to the boil.
- Simmer them for 15 minutes until they are just about cooked.
- Once the potatoes have been drained, place them on a lightly-oiled baking sheet.
- Squash each potato flat, either with a potato masher or a meat mallet. They may break up a little but just squash them back together.
- Drizzle a little olive oil on the top of each potato and sprinkle each one with salt, pepper and thyme leaves.
- Bake for 20 minutes until golden and crisp.

Carrots and broccoli

10g butter
250g carrots, peeled and sliced to 5mm thickness
200g prepared broccoli florets
salt and pepper

- Melt the butter in a saucepan and add the carrots. Turn the heat to low and cook the carrots covered for 10 minutes, stirring occasionally.
- Add the broccoli and two tablespoons of water.
- Bring back to a high heat until you hear the butter and water fizzing.
- Reduce the heat, cover and cook for 10 more minutes.
- Season with salt and pepper and serve.

Lemon meringue pie

Lemon meringue pie has gone out of fashion recently, and I have to admit that I don't cook it very often. It is always a surprise, however, when I do make it as we all really enjoy it.

For the pastry

180g butter, cold from the fridge and cut into cubes
75g icing sugar
2 egg yolks
225g plain flour

For the lemon filling

3 lemons, zested and juiced
40g cornflour
300ml water
2 egg yolks
85g caster sugar
50g butter, diced

For the topping

4 egg whites
150g caster sugar

To make the pastry case

- Preheat the oven to 200°C/400°F/gas 6.
- Place all the pastry ingredients in the bowl of a food processor.
- Process the ingredients together until they begin to form a ball of dough.
- Turn the dough out onto a floured surface and combine into a smooth ball.
- Wrap in cling-film and chill in the fridge for 30 minutes.
- Grease a 22cm loose-based flan tin.
- Roll out the chilled pastry and line the flan tin with it.
- Place a sheet of greaseproof paper on top of the pastry and on top of this pour some baking beans.
- Bake for 15 minutes.
- Remove the beans and the greaseproof paper and bake the pastry case for a further 5 minutes.
- Remove the pastry case from the oven and set aside.
- Reduce the oven temperature to 180°C/350°F/ gas 4.

To prepare the filling

- Place the grated zest and lemon juice in a saucepan.
- Add the cornflour and 2 tablespoons of the water and stir.
- Bring the rest of the water to the boil in a saucepan.
- Stir the boiling water into the lemon and cornflour mixture.
- Keep on the heat, stirring constantly, until the mixture boils again.
- Reduce the heat and simmer for 1 minute.
- Remove the pan from the heat and stir in the egg yolks, sugar and then the diced butter.
- Spoon the filling into the pastry case.
- Whisk the egg whites until you have soft peaks forming.
- Add the sugar a tablespoon at a time and whisk until you have a stiff shiny meringue.
- Spread the meringue over the lemon filling and bake for 15 minutes.

TIP

To make the topping: *The key to whisking egg whites successfully is to make sure your whisk and the bowl you are using are grease free. If you are not sure, wipe the whisk and the bowl with a cut half of lemon.*

Chocolate sponge with white chocolate filling

White chocolate makes a lovely filling for this cake. The contrasting colours are quite striking too. There's nothing quite like the sight of a home-made chocolate cake waiting to be sliced.

For the sponge
200g plain flour
a scant teaspoon of baking powder
200g butter, softened
200g caster sugar
3 eggs
100g good quality dark chocolate
2 teaspoons vanilla essence
1 dessertspoon instant coffee, dissolved in 4 tablespoons boiling water

For the filling
50g butter
100g white chocolate
75g icing sugar, sifted
1 teaspoon vanilla essence

To make the sponge

- Preheat oven to 180°C/350°F/gas 4.
- Grease and line two 20cm sandwich cake tins.
- Sift the flour and baking powder together in a bowl and set aside.
- Beat the butter and sugar together in a food processor or electric mixer for 5 minutes, until white and fluffy.
- Add one tablespoon of the sifted flour and baking powder and one of the eggs.
- Mix together.
- Add each of the remaining eggs in the same manner with a tablespoon of flour each time.
- Add the remaining flour and gently fold it in with a metal spoon.
- Melt the chocolate over a small saucepan of simmering water.
- Add the melted chocolate, vanilla and coffee to the cake mixture and fold in gently.
- Spoon the mixture evenly between the cake tins and bake for 20 minutes.
- Remove the cakes from the oven, checking that they are cooked by inserting a skewer into the middle of each. If the skewer comes away cleanly then the cakes are cooked.
- Remove the cakes from the tins and place on a cooling rack.
- When cool fill with the mixture below.

To make the filling

- Place the butter and chocolate in a small glass bowl.
- Put the glass bowl over a saucepan of simmering water and let both melt, stirring occasionally.
- Remove the glass bowl from the heat and add the icing sugar and vanilla essence.
- Spread the filling on the top of one of the cakes and make a sandwich with the other cake.
- Decorate the top of the cake with some sifted icing sugar.

FEBRUARY

Week 1

Monday p72	Chicken and chickpea stew
Tuesday p73	Coconut marinated sea bream + sautéed potatoes + tomato and cucumber salad
Wednesday p74	Red pepper soup + smoked mackerel paté on toast
Thursday p75	Macaroni with crème fraîche and pancetta + green salad
Friday p76	Chicken tikka + yellow rice
Saturday p78	Provençal meat stew + mashed potato + purple sprouting broccoli
Sunday p79	Ham baked in Madeira + buttered celeriac and swede + baked potatoes
Sunday pudding p80	Baked mocha cheesecake
Extra tasty treat p81	Coffee walnut puddings

Shopping list

MEAT

- ☐ 1.5kg gammon joint
- ☐ 1.5kg shin beef
- ☐ 22 pieces chicken

FISH

- ☐ 3 whole sea bream

VEGETABLES

- ☐ 500g carrots
- ☐ 3kg potatoes
- ☐ 6 baking potatoes
- ☐ 1 garlic bulb
- ☐ 1 small celeriac
- ☐ 1 small swede
- ☐ 7 onions
- ☐ 2 red onions
- ☐ 2 green chillies
- ☐ 250g purple sprouting broccoli
- ☐ fresh ginger
- ☐ 23 tomatoes
- ☐ 1 cucumber
- ☐ 1 avocado pear
- ☐ 200g young spinach leaves
- ☐ 6 red peppers

FRUIT

- ☐ 1 orange
- ☐ 1 lemon

FRESH HERBS

- ☐ thyme
- ☐ bay leaves
- ☐ flat-leaf parsley
- ☐ basil
- ☐ rosemary

FRIDGE ITEMS

- ☐ 2 packs butter
- ☐ 230g mascarpone cheese
- ☐ 100g Parmesan cheese
- ☐ 150ml double cream
- ☐ 300ml milk
- ☐ 525ml natural yoghurt
- ☐ 4 eggs
- ☐ 600ml fresh beef stock
- ☐ 100g chopped pancetta
- ☐ 150g frozen petits pois
- ☐ 325g crème fraîche
- ☐ 140g smoked mackerel
- ☐ 200g cream cheese
- ☐ 100g chorizo sausage

KITCHEN CUPBOARD ITEMS

- ☐ 150g self-raising flour
- ☐ 1 jar instant coffee
- ☐ salt
- ☐ olive oil
- ☐ extra virgin olive oil
- ☐ balsamic vinegar
- ☐ 200g light brown muscovado sugar
- ☐ 85g caster sugar
- ☐ 50g broken walnut pieces
- ☐ 45g ground almonds
- ☐ 50g good quality milk chocolate
- ☐ 60g plain chocolate
- ☐ cocoa powder
- ☐ 1 tablespoon amaretto liqueur
- ☐ 100ml dry sherry
- ☐ 200ml Madeira wine
- ☐ 225g digestive biscuits
- ☐ 400ml tin coconut milk
- ☐ 500g basmati rice
- ☐ 50g sultanas
- ☐ 1 bottle red table wine
- ☐ 400g tin chopped tomatoes
- ☐ 2 x 400g tins chickpeas
- ☐ tomato purée
- ☐ pumpkin seeds
- ☐ 100g raisins
- ☐ 500g macaroni
- ☐ Dijon mustard
- ☐ horseradish sauce
- ☐ 1 loaf brown bread

SPICES

- ☐ paprika
- ☐ allspice
- ☐ cardamom pods
- ☐ cinnamon sticks
- ☐ cloves
- ☐ fennel seeds
- ☐ saffron threads
- ☐ coriander seeds
- ☐ cumin seeds
- ☐ fennel seeds
- ☐ fenugreek
- ☐ turmeric
- ☐ cayenne pepper
- ☐ black mustard seeds
- ☐ black pepper
- ☐ curry powder

Chicken and chickpea stew

This is an incredibly easy recipe. The meal will be ready and on the table within about 50 minutes of starting it.

1 tablespoon olive oil
25g butter
10 chicken pieces, thighs or drumsticks, skin removed
100g chorizo sausage, sliced into 5mm thick pieces
300g carrots, peeled and chopped into bite-size pieces
500g potatoes, peeled and chopped into bite-size pieces
2 cloves garlic, peeled and smashed with the flat of a knife
2 x 400g tins chickpeas, drained
1 sprig fresh thyme
1 bay leaf
1 teaspoon paprika
100ml dry sherry
250ml water
salt and pepper

- Heat the olive oil and butter in a large saucepan.
- Add the chicken pieces and brown them all over.
- Set the chicken pieces aside but keep the saucepan on the heat.
- Fry the chorizo in the oil and butter.
- Add the vegetables, chickpeas, herbs, paprika and the sherry.
- Let the sherry sizzle away for 1 minute.
- Return the chicken to the pan and add the water.
- Bring to a simmer, season and cook covered on a slow simmer for 40 minutes.
- Check for seasoning once more before serving.

Coconut marinated sea bream + sautéed potatoes + tomato and cucumber salad

This recipe comes from Sophie Grigson's *Fish* book (with some small alterations). Its simplicity appeals, as do the refreshing flavours at this time of year, when one's palate is becoming jaded by winter comfort foods.

Coconut marinated sea bream

2 medium onions, finely chopped
4 cloves garlic, peeled and finely chopped
1 green chilli, deseeded and halved
400ml tin coconut milk
2 tablespoons natural yoghurt
3 whole sea bream, descaled with fins removed

- To make the marinade place the onions, garlic, green chilli, coconut milk and yoghurt into a roasting tin and mix to combine.
- Cut 2 deep slashes into each side of the fish.
- Place the fish in the marinade and using your hands or a wooden spoon make sure the fish get completely coated in the liquid.
- Set aside for 1–3 hours, turning the fish occasionally in the marinade.
- Preheat the grill and when hot place the fish under it, quite close to the heat. Cook each side of the fish until the skin crisps and browns. With an average sized bream this takes about 7 minutes on each side. To see whether the fish is cooked test it with the tip of a knife and if the fish comes away easily from the bone then it is done. If the inside needs more cooking, lower the shelf in the grill and continue to cook for a minute or two longer, but be careful, as there is little worse than overcooked fish.

Sautéed potatoes

1 tablespoon olive oil
1kg potatoes, peeled and cut into 1cm cubes
1 teaspoon black mustard seeds
½ teaspoon curry powder (shop-bought will do)
1 teaspoon salt

- Heat the oil in a large frying pan.
- When hot add the potatoes and cook them on a medium heat until tender on the inside and brown on the outside. This takes about 25–30 minutes.
- Add the mustard seeds, curry powder and salt and when you hear the first pop of the mustard seeds, the potatoes are ready to serve.

Tomato and cucumber salad

4 tomatoes, finely sliced
½ cucumber, finely sliced
squeeze of lemon juice
salt and pepper

- Combine the tomatoes and cucmber in a small serving bowl.
- Squeeze on the lemon juice and season with salt and pepper.

Red pepper soup
+ smoked mackerel paté on toast

This is a soup full of goodness, which children should like due to the sweetness of the peppers.

Red pepper soup

1 tablespoon olive oil
6 red peppers, cored and deseeded
15 medium tomatoes, chopped
2 red onions, sliced
1 teaspoon fresh rosemary leaves, finely chopped
2 cloves garlic, peeled and smashed with the flat of a knife
water
salt and pepper
1 tablespoon crème fraîche

- Heat the olive oil in a large saucepan.
- Add the peppers, tomatoes, onions, rosemary and garlic and sauté on a gentle heat for 15 minutes.
- Add enough water to just cover everything and bring the pan to a simmer.
- Cover and simmer the soup gently for 20 minutes.
- Blitz the soup with a hand blender or food processor and then pass it through a sieve with the help of a wooden spoon.
- Return the soup to the saucepan and season with salt and pepper to taste.
- Warm through and add the crème fraîche.

Smoked mackerel paté

140g smoked mackerel, skin removed
200g cream cheese
1 dessertspoon horseradish sauce
1 tablespoon flat-leaf parsley, chopped

- Place the mackerel in the bowl of a food processor and process until the fish is paste-like.
- Add the cream cheese, horseradish sauce and the parsley and serve on warm brown toast.

Macaroni with crème fraîche and pancetta + green salad

This is a great recipe when you are pushed for time, which we all are at some point. It takes no longer to make than a saucepan of macaroni takes to cook. Serve it with a fresh green salad.

Macaroni with crème fraîche and pancetta

500g macaroni
1 tablespoon olive oil
100g chopped pancetta
150g frozen petits pois
300g crème fraîche
1 teaspoon Dijon mustard
100g Parmesan cheese, freshly grated
salt and pepper

- Boil a large saucepan of well-salted water.
- Cook the macaroni according to the packet instructions, checking to see whether it is cooked 1 minute before the time stated on the packet.
- Take a frying pan and warm the olive oil on a medium heat.
- Add the pancetta and fry until golden brown.
- Add the frozen peas and stir round.
- Add 4 tablespoons of water and simmer for 1 minute or until the water has boiled away.
- Remove the saucepan from the heat and stir in the crème fraîche, Dijon mustard and all but a handful of the Parmesan cheese.
- When the macaroni is cooked pour the sauce over it and spoon the entire mixture into a gratin dish.
- Season with a good grinding of pepper and a little more salt.
- Sprinkle with the remaining Parmesan cheese, drizzle with a little more olive oil and place under a hot grill for 5 minutes when you are ready to serve.

Green salad

a few handfuls young spinach leaves
5 or 6 fresh basil leaves, torn
4 tomatoes, quartered
½ cucumber, sliced
1 avocado pear, de-stoned and chopped up into chunks
1 handful pumpkin seeds
1 handful raisins

For the dressing

2 dessertspoons extra virgin olive oil
2 teaspoons balsamic vinegar
salt and pepper

- Place the salad ingredients in a serving bowl.
- Mix the dressing ingredients together in a small bowl and then pour the dressing over the salad when you are ready to eat.

Chicken tikka
+ yellow rice

This well known chicken dish has two parts to its cooking process. First, the tandoori stage and then the tikka stage. It takes a while but is worth it.

Chicken tikka

First Part

For the marinade

1 onion, roughly chopped
1 clove garlic, peeled and chopped
1 green chilli, deseeded and roughly chopped
500ml natural yoghurt
2 teaspoons curry powder*
12 pieces chicken, i.e. thighs and drumsticks, with skin removed

Second Part

2 tablespoons olive oil
5 cardamom pods
2cm piece cinnamon stick
1 onion, finely chopped
2cm piece fresh ginger, peeled and finely chopped
1 clove garlic, peeled and finely chopped
1 teaspoon ground cumin
1 teaspoon ground coriander
¼ teaspoon turmeric
¼ teaspoon cayenne pepper
1 tablespoon ground paprika
2 tablespoons tinned chopped tomatoes
1 teaspoon tomato purée
1 teaspoon curry powder*
200ml water
salt

To prepare the first part

- Whizz the onion, garlic, chilli, yoghurt and curry powder in a food processor to a smooth paste to make the marinade.
- Cut a couple of slashes in each piece of chicken with a sharp knife.
- Place the chicken in a large bowl and pour the marinade over it.
- Put in the fridge for at least an hour, the longer the better.
- Preheat the oven to its maximum temperature 30 minutes before the chicken is ready.

To prepare the second part

- Heat the olive oil in a large frying pan until hot and then add the cardamom pods and the cinnamon stick.
- Stir once and add the onion.
- Fry the onion for 3 minutes on a medium heat until the edges of the onion start to brown.
- Add the ginger and garlic and fry for 1 minute.
- Add the cumin, coriander, turmeric, cayenne and paprika and stir round for 30 seconds. Remove from the heat and set aside for a moment.
- Remove the chicken pieces from the marinade, making sure you retain the marinade.
- Place the chicken pieces on a shallow roasting tin and bake for 25 minutes.
- Add the remaining marinade to the onion and spice mixture. Return the frying pan to the heat and cook for 1 minute.
- Add the tinned tomatoes, tomato purée and curry powder. Stir to combine.
- Add the water.
- Bring to a simmer and then cover and cook gently for 10 minutes.
- Season with salt.
- Add the cooked chicken and the juices from the roasting tin. Stir round to coat the chicken and serve with the rice below.

Yellow rice

500ml basmati rice
50g sultanas
2 cardamom pods
2cm piece cinnamon stick
2 cloves
¼ teaspoon fennel seeds
½ teaspoon salt
½ teaspoon saffron threads soaked in one tablespoon warm boiled water
750ml water

- Put the rice and all the other ingredients in a medium-sized saucepan.
- Bring to the boil.
- Reduce the heat to very low, cover the saucepan and cook for 15 minutes, without removing the lid.
- Remove the saucepan from the heat and leave covered for 10 minutes.
- Serve with the chicken.

***** To make your own curry powder**
1 tablespoon coriander seeds
1 dessertspoon cumin seeds
1 teaspoon fennel seeds
½ teaspoon fenugreek

- *Place the coriander seeds into a small, heavy-bottomed pan and heat through for 30 seconds.*
- *Add the other ingredients and toast until you smell the lovely aroma of the spices.*
- *Transfer the spices to a coffee grinder, a small processor or grind them in a pestle and mortar.*

Provençal meat stew + mashed potato + purple sprouting broccoli

This is a lovely warming winter stew based on a recipe in Claudia Roden's *Mediterranean Cookery*. She suggests marinating the beef but because of time constraints I miss this bit out. It takes a long time to cook which is why I have suggested that you make it on a Saturday. Saturdays nights are perfect for stews. You can make it in the morning and then get on with the rest of the day, knowing that dinner is already made.

Provençal meat stew

1.5kg shin beef cut into chunks for stewing
2 large onions, thinly sliced
3 carrots, thinly sliced
4 garlic cloves, peeled and crushed
1 bottle red table wine
2 bay leaves
1 teaspoon allspice
1 bunch parsley stalks, tied together
2 sprigs thyme
salt and pepper

- Put all the ingredients in a large saucepan, bring to a simmer and remove any scum that appears.
- Reduce the heat so that there is the merest hint of a simmer.
- Season with plenty of salt and pepper.
- Cover the saucepan with tin foil and then place a lid on top and simmer on a low heat for 3 hours.

Mashed potato

1.5kg potatoes, peeled and chopped for boiling
salt and pepper
50g butter
300ml milk

- Place the potatoes in a saucepan of salted water and bring to the boil.
- Simmer for about 15 minutes until the potatoes are tender to the tip of a sharp knife.
- Drain them and put them through a potato ricer if you have one. If not, mash in the usual way.
- Once you have mashed the potato place it back in the pan over a low heat for 1 minute to dry it out.
- Add the butter and milk and mix gently until these are combined.

Purple sprouting broccoli

250g purple sprouting broccoli
salt and pepper
a little butter

- Boil a saucepan of water.
- Add the broccoli and simmer for 3 minutes.
- Season with salt, pepper and a little butter.

Ham baked in Madeira + buttered celeriac and swede + baked potatoes

This gammon joint is more than enough for 6 people, but I find that if you are going to the trouble of cooking gammon then it is nice to have some left over in the fridge for sandwiches later on in the week. The smell that emanates from the oven while this meal is cooking would warm even the coldest heart to home-cooked food.

Ham baked in Madeira

1 tablespoon olive oil
30g butter
1 onion, sliced
150g carrots, chopped roughly
1.5kg gammon joint
1 bouquet garni of bay, thyme and parsley
200ml Madeira wine
600ml beef stock
1 tablespoon soft brown sugar
25g butter
grated zest ½ orange

- Preheat the oven to 180°C/350°F/gas 4.
- Warm the oil and butter in a casserole pan large enough to hold the gammon joint and gently brown the onions and carrots for 5 minutes.
- Place the gammon in the casserole pan with the onions and carrots.
- Add the herbs, wine and the stock.
- Bring to the boil and then place the casserole pan in the oven to bake for 2 hours, basting the gammon every 40 minutes or so.
- Remove the gammon from the casserole pan, leaving all the sauce behind. Cut the rind away and place the gammon in a roasting tin.
- Sprinkle the joint with the brown sugar and return it to the oven for 10 minutes.
- Remove the joint from the oven and pour any melted sugar that has run into the bottom of the tin back over the ham.
- Set aside to rest for 15 minutes.
- Meanwhile reduce the sauce in which the gammon was cooked by placing the casserole pan on the hob and bringing it to a rapid boil for 5 minutes.
- Whisk in the last of the butter and the orange zest and serve with the ham, which you can carve as you like.

Buttered celeriac and swede

1 small celeriac, peeled and cut into 2cm cubes
1 small swede, peeled and cut into 2cm cubes
20g butter
salt and pepper
2 tablespoons flat-leaf parsley, chopped

- Place the swede, celeriac and butter in a saucepan.
- Place the saucepan on the hob on a medium heat.
- When you hear the butter sizzling reduce the heat to low and cook covered for 15 minutes until the vegetables are tender.
- Season with salt, pepper and the parsley.

Baked potatoes

6 baking potatoes
butter for serving
salt and pepper

- Preheat the oven to 220°C/425°F/gas 7.
- Pierce the potato skins with a sharp knife and bake for 1 hour 30 minutes.
- Split each one and serve with butter, salt and pepper.

Baked mocha cheesecake

This is a lovely chocolate concoction with a hint of coffee, hence the 'mocha' flavour. This is a baked variety of cheesecake. Cheesecake connoisseurs will argue that a baked cheesecake is the only true cheesecake, but I like both kinds.

For the biscuit base

225g digestive biscuits
60g butter
60g plain chocolate

For the filling

2 large eggs, separated (you will need both the yolks and the whites)
85g caster sugar
230g mascarpone cheese
150ml double cream, lightly whipped
50g good quality milk chocolate, finely chopped
3 tablespoons cocoa powder, sifted
1 tablespoon instant coffee granules, dissolved in 1 tablespoon boiled water
45g ground almonds
1 tablespoon amaretto liqueur

- Preheat the oven to 170°C/325°F/gas 3.
- Grease a springform tin with a diameter of 23cm.

To make the biscuit base

- Grind the biscuits to fine crumbs in a food processor or by placing the biscuits in a plastic bag and bashing them with a rolling pin.
- Place the butter and chocolate in a glass bowl above a saucepan of gently simmering water.
- Stir occasionally until the chocolate and butter have melted. Remove from the heat.
- Tip the biscuit crumbs into the chocolate and butter mixture and combine.
- Spread the mixture onto the base of the springform tin and press down until the base is even and firm.
- Chill in the fridge while you prepare the filling.

To make the filling

- Put the egg yolks into a bowl with the sugar and mix with an electric mixer until the mixture is pale in colour and when the whisk is lifted a ribbon-like trail is left on the top of the mixture.
- Beat the mascarpone cheese in another bowl until smooth.
- Fold the whipped double cream into the mascarpone cheese.
- Spoon the mascarpone and cream into the egg yolk and sugar mixture.
- Add the chopped chocolate, cocoa, coffee, almonds and liqueur and mix gently until combined.
- Whisk the egg whites until stiff and then fold these into the chocolate mixture.
- Pour the filling onto the biscuit base and bake for 1 hour.
- Serve with cream.

Coffee walnut puddings

These puddings are nice and moist and who wouldn't love the partnership of the coffee and walnut flavours? Note, too, that mini steamed puddings cook in half the time of a large pudding.

For the topping
50g melted butter
75g light brown muscovado sugar
50g broken walnut pieces
For the puddings
110g softened butter
110g light muscovado sugar
2 large eggs beaten together
150g self-raising flour
small pinch of salt
1 level tablespoon instant coffee granules dissolved in 2 tablespoons boiling water

- Preheat the oven to 190°C/375°F/gas 5.

To make the topping

- Melt the butter in a small saucepan and use some of it to grease the pudding moulds with a pastry brush.
- Add the sugar and walnuts to the rest of the melted butter and mix together.
- Spoon the mixture equally into the bottom of the pudding moulds and then set aside.

To make the puddings

- Cream the butter with the sugar in a mixing bowl using an electric hand-held mixer.
- Gradually add the beaten eggs to the butter and sugar, incorporating each addition before making the next one.
- Fold in the flour, the pinch of salt and the coffee mixture.
- Spoon the mixture equally into the pudding moulds and cover each one with a piece of tin foil.
- Place the moulds into a roasting tin and pour 2cm of boiling water into the tin.
- Cover the whole roasting tin with tin foil and place in the oven to cook for 40 minutes.
- When the puddings have cooled slightly, turn them out and serve with cream.

Week 2

Monday p84	Sirloin steak + Parmesan mash + celeriac, carrots and swede
Tuesday p85	Orecchiette with tomato sauce
Wednesday p86	Chinese chicken with pilaf rice
Thursday p87	Cod and prawns in white wine + garlic mayonnaise + sautéed potatoes + broccoli
Friday p88	Ham cakes + tomato salad + poached eggs
Saturday p89	Duck and sausage stew
Sunday p90	Roast chicken with thyme and lemon + bread sauce + potatoes with chorizo
Sunday pudding p92	Apple crumble + custard
Extra tasty treat p93	Banana loaf

Shopping list

MEAT
- ☐ 4 sirloin steaks
- ☐ 6 chicken drumsticks
- ☐ 6 chicken thighs
- ☐ 225g minced pork
- ☐ 6 duck legs
- ☐ 8 pork sausages
- ☐ 2 x 1.5kg chickens

FISH
- ☐ 1kg cod fillets, skinless
- ☐ 200g cooked prawns

VEGETABLES
- ☐ 2 shallots
- ☐ 3.5kg potatoes
- ☐ 200g swede
- ☐ 200g celeriac
- ☐ 400g carrots
- ☐ 4 onions
- ☐ 1 garlic bulb
- ☐ 1 bunch celery
- ☐ 1 whole broccoli
- ☐ 4 plum tomatoes
- ☐ 1 fennel bulb
- ☐ 3 spring onions
- ☐ fresh ginger

FRUIT
- ☐ 2 lemons
- ☐ 2 cooking apples
- ☐ 2 large bananas

FRESH HERBS
- ☐ thyme
- ☐ rosemary
- ☐ sage
- ☐ chives
- ☐ bay leaf
- ☐ flat-leaf parsley

FRIDGE ITEMS
- ☐ 3 packs butter
- ☐ 1.2 litres milk
- ☐ 50g Parmesan cheese
- ☐ 250g mascarpone cheese
- ☐ 100g salami
- ☐ 300g frozen peas
- ☐ 16 eggs
- ☐ 8 slices pancetta
- ☐ 1 medium-sized pot double cream
- ☐ 175ml crème fraîche
- ☐ 150g chorizo
- ☐ 400ml chicken stock
- ☐ 450g cooked ham for mincing

KITCHEN CUPBOARD ITEMS
- ☐ olive oil
- ☐ salt
- ☐ 2 x 400g tins chopped tomatoes
- ☐ 500g Orecchiette pasta
- ☐ 250g basmati rice
- ☐ dry sherry
- ☐ soy sauce
- ☐ sesame oil
- ☐ 1 bottle dry white wine
- ☐ Dijon mustard
- ☐ groundnut oil
- ☐ light olive oil
- ☐ extra virgin olive oil
- ☐ white wine vinegar
- ☐ 1 small white loaf for breadcrumbs
- ☐ 345g plain flour
- ☐ 75g soft brown sugar
- ☐ 175g caster sugar
- ☐ 1 vanilla pod
- ☐ baking powder
- ☐ bicarbonate of soda
- ☐ 50g raisins
- ☐ 50g pecan nuts
- ☐ chicken stock cubes
- ☐ 1 loaf crusty bread

SPICES
- ☐ black pepper
- ☐ paprika
- ☐ cloves
- ☐ ground cinnamon

Sirloin steak + Parmesan mash + celeriac, carrots and swede

This meal is obviously a bit of a treat due to the cost of good sirloin. The children can share a steak and so you should be able to get by with just four steaks, thereby making the meal slightly cheaper. Prepare the vegetables first as the steaks only take a few minutes to cook.

Sirloin steak

4 sirloin steaks
olive oil
salt and pepper
30g butter
1 shallot, finely chopped
3 sprigs fresh thyme

- Brush the steaks with a little olive oil.
- Heat a frying pan until hot and then place the steaks in the pan two at a time.
- Fry the steaks for approximately 4–6 minutes altogether, depending on how well done you like your steak and how thick they are. Turn the steaks once during this cooking time.
- Season each steak with salt and pepper and keep them warm while you fry the remaining two.
- Place all 4 steaks together to keep warm and return the pan to the heat.
- Deglaze the pan with a knob of butter, the shallots and thyme on a medium heat.
- Add any juices that have escaped from the steaks and then pour the sauce over the steaks and serve.

Parmesan mash

1kg potatoes, peeled and chopped for boiling
50g butter
300ml milk
3 tablespoons Parmesan, grated
salt and pepper

- Place the potatoes in a saucepan of salted water and bring to the boil.
- Simmer for about 15 minutes until the potatoes are tender.
- Drain them and mash them by putting them through a potato ricer, which is quick and easy, or use a regular masher.
- Once you have mashed the potato place it back in the pan over a low heat and add the butter, milk and cheese.
- Stir to combine and then remove from the heat.
- Check for seasoning.

Celeriac, carrots and swede

200g swede, peeled and cut into 1cm cubes
200g celeriac, peeled and cut into 1cm cubes
200g carrot, peeled and cut into 1cm cubes
30g butter
1 sprig rosemary
salt and pepper

- Put the vegetables in a saucepan with the butter and rosemary.
- Place on a medium heat and once you hear the butter sizzling reduce the heat to low, cover the saucepan and cook the vegetables for 20 minutes until tender.
- Season with salt and pepper.

Orecchiette with tomato sauce

Pasta is a must in a weekly menu if you want to regulate the amount of meat you are eating, as there are so many vegetarian pasta sauces. It is also very quick to get from hob to table.

2 tablespoons olive oil
1 onion, finely chopped
1 clove garlic, peeled and finely chopped
1 carrot, peeled and chopped
1 stick celery, chopped
2 x 400g tins chopped tomatoes
1 teaspoon sugar
salt and pepper
500g Orecchiette pasta
2 tablespoons mascarpone cheese
Parmesan cheese, freshly grated for serving

- Heat the olive oil in a saucepan.
- Add the onion, garlic, carrot and celery.
- Gently fry the vegetables for 10 minutes until soft.
- Add the tomatoes and season with the sugar, salt and pepper.
- Cook uncovered on a very low heat for about 45 minutes.
- Bring some water to the boil and cook the pasta following the instructions on the packet.
- Add the mascarpone cheese to the tomato sauce and stir in.
- Serve with the cooked Orecchiette and liberal gratings of Parmesan cheese.

Chinese chicken with pilaf rice

I have been cooking this dish for my children for years and they love it. I think I first discovered a version of it in *Sainsbury's Magazine*, but it is now firmly set in my mind. It's really easy as it's a one-dish meal, which is a real bonus at the end of a busy day. You can also do all the preparation in advance.

6 chicken drumsticks, skin removed
6 chicken thighs, skin removed
salt and pepper
2 tablespoons olive oil
1 onion, diced
100g salami, chopped
250g basmati rice
4 tablespoons frozen peas
545ml chicken stock (a stock cube is fine)
3 tablespoons dry sherry
3 tablespoons soy sauce
1 teaspoon sesame oil
1 clove garlic, crushed
2.5cm cube fresh ginger, peeled and chopped

- Preheat the oven to 200°C/400°F/gas 6.
- Season the chicken pieces with salt and pepper.
- Heat the olive oil in a large frying pan and sauté the chicken pieces for 5 minutes in batches over a medium heat until lightly browned all over.
- Meanwhile place the chopped onion into a high-sided roasting tin along with the salami, rice and peas.
- On top of these place the browned chicken pieces, in a single layer.
- In a measuring jug combine the stock, sherry, soy sauce, sesame oil, garlic and ginger and pour over the chicken.
- Place the dish in the oven and leave to cook, completely undisturbed for 1 hour.

Cod and prawns in white wine + garlic mayonnaise + sautéed potatoes + broccoli

For this meal cook the potatoes first, up until the sautéeing stage. Then get the mayonnaise done and set aside. Place the fish in the dish ready for the oven and then finish off the potatoes. Cook the broccoli while the fish is cooking.

Cod and prawns in white wine

1 shallot, finely chopped
1kg cod fillets, skinless
200g cooked prawns
salt and pepper
30g butter, cubed
1 sprig fresh thyme
2–3 stalks parsley
200ml dry white wine mixed with 100ml water

- Preheat the oven to 200°C/400°F/gas 6.
- Butter an ovenproof dish that will hold the fish in overlapping layers.
- Sprinkle the shallot on the bottom of the dish.
- Put in the cod and the prawns and season with salt and pepper.
- Dot with the butter and place the herbs on top.
- Pour on the wine and water.
- Cover the fish with butter paper or baking parchment and cook for 18 minutes.

Garlic mayonnaise

2 egg yolks
1 teaspoon Dijon mustard
150ml groundnut oil
150ml light olive oil
2 cloves garlic, crushed
salt

- Put the egg yolks and mustard in a bowl and whisk until thoroughly combined.
- Combine the olive and groundnut oil in a measuring jug.
- Start adding the oil to the eggs and mustard, literally a drop at a time. This will avoid the mayonnaise curdling.
- Once you have added about 50ml of the oil you can start adding it a bit more quickly but still take care that each addition is fully incorporated before adding the next lot.
- The mayonnaise will become thick. It may seem too thick but add a tablespoon of cold water, which instantly creates the right consistency by emulsifying the mixture.
- Add the garlic and season with a pinch of salt.

Sautéed potatoes

1kg potatoes, peeled and cut into 3cm chunks
2 tablespoons olive oil
salt and pepper

- Boil the potatoes in salted water until tender.
- Drain them.
- Heat the oil in a large sauté pan, add the potatoes and sauté them on a medium heat for 20 minutes until golden brown all over.

Broccoli

1 whole broccoli, trimmed and cut into florets
salt
black pepper
squeeze of fresh lemon

- Place a saucepan of slightly salted water on the hob and bring it to the boil.
- Add the broccoli and cook for 3 minutes.
- Season with pepper and lemon juice.

Ham cakes
+ tomato salad + poached eggs

Use a food processor to chop the ham very finely, unless you prefer to use a mincer. I used leftover roasted gammon when I first made these, but otherwise buy a joint of cooked ham.

Ham cakes

450g minced ham
225g minced pork
100g fresh white breadcrumbs
½ teaspoon paprika
1 tablespoon sage leaves, chopped
1 tablespoon chives, snipped
2 eggs, beaten
pepper (you probably won't need salt as the ham is salty enough)
3 tablespoons olive oil
flour for dusting

- Place the ham, pork, breadcrumbs, paprika and herbs in a mixing bowl and then add the beaten eggs.
- Mix together gently and then form the mixture into patties weighing approximately 100g each.
- Heat the olive oil in a frying pan.
- Dip each pattie into some flour and fry over a moderate heat until golden brown on each side.

Tomato salad

4 plum tomatoes, sliced
salt and pepper
1 tablespoon extra virgin olive oil

- Lay the tomatoes on a serving dish and pour the olive oil over them.
- Season with salt and pepper.

Poached eggs

6 eggs
1 teaspoon white wine vinegar

- Pour water into a deep frying pan or saucepan until you have a depth of 3cm. Add the vinegar.
- Bring the water to a simmer.
- Break 3 eggs into the pan, without breaking the yolks.
- Using a spoon try and keep each egg compact by spooning the white back onto the egg as it cooks.
- Simmer the eggs for 2 minutes.
- Cook the other 3 eggs in the same manner.
- Serve the eggs on top of the ham cakes with the tomato salad.

Duck and sausage stew

This stew is wonderful and is perfect for a winter's evening. The key to cooking duck successfully is to make sure you remove most of the fat from the bird before the finished dish gets to the table. This is done by cooking the duck to release the fat before it meets the other ingredients, by which time it would be too late.

a small splash vegetable oil
6 duck legs
salt and pepper
8 pork sausages
1 tablespoon flour
200ml white wine
600ml water
200g frozen peas
100g carrots, peeled and sliced
1 fennel bulb, roughly chopped
6 medium potatoes, peeled and halved
6 or 7 sage leaves, roughly torn

- Heat the vegetable oil in a large saucepan on a medium heat.
- Lay all the duck legs skin side down in the pan and season them with salt and pepper.
- Cook the legs on a low heat for 10 minutes and you will see the fat begin to leave the meat.
- Remove the duck legs to a plate.
- Drain off the fat. (Remember that duck fat is great for roasting potatoes so drain it into something that will fit in the fridge.)
- Return the duck legs to the pan and return the pan to the hob.
- Increase the heat and brown the duck legs all over for 10 minutes.
- Remove the duck legs again and set aside.
- Pour off most of the fat, retaining a tablespoon in the saucepan.
- Place the sausages in the pan, brown them all over and then set aside with the duck legs.
- Add the flour to the saucepan, and stir with a wooden spoon until all the fat is absorbed.
- Gradually add the wine to the flour and fat, stirring as you do so to avoid any lumps forming.
- Return the duck and sausages to the pan.
- Pour on the water.
- Add the peas, carrots, fennel, potatoes and sage leaves.
- Season well with salt and pepper.
- Bring to a simmer, cover and cook for 45 minutes.
- Remove the lid and cook for a further 20 minutes.
- Serve with crusty bread.

Roast chicken with thyme and lemon + bread sauce + potatoes with chorizo

Roast chicken and bread sauce is an unbeatable combination. The potato recipe is different from the roast potatoes one would normally have for Sunday lunch but a change is as good as a rest.

Roast chicken with thyme and lemon

2 x 1.5kg chickens
1 onion, sliced
1 lemon, halved
1 bunch fresh thyme
30g butter
salt and pepper
8 slices pancetta
for the gravy
1 tablespoon flour
400ml chicken or vegetable stock

- Preheat the oven to 180°C/350°F/gas 4.
- Place the chickens on top of the sliced onion in a roasting tin.
- Stuff the neck cavity of each chicken with half a lemon and half the thyme.
- Smear the skin of each chicken with butter and then season them with salt and pepper.
- Lay the pancetta slices over the breasts of each bird.
- Roast the chickens in the oven for 1 hour 30 minutes.
- Once the pancetta is brown remove it from the chickens and leave it in the bottom of the roasting tin to add to the flavour of the juices.
- Remove the chickens from the roasting tin and set aside.
- Place the roasting tin on the hob on a medium heat.
- Sprinkle the flour into the tin and scrape round with a wooden spoon so that all the fat is absorbed into the flour.
- Add the stock and bring to a simmer.
- Simmer very gently, stirring occasionally until ready to serve.

Bread sauce

2 cloves
1 onion, peeled and left whole
1 bay leaf
300ml milk
4 heaped tablespoons fresh white breadcrumbs
salt and pepper
20g butter
1 tablespoon double cream

- Stick the cloves into the onion.
- Place the onion and the bay leaf in a small saucepan with the milk.
- Warm on a low heat for 10 minutes.
- Remove the onion and bay leaf and spoon in the breadcrumbs.
- Simmer for 3 minutes.
- Remove from the heat and add the seasoning, butter and cream.
- Reheat when you are ready to serve the chicken.

Potatoes with chorizo

2 tablespoons olive oil
3 spring onions, peeled and sliced
150g chorizo, sliced into thick pieces
800g potatoes, peeled, quartered and cooked until tender
handful fresh flat-leaf parsley, roughly chopped

- Heat the olive oil in a frying pan.
- Add the spring onions and the chorizo and fry until the chorizo starts to turn golden at the edges.
- Add the potatoes to the pan and stir them around so they get coated in the chorizo oil.
- Scatter over the parsley and season with pepper and salt if necessary.
- Serve with the chicken and bread sauce.

Apple crumble + custard

The secret to a good crumble, and one that my children will eat, is to have a substantial layer of crumble. This recipe captures the proportion of sugary crumble to fruit perfectly. I use a food processor for the crumble but you can do it by hand, which is slightly more time-consuming. Don't be scared of making custard. It is not difficult and it tastes so much better than the cloying supermarket sauce. I use a double saucepan, but you can easily manage with a glass bowl over a saucepan. Either method averts the risk of curdling. If you want to make the custard in a saucepan directly over heat, either watch it like a hawk or add a teaspoon of cornflour, which will prevent curdling. It takes a good 10–15 minutes to make from start to finish, but this is a Sunday recipe so time is not so precious.

Apple crumble

2 cooking apples
120g plain flour
90g butter, straight from the fridge and cut into cubes
3 tablespoons soft brown sugar
3 tablespoons caster sugar
small knob of butter
sprinkling ground cinnamon

- Preheat the oven to 190°C/375°F/gas 5.
- Peel and core the cooking apples. Cut them into eighths and set aside.
- Place the flour in a food processor with the butter and whizz for a few seconds until like coarse breadcrumbs.
- Add both sugars and mix briefly.
- Place a small knob of butter in a frying pan and, when melted, add the apples and the sprinkling of ground cinnamon.
- Cook for 3–4 minutes until the apples are nicely coated.
- Place the apples in a pie dish, cover with the crumble mixture and bake for 35 minutes.

Custard

2 whole eggs
2 egg yolks
2 tablespoons caster sugar
600ml milk and double cream mixed
1 vanilla pod or a drop or two vanilla extract

- Place the eggs, egg yolks and the sugar in a glass bowl.
- Whisk the eggs and sugar with a hand whisk for 2 minutes.
- Pour the milk and cream into a measuring jug.
- Add the vanilla pod or extract.
- Heat the milk and cream in a microwave on high for 2 minutes. You want the milk and cream to be almost at boiling point.
- Place the glass bowl with the eggs and sugar over a saucepan of simmering water. Make sure the water does not touch the bottom of the bowl.
- Add the milk and cream to the egg mixture, stirring all the time with a wooden spoon to avoid lumps. If you are using a vanilla pod then split it open and scrape the seeds into the custard.
- Keep stirring for 10 minutes by which time you should have a good consistency. An indication of when the custard is thick enough is that it will coat the back of your wooden spoon. It will not be as thick as shop-bought custard.
- Avoid reheating home-made custard, as it may curdle.

Banana loaf

Everyone ends up with bananas that are just a little too ripe to eat and this cake is a great way to make use of them.

50g butter, softened
50g caster sugar
2 large bananas
175ml crème fraîche
225g plain flour
1 teaspoon baking powder
½ teaspoon bicarbonate of soda
2 eggs
50g carrots, grated
50g raisins
50g pecan nuts, chopped

- Grease and line a 900g loaf tin.
- Preheat the oven to 180°C/350°F/gas 4.
- Cream the butter and sugar in a mixer until white and fluffy.
- In a small bowl mix the bananas with the crème fraîche until combined.
- Add the banana and crème fraîche mixture to the butter and sugar, along with the flour, baking powder, bicarbonate of soda, eggs, carrot, raisins and nuts.
- Mix together gently but thoroughly and spoon the mixture into the cake tin.
- Bake for 1 hour.
- Leave to cool and then turn out onto a cooling rack.
- Serve in slices with butter if desired.

Week 3

Shopping list

MEAT

- ☐ 1kg pork shoulder
- ☐ 8 boneless chicken thighs
- ☐ 8–9 lamb loin chops
- ☐ 2 x 1.5kg chickens

FISH

- ☐ 750g smoked haddock
- ☐ 6 trout

VEGETABLES

- ☐ 1 garlic bulb
- ☐ 500g new potatoes
- ☐ 3 onions
- ☐ 1 bunch celery
- ☐ 5 carrots
- ☐ 1 cucumber
- ☐ 6 spring onions
- ☐ 1 shallot
- ☐ 2 tomatoes
- ☐ 1kg cauliflower
- ☐ 1.6kg potatoes
- ☐ fresh ginger

FRUIT

- ☐ 1 lemon

FRESH HERBS

- ☐ chives
- ☐ basil
- ☐ mint
- ☐ flat-leaf parsley
- ☐ bay leaves
- ☐ thyme
- ☐ 2 bunches coriander

FRIDGE ITEMS

- ☐ 725g frozen petits pois
- ☐ 400g crème fraîche
- ☐ 140g sliced pancetta
- ☐ 50g Parma ham
- ☐ 50g Parmesan cheese
- ☐ 1.7 litres chicken stock
- ☐ 9 eggs
- ☐ 2 packs butter
- ☐ 500ml milk
- ☐ 100g Gruyère cheese
- ☐ 50g Cheddar cheese
- ☐ 1 medium-sized pot double cream

KITCHEN CUPBOARD ITEMS

- ☐ vanilla extract
- ☐ almond essence
- ☐ 225g raisins
- ☐ 225g sultanas
- ☐ 50g chopped walnuts
- ☐ 200g plain flour
- ☐ 325g self-raising flour
- ☐ baking powder
- ☐ 50g cocoa powder
- ☐ 50g dark chocolate
- ☐ 110g soft brown sugar
- ☐ 250g demerara sugar
- ☐ 200g caster sugar
- ☐ 100ml coconut milk
- ☐ 2 x 400g tin flageolet beans
- ☐ 1 bottle red wine
- ☐ olive oil
- ☐ salt
- ☐ 410g tin borlotti beans
- ☐ 150g penne
- ☐ fish sauce
- ☐ dry sherry
- ☐ vegetable oil
- ☐ sesame oil
- ☐ light soy sauce
- ☐ 300g medium egg noodles
- ☐ 75g cashew nuts
- ☐ 1kg basmati rice
- ☐ 50g cashew nuts
- ☐ Dijon mustard
- ☐ 1 loaf bread
- ☐ mango chutney
- ☐ poppadums

☐ SPICES

- ☐ coriander seeds
- ☐ star anise
- ☐ ground cinnamon
- ☐ cinnamon stick
- ☐ cumin seeds
- ☐ fennel seeds
- ☐ fenugreek
- ☐ turmeric
- ☐ dried curry leaves
- ☐ cayenne pepper
- ☐ black mustard seeds
- ☐ black peper

Minestrone soup

There are various minestrone soups in this book. They make such a hearty, healthy meal and there are plenty of variations. This particular variation is based on an Antonio Carluccio recipe.

Although minestrone soup has its origins in peasant food this is to underestimate the luxuriousness it offers when one tucks into it. It is a feast for the senses in terms of it's aroma, colour and, most importantly, it's taste. As Italian food has become more popular in Britain as everyday food minestrone has lost the drab image it acquired in the 1970s when it was only really available as a variety of tinned soup.

3 tablespoons olive oil
1 large onion, chopped
2 cloves garlic, peeled and chopped
4 slices pancetta, chopped
50g Parma ham, finely chopped
4 sticks celery, diced
2 carrots, peeled and diced
4 medium potatoes, diced
5 basil leaves, shredded by hand
1.5 litres chicken stock
410g tin borlotti beans, drained
150g penne
Parmesan cheese, grated for serving

- Heat the olive oil in a large saucepan.
- Sauté the onion, garlic, pancetta and Parma ham for 5 minutes until the onion is soft.
- Add the celery, carrots, potatoes, basil and stock and cook, covered, on a gentle simmer for 10 minutes.
- Add the borlotti beans and pasta and season well with salt and pepper.
- Bring to a simmer, cover and cook for a further 8–10 minutes, depending on how long the pasta takes to cook according to the packet instructions.
- Serve with freshly grated Parmesan cheese and hunks of bread and Cheddar cheese.

Pork in red wine + sautéed potatoes and sour chive cream + petits pois

Cubed pork is often overlooked in this country as a basis for a casserole or stew, which is a shame as it is extremely tasty and maintains a good texture in a stew.

Pork in red wine

1kg pork shoulder, cut into 3cm chunks
500ml red wine
3 teaspoons coriander seeds
¼ star anise
¼ teaspoon ground cinnamon
2 tablespoons olive oil
3 cloves garlic, peeled and finely chopped
salt and pepper
200ml water

- Put the pork in a large bowl with the wine and place in the fridge for 1–2 hours.
- Roughly grind the coriander, star anise and cinnamon using a pestle and mortar. A fine powder is not necessary; just break up the shells of the coriander seeds.
- Heat the olive oil in a large saucepan.
- When hot, scoop up a couple of tablespoons of the pork in a slotted spoon and brown it for a minute in the olive oil. Retain the red wine marinade for later.
- Brown the pork in batches and then return it all to the saucepan on a medium heat.
- Add the spices, garlic and a good teaspoon of salt and a grinding of black pepper.
- Cook for 2 minutes and then pour over the reserved red wine and the water.
- Bring to a simmer and cook uncovered for an hour, until the pork is tender.
- Check the seasoning and adjust if necessary.

Sautéed potatoes and sour chive cream

500g new potatoes, halved if large
salt
200g crème fraîche
1 small bunch fresh chives
2 tablespoons olive oil

- Boil the potatoes with their skins on in salted water for 10–15 minutes until tender.
- Place the crème fraîche in a small serving bowl and snip the chives into it.
- Heat the olive oil in a large frying pan until hot and then add the potatoes.
- Sauté until brown all over.
- Sprinkle with sea salt and serve with the crème fraîche and chives.

Petits pois

300g frozen petits pois
salt

- Place the peas in a pan of slightly salted boiling water and simmer for 3 minutes.
- Serve with the pork and potatoes.

Thai-style chicken
+ cucumber noodle salad

This is the simplest of meals. The chicken thighs, being boneless, cook quickly. One word of warning though; don't season the chicken once it has cooked as the Thai fish sauce is very salty and there is also salt in the marinade.

Thai-style chicken

3 tablespoons fish sauce
1 tablespoon dry sherry
2 garlic cloves, peeled and crushed
2 teaspoons caster sugar
1 teaspoon salt
8 chicken thighs, boneless and skin removed
2 tablespoons vegetable oil

- Mix the fish sauce, sherry, garlic, sugar and salt together in a medium-sized bowl.
- Place the chicken thighs in the bowl and coat them with the mixture. Leave in a cool place for 30 minutes.
- To cook the chicken heat the vegetable oil in a frying pan.
- Cook the chicken thighs in two batches for 5 minutes on each side at a medium heat to brown the meat well.
- Serve the chicken on top of the salad below.

Cucumber noodle salad

For the dressing
2 tablespoons lemon juice
1 teaspoon caster sugar
1 teaspoon salt
2 tablespoons dry sherry
1 tablespoon olive oil
4 teaspoons sesame oil
1 tablespoon light soy sauce

For the salad
300g medium egg noodles, cooked following the packet instructions
1 large cucumber, halved and cut into strips lengthways and then chopped into matchstick shapes
3 tablespoons cashew nuts, roughly chopped
1 large handful mint leaves, finely shredded
6 spring onions, peeled and finely sliced

- To make the dressing mix the lemon juice, sugar, salt, sherry, oils and soy sauce together in a small bowl and set aside.
- Place the cooked noodles in a serving dish along with the cucumber, nuts, mint leaves and spring onions.
- Pour the lemon dressing over and serve.

Kedgeree

We often had kedgeree when we were young and it was always at dinner time, never for breakfast, which is the more traditional time to eat it.

500ml basmati rice
750ml water
½ teaspoon salt
2cm piece cinnamon stick
25g butter
750g smoked haddock
milk
2 tablespoons vegetable oil
1 onion, finely chopped
1 tablespoon curry powder*
6 hard-boiled eggs, peeled and quartered
2 tablespoons flat-leaf parsley, chopped

- Place the rice in a saucepan with the water, salt and cinnamon stick on a high heat and bring to the boil.
- Reduce the heat to very low, cover and cook for 15 minutes without removing the lid.
- Remove from the heat and leave undisturbed, with the lid on, for 10 minutes.
- Then remove the lid, add the butter and stir briefly. Replace the lid.
- Meanwhile, place the haddock skin side down in a large meat tin. Cover it with milk. Cover the meat tin with a large sheet of tin foil leaving one corner open.
- Place the meat tray on the hob and bring the milk to the boil.
- Remove the tray from the heat, seal the open corner and leave it covered for 5 minutes, by which time the fish will be cooked.
- Remove and discard the skin, then flake the fish into a serving dish.
- Heat the vegetable oil in a sauté pan.
- Add the onion and sauté gently for 10 minutes until soft.
- Sprinkle on the curry powder and stir so that the onion is completely coated.
- Spoon the onion into the dish with the rice, fish, eggs and parsley.
- Serve with mango chutney and some poppadums if you like.

To make your own curry powder
1 tablespoon coriander seeds
1 dessertspoon cumin seeds
1 teaspoon fennel seeds
½ teaspoon fenugreek

- *Place the coriander seeds into a small, heavy-bottomed pan and heat through for 30 seconds.*
- *Add the other ingredients and toast until you smell the lovely aroma of the spices.*
- *Transfer the spices to a coffee grinder, a small processor or grind them in a pestle and mortar.*

Fried lamb loin chops + flageolet and pea stew

This is a slightly altered version of a Rick Stein recipe. Flageolet beans go very well with lamb; as do most pulses. Make the flageolet and pea stew first and reheat when the chops are ready.

For the loin chops

8–9 lamb loin chops
salt and pepper

For the flageolet and pea stew

2 tablespoons olive oil
2 cloves garlic, peeled and finely chopped
1 shallot, finely chopped
1 carrot, peeled and diced
2 x 400g tins flageolet beans, drained
1 bay leaf
1 sprig thyme
225g frozen petits pois
150ml water
salt and pepper
3 tablespoons flat-leaf parsley, chopped

To cook the loin chops

- First remove the slightly tough, outer skin that covers the fat on loin chops. You can do this with a sharp knife or a pair of scissors.
- Season the chops with salt and pepper.
- Heat a large frying pan.
- When hot put four chops in the pan and cook on a high temperature. Try and brown the fat first by balancing the chops on their sides. Then quickly brown the chops on each side.
- Reduce the heat and cook for a further 3 minutes. The chops should then be medium rare.

To make the flageolet and pea stew

- Heat the olive oil in a medium-sized saucepan and gently sauté the garlic, shallot and carrot for 5 minutes.
- Add the flageolet beans, bay leaf, thyme, peas and the water to the pan and cook uncovered on a gentle simmer for 8 minutes.
- Season with salt and pepper, the parsley and a drizzle of olive oil.
- Reheat when the chops are ready.

Spiced trout + vegetables in coconut gravy + boiled rice

I find it very satisfying to eat trout as it is so plentiful and always available. You feel you are making use of what the environment offers, rather than pandering to tastes and whims that often involve flying ingredients halfway across the world.

Spiced trout

1 teaspoon turmeric
3 teaspoons dried curry leaves
¼ teaspoon cayenne pepper
2 teaspoons coriander seeds
2 teaspoons cumin seeds
½ teaspoon fenugreek
2 teaspoons salt
6 trout, gutted
1 large bunch fresh coriander

- Grind the turmeric, curry leaves, cayenne, coriander, cumin, fenugreek and salt together using a pestle and mortar, so that the seeds are as fine as possible without too much effort.
- Slash the fish with a sharp knife, making three incisions on each side.
- Rub the ground spices into the fish.
- Cut a deep incision into the bottom of the fish and stuff the cavity with the coriander leaves.
- Place the fish in the fridge for a couple of hours if you have time.
- Preheat the grill and place the fish under it for 5 minutes. Then turn the fish over and grill for 5 minutes on the other side. Make sure the skin does not burn and adjust the height of the grill pan if the fish is darkening too quickly.

Vegetables in coconut gravy

400g potatoes, peeled and cut into quarters
2 carrots, peeled and chopped into 2cm pieces
200g frozen peas
1 tablespoon vegetable oil
1 clove garlic, peeled and finely chopped
1 onion, finely chopped
1cm fresh ginger, peeled and finely chopped
5 curry leaves
1 teaspoon coriander seeds
¼ teaspoon turmeric
¼ teaspoon cayenne pepper
2 tomatoes, each cut into 8 pieces
100ml water
100ml coconut milk
salt and pepper
50g cashew nuts
½ teaspoon mustard seeds
1 tablespoon fresh coriander, chopped

- Cook the potatoes, carrots and peas in boiling salted water until tender and then drain them and set aside.
- Heat the oil in a large frying pan or saucepan.
- Add the garlic, onion, ginger and curry leaves and sauté for 3 minutes.
- Grind the coriander seeds in a pestle and mortar, until you have a reasonably fine powder.
- Add the coriander powder, turmeric and cayenne to the onions, garlic, curry leaves and ginger and stir for 30 seconds.
- Add the cooked vegetables and tomatoes and sauté for 2 minutes.
- Pour on the water and simmer for 30 seconds.
- Add the coconut milk and bring to a gentle simmer.
- Remove from the heat and check the seasoning.
- When you are ready to serve take a small frying pan and heat one teaspoon of vegetable oil.
- Gently fry the cashew nuts and mustard seeds.
- Garnish the vegetables with the nuts, seeds and fresh coriander and serve.

Boiled rice

500ml basmati rice
750ml water
salt

- Put the rice in a saucepan with the water and a pinch of salt.
- Place on a high heat and as soon as it comes to the boil, cover the saucepan with a lid and turn the heat right down to very low. Leave it for 15 minutes, giving it one stir only during the cooking time.
- Then remove from the heat and leave it covered for a further 10 minutes before you remove the lid.

Coriander roast chicken
+ cauliflower cheese + roast potatoes

This is a slight variation on the traditional roast chicken that you might normally have on a Sunday, although the vegetables are very conventional.

Coriander roasted chicken

150g butter, softened
40g fresh coriander, finely chopped
2 cloves garlic, peeled and finely chopped
1 teaspoon dry sherry
salt and pepper
2 x 1.5kg chickens
8 slices pancetta
For the gravy
1 tablespoon flour
200ml vegetable/chicken stock

- Preheat the oven to 190°C/375°F/gas 5.
- In a small bowl mix together the butter, coriander, garlic and sherry and season well with salt and pepper.
- Place the chickens in a roasting tin.
- Smear the butter mixture between the skin of the chickens and the breast meat, saving a little dollop for between each leg and the breast.
- Cover the breasts of each chicken with sliced pancetta.
- Roast the chickens for 1 hour 30 minutes.

To make the gravy

- Take the chickens out of the oven, remove them from the roasting tin and leave them to rest for 20 minutes before carving.
- Put the roasting tin on the hob on a medium heat.
- Sprinkle the flour into the tin and scrape it round with a wooden spoon so that all the fat is absorbed into the flour.
- Add the vegetable/chicken stock and bring to a simmer.
- Simmer very gently until you are ready to eat.

Cauliflower cheese

1 cauliflower, weighing approximately 1kg
50g butter
30g flour
500ml milk
1 teaspoon Dijon mustard
100g Gruyère cheese, grated
salt and pepper
50g Cheddar cheese, grated

- Prepare the cauliflower by removing the outer green leaves and cutting the white part into reasonably large florets.
- Place the cauliflower in a large saucepan of salted water and bring it to the boil.
- Reduce the heat, cook on a steady simmer for 6 minutes, then drain and set aside in a gratin dish.
- Meanwhile, melt the butter in a small saucepan.
- Add the flour and stir on a low heat for 30 seconds.
- Remove the saucepan from the heat and add the milk gradually, stirring all the time to avoid lumps.
- Return the saucepan to the heat and continue stirring until the sauce comes to the boil.
- Reduce the heat and simmer for 10 minutes.
- Remove the saucepan from the heat, add the Dijon mustard and stir in the Gruyère cheese.
- Season with salt and pepper.
- Pour the sauce over the cooked cauliflower and sprinkle on the Cheddar cheese.
- Place the cauliflower cheese under a hot grill until it is bubbling and golden brown.

Roast potatoes

1kg roasting potatoes, peeled
2 tablespoons olive oil
salt and pepper

- Preheat the oven to 220°C/425°F/gas 7.
- Parboil the potatoes in boiling salted water for 5 minutes.
- Drain and place them in a roasting tin.
- Pour the olive oil over the potatoes and then roast them for 50 minutes until golden brown.

Hot chocolate pudding

This recipe came from an old magazine cutting I have kept since 1998, but have not used for many years. Now it has come to light, it is included here, never to be forgotten again. The pudding does not look particularly delectable before it is cooked, but in the oven something magical happens and a beautiful pudding emerges.

For the hot chocolate sauce
50g dark chocolate
110g soft brown sugar
25g cocoa powder
2 teaspoons vanilla extract
310ml water

For the sponge
125g plain flour
2 level teaspoons baking powder
25g cocoa powder
150g caster sugar
small pinch of salt
200ml crème fraîche
50g butter, melted
50g walnuts, chopped into pieces
1 teaspoon vanilla extract

- Preheat the oven to 170°C/325°F/gas 3.

To make the hot chocolate sauce
- Place all the sauce ingredients in a saucepan and bring to the boil.
- Reduce the heat and simmer, stirring continuously for 2 minutes.
- Remove the saucepan from the heat and set aside.

To make the sponge
- Grease a small soufflé dish. A deep pie dish would work as well.
- Sift the flour, baking powder and cocoa into a mixing bowl.
- Add the sugar, salt, crème fraîche, melted butter, walnuts and the vanilla extract and mix until all the ingredients are combined.
- Spoon the mixture into the dish and spread out evenly.
- Pour the sauce over the sponge mixture and bake for 40 minutes.
- Serve with cream.

Fruit cake

This is an extremely quick fruit cake to make. The recipe came from a friend who made one like this for a village hall fête. The cake was much praised.

225g raisins
225g sultanas
225g butter, softened
225g demerara sugar
3 eggs, beaten
1 teaspoon vanilla essence
1 teaspoon almond essence
325g self-raising flour
salt
1 tablespoon demerara sugar for sprinkling

- Grease and line a 20cm fruit cake tin.
- Preheat the oven to 170°C/325°F/gas 3.
- Place the raisins and sultanas in a saucepan of cold water and bring to the boil.
- Reduce the heat and simmer for 5 minutes.
- Strain the fruit and set aside.
- Cream the butter with the sugar, using an electric mixer, until light and fluffy.
- Add the beaten eggs a little at a time, combining each addition with the mixer before you make the next.
- Add the vanilla and almond essences and then sift in the flour and a pinch of salt.
- Fold the flour into the mixture with a metal spoon, followed by the fruit.
- Spoon the mixture into the cake tin.
- Sprinkle the top of the cake with the demerara sugar.
- Bake for 1 hour 30 minutes.
- Turn out once cooled.

Week 4

Monday p110	Curried chicken soup
Tuesday p111	Navarin of lamb
Wednesday p112	Cheese, bacon and onion flan + baked potatoes + salad
Thursday p114	Cumberland pie + green peas
Friday p115	Fried sea bass with curry sauce + sautéed potatoes + roast cherry tomatoes
Saturday p116	Pasta with peas and sausages
Sunday p117	Beef and Guinness pie + savoy cabbage
Sunday pudding p118	Baked chocolate tart
Extra tasty treat p119	Pancakes with chocolate sauce

Shopping list

MEAT
- ☐ 1kg diced leg lamb
- ☐ 1kg minced beef
- ☐ 4 sausages
- ☐ 1kg shin beef

FISH
- ☐ 6 sea bass fillets

VEGETABLES
- ☐ 6 onions
- ☐ 300g carrots
- ☐ 1 garlic bulb
- ☐ 1 bunch celery
- ☐ 6 shallots
- ☐ 2 parsnips
- ☐ 1.3kg potatoes
- ☐ 700g new potatoes
- ☐ 6 baking potatoes
- ☐ 200g green beans
- ☐ ½ cucumber
- ☐ 1 lettuce
- ☐ 4 spring onions
- ☐ 12 cherry tomatoes
- ☐ 100g button mushrooms
- ☐ 1 savoy cabbage
- ☐ 4 tomatoes

FRESH HERBS
- ☐ thyme
- ☐ bay leaves
- ☐ flat-leaf parsley
- ☐ basil
- ☐ rosemary

FRIDGE ITEMS
- ☐ 3 packs butter
- ☐ 3.4 litres chicken stock
- ☐ 500g frozen peas
- ☐ 250g cooked chicken
- ☐ 140g cubed pancetta
- ☐ 18 eggs
- ☐ 600ml double cream
- ☐ 150g Cheddar cheese
- ☐ 50g Parmesan cheese
- ☐ 725ml milk
- ☐ 200g crème fraîche
- ☐ 750g frozen or fresh peas
- ☐ 375g pack ready-made puff pastry
- ☐ vanilla ice cream
- ☐ 250g cooked chicken (see p.110)

KITCHEN CUPBOARD ITEMS
- ☐ 50g basmati rice
- ☐ salt
- ☐ olive oil
- ☐ balsamic vinegar
- ☐ extra virgin olive oil
- ☐ 400g tin chopped tomatoes
- ☐ beef stock cubes
- ☐ Worcestershire sauce
- ☐ 1 teaspoon mango chutney
- ☐ 200g Pappardelle pasta
- ☐ tomato purée
- ☐ 400ml Guinness
- ☐ sesame oil
- ☐ caraway seeds
- ☐ light soy sauce
- ☐ 75g icing sugar
- ☐ 625g plain flour
- ☐ 70g caster sugar
- ☐ 225g dark chocolate
- ☐ 225g best milk chocolate
- ☐ golden syrup
- ☐ 2 loaves white bread

SPICES
- ☐ black pepper
- ☐ coriander seeds
- ☐ cumin seeds
- ☐ fennel seeds
- ☐ fenugreek
- ☐ paprika

Curried chicken soup

The first time I made this soup was one cold spring evening when the children had just broken up from school and they had coughs and colds. It revitalised them almost immediately. If you have the chicken carcasses from Sunday's lunch then boil them and use the stock and meat, otherwise buy fresh chicken stock.

50g butter
1 onion, finely diced
2 carrots, peeled and finely diced
2 tablespoons curry powder*
50g basmati rice
2 litres chicken stock
100g frozen peas
250g cooked chicken, roughly chopped into small pieces
salt and pepper

- Heat the butter in a large saucepan, and gently sauté the onion and carrots for 10 minutes.
- Sprinkle on the curry powder and stir.
- Add the rice next, stirring it to coat it in the melted butter and curry powder.
- Add the stock, peas and the chicken and cook on a gentle simmer for 20 minutes.
- Season well with salt and pepper.
- Serve with thinly sliced, hot, crispy, buttered toast.

To make your own curry powder
1 tablespoon coriander seeds
1 dessertspoon cumin seeds
1 teaspoon fennel seeds
½ teaspoon fenugreek

- *Place the coriander seeds into a small, heavy-bottomed pan and heat through for 30 seconds.*
- *Add the other ingredients and toast until you smell the lovely aroma of the spices.*
- *Transfer the spices to a coffee grinder, a small processor or grind them in a pestle and mortar.*

Navarin of lamb

This is a spring stew. Serve it with chunks of bread to soak up the lovely thick gravy.

3 tablespoons olive oil
1kg diced leg lamb
1 tablespoon flour, seasoned
2 cloves garlic, peeled and crushed
1 onion, finely chopped
2 sticks celery, finely chopped
4 shallots, peeled and halved
4 carrots, peeled and cut into 1cm thick, 2cm long batons
2 parsnips, peeled and cut into 2cm chunks
4 medium potatoes, peeled and cut in half
400g tin chopped tomatoes
1 sprig thyme
2 tablespoons flat-leaf parsley, chopped
1 bay leaf
salt and pepper
approximately 200ml chicken stock
200g green beans

- Preheat the oven to 170°C/325°F/gas 3.
- Heat 1 tablespoon of the olive oil in a casserole pan over a medium heat.
- Brown the lamb in the oil in three batches. As you add the last batch of lamb sprinkle it with the flour.
- Return all the lamb to the pan and stir it round for 1 minute.
- Remove the lamb from the pan and set aside.
- Keep the pan on the heat and add the remaining olive oil, garlic and onions and cook for 3 minutes.
- Add the celery, shallots and carrots and cook for 5 minutes on a medium heat.
- Return the meat to the pan with the parsnips, potatoes, tomatoes, thyme, parsley and bay leaf. Season well with salt and pepper.
- Next add some chicken stock, just enough to come 2cm below the meat and vegetables.
- Bake in the oven for 1 hour 25 minutes.
- Remove the pan from the oven, add the green beans and return to the oven for 10 more minutes.
- Serve with chunks of bread.

Cheese, bacon and onion flan + baked potatoes + salad

I used to panic about making shortcrust pastry as it would turn out differently every time I made it. Stick to this recipe and I promise you that the pastry will work. If you use a food processor to make the pastry it is almost as quick as opening a shop-bought packet of pre-prepared pastry.

Cheese, bacon and onion flan

For the pastry

225g plain flour
150g butter
salt
1 egg yolk
2 tablespoons cold water

For the filling

1 tablespoon olive oil
1 large onion, diced
140g cubed pancetta
2 eggs
300ml double cream
salt and pepper
100g Cheddar cheese, grated

To make the pastry

- Put the flour and butter in the bowl of a food processor and incorporate them so that the resulting mixture looks like fine breadcrumbs.
- Add a pinch of salt.
- Mix the egg yolk with the cold water in a small bowl and then add this liquid to the flour and fat.
- Turn on the food processor and mix until a dough just begins to form. Turn the mixture onto a floured work surface and combine thoroughly, with a light hand, until you have a smooth dough.
- Wrap the dough in cling-film and place it in the fridge to chill for 20 minutes.

To make the flan base

- Preheat the oven to 200°C/400°F/gas 6 and grease a 24cm diameter, 3½cm deep flan tin.
- Roll out the pastry on a lightly floured surface and line the flan tin with it. Place a sheet of baking parchment over the pastry case and then pour on some baking beans. Place the flan tin on a baking sheet and put it in the oven for 15 minutes.
- Take the flan tin from the oven and remove the parchment and baking beans. Return the flan tin to the oven for a further 5 minutes.
- Remove the flan tin from the oven and reduce the oven temperature to 190°C/375°F /gas 5.

To make the filling

- Warm the olive oil in a heavy-bottomed frying pan.
- Add the onion and fry for 5 minutes on a medium heat until soft and translucent.
- Add the pancetta and cook for 3 minutes until golden.
- In a small bowl combine the eggs with the cream and season with salt and pepper.
- Spoon the onion and pancetta onto the base of the flan case.
- Sprinkle on the cheese and carefully pour on the egg and cream mixture.
- Place the flan tin on a baking sheet and cook for 30 minutes.

Baked potatoes

6 baking potatoes
salt and pepper
butter for serving

- Preheat the oven to 220˚C/425˚F/gas 7.
- Pierce the potato skins with a sharp knife and bake for 1 hour 30 minutes.
- Split each one and serve with butter, salt and pepper.

Salad

½ cucumber, sliced
1 lettuce, washed
4 spring onions, sliced
4 tomatoes, sliced
For the dressing
2 tablespoons extra virgin olive oil
½ tablespoon balsamic vinegar
salt and pepper

- Combine the salad ingredients in a serving bowl.
- Mix the dressing ingredients together and pour over the salad.

Cumberland pie
+ green peas

Cumberland pie is really a cottage pie with cheese added to the topping. It is just the kind of food to eat on cosy winter evenings, when one requires some solace from the elements.

Cumberland pie

1 tablespoon olive oil
1 onion, finely chopped
1kg minced beef
1 tablespoon flour
150g carrots, peeled and sliced
500ml beef stock (a stock cube is fine)
1 tablespoon Worcestershire sauce
salt and pepper
900g potatoes, peeled and quartered
30g butter
300ml milk
3 tablespoons Parmesan cheese, grated
50g Cheddar cheese, grated

- Warm the olive oil in a large saucepan.
- Add the onion and sauté it for 5 minutes on a medium heat stirring occasionally.
- Increase the heat, add the mince and brown it all over, turning the meat and crumbling it with a wooden spoon as you do so.
- Sprinkle on the flour and stir round to incorporate.
- Add the carrot and stock and bring to a simmer.
- Add the Worcestershire sauce and season sparingly with salt and pepper as you can always add more later.
- Cover the saucepan and simmer gently for 1 hour. Check the meat, occasionally, while it is cooking and if there is too much liquid remove the lid for 10 minutes or so, to reduce it.
- Meanwhile, boil the potatoes in salted water until tender enough to mash.
- Mash the potatoes, add the butter and milk and mix round until it is smooth.
- Add the Parmesan cheese to the potato and stir to combine.
- Spoon the meat into an ovenproof dish.
- Spoon the potato over the meat and smooth it with a knife.
- Sprinkle the Cheddar cheese over the top and then place under a hot grill for 5 minutes to brown.

Green peas

400g frozen peas
salt

- Bring a saucepan of salted water to the boil and add the peas, boiling them for 3 minutes until tender.

Fried sea bass with curry sauce + sautéed potatoes + roast cherry tomatoes

Sea bass is a wonderfully meaty fish that most children enjoy. It copes well on its own or with a sauce. Prepare the sauce, the potatoes and tomatoes first and then cook the fish just before you want to eat.

Fried sea bass with curry sauce

For the curry sauce

1 dessertspoon olive oil
1 shallot, finely chopped
½ teaspoon curry powder
200g crème fraîche
1 teaspoon mango chutney
salt and pepper

For the fried sea bass

1 tablespoon olive oil
6 sea bass fillets
salt and pepper

To make the curry sauce

- Heat the olive oil in a frying pan.
- Gently fry the shallot in the olive oil until golden brown.
- Stir in the curry powder.
- Remove from the heat, add the crème fraîche, mango chutney and season with salt and pepper.
- Then set aside.

To prepare the fish

- Season the fish.
- Heat the olive oil in a frying pan until hot.
- Place the sea bass fillets in the pan, skin side down.
- If you have thick fillets of fish then they will probably take 4 minutes to cook through, 2 minutes each side. Thin fillets will take about 1 minute each side.

Sautéed potatoes

700g new potatoes, halved
salt
2 tablespoons olive oil
1 tablespoon balsamic vinegar
black pepper

- Boil the potatoes in salted water until tender, then drain.
- Heat the olive oil in a large frying pan and sauté the potatoes until golden brown.
- Place the potatoes in a serving bowl and dress them with the balsamic vinegar, more salt, if necessary, and black pepper.

Roast cherry tomatoes

12 cherry tomatoes, halved
2 tablespoons olive oil
salt and pepper

- Preheat the oven to 200°C/400°F/gas 6.
- Place the tomatoes in a roasting tray.
- Drizzle them with olive oil and season with salt and pepper.
- Roast them for 15 minutes.

Pasta with peas and sausages

I have adapted the classic Italian pea and pasta recipe by adding sausages. In this instance I used sweet chilli sausages but you can choose whichever type you prefer.

3 tablespoons olive oil
1 shallot, peeled and finely diced
4 sausages, sliced into 1cm pieces
250g frozen or fresh peas
1.2 litres chicken stock
salt and pepper
200g Pappardelle pasta
5 basil leaves, chopped
fresh Parmesan cheese, grated for serving

- Heat the oil in a large pan and gently fry the shallot and sausage for 5 minutes.
- Add the peas and the stock and bring to a simmer.
- Check the seasoning.
- Add the pasta and basil and cook, covered, following the packet instructions for the pasta.
- Serve with grated Parmesan.

Beef and Guinness pie
+ savoy cabbage

This recipe comes, in part, from Sophie Grigson's *The Complete Sophie Grigson Cookbook*. Using shin of beef, which is one of the cheaper cuts, ensures that the beef filling for the pie becomes tender but remains full of flavour, so much more so than if you use braising or stewing steak. The only downside is that it takes longer to cook, but as it is Sunday time is not so much of the essence.

Beef and Guinness pie

1kg shin beef, trimmed
4 tablespoons flour seasoned with a teaspoon salt, a good grinding black pepper and 1 teaspoon paprika
50g butter
2 tablespoons olive oil
2 onions, chopped
100g button mushrooms
400ml Guinness
350ml boiling water
2 tablespoons tomato purée
½ tablespoon sugar
1 bouquet garni (2 sprigs thyme, 1 sprig rosemary and 2 sprigs parsley)
salt and pepper
375g pack ready-made puff pastry

- Preheat the oven to170°C/325°F/gas 3.
- Place the meat in a bowl and toss it in the seasoned flour.
- Heat half the butter and 1 tablespoon of the olive oil in a large saucepan.
- Brown the meat in batches and as it browns put it into a casserole dish.
- Add the rest of the butter and oil to the saucepan and brown the onions for 3 minutes.
- Transfer the onions to the casserole dish.
- Using the same saucepan fry the mushrooms for 3 minutes and add to the casserole dish.
- Keep the saucepan on the heat, pour the Guinness into it and bring to the boil.
- Stir in 350ml of boiling water, the tomato purée and sugar and then pour the liquid over the other ingredients in the casserole dish.
- Add the bouquet garni and season well with salt and pepper.
- Cover the casserole dish with a lid and cook in the oven for 2 hours.
- Once cooked turn the meat into a pie dish and leave it to cool for 15 minutes.
- Increase the oven temperature to 200°C/400°F/gas 6.
- Cover the pie dish with the pastry and bake for 20 minutes until the pastry is golden.

Savoy cabbage

1 savoy cabbage
2 teaspoons sesame oil
1 clove garlic, peeled and finely chopped
100ml water
1 teaspoon caraway seeds
1 tablespoon light soy sauce
salt and pepper

- Quarter the cabbage, remove the hard core and slice it finely.
- Heat the sesame oil in a saucepan and gently fry the garlic.
- Add the cabbage and the water.
- Cover and cook on a low heat for 10 minutes.
- Sprinkle on the caraway seeds and the soy sauce.
- Season with a little salt and pepper and serve with the pie.

Baked chocolate tart

This chocolate tart is really Simon Hopkinson's recipe but I have changed it slightly and used half milk chocolate and half dark chocolate. This ensures that my children eat it. I am sure gourmets will gasp in horror but I prefer to risk their disapproval rather than my children's.

For the pastry
180g cold butter
75g icing sugar
2 egg yolks
225g plain flour
For the filling
2 whole eggs
3 egg yolks
45g caster sugar
150g butter
100g dark chocolate
100g best milk chocolate

To make the pastry

- Place the butter, sugar, eggs and flour in a food processor and mix until everything is evenly combined. Turn the mixture out onto the work surface. It will look as though it will never combine but with a little work it will form into a ball of pastry dough.
- Cover with cling-film and chill in the fridge for 30 minutes.

To make the tart

- Preheat the oven to 190°C/375°F/gas 5.
- Grease a 25cm tart tin.
- Roll out the pastry and line the tart tin with it. Cover the pastry with a sheet of baking parchment and pour some baking beans on top of the paper.
- Place the tart tin on a baking sheet and bake for 15 minutes.
- Remove the parchment paper and beans from the tart tin and place it back in the oven for 5 minutes.
- Remove the tart tin from the oven.
- With an electric mixer, beat the whole eggs, yolks and sugar together in a bowl for 5 minutes, until thick and creamy.
- Place the butter and chocolate in a glass bowl and gently melt them over a saucepan of simmering water.
- Pour the chocolate mixture into the egg mixture and beat to combine.
- Pour this mixture into the pastry case and place in the oven for 5 minutes.
- Allow the tart to cool, then chill and serve with thick cream.

Pancakes with chocolate sauce

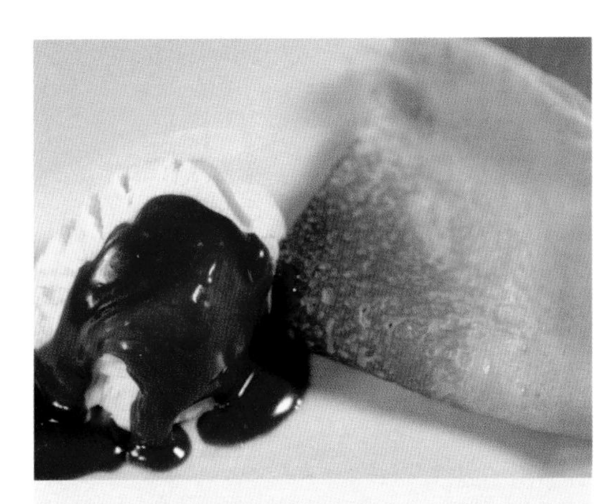

My children are crazy about pancakes, as are most adults I know. I am pretty ambivalent about them myself, but I think I am in the minority.

For the pancakes

175g plain sifted flour
pinch of salt
1 dessertspoon caster sugar
2 large eggs
1 egg yolk
425ml milk
3 tablespoons melted butter

For the chocolate sauce

300ml double cream
125g good quality milk chocolate
125g dark chocolate
1 tablespoon golden syrup
30g butter

To make the pancakes

- Combine the dry ingredients in a mixing bowl.
- Combine the whole eggs, yolk and milk in a measuring jug.
- Beating the whole time, add the wet ingredients to the centre of the dry ingredients. You should end up with small bubbles on top of the batter when you have finished.
- Set aside for 1 hour.
- Just before using the batter add the melted butter to it.
- Lightly grease a small frying pan. You won't need to grease it again because of the butter in the batter.
- For thin pancakes use about 3 tablespoons of batter at the most for each one. Spoon the batter into the frying pan once it is hot. Immediately tilt the pan away from you, so that the batter spreads across the whole of the pan. As soon as the pancake moves when you shake the pan, it is time to turn it over. Either toss it if you are confident, or use a palette knife.

To make the chocolate sauce

- Pour the cream into a small saucepan and, watching it like a hawk, bring it to just below boiling point.
- Remove the saucepan from the heat and add the chocolate, golden syrup and butter.
- Stir until everything has melted.
- Serve with the pancakes and some ice cream.

TIP

Cooking pancakes: *A good tip about pancakes is that you can make them in advance and then reheat them in the microwave.*

Week 1

Monday p122	Corned beef hash with fried eggs
Tuesday p123	Vegetable cannelloni + green salad
Wednesday p125	Fishcakes with tartare mayonnaise + green salad
Thursday p126	Leftover meat pie + salad leaf salad
Friday p127	Salmon with pepper sauce + potatoes with garlic and lemon + spinach
Saturday p128	Beef in red wine + boiled potatoes + carrots and peas
Sunday p129	Spring chicken
Sunday pudding p130	Apricot and cinnamon cake + custard
Extra tasty treat p131	Mincemeat tart

Shopping list

MEAT

- ☐ 4 pork sausages
- ☐ 1.5kg cubed stewing beef
- ☐ 1.5kg chicken

FISH

- ☐ 6 pieces salmon fillet
- ☐ 200g salmon fillet, lightly smoked (not smoked salmon)
- ☐ 750g undyed smoked haddock

VEGETABLES

- ☐ 4 onions
- ☐ 4 spring onions
- ☐ 5 shallots
- ☐ 10 baby onions
- ☐ 3.5kg potatoes
- ☐ 500g new potatoes
- ☐ 3 plum tomatoes
- ☐ 1 orange pepper
- ☐ 1 green pepper
- ☐ 2 red peppers
- ☐ 1 garlic bulb
- ☐ 1 cucumber
- ☐ 2 lettuces
- ☐ 50g rocket leaves
- ☐ 50g watercress
- ☐ 300g baby spinach leaves
- ☐ 150g button mushrooms
- ☐ 325g carrots
- ☐ 100g green beans

FRUIT

- ☐ 1 lemon
- ☐ 6 apricots

FRESH HERBS

- ☐ flat-leaf parsley
- ☐ basil
- ☐ chives
- ☐ coriander
- ☐ dill
- ☐ thyme
- ☐ bay leaves

FRIDGE ITEMS

- ☐ 24 eggs
- ☐ 500g ricotta cheese
- ☐ 275g pecorino cheese
- ☐ 125g mascarpone cheese
- ☐ 50g Parmesan cheese
- ☐ 1.15 litres full fat milk
- ☐ 200g crème fraîche
- ☐ 475ml double cream
- ☐ 2 packs butter
- ☐ 500g cooked chicken and ham mixed
- ☐ 1 pack ready-made puff pastry
- ☐ 100g sliced pancetta
- ☐ 250g frozen petits pois
- ☐ 1.5 litres chicken stock
- ☐ 300ml fish stock
- ☐ 12 sheets fresh lasagne

KITCHEN CUPBOARD ITEMS

- ☐ olive oil
- ☐ extra virgin olive oil
- ☐ groundnut oil
- ☐ light olive oil
- ☐ balsamic vinegar
- ☐ white wine vinegar
- ☐ salt
- ☐ 450g can corned beef
- ☐ 275g cooked, pickled beetroot
- ☐ Worcestershire sauce
- ☐ 400g tin tomatoes
- ☐ 480g plain flour
- ☐ 130g tinned tuna fish
- ☐ capers
- ☐ cornichons
- ☐ brandy
- ☐ 600ml red wine
- ☐ tomato purée
- ☐ 150g caster sugar
- ☐ baking powder
- ☐ vanilla essence
- ☐ 1 vanilla pod
- ☐ 75g icing sugar
- ☐ 1 jar mincemeat (unless you have made your own)

SPICES

- ☐ black pepper
- ☐ whole nutmeg
- ☐ ground cinnamon
- ☐ cloves

Corned beef hash with fried eggs

Tinned corned beef has a bad reputation as a result, I presume, of its use as a 1970s accompaniment to salad dressed with salad cream. This recipe may go some of the way to re-establishing its reputation.

450g can corned beef, diced
1 onion, finely diced
500g cooked potatoes, peeled and diced
275g cooked, pickled beetroot, drained, rinsed and diced
1 tablespoon Worcestershire sauce
salt and pepper
50g butter
flat-leaf parsley, chopped to serve
6 eggs

- In a bowl mix together the corned beef, onion, potatoes, beetroot and Worcestershire sauce.
- Season with a scant amount of salt and a few grindings of black pepper.
- Melt the butter in a wide, heavy-bottomed frying pan until it is foaming.
- Add the corned beef mixture.
- Stir it round and then press it down firmly with a wooden spoon.
- Turn the heat down to low and cook for 15 minutes, during which time a crust will form on the bottom of the mixture.
- Stir the hash, breaking it up, so that some of the crust gets mixed up with the rest.
- Add 4 tablespoons of hot boiled water.
- Press the hash down again and cook it for a further 15 minutes, until a second crust has formed.
- Sprinkle on the parsley and then serve spoonfuls of it with a fried egg for each person.

Vegetable cannelloni + green salad

This is a very satisfying pasta dish. It takes a little while to assemble but it is worth it. One huge plus is that you can get it ready for the oven a few hours before you want to eat.

Vegetable cannelloni

For the filling

2 tablespoons olive oil
1 shallot, finely chopped
3 plum tomatoes, finely chopped
1 orange pepper, very finely chopped
250g ricotta cheese
200g pecorino cheese, grated
1 tablespoon basil leaves, finely chopped
3 tablespoons frozen petits pois, defrosted
1 egg
salt and pepper
12 sheets fresh lasagne

For the tomato sauce

1 tablespoon olive oil
1 onion, finely chopped
1 clove garlic, peeled and finely chopped
400g tin tomatoes
1 teaspoon sugar
salt and pepper

For the cheese sauce

450ml full fat milk
1 onion, peeled and studded with 3 cloves
30g butter
30g flour
salt and pepper
2 tablespoons Parmesan cheese, grated
2 tablespoons double cream

- Preheat the oven to 200°C/400°F/gas 6.

To make the filling

- Heat the olive oil in a sauté pan.
- Add the shallot, tomatoes and pepper and sauté for 5 minutes on a medium heat until soft.
- Remove from the heat and stir in the ricotta cheese, the pecorino, basil, peas and egg.
- Season well with salt and pepper and set aside.
- Place a large pan of salted water to boil.
- Once you have a good rolling boil add the lasagne sheets, one at a time.
- Take the pan off the heat and leave the lasagne sheets for 2 minutes.
- Drain the sheets and then lay them out separately on a clean tea towel to avoid them sticking together.

To make the tomato sauce

- Heat the olive oil in a small saucepan.
- Add the onion and garlic and sauté on a low heat for 10 minutes.
- Add the tomatoes and sugar and season with salt and pepper.
- Bring to a simmer.
- Reduce the heat and cook uncovered for 30 minutes.

To make the cheese sauce

- Place the milk in a saucepan with the clove-studded onion.
- Bring to the boil and then cover the saucepan with a lid and remove from the heat.
- Set aside, while you prepare the rest of the cheese sauce.
- Melt the butter in a small saucepan.
- Add the flour and stir to combine.
- Remove from the heat and gradually add the infused milk, stirring continuously.
- Return the sauce to the heat, stirring continuously.
- Bring to the boil, reduce the heat to low and cook on a very slow simmer for 10 minutes.
- Season with salt and pepper.
- Add the cream and the Parmesan and set aside.

continues

To assemble

- Take an ovenproof lasagne dish.
- Spread the tomato sauce on the bottom of the dish.
- Place a large spoonful of the filling on one end of a sheet of lasagne and roll it up.
- Place it seam side down on top of the sauce.
- Repeat with all the lasagne sheets.
- Spoon the cheese sauce over the top of the rolled cannelloni.
- Sprinkle a couple of tablespoons of grated Parmesan cheese over the top of the dish and bake for 30 minutes, until golden brown and bubbling away.

Green salad

½ cucumber, sliced
1 lettuce, washed
4 spring onions, sliced

For the dressing

2 tablespoons extra virgin olive oil
½ tablespoon balsamic vinegar
salt and pepper

- Combine the salad ingredients in a serving bowl.
- Combine the dressing in a small bowl and then pour it over the salad when you are ready to eat.

Fishcakes with tartare mayonnaise + green salad

Unlike many fishcake recipes, this is both quick and tasty. It makes about 12 cakes.

Fishcakes with tartare mayonnaise

For the fishcakes

200g salmon fillet, lightly smoked (not smoked salmon)
750g undyed smoked haddock
400ml milk
200g potatoes, peeled, boiled and lightly mashed
1 shallot, finely chopped
1 dessertspoon Worcestershire sauce
130g tinned tuna fish, drained
3 tablespoons flat-leaf parsley, finely chopped
250g ricotta cheese
salt and pepper
2 tablespoons olive oil
flour for dusting

For the tartare mayonnaise

2 egg yolks
1 teaspoon Dijon mustard
150ml groundnut oil
150ml light olive oil
salt
1 shallot, finely chopped
1 tablespoon flat leafed parsley, chopped
½ tablespoon chives, chopped
½ tablespoon capers, rinsed and chopped
1 tablespoon cornichons, chopped

To make the fishcakes

- Place the salmon and the haddock in a large wide-bottomed pan and cover with milk.
- Place on the the hob on a medium heat and bring to a simmer, taking care not to let the milk boil over. Cook for 2 minutes.
- Turn the fillets over and cook for a further 2 minutes.
- Remove the fish from the pan and remove any skin.
- Leave the fish to cool for 20 minutes or so.
- Then place it in a bowl with the potatoes, shallot, Worcestershire sauce, tuna fish, parsley and ricotta cheese.
- Season well and mix gently until combined.
- Shape the mixture into cakes weighing approximately 100g each.
- Chill them in the fridge for 15 minutes.
- Heat the oil in a frying pan.
- Dip each fishcake in a little flour and fry on a medium heat for 2 minutes on each side.

To make the tartare mayonnaise

- Put the egg yolks in a bowl with the mustard and whisk until thoroughly combined.
- Pour the olive oil and groundnut oil into a measuring jug.
- Start adding the oil to the egg yolks, a drop at a time to prevent the mayonnaise from curdling. Once you have added about 50ml of the oil you can start adding it a bit more quickly but take care that each addition is fully incorporated before adding the next. Once the mayonnaise becomes thick add a tablespoon of cold water, which instantly creates the right consistency by emulsifying the mixture.
- Add salt to taste.
- Add the other ingredients and mix in.
- Serve with the fishcakes, the green salad and some brown bread and butter.

Green salad

1 lettuce, shredded
½ cucumber, sliced
1 green pepper, finely diced

For the dressing

2 tablespoons extra virgin olive oil
½ tablespoon balsamic vinegar
salt and pepper

- Combine the salad in a serving bowl.
- Combine the dressing ingredients and drizzle over the salad.

Leftover meat pie + salad leaf salad

I first made this pie when I had a lot of leftover cold meat in the fridge. It was very satisfying to find a way to use it up rather than slicing it and serving it with salad. Mrs Beeton would have been proud of me.

Leftover meat pie

125g mascarpone cheese
3 eggs
2 tablespoons parsley, freshly chopped
1 tablespoon chives, snipped
75g pecorino cheese, grated
1 tablespoon brandy
2 teaspoons Dijon mustard
salt and pepper
500g cooked chicken and ham mixed, chopped into bite-sized pieces
4 pork sausages, skins removed
1 shallot, finely chopped
1 pack ready-made puff pastry

- Preheat the oven to 220°C/425°F/gas 7.
- You will need a flan tin with a diameter of 24cm and a depth of about 4cm.
- In a large bowl mix together the mascarpone cheese, eggs, herbs, pecorino, brandy and mustard.
- Season with salt and pepper.
- In a separate bowl combine the cooked meats, the sausage meat and the shallot and mix in well.
- Take the puff pastry and roll it out to a rectangle of about 45cm long and 24cm wide. Keeping the pastry in one piece, line the flan tin from the end of the length so you have a long piece hanging over. Press the pastry into the round tin. You will have some pastry hanging over the sides of the flan tin.
- Fill the flan tin with half of the cheese mixture and then pile on the meat.
- Add the remaining cheese mixture and then fold over the sides of the pastry hanging over and the remaining length of pastry. Press together so you have a neat, compact pie.
- Pierce the top of the pie with a knife to allow steam to escape.
- Using a pastry brush, glaze the pastry with an egg yolk and bake for 35 minutes until golden brown.
- Turn out the pie from the flan tin on to a baking sheet and cook the underneath for 10 minutes.
- Turn back the right way to serve.

Salad leaf salad

50g rocket leaves
50g watercress
50g flat-leaf parsley and fresh coriander leaves, roughly chopped
50g baby spinach leaves

For the dressing

2 tablespoons extra virgin olive oil
1 dessertspoon white wine vinegar
salt and pepper

- Place the salad ingredients in a serving bowl.
- Combine the dressing in a small bowl and then spoon it over the salad when you are ready to eat.

Salmon with pepper sauce + potatoes with garlic and lemon + spinach

The pepper sauce here complements the richness of the salmon very well and is very simple to make. The potato recipe makes a change from boiled potatoes.

Salmon with pepper sauce

For the pepper sauce
1 tablespoon olive oil
1 shallot, finely chopped
2 cloves garlic, peeled and finely chopped
300ml fish stock
2 peppers any colour, deseeded and roughly chopped
salt and pepper
75ml double cream
1 teaspoon dill leaves, finely chopped

For the grilled salmon
6 pieces salmon fillet with skin
1 tablespoon olive oil
salt and pepper

To make the pepper sauce
- Warm the oil in a frying pan and gently cook the shallot and garlic for a minute or two, stirring continuously so as not to burn the garlic.
- Add the stock and peppers and season.
- Bring to a simmer and cook covered for 15 minutes until the peppers are soft.
- Liquidize the mixture until smooth and then pass it through a sieve.
- Add the cream and dill, reheat the sauce and check the seasoning.

To grill the salmon
- Preheat the grill.
- Brush the salmon fillets with olive oil and season them with salt and pepper.
- Grill them for 2 minutes on each side.

Potatoes with garlic and lemon

1kg new potatoes
2 tablespoons olive oil
salt
grated zest 1 lemon
2 cloves garlic, peeled and finely chopped
milk

- Preheat the oven to 200°C/400°F/gas 6.
- Slice the potatoes to a 1cm thickness, lengthways.
- Place them in a bowl with olive oil and toss them in the oil.
- Arrange the potatoes in layers in an ovenproof dish.
- Sprinkle them with salt, grated lemon zest and chopped garlic.
- Pour in enough milk to reach just to the top layer of potatoes.
- Bake for 40 minutes until the potatoes are cooked and golden brown.

Spinach

250g spinach leaves, rinsed
1 tablespoon water
salt
small knob of butter
nutmeg
pepper

- Place the spinach in a large saucepan with the water and a pinch of salt.
- Cover and place the saucepan on a low heat.
- Gradually wilt the spinach for 10 minutes, until the leaves are a glossy dark green.
- As soon as the leaves have wilted remove the lid and stir for a few seconds to get rid of any excess water. Drain if there is still too much.
- Add the butter, a tiny grating of nutmeg and a generous grinding of black pepper.

Beef in red wine
+ boiled potatoes + carrots and peas

This is another easy, meaty stew. Although March means early spring there are still plenty of chilly evenings to come when only heart-warming food will do.

Beef in red wine

2 tablespoons olive oil
100g sliced pancetta, chopped
1.5kg cubed stewing beef
10 baby onions
1 onion, diced
1 carrot, peeled and sliced
150g button mushrooms, left whole
1 tablespoon flour
600ml red wine
1 tablespoon tomato purée
2 cloves garlic, peeled and crushed
2 sprigs thyme
1 bay leaf
1½ teaspoons salt
black pepper

- Preheat the oven to 160°C/320°F/gas 2½.
- Heat the olive oil in a large casserole pan.
- Add the pancetta and cook for 2 minutes.
- Remove the pancetta from the pan and set aside.
- Brown the beef in the same oil, in small batches, setting each batch aside while you brown the rest.
- Keep the pan on the heat while you brown the baby onions and then set aside.
- Add the onion, carrot and mushrooms and sauté for 3 minutes on a high heat, stirring continuously.
- Return the beef, pancetta and baby onions to the pan and sprinkle over the flour, coating the vegetables and the meat.
- Stir in the wine, tomato purée, garlic and herbs.
- Season with salt and pepper.
- Bring to a simmer on the hob, then cover and cook in the oven for 2 hours.

Boiled potatoes

800g potatoes, peeled and quartered
salt
butter for serving
black pepper

- Boil the potatoes in plenty of salted water until tender.
- Drain the potatoes and then return them to the saucepan, along with the butter.
- Season with a good grinding of black pepper

Carrots and peas

15g butter
300g carrots, peeled and chopped widthways 1cm thick
200g frozen petits pois
salt and pepper

- Melt the butter in a small saucepan and add the carrots.
- Turn the heat down to very low and cover the saucepan with a lid.
- Cook the carrots for 15 minutes and then add the peas with 2 tablespoons of water.
- Cook, covered, on a low heat for 3 minutes.
- Season with salt and pepper.

Spring chicken

This recipe has lots of early summer flavours in it and is very tasty just as one's palette is becoming jaded with winter comfort food.

1 bunch fresh basil
1.5kg whole chicken
1.5 litres chicken stock
500g new potatoes
salt and pepper
100g green beans
50g butter
1 tablespoon olive oil
1 tablespoon flour
1 tablespoon crème fraîche
1 dessertspoon Dijon mustard
2 tablespoons flat-leaf parsley, chopped

- Stuff the basil into the neck cavity of the chicken.
- Place the chicken in a large saucepan, breast side up, and pour over the stock.
- Add the new potatoes.
- Season generously with salt and pepper.
- Bring the stock to a simmer on the hob and then cook, partially covered, for 20 minutes.
- Turn the chicken over in the stock and cook for another 20 minutes.
- Add the green beans and cook for a further 10 minutes.
- Remove the chicken and vegetables from the stock, keeping them warm by covering them with tin foil. Pour the stock into a jug.
- Remove the basil from the cavity of the chicken and chop it up finely.
- Heat the butter and oil in a medium saucepan.
- Add the flour and stir on a low heat for 2 minutes.
- Pour the stock into the butter and flour, gradually, stirring all the time and cook on a low simmer for 5 minutes.
- Remove from the heat and stir in the crème fraîche, mustard, chopped basil and parsley.
- Carve the chicken and serve it with the vegetables and sauce.

Apricot and cinnamon cake + custard

To get the perfect light sponge you should weigh all the eggs you are going to use and use the same weight in caster sugar, butter and flour as I have done below.

Apricot and cinnamon cake

3 eggs
the weight of the 3 eggs in caster sugar
the weight of the 3 eggs in softened butter
the weight of the 3 eggs in plain flour
1 scant teaspoon baking powder
1 teaspoon vanilla essence
½ teaspoon ground cinnamon
6 fresh ripe apricots, halved and stoned

- Preheat the oven to 180°C/350°F/gas 4.
- Grease a 27cm flan tin with a removable base.
- Using an electric mixer cream the butter and sugar together for 5 minutes, until light and fluffy.
- Sift the flour and the baking powder together.
- Add one egg and a tablespoon of flour to the butter and sugar and mix in thoroughly.
- Add the remaining eggs in exactly the same way.
- Add the remaining flour and fold it in gently.
- Add the vanilla essence and cinnamon.
- Spoon the mixture into the flan tin and then press the apricot halves into the mixture, cut side down.
- Bake for 25 minutes until brown on the top and firm in the centre so that when you pierce the cake with a skewer it comes away clean.

Custard

2 whole eggs
2 egg yolks
2 tablespoons caster sugar
600ml milk and double cream mixed
1 vanilla pod or a drop or two vanilla extract

- In a glass bowl beat the whole eggs, yolks and sugar with a wooden spoon for 2 minutes.
- Measure the milk and cream into a measuring jug, add the vanilla pod or the extract and microwave on high for 2 minutes. The milk and cream should be almost at boiling point.
- Place the glass bowl over a saucepan of gently simmering water.
- Add the milk and cream, stirring all the time to avoid lumps.
- If you are using the vanilla pod, scrape out the seeds into the mixture.
- Keep stirring for 10 minutes, by which time you should have a good consistency. An indication of when the custard is thick enough is that it will coat the back of the wooden spoon.
- You can make custard ahead of time but avoid reheating it, as it may curdle.

Mincemeat tart

I think it is a shame that people only tend to eat mincemeat at Christmas. If you have some mincemeat left over from Christmas, then this is a good way of making use of it later in the year.

For the sweet pastry

180g butter

75g icing sugar

2 egg yolks

225g plain flour

For the mincemeat filling

1 jar mincemeat

To make the pastry

- Mix the butter, icing sugar, egg yolks and flour together in a food processor until the mixture starts to combine.
- Turn out onto a floured surface and form into a ball.
- Wrap in cling-film and chill in the fridge for 30 minutes.

To make the tart

- Preheat the oven to 190°C/375°F/gas 5.
- Grease a 20cm diameter tart tin.
- Roll out the pastry and line the tart tin.
- Fill the pastry case with the mincemeat and with some of the left-over pastry make a lattice of pastry strips on top of the mincemeat.
- Place the tart tin on a baking sheet and bake for 20 minutes.
- Serve with whipped cream.

MARCH

Week 2

Monday p134	Sesame chicken + salad + baked potatoes
Tuesday p135	Tomato risotto + sausages
Wednesday p136	Spaghetti with pea sauce
Thursday p137	Steak Victor Hugo + grilled plum tomatoes + mushrooms + watercress salad
Friday p138	Tuna fish curry + boiled rice + lentil curry
Saturday p140	Lamb hotpot
Sunday p141	Pork with sage pesto stuffing and red onion potatoes + buttered spinach
Sunday pudding p142	Frangipane and marzipan tart
Extra tasty treat p143	Carrot cake

Shopping list

MEAT

- ☐ 6 sausages
- ☐ 6 chicken breasts, boneless
- ☐ 6 beef fillet steaks
- ☐ 700g lamb neck fillet
- ☐ 2kg piece rolled belly pork

FISH

- ☐ 700g tuna steaks

VEGETABLES

- ☐ 5 red onions
- ☐ 3 shallots
- ☐ 3 onions
- ☐ 10 radishes
- ☐ 6 baking potatoes
- ☐ 2kg potatoes
- ☐ 3 plum tomatoes
- ☐ 250g chestnut mushrooms
- ☐ 200g watercress
- ☐ 1 garlic bulb
- ☐ 550g carrots
- ☐ fresh ginger
- ☐ 1 bunch celery
- ☐ 250g spinach leaves

FRUIT

- ☐ 2 oranges
- ☐ 2 lemons

FRESH HERBS

- ☐ basil
- ☐ flat-leaf parsley
- ☐ bay leaves
- ☐ sage
- ☐ rosemary
- ☐ mint
- ☐ tarragon

FRIDGE ITEMS

- ☐ 3 packs butter
- ☐ 250g mascarpone cheese
- ☐ 50g Parmesan cheese
- ☐ 200g cubed pancetta
- ☐ 1.9 litres fresh chicken stock
- ☐ 200g fromage frais
- ☐ 500g frozen peas
- ☐ 250ml single cream
- ☐ 10 eggs
- ☐ 70g sliced pancetta
- ☐ 284ml buttermilk

KITCHEN CUPBOARD ITEMS

- ☐ olive oil
- ☐ extra virgin olive oil
- ☐ groundnut oil
- ☐ vegetable oil
- ☐ sunflower oil
- ☐ white wine vinegar
- ☐ salt
- ☐ 400g Arborio rice
- ☐ 400g tin chopped tomatoes
- ☐ 500g spaghetti
- ☐ 600ml coconut milk
- ☐ 500g basmati rice
- ☐ 200g red lentils
- ☐ 150ml dry white wine
- ☐ 75g icing sugar
- ☐ 285g plain flour
- ☐ 200g wholemeal self-raising flour
- ☐ 250g ground almonds
- ☐ almond extract
- ☐ 150g caster sugar
- ☐ 175g soft brown sugar
- ☐ amaretto liqueur
- ☐ 1 jar raspberry jam
- ☐ 200g white marzipan
- ☐ 100g pecan nuts
- ☐ bicarbonate of soda
- ☐ 100g sultanas
- ☐ 75g raisins
- ☐ 50g desiccated coconut
- ☐ horseradish sauce
- ☐ 1 white loaf for breadcrumbs
- ☐ 100g sesame seeds
- ☐ dried mustard powder

SPICES

- ☐ ground cinnamon
- ☐ dried oregano
- ☐ turmeric
- ☐ mixed spice
- ☐ black pepper
- ☐ whole coriander seeds
- ☐ fennel seeds
- ☐ cumin seeds
- ☐ cinnamon sticks
- ☐ curry leaves
- ☐ cayenne pepper
- ☐ fenugreek
- ☐ dried red chillies
- ☐ tamarind paste
- ☐ black mustard seeds
- ☐ whole nutmeg

Sesame chicken + salad + baked potatoes

Sesame seeds have a special flavour all of their own. They make a great crispy coating for chicken.

Sesame chicken

6 chicken breast fillets, skinless
1 teaspoon dried oregano
salt and pepper
284ml buttermilk
100g white breadcrumbs
100g sesame seeds
1 teaspoon dried mustard powder
2 tablespoons fresh flat-leaf parsley, chopped
2 tablespoons olive oil

- Preheat the oven to 200°C/400°F/gas 6.
- Place the chicken breasts in a large bowl along with the dried oregano, salt, pepper and buttermilk.
- Leave to marinate for at least 30 minutes.
- Mix the breadcrumbs in a bowl with the sesame seeds, mustard powder and chopped parsley. Season with salt and pepper.
- Remove the chicken breasts from the marinade and coat each one with the breadcrumb and sesame seed mix.
- Heat the olive oil in a frying pan and add two breasts at a time, browning them on each side.
- As soon as they are brown arrange the breasts on a shallow baking tin and bake for 20 minutes.
- Serve with the salad and baked potatoes.

Salad

5 carrots, peeled and grated, or finely chopped
1 red onion, finely sliced
3 tablespoons raisins
10 radishes, sliced
For the dressing
juice 1 lemon and 1 orange
freshly ground black pepper
20g fresh mint, chopped
2 tablespoons extra virgin olive oil

- Place the salad ingredients in a serving bowl.
- Combine the dressing ingredients in a small bowl and when ready pour over the salad.

Baked potatoes

6 baking potatoes
butter for serving
salt and pepper

- Preheat the oven to 220°C/425°F/gas 7.
- Pierce the potato skins with a sharp knife and put them in the oven for 1 hour 30 minutes.
- Split each one and serve with butter, salt and pepper.

Tomato risotto
+ sausages

This is one of my favourite risotto recipes as it has such a lovely rich flavour. To make it more of a meal that children will enjoy, I sometimes serve it with sausages, which is what I recommend here. I do use fresh chicken stock, as opposed to a cube, so as not to over-season the risotto.

Tomato risotto

3 tablespoons olive oil
50g unsalted butter
2 shallots, peeled and finely chopped
200g cubed pancetta
400g Arborio rice
400g tin chopped tomatoes
1.25 litres hot chicken stock
2 tablespoons Parmesan cheese, grated
5 fresh basil leaves, freshy torn
knob of butter
salt and pepper

- Warm the olive oil and butter in a heavy-bottomed saucepan.
- Add the shallots and sauté them for 5 minutes until soft and transparent.
- Add the pancetta and sauté for a further 2 minutes.
- Add the rice and stir to coat it in the oil and butter. Keep stirring and cooking the rice for 2 minutes.
- Add the tomatoes and cook the mixture for 2 minutes, stirring continuously.
- You now need to start adding the hot stock, a ladle at a time. Keep cooking and stirring the rice until the hot stock has been incorporated. Using this method the risotto will be ready in 20 minutes and you will find that you have used most, if not all, of the stock.
- Add the Parmesan cheese, basil and a knob of butter.
- Season to taste. You will definitely want black pepper but add according to your taste.

Sausages

6 sausages
olive oil

- Fry the sausages in a little olive oil in a large frying pan. Brown them on a reasonably high heat and then reduce the heat until they are cooked through, which should take about 20 minutes.

Spaghetti with pea sauce

As ever with pasta sauces, this one is supremely easy.

40g butter
1 large onion, finely chopped
2 cloves garlic, peeled and finely chopped
500g frozen peas
300ml chicken stock
salt and pepper
½ teaspoon sugar
250ml single cream
1 handful torn basil leaves
Parmesan cheese, grated for serving
500g spaghetti

- Gently warm the butter in a saucepan.
- Add the onion and garlic and fry gently on a low heat for 10 minutes until soft, stirring occasionally.
- Add the peas, stock, salt, pepper and sugar and bring to a simmer.
- Simmer covered for 20 minutes.
- Pour the cream onto the cooked peas. Bring to a simmer and cook for 1 minute.
- Adjust the seasoning.
- Sprinkle on the basil leaves and serve with lots of grated Parmesan.
- Bring a large saucepan of salted water to the boil and cook the spaghetti according to the packet instructions.

Steak Victor Hugo + grilled plum tomatoes + mushrooms + watercress salad

I found this recipe in a very old 1930s cook book that I bought by Elizabeth Craig, but, unfortunately, she makes no reference to the origins of the name. The sauce is rather like a béarnaise. I suggest you prepare the sauce first and fry the steaks just before you are ready to eat.

Steak Victor Hugo

For the sauce

1 shallot, finely diced
½ teaspoon tarragon, chopped
2 tablespoons white wine vinegar
2 egg yolks
150g butter, cubed and slightly softened
3 teaspoons horseradish sauce
salt and pepper

For the steaks

olive oil
6 beef fillet steaks

To make the sauce

- In a small saucepan simmer the shallot, tarragon and white wine vinegar for 2 minutes.
- Remove the saucepan from the heat and set aside.
- Place the egg yolks in a glass bowl over a pan of simmering water and beat for a few seconds.
- Pour the reduced vinegar, tarragon and shallots into the egg yolks.
- Keeping the egg yolks and vinegar mixture over the pan of simmering water, add the butter a cube at a time, whisking after each addition, while the butter slowly melts into the egg yolks and vinegar. You will end up with a thick, pale yellow sauce.
- Remove the glass bowl from the heat.
- Now add the horseradish to the sauce and season with salt and pepper.

To fry the steaks

- Rub the steaks with a little olive oil and season them with pepper.
- Heat a frying pan until it is very hot and then sear each steak for 2 minutes, without moving it. Turn them and cook for another 2 minutes on the other side. Adjust these cooking times depending on how you like your steak cooked. If you press your finger into the steak and a gentle impression is left, this usually means that the steak is medium rare.

Grilled plum tomatoes

3 plum tomatoes, halved
salt and pepper
1 tablespoon extra virgin olive oil

- Preheat the grill.
- Place the tomatoes on a baking tray and season them with salt and pepper.
- Grill the tomatoes for 10 minutes and then drizzle them with the olive oil.

Fried mushrooms

25g butter
250g chestnuts mushrooms, thinly sliced
salt and pepper

- Melt the butter in a frying pan and fry the mushrooms on a medium heat for 5 minutes until they are nice and brown.
- Season them with salt and pepper.

Watercress salad

200g watercress
salt and pepper
1 tablespoon extra virgin olive oil

- Place the watercress in a serving bowl and dress with the salt, pepper and olive oil.

Tuna fish curry + boiled rice + lentil curry

Tuna is a great fish to curry as it remains firm in texture once it is cooked.

Tuna fish curry

1 teaspoon turmeric
1 teaspoon salt
½ teaspoon black pepper
700g fresh tuna steaks
2 tablespoons groundnut oil
1 dessertspoon whole coriander seeds
1 teaspoon fennel seeds
½ teaspoon cumin seeds
1 red onion, sliced
2cm piece fresh ginger, peeled and finely chopped
2 cloves garlic, peeled and finely chopped
3cm piece cinnamon stick
10 curry leaves
¼ teaspoon cayenne pepper
pinch fenugreek
1 dried red chilli
1 dessertspoon tamarind paste
400ml tin coconut milk

- Mix the turmeric, salt and pepper on a plate and rub into each side of the fish steaks.
- Heat the groundnut oil in a large saucepan.
- When hot add the fish pieces and brown them on each side for a few seconds only.
- Remove the fish and set aside. Keep the saucepan with the oil, as you will need this in a minute.
- In a small frying pan toast the coriander seeds, fennel seeds and cumin seeds until you smell the aroma of their toasting. Grind the spices into a powder using a pestle and mortar.
- In the saucepan reheat the oil and add the red onion, ginger, garlic, cinnamon stick, curry leaves, cayenne, fenugreek and red chilli.
- Fry for 4 minutes until the onion is soft, stirring as you go.
- Add the ground spices and stir for 1 minute.
- Add the tamarind paste and stir for 30 seconds.
- Add the coconut milk and return the fish to the pan.
- Bring the fish to a simmer and cook, covered, for 3 minutes, moving the fish around so that it all cooks evenly.

Boiled rice

500ml basmati rice
750ml water
salt

- Put the rice in a saucepan with the water and a pinch of salt.
- Place the rice on a high heat and as soon as it comes to the boil cover the saucepan with a lid and turn the heat right down to very low. Leave it like this for 15 minutes, giving it one stir only during the cooking time.
- Then remove from the heat and leave it covered for a further 10 minutes, before you remove the lid.

Lentil curry

1 tablespoon vegetable oil
1 medium onion, diced finely
6 curry leaves
½ teaspoon cumin seeds
½ teaspoon turmeric
½ teaspoon black mustard seeds
200g red lentils
600ml water
200ml coconut milk
1 teaspoon salt

- Heat the vegetable oil in a medium saucepan.
- Add the onion, curry leaves, cumin seeds, turmeric and black mustard seeds and cook until the onion starts to turn a golden brown. This should take about 5 minutes.
- Add the lentils and water and bring to the boil.

- Reduce the heat to the slightest simmer and cook uncovered for about 40 minutes.
- Try the lentils and if there is still the slightest hardness to them, then cook for a few minutes longer.
- Add the coconut milk and bring to a simmer again.
- Add the salt and set aside. You can reheat it when you are ready to serve.

Lamb hotpot

This is a classic English dish and, as with so many English classics, it is pure comfort food. It is perfect for a Saturday evening.

1 tablespoon olive oil
20g butter
2 carrots, finely diced
2 sticks celery, finely sliced
1 onion, finely diced
70g sliced pancetta, chopped into small pieces
150ml dry white wine
300ml chicken stock
2 bay leaves
1kg potatoes, peeled and sliced into 1cm thick discs
700g lamb neck fillet, sliced into 2cm slices
1 sprig rosemary
salt and pepper
20g butter, cut into little cubes

- Preheat oven to 170°C/325°F/gas 3.
- Heat the oil and butter in a large saucepan.
- Add the carrots, celery, onion and pancetta and cook for 10 minutes on a medium heat.
- Add the wine and let it bubble away for 2 minutes.
- Add the stock and bay leaves and simmer for 2 minutes.
- Place half the potatoes in a layer on the bottom of a large casserole pan.
- Put the lamb and rosemary on top and season with salt and pepper.
- Pour over the stock and vegetables and finish with the remaining potatoes in a layer. The liquid should come up to just below the last layer of potatoes.
- Dot the potatoes with the small cubes of butter and season again with salt and pepper.
- Place the lid on the casserole and cook in the oven for 1 hour 30 minutes.
- Remove the lid and cook the hotpot for another 30 minutes so that the potatoes become nice and brown.

Pork with sage pesto stuffing and red onion potatoes + buttered spinach

Pork and sage is a classic combination. This dish is quite spring-like in flavour, although one usually associates pork with the winter months. Serve with buttered spinach or green beans as above.

Pork with sage pesto stuffing and red onion potatoes

2kg piece rolled belly pork
juice 1 lemon

For the sage pesto stuffing

2 cloves garlic, peeled and crushed
1 tablespoon salt
3 tablespoons olive oil
10–12 fresh sage leaves
black pepper

For the potatoes with red onions

1kg peeled, quartered potatoes, parboiled in salted water for 5 minutes
3 red onions, peeled and quartered
1 tablespoon olive oil

- Unroll the belly pork and put it on a plate uncovered in the fridge to dry out overnight. If you don't get around to doing this pat it dry with a piece of kitchen roll.
- Preheat the oven to 230°C/450°F/gas 8.
- If your butcher has not already done so, score the pork rind with a sharp knife making sure you go through the rind and fat. Set the pork aside while you prepare the stuffing.
- To make the sage pesto place the garlic, salt, 2 tablespoons of the olive oil, the sage leaves and some black pepper in a food processor or liquidizer and blitz until you have a rough paste.
- Rub the pesto onto the inside of the unrolled pork.
- Roll up the pork and retie tightly with string.
- Rub the remaining tablespoon of olive oil and the lemon juice into the rind of the pork and sprinkle with salt.
- Place the pork joint in a large roasting tin with the parboiled potatoes and red onions around it.
- Drizzle the onions and potatoes with one tablespoon of olive oil.
- Roast for 30 minutes.
- Reduce the oven temperature to 190°C/375°F/gas 5 and roast for a further 1 hour and 30 minutes.
- Remove the pork and let it rest on a heated serving dish for 15 minutes, while keeping the potatoes warm in a low oven.

Buttered spinach

250g spinach leaves, rinsed
1 tablespoon water
salt
pepper
small knob of butter
nutmeg

- Place the spinach in a large saucepan with the water and a pinch of salt.
- Cover and place the saucepan on a low heat.
- Gradually wilt the spinach for 10 minutes, until all the leaves are a glossy dark green.
- Remove the lid and stir around for a few seconds to get rid of any excess water. You may want to drain any extra off if you feel there is too much.
- Add the butter, a tiny grating of nutmeg and a good grinding of black pepper.

Frangipane and marzipan tart

This recipe originally came from an old magazine cutting. It is a fabulous almond concoction that is well worth the effort.

For the pastry
180g butter, chilled and cubed
75g icing sugar
2 egg yolks
225g plain flour
For the filling
250g ground almonds
few drops almond extract
175g butter, softened
150g caster sugar
60g plain flour
1 tablespoon amaretto
4 eggs
½ jar raspberry jam
200g white marzipan

- Grease a 24cm tart tin.
- Preheat the oven to 200°C/400°F/gas 6.

To make the pastry case

- Place the butter, icing sugar, egg yolks and flour together in a food processor and process until the mixture just starts to combine.
- Turn out onto a floured surface and form into a ball.
- Wrap in cling-film and chill in the fridge for 30 minutes.
- When ready, roll out the pastry and line the tart tin with it.
- Lay a sheet of baking parchment on top of the pastry case and pour some baking beans on top of the paper.
- Place in the oven for 15 minutes and then remove the pastry case from the oven and discard the paper and baking beans.
- Reduce the oven temperature to 180°C/350°F/gas 4.

To make the filling

- Put the almonds, almond extract, butter, sugar, flour, amaretto and eggs in a food mixer or food processor and mix until smooth.
- Spread the raspberry jam onto the bottom of the pastry case.
- Spoon the almond filling on top of the jam and place the tart in the oven to bake for 40 minutes, until firm to the touch.
- Leave to cool for 30 minutes.
- Preheat the grill.
- Roll out the marzipan to a thin round the size of the tart and lay it on top of the tart.
- Place the tart under the grill for a few minutes, watching it the whole time, until the marzipan browns.
- Serve with crème fraîche.

Carrot cake

Carrot cake is American in origin. Its moist texture accounts for its popularity.

For the cake
50g pecan nuts
175g soft brown sugar
2 eggs
150ml sunflower oil
200g wholemeal self-raising flour
3 level teaspoons mixed spice
1 level teaspoon bicarbonate of soda
grated zest 1 orange
200g carrots, grated
100g sultanas
50g desiccated coconut
For the filling and topping
250g mascarpone cheese
200g fromage frais
1 tablespoon caster sugar
1 teaspoon ground cinnamon
For the decoration
pecan nut halves

To make the cake

- Preheat the oven to 200°C/400°F/gas 6.
- Grease and line two 20cm sandwich cake tins.
- Place the pecan nuts on a baking sheet and toast them in the oven for 7 minutes.
- Then chop the nuts roughly and set aside.
- Reduce the oven temperature to 170°C/325°F/gas 3.
- Whisk the sugar, eggs and oil together in an electric mixer or with an electric hand whisk for 2 minutes.
- Sift in the flour, mixed spice and bicarbonate of soda and stir in gently.
- Add the rest of the cake ingredients and stir gently.
- Spoon the batter equally between the two cake tins.
- Bake for 30 minutes.

To make the filling and topping

- Whisk all the topping ingredients together in a mixing bowl until light and fluffy.
- Once the cakes have cooled fill them with some of the topping and then spread the remainder round the sides and on the top.

To decorate

- Lay the pecan nut halves in an attractive pattern on top of the cake.

Week 3

Monday p146	Meatloaf + potato salad + tomato salad
Tuesday p147	Fusilli with mushroom and tomato sauce
Wednesday p148	Pork schnitzel + boiled potatoes with parsley + carrots and peas
Thursday p149	Curried eggs + boiled rice + dry potato curry + tomato salad
Friday p151	Poached cod and salmon with egg, chickpeas and leeks
Saturday p152	Irish stew
Sunday p153	Daube de porc + boiled potatoes
Sunday pudding p154	Stewed apple + rice pudding
Extra tasty treat p155	Victoria sandwich with vanilla and raspberry filling

Shopping list

MEAT

- ☐ 350g sausage meat
- ☐ 1.5kg lamb shoulder chops, on the bone
- ☐ 6 boneless pork steaks
- ☐ 1.2kg pork shoulder
- ☐ 675g minced beef

FISH

- ☐ 250g smoked cod fillet
- ☐ 500g salmon fillets
- ☐ 250g cooked prawns

VEGETABLES

- ☐ 150g leeks
- ☐ 1 garlic bulb
- ☐ 6 onions
- ☐ 1kg carrots
- ☐ 3kg potatoes
- ☐ 500g new potatoes
- ☐ 450g chestnut mushrooms
- ☐ fresh ginger
- ☐ 12 medium tomatoes

FRUIT

- ☐ 2 lemons
- ☐ 900g cooking apples

FRESH HERBS

- ☐ rosemary
- ☐ chives
- ☐ bay leaves
- ☐ sage
- ☐ flat-leaf parsley
- ☐ coriander

FRIDGE ITEMS

- ☐ 2 packs butter
- ☐ 18 eggs
- ☐ 1550ml full fat milk
- ☐ 400ml single cream
- ☐ 200g sliced pancetta
- ☐ 50g Parmesan cheese
- ☐ 200g frozen petits pois
- ☐ 300ml chicken stock
- ☐ 150ml apple juice
- ☐ 250ml double cream

KITCHEN CUPBOARD ITEMS

- ☐ olive oil
- ☐ vegetable oil
- ☐ balsamic vinegar
- ☐ 1 tin chickpeas
- ☐ 1 bottle red wine
- ☐ 2 x 400g tins chopped tomatoes
- ☐ salt
- ☐ light soy sauce
- ☐ vegetable stock cubes
- ☐ 2 loaves white bread
- ☐ 10 cornichons
- ☐ 1 jar mayonnaise
- ☐ tomato purée
- ☐ 500g basmati rice
- ☐ dried porcini mushrooms
- ☐ 250g caster sugar
- ☐ 500g fusilli pasta
- ☐ 50g sultanas
- ☐ 100g soft brown sugar
- ☐ 110g short-grain pudding rice
- ☐ 1 tin condensed milk
- ☐ 200g plain flour
- ☐ vanilla essence
- ☐ 125g icing sugar
- ☐ raspberry jam
- ☐ mustard powder
- ☐ baking powder
- ☐ 1 jar chutney

SPICES

- ☐ paprika
- ☐ black pepper
- ☐ ground coriander
- ☐ cayenne pepper
- ☐ ground cumin
- ☐ dried oregano
- ☐ cumin seeds
- ☐ coriander seeds
- ☐ fennel seeds
- ☐ fenugreek
- ☐ cinnamon sticks

Meatloaf
+ potato salad + tomato salad

My husband, being half-German, was brought up eating meatloaf. It is such an easy meal to prepare and the taste is lovely, especially if you can get good quality sausage meat.

Meatloaf

15g butter
1 tablespoon olive oil
1 large onion, finely diced
2 garlic cloves, finely chopped
30g white breadcrumbs
675g minced beef
350g sausage meat
2 eggs, lightly beaten
2 tablespoons flat-leaf parsley, chopped
1 teaspoon dried oregano
salt and freshly-ground pepper

- Preheat the oven to 180°C/350°F/gas 4.
- Place the butter and oil in a heavy-bottomed frying pan, on a medium heat and gently cook the onion and garlic for 10 minutes until soft, taking care not to burn the garlic. Scrape the onion and garlic into a mixing bowl.
- Add the remaining ingredients to the mixing bowl and mix thoroughly.
- To make a successful meatloaf the seasoning must be right, so while taking care not to add too much salt, be generous with the freshly-ground black pepper. The best way to ensure a good taste is to fry a small knob of the mixture and add more seasoning if required.
- Next, spoon the mixture into a buttered loaf tin, which is 6.5cm deep, 23cm long and 12.5cm wide, smoothing and pressing down the mixture. Bang the filled loaf tin hard on a solid surface to ensure that there are no air bubbles in the mixture. Any air bubbles will appear as holes and make the loaf crumble on slicing.
- Bake for 1 hour 30 minutes.
- Leave to cool and then turn out onto a serving plate.
- Serve with a good chutney and the potato and tomato salads below.

Potato salad

500g new potatoes
small bunch fresh chives, finely snipped
10 cornichons, chopped into small rounds
3 tablespoons mayonnaise (good quality shop-bought mayonnaise will do unless you want to make your own, see p.125 tartare mayonnaise)

- Boil the potatoes with their skins on in salted water until tender. This should take about 15 minutes once the water has reached boiling point.
- When they're cooled, cut the potatoes in half. You can peel them if you prefer, or leave the skins on. Place them in a serving bowl.
- Add the rest of the ingredients and serve.

Tomato salad

6 ripe tomatoes
For the dressing
1 dessertspoon olive oil
1 teaspoon balsamic vinegar
salt and pepper

- Slice the tomatoes and lay them on a serving plate.
- Mix the dressing in a small bowl and drizzle it over the tomatoes.

Fusilli with mushroom and tomato sauce

This is based on a recipe in Sophie Grigson's book *Organic*. The sauce in her recipe accompanies gnocchi but I find the sauce more popular with fusilli in my household. I have altered the quantities slightly.

1 handful dried porcini mushrooms, soaked in warm water for 10 minutes
3 tablespoons olive oil
1 onion, finely diced
1 clove garlic, peeled and finely chopped
8 sage leaves, shredded
250g chestnut mushrooms, thickly sliced
400g tin chopped Italian tomatoes
1 tablespoon tomato purée
1 teaspoon caster sugar
2 tablespoons flat-leaf parsley, chopped
salt and pepper
500g fusilli pasta
Parmesan cheese, grated for serving

- Drain the porcini mushrooms, retaining the water.
- Finely chop the porcini mushrooms and set aside.
- Warm the olive oil in a large sauté pan and gently fry the onion for 10 minutes.
- Add the garlic and sage and fry for 2 minutes.
- Add the chestnut mushrooms and the porcini mushrooms and fry them together on a high heat until the mushrooms start to turn a beautiful golden brown.
- Pour on the tomatoes.
- Add the tomato purée, sugar, parsley and the mushroom water.
- Simmer the sauce, uncovered, very gently for 30 minutes.
- The sauce is quite a glutinous one and so shouldn't be runny. If the sauce starts to stick while it cooks add a little water, but be careful not to add too much. If you simmer it at a very low heat this should not happen.
- Once the sauce is cooked, season with salt and pepper.
- Next cook the fusilli according to the packet instructions.
- Pour the sauce over the drained pasta and serve with Parmesan cheese.

Pork schnitzel + boiled potatoes with parsley + carrots and peas

My husband's mother makes a very good schnitzel; being German, she should do as it is definitely everyday food in Germany. Cook the vegetables first, as they take longer than the pork.

Pork schnitzel

6 boneless pork steaks
200g white breadcrumbs
1 teaspoon salt
black pepper
1 teaspoon mustard powder
½ teaspoon paprika
2 eggs, beaten
20g butter
1 tablespoon olive oil

- Preheat the oven to 100°C.
- Take a steak mallet or a rolling pin and give the pork steaks a good pounding until they are half their original thickness.
- Season the breadcrumbs with the salt, pepper, mustard and paprika.
- Dip each steak in the beaten egg and then coat each one in the breadcrumbs and set aside.
- When the vegetables are almost cooked, start to cook the schnitzel.
- Heat the butter and oil in a frying pan.
- When the fat starts to foam, fry each schnitzel for 2–3 minutes on each side. Place the cooked schnitzel in the oven to keep warm while you cook the rest.

Boiled potatoes with parsley

800g potatoes, peeled and quartered
salt
butter for serving
2 tablespoons finely chopped flat-leaf parsley
black pepper

- Boil the potatoes in salted water until tender.
- Drain the potatoes and then return them to the saucepan, along with the butter.
- Sprinkle them with parsley and a good grinding of black pepper.

Carrots and peas

15g butter
300g carrots, peeled and chopped widthways to a 1cm thickness
200g frozen petits pois
salt and pepper

- Melt the butter in a small saucepan and add the carrots.
- Turn the heat down to very low and cover the saucepan with a lid.
- Cook the carrots for 10 minutes and then add the peas with 2 tablespoons of water.
- Cook, covered on a low heat for 3 minutes.
- Season with salt and pepper.

Curried eggs + boiled rice + dry potato curry + tomato salad

We used to have curried eggs when we were little. It was never a very glamorous meal but I always loved it and I expect my mother made it because it was cheap and quick to produce. For similar reasons, my husband used to have mustard eggs when he was growing up in Germany.

Curried eggs

¼ teaspoon cayenne pepper
½ teaspoon ground cumin
1 teaspoon curry powder*
1 teaspoon ground coriander
1 tablespoon lemon juice
½ teaspoon salt
pepper
1 tablespoon vegetable oil
1 medium onion, finely diced
2.5cm piece fresh ginger, peeled and finely chopped
2 teaspoons tomato purée
150ml chicken stock
250ml single cream
2 tablespoons fresh coriander, chopped
7 eggs, hard boiled, peeled and halved
black pepper

- Mix the cayenne, cumin, curry powder, ground coriander, lemon juice, salt and pepper in a small bowl with one tablespoon of water and set aside.
- Warm the oil in a large frying pan and on a medium heat fry the onion until it starts to brown. Add the ginger and stir for 10 seconds.

continues

- Stir in the tomato purée, chicken stock, cream and the spice mixture and bring to a simmer.
- Cover and simmer gently for 2 minutes.
- Remove from the heat and add the fresh coriander.
- Lay the egg halves in the sauce so the yolks face upwards and spoon the sauce over them. Set aside while you prepare the rice, potatoes and tomatoes.
- When ready to serve, cover and simmer gently for 2 minutes.

Boiled rice

500g basmati rice
750ml water
salt

- Put the rice in a saucepan with the water and a pinch of salt.
- Place the rice on a high heat and as soon as it comes to the boil cover the saucepan with a lid and turn the heat right down to very low. Leave it for 15 minutes, giving it one stir only during the cooking time.
- Then take it off the heat and leave it covered for a further 10 minutes before removing the lid.

Dry potato curry

450g potatoes, peeled and quartered
2 tablespoons vegetable oil
½ teaspoon cumin seeds
2 teaspoons peeled and grated fresh ginger
1 teaspoon salt
1 teaspoon ground cumin
¼ teaspoon cayenne pepper
freshly ground black pepper
2 tablespoons fresh coriander, chopped

- Cook the potatoes in boiling salted water until tender. Drain them and set aside to cool.
- Put the oil in a large, heavy-bottomed frying pan and set the pan over a medium heat.
- When the oil is hot add the cumin seeds and fry them for 10 seconds.
- Add the potatoes, ginger, salt, ground cumin, cayenne and black pepper.
- Brown the potatoes on a medium heat for about 10 minutes.
- Stir in the coriander and serve.

Tomato salad

6 medium tomatoes, cut into eights
salt
lemon juice

- Place the tomatoes in a serving bowl.
- Sprinkle with salt and pour the lemon juice over them.

**** To make your own curry powder***
1 tablespoon coriander seeds
1 dessertspoon cumin seeds
1 teaspoon fennel seeds
½ teaspoon fenugreek

- *Place the coriander seeds into a small, heavy-bottomed pan and heat through for 30 seconds.*
- *Add the other ingredients and toast until you smell the lovely aroma of the spices.*
- *Transfer the spices to a coffee grinder, a small processor or grind them in a pestle and mortar.*

Poached cod and salmon with egg, chickpeas and leeks

Fish and eggs make a great combination. This is a light meal that is full of protein. Anyone who feels ambivalent about fish might be more enthusiastic after this meal.

3 eggs
25g butter
150g leeks, washed and finely sliced
410g tin chickpeas, drained
400ml full fat milk
250g smoked cod fillet
500g salmon fillets
250g cooked prawns
150ml single cream
small bunch chives, snipped

- Boil the eggs for 3 minutes and leave in their shells.
- Heat the butter in a large saucepan and gently cook the leeks for 3 minutes.
- Add the chickpeas to the leeks and cook, covered, for 5 minutes on a gentle heat.
- Add the milk and bring to a simmer.
- Add the cod and salmon fillets, reduce the heat, cover and cook for 3 minutes.
- Turn the fish fillets over and then cook them for a further 2 minutes.
- Remove the skin, if any, from the fish and then flake the fish up slightly in the saucepan with a fork.
- Add the prawns and the cream and stir in.
- Warm the prawns and cream through on a gentle heat for 2 minutes.
- Shell the eggs, halve each one and serve each half on top of each serving of the fish.
- Snip the chives over the top and serve with thinly sliced, hot, buttered toast.

Irish stew

This is a simple, understated meal that is welcome on a cold night. It can be served with dumplings but I have chosen not to on this occasion.

50g butter
1.5kg lamb shoulder chops, on the bone
2 large onions, sliced
700g carrots, peeled and cut into chunks
1kg potatoes, peeled and halved
1 bay leaf
1 sprig rosemary
1 tablespoon light soy sauce
salt and pepper
500ml vegetable stock (a stock cube will do)

- Warm the butter in a large saucepan on a medium heat.
- Brown the lamb in the butter in manageable batches.
- Set the lamb aside.
- In the same saucepan cook the onion and carrots for 4 minutes, until lightly browned.
- Return the meat to the pan along with the potatoes, herbs, soy sauce, salt, pepper and the stock.
- Cover and simmer on a very low heat for 2 hours.
- Check the seasoning and serve.

Daube de porc
+ buttered boiled potatoes

Though this dish is very straightforward to make, the mouthwatering smell when it is cooking in the oven and the huge flavours you experience when you tuck in make it a meal to remember. I am sure you will want to serve it up more than once a year.

Daube de porc

1.2kg pork shoulder, diced
300ml red wine
2 tablespoons olive oil
2 teaspoons salt
a good grinding black pepper
4 sage leaves, finely chopped
1 bay leaf
2 cloves garlic, peeled and crushed
1 large onion, finely sliced
2 carrots, thinly sliced
200g sliced pancetta
200g chestnut mushrooms, sliced
400g tin chopped tomatoes
150ml chicken stock

- Preheat the oven to170°C/325°F/gas 3.
- Place the pork in a bowl with the wine, oil, salt, pepper, herbs, garlic, onion and carrots and stir well.
- Lay one third of the sliced pancetta on the bottom of a casserole dish.
- On top of the pancetta scatter half the mushrooms along with half the tinned tomatoes.
- Spoon half of the meat mixture on top of the mushrooms and tomatoes.
- Layer another third of the pancetta on top of the meat. Then scatter over the remaining mushrooms and tomatoes.
- Next, spoon on the remaining meat and end with a layer of the remaining pancetta.
- Pour the marinade into the casserole dish and pour on enough of the chicken stock to bring the liquid up to just below the level of the meat.
- Season with more salt and a good grinding of pepper.
- Bring to a simmer on the hob and then place in the oven and cook for 2 hours.

Buttered boiled potatoes

700g potatoes, peeled and quartered
salt and pepper
knob of butter

- Boil the potatoes in salted water for 15 minutes or so until tender.
- Season with pepper.
- Serve with a knob of butter.

Stewed apple + rice pudding

This is a quick, easy rice pudding and I think it is every bit as good as the traditional baked variety. Stewed apples go beautifully with rice pudding.

Stewed apple

900g cooking apples, peeled, cored and cut into 8 pieces
50g sultanas
10g soft brown sugar
2cm piece cinnamon stick
150ml apple juice

- Place all the ingredients in a saucepan.
- Cover with a lid and stew on a low heat without stirring for 30 minutes, until the apples are soft but still maintain their shape.

Rice pudding

110g short-grain pudding rice
60g butter
2 teaspoons sugar
1.15 litres full fat milk
4 tablespoons double cream
4 tablespoons condensed milk
pinch of salt

- Put all the ingredients together in a saucepan.
- Slowly bring the pan to the boil.
- Lower the heat and simmer on a very low heat for 40 minutes, stirring regularly, until the pudding has thickened and the rice is tender. There will appear to be too much milk when you start to cook the rice, but suddenly the rice will expand and you will have a lovely creamy dessert.

Victoria sandwich with vanilla and raspberry filling

The key to a good Victoria sandwich is to cream the sugar and butter for a sufficient length of time and to sieve the flour before adding it to the mixture. I recommend using plain flour with baking powder instead of self-raising, as I think that self-raising flour contains too much baking powder. You will need an electric mixer or hand-held electric mixer to make this cake.

For the sponge cakes

4 eggs (weigh the eggs together and then use the same weight in sugar, butter and flour)
caster sugar
butter, softened
plain flour sifted with 1½ teaspoons baking powder
1 teaspoon vanilla essence
salt

For the filling

40g butter, very soft
125g icing sugar, sieved
40g sweetened condensed milk
40ml double cream
3 tablespoons raspberry jam

To make the sponge cakes

- Preheat the oven to 180°C/350°F/gas 4.
- Grease and line two 21cm cake tins.
- Cream the butter and sugar together with a mixer until white and fluffy. This will take at least 5 minutes.
- Add one egg to the butter and sugar with one tablespoon of flour and beat to combine.
- Add the remaining three eggs, one at a time with a tablespoon of flour, making sure each egg is combined before adding the next.
- Once all the eggs have been added, fold in the remaining flour with a metal spoon.
- Add the vanilla essence and a pinch of salt.
- Spoon the mixture equally between the two cake tins and then bake the cakes for 25 minutes until firm to the touch or until a skewer placed into the centre of the cakes comes out clean.
- Let the cakes cool slightly and then turn them out onto a cooling rack.

To make the filling

- Cream the butter for 5 minutes.
- Add the icing sugar and mix until combined.
- Now add the condensed milk and the cream and mix in.
- When the cakes have completely cooled, spread the raspberry jam onto one of the cakes and the frosting onto the other and then sandwich them together.
- Dust the top of the cake with sifted icing sugar.

MARCH

Week 4

Monday p158	Pork and prawns with noodles
Tuesday p159	Smoky chicken stew
Wednesday p160	Roast monkfish + roast potatoes + watercress and rocket
Thursday p161	Chickpea and vegetable stew + buttered couscous
Friday p162	Herby cream cheese chicken breasts with leeks + roast potatoes
Saturday p163	Calves' liver with pancetta + mashed potato + buttered spinach
Sunday p164	Shin of beef stew with chive and horseradish dumplings
Sunday pudding p166	Baked honeyed custard tart
Extra tasty treat p167	Ice cream with hot toffee sauce

Shopping list

MEAT

- ☐ 500g minced pork
- ☐ 6 chicken legs
- ☐ 6 chicken breasts, boneless
- ☐ 4-6 pieces calves' liver
- ☐ 1kg shin beef

FISH

- ☐ 250g cooked prawns
- ☐ 1kg monkfish tail, removed from the bone

VEGETABLES

- ☐ 6 spring onions
- ☐ 1 garlic bulb
- ☐ fresh ginger
- ☐ 1 red pepper
- ☐ 1 red onion
- ☐ 4.1kg potatoes
- ☐ 70g watercress
- ☐ 70g rocket
- ☐ 225g onions
- ☐ 140g sweet potatoes
- ☐ 8 carrots
- ☐ 180g courgettes
- ☐ 4 leeks
- ☐ 250g spinach leaves
- ☐ 1 swede
- ☐ 6 shallots

FRESH HERBS

- ☐ mint
- ☐ coriander
- ☐ flat-leaf parsley
- ☐ sage
- ☐ rosemary
- ☐ thyme
- ☐ bay leaves
- ☐ chives

FRIDGE ITEMS

- ☐ 2 packs butter
- ☐ 8 frankfurter sausages
- ☐ 300ml chicken stock
- ☐ 600ml vegetable stock
- ☐ 500ml beef stock
- ☐ 200g cream cheese
- ☐ 210g sliced pancetta
- ☐ 7 eggs
- ☐ 500ml full fat milk

KITCHEN CUPBOARD ITEMS

- ☐ 400g medium Chinese egg noodles
- ☐ vegetable oil
- ☐ olive oil
- ☐ extra virgin olive oil
- ☐ fish sauce
- ☐ 2 tablespoons soy sauce
- ☐ 200ml coconut milk
- ☐ salt
- ☐ 510ml white wine
- ☐ balsamic vinegar
- ☐ 1 tin chickpeas
- ☐ 2 x 400g tins chopped tomatoes
- ☐ 250g couscous
- ☐ 300g plain flour
- ☐ 175g self-raising flour
- ☐ 500ml pale ale
- ☐ 75g shredded vegetable suet
- ☐ mustard powder
- ☐ runny honey
- ☐ horseradish sauce
- ☐ grain mustard
- ☐ 150ml maple syrup
- ☐ 225g soft brown sugar
- ☐ vanilla extract
- ☐ 75g icing sugar
- ☐ a handful dried porcini mushrooms

SPICES

- ☐ cumin seeds
- ☐ turmeric
- ☐ ground ginger
- ☐ whole nutmeg
- ☐ black pepper
- ☐ paprika

Pork and prawns with noodles

For busy people it is difficult trying to think of different things to cook for the family every day, which was one of the reasons I began this book. It is easy to fall into the habit of producing 'meat and two veg' type meals which, although great to eat, can quickly become boring. This meal is full of different flavours and at the same time is relatively quick to make.

400g medium Chinese egg noodles
2 tablespoons vegetable oil
6 spring onions, finely chopped
2 cloves garlic, peeled and finely chopped
2cm piece fresh ginger, peeled and finely chopped
500g minced pork
3 tablespoons fish sauce
1 teaspoon sugar
1 teaspoon paprika
2 tablespoons soy sauce
200ml coconut milk
250g cooked prawns
salt and pepper
10 mint leaves, finely chopped

- Cook the egg noodles following the packet instructions and then set aside.
- Heat the oil in a frying pan.
- Add the onions, garlic and ginger and fry on a low heat for 3 minutes until soft.
- Add the pork and fry on a high heat until browned all over, stirring continuously.
- Pour on the fish sauce, sugar, paprika and the soy sauce and stir until combined.
- Add the coconut milk and the prawns and heat through, bringing the pan to a simmer. Once a simmer is reached, remove the pan from the heat, otherwise the prawns will become rubbery.
- Taste and then season with salt and pepper, if necessary.
- Sprinkle on the chopped mint.
- Combine the meat and prawn mixture with the noodles and serve.

Smoky chicken stew

Chicken legs make the basis of a great stew as they don't lose their flavour when they are cooked. This is one of those meals that was thrown together in desperation one evening when I was trying to think of something different to make. It worked quite well so I've included it here.

20g butter
6 chicken legs, skin removed
salt and pepper
8 frankfurter sausages, chopped into 2cm chunks
1 tablespoon flour
200ml white wine
1 red pepper, deseeded and roughly chopped
1 handful dried porcini mushrooms
6 medium potatoes, peeled and halved
300ml chicken stock
a small bunch flat-leaf parsley, chopped

- Melt the butter in large saucepan.
- Brown the chicken legs all over in the butter for 10 minutes and season them with salt and pepper.
- Remove the legs and set aside, keeping the pan on the heat.
- Brown the frankfurters and set them aside.
- Add the flour to the pan and stir it around to soak up the fat.
- Add the wine and stir until the lumps have disappeared.
- Return the meat to the pan.
- Add the vegetables.
- Pour over the stock and cook, covered, on a gentle simmer for 40 minutes.
- Check the seasoning and sprinkle over the parsley before serving.

Roast monkfish + roast potatoes + watercress and rocket

Monkfish roasts well and goes brilliantly with rosemary and garlic. This recipe is simplicity itself.

Roast monkfish tail

1kg monkfish tail, removed from the bone
2 cloves garlic, cut into thin slivers
1 sprig rosemary
1 red onion, thinly sliced
110ml dry white wine
110ml olive oil
salt and pepper

- Once the monkfish has been removed from the bone it should be in two long pieces. Keep it like this. If the tail is small, then use two tails.
- With a sharp knife cut 7 or 8 slits all over the fish and into each one insert a sliver of garlic and a piece of rosemary.
- Lay the fish in an ovenproof dish with the onion, pour over the wine and oil and season with salt and a generous amount of pepper.
- Leave to marinate for 30 minutes.
- Preheat the oven to 190°C/375°F/gas 5.
- Roast the fish for 30 minutes, basting intermittently with the juices.

Roast potatoes

1kg potatoes, peeled and quartered
salt
1 sprig rosemary
2 tablespoons olive oil

- Preheat the oven to 220°C/425°F/gas 7.
- Parboil the potatoes in salted water for 4 minutes.
- Drain and place them in a roasting tin with the rosemary sprigs.
- Drizzle with the olive oil and roast for 45–60 minutes until golden brown.

Watercress and rocket

70g watercress
70g rocket
For the dressing
3 dessertspoons extra virgin olive oil
1 dessertspoon balsamic vinegar
good grinding salt and pepper

- Place the leaves in a serving dish.
- Mix the ingredients for the dressing together in a small bowl and drizzle it over the leaves when you are ready to serve.

Chickpea and vegetable stew + buttered couscous

This fragrant stew is based on a recipe from Madhur Jaffrey's book *World Vegetarian*, which is a treasure trove of interesting vegetable dishes. I sometimes worry about serving something so obviously vegetarian to the children, but you have to weigh this anxiety against the benefit they derive from not consuming meat every single day of the week. This meal is so tasty and filling that the children tuck in with no complaints.

Chickpea and vegetable stew

2 tablespoons olive oil
225g onion, finely chopped
2 cloves garlic, peeled and finely chopped
1 tin chickpeas, drained
2 x 400g tins chopped tomatoes
300g potatoes, peeled and chopped into 2.5cm pieces
5 tablespoons flat-leaf parsley, finely chopped
5 tablespoons fresh coriander, finely chopped
2 teaspoons salt
2 teaspoons ground cumin seeds
¼ teaspoon turmeric
1 teaspoon ground ginger
600ml vegetable stock
140g sweet potatoes, peeled and cut into 2.5cm chinks
3 carrots, peeled and cut into 2.5cm chunks
180g courgettes, cut into 2.5cm chunks

- Put the oil in a large saucepan and heat it until warm.
- Add the onion and fry for 5 minutes until the onion starts to turn golden brown.
- Add the garlic and fry for 1 minute.
- Add the chickpeas, tomatoes, potatoes, parsley, coriander, salt, cumin, turmeric, ginger and the vegetable stock.
- Bring to the boil and simmer, covered, for 20 minutes.
- Add the sweet potatoes and carrots.
- Bring back to a simmer and cook, covered, for 10 minutes more.
- Add the courgettes and simmer for a final 7 minutes.
- Serve hot with buttered couscous.

Buttered couscous

250g couscous, prepared following the packet instructions
salt
40g butter
2 tablespoons flat-leaf parsley, finely chopped

- Place the warm couscous in a serving bowl.
- Season with the salt.
- Add the butter and parsley.
- Mix and serve.

Herby cream cheese chicken breasts with leeks + roast potatoes

This is about as fussy as food gets in my house, but it is only fussy in terms of wrapping the pancetta round each chicken breast. The cooking is very straightforward.

Herby cream cheese chicken breasts with leeks

4 leeks, washed and finely sliced
200g cream cheese
1 tablespoon flat-leaf parsley, chopped
1 tablespoon chives, snipped
salt and pepper
6 chicken breasts, boneless
125g pancetta (about 18 slices)
200ml white wine
salt and pepper

- Preheat the oven to 200°C/400°F/gas 6.
- Scatter the leeks in an ovenproof dish and set aside.
- In a small bowl mix the cream cheese with the herbs and season with salt and pepper.
- Spread a small amount of the herby cream cheese between the main part of the breast and the loosely attached fillet.
- Wrap each chicken breast up in 2 to 3 slices of pancetta.
- Place the breasts on top of the leeks in the ovenproof dish.
- Pour over the white wine.
- Season with salt and pepper and dot the remaining cream cheese in among the leeks.
- Bake in the oven for 40 minutes.

Roast potatoes

1kg potatoes, peeled and quartered
salt
1 sprig rosemary
olive oil

- Preheat the oven to 220°C/425°F/gas 7.
- Parboil the potatoes, in salted water, for 4 minutes.
- Drain and place them in a roasting tin with the rosemary sprigs.
- Drizzle with the olive oil and roast for 45–60 minutes until golden brown.

Calves' liver with pancetta + mashed potato + buttered spinach

It is a tall order getting children to eat spinach so it may be better to give them broccoli and leave the spinach for the grown-ups. I find that liver is also a problem area when it comes to children but I very much hold the view, as I have expressed elsewhere in this book, that unless you stretch and expand your children's experiences, their tastes will not develop.

Calves' liver with pancetta

4 pieces calves' liver (one piece per adult and one piece divided between two children)
a little flour for dusting
2 tablespoons olive oil
4 or 5 fresh sage leaves
salt and pepper
85g sliced pancetta, chopped into small pieces

- Dust each piece of calves' liver with some flour and set aside.
- Heat one tablespoon of olive oil in a frying pan and when moderately warm add the sage leaves.
- Next add two pieces of liver and fry them for 1 minute on each side. Liver becomes tough if it is overcooked.
- Season each side of the liver with pepper as it cooks. When the liver is cooked, remove from the heat, sprinkle each one with salt and put in a low oven to keep warm.
- Cook the other pieces in the same way.
- When the liver has finished cooking, throw in the pancetta for a few moments until golden brown.
- Add the pancetta to the liver and serve.

Mashed potato

1.5kg potatoes, peeled and chopped for boiling
salt and pepper
50g butter
300ml milk

- Place the potatoes in a saucepan of salted water and bring to the boil.
- Simmer for about 15 minutes until the potatoes are tender to the tip of a sharp knife.
- Drain and mash them with a potato ricer, if you have one, or a regular masher if not.
- Once you have mashed the potato put it back in the saucepan over a low heat for 1 minute, to dry it out and then add the butter and milk and gently stir in.

Buttered spinach

250g spinach leaves, rinsed
1 tablespoon water
salt
small knob of butter
grating of nutmeg
pepper

- Place the spinach in a large saucepan with the water and a pinch of salt.
- Cover and place the saucepan on a low heat.
- Gradually wilt the spinach for 10 minutes until all the leaves are a glossy dark green.
- As soon as the leaves have wilted remove the lid and stir for a few seconds to get rid of any excess water. Drain any extra off if there is too much.
- Add the butter, a tiny grating of nutmeg and a good grinding of black pepper.

TIP

Potato ricers: *Potato ricers can be found in most cookware catalogues or shops and make mashed potato less of a chore.*

Shin of beef stew with chive and horseradish dumplings

I take great satisfaction in the fact that the cheaper cuts of meat often make the tasiest stews. Shin of beef makes the most delicious beef stew, with very little effort.

For the stew

1kg shin beef, chopped into 2cm cubes and trimmed of the obvious fatty bits
4 tablespoons flour, seasoned with a teaspoon salt and a good grinding pepper
2 tablespoons olive oil
5 carrots, peeled and chopped into chunks
1 swede, peeled and cut into chunks
6 shallots, peeled and cut into halves
500ml pale ale
500ml beef stock
1 sprig fresh thyme
1 bay leaf
salt and pepper

For the dumplings

175g self-raising flour
75g shredded vegetable suet
1 teaspoon mustard powder
1 tablespoon chives, snipped
1 tablespoon horseradish sauce
1 teaspoon grain mustard
salt and pepper

To make the stew

- Preheat heat the oven to 150°C/300°F/gas 2.
- Coat the meat in the seasoned flour.
- Heat the olive oil in a large saucepan and when hot, add the meat in batches to brown.
- When all the meat has browned return it to the pan along with the vegetables and pour over the ale and stock.
- Add the herbs and season with salt and pepper.
- Bring to a simmer and then place in the oven for 1 hour 30 minutes.

To prepare the dumplings

- Mix all the ingredients together in a mixing bowl.
- Add enough cold water to combine the ingredients together without becoming too wet.
- Form the mixture into rounds the size of golf balls.
- When the stew has finished cooking in the oven lay the dumplings gently on top.
  Try to keep the dumplings from touching.
- Bring the stew to a simmer on top of the hob and cook, covered, for 25 minutes.

Baked honeyed custard tart

This lovely pudding is simplicity itself. Once you have done the pastry, which is very easy, the filling can be made in minutes.

For the pastry
180g butter
75g icing sugar
2 egg yolks
225g plain flour
For the custard filling
500ml full fat milk
2 tablespoons runny honey
5 eggs
nutmeg

To make the pastry case

- Place the butter, icing sugar, egg yolks and flour together in a food processor and process until the mixture just starts to combine.
- Turn out onto a floured surface, form into a ball then wrap in cling-film and chill in the fridge for 30 minutes.
- Grease a 24cm tart tin and preheat the oven to 200°C/400°F/gas 6.
- Once the pastry has chilled roll it out and line the tart tin.
- Lay a sheet of baking parchment on top of the pastry case and pour some baking beans on top of the paper.
- Bake for 15 minutes, then remove the pastry case from the oven and discard the paper and baking beans.
- Reduce the oven temperature to 180°C/350°F/ gas 4.

To make the filling

- Heat the milk and honey in a saucepan until it reaches boiling point.
- Leave to cool for 10 minutes.
- Beat the eggs in a mixing bowl.
- Slowly pour the milk and honey into the eggs, whisking until well mixed.
- Place the tart case on a baking sheet close to the oven.
- Pour the custard mixture into the pastry case.
- Grate over a sprinkling of nutmeg and bake for 30 minutes.

Ice cream with hot toffee sauce

I suggest you buy some good quality vanilla ice cream to partner this sauce, unless you prefer to make your own. I have not included a recipe for home-made ice cream here as this is supposed to be a quick tea-time treat. Good quality shop-bought ice cream is a great source of calcium for growing children.

150ml maple syrup
225g soft brown sugar
25g butter
2 drops vanilla extract
small pinch of salt
1 tub vanilla ice cream

- Place all the ingredients in a saucepan and heat through to a gentle simmer.
- Simmer gently, uncovered, for 30 minutes.
- Serve dribbled over the ice cream.

MARCH

Week 5

Monday p170	Chicken curry + boiled rice
Tuesday p171	Open-faced salmon omelette + watercress salad
Wednesday p172	Sausages + red wine sauce + cheesy mash + savoy cabbage
Thursday p173	Minced beef with baked potatoes + broccoli
Friday p174	Spicy fishcakes + eggs cooked in cumin and tomatoes + green salad
Saturday p176	Garlic prawns + stir-fried beef with shallots + egg fried rice + tomato salad
Sunday p177	Braised lamb shanks + cabbage mashed potato
Sunday pudding p178	Orange and almond tart
Extra tasty treat p179	Treacle tart

Shopping list

MEAT

- ☐ 1.5kg chicken pieces on the bone
- ☐ 1kg minced beef
- ☐ 200g sirloin steak
- ☐ 8–10 sausages
- ☐ 4 lamb shanks weighing about 450g each

FISH

- ☐ 400g salmon fillets
- ☐ 300g cooked prawns

VEGETABLES

- ☐ 3 onions
- ☐ 1 garlic bulb
- ☐ fresh ginger
- ☐ 2 carrots
- ☐ 5 shallots
- ☐ 1 bunch celery
- ☐ 1 leek
- ☐ 500g green cabbage
- ☐ 2.3kg potatoes
- ☐ 2 green chillies
- ☐ 1 green pepper
- ☐ 6 baking potatoes
- ☐ 1 savoy cabbage
- ☐ 400g broccoli
- ☐ 300g sweet potatoes
- ☐ 20 spring onions
- ☐ ½ cucumber
- ☐ 1 lettuce
- ☐ 700g tomatoes
- ☐ 1 big bunch watercress

FRUIT

- ☐ 5 lemons
- ☐ 1 orange

FRESH HERBS

- ☐ flat-leaf parsley
- ☐ thyme
- ☐ coriander
- ☐ rosemary
- ☐ bay leaves

FRIDGE ITEMS

- ☐ 3 packs butter
- ☐ 275ml double cream
- ☐ 1 small tub plain yoghurt
- ☐ 28 eggs
- ☐ 350ml milk
- ☐ 150g Cheddar cheese
- ☐ 100g Parmesan cheese
- ☐ 100g frozen peas
- ☐ 1 litre chicken stock

KITCHEN CUPBOARD ITEMS

- ☐ salt
- ☐ 200ml coconut milk
- ☐ 800g basmati rice
- ☐ beef stock cubes
- ☐ Worcestershire sauce
- ☐ tomato ketchup
- ☐ 400g canned yellow fin tuna
- ☐ olive oil
- ☐ extra virgin olive oil
- ☐ vegetable oil
- ☐ balsamic vinegar
- ☐ fish sauce
- ☐ sesame oil
- ☐ 350ml dry white wine
- ☐ 100ml red wine
- ☐ 75g icing sugar
- ☐ 450g plain flour
- ☐ 100g caster sugar
- ☐ 75g ground almonds
- ☐ Disaronno liqueur
- ☐ 450g golden syrup
- ☐ 1 loaf brown bread for breadcrumbs
- ☐ light soy sauce
- ☐ tomato purée
- ☐ 1 loaf white bread

SPICES

- ☐ cumin seeds
- ☐ ground coriander
- ☐ black pepper
- ☐ dried chilli flakes
- ☐ coriander seeds
- ☐ fennel seeds
- ☐ fenugreek

Chicken curry
+ boiled rice

This is a coconut curry that is very mild and, therefore, more than suitable for younger children.

Chicken curry

1.5kg chicken pieces on the bone, skin removed
300ml water
2 tablespoons vegetable oil
1 teaspoon cumin seeds
1 onion, very finely chopped
2 cloves garlic, peeled and finely chopped
2cms fresh ginger, peeled and finely chopped
1 tablespoon ground coriander
1½ teaspoons salt
1 green chilli, deseeded and finely chopped
2 tablespoons plain yoghurt
200ml coconut milk

- Place the chicken and water in a saucepan and bring it to a simmer.
- Simmer gently, covered, for 30 minutes.
- Remove the chicken, set it aside and pour the liquid into a bowl.
- Clean the saucepan and place it back on a medium heat.
- Add the oil and when it is hot add the cumin seeds.
- Once you hear them sizzling add the onion, garlic and ginger.
- Stir and cook on a low heat for 10 minutes.
- Sprinkle in the ground coriander, salt and chilli.
- Stir and cook for a further 3 minutes.
- Stir in the yoghurt, coconut milk and the chicken water.
- Return the chicken to the pan.
- Bring the pan to a simmer and cook, uncovered, for 15 minutes.

Boiled rice

500ml basmati rice
750ml water
salt

- Put the rice in a saucepan with the water and a pinch of salt.
- Place the rice on a high heat and as soon as it comes to the boil cover the saucepan with a lid and turn the heat right down to very low. Leave it for 15 minutes, giving it one stir only during the cooking time.
- Take it off the heat and leave it covered for a further 10 minutes before removing the lid.

Open-faced salmon omelette + watercress salad

Open-faced omelettes are a doddle as you don't have to worry about folding them over and creating the masterpiece that is a French omelette. If you have a very wide frying pan and you are all eating at the same time, make one big omelette; otherwise just divide the mixture into two and cook two separate omelettes.

Open-faced salmon omelette

400g salmon fillets
milk for cooking the fish
12 eggs
black pepper
100g Parmesan cheese, grated
30g butter
200ml double cream
2 tablespoons flat-leaf parsley, chopped

- Place the fish in a saucepan and pour in enough milk to cover it. Bring the milk to a simmer and cook the fish for 2 minutes only. The fish needs to have a certain pink rawness to it in the middle.
- Discard the milk and remove any skin there may be from the fish fillets.
- Roughly chop the cooked salmon and set aside.
- Preheat the grill.
- Whisk the eggs in a bowl with some black pepper, until the eggs are frothy.
- Stir the salmon and half the cheese into the eggs.
- Heat the butter in a frying pan on a medium heat.
- Once the butter starts to foam and becomes slightly tinged with brown, pour in the egg mixture.
- Stir the eggs with a fork for a few seconds until the egg starts to set. Using the fork, pull the egg away from the edge of the pan, tilting it as you do so, so that uncooked egg flows to the edge of the pan. Continue until the eggs are just set on the bottom.
- Pour the cream over the egg and sprinkle on the rest of the cheese and the parsley.
- Place the pan under the hot grill and heat for 1 minute. Don't leave the pan under the grill for too long as you want a bit of runniness to the egg. The omelette will be too dry if it is completely set.
- Serve with the watercress salad and plenty of bread and butter.

Watercress salad

big bunch watercress
1 dessertspoon olive oil
1 teaspoon balsamic vinegar
salt and pepper

- Take a big bunch of watercress, place it in a serving bowl and dress it with the olive oil, balsamic vinegar, salt and pepper.

Sausages + red wine sauce + cheesy mash + savoy cabbage

There are some nights when only sausages will do. They are, of course, a great mid-week meal because they are so quick to get on the table. Prepare the sauce and mash first.

Sausages

8–10 sausages
olive oil

- Fry the sausages in a little olive oil in a frying pan on a medium heat to brown them all over.
- Then turn the heat down to cook them through.
- This will take about 12–15 minutes .

Red wine sauce

2 shallots, finely sliced
30g butter
1 tablespoon flour
100ml red wine
300ml beef stock (a stock cube will do)
salt and pepper
1 sprig thyme

- Gently sauté the shallot with the butter in a small saucepan until soft for about 5 minutes.
- Add the flour and stir for 30 seconds.
- Add the wine and simmer on a low heat for 10 minutes.
- Add the beef stock and season with the salt, pepper and thyme.
- Simmer on a very low heat while you prepare the rest of the meal.

Cheesy mash

1kg potatoes, peeled and quartered
salt
30g butter
300ml milk
2 tablespoons flat-leaf parsley, chopped
100g Cheddar cheese

- Boil the potatoes in salted water, until tender.
- Mash the potatoes with the milk and butter and add the parsley.
- Taste for seasoning, bearing in mind it will have some cheese, which is quite salty, with it.
- Spread the potato in a gratin dish and then sprinkle with the cheese.
- Heat the grill.
- Place the gratin dish under the grill until the cheese has bubbled and turned golden brown.

Savoy cabbage

1 savoy cabbage, shredded finely
small knob of butter
salt and pepper
squeeze of lemon juice

- Place the cabbage in a large saucepan with a dessertspoon of water and the butter.
- Cover the cabbage and cook on a low heat, stirring occasionally, for 5 minutes.
- Season to taste with salt, freshly-ground black pepper and a squeeze of lemon juice and serve with the sausages and mash.

Minced beef with baked potatoes + broccoli

There are probably 1001 things to do with mince and this could be one of them.

Minced beef with baked potatoes

30g butter
1 large onion, finely chopped
3 sticks celery, finely chopped
1 green pepper, diced
1kg minced beef
2 tablespoons Worcestershire sauce
6 tablespoons tomato ketchup
170ml water
salt and pepper
6 baking potatoes
Cheddar cheese, grated for serving

- Preheat the oven to 200°C/400°F/gas 6.
- Warm the butter in a large saucepan on a medium heat.
- Add the onion, celery and green pepper and fry for 10 minutes until soft.
- Add the minced beef and brown it all over.
- Add the Worcestershire sauce, ketchup and water and stir.
- Season with salt and pepper.
- Cover and simmer for 1 hour.
- Remove the lid from the saucepan and simmer for a further 30 minutes uncovered.
- Place the potatoes in the oven for 1 hour 30 minutes.
- Split the baked potatoes in two, fill each one with the beef and serve with a sprinkling of cheese on top.

Broccoli

400g broccoli
salt
lemon juice
black pepper

- Trim the broccoli into florets. If the stalks are very thick trim them down a little.
- Bring a pan of slightly salted water to the boil.
- Add the broccoli florets and cook on a simmer for 3 minutes.
- Season with a squeeze of lemon and a grinding of black pepper.

Spicy fishcakes + eggs cooked in cumin and tomatoes + green salad

These fishcakes appear elsewhere in this book, but here I have teamed them with spicy eggs and a salad, which I think works really well.

Spicy fishcakes

300g potatoes, peeled and cut into quarters for boiling

300g sweet potatoes, peeled and cut into chunks for boiling

1 tablespoon vegetable oil

7 spring onions, finely chopped

2.5cm fresh ginger, peeled and finely chopped

2 cloves garlic, peeled and finely chopped

1 tablespoon curry powder*

400g canned yellow fin tuna

100g frozen peas, defrosted

¼ fresh green chilli, deseeded and finely chopped (optional)

salt and pepper

seasoned flour for coating the fishcakes

1 tablespoon vegetable oil for frying the fishcakes

- Boil all the potatoes until tender. The sweet potatoes may cook a fraction before the ordinary ones, in which case remove them first to avoid them becoming mushy.
- Drain the potatoes, place them in a mixing bowl and mash them roughly with a fork.
- Heat the vegetable oil in a frying pan on a medium heat.
- Add the spring onions, ginger and garlic and fry for 2 minutes, stirring continuously to avoid the garlic burning.
- Add the curry powder and fry for a 1 minute.
- Put this mixture in the bowl with the potatoes and add the tuna, peas and green chilli (if using).
- Season well with salt and pepper.
- Form the mixture into approximately 14 fishcakes.
- Coat each fishcake in seasoned flour.
- Heat the vegetable oil in a frying pan.
- When hot, add 3 or 4 fishcakes at a time and cook for 1 minute on each side until golden brown.

**** To make your own curry powder***
1 tablespoon coriander seeds
1 dessertspoon cumin seeds
1 teaspoon fennel seeds
½ teaspoon fenugreek

- *Place the coriander seeds into a small, heavy-bottomed pan and heat through for 30 seconds.*
- *Add the other ingredients and toast until you smell the lovely aroma of the spices.*
- *Transfer the spices to a coffee grinder, a small processor or grind them in a pestle and mortar.*

Eggs cooked in cumin and tomatoes

3 tablespoons olive oil
6 spring onions, peeled and finely chopped
2 cloves garlic, peeled and finely chopped
1 teaspoon cumin seeds, roughly ground in a pestle and mortar
600g tomatoes, roughly chopped
1 pinch dried chilli flakes
salt and pepper
6 eggs
2 tablespoons fresh coriander, chopped

- Heat the olive oil in a frying pan and fry the spring onion, garlic and cumin on a medium heat for 3 minutes, stirring occasionally.
- Add the tomatoes and chilli, season with salt and pepper and simmer for 10 minutes, uncovered.
- Crack all the eggs into the pan, spacing them apart as much as you can.
- Let the tomatoes simmer until the eggs are cooked.
- Sprinkle with coriander and serve with the salad and fishcakes.

Green salad

½ cucumber, sliced
1 lettuce, washed
1 bunch 6 or 7 spring onions, sliced
To dress
2 tablespoons extra virgin olive oil
½ tablespoon balsamic vinegar
salt and pepper

- Combine the salad ingredients in a serving bowl.
- Mix the dressing in a small bowl and pour over the salad just before serving.

Garlic prawns + stir-fried beef with shallots + egg fried rice + tomato salad

With this dish you can prepare the rice in advance. The beef and prawns only take a few minutes to cook, so there is no last-minute panic about getting everything ready at the same time and the ingredients make a delicious combination.

Garlic prawns

50g butter
2 cloves garlic, peeled and finely chopped
300g cooked prawns
2 tablespoons chopped flat-leaf parsley
juice ½ lemon
salt and pepper

- Heat the butter in a frying pan.
- Add the garlic and cook for 1 minute, stirring and keeping an eye on the heat so that the garlic does not brown.
- Add the prawns and stir for 1 minute to warm through.
- Add the parsley and squeeze over the lemon juice.
- Season with salt and pepper.

Stir-fried beef with shallots

1 tablespoon vegetable oil
2 shallots, finely sliced
200g sirloin steak, sliced into thin strips
1 teaspoon thai fish sauce
½ teaspoon sugar
1 teaspoon sesame oil

- Heat the oil in a wok or small frying pan.
- When hot add the shallot and beef and stir-fry for a few seconds.
- Add the fish sauce, sugar and sesame oil and cook for 1 minute.
- This is now ready to serve.

Egg fried rice

300g basmati rice
450ml water
salt
1 tablespoon vegetable oil
2 eggs, beaten
1 carrot, finely diced
1 shallot, finely chopped
1 tablespoon light soy sauce

- Put the rice in a saucepan with the water and a pinch of salt.
- Place the rice on a high heat and as soon as it comes to the boil cover the saucepan with a lid and turn the heat right down to very low. Leave it for 15 minutes, giving it one stir only during the cooking time.
- Then remove from the heat and leave it covered for a further 10 minutes, before removing the lid, then set aside.
- Heat the oil in a large frying pan or a wok.
- Add the beaten eggs and cook as though you are cooking an omelette.
- Remove the egg from the pan and chop it up. Set aside.
- Keeping the pan on the heat, add the carrot and shallot and fry for 2 minutes.
- Add the cooked rice with the soy sauce.
- Lastly, add the chopped egg.

Tomato salad

4 tomatoes, chopped
salt and pepper
squeeze of fresh lemon juice

- Combine all the ingredients and serve with the other dishes.

Braised lamb shanks + cabbage mashed potato

This is great comfort food. I always used to think that braising lamb shanks was complicated, but it really is quite easy. I have, however, included this as a weekend meal as the shanks take a good 2 hours 30 minutes to cook, so it's not quick mid-week fare.

Braised lamb shanks

4 lamb shanks weighing about 450g each
salt and pepper
3 tablespoons olive oil
1 large onion, chopped
2 garlic cloves, peeled and crushed
1 carrot, chopped
1 stick celery, finely chopped
1 leek, finely chopped
1 sprig thyme
1 sprig rosemary
1 bay leaf
1 tablespoon tomato purée
1 tablespoon flour
350ml dry white wine
1 litre chicken stock

- Preheat the oven to 160°C/320°F/gas 2½.
- Season the lamb shanks with salt and pepper.
- Heat the olive oil in a large heavy-bottomed saucepan and brown the lamb shanks two at a time all over. To brown two shanks will take about 7 minutes.
- Remove the lamb shanks and set aside. Keep the saucepan on the heat.
- Add the chopped vegetables to the saucepan and cook them for 5 minutes.
- Add the thyme, rosemary and bay leaf and stir.
- Next add the tomato purée and the flour, stir and cook for 2 minutes.
- Add the wine, stir and bring to a simmer for 5 minutes.
- Now return the lamb to the pan, add the stock and bring to a simmer.
- Cover the saucepan and then place it in the oven for 2 hours 30 minutes.
- Next, remove the lamb shanks from the pot and reduce the gravy by half, by rapidly boiling the liquid on the hob for 3–5 minutes.
- Return the shanks to the pot and serve.

Cabbage mashed potato

500g green cabbage, finely chopped
milk
1kg potatoes, peeled and quartered
salt
butter
black pepper

- Place the cabbage in a saucepan and barely cover it with milk.
- Bring to the boil and then reduce the heat and simmer for 2 minutes, by which time the cabbage should be soft.
- In a separate pan boil the potatoes in salted water until soft enough to mash. The length of time depends on the size of the cut potatoes, but it should take about 15 minutes from when the potatoes first come to the boil.
- Once cooked, drain the potatoes and mash them.
- Pour in the cabbage, milk (add extra milk if too dry) and a large knob of butter.
- Add a good grinding of black pepper and more salt if necessary.

Orange and almond tart

The combination of orange and almond is excellent and this tart makes a very elegant dinner party dessert.

For the sweet pastry
180g butter
75g icing sugar
2 egg yolks
225g plain flour
For the filling
100g caster sugar
25g flour
75g ground almonds
100g butter, softened
4 egg yolks
grated zest 1 orange
juice 1 lemon
2 tablespoons Disaronno liqueur

- Place the butter, icing sugar, egg yolks and flour together in a food processor and process until the mixture just starts to combine.
- Turn out onto a floured surface and form into a ball.
- Wrap in cling-film and chill in the fridge for 30 minutes.
- Preheat the oven to 190°C/375°F/gas 5.
- Grease a 23cm tart tin.
- Roll out the pastry and line the tart tin with it.
- Beat together all the filling ingredients and pour them into the uncooked tart case.
- Bake for 40 minutes until the filling is firm and has turned a golden brown.
- Serve with double cream.

Treacle tart

I got this recipe from a friend of mine as her treacle tart tasted so good.

For the pastry
180g plain flour
120g butter, chilled and cubed
salt
1 egg yolk
2 tablespoons cold water
For the filling
450g golden syrup
30g butter
1 egg
3 tablespoons double cream
grated zest 1 lemon
5 heaped tablespoons brown breadcrumbs

- Preheat the oven to 190°C/375°F/gas 5.

To make the pastry

- Put the flour and butter in the bowl of a food processor and incorporate them so that the resulting mixture looks like fine breadcrumbs.
- Add a small pinch of salt.
- Mix the egg yolk with the cold water in a small bowl and add this liquid to the flour and fat.
- Turn on the food processor and mix until a dough just begins to form. Turn the mixture onto a floured work surface and combine thoroughly, with a light hand, until you have a smooth dough. Wrap the dough in cling-film and chill in the fridge for 20 minutes.

To make the tart

- Grease a 21–22cm tart tin.
- Roll out the pastry and line the tart tin with it.
- Lay a sheet of baking parchment on top of the pastry case and pour some baking beans on top of the paper.
- Bake for 15 minutes and then remove the pastry case from the oven and discard the paper and baking beans.
- Prick the base of the pastry case with a fork.
- Return the pastry case to the oven and cook for 5 minutes more. Remove from the oven and set aside.
- Reduce the oven temperature to 180°C/350°F/gas 4.
- Warm the syrup in a small saucepan.
- Remove the syrup from the heat and add the butter, stirring until it has melted.
- In a small bowl beat together the cream and eggs and then add these to the syrup and butter mixture.
- Add the lemon zest and the breadcrumbs and stir to combine.
- Pour the mixture into the pastry case.
- Bake for 35 minutes.
- Let the tart cool for 20 minutes before serving with cream.

Week 1

Monday p182	Shepherd's pie + savoy cabbage
Tuesday p183	Creamy chicken and vegetable tarts + broccoli
Wednesday p184	Spicy king prawns + fried rice
Thursday p185	Tortilla wraps with beans + salad
Friday p186	Smoked haddock pie + purple sprouting broccoli
Saturday p187	Roast duck breasts + noodles
Sunday p188	Coq au vin + buttered new potatoes + green peas
Sunday pudding p190	Almond macaroon cake + rhubarb and orange compote
Extra tasty treat p191	White chocolate mousse with banana

Shopping list

MEAT

- ☐ 4 boned duck breasts
- ☐ 1kg minced lamb
- ☐ 6 chicken breasts
- ☐ 10 chicken thighs on the bone

FISH

- ☐ 800g smoked haddock
- ☐ 500g cooked king prawns

VEGETABLES

- ☐ 1 garlic bulb
- ☐ 300g shallots
- ☐ 1 onion
- ☐ 1 red onion
- ☐ 3 spring onions
- ☐ fresh ginger
- ☐ 1 cucumber
- ☐ 325g button mushrooms
- ☐ 6 carrots
- ☐ 400g broccoli
- ☐ 1 avocado
- ☐ 4 tomatoes
- ☐ 250g purple sprouting broccoli
- ☐ 1.75kg potatoes
- ☐ 700g new potatoes
- ☐ 1 savoy cabbage

FRUIT

- ☐ 2 lemons
- ☐ 450g fresh rhubarb
- ☐ 1 orange
- ☐ 3 bananas

FRESH HERBS

- ☐ thyme
- ☐ rosemary
- ☐ bay leaves
- ☐ flat-leaf parsley
- ☐ mint
- ☐ coriander

FRIDGE ITEMS

- ☐ 530g frozen petits pois
- ☐ 10 eggs
- ☐ 3 packs butter
- ☐ 450ml double cream
- ☐ 400ml milk
- ☐ 100g Cheddar cheese
- ☐ 300g crème fraîche
- ☐ 140g chopped pancetta
- ☐ 1 small carton soured cream
- ☐ 500ml chicken stock

KITCHEN CUPBOARD ITEMS

- ☐ clear honey
- ☐ dark soy sauce
- ☐ 350g Chinese egg noodles
- ☐ groundnut oil
- ☐ sesame oil
- ☐ olive oil
- ☐ extra virgin olive oil
- ☐ 2 packets tortilla wraps
- ☐ 1 tin pinto beans
- ☐ 2 tins haricot beans
- ☐ 1 jar passata
- ☐ tomato purée
- ☐ chicken stock cubes
- ☐ brandy
- ☐ 450ml red wine
- ☐ dry sherry
- ☐ sesame seeds
- ☐ salt
- ☐ 225g plain flour
- ☐ 150g self-raising flour
- ☐ 400g basmati rice
- ☐ 360g caster sugar
- ☐ 170g ground almonds
- ☐ 150g white chocolate

SPICES

- ☐ Chinese 5-spice powder
- ☐ black pepper
- ☐ paprika
- ☐ ground cumin
- ☐ ground ginger
- ☐ cayenne
- ☐ whole nutmeg

Shepherd's pie
+ savoy cabbage

Everyone likes a traditional shepherd's pie. It's a great meal to prepare in advance and then heat up when you are ready to eat.

Shepherd's pie

2 tablespoons olive oil
1 onion, finely chopped
3 carrots, finely chopped
1kg minced lamb
salt and pepper
1 tablespoon flour
450ml chicken stock (a cube will do)
2 teaspoons tomato purée
1kg potatoes, peeled and quartered
30g butter plus a little melted butter
200ml milk

- Heat the olive oil in a large saucepan.
- Add the onions and carrots and sauté for 10 minutes on a medium heat until soft.
- Add the lamb and brown all over, stirring continuously.
- Season well with salt and pepper.
- Sprinkle over the flour and stir to combine.
- Pour on the stock and stir in the tomato purée.
- Bring to a simmer and cook uncovered for 30 minutes. Then cover the pan and simmer for a further 30 minutes.
- Meanwhile boil the potatoes in plenty of salted water until tender enough to mash.
- Mash using a potato ricer or a fork.
- Stir the butter and milk into the mashed potato until combined.
- Check the seasoning.
- Tip the mince into an ovenproof dish and spoon the potato over the top.
- Run a fork along the top of the potato and brush with melted butter.
- Just before serving place under a hot grill until golden brown.

Savoy cabbage

1 Savoy cabbage, shredded finely
small knob of butter
salt and pepper
squeeze of lemon juice

- Place the cabbage in a large saucepan with the butter and a dessertspoon of water.
- Cover the cabbage and cook on a low heat, stirring occasionally, for 5 minutes.
- Season to taste with salt, freshly-ground black pepper and a squeeze of lemon juice.

Creamy chicken and vegetable tarts + broccoli

This recipe is based on a recipe in Michael Smith's *New English Cookery*. I have made some minor changes to make the dish more appropriate for an everyday family meal. It's easy enough to make and fine to warm up if you have different sittings in your home, as I often do in mine.

Creamy chicken and vegetable tarts

For the pastry

225g plain flour

150g butter

salt

2 egg yolks

2 tablespoons cold water

For the creamy chicken and vegetable

50g butter

6 chicken breasts, sliced diagonally into 4 or 5 pieces

4 shallots, peeled and chopped into quarters

100g button mushrooms (halve any big ones)

50ml dry sherry

salt and pepper

nutmeg

300ml double cream

2 carrots, peeled and cut into small dice and cooked

100g frozen petits pois, defrosted

handful flat-leaf parsley, finely chopped

To make the pastry

- Mix the flour and butter in a food processor so that the result looks like fine breadcrumbs.
- Add a pinch of salt.
- Mix the egg yolks with the cold water in a small bowl and add this liquid to the flour and fat.
- Mix again in the processor until a dough just begins to form. Turn the dough onto a floured work surface and combine thoroughly, with a light hand, until you have a smooth dough.
- Wrap it in cling-film and chill in the fridge for 20 minutes.
- Preheat the oven to 200°C/400°F/gas 6 and lightly grease a baking sheet.
- Roll out the pastry and then cut it into six 13cm discs. Place the pastry discs on the baking sheet and bake them for 15 minutes until golden brown. You will place the chicken mixture on top of these rounds when you come to serve the meal.

To make the creamy chicken and vegetable

- Heat the butter in a sauté pan.
- Fry the chicken pieces in four separate batches in the butter until they are nicely browned all over, and then set aside.
- In the same pan fry the shallots and mushrooms for 5 minutes.
- Place the chicken back in the saucepan with the shallots and mushrooms and add the sherry.
- Season with salt, pepper and a grating of nutmeg.
- Add the cream and cook, uncovered, on a gentle simmer for 5 minutes, stirring occasionally.
- Add the carrots and peas and cook for 1 minute.
- Finally, spoon the creamy mixture onto the pastry discs and serve with a sprinkling of parsley and the broccoli.

Broccoli

400g broccoli

salt

lemon juice

black pepper

- Trim the broccoli into florets. If the stalks are very thick trim them down a little.
- Bring a pan of slightly salted water to the boil.
- Add the broccoli florets and cook on a simmer for 3 minutes.
- Drain and season with a squeeze of lemon and a grinding of black pepper.

Spicy king prawns + fried rice

This recipe is very quick once the rice is cooked. My children love it and you can pretty much add what you like to the rice. The carrot works well as you only cook it briefly, so it retains a satisfying crunch.

Spicy king prawns

2 tablespoons olive oil
2 cloves garlic, peeled and crushed
1 teaspoon paprika
½ teaspoon ground cumin
¼ teaspoon ground ginger
pinch cayenne
500g king prawns, cooked
salt and pepper
1 large bunch coriander, finely chopped

- Warm the oil in a frying pan and add the garlic. Fry it for a few seconds only, keeping it moving around the pan.
- Stir in the spices and add the prawns.
- Warm the prawns through carefully, but don't overcook them as they will become rubbery.
- Season with salt and pepper and add the coriander.
- Serve with the fried rice.

Fried rice

400g basmati rice
600ml water
salt
2 tablespoons groundnut oil
1 shallot, very finely diced
1 carrot, very finely diced
100g frozen petits pois, cooked
2 tablespoons dark soy sauce

- Put the rice in a saucepan with the water and a pinch of salt.
- Place the rice on a high heat and as soon as it comes to the boil, cover the saucepan with a lid and turn the heat right down to very low. Leave it for 15 minutes, giving it one stir only during the cooking time.
- Then remove from the heat and set aside, covered, for a further 10 minutes.
- Heat the oil in a frying pan until hot.
- Add the shallot and carrot and cook, stirring continuously for 3 minutes.
- Now add the cooked rice, peas and the soy sauce and stir.

Tortilla wraps with beans + salad

I try not to use processed food, but tortilla wraps are an exception, especially if you only have them occasionally. This is a very tasty and satisfying meal. If I had an unlimited amount of time then I probably would attempt to make homemade wraps but to suggest this here would, I think, turn people against the idea of home-produced food.

Tortilla wraps with beans

1 tablespoon olive oil
1 shallot, finely chopped
2 tins haricot beans, drained
1 tin pinto beans, drained
1 sprig thyme
1 bay leaf
1 jar passata
salt and pepper
2 packets tortilla wraps

For serving

soured cream
Cheddar cheese, grated

- Warm the olive oil in a shallow pan and gently sauté the shallot for 2 minutes.
- Add the haricot and pinto beans, the thyme, bay leaf and the passata.
- Cook on a slight simmer, covered, for 1 hour.
- Season to taste.
- If the mixture becomes too thick or dry, add a bit more passata or a little water. The mixture should be quite thick so that it is held by the tortilla wrap and doesn't slop out of the sides.
- Warm the wraps in the microwave following the packet instructions.
- Place the beans on the table with the tortilla wraps, soured cream and cheese and serve with the salad.

Salad

1 red onion, finely diced
1 avocado, peeled and chopped
4 tomatoes, chopped
½ cucumber, diced

For the dressing

1 tablespoon extra virgin olive oil
squeeze of fresh lemon juice
salt and pepper

- Place the salad ingredients in a serving bowl.
- Mix the dressing in a small bowl and then pour it over the salad when you are ready to serve.

Smoked haddock pie
+ purple sprouting broccoli

Fish pie holds an esteemed place in the heart of the British nation. You can find it on the most elegant of restaurant menus and in the pre-prepared sections of supermarkets. It's simple to make and full of flavour, especially if you use smoked fish, as I have done in this recipe.

Smoked haddock pie

800g smoked haddock
568ml milk for the fish
750g potatoes, peeled and quartered
50g butter for the potatoes
200ml milk for the potatoes
salt and pepper
40g butter
25g flour
1 teaspoon lemon juice
50g Cheddar cheese, grated

- Slice the fish into large chunks so that it fits inside a medium-sized saucepan.
- Cover the fish with the milk.
- Bring the milk to a simmer, reduce the heat and cook, covered, for 5 minutes.
- Drain the milk off, retaining it for later, and place the fish in an ovenproof dish, removing the skin and any remaining bones.
- Boil the potatoes in plenty of salted water for 15 minutes until tender enough to mash.
- Pass the potatoes through a potato ricer or mash with a fork.
- Place the potatoes back on a low heat in a saucepan with the butter and milk and mix until the butter has melted and has been incorporated into the mashed potato.
- Season and set aside.
- Melt the 40g of butter in a small saucepan.
- Add the flour and stir until combined with the butter on a low heat.
- Remove the pan from the heat and gradually add the reserved fish milk and lemon juice and stir until all the liquid has been incorporated and the sauce is smooth.
- Return the pan to the hob and simmer on a low heat for 5 minutes.
- Season with salt and pepper.
- Remove from the heat and sprinkle in the cheese.
- Pour the sauce over the fish.
- Cover with the mashed potato and sprinkle a handful of grated Cheddar on top.
- Place under a hot grill until golden brown.

Purple sprouting broccoli

250g purple sprouting broccoli
salt and pepper
a little butter

- Boil a saucepan of water.
- Add the broccoli and simmer for 3 minutes.
- Season with salt and pepper and a little butter.

Roast duck breasts + noodles

I must admit that on the various occasions I have attempted to cook duck I have always been a little disappointed. This recipe, however, works perfectly and is simplicity itself.

Roast duck breasts

2 tablespoons clear honey
1½ tablespoons soy sauce
½ teaspoon Chinese 5-spice powder
4 boned duck breasts (based on 1 breast per adult and 2 children sharing 1 breast)
salt and pepper

- Preheat the oven to 230°C/450°F/gas 8.
- Mix the honey, soy sauce and 5-spice powder together in a small bowl.
- Using a pastry brush, coat the skin of each duck breast liberally with the mixture.
- Leave for 30 minutes and then coat the skin of the breasts again.
- Season with salt and pepper.
- Place the breasts on a small rack in a roasting tin and roast them for 15 minutes. This will cook the meat to medium rare, so increase the cooking time if you prefer your duck well done.
- Remove the duck from the oven and rest for 5 minutes.
- Cut each breast into slices and serve with the noodles below.

Noodles

1 tablespoon groundnut oil
1 clove garlic, peeled and finely chopped
1 shallot, finely chopped
1cm piece fresh ginger, peeled and finely chopped
80g frozen petits pois, cooked
3 spring onions, chopped into chunks
½ cucumber, chopped into small batons
350g Chinese egg noodles, cooked according to the packet instructions
1 tablespoon soy sauce
2 teaspoons sesame oil
1 dessertspoon sesame seeds
salt

- Heat the groundnut oil in a large frying pan or wok.
- When hot add the garlic, shallot and ginger and fry for 1 minute.
- Add the peas, spring onions, cucumber and noodles and stir for 1 minute.
- Add the soy sauce and sesame oil and stir.
- Sprinkle on the sesame seeds, season with a little salt and serve.

Coq au vin + buttered new potatoes + green peas

Coq au vin had gone out of fashion a few years ago but it seems to have had a resurgence in its popularity. It's reasonably straightforward to make and the combination of robust flavours is wonderful.

Coq au vin

10 chicken thighs on the bone, skin removed
flour for dusting
1 tablespoon olive oil
40g butter
140g chopped pancetta
100g small shallots, peeled and left whole
2 tablespoons brandy
450ml red wine
500ml chicken stock
salt and pepper
a bouquet garni made with 1 sprig rosemary, bay leaf and a parsley stalk
2 cloves garlic, peeled and finely chopped
½ tablespoon tomato purée
225g button mushrooms

- Dust the chicken pieces with the flour and then set them aside.
- Heat the oil and 15g of butter in a frying pan.
- Fry the chopped pancetta for 3 minutes until golden brown, then transfer the pancetta to a casserole, leaving the fat in the frying pan.
- Brown the shallots in the frying pan for 4 minutes and then transfer the shallots to the casserole.
- Add 10g of butter to the frying pan.
- Brown the chicken pieces in the butter until lightly browned.
- Pour the brandy over the chicken and then set light to it with a match. This is great fun!
- Once the flames have died down, tip the juices and the chicken pieces into the casserole dish.
- Pour the wine into the frying pan. Bring it to a simmer and leave to bubble gently for 3 minutes. Then pour it into the casserole dish.
- Bring the stock to the boil in the frying pan and then pour this over the chicken too.
- Season with salt and pepper.
- Add the bouquet garni, garlic, tomato purée and stir thoroughly.
- Cover and simmer gently for 40 minutes.
- Meanwhile fry the mushrooms in the remaining butter and then add them to the casserole dish and cook for a further 5 minutes.
- Taste and adjust the seasoning if necessary.

Buttered new potatoes

700g new potatoes
salt
a little butter
pepper

- Boil the potatoes in salted water for 20 minutes until tender.
- Drain them and peel them if you prefer them peeled.
- Toss the potatoes in the butter and season them with some black pepper.

Green peas

250g frozen petits pois
fresh mint and butter for serving

- Place the peas in boiling water for about 3 minutes and drain them once cooked.
- Serve with a little butter and chopped mint.

Almond macaroon cake + rhubarb and orange compote

This cake is very popular in my household and it goes beautifully with the rhubarb and orange.

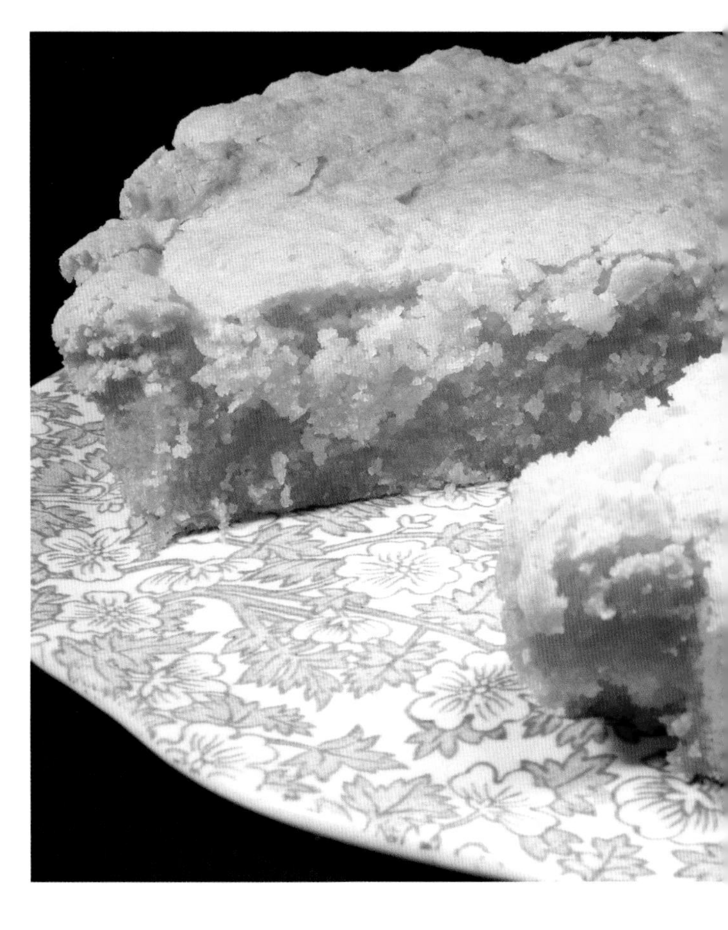

Almond macaroon cake

175g butter, softened
150g caster sugar
salt
grated zest 1 lemon
2 eggs
200g crème fraîche
150g self-raising flour
85g ground almonds

For the topping

2 egg whites
125g caster sugar
85g ground almonds

- Preheat the oven to 180°C/350°F/gas 4.
- Grease a 24cm cake tin and line the bottom of the tin with greaseproof paper.
- Cream the butter and sugar together.
- Add a pinch of salt, the lemon zest and then the eggs one by one, beating thoroughly between the addition of each egg.
- Fold in the crème fraîche, flour and almonds.
- Spoon the mixture into the cake tin and bake for 30 minutes.

To make the topping

- Whisk the egg whites in a clean bowl until they are stiff.
- Add half the sugar and whisk until stiff again.
- Fold in the almonds and the rest of the sugar.
- When the cake is ready spread the topping on the top of it.
- Return the cake to the oven for 20 minutes.
- Once cooled, serve with the fruit compote and crème fraîche.

Rhubarb and orange compote

85g caster sugar
450g fresh rhubarb, trimmed and cut into 2.5cm chunks
grated zest and juice 1 orange

- Put 150ml water into a saucepan, add the sugar and stir over a low heat until dissolved.
- Bring to the boil and add the rhubarb.
- Lower the heat and bring to a simmer. Cook for 1 minute.
- Remove from the heat straightaway, cover with a lid and leave undisturbed for 15 minutes.
- Grate the orange zest onto the rhubarb and add the juice.

White chocolate mousse with banana

This chocolate mousse is very quick to make and is rich and delicious in flavour. It contains uncooked eggs so do make sure that you buy fresh, good quality eggs.

3 bananas, peeled and sliced into discs
150g white chocolate, broken into pieces
150ml double cream, lightly whipped
4 egg yolks
4 egg whites

- Place the sliced bananas into six dessert glasses or bowls in equal amounts.
- Put the white chocolate in a glass bowl over a saucepan of gently simmering water.
- Stir the chocolate until melted.
- Remove the glass bowl from the heat and stir the cream and the egg yolks into the chocolate.
- Whisk the egg whites in a clean, grease-free bowl until they form stiff peaks.
- Fold the egg whites into the chocolate mixture.
- Spoon the resulting mousse into the dessert bowls on top of the banana and chill in the fridge for 2 hours before serving.

Week 2

Shopping list

MEAT

- 6 sausages
- 300g minced pork
- 600g diced leg lamb
- 2kg leg lamb
- 4–6 pork chops

VEGETABLES

- 1 cucumber
- 2 Cos or Romaine lettuces
- 12 spring onions
- 3 onions
- 4 red onions
- 1kg tomatoes
- 1 orange pepper
- 1 garlic bulb
- 3 shallots
- 200g courgettes
- 300g butternut squash
- 300g carrots
- 100g watercress
- 2kg potatoes
- 6 large baking potatoes
- 400g spring cabbage
- fresh ginger

FRUIT

- 1 orange
- 5 lemons
- 500g rhubarb

FRESH HERBS

- bay leaves
- coriander
- flat-leaf parsley
- chives
- rosemary
- thyme
- sage

FRIDGE ITEMS

- 700ml milk
- 300ml double cream
- 200ml single cream
- 13 eggs
- 140g sliced pancetta
- 50g pecorino cheese
- 200g ricotta cheese
- 300g cream cheese
- 200g Cheddar cheese
- 200g cooked ham
- 2 packs butter
- 1.5 litres fresh chicken stock

KITCHEN CUPBOARD ITEMS

- 1 loaf brown bread
- mango chutney
- English mustard
- mustard powder
- pitted green olives
- 325ml dry white wine
- 1 jar stem ginger
- 1kg strong white bread flour
- 140g self-raising flour
- 400g plain flour
- 85g raisins
- 400g tin chickpeas
- 500g basmati rice
- 400g caster sugar
- 1 vanilla pod or vanilla extract
- 2 x 400g tins chopped tomatoes
- fast-action dried yeast
- salt
- olive oil
- vegetable oil
- extra virgin olive oil
- balsamic vinegar
- white wine vinegar

SPICES

- ground cinnamon
- ground nutmeg
- cardamom pods
- cloves
- ground coriander
- ground cumin
- dried oregano
- black peppercorns

Lamb and chickpea curry + tomato salad + boiled rice

Lamb and chickpeas are two very well matched ingredients. Diced leg of lamb is great as it tolerates being cooked without too much care and attention, has a great flavour and holds its shape well.

Lamb and chickpea curry

2 tablespoons vegetable oil
1 bay leaf
1 cardamom pod
2 cloves
1 onion, diced
2 cloves garlic, peeled and finely chopped
2cm piece fresh ginger, peeled and finely chopped
1 teaspoon ground coriander
1 teaspoon ground cumin
1 teaspoon salt
600g diced leg lamb
400g tin chopped tomatoes
200ml water
400g tin chickpeas, drained

- Heat the oil in a large, heavy-bottomed saucepan.
- Place the bay leaf, cardamom pod and cloves in the oil and fry for 1 minute on a medium heat.
- Next, add the onion and fry for 5 minutes until soft but not browned.
- Add the garlic and ginger and fry for 2 minutes.
- Then add the coriander, cumin and salt and stir everything thoroughly.
- Increase the heat and then add the lamb, browning it for 2 minutes, stirring continuously.
- Add the tomatoes, water and chickpeas and simmer partially covered for 1 hour. Then cover the saucepan and simmer for 30 minutes more.

Tomato salad

6 tomatoes
For the dressing
2 tablespoons extra virgin olive oil
¼ tablespoon balsamic vinegar
salt and pepper

- Slice the tomatoes and place on a serving plate.
- Mix the dressing together in a small bowl and pour over the tomatoes.

Boiled rice

500ml basmati rice
750ml water
salt

- Put the rice in a saucepan with the water and a pinch of salt.
- Place on a high heat and as soon as it comes to the boil, cover the saucepan with a lid and turn the heat right down to very low. Leave it for 15 minutes, giving it one stir only during cooking.
- Take off the heat and leave it covered for 10 minutes before you remove the lid and serve.

Stuffed baked potatoes

This is a really straightforward quick meal that is all the more enjoyable for that.

6 large baking potatoes

For the filling

6 slices pancetta

1 orange pepper, very finely chopped

1 shallot, very finely chopped

1 small bunch chives, snipped

salt and pepper

300g cream cheese

100g Cheddar, grated

- Preheat the oven to 200°C/400°F/gas 6.
- Pierce the potatoes and bake them for 1 hour 30 minutes.

To prepare the filling

- Fry the pancetta slices and then, using kitchen scissors, snip them into a bowl along with all the other ingredients.
- Stir well to combine.
- Once the potatoes are cooked cut them open, fluff up the insides a little with a fork and stuff them with the filling.

Spicy garlic tomatoes on toast

This is beautifully simple. It is so pleasing to be able to make a good meal out of a few limited ingredients.

2 tablespoons olive oil
1 clove garlic, peeled and finely chopped
1 teaspoon cumin, ground
1 teaspoon coriander, ground
6–8 plum tomatoes, each sliced in half lengthways
12 slices pancetta
6 thickish slices brown bread
mango chutney
salt and pepper
a little extra virgin olive oil
1 handful fresh coriander, roughly chopped

- Preheat the oven to 110°C/225°F/gas ¼, so you have somewhere to keep the tomatoes warm once they are cooked.
- Warm the olive oil in a frying pan.
- On a very low heat fry the garlic for a few seconds so as not to burn it.
- Add the ground cumin and coriander and stir for a few seconds.
- Place half the tomatoes, cut side down, in the frying pan and cook for 1 minute.
- Turn them over and cook them for another minute.
- Remove the tomatoes and keep them warm in a dish in the low oven, while you cook the rest.
- Fry the pancetta in the frying pan and start to toast the bread.
- Spread each slice of toast with mango chutney.
- Serve by placing the tomatoes on top of the mango chutneyed pieces of toast.
- Season with salt and pepper and a drizzle of extra virgin olive oil.
- Place the pancetta on top of each serving and sprinkle with a little freshly chopped coriander.

Pork and ham pie + green salad

This is an Italian-inspired pie and it looks like a huge Cornish pasty when it is cooked, which pleases the children. The pastry is very different from the English shortcrust you may be used to eating, but give this a try, as it makes a nice change and the lack of richness complements the rich flavours of the filling.

Pork and ham pie

For the pastry

400g plain flour
1 tablespoon olive oil
1 tablespoon cold water
1 egg
salt
100ml dry white wine

For the filling

1 tablespoon olive oil
1 onion, finely chopped
300g minced pork
50g pecorino cheese, grated
200g ricotta cheese
200g cooked ham, finely chopped
4 sage leaves, finely chopped
4 eggs
salt and pepper
1 egg yolk mixed with 1 tablespoon water to glaze

To make the pastry

- Put the flour in a mixing bowl, making a well in the centre.
- Add the olive oil, water, egg, salt and white wine and gradually mix to a dough with your hands, turning the dough out onto a lightly floured work surface.
- Be light-handed with the dough and once it is combined, wrap it in cling-film and chill in the fridge for 30 minutes.

To make the filling

- Heat the oven to 200°C/400°F/gas 6.
- Heat the olive oil in a sauté pan.
- Add the onion and fry for 10 minutes on a low heat until soft.
- Add the minced pork and fry until it has lost its pinkness, which will take 5 minutes.
- Remove the pan from the heat and add the cheeses, ham, sage and eggs.
- Check the seasoning and adjust if necessary.
- Roll out the chilled pastry into a circle with a diameter of 35cm and a thickness of approximately 3mm.
- Place the pastry on a lightly greased baking tray.
- Pile the filling onto one half of the circle and fold the other half over.
- Seal it with your fingertips.
- Brush the huge pasty all over with an egg yolk mixed with a tablespoon of water and bake for 30 minutes.

Green salad

½ cucumber, sliced
1 lettuce, washed
1 bunch of 6 or 7 spring onions, sliced

To dress

2 tablespoons extra virgin olive oil
½ tablespoon balsamic vinegar
salt and pepper

- Combine the salad ingredients in a serving bowl and pour over the salad just before serving.

Vegetable soup + sausage and mustard filled bread rolls

This is a hearty and warming vegetable soup that goes well with the rolls. Try these bread rolls, as they will not disappoint. This recipe makes about 12 small ones. Get the rolls started first and then make the soup.

Vegetable soup

200g courgettes, roughly chopped
300g butternut squash, peeled and roughly chopped
1 onion, peeled and roughly chopped
300g carrots, peeled and roughly chopped
100g watercress
50g butter
1.5 litres chicken stock
salt and pepper
1 tablespoon chives, snipped
200ml single cream

- Place all the vegetables in a large saucepan with the butter.
- Cover with a lid and cook over a low heat for 15 minutes, stirring occasionally.
- Pour over the stock.
- Bring to a good simmer, cover and cook gently for 35 minutes.
- Once cooled, blend the soup in a food processor or blender.
- Warm the soup through on the hob.
- Check the seasoning, add the herbs and cream and serve with the filled rolls.

Sausage and mustard filled bread rolls

For the cheese and onion bread rolls

325g white bread flour
1 teaspoon salt
½ teaspoon mustard powder
75g Cheddar cheese, grated
2 spring onions, peeled and finely chopped
100ml milk, warmed
100ml water, warmed
one sachet fast-action dried yeast
a little milk for glazing
a little Cheddar cheese for sprinkling

For the sausages

6 sausages
teaspoon or two olive oil
good English mustard for serving

To make the bread rolls

- Mix the flour, salt, mustard powder, cheese and onions in a mixing bowl.
- Combine the milk and water in a measuring jug.
- Mix the yeast with a little of the milk and water, in a small bowl and leave for 3 minutes.
- Pour the yeasty milk and water onto the flour mixture and then pour on the rest of the liquid.
- Mix to a rough dough.
- Turn the dough out onto a floured surface and work together, kneading for 10 minutes by hand, or 5 if you are using a food mixer.
- Return to the bowl, cover with a clean tea towel and leave to rise for 1 hour 30 minutes.
- Turn out and divide the dough into 12 small pieces weighing approximately 50g each.
- Shape the pieces into rolls and lay on a greased baking sheet.
- Brush each roll with milk and sprinkle with a little grated cheese.
- Preheat the oven to 220°C/425°F/gas 7.
- Leave the rolls to rise again for 30 minutes and then bake in the oven for 15 minutes.

To fry the sausages

- Fry the sausages in a little olive oil in a frying pan on a medium heat to brown them all over.
- Turn the heat down and cook for 12–15 minutes.

To serve

- Split the rolls and fill them with sausages and mustard.

Marinated pork chops
+ roast potatoes + spring cabbage

Marinating pork chops transforms them from an everyday meal into something rather special.

Marinated pork chops

4–6 pork chops (if your children eat adult portions 6 chops is more realistic)
4 garlic cloves, peeled
3 tablespoons sea salt
2 tablespoons black peppercorns
leaves from six sprigs rosemary, roughly chopped
juice 3 fresh lemons
6 tablespoons olive oil
fresh lemon for serving

- Place each chop between two sheets of cling-film and bash them until they are 1cm thick.
- Place all the chops in a dish large enough to hold them in one layer.
- Using a pestle and mortar, roughly pound the garlic cloves, salt, peppercorns and fresh rosemary leaves.
- Add the lemon juice and olive oil and stir.
- Pour this mixture over the pork chops and leave them to marinate for 1 hour in the fridge.
- Preheat the grill until very hot and then grill each chop for 5 minutes on each side.
- Serve with a squeeze of lemon and the potatoes and cabbage.

Roast potatoes

1kg potatoes, peeled and quartered
salt
2 sprigs rosemary
2 tablespoons olive oil

- Preheat the oven to 220°C/425°F/gas 7.
- Parboil the potatoes in salted water for about 4 minutes.
- Drain and place the potatoes in a roasting tin with the rosemary sprigs.
- Drizzle with olive oil and roast them for 45–60 minutes until golden brown.

Spring cabbage

1 tablespoon olive oil
2 shallots, finely sliced
1 clove garlic, finely chopped
1cm piece fresh ginger, peeled and finely chopped
400g tin tomatoes
400g spring cabbage, sliced to a 1cm thickness
200ml water
salt and pepper

- Heat the olive oil in a saucepan and fry the shallots for 2 minutes.
- Add the garlic and ginger and stir, cooking for about 1 minute.
- Then add the tomatoes and cook for a further minute.
- Next, add the cabbage and water.
- Season and cook, covered, on a low simmer for 15 minutes and then uncovered for another 15 minutes.

Roast marinated lamb with vegetables + green salad

This is roast lamb as the Greeks do it, and it is very simple. If possible, prepare the lamb the night before you intend to cook it.

Roast marinated lamb with vegetables

150ml olive oil
juice 1 lemon
leaves from two sprigs fresh thyme
1 teaspoon dried oregano
salt and pepper
2kg leg lamb
2 cloves garlic, peeled and cut into thin slivers
4 small red onions, peeled and quartered
1kg potatoes, peeled and quartered
225g plum tomatoes
225ml dry white wine

- Preheat the oven to 200°C/400°F/gas 6.
- To make the marinade place the olive oil, lemon juice, thyme and dried oregano in a small bowl and mix well.
- Add salt and pepper in generous quantities.
- Place the leg of lamb in a large roasting tin.
- Make several small incisions in the leg of lamb using a sharp knife.
- Rub ⅔ of the marinade over the lamb, making sure it goes into the incisions.
- Fill each incision with slivers of garlic and season the lamb with more salt and pepper.
- Set aside for as long as you can before cooking.
- Place the onions, potatoes and tomatoes in the meat tray around the lamb.
- Pour on the remaining marinade and roast for 35 minutes.
- Remove the roasting tin from the oven and pour the wine over the lamb and vegetables.
- Return the roasting tin to the oven for a further 50 minutes.
- Remove the meat from the roasting tin and set it aside to rest for 20 minutes.
- Reduce the oven to 140°C/275°F/gas 1 and return the vegetables to the oven to keep warm while the lamb rests.
- Carve the lamb and serve with the juices, the vegetables, and the green salad.

Green salad

1 lettuce, either Cos or Romaine, washed and roughly sliced
½ cucumber, sliced
4 spring onions, peeled and sliced
2 tablespoons flat-leaf parsley, roughly chopped
1 bunch chives, snipped
1 tablespoon pitted green olives

For the dressing

3 tablespoons extra virgin olive oil
1 tablespoon white wine vinegar
salt and pepper

- Place the salad ingredients in a serving bowl.
- Mix the dressing in a small bowl and pour it over the salad when you are ready to eat.

Steamed ginger and rhubarb pudding + custard

The basic steamed sponge in this recipe, without the rhubarb and ginger, can form the basis of any steamed pudding, whether you use strawberry jam, dried fruit compote or a summer fruit concoction. The pudding is wonderfully light and does not have that heavy denseness that some steamed puddings tend to have. I have chosen rhubarb, as it is seasonal in April and should be easy to obtain.

Steamed ginger and rhubarb pudding

For the rhubarb

100g caster sugar

200ml water

500g rhubarb, trimmed and cut into 5cm lengths

For the steamed pudding

1 tablespoon stem ginger and 1 tablespoon of the syrup

2 teaspoons grated orange zest

115g butter, softened

115g caster sugar

2 eggs, beaten

140g self-raising flour

salt

2 tablespoons milk or a little more

To cook the rhubarb

- Boil the water and caster sugar rapidly for 5 minutes.
- Add the rhubarb, cover the pan and bring the syrupy water very slowly up to simmering point. Avoid stirring.
- As soon as the syrup begins to simmer, take the pan off the heat as the rhubarb will be ready.

continues

To make the pudding

- Grease a 1 litre pudding basin.
- Finely chop the stem ginger and put it with the accompanying syrup in the bottom of the pudding basin.
- Add the grated orange zest and two tablespoons of the cooked rhubarb. Serve the rest of the rhubarb with the pudding once it has steamed.
- Cream the butter and sugar in a mixing bowl with an electric hand whisk, until it is white and fluffy in texture. This takes at least 5 minutes.
- Add the beaten eggs and then stir in the flour and a pinch of salt.
- Next, add the milk and mix to combine.
- If the batter seems too stiff add a splash more milk and mix it in.
- Spoon the batter into the pudding basin on top of the rhubarb and ginger mixture.
- Cover the basin securely with greaseproof paper tied on with string. Take a large saucepan and pour 2cm of water into it. Place the pudding basin in the saucepan. Place a lid on the saucepan and simmer for 2 hours.
- Serve the pudding with more of the rhubarb sauce and custard.

Custard

600ml milk and double cream mixed
2 whole eggs
2 egg yolks
2 tablespoons caster sugar
1 vanilla pod or a drop or two vanilla extract

- In a glass bowl whisk the whole eggs, yolks and the sugar with a hand whisk for 2 minutes. Set aside.
- Measure the milk and cream in a measuring jug, add the vanilla pod or the extract and microwave it on high for 2 minutes. The milk and cream should be just at boiling point but not actually boiling.
- Place the glass bowl, containing the eggs and sugar, over a saucepan of simmering water.
- Add the milk and cream to the eggs and sugar, whisking continuously to avoid lumps.
- If you used a vanilla pod, scrape out the seeds into the mixture.
- Keep stirring for 10 minutes, by which time the custard will have a good consistency. An indication of when the custard is thick enough is that it will coat the back of a wooden spoon as you lift it out of the mixture.
- You can make custard ahead of time, but avoid reheating it, as it may curdle.

Hot cross buns

Unlike Christmas time, there are not many things that we still cook to celebrate Easter. Hot cross buns remain a favourite, though, and are well worth the effort of making yourself.

1 sachet fast-action dried yeast
300ml warm milk and water mixed
sugar
600g strong white bread flour
1 teaspoon ground cinnamon
1 teaspoon ground nutmeg
85g raisins
55g caster sugar
1 teaspoon salt
55g melted butter
1 egg, beaten
For the glaze
2 tablespoons sugar and 2 tablespoons warm water mixed together

- In a small bowl blend the yeast with a little of the milk and water and a pinch of sugar.
- Then set aside.
- Sift half the flour into a mixing bowl and make a well in the centre.
- Pour in the yeast mixture and the rest of the milk and water and combine.
- Cover with a clean tea towel and leave in a draught-free place for 40 minutes.
- Next, add the rest of the flour, the spices, raisins, sugar, salt, butter and egg.
- Mix really well and then turn out onto a floured surface and knead for 5 minutes.
- Place back in the mixing bowl, cover with a tea towel and leave to rise for 1 hour.
- Then turn the dough out onto a floured surface and divide it into 16 pieces.
- Shape each piece into a round and place on a greased baking sheet.
- Mark each bun with a cross, using a sharp knife.
- Heat the oven to 220°C/425°F/gas 7. Cover the buns with the tea towel and leave them to rise again for 15 minutes.
- Then bake the buns for 15 minutes.
- Immediately they come out of the oven, brush the buns with the glaze for a lovely shiny finish.

TIP

The cross is symbolic of the crucifixion at Easter, but these buns are so good, you could just not cut the cross into the dough and bake them at any time of year.

Week 3

Monday p206	Meat and vegetable pie + broccoli
Tuesday p207	Spinach and watercress soup + smoked salmon paté and toast
Wednesday p208	Pasta Puttanesca
Thursday p209	Fish gratin + spinach
Friday p210	Chicken and mushrooms in Marsala + pommes boulangère + white cabbage
Saturday p211	Grilled salmon fillets with pea and parsley cream sauce + boiled potatoes
Sunday p212	Leg of lamb in white wine + roast sweet potatoes, potatoes and parsnips
Sunday pudding p213	Rhubarb, orange and almond tart
Extra tasty treat p214	Madeira cake

Shopping list

MEAT

- ☐ 1kg shin beef
- ☐ 6 chicken breasts, boneless and skinless
- ☐ 2kg leg lamb on the bone

FISH

- ☐ 6 salmon fillets
- ☐ 900g cod fillet
- ☐ 200g cooked prawns
- ☐ 150g smoked salmon

VEGETABLES

- ☐ 1 onion
- ☐ 4 shallots
- ☐ 1 carrot
- ☐ 1 bunch celery
- ☐ 400g broccoli
- ☐ 3kg potatoes
- ☐ 300g sweet potatoes
- ☐ 200g watercress
- ☐ 385g spinach
- ☐ 100g chestnut mushrooms
- ☐ 1 garlic bulb
- ☐ 1 white cabbage
- ☐ 4 parsnips

FRUIT

- ☐ 4 lemons
- ☐ 1 orange
- ☐ 2–3 stalks forced rhubarb

FRESH HERBS

- ☐ thyme
- ☐ bay leaves
- ☐ flat-leaf parsley
- ☐ basil
- ☐ chives
- ☐ rosemary

FRIDGE ITEMS

- ☐ 400g frozen petits pois
- ☐ 4 packs butter
- ☐ 11 eggs
- ☐ 300ml single cream
- ☐ 150ml double cream
- ☐ 600ml milk
- ☐ 1 litre chicken stock
- ☐ 1 tub Greek yoghurt
- ☐ 50g Parmesan cheese
- ☐ 150g chopped pancetta
- ☐ 100ml fish stock

KITCHEN CUPBOARD ITEMS

- ☐ olive oil
- ☐ extra virgin olive oil
- ☐ beef stock cubes
- ☐ chicken stock cubes
- ☐ 300ml pale ale
- ☐ anchovy fillets
- ☐ black pitted olives
- ☐ 2 x 400g tins chopped tomatoes
- ☐ 1 wholemeal loaf
- ☐ capers
- ☐ 250ml Marsala wine
- ☐ 450ml dry white wine
- ☐ Dijon mustard
- ☐ salt
- ☐ 80g icing sugar
- ☐ 225g white marzipan
- ☐ cointreau
- ☐ 410g tin cannellini beans
- ☐ 410g tin butter beans
- ☐ 500g spaghetti
- ☐ 175g caster sugar
- ☐ 175g self-raising flour
- ☐ 700g plain flour

SPICES

- ☐ whole nutmeg
- ☐ black pepper
- ☐ paprika

Meat and vegetable pie + broccoli

Nobody can resist a hearty meat and vegetable pie after a busy day. The filling can, if you prefer, be prepared the day before and kept in the fridge to save time.

Meat and vegetable pie

For the filling

2 tablespoons olive oil
1 onion, diced
1 carrot, peeled and chopped
1 stick celery, chopped
1kg shin beef, diced and trimmed of any excess fat
30g plain flour
½ beef stock cube
200ml hot water
300ml pale ale
4 medium potatoes, peeled and diced into 2cm chunks
1 sprig thyme and a bay leaf
100g frozen peas
salt and pepper

For the pastry

225g plain flour
140g butter, chilled and cubed
salt
1 egg yolk
2 tablespoons cold water
1 beaten egg

To make the filling

- Place the oil in a heavy-bottomed saucepan and warm through on a medium heat.
- Add the onion, carrot and celery and cook for 10 minutes until soft.
- Raise the heat to high and add the beef, browning it all over.
- Reduce the heat once browned, add the flour and stir until absorbed.
- Dissolve the stock cube in the water and pale ale, then add to the beef and vegetables.
- Add the potatoes and herbs and bring to a gentle simmer.
- Simmer gently, uncovered, for 1 hour 30 minutes.
- Add the peas and cook, uncovered, for another 10 minutes.
- Season and set aside to cool.

To make the pastry

- Put the flour and butter in the bowl of a food processor and incorporate them so that the resulting mixture resembles fine breadcrumbs.
- Add a pinch of salt.
- Mix the egg yolk with the cold water in a small bowl and add this liquid to the flour and fat.
- Turn on the food processor and mix until a dough just begins to form. Turn the mixture onto a floured work surface and combine thoroughly, with a light hand, until you have a smooth dough.
- Wrap the dough in cling-film and chill in the fridge for 20 minutes.

To assemble the pie

- Preheat the oven to 200°C/400°F/gas 6.
- Roll out the pastry into a thick circle.
- Pile the meat and vegetables into a pie dish and cover with the pastry, cutting a few slits in the top to let the steam escape.
- Brush the pastry with a beaten egg.
- Bake for 30 minutes.

Broccoli

400g broccoli
salt
lemon juice
black pepper

- Trim the broccoli into florets. If the stalks are very thick trim them down a little.
- Add the broccoli to a pan of salted, boiling water and simmer for 3 minutes.
- Drain and season with a squeeze of lemon and a grinding of black pepper.

Spinach and watercress soup + smoked salmon paté and toast

This is a particularly uncomplicated meal full of natural, unprocessed flavours. The fish paté goes really well with the soup.

Spinach and watercress soup

30g butter
200g potatoes, peeled and cut into chunks
1 litre chicken stock
200g watercress
150g spinach
salt and pepper
nutmeg
150ml single cream

- Heat the butter in a large saucepan.
- Add the potato and stir.
- Reduce the heat, cover the saucepan and cook the potato for 10 minutes.
- Add the stock, watercress and spinach and bring to a simmer.
- Reduce the heat and simmer gently, covered, for 30 minutes.
- Using a hand-held blender or food processor, blend the soup until smooth.
- To get rid of any stringy bits, pass the soup through a sieve.
- Just before serving bring the soup to a simmer.
- Season with salt, pepper and a grating of nutmeg and stir in the cream.

Smoked salmon paté

150g smoked salmon
1 tablespoon fresh chives, chopped
juice ½ lemon
grated zest 1 lemon
55g butter, softened
1 tablespoon extra virgin olive oil
4 tablespoons Greek yoghurt
½ teaspoon paprika
pepper
wholemeal toast for serving

- Whizz the salmon, chives, lemon juice and zest in a food processor until the salmon is reasonably fine.
- Add the butter, oil and yoghurt and blitz again until you have a smooth paste.
- Season with the paprika and pepper and serve on hot, buttered toast.

Pasta Puttanesca

This sauce is full of robust Mediterranean flavours and is very easy to put together. Although it's only April, it will conjure up thoughts of warm summer evenings.

2 cloves garlic, peeled and chopped finely
2 tablespoons olive oil
3 anchovy fillets
1 tablespoon capers, rinsed
16 black, pitted olives
2 x 400g tins chopped tomatoes
salt and pepper
small bunch flat-leaf parsley, finely chopped
6 basil leaves, roughly torn
500g spaghetti

- Gently fry the garlic in olive oil on a low heat for a few minutes until you can smell the garlic, taking care not to burn it.
- Add the anchovies and stir, crushing them with the back of a wooden spoon as you stir.
- Add the capers, olives and tomatoes and season with salt and pepper.
- Cook on a gentle simmer for 30 minutes.
- Cook the pasta following the packet instructions.
- Add the herbs to the sauce, stir in well and serve with the cooked spaghetti.

Fish gratin + spinach

This recipe with some modification comes from *The Complete Sophie Grigson Cookbook*, published by the BBC, which is full of really useful and tasty recipes. I have changed the quantities slightly. My children, angels though they are, do not stretch to spinach. My husband and I love it, though, so I usually cook a different green vegetable for the children when we have spinach. For two spinach eaters I would use about 235g of young leaf spinach. Increase the quantities for more than two spinach lovers.

Fish gratin

900g cod fillet
salt and pepper
1 tablespoon lemon juice
45g butter
25g plain flour
300ml milk
150ml single cream
200g cooked prawns
2 egg yolks
50g freshly grated Parmesan cheese

- Preheat the oven to 180°C/350°F/gas 4.
- Put the fish fillets into a lightly buttered, ovenproof gratin dish and season with salt, pepper and lemon juice.
- Cover with tin foil and bake in the oven for 20 minutes.
- Remove from the oven and drain any liquid from the dish.
- In the meantime, heat the butter in a saucepan and stir in the flour.
- Stir for a minute and then remove from the heat and add the milk, stirring until combined.
- Add the cream and bring to the boil.
- Simmer for 10 minutes, on a very low heat, stirring occasionally.
- Remove from the heat and add the prawns and the egg yolks. Check the seasoning. Pour the sauce over the fish and sprinkle with the cheese.
- Place under a preheated grill for 5 minutes until nicely browned.

Spinach

1 shallot, finely diced
knob of butter
1 dessertspoon olive oil
235g spinach
salt and pepper

- Over a gentle heat sauté the shallot in the butter and oil until soft. Add the spinach and let it wilt, stirring it occasionally. The spinach is cooked when it is soft and dark green.
- Season with salt and pepper and serve with the fish gratin.

Chicken and mushrooms in Marsala + pommes boulangère + white cabbage

This is such a quick, easy dish to make and the Marsala makes it taste very special. The pommes boulangère add a lovely garlic flavour, and the aroma from the oven while they are cooking is wonderful. White cabbage is a good buy at this time of year, because it is home-grown rather than imported. Make the pommes boulangère first.

Chicken and mushrooms in Marsala

1 tablespoon olive oil
25g butter
6 chicken breasts, boneless and skinless
2 shallots, thinly sliced
150g chopped pancetta
100g chestnut mushrooms, sliced
250ml Marsala wine

- Heat the oil and butter gently in a heavy-bottomed frying pan.
- Add the chicken breasts, two at a time, browning them on each side for a few minutes.
- Set the chicken aside, retaining the juices in the pan on a medium heat.
- Add the shallots, chopped pancetta and mushrooms to the pan and cook until nice and brown. This will take about 3 minutes.
- With the heat still high add the Marsala wine and stir round for a few seconds, scraping off the bits from the side of the pan.
- Reduce the heat and return the chicken breasts to the pan.
- Cook for 15 minutes on a low simmer, with the pan slightly covered, as you don't want too much sauce with this recipe. The potatoes are cooked in stock and provide most of the liquid the meal will need. Check that the chicken is cooked through and serve with the pommes boulangère and white cabbage.

Pommes boulangère

1kg potatoes, peeled and cut slightly thinner than a pound coin
salt and pepper
3 cloves garlic, peeled and crushed
1 sprig rosemary
600ml chicken stock, fresh or cube

- Preheat the oven to 180°C/350°F/gas 4.
- Place the potatoes in a shallow baking dish and season them with salt and pepper.
- Add the garlic and rosemary to the potatoes and pour over the stock. The stock should come just to the top of the potatoes.
- Bake in the oven for 1 hour until the potatoes are tender.

White cabbage

1 white cabbage, cored and thinly sliced
15g butter
1 dessertspoon olive oil
salt and pepper
squeeze of lemon juice

- Heat the butter and oil in a saucepan.
- Add the cabbage and cook gently for 4 minutes.
- Season with salt, pepper and lemon juice.

Grilled salmon fillets with pea and parsley cream sauce + boiled potatoes

Salmon is good for you as it is rich in oil. Like most fish it's great with a good sauce, and the peas and parsley add a freshness that complements the salmon well.

Grilled salmon fillets with pea and parsley cream sauce

For the sauce

1 shallot, peeled and finely chopped
150ml dry white wine
100ml fish stock, shop-bought is the best option here
300g frozen petits pois, cooked
2 tablespoons flat-leaf parsley, chopped
150ml double cream
1 teaspoon Dijon mustard
salt and pepper

For the salmon

6 salmon fillets
olive oil
salt and pepper
squeeze of lemon juice

To make the sauce

- Put the shallot, wine, stock and petits pois into a small saucepan and bring to the boil.
- Reduce the heat and simmer for 3 minutes.
- Add the parsley, cream and mustard and season with salt and pepper.
- Bring to the boil and then reduce the heat and simmer for 2 minutes.
- Remove from the heat and set aside.

To cook the fish

- Preheat the grill and line the grill pan with a sheet of aluminium foil.
- Brush the salmon fillets with a little olive oil and place them under the hot grill for 2 minutes or so before turning them and grilling them for a further 2 minutes.
- Season with salt, pepper and a squeeze of lemon juice.
- Serve with the sauce and boiled potatoes.

Boiled potatoes

750g potatoes, peeled and quartered
salt
butter
black pepper

- Place the potatoes in a large saucepan of salted water.
- Bring to the boil and then reduce the heat to a simmer until the potatoes are tender.
- Serve with a dab of butter and a few grindings of black pepper.

Leg of lamb in white wine + roast sweet potatoes, potatoes and parsnips

This recipe is Italian in taste and method. It is very simple and perfect for a spring Sunday lunch. You will need a very large saucepan with a lid that will hold the whole leg. Alternatively, get your butcher to cut the leg in half, or buy two smaller legs of lamb.

Leg of lamb in white wine

3 tablespoons olive oil
30g butter
2kg leg lamb on the bone
3 cloves garlic, peeled and left whole
1 large sprig rosemary
salt and pepper
300ml dry white wine
410g tin cannellini beans, drained
410g tin butter beans, drained

- Heat the olive oil and butter in a large saucepan.
- Place the leg of lamb in the saucepan along with the garlic and rosemary and brown the lamb all over. By the time you have finished, the lamb should be a good dark brown colour. To achieve this the heat will have to be reasonably high.
- Once this is done, add a good seasoning of salt and pepper.
- Then, add the wine to the pan and let it bubble away for 15 minutes, turning the joint once during this time.
- Reduce the heat, cover the pan and cook the lamb on a gentle simmer for 2 hours.
- Add the tins of beans and cook for a further hour.
- Remove the lamb from the saucepan. It needs to be served straightaway and the meat should just fall off the bone.
- There should be plenty of juices left in the pan to serve as a gravy.

Roast sweet potatoes, potatoes and parsnips

800g roasting potatoes, peeled and quartered
300g sweet potatoes, peeled and quartered
4 parsnips, peeled and quartered
2 tablespoons olive oil
salt and pepper

- Preheat the oven to 220°C/425°F/gas 7.
- Parboil the potatoes and parsnips in salted water for 4 minutes.
- Drain the potatoes and parsnips and place them with the sweet potatoes in a roasting tray.
- Pour over the olive oil and roast the vegetables for 1 hour.
- Season with salt and pepper and serve.

Rhubarb, orange and almond tart

Rhubarb and orange go superbly well together in this lovely, elegant pudding.

For the pastry

180g butter, chilled and cubed
75g icing sugar
2 egg yolks
225g plain flour

For the filling

110g butter, softened
225g white marzipan, cut into small pieces
2 tablespoons plain flour
1 dessertspoon cointreau
grated zest 1 orange
2 eggs
2–3 stalks forced rhubarb, chopped into 1.5cm chunks

To make the pastry

- Put the butter, sugar, flour and egg yolks in a food processor and pulse together quickly.
- As soon as a dough starts to form, turn it out onto a floured work surface and knead gently into a ball.
- Wrap in cling-film and chill in the fridge for 30 minutes.

To make the filling

- Preheat the oven to 190°C/375°F/gas 5.
- Grease a 23cm tart tin.
- Cream the butter with the marzipan until combined into a smooth mixture.
- Add the flour, eggs, cointreau and orange zest.
- Mix until smooth.
- Roll out the chilled pastry and line the tart tin with it.
- Spoon the cake mixture onto the pastry and smooth it out gently.
- Press the rhubarb chunks into the cake mixture in an attractive pattern.
- Place the tart on a baking tray and bake for 45 minutes.
- Serve with cream.

Madeira cake

Madeira cake reminds me of childhood holidays to Wales or the Lake District, with all of us squashed into our car. My mother would always pack two Madeira cakes to last the whole holiday. You can't beat the smell of a Madeira cake baking in the oven.

175g butter, softened
175g caster sugar
3 eggs
175g self-raising flour, sieved
80g plain flour, sieved
grated zest and juice 1 lemon
icing sugar

- Grease and line a 20cm round cake tin.
- Preheat the oven to 160°C/320°F/gas 2½.
- Cream the butter and sugar together in an electric mixer until white and fluffy.
- Beat the eggs into the mixture one at a time, incorporating each one thoroughly before adding the next.
- Then, using a metal spoon, fold in both flours along with the zest and juice of the lemon.
- Spoon the mixture into the cake tin and bake for 60 minutes.
- When cooled, dust the top with icing sugar.

APRIL

Week 4

Monday p218	Spaghetti with tomato and basil sauce
Tuesday p219	Fish pie + purple sprouting broccoli
Wednesday p220	Oregano lamb chops with roasted new potatoes and roasted courgettes
Thursday p221	Peasant vegetable soup + wholemeal bread
Friday p222	Chicken and cashew nut curry + carrots, potatoes and peas
Saturday p224	Steak pudding + leeks
Sunday p225	Roast chicken with curry sauce + roast potatoes + watercress and rocket salad
Sunday pudding p226	Coconut rice pudding + warm pineapple
Extra tasty treat p227	Scones with raspberry jam

Shopping list

MEAT

- ☐ 2 x 1.5kg chickens
- ☐ 700g shin beef
- ☐ 1 unsmoked gammon joint about 500g
- ☐ 1.5kg chicken pieces, on the bone
- ☐ 10–12 lamb chops

FISH

- ☐ 400g smoked haddock
- ☐ 400g salmon
- ☐ 150g cooked prawns

VEGETABLES

- ☐ 1 bunch celery
- ☐ 5 onions
- ☐ 400g carrots
- ☐ 1 bulb garlic
- ☐ 2.5kg potatoes
- ☐ 1kg new potatoes
- ☐ 4-5 courgettes
- ☐ 7 leeks
- ☐ 200g watercress
- ☐ 100g rocket leaves
- ☐ fresh ginger
- ☐ 2 tomatoes
- ☐ 1 green chilli
- ☐ 3 parsnips
- ☐ ½ small white cabbage
- ☐ 250g purple sprouting broccoli

FRUIT

- ☐ 400g fresh pineapple
- ☐ 1 lemon

HERBS

- ☐ basil
- ☐ thyme
- ☐ coriander
- ☐ bay leaves
- ☐ flat-leaf parsley

FRIDGE ITEMS

- ☐ 1 pack butter
- ☐ 400ml double cream
- ☐ 700ml full fat milk
- ☐ 200ml beef stock
- ☐ 2 litres chicken stock
- ☐ 4 eggs
- ☐ 50g Parmesan cheese
- ☐ 50g Cheddar cheese
- ☐ 650g frozen peas
- ☐ 200ml crème fraîche

KITCHEN CUPBOARD ITEMS

- ☐ 600g plain flour
- ☐ English mustard powder
- ☐ salt
- ☐ 410g tin cannellini beans
- ☐ extra virgin olive oil
- ☐ olive oil
- ☐ vegetable oil
- ☐ white wine vinegar
- ☐ Dijon mustard
- ☐ 270g risotto rice
- ☐ 2 tins coconut milk
- ☐ 100g caster sugar
- ☐ raspberry jam
- ☐ desiccated coconut
- ☐ bicarbonate of soda
- ☐ cream of tartar
- ☐ 120g cashew nuts
- ☐ Worcestershire sauce
- ☐ 500g spaghetti
- ☐ 2 x 400g tins chopped Italian tomatoes
- ☐ 400g self-raising flour
- ☐ 400g wholemeal flour
- ☐ 100g strong white bread flour
- ☐ 200g vegetable suet
- ☐ fast-action dried yeast
- ☐ black treacle

SPICES

- ☐ cinnamon sticks
- ☐ turmeric
- ☐ black peppercorns
- ☐ coriander seeds
- ☐ cumin seeds
- ☐ fennel seeds
- ☐ fenugreek
- ☐ black mustard seeds
- ☐ cloves
- ☐ dried oregano

Spaghetti with tomato and basil sauce

This is a quick, fresh-tasting pasta sauce, a great meal for a Monday evening. It's healthy and only takes 30 minutes or so.

2 tablespoons olive oil
½ stick celery, finely chopped
1 onion, peeled and finely chopped
1 carrot, peeled and finely chopped
2 x 400g tins chopped Italian tomatoes
3 cloves garlic, peeled and finely chopped
salt and pepper
100ml double cream
1 bunch fresh basil, torn into shreds
Parmesan cheese, freshly grated for serving
500g spaghetti cooked in plenty of salted water, following the packet instructions

- Heat the olive oil in a saucepan.
- Add the celery, onion and carrot and sauté for 5 minutes on a low heat until soft.
- Add the tinned tomatoes and the garlic and another tablespoon of olive oil.
- Cook, uncovered, on a slow simmer for 25 minutes.
- Season with salt and pepper.
- Add the cream.
- Stir in and then throw in the basil leaves.
- Serve with the spaghetti and some Parmesan sprinkled over the top.

Fish pie
+ purple sprouting broccoli

There are an enormous number of fish pie recipes in various cookery books and it's difficult to know which one to use. There's nothing wrong with cooking a different fish pie every time you make one, but when time is of the essence it helps if you have a recipe you know and consequently can produce quickly. This one is good because it is relatively easy and makes use of smoked fish, thereby guaranteeing a good flavour. It's also child friendly.

Fish pie

400g smoked haddock
400g salmon
300ml milk
200ml water
1kg potatoes, peeled and cut into quarters
40g butter
30g flour
150g frozen peas, cooked
150g cooked prawns
4 eggs, hard boiled and sliced
Worcestershire sauce
handful flat-leaf parsley, finely chopped
black pepper
50g Cheddar cheese, grated

- Preheat the oven to 190°C/375°F/gas 5.
- Place the haddock and salmon in an ovenproof dish and pour over the milk and water. The liquid should just cover the fish.
- Cover the dish with tin foil and bake for 20 minutes on the middle shelf.
- Then drain the fish but keep the milk and water.
- Remove any skin from the fish and then flake the fish, setting it aside in the ovenproof dish.
- Place the potatoes in a saucepan of salted water, bring to the boil and simmer for 20 minutes or so until soft enough to mash with a little milk and butter.
- Set the potatoes aside.
- To make the white sauce heat the butter in a small saucepan on a very low heat.
- Add the flour and stir to incorporate.
- Remove from the heat and add the milk and water mixture very slowly at first, incorporating each addition as you go to avoid lumps.
- Place the sauce back on the heat and stir until it comes to a simmer.
- Reduce the heat to very low and cook for 5 minutes.
- Once cooked pour the sauce over the fish and add the peas, prawns, eggs, a splash of Worcestershire sauce and the parsley.
- Season with pepper. Taste at this stage to see if any salt is necessary, as often with smoked fish it won't be.
- Top the fish mixture with the mashed potato and grated Cheddar and place in the oven for 15 minutes to warm through.
- To get a nice crispy, cheesy look to the top place the dish under a hot grill for a few minutes.

Purple sprouting broccoli

250g purple sprouting broccoli
salt and pepper
a little butter

- Boil a saucepan of water.
- Add the broccoli and simmer for 3 minutes.
- Drain well, then season with salt, pepper and a little butter.

Oregano lamb chops with roasted new potatoes and roasted courgettes

This meal is very simple as you can put everything in the same tray in the oven, *à la* Jamie Oliver. The chops are well done and the combination of lamb, oregano and lemon is very much in the Greek style.

1kg new potatoes, halved lengthways with skins on
10–12 lamb chops (depending on the appetites of you and your children)
salt
2 teaspoons dried oregano
black pepper
juice 1 lemon
1 tablespoon olive oil
4–5 courgettes, sliced into 5mm thick discs

- Preheat the oven to 200°C/400°F/gas 6.
- Parboil the potatoes in salted water for 5 minutes.
- Drain the potatoes and place them in a roasting tin with the lamb chops.
- Season both the potatoes and chops with the oregano, salt, pepper, lemon juice and olive oil.
- Place the chops and potatoes in the oven for 35 minutes, turning the potatoes occasionally as they brown.
- Increase the oven temperature to 220°C/425°F/gas 7 and add the courgettes to the roasting tin.
- Roast for a further 15 minutes.
- Remove from the oven and serve.

Peasant vegetable soup + wholemeal bread

Making bread can be time-consuming and, therefore, not very practical for working people, hence the small number of bread recipes in this book. This bread, however, is quick to make as it requires no kneading and only takes 30 minutes to rise. The recipe originates from the Ballymaloe House Cookery School but I have changed it slightly by adding a little white flour. The soup is very hearty so you can always forgo the bread. You will need a saucepan large enough to accommodate the soup and a small joint of ham.

Peasant vegetable soup

50g butter
1 onion, finely chopped
3 leeks, finely sliced
2 sticks celery, roughly chopped
3 carrots, peeled and sliced
1 sprig thyme
1 bay leaf
1.5 litres chicken stock
3 parsnips, peeled and chopped into small chunks
1 unsmoked gammon joint, weighing approximately 500g
410g tin cannellini beans, drained
300g frozen peas
½ small white cabbage
3 cloves garlic, peeled and finely chopped
3 tablespoons flat-leaf parsley, chopped
salt and pepper

- Heat the butter in the saucepan and add the onion, leeks, celery and carrots.
- Reduce the heat to low, cover the saucepan with a lid, and cook the vegetables for 10 minutes.
- Stir in the thyme and the bay leaf and pour in the stock.
- Add the parsnips, gammon joint, cannellini beans, peas, cabbage and garlic.
- Bring the soup to a simmer, cover, and cook gently for 40 minutes.
- Remove the ham to a carving board and add the parsley to the soup.
- Taste to check the seasoning. It will need pepper but it may not need a lot of salt.
- Cut the ham into bite-sized chunks, return it to the soup and serve with the bread.

Wholemeal bread

1 sachet dried yeast
400ml water
1 teaspoon black treacle
400g wholemeal flour
100g strong white bread flour
1 heaped teaspoon salt

- Preheat the oven to 120°C/250°F/gas ½.
- Grease a 500g loaf tin and warm it in the preheated oven for 10 minutes.
- Mix the yeast with 150ml of the water in a small mixing bowl.
- Add the treacle and the remaining water and stir.
- Mix the flours and salt together in a large mixing bowl, making a well in the centre, then add the liquid and stir in.
- Use your hand to mix the batter gently in the bowl for 1 minute.
- Place the dough in the loaf tin, cover with a tea towel and leave to rise for 30 minutes.
- Meanwhile increase the oven temperature to 220°C/425°F/gas 7.
- Bake the dough for 30 minutes.
- Reduce the temperature to 200°C/400°F/gas 6 and bake for a further 15 minutes.
- Turn the loaf out of the tin and return it to the oven, bottom side up, for 10 minutes.
- Cool on a rack.

Chicken and cashew nut curry
+ carrots, potatoes and peas

The vegetable is based on a recipe from Madhur Jaffrey's *World Vegetarian* book, which is a treasure trove of interesting culinary things to do with vegetables. I think the vegetables make a nice change from the boiled rice one usually eats with curry.

Chicken and cashew nut curry

1 teaspoon coriander seeds
1 teaspoon cumin seeds
½ teaspoon black mustard seeds
2 cloves
10 black peppercorns
50g fresh ginger, peeled
2 cloves garlic, peeled
½ teaspoon turmeric
120g cashew nuts
1 green chilli, deseeded
125ml water
2 tablespoons vegetable oil
1.5kg chicken pieces, on the bone, skin removed
1 onion, finely chopped
1 teaspoon salt
400ml tin coconut milk
1 tablespoon fresh coriander, chopped

- Over a medium heat toast the coriander, cumin, black mustard seeds, cloves and peppercorns in a frying pan, until you smell the aroma and they start to smoke a little.
- Place the spices in a food processor along with the ginger, garlic, turmeric, cashew nuts, green chilli and water.
- Whizz to a smoothish paste and set aside.
- Meanwhile heat the oil in a large saucepan.
- Brown the chicken pieces in batches and set aside.
- Add the onion to the same pan and sauté for 10 minutes until soft but not browned.
- Return the chicken to the pan.
- Season with salt.
- Add the spice mixture and the tin of coconut milk.
- Bring to a good simmer and then reduce the heat and cook gently, covered, for 40 minutes.
- Garnish with the coriander.

To make your own curry powder:

1 tablespoon coriander seeds
1 dessertspoon cumin seeds
1 teaspoon fennel seeds
½ teaspoon fenugreek

- *Place the coriander seeds into a small, heavy-bottomed pan and heat through for 30 seconds.*
- *Add the other ingredients and toast until you smell the lovely aroma of the spices.*
- *Transfer the spices to a coffee grinder, a small processor or grind them in a pestle and mortar.*

Carrots, potatoes and peas

1 tablespoon vegetable oil
1 onion, finely diced
2.5cm piece fresh ginger, peeled and finely chopped
2 tomatoes, chopped
1 teaspoon salt
1 teaspoon curry powder*
¼ teaspoon turmeric
300g carrots, peeled and diced
450g potatoes, peeled and diced
120ml water
200g frozen peas

- Heat the oil in a frying pan over a medium heat.
- When hot, fry the onion for 5 minutes until softened and tinged with brown.
- Add the ginger and fry for 1 minute.
- Next, put in the tomatoes, salt, curry powder and turmeric.
- Increase the heat and cook for 3 minutes, stirring continuously.
- Add the carrots, potatoes and water and bring to a gentle simmer.
- Cover and simmer for 20 minutes.
- Add the peas, cover and simmer for another 4 minutes.

Steak pudding + leeks

You could easily make this a steak and kidney pudding if you care to. My children aren't too keen on kidneys so I tend to leave them out. Note this dish takes 4 hours to cook which is why I have suggested it for a Saturday,

Steak pudding

For the suet crust

400g self-raising flour
200g vegetable suet
1 teaspoon salt
½ teaspoon fresh thyme
150–200ml water

For the filling

700g shin beef, chopped in to 2cm chunks and trimmed of excess fat
2 tablespoons flour
1 teaspoon English mustard powder
1 large onion, peeled and thinly sliced
salt and pepper
200ml beef stock
1 tablespoon Worcestershire sauce
1 bay leaf

To make the suet crust

- Grease a 1.2 litre pudding basin.
- Mix the flour, suet, salt and thyme together in a mixing bowl.
- Add the water gradually until a rough dough is formed.
- Turn out and knead briefly on a floured work top.
- Set half of the dough aside.
- Roll out the remaining dough to a thickness of about 1cm.
- Line the basin with the dough, leaving an overhang of 1cm.

To make the filling

- In a mixing bowl, toss the shin of beef in the flour and mustard powder.
- Stir in the onion and season with salt and pepper.
- Spoon the meat and onions into the pudding basin and add half the stock, the Worcestershire sauce and the bay leaf.
- Fold over the overhanging pastry and brush it with some water, using a pastry brush.
- Roll out the remaining piece of dough and press this down on top of the pudding.
- Cover the top of the pudding with a circle of greaseproof paper and then cover the bowl completely with tin foil.
- Pour 3–4cm of boiling water into a large saucepan and place the basin in the saucepan. Cover the saucepan with a lid and simmer on a very low heat for 4 hours. You may need to add more hot water during this time.
- Once the pudding is cool enough to handle, unwrap the foil and greaseproof paper.
- Invert onto a plate.
- Reheat the remaining stock. Make a small hole in the top of the pudding and pour in as much warm stock as will fit.

Leeks

4 leeks
salt and pepper
200ml crème fraîche

- Prepare the leeks by cutting them lengthways, stopping about 1cm from the bottom of the leek so it's still in one piece. Wash them under the tap, fanning each leek out as you wash them, to get rid of any grit between the leaves.
- Slice the leeks as thinly as possible and then place them in a sauté pan with a sprinkling of salt.
- Gently sauté the leeks on a medium heat for 3 minutes, until they are soft. Try not to brown them.
- Stir in the crème fraîche and remove from the heat.

Roast chicken with curry sauce + roast potatoes + watercress and rocket salad

I don't think you can do much better than chicken, roast potatoes and a watercress salad. The curry sauce adds a twist to a traditional meal and is easy to make once you have prepared the curry powder. It is worth acknowledging that not everyone has two ovens and I get irritated by cookbooks that assume that everyone has a large designer kitchen. If you do have just one oven, put the potatoes round the chicken to start roasting and then finish them off in a different roasting tin once the chickens have cooked and you are making the gravy.

Roast chicken with curry sauce

2 x 1.5kg chickens
a little butter
salt and pepper
1 tablespoon plain flour
2 teaspoons curry powder*
500ml chicken stock
2 tablespoons double cream

- Preheat the oven to 180°C/350°F/gas 4.
- Place the chickens in a high-sided roasting tin and smear each one with a little butter.
- Season each chicken with salt and pepper and then roast for 1 hour 20 minutes.
- Remove the chickens from the meat tray, placing them under foil to keep warm.
- Take the roasting tin and place it on the hob.
- Sprinkle in the flour and stir round with a wooden spoon scraping up all the tasty caramelised bits and combining the flour with the juices.
- Add the curry powder and stir round.
- Pour on the chicken stock and bring to a simmer.
- Simmer for 10 minutes, add the cream and remove from the heat.

Roast potatoes

1kg potatoes, peeled and quartered
salt
2 tablespoons olive oil

- Preheat the oven to 220°C/425°F/gas 7.
- Parboil the potatoes in boiling salted water for about 5 minutes.
- Drain and place them in a roasting tin.
- Pour the olive oil over the potatoes and then roast in the oven for 50 minutes until brown.

To make your own curry powder:
1 tablespoon coriander seeds
1 dessertspoon cumin seeds
1 teaspoon fennel seeds
½ teaspoon fenugreek

- *Place the coriander seeds into a small, heavy-bottomed pan and heat through for 30 seconds.*
- *Add the other ingredients and toast until you smell the lovely aroma of the spices.*
- *Transfer the spices to a coffee grinder, a small processor or grind them in a pestle and mortar.*

Watercress and rocket salad

200g watercress
100g rocket leaves
For the dressing
2 tablespoons extra virgin olive oil
½ tablespoon white wine vinegar
1 teaspoon Dijon mustard
salt and pepper

- Place the watercress and rocket in a serving bowl.
- Mix the dressing ingredients together in a small bowl and then pour over the salad when ready to eat.

Coconut rice pudding + warm pineapple

Coconut milk adds a different flavour to a traditional rice pudding. The pineapple adds a tropical theme.

Coconut rice pudding

270g risotto rice
salt
400ml coconut milk
300ml milk
225ml water
1 cinnamon stick
1 teaspoon butter
2 tablespoons caster sugar

- Place the rice, a pinch of salt, the coconut milk, milk, water and cinnamon stick in a heavy-bottomed saucepan.
- Bring to a simmer and cook gently for 20–25 minutes, partially covered, stirring from time to time.
- Remove the cinnamon stick.
- Add the butter and sugar and stir in.
- Serve with the pineapple below.

Warm pineapple

20g butter
1 dessertspoon sugar
400g fresh pineapple, prepared and chopped into chunks
1 dessertspoon desiccated coconut

- Heat the butter with the sugar in a small sauté pan until the butter starts to sizzle.
- Add the pineapple and the desiccated coconut and fry gently for 5 minutes.

Scones with raspberry jam

Scones are a great teatime treat as they are so quick to make. There must be hundreds of scone recipes in the world, and some are very dry and disappointing. This one, I think, hits the mark.

450g plain flour
2 level teaspoons bicarbonate of soda
2 level teaspoons cream tartar
½ teaspoon salt
90g cold butter, cut into cubes
200ml double cream and 100ml full fat milk, combined
butter and raspberry jam for serving

- Preheat the oven to 220°C/425°F/gas 7.
- Grease a baking tray.
- Place the flour, bicarbonate of soda, cream of tartar and salt in a mixing bowl.
- Add the butter and rub it into the flour using your fingertips, as quickly as you can.
- Add the liquid and mix it in quickly with your hands to form a rough dough. Don't over-mix.
- Roll out the dough on a floured surface to a 2cm thickness, using a rolling pin.
- Cut into 5cm rounds using a pastry cutter.
- Place each scone onto the baking sheet and bake for approximately 12 minutes.
- Serve creamy butter and raspberry jam.

Week 1

Monday p230	Fried lamb cutlets + sugared new potatoes + watercress salad
Tuesday p231	Gruyère clafoutis + green salad
Wednesday p232	Chicken pasta
Thursday p233	Rarebit with red onion relish + salad
Friday p234	Smoked cod + puy lentils
Saturday p235	Chicken Anjou style + rice + peas
Sunday p236	Roast pork belly with apple, fennel and roast potatoes + purple sprouting broccoli
Sunday pudding p237	Bakewell tart + custard
Extra tasty treat p239	Coconut, cashew and sultana cake

Shopping list

MEAT

- ☐ 10–12 lamb cutlets
- ☐ 1.5kg whole chicken
- ☐ 2 chicken legs
- ☐ 2 chicken breasts
- ☐ 2 chicken thighs
- ☐ 2kg joint pork belly

FISH

- ☐ 6 pieces smoked cod fillet

VEGETABLES

- ☐ 200g watercress
- ☐ 1 carrot
- ☐ 1 bunch celery
- ☐ 1 onion
- ☐ 1 cucumber
- ☐ 2 lettuces
- ☐ 14 spring onions
- ☐ 1 red pepper
- ☐ 4 red onions
- ☐ 1.5kg potatoes
- ☐ 750g new potatoes
- ☐ 2 fennel bulbs
- ☐ 250g purple sprouting broccoli
- ☐ 200g shallots

FRUIT

- ☐ 1 lemon
- ☐ 2 eating apples

FRESH HERBS

- ☐ thyme
- ☐ mint
- ☐ flat-leaf parsley

FRIDGE ITEMS

- ☐ 200g diced pancetta
- ☐ 3 slices cooked ham
- ☐ 100g sliced pancetta
- ☐ 210g Gruyère cheese
- ☐ 50g Parmesan cheese
- ☐ 225g Cheddar cheese
- ☐ 250g frozen petits pois
- ☐ 200g crème fraîche
- ☐ 975ml milk
- ☐ 300ml double cream
- ☐ 16 eggs
- ☐ 2 packs butter

KITCHEN CUPBOARD ITEMS

- ☐ 50g desiccated coconut
- ☐ 75g sultanas
- ☐ 400g linguine
- ☐ 100g granulated sugar
- ☐ redcurrant jelly
- ☐ 1 loaf white bread for breadcrumbs
- ☐ 1 loaf wholemeal bread
- ☐ 1 loaf crusty white bread
- ☐ English mustard powder
- ☐ Worcestershire sauce
- ☐ extra virgin olive oil
- ☐ olive oil
- ☐ sherry or cider vinegar
- ☐ balsamic vinegar
- ☐ 200g Puy lentils
- ☐ 500g basmati rice
- ☐ 400ml dry white wine
- ☐ 100ml red wine
- ☐ 100g ground almonds
- ☐ raspberry jam
- ☐ 3 vanilla pods
- ☐ 100g unsalted cashew nuts
- ☐ 500g caster sugar
- ☐ 700g plain flour
- ☐ 25g ground rice
- ☐ baking powder
- ☐ salt

SPICES

- ☐ dried oregano
- ☐ black pepper
- ☐ cardamom pods
- ☐ ground cinnamon

Fried lamb cutlets + sugared new potatoes + watercress salad

There are various ways to cook lamb cutlets; under the grill or in the oven, but I think the best way is to pan-fry them with a tiny amount of olive oil brushed on each side of the cutlet and with plenty of salt and pepper. The potatoes with this meal accompany the lamb very well because of their sweetness. The recipe for the potatoes is Danish in origin.

Fried lamb cutlets

10–12 lamb cutlets (quantity depending upon your family's appetite)
salt and pepper
brushing of olive oil

- Heat a heavy griddle or frying pan.
- Brush each cutlet sparingly on each side with olive oil and season them with salt and pepper.
- When the pan is hot put in the cutlets and cook them on each side for 4–5 minutes.
- If you prefer lamb very rare then cook them for 3 minutes on each side.

Sugared new potatoes

750g new potatoes
50g butter
50g granulated sugar
salt

- Cut the potatoes so that they are all approximately the same size.
- Boil them in unsalted water until just tender.
- Let the potatoes cool slightly and then peel them. This is a little fiddly but quicker than trying to peel them before they are cooked.
- Heat the butter in a frying pan and then add the sugar.
- Stir the sugar and butter around a few times and then add the potatoes. Do this on a medium heat, as you want the sugar to brown around the potatoes, but not to burn.
- Once the potatoes have a sugary brown coating, salt them generously with sea salt and serve.

Watercress salad

200g watercress
For the dressing
1 dessertspoon olive oil
1 teaspoon balsamic vinegar
salt and pepper

- Put the watercress in a serving bowl.
- Mix the dressing ingredients in a small bowl and then pour over the watercress when you are ready to eat.

Gruyère clafoutis + green salad

This is a simple French recipe that is rather like a quiche lorraine but without the pastry.

Gruyère Clafoutis

1 dessertspoon olive oil
200g diced pancetta
4 spring onions, sliced
3 slices cooked ham, cut into strips
4 large eggs
600ml milk
2 sprigs fresh thyme, leaves only
dried oregano
110g plain flour
210g Gruyère cheese, grated
1 tablespoon flat-leaf parsley, chopped
black pepper

- Preheat the oven to 200°C/400°F/gas 6 and place a baking sheet in the oven to heat up.
- Grease an ovenproof dish approximately 30cm long and 24cm wide.
- Heat the olive oil in a sauté pan.
- Add the pancetta and sauté for 2 minutes until golden brown.
- Add the spring onions and ham and turn the heat down very low, gradually warming them through while you prepare the rest of the ingredients.
- Beat the eggs in a bowl with a fork until frothy.
- Add the milk to the eggs and beat again.
- Sprinkle in the thyme and a pinch of dried oregano.
- Sift in the flour, gradually whisking as you go to avoid lumps.
- Stir in the cheese and parsley and season with pepper. There is no need to add salt.
- Spoon the pancetta mixture onto the base of the ovenproof dish then pour the milk mixture over the top.
- Place on the hot baking sheet and bake for 30 minutes until set.

Green salad

½ cucumber, sliced
1 lettuce, washed
5 spring onions, sliced
For the dressing
2 tablespoons extra virgin olive oil
½ tablespoon balsamic vinegar
salt and pepper

- Combine the salad ingredients in a serving bowl, mix together the dressing ingredients and dress just before serving.

Chicken pasta

This meal is more a broth than a pasta dish. The chicken can be cooked the night before. Be careful to season the stock well, as the broth will be bland otherwise.

1.5kg whole chicken
1 carrot, peeled and chopped into large chunks
1 stick celery, chopped into thick chunks
1 onion, peeled and left whole
2 sprigs flat-leaf parsley
salt and pepper
400g linguine
3 tablespoons flat-leaf parsley, chopped
Parmesan cheese, grated

- Place the chicken in a saucepan and just cover it with water.
- Add the vegetables and parsley sprigs and season well with salt and pepper.
- Bring to a simmer and cook, covered, for 1 hour 30 minutes.
- Remove the chicken and vegetables and set aside.
- Reduce the stock by boiling it for 20 minutes.
- You only need 500ml of stock for this dish so if you have more than this after 20 minutes, freeze the surplus.
- Season the stock again if it requires more flavour and bring it to the boil.
- Add the linguine and cook in the stock following the packet instructions.
- Meanwhile, remove the chicken meat from the carcass and chop it up into chunks.
- Once the linguine is cooked return the chicken and vegetables to the pot with the linguine.
- Check the seasoning and sprinkle with the flat-leaf parsley.
- Serve with gratings of Parmesan cheese and crusty white bread.

Rarebit with red onion relish + salad

Everyone has heard of rarebit but not everyone has had the pleasure of trying it. It's a real treat and is great served with salad. The relish has a strong flavour but is a good accompaniment to the cheese.

Rarebit with red onion relish

For the red onion relish

45ml olive oil
3 red onions, peeled and thinly sliced
50g granulated sugar
55ml sherry or cider vinegar
1 tablespoon redcurrant jelly
100ml red wine
salt and pepper

For the rarebit

75ml milk
225g Cheddar cheese, grated
1 tablespoon plain flour
1 tablespoon white breadcrumbs
½ teaspoon English mustard powder
½ teaspoon Worcestershire sauce
salt and pepper
1 egg
1 egg yolk
1 loaf wholemeal bread

To make the relish

- Heat the oil in a saucepan and when hot add the sliced onions.
- Cook over a low heat, uncovered, for 30 minutes, stirring frequently.
- Add the sugar, vinegar, redcurrant jelly and red wine and continue to cook gently, uncovered, for a further 30 minutes until the liquid has gone and the onions are soft.
- Season with salt and pepper and set aside.

To make the rarebit

- Stir together the milk and cheese in a medium-sized saucepan over a gentle heat, until melted.
- Add the flour, breadcrumbs and mustard powder and continue to stir for 30 seconds.
- Remove from the heat, beat in the Worcestershire sauce and season to taste.
- Once the mixture has cooled slightly, add the eggs.
- At this stage you can transfer the mixture to a bowl and refrigerate until you need it.
- When you are ready to eat, grill some wholemeal bread on one side.
- Spread a spoon or two of the rarebit mixture on the untoasted side of the bread and then place it under a hot grill until the top of the cheese is brown and bubbling.
- Serve with salad and a spoon of the relish.

Salad

½ cucumber, sliced
1 lettuce, washed
5 spring onions, sliced

For the dressing

2 tablespoons extra virgin olive oil
½ tablespoon balsamic vinegar
salt and pepper

- Combine the salad ingredients in a serving bowl, mix together the dressing ingredients and dress just before serving.

Smoked cod + Puy lentils

I realized as I was cooking this for the first time that the children would pull faces when I put Puy lentils in front of them. I am a firm believer in gradually extending the boundaries of what children will eat by means of perseverance and facing the complaints. The result is that they do like Puy lentils now.

Smoked Cod

6 pieces smoked cod fillet
generous squeeze of lemon juice
black pepper

- Preheat the grill.
- Season the cod pieces with freshly ground black pepper and place them under the grill.
- Grill the fillets for 2 minutes on each side if they are relatively thin, or about 4 minutes on each side for thick fillets.
- Squeeze fresh lemon juice over the fish when ready and serve with the Puy lentils.

Puy lentils

200g Puy lentils
500g potatoes, peeled and quartered
salt
1 small fennel bulb
3 tablespoons olive oil
½ red pepper, diced
½ red onion, sliced finely
black pepper
handful flat-leaf parsley, chopped finely
100g sliced pancetta, cut into pieces

- Rinse the Puy lentils in cold water.
- Place them in a saucepan of unsalted water and bring them to the boil.
- Let them boil for 30 minutes, then drain and set aside.
- Boil the potatoes in salted water for 20 minutes until cooked.
- Remove the tougher outer skin from the fennel bulb and slice the remaining part of the bulb as thinly as possible.
- Warm 2 tablespoons of olive oil in a sauté pan.
- Add the fennel to the frying pan and sauté on a medium heat for 4 minutes.
- Add the red pepper and red onion and sauté for about 10 minutes.
- Next, add the boiled potatoes and sauté them for a further 5 minutes.
- Season the vegetables with a liberal amount of salt and pepper.
- Put the Puy lentils in a serving bowl and add the sautéed vegetables to them.
- Add the remaining tablespoon of olive oil and the chopped parsley.
- Fry the pancetta until crispy and throw this in at the end.

Chicken Anjou style
+ rice + peas

This is a wonderfully quick meal to produce, which fills the kitchen with homely smells as it cooks. The children like to eat it, particularly because of the rice, which I suppose they see as a welcome relief from potatoes.

Chicken Anjou style

2 chicken legs, skin removed
2 chicken breasts, skinless
2 chicken thighs, skin removed
3 tablespoons plain flour, seasoned with salt and pepper
3 tablespoons olive oil
200g shallots, peeled and halved
400ml dry white wine
4 tablespoons crème fraîche
handful flat-leaf parsley, chopped
salt and pepper

- Toss all the chicken pieces in the seasoned flour.
- Heat 2 tablespoons of the olive oil in a large sauté pan and brown 3 pieces of chicken at a time on a reasonably high heat. Remove the chicken as it browns and set aside.
- Clean the pan.
- Heat the last tablespoon of olive oil in the clean pan and sauté the shallots until lightly browned.
- Return the chicken to the pan with the shallots and add the wine.
- Bring to a simmer, reduce the heat and cook gently on a slow simmer, covered, for 40 minutes.
- Next, tip the chicken and shallots into a warm serving dish.
- Return the sauté pan to the heat, add the crème fraîche and let it bubble for 2 minutes.
- Season with salt and pepper and then pour it over the chicken and shallots.
- Sprinkle the parsley on top and serve.

Rice

500g basmati rice
750ml water
salt

- Put the rice in a saucepan with the water and a pinch of salt.
- Place the rice on a high heat and as soon as it comes to the boil, cover the saucepan with a lid and turn the heat right down to very low. Leave it for 15 minutes, giving it one stir only during the cooking time.
- Then take it off the heat and leave it covered for a further 10 minutes, before removing the lid.

Peas

250g frozen petits pois
fresh mint and butter for serving

- Place the peas in boiling water for 3 minutes and then drain them.
- Serve with a little butter and chopped mint.

Roast pork belly with apple, fennel and roast potatoes + purple sprouting broccoli

This recipe uses a rolled joint of pork belly, but you don't need to have the joint rolled. The fat on pork belly is so good that I like to cook the potatoes, fennel and apple in with the meat. This does mean that there's no gravy but it doesn't matter, the meal doesn't suffer as a result. To get a good, crisp crackling you need to start off with a good-quality joint of meat. Be guided by price, local produce and whether the meat is free range or organic.

Roast pork belly with apple, fennel and roast potatoes

1kg roasting potatoes, peeled and quartered
2kg joint rolled pork belly
salt and pepper
olive oil
1 bulb fennel, sliced to a 5mm thickness
2 eating apples, cored and cut into eights

- Preheat the oven to 220°C/425°F/gas 7.
- Parboil the potatoes for about 5 minutes in salted water.
- Dry the skin of the pork with kitchen paper. If your butcher hasn't scored the skin of the joint already, make diagonal score marks using a very sharp knife. Score the skin at 1.5cm intervals going down into the fat, but not the meat.
- Smear the skin with a little olive oil and rub generous amounts of salt and pepper into the score marks and on the skin. It's the delicious salty taste of the crackling that makes it special.
- Place the joint in a roasting tin in the preheated oven for 30 minutes.
- Reduce the heat to 180°C/350°F/gas 4 and cook for a further 20 minutes.
- Next, put the potatoes into the tin around the pork and cook for a further 40 minutes. At this point check that the pork is cooked by inserting a skewer into the meat. If the juices run clear then the pork is ready. If you feel the crackling could be crisper leave the meat in for a little longer, as it won't spoil by doing so. Remove the pork from the oven and leave to rest.
- Increase the temperature of the oven to 200°C/400°F/gas 6.
- Put the apple and fennel into the tin with the potatoes and cook for a further 20 minutes.

Purple sprouting broccoli

250g purple sprouting broccoli
salt and pepper
a little butter

- Boil a saucepan of water.
- Add the broccoli and simmer for 3 minutes.
- Drain well, then season with salt, pepper and a little butter.

Bakewell tart
+ custard

This is one of my favourite desserts. It is very English but would stand up well against any French dessert, in my opinion.

Bakewell tart

For the pastry

125g butter, softened to room temperature
90g caster sugar
2 vanilla pods
1 large egg, beaten
250g plain flour
salt

For the filling

100g butter, softened
100g caster sugar
2 eggs
100g ground almonds
2 tablespoons plain flour
3 tablespoons raspberry jam

continues

To make the pastry

- Using an electric mixer, beat the butter and sugar together until smooth.
- Scrape the seeds from the vanilla pods into the butter and sugar.
- Add the egg and mix to incorporate.
- With the machine on its lowest speed, add the flour and a pinch of salt bit by bit.
- The mixture will start to stick together in a crumbly way and at this point stop the machine and work by hand.
- Knead it with your hands until smooth, but don't be heavy handed.
- Wrap the dough in cling-film and chill in the fridge for 30 minutes.

To make the tart

- Grease a 21cm tart tin.
- Preheat the oven to 190°C/375°F/gas 5.
- Roll out the pastry and line the tart tin with it.
- Place a sheet of baking parchment on top of the pastry case and pour on some baking beans. This method is called 'baking blind'.
- Bake the pastry case for 10 minutes. Then remove the parchment and beans and bake the case for a further 5 minutes. Set aside.

To make the sponge

- Cream the butter and sugar in an electric mixer for 4 minutes until white and fluffy.
- Beat in the eggs one at a time.
- Add the ground almonds and beat.
- Add the flour and beat the mixture again.
- Spread the raspberry jam over the bottom of the pastry case and then spoon the sponge mixture over the top.
- Place in the oven and cook for 30 minutes until the sponge is firm to the touch.

Custard

600ml milk and double cream mixed
2 whole eggs
2 egg yolks
2 tablespoons caster sugar
1 vanilla pod or a drop or two vanilla extract

- In a glass bowl whisk the whole eggs, yolks and sugar with a hand whisk for 2 minutes.
- Measure the milk and cream into a measuring jug, add the vanilla pod or extract and microwave it on high for 2 minutes. The milk and cream should be just at boiling point, but not actually boiling.
- Place the glass bowl of eggs and sugar over a saucepan of simmering water. Make sure that the level of water does not touch the bowl.
- Add the milk and cream, whisking all the time to avoid lumps.
- If you used the vanilla pod, scrape out the seeds into the mixture.
- Keep stirring for 10 minutes, by which time you should have a good consistency. The custard is thick enough when it will coat the back of a wooden spoon as you lift it up.
- You can make custard ahead of time but avoid reheating it, as it may curdle.

TIP

Blind baking is when a pastry case is baked empty. Here I have done this to ensure that the jam and sponge mixture do not soak the pastry during the cooking.

Coconut, cashew and sultana cake

This is a cake with a slight difference, in that it conjures up flavours of Sri Lanka or India without being sickly sweet. It originally came out of an old *Sainsbury Magazine* but I have adapted it slightly.

100g unsalted cashew nuts
seeds from 6 cardamom pods
175g butter, softened
175g caster sugar
175g plain flour
25g ground rice
1 rounded teaspoon baking powder
salt
1 level teaspoon ground cinnamon
3 eggs
50g desiccated coconut
75g sultanas

- Preheat oven to 180°C/350°F/gas 4.
- Grease and line a 4–5cm deep, 21 x 26cm wide square cake tin with baking parchment. Don't worry about getting the base measurement exact, as long as the tin is not too much bigger.
- Place the cashew nuts on a baking sheet and toast in the oven for 4 minutes. Watch them carefully, as they brown so quickly.
- Using a pestle and mortar, grind the cardamom seeds to a rough powder.
- Tip the cardamom seeds into a large mixing bowl with the butter and sugar, and cream them together for 5 minutes with an electric whisk.
- Sift the flour, ground rice, baking powder, a pinch of salt and the cinnamon into the creamed butter and sugar and mix until combined.
- Next, beat in the eggs one at a time, incorporating well between each addition.
- Using a metal spoon, fold in the toasted cashew nuts, desiccated coconut and sultanas.
- Spoon the mixture into the cake tin and bake for 30 minutes.
- Once out of the oven, allow to cool before removing from the tin and cutting the cake into squares. I tend to cut it as I need it, as it stays fresher for longer this way.

Week 2

Shopping list

MEAT
- ☐ 10 lamb loin chops
- ☐ 500g minced turkey
- ☐ 500g minced pork
- ☐ 2kg leg lamb

FISH
- ☐ 2 long salmon fillets, weighing about 500g each

VEGETABLES
- ☐ 4 onions
- ☐ 1 garlic bulb
- ☐ fresh ginger
- ☐ 3 tomatoes
- ☐ 1kg potatoes
- ☐ 1 red pepper
- ☐ 1 green chilli
- ☐ 5 medium courgettes
- ☐ 5 shallots
- ☐ 250g fresh spinach
- ☐ 200g watercress
- ☐ 2 leeks
- ☐ ½ celeriac
- ☐ ½ swede
- ☐ 2 carrots
- ☐ 200g broccoli
- ☐ 700g new potatoes

FRUIT
- ☐ 5 lemons
- ☐ 250g fresh blueberries

FRESH HERBS
- ☐ flat-leaf parsley
- ☐ basil
- ☐ mint
- ☐ dill
- ☐ chives
- ☐ thyme

FRIDGE ITEMS
- ☐ 18 eggs
- ☐ 100g Cheddar cheese
- ☐ 200g cooked ham
- ☐ 400g crème fraîche
- ☐ 2 packs butter
- ☐ 250ml double cream
- ☐ 1.5 litres chicken stock
- ☐ 250g frozen peas
- ☐ 150g Gruyère cheese
- ☐ 150g Parmesan cheese
- ☐ 1kg mascarpone cheese
- ☐ 200g sliced pancetta
- ☐ 150g buffalo mozzarella
- ☐ 100g Taleggio cheese
- ☐ 500ml vegetable stock
- ☐ 450ml soured cream
- ☐ 750ml milk

KITCHEN CUPBOARD ITEMS
- ☐ sesame oil
- ☐ vegetable oil
- ☐ olive oil
- ☐ extra virgin olive oil
- ☐ red wine vinegar
- ☐ salt
- ☐ dark soy sauce
- ☐ light soy sauce
- ☐ orange marmalade
- ☐ Chinese rice wine
- ☐ 2 loaves white bread
- ☐ chicken stock cubes
- ☐ Dijon mustard
- ☐ 325g plain flour
- ☐ 600g medium egg noodles
- ☐ Worcestershire sauce
- ☐ 600g pasta shells
- ☐ goose fat
- ☐ 150g digestive biscuits
- ☐ 550g caster sugar
- ☐ vanilla essence
- ☐ 350g self-raising flour
- ☐ bicarbonate of soda
- ☐ 85g golden syrup
- ☐ 100g good quality milk chocolate
- ☐ 100g dark chocolate

SPICES
- ☐ whole nutmeg
- ☐ allspice
- ☐ black pepper
- ☐ ground ginger

Oriental lamb chops + noodles

My mother always used to serve marrow ginger with lamb chops because the sweetness of the marrow ginger complemented the lamb so well. The marmalade here works along similar lines.

Oriental lamb chops

2 tablespoons sesame oil
10 lamb loin chops
salt
1 large onion, finely diced
2 cloves garlic, peeled and finely chopped
3 tablespoons dark soy sauce
2 tablespoons orange marmalade
2 tablespoons Chinese rice wine
2cm peeled fresh ginger, finely chopped

- Heat the sesame oil in a large frying pan.
- Brown the chops on each side, season them with salt and set aside.
- In the oil that is left in the pan, sauté the onion and garlic on a low heat for 5 minutes until soft.
- Then add the soy sauce, marmalade, rice wine and ginger.
- Simmer for 1 minute, stirring continuously.
- Return the chops to the pan, cover and cook on a low heat for 10 minutes, turning the chops once so that they cook evenly.

Noodles

2 tablespoons vegetable oil
1 large onion, chopped roughly
1 red pepper, finely chopped
2 cloves garlic, peeled and finely chopped
1 green chilli, deseeded and finely chopped
250g medium egg noodles, cooked according to the packet instructions
3 tomatoes, cut into segments
10 basil leaves, roughly torn
1 tablespoon dark soy sauce
4 tablespoons light soy sauce
1 teaspoon sugar

- In a large frying pan or wok, heat the oil until hot and then add the onion, red pepper, garlic and green chilli.
- Stir fry on a low heat for 5 minutes.
- Add the remaining ingredients and cook for 2 minutes, stirring to combine.
- Serve with the lamb.

Cheese and ham omelettes
+ sautéed courgettes

It is slightly too early for courgettes to be seasonal but I usually reach the stage at this time of year when I need something different. Having denied myself courgettes since the end of the previous summer, once May arrives, I do find I can't wait any longer. If your children riot at the idea of courgettes, then serve a salad or green beans with the omelettes as well so they have a choice. If you give them the opportunity to eat different vegetables, they may well become more adventurous.

Cheese and ham omelettes

9 eggs
salt and pepper
1 tablespoon olive oil
6 tablespoons Cheddar cheese, grated
100g cooked ham, chopped

- Crack the eggs into a glass bowl and beat them lightly with a fork. It is best to make two omelettes with this number of eggs.
- Season the eggs with salt and pepper.
- Heat a heavy, medium-sized frying pan on the hob until it is hot.
- Add the olive oil to the frying pan and once it starts to smoke slightly, pour in half the egg mixture.
- Start to gently shake the pan and with a fork or wooden spoon stir the egg very gently, scraping up the bits of the egg that are cooking. Stop for a few seconds while the bottom cooks again and then tilt the pan away from you, causing the uncooked egg to run to the other side of the pan.
- Once the egg has cooked on the underside but is still slightly runny on the top add half the chopped ham and half the grated cheese and fold the omelette over.
- The omelette should be cooked by now but there should be a slight runniness to the centre.
- Make the second omelette in the same way using the rest of the cheese and ham.

Sautéed courgettes

1 tablespoon olive oil
5 medium courgettes, sliced into ½cm pieces
1 shallot, peeled and finely chopped
handful flat-leaf parsley, chopped
salt and pepper

- In a sauté pan heat the olive oil and add the courgettes and shallot.
- Gently cook them until the courgettes start to brown. They should still have a bite to them and not be soggy.
- Sprinkle over the chopped parsley and season with salt and pepper.

Swedish meatballs + mustard noodles

These are different from the usual meatballs and, if you have any left over, they are delicious cold.

Swedish meatballs

150g white breadcrumbs
1 chicken stock cube, dissolved in 275ml water
1 medium onion, finely chopped
grating of nutmeg
1 level teaspoon allspice
1 egg, beaten
500g minced turkey
500g minced pork
salt and pepper
4 tablespoons vegetable oil

- Place the breadcrumbs in a large bowl.
- Pour on the stock and stir until the breadcrumbs have absorbed the liquid.
- Add the onion, spices, egg, turkey and pork and mix thoroughly to combine all the ingredients evenly.
- Season with salt and pepper.
- Chill the mixture in the fridge for 30 minutes.
- Preheat the oven to 200°C/400°F/gas 6.
- Roll the mixture into approximately 48 balls the size of unshelled walnuts. The mixture may become sticky, but keep a bowl of cold water next to you and dip your fingertips into it when you feel the meat is becoming too sticky.
- Roll each meatball in the flour.
- Heat one tablespoon of the oil and fry a quarter of the meatballs, turning them over to get them evenly browned.
- Place the browned meatballs in a meat tray and fry the next quarter in another tablespoon of olive oil. Do the same with the rest of the meatballs.
- Cover the meat tray with tin foil and cook the meatballs in the oven for 25 minutes.

Mustard noodles

400g medium egg noodles
150g crème fraîche
1 tablespoon Dijon mustard

- Mix the crème fraîche with the mustard in a small bowl.
- Cook the noodles according to the packet instructions.
- When cooked, place the noodles in a serving bowl and spoon over the crème fraîche and mustard mixture.
- Serve with the meatballs.

Spinach and pea soup
+ croque-monsieur

This is a great way to get your children to eat spinach. The soup is such a lovely green colour, I defy anyone not to be interested enough to try it.

Spinach and pea soup

40g butter
1 onion, finely diced
250g fresh spinach
250g frozen peas
2 tablespoons fresh mint, chopped
1.5 litres chicken stock
salt and pepper
150ml double cream

- Heat the butter in a large saucepan and gently fry the onion for 10 minutes.
- Add the spinach, peas, mint and stock.
- Bring to a good simmer and then reduce the heat and cook, covered, for 20 minutes.
- Liquidize the soup in a food processor or using a hand-held blender.
- Season with salt and pepper and add the cream just before serving.

Croque-monsieur

9 tablespoons Gruyère cheese, grated
5 tablespoons double cream
freshly ground black pepper
½ teaspoon grated nutmeg
2 teaspoons Worcestershire sauce
2 teaspoons Dijon mustard
12 slices fresh white bread
butter
6 slices good-quality ham

- In a small bowl mix together the cheese, cream, pepper, nutmeg, Worcestershire sauce and mustard until combined.
- Take the slices of bread and butter one side of each slice.
- Turn them butter side down on to a board or surface.
- Cover six of the unbuttered sides with the cheese mixture.
- Place the ham on the unbuttered side of the six remaining slices.
- Sandwich the slices together to make six sandwiches of ham and cheese, buttered on the outside.
- Heat a large frying pan and place two sandwiches at a time in the hot pan.
- Brown each side of each sandwich.
- Keep them warm in a low oven whilst you cook the others and, when they are all ready, serve them with the soup.

Salmon in pastry with crème fraîche sauce + garlic potatoes + watercress salad

The idea for this salmon dish was inspired by the well-known recipe of George Perry-Smith. Without the crème fraîche sauce it is a touch too dry.

Salmon in pastry with crème fraîche sauce

For the pastry

325g plain flour
220g butter
salt
2 tablespoons Parmesan cheese, finely grated
2 egg yolks
2 tablespoons cold water

For the salmon

2 long salmon fillets, about 500g each and roughly the same size
1 teaspoon dill, chopped
1 tablespoon flat-leaf parsley, chopped
5 basil leaves, chopped
1 tablespoon chives, chopped
2 tablespoons mascarpone cheese
1 dessertspoon Dijon mustard
grated zest 1 lemon
salt and pepper
1 beaten egg for glazing

For the sauce

200g crème fraîche
1 teaspoon Dijon mustard
salt and pepper
2 tablespoons chives, chopped

To make the pastry

- Put the flour and butter in the bowl of a food processor and incorporate them so that the resulting mixture looks like fine breadcrumbs.
- Add a pinch of salt and the cheese and mix briefly.
- Mix the egg yolks with the cold water in a small bowl, and then add this liquid to the flour, fat and cheese.
- Turn on the food processor and mix until a dough just begins to form. Turn the mixture onto a floured work surface and combine thoroughly, with a light hand, until you have a smooth dough. Wrap the dough in cling-film and place it in the fridge to chill for 20 minutes.

To prepare the fish

- Preheat the oven to 230°C/450°F/gas 8.
- If your fishmonger has not removed the skin from the salmon then do so with a very sharp knife.
- Check the spine of the fish for pin bones by running your finger down the middle of each fillet. If some remain the best way to remove them is with a pair of tweezers.
- In a small bowl mix together the herbs, mascarpone, mustard, and lemon zest and season well with salt and pepper.
- Spread one piece of fish evenly with this herby cheese mixture and lay the other fillet on top.
- Grease a large roasting tin, which is big enough to hold the fish.
- Roll out the pastry into a large rectangle that will envelope the sandwiched fish fillets.
- Put the pastry in the roasting tin and then place the fish on top. Bring up the sides of the pastry to meet at the top and pinch them together, rather like a Cornish pasty.
- Brush the pastry with a beaten egg and bake for 25–30 minutes.
- Test with a skewer. If it comes out with no resistance then the fish is ready. Remember that salmon is nicer a little underdone than overdone.

To make the sauce

- Place the crème fraîche in a small saucepan and gently bring it to a simmer. Remove from the heat.
- Add the mustard and chives and season with salt and pepper.

Garlic potatoes

700g new potatoes

2 cloves garlic, peeled and crushed

30g butter

juice 1 lemon

salt and pepper

- Boil the potatoes in salted water until tender.
- Drain them and return them to the saucepan, add the crushed garlic and butter and gently warm them on a medium heat for 1 minute.
- Remove from the heat and add the lemon juice and pepper.
- Taste to see whether they need more salt and serve with the salmon and salad.

Watercress salad

200g watercress

For the dressing

2 dessertspoons extra virgin olive oil

½ dessertspoon red wine vinegar

salt and pepper

- Place the watercress in a serving bowl.
- Mix the dressing in a small bowl and pour it over the watercress when ready to serve.

Pasta with three-cheese, broccoli and pancetta sauce

Broccoli makes a colourful addition to pasta sauces, and in this one it goes well with the cheese and pancetta.

4 tablespoons olive oil
4 shallots, peeled and finely sliced
200g sliced pancetta, cut into small pieces
150g buffalo mozarella cheese, diced
100g Taleggio, diced
100g Parmesan, grated
600g pasta shells
200g broccoli, trimmed and cut into florets
handful fresh flat-leaf parsley, chopped

- Place a large saucepan of salted water on the hob to boil.
- Heat 2 tablespoons of olive oil in a frying pan.
- Gently cook the shallots until golden brown.
- Add the chopped pancetta and cook for 3 minutes until golden.
- Put the three cheeses into the bowl in which you are going to serve the pasta.
- Put the pasta into the saucepan of boiling water and cook according to the packet instructions. When there are 4 minutes of cooking time left, add the broccoli to the pasta water.
- Drain the pasta and broccoli and place them in the serving bowl with the cheese.
- Add the remaining 2 tablespoons of olive oil to the pasta in the bowl and gently mix to ensure that the cheese melts and clings to the pasta.
- Throw in the parsley and serve.

Peppered lamb + roast potatoes + root vegetables and leeks with crème fraîche

Sundays don't seem quite right when there is no smell of roasting coming from the kitchen. The pepper in this recipe adds a twist to the usual roast lamb.

Peppered lamb

2kg leg lamb
lemon juice
grated zest 1 lemon
1 tablespoon black peppercorns, crushed roughly in a pestle and mortar
1 tablespoon fresh thyme leaves
salt
olive oil
1 tablespoon flour
500ml vegetable stock

- Preheat the oven to 200°C/400°F/gas 6.
- Place the leg of lamb in a meat tray and wipe one half of the lemon over the skin of the lamb.
- Sprinkle the leg with the lemon zest, peppercorns, thyme leaves, salt and a drizzle of olive oil.
- Roast the joint for 2 hours.
- When the meat is cooked, place it on a warm plate to rest.
- Add a dessertspoon of flour to the empty meat tin and place it on the hob on a low heat.
- Stir the flour into the meat juices, scraping up the bits from the pan.
- Add the vegetable stock and simmer for 15 minutes or so.
- Season with a little salt if necessary.

Roast potatoes

1kg potatoes, peeled, quartered and rinsed in cold water
salt
2 tablespoons olive oil or a spoon of goose or duck fat if you prefer

- Preheat the oven to 220°C/425°F/gas 7.
- Parboil the potatoes in boiling salted water for 5 minutes.
- Drain them, return them to the saucepan and give them a shake to rough up the outsides of the potatoes a little. This helps to give them a lovely crispy crust.
- Place the potatoes in a roasting tin along with your chosen fat.
- Then put them in the oven and roast them for about 50 minutes.

Root vegetables and leeks with crème fraîche

½ celeriac, peeled and chopped into 1cm cubes
½ swede, peeled and chopped into 1cm cubes
2 carrots, peeled and sliced into 1cm slices
20g butter
2 leeks, sliced to a 1cm thickness
2 tablespoons crème fraîche
salt and pepper

- Place the celeriac, swede and carrots into a saucepan with the butter.
- Place the saucepan on the hob and warm through until you hear a nice sizzle.
- Reduce the heat, cover and cook the vegetables for 15 minutes, until they are almost soft.
- Add the leeks and cook, covered, for a further 5 minutes.
- Stir in the crème fraîche and season with salt and pepper.

Blueberry cheesecake

This is a great baked cheesecake recipe. The first time I ever made a baked cheesecake it did not set which was hugely disappointing given the time and effort expended. This one seems to work every time.

For the biscuit base
150g digestive biscuits
40g caster sugar
70g melted butter
For the lemon cheese filling
grated zest 1 lemon
700g mascarpone cheese
1 teaspoon vanilla essence
4 large eggs
150g caster sugar
For the blueberry topping
450ml soured cream
½ teaspoon vanilla essence
1 tablespoon caster sugar
grated zest ½ lemon
250g fresh blueberries

To make the biscuit base
- You will need a 23cm spring form tin.
- Crush the digestive biscuits in a bowl, using the end of a rolling pin.
- Mix the biscuit crumbs with the sugar and melted butter and press into the base of the tin with the back of a wooden spoon.
- Chill in the fridge for 30 minutes.

To make the lemon cheese filling
- Preheat the oven to 180˚C/350˚F/gas 4.
- Mix the mascarpone, vanilla essence and lemon zest with an electric mixer until smooth.
- Beat in the eggs one at a time.
- Then beat in the sugar.
- Pour the filling onto the chilled biscuit base.
- Place the tin on a baking sheet and bake for 45 minutes.

To make the blueberry topping
- Mix the soured cream, vanilla, sugar and lemon zest together in a small bowl.
- When the cheesecake is ready remove it from the oven, spread the topping over the cheesecake, top with the berries and return the cheesecake to the oven for 10 minutes.
- Cool and chill for at least 5 hours, preferably overnight, and then unmould from the tin.

Ginger nuts + hot chocolate

These ginger nuts are a great teatime treat for children. They are crisp on the outside with a slightly chewy centre. Milk is such an excellent source of calcium for children, but they do not seem to drink it like my brothers and I did when we were children. Hot chocolate is a great way to get children to consume milk.

Ginger nuts

350g self-raising flour
salt
200g caster sugar
1 tablespoon ground ginger
1 teaspoon bicarbonate of soda
115g butter
85g golden syrup
1 large egg

- Preheat oven to 170°C/325°F/gas 3.
- Put the flour in a mixing bowl with a pinch of salt, the sugar, ginger and bicarbonate of soda.
- Heat the butter and syrup in a saucepan until the butter has melted.
- Put aside to cool until just warm, and then pour on to the dry ingredients in the mixing bowl. Add the egg and mix thoroughly to form a dough.
- Using your hands, roll the dough into about 30 walnut-sized balls.
- Place these well apart on baking trays and flatten down each one slightly.
- Put the trays in the oven and bake for 15–20 minutes until golden brown.
- Remove from the oven and leave the biscuits on the tray to cool and firm up. Then move them to a wire rack to cool completely.

Hot chocolate

100g good-quality milk chocolate
100g dark chocolate
750ml milk

- Break the chocolate into a glass bowl.
- Place the glass bowl over a saucepan of simmering water and pour on 300ml of the milk.
- Gently melt the chocolate, stirring as you go.
- Heat the rest of the milk in a jug in the microwave until hot and then pour the melted chocolate into the jug, stirring to combine.
- Serve with the ginger nuts.

Week 3

Monday p254	Beef stew with paprika and sage + baked potatoes + spring greens
Tuesday p255	Macaroni with vegetables
Wednesday p256	Feta and mediterranean vegetable tart + baked potatoes + green salad
Thursday p258	Lamb and turnip stew + soda bread
Friday p259	Cold meatloaf + goat's cheese and French bean salad + boiled potatoes
Saturday p260	Fried monkfish with salsa verde + new potato, red onion and chickpea salad
Sunday p261	Garlic and rosemary roasted chicken + roast potatoes + creamy peas and carrots
Sunday pudding p262	Coconut cream and raisin tart
Extra tasty treat p263	Jam sponge puddings with jam sauce

Shopping list

MEAT

- ☐ 900g stewing steak
- ☐ 1kg cubed lamb
- ☐ 250g minced beef
- ☐ 250g minced pork
- ☐ 200g sausage meat
- ☐ 2 whole chickens each weighing 1.4 kg

FISH

- ☐ 1kg filleted monkfish tail

VEGETABLES

- ☐ 5 onions
- ☐ 12 baking potatoes
- ☐ 250g new potatoes
- ☐ 2kg potatoes
- ☐ 250g spring greens
- ☐ 4 courgettes
- ☐ 1 garlic bulb
- ☐ 3 red onions
- ☐ 2 shallots
- ☐ 1 green pepper
- ☐ 250g cherry tomatoes
- ☐ 1 lettuce
- ☐ 7 spring onions
- ☐ 1 cucumber
- ☐ 300g turnips
- ☐ 400g French beans
- ☐ 300g carrots

FRUIT

- ☐ 6 lemons

FRESH HERBS

- ☐ sage
- ☐ 2 bunches flat-leaf parsley
- ☐ thyme
- ☐ rosemary
- ☐ mint
- ☐ basil

FRIDGE ITEMS

- ☐ 3 packs butter
- ☐ 170g chopped pancetta
- ☐ 8 slices pancetta
- ☐ 1.5 litre chicken stock
- ☐ 500g frozen peas
- ☐ 50g Parmesan cheese
- ☐ 11 eggs
- ☐ 150g feta cheese
- ☐ 200g crème fraîche
- ☐ 500ml lamb stock
- ☐ 400ml buttermilk
- ☐ 50g Italian salami
- ☐ 200g soft goat's cheese
- ☐ 200ml single cream
- ☐ 150ml milk

KITCHEN CUPBOARD ITEMS

- ☐ 250ml red wine
- ☐ 400g passata
- ☐ salt
- ☐ 400g tin chopped tomatoes
- ☐ 300g macaroni
- ☐ extra virgin olive oil
- ☐ olive oil
- ☐ balsamic vinegar
- ☐ red wine vinegar
- ☐ 2 tins chickpeas
- ☐ 225g wholemeal flour
- ☐ 1 kg plain flour
- ☐ 150g self-raising flour
- ☐ bicarbonate of soda
- ☐ baking powder
- ☐ 1 loaf white bread for breadcrumbs
- ☐ 1 jar cornichons
- ☐ Dijon mustard
- ☐ 1 tin anchovies
- ☐ capers
- ☐ pitted green olives
- ☐ white wine vinegar
- ☐ raspberry jam
- ☐ 100g block creamed coconut
- ☐ 75g icing sugar
- ☐ 50g raisins
- ☐ 150g caster sugar
- ☐ goose fat

SPICES

- ☐ paprika
- ☐ black pepper

Beef stew with paprika and sage + baked potatoes + spring greens

Although summer is fast approaching and one starts to crave different sorts of food, May still brings its cold days when a warm, comforting stew is the order of the day. There are various stew recipes in this book because 'stew' can mean so many different things. While they may take some time to cook, their preparation time is quite quick. This particular one is from a book by the Italian writer Anna Del Conte. I have made some minor alterations such as reducing the amount of sage, but this was mainly to make it more acceptable to my children.

Beef stew with paprika and sage

1 tablespoon olive oil
25g butter
2 onions, sliced
10 fresh sage leaves
900g stewing steak, cubed
1 teaspoon paprika
250ml red wine
1½ tablespoons plain flour
400g passata
salt and pepper

- Heat the oil and butter in a large saucepan.
- Sauté the onions in the oil and butter for 7 minutes until soft.
- Add the sage leaves and cook for 1 minute.
- Add the meat and brown all over.
- Sprinkle on the paprika and add the red wine.
- Turn up the heat and boil to reduce the wine for 4 minutes, stirring occasionally.
- Sprinkle on the flour, stir in and cook for 1 minute.
- Add the tomato passata and season to taste.
- Bring to a simmer, cover and cook gently on a very low heat for 2 hours.

Baked potatoes

6 baking potatoes
butter for serving
salt and pepper

- Preheat the oven to 220°C/425°F/gas 7.
- Pierce the potato skins with a sharp knife and bake them for 1 hour 30 minutes.
- Split each one and serve with butter, salt and pepper.

Spring greens

250g spring greens
salt
knob of butter
squeeze of fresh lemon juice
black pepper

- Cut the tough stems from the leaves of the spring greens.
- Roll the leaves up into tube shapes and slice them across.
- Bring a saucepan of salted water to the boil.
- Simmer the cabbage for 3 minutes.
- Drain well and toss in butter, lemon juice and black pepper.

Macaroni with vegetables

This recipe is based on an Ursula Ferrigno recipe. She recommends using fresh peas instead of frozen, although the dish is still very tasty with frozen peas if fresh ones are not in season. You can make it using 300g of peas and leave out the courgettes, if you know your children won't eat them.

1 tablespoon olive oil
1 medium onion, finely chopped
2 garlic cloves, finely chopped
100g chopped pancetta
4 tablespoons tinned chopped tomatoes
1 litre chicken stock
4 potatoes, peeled and cut into medium chunks
200g frozen peas
salt
3 courgettes, sliced to a thickness of 5mm
300g macaroni
black pepper
handful flat-leaf parsley, chopped
Parmesan cheese, grated

- In a saucepan heat the oil and sauté the onion and garlic on a low heat for 5 minutes until soft.
- Add the pancetta and cook for 1 minute.
- Add the tomatoes, stock, potatoes and peas and bring to a simmer.
- Cover and cook for 10 minutes.
- Season with salt.
- Add the courgettes and macaroni and cook following the packet instructions for the macaroni.
- Most of the liquid will have disappeared by the end of the cooking time.
- Add some black pepper and parsley and serve with the Parmesan cheese.

Feta and mediterranean vegetable tart + baked potatoes + green salad

Feta cheese is apparently one of the oldest cheeses in the world. It was particularly treasured in Greece as it could be stored for a reasonable time without refrigeration. It has 50 per cent less fat than Cheddar cheese and it makes an interesting tart filling because of its saltiness.

Feta and mediterranean vegetable tart

For the pastry

225g plain flour
150g butter
salt
1 egg yolk
2 tablespoons cold water

For the filling

1 tablespoon olive oil
½ courgette, sliced to a thickness of 5mm
½ a red onion, sliced
½ green pepper, diced
5 cherry tomatoes, quartered
1 dessertspoon fresh thyme leaves
70g chopped pancetta
salt and pepper
2 eggs
150g crème fraîche
1 tablespoon flat-leaf parsley, chopped
150g feta cheese, cubed

To make the pastry

- Put the flour and butter in the bowl of a food processor and incorporate them so that the resulting mixture looks like fine breadcrumbs.
- Add a pinch of salt.
- Mix the egg yolk with the cold water, in a small bowl and then add this liquid to the flour and fat.
- Turn on the food processor and mix until a dough just begins to form. Turn the mixture onto a floured work surface and combine thoroughly, with a light hand, until you have a smooth dough. Wrap the dough in cling-film and chill in the fridge for 20 minutes.

To make the filling

- Preheat oven to 200°C/400°F/gas 6.
- Heat the olive oil in a sauté pan.
- Add the vegetables and thyme and sauté for 4 minutes until soft. The vegetables will brown slightly but do not let them brown too much.
- Add the pancetta and cook for 1 minute.
- Season the vegetables and remove them from the heat to cool.
- Mix the eggs with the crème fraîche in a bowl.
- Then add the parsley, crumble in the feta cheese and mix in thoroughly.
- Season to taste but be cautious if adding salt.

To make the tart

- Grease a 28cm diameter flan tin.
- Roll out the pastry on a lightly floured surface and line the flan tin with it. Place a sheet of baking parchment over the pastry case and pour on some baking beans. Place the flan tin on a baking sheet and bake it for 15 minutes.
- Take the flan tin out of the oven and remove the parchment and baking beans. Then return it to the oven for a further 5 minutes.
- Remove the flan tin from the oven and reduce the oven temperature to 190°C/375°C/gas 5.
- Spoon the sautéed vegetables onto the bottom of the flan case.
- Pour over the crème fraîche and egg mixture.
- Bake for 30 minutes until browned on top.

Baked potatoes

6 baking potatoes
butter for serving
salt and pepper

- Preheat the oven to 220°C/425°F/gas 7.
- Pierce the potato skins with a sharp knife and bake them for 1 hour 30 minutes.
- Split each one and serve with butter, salt and pepper.

Green salad

1 lettuce, prepared for serving
3 spring onions, sliced
1 cucumber, sliced

For the dressing

2 tablespoons extra virgin olive oil
½ tablespoon balsamic vinegar
salt and pepper

- Combine the salad ingredients in a serving dish.
- Mix the dressing ingredients in a small bowl and then pour over the salad when you are ready to eat.

Lamb and turnip stew + soda bread

Turnips go very well with lamb. This is a simple meal and the stew is lovely served with chunks of soda bread.

Lamb and turnip stew

2 tablespoons olive oil
1kg cubed lamb
2 onions, finely chopped
1 tablespoon plain flour
2 sprigs rosemary
500ml lamb stock, shop-bought is ideal
1 tin chickpeas, drained
salt and pepper
300g turnips, peeled and chopped into 2.5cm pieces

- Heat the olive oil in a large saucepan.
- Brown the lamb in the oil in batches, setting each batch aside as you cook the next.
- In the same saucepan, sauté the onions for 5 minutes until soft.
- Then return the lamb to the saucepan with the onions.
- Sprinkle on the flour and stir well.
- Add the chopped rosemary, the stock and chickpeas.
- Season with salt and pepper.
- Bring to a simmer.
- Cover and cook on a slow simmer for 1 hour.
- Add the turnips and cook uncovered for 30 minutes until the turnips are tender.

Soda bread

225g wholemeal flour
225g plain white flour
1½ teaspoons salt
2 teaspoons bicarbonate of soda
45g butter, cubed
1 tablespoon caster sugar
400ml buttermilk

- Preheat the oven to 190°C/375°F/gas 5.
- Lightly grease a baking tray.
- Place both flours, the salt and bicarbonate of soda in the bowl of a food processor.
- Add the butter and whizz in the processor until the butter is combined and you have a breadcrumb consistency, as for pastry.
- Add the sugar and combine.
- Gradually pour in the buttermilk, mixing as you go, until you have a soft dough.
- Turn the dough out onto a lightly floured surface and knead it lightly until you have a smooth round piece of dough.
- Place the round of dough on the baking tray.
- Make a deep cross in the top of the dough with a knife and bake in the oven for 40 minutes.
- Transfer to a wire rack to cool.

Cold meatloaf + goat's cheese and French bean salad + boiled potatoes

This is a really simple meal that can be prepared in advance, so it's ideal if you have to cater for different meal times.

Cold meatloaf

50g white breadcrumbs, soaked in 4 tablespoons milk
250g minced beef
250g minced pork
200g sausage meat
50g Italian salami, finely chopped
1 egg
4 sage leaves, finely chopped
1 tablespoon flat-leaf parsley, chopped
1 sprig rosemary, leaves removed and finely chopped
1 shallot, finely chopped
1 clove garlic, peeled and finely chopped
grated zest 1 lemon
salt and pepper

- Preheat the oven to 200°C/400°F/gas 6.
- Grease a 23cm long, 6cm deep loaf tin.
- Combine all the ingredients in a mixing bowl, taking care not to under season the mixture with the salt and pepper.
- Spoon the mixture into the greased loaf tin.
- Give the loaf tin a good bang on a hard kitchen surface once or twice, as this will get rid of any air bubbles in the meatloaf.
- Bake for 35 minutes. You will know when the meatloaf is ready as it will shrink from the side of the loaf tin.
- Drain off the fat from the tin and leave to cool.
- Slice to serve once cold.

Goat's cheese and French bean salad

For the salad
400g French beans
200g cherry tomatoes, halved
10 cornichons, sliced
4 spring onions, peeled and sliced
200g soft goat's cheese, cut into small lumps
1 tablespoon fresh mint, finely chopped
For the dressing
1 teaspoon Dijon mustard
½ tablespoon red wine vinegar
salt and pepper
3 tablespoons extra virgin olive oil

To make the dressing
- Mix the mustard and red wine vinegar in a small bowl and season with salt and pepper.
- Drizzle the olive oil onto the mustard and vinegar mixture slowly beating with a fork as you do so, so that the dressing starts to emulsify.

To make the salad
- Cook the French beans in salted, boiling water for 6–7 minutes until tender.
- Drain the beans thoroughly and place them in a serving dish.
- Then toss the beans in the dressing while they are still warm.
- Place the tomatoes, cornichons, spring onions, goat's cheese and mint into the same serving dish and gently combine.

Boiled potatoes

750g potatoes, peeled and quartered
salt
butter
black pepper

- Place the potatoes in a saucepan of salted water.
- Bring to the boil and reduce the heat to a simmer for 12–15 minutes, depending on the size of the potatoes.
- Serve with a dab of butter and a few grindings of black pepper.

Fried monkfish with salsa verde + new potato, red onion and chickpea salad

Salsa verde is a versatile sauce that goes well with fish and meat. Here I have teamed it with monkfish.

Fried monkfish with salsa verde

For the salsa verde

bunch flat-leaf parsley, with thicker stalks removed
handful fresh basil leaves
3 tinned anchovies
2 tablespoons capers, rinsed thoroughly
2 cloves garlic, peeled and finely chopped
50g pitted green olives
1 tablespoon white wine vinegar
black pepper
150ml extra virgin olive oil

For the fried monkfish

1kg filleted monkfish tail
2 tablespoons olive oil
salt and pepper
squeeze fresh lemon juice

To make the salsa verde

- Excluding the olive oil, put everything into a food processor and process until finely chopped.
- Gradually add the olive oil, pulsing the processor in short bursts between each addition. The sauce should be quite thick, so add more or less olive oil as you think necessary.

To cook the monkfish

- Slice the monkfish into 1cm thick slices.
- Season with salt and pepper.
- Heat the olive oil in a frying pan.
- Fry the slices in olive oil over a high heat for 1 minute on each side. Monkfish is glorious if not overcooked so take care, as too much cooking makes it rubbery. As you cook it, place it in a warm serving dish and when it's all prepared squeeze over some fresh lemon juice. Serve with the salsa verde and the salad.

New potato, red onion and chickpea salad

250g new potatoes
1 red onion, sliced
400g tin chickpeas, drained
handful flat-leaf parsley, chopped

For the dressing

1 tablespoon extra virgin olive oil
2 teaspoons balsamic vinegar
salt and pepper

- Bring the potatoes to the boil in a saucepan of salted water. Once boiling, cook the potatoes for 20 minutes until tender.
- Drain the potatoes well and place them in a serving dish with the sliced onions, chickpeas and parsley.
- Mix the dressing in a small bowl and then pour it over the salad while the potatoes are still hot.

Garlic and rosemary roasted chicken + roast potatoes + creamy peas and carrots

When roasting chicken for the entire family, I either cook two smaller birds or one big one. There may be some leftovers which you can use to make a good stock.

Garlic and rosemary roasted chicken

2 whole chickens each weighing 1.4 kg
1 or 2 sprigs rosemary
4 cloves garlic
salt and pepper
8 slices pancetta
olive oil

For the gravy

1 tablespoon flour
500ml chicken stock

- Preheat the oven to 180°C/350°F/gas 4.
- Place the chickens in a roasting tray.
- Break the rosemary into mini sprigs and slice each garlic clove into two pieces. Insert the garlic and the rosemary along the gaps between the legs and the body of the chicken.
- Drizzle with olive oil and season well with salt and pepper.
- Cover the breasts lengthways with the pancetta.
- Place the chickens in the oven and roast for 1 hour and 10 minutes. The pancetta will become brown during the cooking time so move it to the bottom of the meat tin to help flavour the gravy.

To make the gravy

- Once the chickens are cooked, set them aside to rest and start the gravy.
- Place the roasting tin in which you roasted the chickens on the hob, on a medium heat.
- Sprinkle a dessertspoon of flour into the tin and mix it into the juices and crusty bits round the tin with a wooden spoon so that you have a paste.
- Turn the heat up high and either add fresh stock or use a stock cube with water.
- Once the gravy is simmering, turn the heat down to very low so that the gravy cooks but does not evaporate.

Roast potatoes

1kg potatoes, peeled, quartered and rinsed in cold water
1 dessertspoon goose fat or 2 tablespoons olive oil
salt

- Preheat the oven to 220°C/425°F/gas 7.
- Parboil the potatoes in salted water for 4 minutes.
- Drain and place them in a roasting tin.
- Drizzle with the goose fat or olive oil and roast for 45–60 minutes until golden brown.

Creamy peas and carrots

15g butter
1 shallot, peeled and finely diced
300g frozen peas
300g carrots, peeled and sliced into pound coin thick slices
2 tablespoons crème fraîche
2 teaspoons Dijon mustard
salt and pepper

- Heat the butter in a saucepan and gently fry the shallot for a few seconds, taking care not to burn it.
- Add the peas and carrots and turn the heat down to low.
- Cover the saucepan with a lid and cook the vegetables for 15 minutes until tender.
- Remove from the heat and stir in the crème fraîche and the mustard.
- Season with salt and pepper.

TIP

For extra crispy roast potatoes rinse the peeled uncooked potatoes in cold water, drain them and then boil them in fresh water.

Coconut cream and raisin tart

I love any dessert that contains coconut and this one has a distinctly Sri Lankan flavour. Raisin and coconut are a great combination in this tart.

For the sweet pastry
180g butter
75g icing sugar
2 egg yolks
225g plain flour
For the filling
200ml single cream
100g block creamed coconut, roughly chopped
1 tablespoon caster sugar
150ml milk
3 eggs, lightly beaten
50g raisins

- Preheat the oven to 190°C/375°F/gas 5.
- Grease a 23cm tart tin.

To make the sweet pastry

- Place the butter, icing sugar, egg yolks and flour together in a food processor, and whizz until the mixture just starts to combine.
- Turn it out onto a floured surface and form into a ball.
- Wrap it in cling-film and chill in the fridge for 30 minutes.

To make the tart

- When the pastry is ready, roll it out and line the tart tin with it.
- Prick the base of the pastry with a fork. Line the case with a sheet of baking parchment and then pour some baking beans on top of the paper.
- Bake the pastry case for 10 minutes.

- Then remove the beans and baking parchment and return the tart case to the oven for about 5 minutes.
- Meanwhile, pour the cream and chopped creamed coconut into a saucepan and stir over a low heat until the coconut has dissolved.
- Remove the saucepan from the heat and stir in the sugar and milk. Let the mixture cool for 5 minutes.
- Next, add the beaten eggs and combine well.
- Sprinkle the raisins on the bottom of the pastry case and pour over the cream mixture.
- Bake on a baking sheet for 30 minutes until the tart is set.
- Serve with cream.

Jam sponge puddings with jam sauce

This is a great midweek pudding as it is quick to make. These are steamed puddings, but because they are cooked in small portions you don't have the usual 2-hour cooking time that you would for one large steamed pudding.

For the sponge pudding
6 teaspoons raspberry jam
110g butter, softened
110g caster sugar
finely grated zest 1 lemon
2 eggs
150g self-raising flour
1 level teaspoon baking powder
salt
juice 1 lemon
For the jam sauce
225g raspberry jam
juice ½ lemon

- Preheat the oven to 190°C/375°F/gas 5.
- Grease 6 small tin pudding moulds.
- Put one teaspoon of raspberry jam in the bottom of each pudding mould.
- In a mixing bowl cream the butter, sugar and lemon zest together until white and fluffy using an electric mixer.
- Add the eggs one at a time, along with a tablespoon of flour, and beat until incorporated.
- Fold in the baking powder, the remaining flour, a pinch of salt and lemon juice with a metal spoon.
- Spoon the mixture into the pudding moulds and cover each one with a square of buttered tin foil.
- Place the puddings in a large roasting tin.
- Pour 1½cm of water into the roasting tin and cover the whole thing with a large piece of tin foil, turning it under the rim of the roasting tin.
- Bake for 55 minutes.
- To make the sauce add the lemon juice to the jam and heat gently on the hob.
- Unmould the puddings when ready and serve with the jam sauce and some cream.

Week 4

Monday p266	Sticky chicken wings + green salad with gorgonzola and walnut dressing
Tuesday p267	Asparagus and pea risotto
Wednesday p268	Chilli con carne + avocado salsa + brown rice
Thursday p269	Herb and cheese omelette on toast + avocado and tomato salad
Friday p270	Tuna fish curry + boiled rice + green salad
Saturday p271	Sausages and lentils + sweet and sour apples + bread
Sunday p272	Leg of pork with rosemary, potatoes and vegetables + watercress salad
Sunday pudding p273	Strawberry and cream sponge
Extra tasty treat p274	Broken biscuit cake

Shopping list

MEAT
- ☐ 20 chicken wings
- ☐ 1kg lean minced beef
- ☐ 12 sausages
- ☐ 1kg pork leg, boned

FISH
- ☐ 700g tuna fish steaks

VEGETABLES
- ☐ 1 Cos or Romaine lettuce
- ☐ 5 red onions
- ☐ 200g asparagus
- ☐ 200g fresh petits pois
- ☐ 1 garlic bulb
- ☐ 2 onions
- ☐ 3 avocadoes
- ☐ 8 plum tomatoes
- ☐ 4 spring onions
- ☐ fresh ginger
- ☐ 1 green chilli
- ☐ 1 green pepper
- ☐ 1 cucumber
- ☐ 1 bunch celery
- ☐ 1kg potatoes
- ☐ 2 whole cobs corn
- ☐ 2 courgettes
- ☐ 12 cherry tomatoes
- ☐ 1 bunch watercress

FRUIT
- ☐ 4 lemons
- ☐ 400g dessert apples
- ☐ 100g strawberries

FRESH HERBS
- ☐ coriander
- ☐ chives
- ☐ flat-leaf parsley
- ☐ mint
- ☐ rosemary

FRIDGE ITEMS
- ☐ 278ml milk
- ☐ 3 packs butter
- ☐ 15 eggs
- ☐ 115g Gorgonzola cheese
- ☐ 1.5 litres chicken stock
- ☐ 50g mascarpone cheese
- ☐ 30g Parmesan cheese
- ☐ 50g Cheddar cheese
- ☐ 70g chopped pancetta
- ☐ 250ml double cream
- ☐ 1 small tub soured cream

KITCHEN CUPBOARD ITEMS
- ☐ 75g walnuts
- ☐ tomato purée
- ☐ 2 x 400g tins kidney beans
- ☐ 2 x 400g tins chopped tomatoes
- ☐ 1 tin cannellini beans
- ☐ salt
- ☐ 1 loaf bread
- ☐ 400ml coconut milk
- ☐ 500g basmati rice
- ☐ 500g brown rice
- ☐ 500g risotto rice
- ☐ extra virgin olive oil
- ☐ vegetable oil
- ☐ olive oil
- ☐ 300g Puy lentils
- ☐ chicken stock cubes
- ☐ 150ml white wine
- ☐ red wine vinegar
- ☐ balsamic vinegar
- ☐ sherry vinegar
- ☐ 175g plain flour
- ☐ baking powder
- ☐ vanilla essence
- ☐ 325g caster sugar
- ☐ 75g dark chocolate
- ☐ 75g good quality milk chocolate
- ☐ 250g digestive biscuits

SPICES
- ☐ cayenne pepper
- ☐ black pepper
- ☐ curry leaves
- ☐ turmeric
- ☐ ground cumin
- ☐ cinnamon sticks

Sticky chicken wings + green salad with gorgonzola and walnut dressing

These wings are truly delicious. Everyone loves them in our family from grandfather down to the youngest child. For my brood I have to buy 20 wings, which makes cooking them a bit tricky, as they should all go into the pan together. I, therefore, use a heavy-bottomed saucepan. I cook the wings in batches of 5 for the high-heat part of the cooking and then throw them all in together at the end for the 30-minute session.

Sticky chicken wings

20 chicken wings
flour for dusting
4 tablespoons olive oil
juice 3 lemons
100g butter

- Dust the chicken wings with flour.
- Heat the olive oil in a heavy-bottomed saucepan until hot.
- Put the wings in the pan. They will spit but resist moving them for 5 minutes, by which time they will be perfectly brown on one side.
- Turn them over and cook for another 5 minutes on the other side. Then set them aside.
- Do the same with all of the wings and when they are browned all over, return them to the saucepan and cook for 10 minutes on a lower heat.
- Give them a turn and then cook them for another 20 minutes or so. It doesn't matter if you cook them for a bit longer, as wings don't get tough like other cuts of chicken.
- Next, season generously with salt.
- Lift them all out and turn up the heat so that the remaining juices sizzle.
- Add the lemon juice and butter and cook for 5 minutes.
- Pour the sauce over the chicken wings when ready to serve.

Green salad with gorgonzola and walnut dressing

1 Cos or Romaine lettuce
5 tablespoons extra virgin olive oil
1 tablespoon red wine vinegar
salt and pepper
115g Gorgonzola cheese, at room temperature
75g walnuts, coarsely chopped

- Prepare the lettuce by tearing it into thick strips.
- Put the olive oil, vinegar, salt and pepper into a serving bowl and blend them with a fork.
- Add half the Gorgonzola and mash it in to the oil and vinegar with the fork.
- Add half the chopped walnuts and the lettuce.
- Toss everything thoroughly.
- Top off with the remaining Gorgonzola and walnuts and serve.

Asparagus and pea risotto

This is an irresistible risotto made with fresh spring ingredients. Make sure the stock is really hot as you add it to the rice.

1.5 litres chicken stock
salt and pepper
200g asparagus
200g fresh petits pois
2 tablespoons olive oil
50g butter
1 red onion, finely chopped
500g risotto rice
1 tablespoon mascarpone cheese
30g Parmesan cheese, grated

- Heat the chicken stock in a large saucepan.
- As it warms check the seasoning.
- Bring it to a simmer and then add the chopped asparagus and petits pois and simmer for about 3 minutes. Remove the vegetables with a slotted spoon and set aside, but keep the stock simmering gently.
- Place the olive oil and butter in a large saucepan and heat it.
- Add the onion and fry gently for about 3 minutes until soft.
- Add the rice and stir for 1 minute.
- After 1 minute start to add the hot stock a ladle or two at a time.
- Don't let all the liquid disappear before adding more hot stock. The key to a good risotto is not to let the rice stick to the pan while it is cooking so keep stirring throughout.
- Keep adding the hot stock until the rice is tender on the outside but still has a slight bite on the inside. A risotto takes about 20 minutes to cook.
- Add the cooked vegetables, mascarpone and the Parmesan cheese.
- Season with pepper and serve.

Chilli con carne + avocado salsa + brown rice

This is almost as popular a midweek meal as spaghetti Bolognaise and makes a nice change. Serve with nutty brown rice.

Chilli con carne

1 tablespoon olive oil
1 clove garlic, peeled and finely chopped
1 onion, diced
1 teaspoon ground cumin
½ teaspoon cayenne pepper
1kg lean minced beef
salt and pepper
2 x 400g tins chopped tomatoes
2 teaspoons tomato purée
2 x 400g tins kidney beans, drained

- Heat the olive oil in a heavy-bottomed saucepan.
- Fry the garlic and onion on a very gentle heat to avoid burning the garlic.
- Once the onion is soft, after about 4 minutes, add the cumin and cayenne.
- Stir to coat the onion and garlic with the spices.
- Add the minced beef and brown it all over, then season with salt and pepper.
- Add the tinned tomatoes and tomato purée and cook on a low simmer, uncovered, for 1 hour.
- Next, add the kidney beans and cook for another 30 minutes uncovered.
- Check the seasoning and adjust as necessary.

Avocado salsa

1 avocado, peeled and cut into small chunks
½ red onion, finely sliced
3 fresh tomatoes, cut into small chunks
handful fresh coriander, roughly chopped
For the dressing
salt and pepper
1 dessertspoon olive oil
squeeze of fresh lemon juice

- Combine the salad ingredients in a serving bowl.
- Mix the oil and lemon juice in a small bowl.
- Season and pour it over the avocado salsa.

Brown rice

500g brown rice
750ml water
salt
20g butter
black pepper

- Put the rice in a saucepan with the water and a pinch of salt.
- Place on a high heat and as soon as it comes to the boil, cover the saucepan with a lid and turn the heat right down to very low. Leave it for 15 minutes, giving it one stir only during the cooking time.
- Take the saucepan off the heat and leave it covered for a further 10 minutes, before removing the lid.
- Stir in the butter while the rice is still hot and season with pepper.
- Serve the chilli on the rice with the salsa and top it with a little soured cream.

Herb and cheese omelette on toast + avocado and tomato salad

If you don't have a large frying pan you can divide the mixture in half and cook two omelettes separately. Omelettes are often thought of as rather unimaginative fare, but if they are cooked well I think they are in a class of their own.

Herb and cheese omelette on toast

8 eggs
4 spring onions, finely chopped
2 tablespoons milk
salt and pepper
25g butter
1 handful fresh chives, snipped
1 tablespoon flat-leaf parsley, chopped
3 tablespoons Cheddar cheese, grated
6 pieces bread for toasting (or more, depending upon your family's appetite)

- Beat the eggs, spring onions and milk together in a mixing bowl and season with salt and pepper.
- Heat the butter in a frying pan and when foaming pour in the egg mixture.
- Move the egg mixture around until it starts to set.
- Sprinkle the chives, parsley and cheese on top of the egg and then fold the omelette over.
- Leave to cook for 2 more minutes and then remove the pan from the heat.
- Make and butter the toast and cut the omelette into six pieces to place on the toast.

Avocado and tomato salad

1 avocado, cut into chunks
3 tomatoes, sliced
1 tin cannellini beans drained
For the dressing
2 dessertspoons olive oil
½ dessertspoon balsamic vinegar
salt and pepper

- Place the avocado, tomatoes and beans in a serving bowl.
- Pour the dressing over the top and serve with the omelette.

Tuna fish curry
+ boiled rice + green salad

This is a typical Sri-Lankan fish curry, which only takes about 30 minutes to create and so is fast food indeed.

Tuna fish curry

2 tablespoons vegetable oil
1 medium onion, finely chopped
1 clove garlic, peeled and finely chopped
2cm piece fresh ginger, peeled and finely chopped
1 green chilli, deseeded and finely chopped
2 small tomatoes, chopped
10 curry leaves
¼ teaspoon turmeric
2 teaspoons ground cumin
400ml coconut milk
100ml water
1 teaspoon salt
2 handfuls coriander, chopped
10 mint leaves, finely chopped
700g tuna fish steaks, cut into 3cm wide strips

- Heat the vegetable oil in a large saucepan.
- Add the onion and fry for 5 minutes.
- Add the garlic, ginger and chilli and fry gently for 5 minutes, so as not to burn the garlic.
- Add the tomatoes and cook for 3 minutes.
- Scatter in the curry leaves, turmeric and cumin.
- Stir well to incorporate.
- Next, add the coconut milk and water and bring to a simmer.
- Season with salt and scatter on the herbs.
- Add the tuna steaks and cook, covered, for about 4 minutes.
- If you are going to reheat the curry later, don't cook the fish for any longer than this, but if you are dishing up immediately then cook for 3 minutes more, turning the fish once or twice so that it cooks through evenly.

Boiled rice

500g basmati rice
750ml water
salt

- Put the rice in a saucepan with the water and a pinch of salt.
- Place on a high heat and as soon as it comes to the boil, cover the saucepan with a lid and turn the heat right down to very low. Leave it for 15 minutes, giving it one stir only during the cooking time.
- Take the pan off the heat and leave it covered for a further 10 minutes before removing the lid.

Green pepper and cucumber salad

1 green pepper, cored, deseeded and diced
1 cucumber, diced
2 plum tomatoes, diced
For the dressing
2 tablespoons extra virgin olive oil
squeeze of fresh lemon juice
salt and pepper

- Combine the salad ingredients in a serving bowl.
- Mix the dressing in a small bowl and once you are ready to eat, pour it over the salad ingredients and toss to coat evenly.

Sausages and lentils + sweet and sour apples + bread

This is a slightly unusual combination, which I think works on two levels. First, it is nice to try different meals and secondly, because the apples work well with the sausages in a sweet and sour kind of way. A completely incidental point is that the meal has a beautiful colour when it is finished. The darkness of the lentils and sauages with the rich colours of the apples makes a hearty meal all the more satisfying.

Sausages and lentils

2 tablespoons olive oil
12 sausages
2 small red onions, finely chopped
1 stick celery, finely chopped
70g chopped pancetta
300g Puy lentils
1 sprig fresh rosemary
450ml chicken stock (a cube will suffice)
150ml white wine
salt and pepper

- On a medium heat, brown the sausages all over in 1 tablespoon of the olive oil in a heavy-bottomed saucepan.
- Set the sausages aside.
- Add the other tablespoon of olive oil to the saucepan and sauté the onions, celery and pancetta for 10 minutes until soft and slightly browned.
- Next, add the lentils and rosemary and stir.
- Pour the stock and wine into the pan and bring to the boil.
- Then reduce to a gentle simmer.
- Return the browned sausages to the pan.
- Season with salt and pepper.
- Cover and simmer for 25 minutes until the lentils are tender.
- Serve with the apples below and hunks of bread.

Sweet and sour apples

400g dessert apples, peeled, cored and quartered
25ml red wine vinegar
25ml balsamic vinegar
25ml sherry vinegar
1 tablespoon sugar
2cm piece cinnamon stick

- Place all the ingredients in a medium-sized saucepan.
- Bring to a simmer slowly.
- Cover the pan and simmer gently for 10 minutes until the apples are soft but maintain their shape.

Leg of pork with rosemary, potatoes and vegetables + watercress salad

This sounds rather a grand meal but it is actually very easy to prepare. The pork and potatoes go in the same meat tray followed by the other vegetables, which soak up lots of the lovely juices, giving a wonderful combination of flavours.

Roast leg of pork with rosemary, potatoes and vegetables

For the pork

1kg pork leg, boned

1 dessertspoon salt

1 tablespoon olive oil

2 sprigs fresh rosemary

For the potatoes

1kg potatoes, peeled, quartered and rinsed in cold water

salt

For the vegetables

1 tablespoon olive oil

1 red onion, peeled and cut into chunks

2 cobs corn, each cut into 4 pieces, and boiled in water for 5 minutes

2 courgettes cut into chunks

10–12 cherry tomatoes

pepper

To prepare the pork

- Preheat the oven to 240°C/475°F/gas 9.
- Pat the pork rind dry with a piece of kitchen paper.
- Score the rind, if your butcher has not already done so, with a very sharp knife.
- Drizzle the rind with olive oil and sprinkle with a generous teaspoon of salt.
- Dot with the rosemary sprigs.

To prepare the potatoes

- Parboil the potatoes in boiling salted water for 5 minutes.
- Drain and place them around the pork joint.
- Roast the potatoes and pork for 20 minutes.
- Reduce the heat to 220°C/425°F/gas 7 and roast for a further 30 minutes.

To prepare the vegetables

- Place the vegetables in the meat tin with the pork and potatoes and roast for a further 20 minutes.
- Serve with the watercress salad below.

Watercress salad

1 bunch watercress

For the dressing

1 dessertspoon extra virgin olive oil

1 teaspoon balsamic vinegar

salt and pepper

- Place the watercress in a serving dish and dress with the oil, vinegar, salt and pepper.

Strawberry and cream sponge

By this time of year you should be able to find English strawberries in the shops, so start to make the most of them.

For the sponge cake
175g butter, softened
175g caster sugar
175g plain flour
½ teaspoon baking powder
3 eggs
4 tablespoons milk
1 teaspoon vanilla essence
For the filling
250ml double cream, whipped to a thick consistency
100g strawberries, sliced

- Grease and line 2 x 20cm sandwich tins.
- Preheat the oven to 180°C/350°F/gas 4.
- Cream the butter and sugar using a food processor or hand-held mixer, until they are light and fluffy.
- Sift together the flour and baking powder.
- Add an egg and a spoonful of flour to the creamed butter and sugar.
- Mix to combine and then do the same with the rest of the eggs.
- Tip in the rest of the flour and fold into the mixture with a metal spoon.
- Add the milk and vanilla essence and mix briefly.
- Then divide the mixture between the two tins and smooth down gently with a knife.
- Bake for 40 minutes until firm to the touch.
- Leave the cakes to cool and then spread one cake with half the cream and half of the strawberries.
- Place the other cake on top, spread with the remaining cream and arrange the rest of the strawberries on top with a sprig of mint.

Broken biscuit cake

This is a favourite teatime treat of my children. There is nothing quite like it.

250g butter
4 egg yolks
2 teaspoons water
125g caster sugar
75g dark chocolate
75g good-quality milk chocolate
250g digestive biscuits broken into small pieces

- Line a small loaf tin with baking parchment.
- Heat the butter in a saucepan until it melts.
- Set aside.
- Blend the egg yolks with the water in a food processor or liquidiser.
- Gradually and slowly add the melted butter to the egg yolks, mixing all the time so that a thick emulsion is formed.
- Then add the sugar and mix until blended.
- Next, add the chocolate a little at a time. It should melt easily as the mixture will still be hot. If it doesn't melt by the last addition of chocolate, heat it gently in the microwave for a few seconds.
- Transfer the mixture to a mixing bowl and add the biscuits, stirring them in.
- Pour the mixture into the loaf tin and chill in the fridge for 2 hours or so.
- Slice into thick pieces and serve.

Week 5

Shopping list

MEAT
- ☐ 1kg diced lamb
- ☐ 600g sausage meat
- ☐ 800g beef fillet
- ☐ 1kg chicken pieces (drumsticks and thighs)

FISH
- ☐ 500g medium cooked prawns
- ☐ 6 lemon sole fillets

VEGETABLES
- ☐ fresh ginger
- ☐ 1 red onion
- ☐ 1 cucumber
- ☐ 18 asparagus spears
- ☐ 50g rocket leaves
- ☐ 2 little gem lettuces
- ☐ 1 avocado
- ☐ 1.4kg potatoes
- ☐ 700g new potatoes
- ☐ 300g fresh peas
- ☐ 300g carrots
- ☐ 5 onions
- ☐ 300g button mushrooms
- ☐ 11 shallots
- ☐ 1 garlic bulb
- ☐ 2 leeks

FRUIT
- ☐ 1 lemon
- ☐ 3 firm eating apples
- ☐ 2 pears

FRESH HERBS
- ☐ bay leaves
- ☐ chives
- ☐ sage
- ☐ 2 bunches flat-leaf parsley
- ☐ thyme

FRIDGE ITEMS
- ☐ 250ml natural yoghurt
- ☐ 140g chopped pancetta
- ☐ 250g frozen peas
- ☐ 500ml milk
- ☐ 10–12 slices pancetta
- ☐ 1 tub vanilla ice cream
- ☐ 2.25 litres chicken stock
- ☐ 1 pack puff pastry
- ☐ 200ml soured cream
- ☐ 1 pack butter
- ☐ 18 eggs
- ☐ 500ml double cream
- ☐ 50g Parmesan cheese

KITCHEN CUPBOARD ITEMS
- ☐ 400g tin chopped tomatoes
- ☐ 500g basmati rice
- ☐ 150g wholemeal flour
- ☐ 100g strong white bread flour
- ☐ 400g tin cannellini beans
- ☐ salt
- ☐ Tabasco sauce
- ☐ 500g red lentils
- ☐ olive oil
- ☐ extra virgin olive oil
- ☐ vegetable oil
- ☐ 1 white loaf for breadcrumbs
- ☐ 2 loaves granary bread
- ☐ Dijon mustard
- ☐ 500g linguine
- ☐ 550ml dry white wine
- ☐ 200ml red wine
- ☐ 125g plain flour
- ☐ 175g ground almonds
- ☐ 185g caster sugar
- ☐ brandy
- ☐ 50g dark chocolate

SPICES
- ☐ cinnamon sticks
- ☐ turmeric
- ☐ ground coriander
- ☐ ground cumin
- ☐ mace
- ☐ whole nutmeg
- ☐ cayenne pepper
- ☐ black pepper
- ☐ cloves
- ☐ cardamom pods
- ☐ curry leaves
- ☐ coriander seeds
- ☐ cumin seeds
- ☐ fennel seeds
- ☐ fenugreek
- ☐ paprika
- ☐ ground cinammon

Lamb pullao
+ chapatis + cucumber raita

Pullao is a traditional Kashmiri dish, with lamb being the meat of choice. This pullao is very straightforward once you have measured out the spices and you can do this while the lamb sits in the salt and pepper. If you don't have time to leave the lamb for 30 minutes in the seasoning, just leave it for as long as it takes to measure the spices. The chapatis are very easy to prepare too.

Lamb pullao

1kg lamb, diced
salt and pepper
2 tablespoons vegetable oil
2 x 2cm pieces cinnamon stick
10 cloves
8 cardamom pods
2 bay leaves
2 tablespoons ginger, finely chopped
1 tablespoon garlic, crushed
2 onions, finely diced
3 teaspoons ground coriander
3 teaspoons ground cumin
½ teaspoon mace
½ teaspoon grated nutmeg
¼ teaspoon cayenne pepper
1 teaspoon freshly ground black pepper
400g tin chopped tomatoes
¼ teaspoon turmeric
2 teaspoons salt
500g basmati rice
550ml water

- Preheat the oven to 160°C/320°F/gas 2½.
- Place the lamb in a bowl with a good sprinkling of salt and pepper.
- Set aside for 30 minutes.
- Heat the vegetable oil in a large, heavy-bottomed saucepan.
- Add the cinnamon, cloves, cardamom and bay leaves and stir.
- When they start to sizzle, add the ginger and garlic and fry for 1 minute until you smell the aromas of both.
- Next, add the onions and fry gently for 10 minutes until soft.
- Mix the coriander, cumin, mace, nutmeg, cayenne and black pepper into the onions and stir-fry for 1 minute.
- Then add the lamb and brown it all over on a medium heat.
- When the lamb is nicely browned add the tomatoes, turmeric and salt.
- Next, add the rice and water and bring to a good simmer.
- Cover the saucepan with a piece of greaseproof paper, place the lid on top and cook in the oven for 55 minutes.
- You can now get on with the chapatis.

Chapatis

150g wholemeal flour
100g strong white bread flour
salt
175ml water

- Place the flours and a pinch of salt in a bowl, make a well and add the water.
- Stir to combine and then knead for 5 minutes.
- Leave to rest for 20–30 minutes.
- Then divide the mixture into 12 pieces.
- Shape each one into a ball and then roll them out as thinly as they will go with a rolling pin.
- Next, place an iron frying pan on the hob and heat it up.
- Add the first chapati and press it down with your hand wrapped in a clean tea towel. As you do this it will puff up. Leave for 1 minute and then turn for another minute, pressing down again with the tea towel.
- Keep the chapatis warm in a tea towel while you cook the rest.

Cucumber raita

½ red onion, finely diced
1 cucumber, diced
250ml natural yoghurt
salt

- Place all the ingredients in a serving bowl with the yoghurt and season with a little salt.

Scrambled eggs, asparagus and pancetta on toast

Asparagus can be expensive and I don't want to advocate food items that are out of reach of most people's pockets. However, if there is one time of year to eat asparagus, it is during May and June when it is seasonal in this country and is, therefore, more affordable. This recipe uses only a small amount, and served with eggs, it works out to be a relatively inexpensive but delicious meal.

10–12 eggs, depending on the appetites of your children
25g butter
salt and pepper
150ml double cream
6 slices granary bread
10–12 slices pancetta
12 or so asparagus spears, depending on your budget

- Prepare the asparagus by holding each stalk between your left thumb and index finger. Take the tip of the spear between your right thumb and index finger and bend down so that it snaps off the tough end section. Discard these.
- Bring a large saucepan of water to a simmer. If the asparagus is very fresh there is no need to salt the water.
- Break the eggs into a large bowl and mix them with a wooden spoon to incorporate the whites with the yolks.
- Season well with salt and pepper.
- Then melt the butter in a large pan.
- Add the eggs but keep the heat low, stirring occasionally. The key to good scrambled eggs is to cook them slowly, season properly and not to overcook them.
- Stir the eggs round and as they begin to cook add the cream.
- Put the asparagus into the saucepan and simmer for 3 minutes.
- In a small frying pan start to fry the pancetta slices until golden brown.
- Remove the eggs from the heat when they are ready.
- Toast and butter the bread.
- Pile the toast with the scrambled eggs, lay the asparagus on top and then adorn with the crispy pancetta.

Prawn and avocado salad

Whoever first married prawn and avocado together in a recipe knew what they were doing; it is a sublime combination.

50g rocket leaves
2 little gem lettuces, washed and sliced
400g tin cannellini beans, drained
500g medium prawns, cooked and peeled
1 tablespoon chives, snipped
6 spears asparagus, trimmed
3 tablespoon extra virgin olive oil
salt and pepper
1 avocado
1 tablespoon lemon juice
Tabasco sauce

- Preheat the oven to 200°C/400°F/gas 6.
- Place the salad leaves in a serving bowl with the beans, prawns and chives.
- Place the asparagus on a baking sheet, drizzle with olive oil and sprinkle with salt and pepper.
- Put the asparagus in the oven and roast for 6 minutes.
- Meanwhile, peel and slice the avocado.
- Put this and the cooked asparagus in the serving bowl with the other ingredients.
- Dress the salad using the olive oil, lemon juice, salt and pepper and a few drops of Tabasco.
- Serve with hunks of brown bread and butter.

Sausage patties
+ spicy red lentils and potatoes

This is a very tasty combination full of robust flavours. It is also a healthy meal that children seem to enjoy.

Sausage patties

600g sausage meat
20g flat-leaf parsley, chopped
black pepper
75g white breadcrumbs
2 tablespoons olive oil
200ml red wine

- Place the sausage meat in a bowl.
- Add the parsley and season with black pepper.
- Form the mixture into about 18 patties.
- Roll each one in the breadcrumbs.
- Heat the olive oil in a frying pan and brown the patties all over in batches.
- Once all the patties are brown return them to the frying pan and cook thoroughly on a low heat for about 15 minutes.
- Increase the heat and add the red wine.
- Let it bubble away for 1 minute and then reduce the heat and cook for a further 3 minutes.
- Serve the patties with the spicy red lentils and potatoes.

Spicy red lentil and potatoes

2 tablespoons olive oil
1 onion, finely chopped
6 sage leaves, finely chopped
3 curry leaves
1 dessertspoon curry powder*
500g red lentils
400g potatoes, peeled and quartered
1.75 litres chicken stock
salt and pepper

- Heat the olive oil in a large saucepan.
- Fry the onion with the sage and curry leaves for 5 minutes until the onions are soft.
- Sprinkle on the curry powder and stir.
- Add the lentils and potatoes and then pour on the stock.
- Bring to a simmer and cook, partly covered, on a gentle heat for 45 minutes.
- Season with salt and pepper.

***** To make your own curry powder:**
1 tablespoon coriander seeds
1 dessertspoon cumin seeds
1 teaspoon fennel seeds
½ teaspoon fenugreek

- *Place the coriander seeds into a small, heavy-bottomed pan and heat through for 30 seconds.*
- *Add the other ingredients and toast until you smell the lovely aroma of the spices.*
- *Transfer the spices to a coffee grinder, a small processor or grind them in a pestle and mortar.*

Gratin of lemon sole + buttered new potatoes + peas and carrots

Lemon sole has a subtle yet beautiful flavour. Fish is so easy to prepare I am surprised people don't make use of it more in their weekly menus.

Gratin of lemon sole

6 lemon sole fillets
1 shallot, finely chopped
salt and pepper
1 sprig parsley
300ml dry white wine
100ml double cream
½ teaspoon Dijon mustard
1 tablespoon flat-leaf parsley parsley, chopped
2 tablespoons white breadcrumbs mixed with 1 tablespoon Parmesan cheese, grated

- Preheat the oven to 200°C/400°F/gas 6.
- Place the sole fillets in a large oven-proof dish, along with the shallot. Don't worry if the fillets are overlapping slightly.
- Season with salt and pepper.
- Place the sprig of parsley in the dish and pour over the wine.
- Cover the fillets with butter papers or baking parchment and poach for 8 minutes in the oven.
- Meanwhile heat the cream in a small saucepan.
- Add the mustard and parsley, season with salt and pepper and place to one side.
- Once the fish is ready, drain off the wine into a small saucepan.
- Preheat the grill.
- Rapidly boil the wine in the small saucepan for 1 minute.
- Slowly add the reduced wine to the cream and pour this over the fish.
- Sprinkle over the breadcrumbs and cheese and brown under the grill for 3 minutes.

Buttered new potatoes

700g new potatoes
salt
a little butter
black pepper

- Boil the potatoes in salted water for 20 minutes, until tender.
- Drain and peel them.
- Toss the potatoes in the butter and season them with salt and pepper.

Peas and carrots

300g fresh peas
300g carrots, peeled and thinly sliced
30g butter

- Place the vegetables in a small saucepan along with the butter.
- As the butter melts reduce the heat, cover and cook the peas and carrots for 10 minutes until tender, stirring them occasionally.
- Season with salt and pepper and serve.

Beef stroganoff + buttered linguine

This dish went out of favour in England in the late 1980s, when the fashion for more flamboyantly cooked food took hold. I see its simplicity as a distinct advantage when I want to create a quick and tasty midweek family meal.

Beef stroganoff

70g butter
2 medium onions, thinly sliced
300g button mushrooms, sliced
800g beef fillet, cut into ½cm strips
salt and pepper
200ml soured cream
¼ teaspoon paprika
1 dessertspoon Dijon mustard
2 tablespoons flat-leaf parsley, chopped

- Heat half the butter in a sauté pan and fry the onions on a low heat until nicely golden.
- Add the mushrooms and fry for 3 minutes.
- Remove the onions and mushrooms from the pan and set aside.
- Add the other half of the butter and, when foaming, add the beef.
- Stir-fry for 2 minutes.
- Return the onions and mushrooms to the pan and season well.
- Add the cream, paprika, mustard and parsley and cook for 1 minute.
- Serve immediately with the buttered linguine.

Buttered linguine

500g linguine
salt
25g butter
black pepper

- Cook the linguine in boiling salted water according to the packet directions.
- As soon as it is cooked, toss the pasta in the butter and season generously with pepper.

Chicken pieces with peas and pancetta + mashed potato

Unless you can get freshly picked English peas, it's not worth using the expensive imported fresh peas; use frozen ones, which taste just as good.

Chicken pieces with peas and pancetta

1kg chicken pieces, skin removed (drumsticks and thighs)
flour for dusting
2 tablespoons olive oil
salt and pepper
10 small shallots, peeled and left whole
2 cloves garlic, peeled and finely chopped
2 leeks, trimmed, washed and sliced
140g chopped pancetta
250ml dry white wine
500ml chicken stock
250g frozen peas
1 sprig fresh thyme

- Preheat the oven to 180°C/350°F/gas 4.
- Dust the chicken pieces with a little flour.
- Heat the oil in a large frying and brown the chicken pieces in manageable batches.
- As the pieces brown, transfer them to a casserole dish and season with salt and pepper.
- Add a little more oil to the frying pan if needed and sauté the shallots for 5 minutes until golden brown.
- Turn the shallots into the casserole with the chicken and return the frying pan to the heat.
- Next brown the garlic, leeks and pancetta for about 3 minutes.
- Add these to the casserole and return the frying pan to the heat.
- Next, add the wine and, as it bubbles, pour it over the chicken, vegetables and pancetta in the casserole dish.
- Then add the chicken stock, peas and thyme to the casserole.
- Season with salt and pepper.
- Bring the casserole to a gentle simmer on the hob and transfer to the oven for 1 hour.

Mashed potato

1.5kg potatoes, peeled and chopped for boiling
salt and pepper
50g butter
300ml milk

- Place the potatoes in a saucepan of salted water and bring to the boil.
- Simmer for about 15 minutes until the potatoes are tender to the tip of a sharp knife.
- Drain them and put them through a potato ricer if you have one. If not, mash in the usual way.
- Once you have mashed the potato place it back in the pan over a low heat for 1 minute to dry it out.
- Add the butter and milk and mix gently until these are combined.

Apple and pear batter pudding
+ cinnamon ice cream

This is really a sweet Yorkshire pudding, served as a dessert pudding with apples and pears. It is delicious straight from the oven but does not keep well.

Apple and pear batter pudding

3 firm eating apples, peeled, cored and sliced
2 pears, peeled, cored and sliced
60g caster sugar
3 eggs
125g plain flour
300ml milk
a little caster sugar for serving
vanilla ice cream
ground cinnamon

- Preheat the oven to 200°C/400°F/gas 6.
- Grease an ovenproof gratin dish.
- Place the apples and pears in the dish as evenly as you can.
- Sprinkle the sugar over the fruit and bake for 5 minutes.
- Remove the fruit from the oven and increase the oven temperature to 230°C/450°F/gas 8.
- Separate the whites of the eggs from the yolks.
- Place the yolks in a bowl with the flour and a little of the milk and beat them well to make a smooth batter.
- Add the rest of the milk, stirring as you do so.
- Whisk the egg whites in a clean, grease-free bowl until they form stiff peaks and then fold these into the batter.
- Pour the batter over the apples and pears and bake for 25 minutes.
- Sprinkle the pudding with more caster sugar and serve immediately with the ice cream.

Cinnamon ice cream

- Take a tub of vanilla ice cream from the freezer and, when soft enough, fold in half a teaspoon of ground cinnamon. Return to the freezer until you are ready to serve with the pudding.

Almond chocolate cake

This is more a pie than a cake, along the lines of a pithivier. It is nicest when cold, served in thin slices and goes very well with a cup of coffee in the morning.

Almond chocolate cake

1 pack puff pastry
beaten egg to glaze
For the filling
175g ground almonds
125g caster sugar
60g melted butter
2 egg yolks
2 tablespoons double cream
1 tablespoon brandy
50g dark chocolate, cut into 1.5cm pieces

- Preheat the oven to 220°C/425°F/gas 7.
- Mix all the filling ingredients, except the chocolate, in a small bowl and set aside.
- Divide the pastry into two pieces and roll out two circles, one measuring 25cm in diameter and the other about 26cm in diameter.
- Place the smaller circle on a baking sheet and brush the rim of the pastry with beaten egg.
- Pile the filling onto the circle of pastry spreading it up to the beaten egg.
- Then lay the chocolate pieces on top of the filling mixture.
- Place the slightly bigger circle of pastry on top, pressing down the edges. Trim the edges with a sharp knife to make it a bit more circular if it has lost its shape.
- Brush the top of the pie with some more beaten egg and bake for 20 minutes until the pie has a dark, but not burnt appearance.

Week 1

Shopping list

MEAT

- ☐ 800g minced beef
- ☐ 1.5kg chicken joints (thighs and drumsticks)
- ☐ 1.5kg leg of lamb on the bone

FISH

- ☐ 6 halibut steaks
- ☐ 6 salmon fillets, with skin on

VEGETABLES

- ☐ 4 shallots
- ☐ 3 onions
- ☐ 2.5kg potatoes
- ☐ 1 garlic bulb
- ☐ 2 green chillies
- ☐ 2 avocadoes
- ☐ 3 tomatoes
- ☐ 6 spring onions
- ☐ 2 green peppers
- ☐ 12 cherry tomatoes
- ☐ 1 red onion
- ☐ fresh ginger
- ☐ 18–20 asparagus spears
- ☐ 1 lettuce
- ☐ ½ cucumber
- ☐ 225g courgettes

FRUIT

- ☐ 4 lemons
- ☐ 450g strawberries

FRESH HERBS

- ☐ coriander
- ☐ flat-leaf parsley
- ☐ dill

FRIDGE ITEMS

- ☐ 1 pack of butter
- ☐ 23 eggs
- ☐ 50g Parmesan cheese
- ☐ 250g mascarpone cheese
- ☐ 150ml natural yoghurt
- ☐ 100ml single cream
- ☐ 1 tub of tzatziki
- ☐ 100ml milk
- ☐ 450ml double cream

KITCHEN CUPBOARD ITEMS

- ☐ tomato ketchup
- ☐ Worcestershire sauce
- ☐ salt
- ☐ cornichons
- ☐ olive oil
- ☐ extra virgin olive oil
- ☐ vegetable oil
- ☐ groundnut oil
- ☐ sunflower oil
- ☐ walnut oil
- ☐ balsamic vinegar
- ☐ 500g linguine
- ☐ 2 x 400g tins chopped tomatoes
- ☐ tomato purée
- ☐ dried porcini mushrooms
- ☐ 100g sun-dried tomatoes
- ☐ 1 loaf wholemeal bread
- ☐ 600ml tinned coconut milk
- ☐ 200g red lentils
- ☐ 500g basmati rice
- ☐ 1 tin flageolet beans
- ☐ 250g plain flour
- ☐ 275g self-raising flour
- ☐ baking powder
- ☐ 100g hazelnuts
- ☐ 250g caster sugar

SPICES

- ☐ paprika
- ☐ black pepper
- ☐ turmeric
- ☐ fenugreek seeds
- ☐ curry leaves
- ☐ chilli powder
- ☐ cinnamon sticks
- ☐ ground cumin
- ☐ cardamom pods
- ☐ cloves
- ☐ coriander seeds
- ☐ cumin seeds
- ☐ fennel seeds
- ☐ black mustard seeds
- ☐ dried oregano
- ☐ ground cinnamon

Minced beef steaks with fried eggs + boiled potatoes

This recipe came from a Danish cookbook that I bought for my mother in 1971. It is a very simple, unfussy meal.

Minced beef steaks with fried eggs

800g minced beef
2 shallots, very finely chopped
1 tablespoon tomato ketchup
1 tablespoon Worcestershire sauce
1 teaspoon paprika
2 teaspoons salt
black pepper
a little flour for dusting
50g butter and 1 tablespoon of olive oil for frying
1 onion, sliced for serving
6 eggs
12–18 cornichons

- Preheat the oven to a low temperature to keep the patties warm while the eggs are being fried.
- Place the minced beef, shallots, ketchup, Worcester sauce and paprika in a mixing bowl.
- Season well with the salt and pepper and mix to combine.
- Shape the meat mixture into patties weighing about 150g each.
- Dust each pattie with a little flour.
- Heat the butter and olive oil in a frying pan and when reasonably hot add the patties.
- Brown them for 5 minutes without moving them. Reduce the heat after a minute or two to avoid the meat from over-browning. Don't be tempted to move the patties around the pan too much as they will start to crumble.
- After 5 minutes, flip them over and fry them for 5 minutes on the other side.
- Keep the patties warm in the oven while you fry the eggs and onions.
- Fry the onions first, remove from the pan and then fry the eggs.
- Serve the patties with the eggs, potatoes, cornichons and fried onions.

Boiled potatoes

750g potatoes, peeled and quartered
salt
butter
black pepper

- Place the potatoes in a saucepan of salted water.
- Bring to the boil and reduce the heat to a simmer.
- Simmer the potatoes until tender.
- Serve with a dab of butter and a few grindings of black pepper.

Linguine with tomato sauce

Sometimes a simple, home-made pasta sauce is exactly what is needed at the end of a day. The flavour of this tomato sauce is deepened by the addition of sun-dried tomatoes.

2 tablespoons olive oil
1 onion, peeled and finely diced
1 clove of garlic, peeled and finely chopped
30g dried porcini mushrooms, soaked in warm water
100g sun-dried tomatoes
2 x 400g tins chopped tomatoes
salt and pepper
2 tablespoons mascarpone cheese
500g linguine, cooked according to the packet instructions
Parmesan cheese, grated for serving

- Warm the olive oil in a saucepan on a low heat.
- Gently sauté the onion and garlic for 10 minutes, until soft.
- Drain the porcini mushrooms and then add them to the pan with the sun-dried tomatoes and cook for 10 minutes.
- Add the tinned tomatoes and season with salt and pepper.
- Cook on a gentle simmer, covered, for 45 minutes.
- Blitz with a hand-held blender or in a food processor.
- Stir in the mascarpone cheese.
- Serve with the linguine and freshly grated Parmesan cheese.

Baked halibut + white potato curry + avocado and tomato salad

If you can't get halibut steaks for this recipe, get 1kg of fillet and simply slice it up once it is cooked. Remember to adjust the cooking times accordingly, as there is nothing worse than overcooked fish. Prepare the potatoes first, as you can reheat these once the fish is ready.

Baked halibut

6 halibut steaks
salt and pepper
2 tablespoons olive oil
squeeze of fresh lemon

- Preheat the oven to 200°C/400°F/gas 6.
- Place the halibut steaks or fillets in a large roasting tin.
- Season with salt and pepper and drizzle with olive oil and lemon juice.
- Bake for 15 minutes. If the fillet has skin on it remove it after the fish has cooked, prior to serving.

White potato curry

750g potatoes, peeled and cut into 2cm cubes
½ teaspoon turmeric
¾ teaspoon fenugreek
2 shallots, peeled and finely chopped
1 green chilli, seeds removed and thinly sliced
12 curry leaves
1 teaspoon salt
450ml water
150ml natural yoghurt
squeeze of fresh lemon juice

- Combine the potatoes, turmeric, fenugreek, shallots, green chillies, curry leaves and salt in a medium saucepan.
- Pour on the water and bring to a good simmer.
- Reduce the heat and cook for 15 minutes, until the potatoes are tender.
- Remove from the heat.
- Stir in the yoghurt and lemon juice.

Avocado and tomato salad

2 avocadoes, cut into chunks
3 tomatoes, sliced
For the dressing
2 dessertspoons olive oil
½ dessertspoon balsamic vinegar
1 tablespoon fresh coriander, chopped
salt and pepper

- Place the avocadoes and tomatoes in a serving dish.
- In a small bowl mix together the dressing ingredients and pour over the salad when you are ready to eat.

Spicy scrambled eggs on toast

It is nice on occasion to have a very simple supper to look forward to, which requires almost no effort in the kitchen, but that is, nevertheless, very nutritional. The key to good scrambled eggs is to ensure that you cook them quite slowly and that you don't overcook them.

40g butter
6 spring onions, finely sliced
1 green pepper, diced
12 cherry tomatoes, whole
10–12 eggs
1 loaf wholemeal bread for toast
100ml single cream
½ teaspoon curry powder*
salt and pepper
1 tablespoon chopped parsley

- Heat the butter in a large frying pan or saucepan.
- Add the onions and pepper and sauté on a gentle heat for 2 minutes.
- Add the tomatoes, stir round and sauté for 1 minute.
- Remove the pan from the heat and let the contents cool for a minute or two before you start cracking the eggs into the pan.
- Add one egg at a time stirring it in before you add the next one.
- Once all the eggs have been added, return the pan to a low heat to cook the eggs, stirring constantly.
- Meanwhile, make the toast.
- Add the cream and curry powder to the eggs and season well with salt and pepper.
- Once the eggs start to thicken they will finish off cooking very quickly. Aim for a thick, creamy consistency and take the pan off the heat while the eggs are still slightly runny on top. This will avoid overcooking.
- Sprinkle over the parsley.
- Butter the toast and serve the scrambled eggs on top of the buttered toast immediately.

**** To make your own curry powder:***
1 tablespoon coriander seeds
1 dessertspoon cumin seeds
1 teaspoon fennel seeds
½ teaspoon fenugreek

- *Place the coriander seeds into a small, heavy-bottomed pan and heat through for 30 seconds.*
- *Add the other ingredients and toast until you smell the lovely aroma of the spices.*
- *Transfer the spices to a coffee grinder, a small processor or grind them in a pestle and mortar.*

Maldivian chicken curry + lentil curry + boiled rice

Everyone should know how to cook a curry. Once you have mastered this recipe you can vary the meat to pork, beef or fish. I was brought up on Sri Lankan curries and this is very similar.

Maldivian chicken curry

1 tablespoon vegetable oil
1 red onion, thinly sliced
2 cloves garlic, peeled and finely chopped
10 curry leaves
2½cm fresh ginger, finely chopped
1 green chilli, finely chopped
½ teaspoon chilli powder
4 heaped dessertspoons curry powder*
½ teaspoon turmeric
1 teaspoon ground cumin
10 cardamom pods
5 cloves
3 x 3cm pieces cinnamon stick
2 level dessertspoons tomato purée
400ml tin coconut milk
1.5kg chicken joints (thighs and drumsticks), skin removed
salt
water

- Heat the oil in a large saucepan.
- Add the onion and sauté for 2–3 minutes on a medium heat.
- Sprinkle in the chopped garlic, curry leaves and ginger and cook for 1 minute, stirring.
- Next, add the chopped chilli, chilli powder, curry powder, turmeric, cumin, cardamom, cloves and cinnamon stick and stir constantly until the mixture is incorporated with the onions and looks dry.
- Stir in the tomato purée and cook for 1 minute.
- Add half the coconut milk so the mixture forms a thick paste.
- Then add the chicken pieces, stirring well to coat them with the spice paste.
- Pour in the rest of the coconut milk and a heaped teaspoon of salt.
- Next, add enough water to make sure the chicken is just covered with liquid.
- Bring to the boil and then simmer, covered, for 40 minutes.

To make your own curry powder:
1 tablespoon coriander seeds
1 dessertspoon cumin seeds
1 teaspoon fennel seeds
½ teaspoon fenugreek

- *Place the coriander seeds into a small, heavy-bottomed pan and heat through for 30 seconds.*
- *Add the other ingredients and toast until you smell the lovely aroma of the spices.*
- *Transfer the spices to a coffee grinder, a small processor or grind them in a pestle and mortar.*

Lentil curry

1 tablespoon vegetable oil
1 medium onion, finely diced
6 curry leaves
½ teaspoon cumin seeds
½ teaspoon turmeric
½ teaspoon black mustard seeds
200g red lentils
600ml water
200ml coconut milk
1 teaspoon salt

- Heat the vegetable oil in a medium saucepan.
- Add the onion, curry leaves, cumin seeds, turmeric and black mustard seeds and cook until the onion starts to turn a golden brown. This should take 5 minutes.
- Add the lentils and water and bring to a simmer.

- Reduce the heat to the slightest simmer and cook uncovered for 40 minutes.
- Try the lentils and if there is still the slightest hardness to them, cook for a few minutes longer.
- Add the coconut milk, stir and bring to a simmer again.
- Then add the salt and set aside. Reheat it when you are ready to serve.

Boiled rice

500g basmati rice
750ml water
salt

- Put the rice in a saucepan with the water and a pinch of salt.
- Place on a high heat and as soon as it comes to the boil, cover the saucepan with a lid and turn the heat right down to very low. Leave it for 15 minutes, giving it one stir only during the cooking time.
- Take the pan off the heat and leave it covered for a further 10 minutes, before removing the lid.

Salmon fillets with dill and lemon mayonnaise + asparagus

If you can't stretch to asparagus or your children won't eat it, a nice alternative is to cook some tagliatelle and peas and serve the salmon on a bed of pasta and peas.

Salmon fillets with dill and lemon mayonnaise

For the mayonnaise

2 egg yolks
juice ½ lemon
2 tablespoons water
120ml groundnut oil
3 tablespoons olive oil
salt and pepper
1 dessertspoon fresh dill, chopped

For the salmon fillets

olive oil
6 salmon fillets, with skin
salt and pepper

To make the mayonnaise

- In a small glass bowl mix the eggs with the lemon juice and water.
- Place the glass bowl over a saucepan of simmering water, making sure that the bowl does not touch the water.
- Whisk the egg yolks continuously, checking that the water keeps to a gentle simmer. The egg will become frothy and then gradually will thicken to the consistency of single cream. Remove the bowl from the heat at this stage.
- Measure the groundnut oil in a measuring jug with the olive oil.
- Place the oils in the microwave for 30 seconds on full power.
- Gradually drizzle the warm oils onto the egg mixture, stirring all the time, until you have quite a thick mayonnaise.
- Add 2 tablespoons of water to loosen the mayonnaise slightly.
- Then season with salt, pepper and dill.

To cook the salmon

- Rub some olive oil on the skin side of each salmon portion and then heat a heavy frying pan.
- Once the pan is hot, add the salmon portions skin side down. Cook two fillets at a time and once they are in the pan refrain from moving them for 4 minutes.
- Turn the fillets over and cook for a further 3 minutes.
- Season and serve with the mayonnaise and asparagus.

Asparagus

18–20 asparagus spears
salt and pepper

- To prepare the asparagus, hold the end of the stalk between your left thumb and index finger. Take the tip of the spear in your right thumb and index finger and bend down. The tip will snap where the stem is becoming woody and tough, so discard the thicker end piece.
- Bring a pan of salted water to the boil.
- Cook the asparagus for 3 minutes.
- Drain well and serve with black pepper.

Leg of lamb with oregano, potatoes and flageolet beans + green salad

This lamb is cooked in the Greek style. One has to take a leap of faith to a certain extent with it as, to all intents and purposes, it is overcooked. I would normally eat pink lamb, but this makes a nice change. I have used the potatoes and beans as they add a bit of moisture to what would otherwise be a slightly dry meal. The oregano and lemon partner the lamb perfectly.

Leg of lamb with oregano, potatoes and flageolet beans

1.5kg leg of lamb on the bone
1 lemon, halved
salt and pepper
a good sprinkling of dried oregano
a knob of butter
2 tablespoons of olive oil
1kg of potatoes, peeled and cut into 2cm chunks
1 tin flageolet beans, drained
salt and pepper
1 tub of tzatziki

- Preheat the oven to 220°C/425°F/gas 7.
- Place the lamb in a meat tin.
- Rub the lamb with the halves of lemon.
- Season the lamb with salt and pepper and sprinkle with the oregano.
- Spread the butter over the lamb.
- Pour 250ml of water into the meat tin.
- Drizzle the olive oil over the lamb and then place it in the oven for 30 minutes.
- Remove the lamb from the oven and place the potatoes and flageolet beans around it, seasoning them with a little salt.
- Reduce the oven temperature to 180°C/350°F/gas 4.
- Then cover the tin with tin foil and return to the oven for 2 hours.
- Remove the foil and cook for a further 30 minutes.
- Remove from the oven and leave to rest for 10 minutes.
- Carve and serve with the potatoes and beans, some tzatziki on the side and the green salad.

Green salad

1 lettuce, washed
½ cucumber, sliced
1 green pepper, finely diced
For the dressing
2 tablespoons extra virgin olive oil
½ tablespoon balsamic vinegar
salt and pepper

- Combine the salad in a serving bowl.
- Combine the dressing ingredients and drizzle over the salad when ready to serve.

Strawberry shortcake

This is a light American dessert, great for early summer. Don't be confused by the name; shortcake is not like shortbread. It looks and tastes more like a scone.

225g plain flour
1 teaspoon baking powder
1 tablespoon caster sugar
salt
100g butter
100ml milk
50ml double cream
450g strawberries
400ml double cream, whipped until thick

- Preheat the oven to 200°C/400°F/gas 6.
- Grease and line two 23cm flan tins.
- Put the flour, baking powder, sugar, a pinch of salt and the butter into the bowl of a food processor and process until you have a breadcrumb-like consistency.
- Add the milk and cream and mix until a dough starts to form.
- Turn out onto a floured surface and knead very gently until you have a ball of dough.
- Divide into 2 pieces and roll out a circle of dough to place in the bottom of each flan tin.
- Bake the shortcake for 15 minutes.
- Cool and then turn out.
- Sandwich the two pieces together with the fruit and cream, retaining some of each for the top of the shortcake.

Courgette and roasted hazelnut cake

This cake is great at this time of year. It must have originated from Italy where, during the summer, the shops are full of hazelnuts and courgettes. It's a good moist cake that is simple to make.

100g hazelnuts
225g caster sugar
3 eggs
190ml sunflower oil
35ml walnut oil
225g courgettes, grated and patted dry with kitchen roll
275g self-raising flour
salt
1 teaspoon ground cinnamon

- Preheat the oven to 200°C/400°F/gas 6.
- Grease a 23cm springform tin.
- Lay the hazelnuts on a baking sheet and roast them in the oven for 8 minutes.
- Tip the hazelnuts onto a chopping board and allow them to cool.
- Reduce the oven temperature to 180°C/350°F/gas 4.
- Place the sugar, eggs and oils into a mixing bowl and give them a thorough whisk for at least 2 minutes.
- Add the courgettes to the egg and oil and mix to combine well.
- Then sift the flour, a pinch of salt and the cinnamon into the mixture and gently fold them in.
- Next, chop the hazelnuts roughly, tip them into the mixing bowl and fold in.
- Spoon the mixture into the cake tin and bake for 50 minutes until a skewer inserted into the middle of the cake comes out clean.
- Leave to cool before turning out.

JUNE

Week 2

Monday p302	Dijon chicken + roasted new potatoes + warm tomato salad
Tuesday p303	Souffléed omelettes + sautéed potatoes + tomato salad
Wednesday p304	Lamb kebabs + chickpea pullao + yoghurt and mint dressing
Thursday p306	Grilled goat's cheese and asparagus salad
Friday p307	Chef's salad
Saturday p308	Pea and broad bean risotto
Sunday p309	Slow-roasted duck with fennel and roast potatoes
Sunday pudding p310	Orange and lemon spiced tart
Extra tasty treat p311	Cinnamon buns with almond filling

Shopping list

MEAT

- ☐ 1kg chicken thighs on the bone
- ☐ 900g boneless lamb shoulder
- ☐ 2 chicken breasts
- ☐ 3kg duck

VEGETABLES

- ☐ 16 tomatoes
- ☐ 2 plum tomatoes
- ☐ 1.5kg new potatoes
- ☐ 1kg potatoes
- ☐ 1 garlic bulb
- ☐ fresh ginger
- ☐ 1 onion
- ☐ 100g rocket leaves
- ☐ 6 asparagus spears
- ☐ 300g fresh salad leaves
- ☐ 1 Romaine lettuce
- ☐ 50g watercress
- ☐ 1 cucumber
- ☐ 1 red pepper
- ☐ 1 green pepper
- ☐ 2 shallots
- ☐ 500g broad beans
- ☐ 500g garden peas
- ☐ 1 fennel bulb

FRUIT

- ☐ 3 lemons
- ☐ 2 eating apples
- ☐ 1 orange

FRESH HERBS

- ☐ thyme
- ☐ bay leaves
- ☐ chives
- ☐ 2 packs mint
- ☐ flat-leaf parsley

FRIDGE ITEMS

- ☐ 3 packs of butter
- ☐ 23 eggs
- ☐ 335ml double cream
- ☐ 250ml milk
- ☐ 380g Gruyère cheese
- ☐ 100g Taleggio cheese
- ☐ 250g goat's cheese
- ☐ 250g ricotta cheese
- ☐ 200g Parmesan cheese
- ☐ 300ml natural yoghurt
- ☐ 70g sliced pancetta
- ☐ 140g chopped pancetta
- ☐ 80g sliced prosciutto
- ☐ 70g salami
- ☐ 90g cooked ham
- ☐ 1.5 litres chicken stock
- ☐ 75ml orange juice

KITCHEN CUPBOARD ITEMS

- ☐ 150ml white wine
- ☐ Dijon mustard
- ☐ 1 loaf white bread for breadcrumbs
- ☐ olive oil
- ☐ extra virgin olive oil
- ☐ balsamic vinegar
- ☐ red wine vinegar
- ☐ vegetable oil
- ☐ 6 sun-dried tomatoes
- ☐ 400g basmati rice
- ☐ 1 tin chickpeas
- ☐ 1 French baguette
- ☐ salt
- ☐ 25g raisins
- ☐ tinned artichoke hearts
- ☐ 1 tin pitted black olives
- ☐ 400g risotto rice
- ☐ 75g icing sugar
- ☐ 225g plain flour
- ☐ 650g strong white bread flour
- ☐ 370g caster sugar
- ☐ fast-action dried yeast
- ☐ 100g ground almonds
- ☐ granulated sugar

SPICES

- ☐ black pepper
- ☐ dried oregano
- ☐ ground coriander
- ☐ cinnamon sticks
- ☐ cloves
- ☐ cardamom pods
- ☐ coriander seeds
- ☐ cumin seeds
- ☐ cayenne pepper
- ☐ turmeric
- ☐ ground ginger
- ☐ ground cinnamon

Dijon chicken + roasted new potatoes + warm tomato salad

This chicken dish is French in style, hence the name 'Dijon Chicken'. It's a cinch to make and you can prepare it beforehand right up to the grilling stage, which is a real bonus with any dish.

Dijon chicken

70g butter
1kg chicken thighs on the bone, skin removed
2 sprigs fresh thyme
2 bay leaves
salt and pepper
150ml white wine
200ml double cream
100g Gruyère cheese, grated
1 tablespoon Dijon mustard
1 tablespoon white breadcrumbs

- Heat 40g of the butter in a large saucepan.
- Add half the chicken pieces with the thyme and bay leaves.
- Season well with salt and pepper and brown the chicken thoroughly all over.
- Remove the chicken, set aside and brown the rest of the chicken pieces.
- Return all the chicken to the pan, cover and cook on a medium heat for 20 minutes, moving the chicken pieces around during this time.
- Next, remove the chicken from the pan and place it in an ovenproof serving dish.
- Place the saucepan on a high heat and add the wine and the rest of the butter.
- Simmer for 3 minutes.
- Add the cream and cook for 1 minute.
- Remove from the heat and add the cheese (retaining a small amount for sprinkling over the top of the chicken at the end) and mustard.
- Pour the sauce over the chicken.
- Sprinkle with the remaining cheese and breadcrumbs and place under a hot grill to brown.

Roasted new potatoes

1kg new potatoes, washed and halved
salt
2 tablespoons olive oil

- Preheat the oven to 220°C/425°F/gas 7.
- Boil the potatoes in salted water for 5 minutes.
- Drain and place them in a roasting tin.
- Drizzle with olive oil and season with pepper.
- Roast the potatoes for 40 minutes.

Warm tomato salad

5 medium tomatoes, sliced
1 tablespoon olive oil
½ teaspoon dried oregano
salt and pepper

- Preheat the oven to 150°C/300°F/gas 2.
- Place the tomatoes on a baking sheet and drizzle with olive oil.
- Season with oregano, salt and pepper.
- Place in the oven to warm for 10 minutes.

Souffléed omelettes
+ sautéed potatoes + tomato salad

This is an omelette with a difference. Prepare the potatoes and tomatoes first, then get the eggs ready for cooking. You will have to cook the eggs in two batches, so preheat the oven to keep one batch warm while you prepare the other. With a large family there is no way round this, but don't be put off. I find preparing omelettes quite relaxing. You will need a frying pan with a lid for these omelettes. If you don't have one, cover the pan with a plate.

Souffléed omelettes

10–12 eggs, depending on the appetite of your family
100g Taleggio cheese, cut into 1cm cubes
6 tablespoons Parmesan cheese, grated
2 tablespoons chives, snipped finely
salt and pepper
2 x 20g portions of butter

- Preheat the oven to 110C/225F/gas ¼.
- In a bowl mix the eggs with the cheeses and chives and season well with salt and pepper.
- Heat one portion of the butter in a frying pan.
- Once the butter starts to foam add half the egg mixture and cook for 1 minute, while the base of the omelette sets.
- Place a lid or plate over the pan and turn the heat down to very low for 10 minutes.
- The omelette will puff up beautifully when it is ready and should be served immediately if possible. If you have to cook the second one straightaway, place the first one in the preheated oven to keep warm. Alternatively, you could all tuck into the first omelette and then sit around the table while the second one is cooking.

Sautéed potatoes

800g potatoes, peeled and quartered
salt
2 tablespoons olive oil
pepper

- Boil the potatoes in salted water for 12–15 minutes until tender.
- Drain them well.
- Heat the olive oil in a sauté pan and when it is reasonably hot, add the potatoes.
- Brown them all over in the oil. This is made easier if you don't move them around too much, and once they are browned all over turn the heat down to medium.
- Sprinkle on some extra salt and pepper just before serving.

Tomato salad

6 tomatoes, sliced
2 tablespoons extra virgin olive oil
¼ tablespoon balsamic vinegar
salt and pepper

- Lay the tomatoes on a serving plate.
- Dress with the oil, vinegar, salt and pepper.

Lamb kebabs + chickpea pullao + yoghurt and mint dressing

Skewered lamb shoulder cooks really well under a hot grill. The rice is very simple despite the list of ingredients.

Lamb kebabs

4 tablespoons natural yoghurt
2 cloves garlic, peeled and crushed
1 teaspoon ground coriander
juice ½ lemon
1 tablespoon vegetable oil
1 teaspoon salt
good grinding of black pepper
¼ teaspoon cayenne
900g boneless lamb shoulder, diced into 2cm dice

- In a large bowl mix together the yoghurt, garlic, coriander, lemon juice, oil, salt, pepper and cayenne.
- Add the lamb and coat it all over with the yoghurt mixture.
- Place in the fridge for 1 hour.
- Preheat the grill.
- Thread the lamb pieces onto wooden skewers.
- Cook the kebabs under the grill until the lamb is brown all over.

Chickpea pullao

3 tablespoons vegetable oil
1 x 2cm piece cinnamon stick
2 cloves
2 cardamom pods
2 bay leaves
3 cloves garlic, peeled and crushed
1 tablespoon fresh ginger, finely chopped
1 onion, finely sliced
1 tin chickpeas, drained
2 teaspoons coriander seeds, ground
1 teaspoon cumin seeds, ground
¼ teaspoon cayenne pepper
black pepper
2 large tomatoes, roughly chopped
¼ teaspoon turmeric
1½ teaspoons salt
400ml water
400g basmati rice

- Preheat the oven to 160°C/320°F/gas 2½.
- Heat the oil in an ovenproof pot or casserole dish with a tight-fitting lid.
- Throw in the cinnamon stick, cloves, cardamom and bay leaves and stir for a few seconds.
- Next, add the garlic and ginger and stir-fry for 2 minutes.
- Then add the onions and fry for 5 minutes on a medium heat.
- Stir in the chickpeas, then the coriander, cumin, cayenne and black pepper and stir fry for 30 seconds or so.
- Add the tomatoes, turmeric, salt and water and bring to a simmer.
- Add the rice and bring back to a simmer.
- Cover the pot with a piece of greaseproof paper and place the lid on top.
- Bake for 45 minutes in the oven, removing the lid once during the cooking time to give the rice a stir.
- Serve with the hot lamb kebabs and yoghurt mint dressing.

Yoghurt and mint dressing

4 tablespoons natural yoghurt
sprig of fresh mint, finely chopped
salt and pepper

- Mix the yoghurt with the mint and season with a little salt and pepper.

Grilled goat's cheese and asparagus salad

Asparagus is expensive, but this recipe uses only a small amount and it goes so well with the grilled goat's cheese.

200g salad leaves
1 tablespoon flat-leaf parsley, chopped
5 fresh mint leaves, chopped
100g rocket leaves
6 sun-dried tomatoes, chopped
2 fresh plum tomatoes, sliced
1 tablespoon raisins
6 asparagus spears, cooked until tender
70g sliced pancetta
½ French baguette
250g goat's cheese, sliced into 1cm thick slices

For the dressing
1 clove garlic, peeled and fnely chopped
3 tablespoons extra virgin olive oil
1 tablespoon red wine vinegar
1 teaspoon Dijon mustard
salt and pepper

- Preheat the grill.
- Place the salad leaves, herbs, rocket, both kinds of tomato, raisins and asparagus in a serving bowl.
- Fry the pancetta in a frying pan, until it is golden brown.
- Cut the pancetta into smallish pieces and sprinkle these into the serving bowl with the other salad ingredients.
- Slice the French bread into 1cm thick slices, widthways.
- Toast the slices of bread on one side only and then place a slice of goat's cheese on the untoasted side of each slice of bread.
- Place the bread and cheese under the grill until the cheese starts to melt.
- Mix the dressing ingredients together in a small bowl.
- Pour the dressing over the salad and then place the pieces of goat's cheese on toast on top of the salad and serve.

Chef's salad

Chef's salad originated in America and traditionally contained hard-boiled eggs and cooked meat, such as turkey. Since the evolution of salad in recent times into a dish that is so much more than leaves, cucumber and tomato, the Chef's salad has disappeared from menus to a large extent, which is a shame as it makes a great meal.

100g fresh salad leaves
1 Romaine lettuce, torn into strips
50g watercress
1 cucumber, sliced into semicircles
3 tomatoes, cut into 6 pieces
½ red pepper, cut into julienne strips
½ green pepper, cut into julienne strips
3 or 4 tinned artichoke hearts, halved
200g Gruyère cheese, cut into julienne strips
80g sliced prosciutto, cut into strips
70g salami, cut into strips
2 chicken breasts, cooked and cut into strips
90g cooked ham, cut into strips
3 hard-boiled eggs, chopped into chunks
15 pitted black olives

The dressing

1 tablespoon Dijon mustard
2 tablespoons red wine vinegar
6 tablespoons extra virgin olive oil
½ teaspoon sugar
generous amount of salt and pepper

- Arrange all the salad ingredients in an attractive fashion on a large serving plate.
- Mix the dressing in a small bowl and pour over the salad when you are ready to eat.
- Serve with bread.

Pea and broad bean risotto

Peas and broad beans are in season and this is the perfect risotto for this time of year, fresh and light.

1.5 litres fresh or homemade chicken stock
500g broad beans, podded
500g garden peas, podded (use frozen if you can't get fresh peas)
salt and pepper
50g butter
2 tablespoons olive oil
2 shallots, peeled and finely chopped
140g pancetta, chopped
400g risotto rice
100g Parmesan cheese, freshly grated
2 tablespoons ricotta cheese
2 tablespoons fresh mint, chopped

- Heat the chicken stock in a large saucepan.
- When it reaches a good simmer add the broad beans and cook them for 2–4 minutes, depending on the size of the beans.
- Remove the beans with a slotted spoon and set aside in a bowl.
- Now add the peas to the simmering stock and cook them for 4 minutes. Remove with a slotted spoon and place with the beans.
- Season the stock with salt and pepper and keep it simmering constantly.
- Heat the butter with the olive oil in another large saucepan.
- Add the shallots and pancetta and fry gently for 1 minute on a low heat.
- Then add the rice and stir gently, coating all the grains in olive oil and butter.
- Start adding the stock a ladle or two at a time. The rice will gradually absorb the stock, but keep the rice quite wet between each addition.
- Keep this up until the rice is cooked but still has a slight bite to it.
- Remove from the heat.
- Fold in the beans, peas, Parmesan cheese, ricotta and mint.
- Check the seasoning and adjust if necessary.
- Serve immediately.

Slow-roasted duck with fennel and roast potatoes

I used to panic at the idea of cooking duck, but if you buy a free-range bird and drain off the fat during the cooking process, you are pretty much guaranteed a meal to remember. This duck dish is very straightforward as you can just put everything into the same roasting tin.

3kg duck, giblets removed
salt and pepper
1 orange, cut into quarters
500g potatoes, peeled and quartered
2 eating apples, peeled, cored and quartered
1 fennel bulb, cut into 2cm chunks

- Preheat the oven to 180°C/350°F/gas 4.
- Place the duck on a wire rack in a roasting tin.
- Score the duck on the top with a sharp knife.
- Season very generously with salt and pepper.
- Place the orange into the duck cavity.
- Roast the duck for 60 minutes.
- Meanwhile, parboil the potatoes in salted boiling water for 5 minutes.
- Drain them well and set aside.
- Reduce the oven temperature to 150°C/300°F/gas 2.
- Take the duck out of the oven.
- Spoon off the fat at the bottom of the roasting tin. You can store this in the fridge and use it for roasting potatoes another time.
- Return the duck to the oven and roast for a further 30 minutes.
- Remove the duck from the oven and spoon off the fat at the bottom of the roasting tin.
- Place the potatoes, apple and fennel around the duck and return to the oven for 1 hour.
- Serve straight from the roasting tin and by the end of the meal everyone will be tucking in with their fingers.

Orange and lemon spiced tart

This is a citrus tart with a hint of ginger and cinnamon, which makes a nice change from the more traditional lemon tart.

For the pastry
180g butter
75g icing sugar
2 egg yolks
225g plain flour
For the filling
5 eggs
170g caster sugar
juice 2 lemons
75ml orange juice
1 teaspoon ground ginger
¼ teaspoon ground cinnamon
135ml double cream

- Grease a 24cm tart tin.
- Preheat the oven to 200°C/400°F/gas 6.

To make the pastry

- Place the butter, icing sugar, egg yolks and flour together in a food processor and mix until the ingredients are just beginning to combine.
- Turn out onto a floured surface and form into a ball.
- Wrap in cling-film and chill in the fridge for 30 minutes.
- When ready, roll out the pastry and line the tart tin with it.
- Bake the pastry case blind by lining it with greaseproof paper and baking beans (see p.238)
- Place in the oven for 15 minutes.
- Remove the greaseproof paper and set aside while you prepare the filling.
- Reduce the oven temperature to 170°C/325°F/gas 3.

For the filling

- Mix the eggs and sugar in a mixing bowl.
- Add the lemon juice, orange juice and spices and stir to combine.
- Finally, stir in the double cream.
- Pour the filling into the pastry case and place on a baking sheet.
- Bake for 30 minutes. When ready, the tart filling should still have a slight wobble to it.
- Serve with cream.

Cinnamon buns with almond filling

This recipe makes about 30 buns, which sounds rather a lot, but my children munch their way through them quickly. You can freeze any that are left over.

For the buns

250ml milk, warmed
1 sachet fast-action dried yeast
100g caster sugar
1 egg
1 teaspoon ground cinnamon
1 teaspoon salt
125g butter, melted
650g strong white bread flour

For the filling

100g caster sugar
100g ground almonds
160g butter, softened

To make the buns

- Pour the milk into a large mixing bowl.
- Add the yeast and sugar and stir.
- Leave for 3 minutes.
- Add the egg, cinnamon, salt and melted butter and stir to combine.
- Then add the flour and combine to a soft dough.
- Turn onto a floured surface and knead for 5–10 minutes until you have a silky, soft dough.
- Place in the bowl, cover with a clean cloth and leave for 2 hours to rise.

To make the filling

- Place the ingredients in a small bowl and mix to a smooth paste using a wooden spoon.

To get the buns ready for the oven

- Preheat the oven to 180°C/350°F/gas 4.
- Divide the dough into 4 equal pieces.
- Roll each piece into a 5mm thick rectangle. Don't worry too much about straight edges; you just need a rectangle that can be rolled into a long sausage shape.
- Spread each rectangle with a quarter of the filling.
- Roll each one up into a long sausage shape.
- Cut each sausage into 3cm thick pieces, laying each one on a greased baking tray, cut side up.
- Brush each bun with some beaten egg and sprinkle with caster sugar.
- Leave to rise for a further 30 minutes.
- Then bake for 20 minutes until golden brown.

Week 3

Monday p314	Chicken and tomatoes + rice
Tuesday p315	Prawn risotto
Wednesday p316	Roast chicken, pancetta and haloumi salad
Thursday p317	Pea, ricotta and herb tart + summer salad
Friday p318	Salmon salade Niçoise
Saturday p320	Fried lamb chops + peas and broad beans à la Française + roasted rosemary potatoes
Sunday p321	Turkey breasts with ham and cheese + sautéed potatoes + buttered broad beans
Sunday pudding p322	Lemon posset + baked summer fruits
Extra tasty treat p323	Seed cake

Shopping list

MEAT

- 1kg chicken pieces on the bone (drumsticks and thighs)
- 1 x 2.5kg chicken
- 8–10 lamb chops
- 6 turkey breasts

FISH

- 300g cooked prawns
- 400g salmon fillet

VEGETABLES

- 1 green pepper
- 1 bunch celery
- 2 onions
- 100g watercress
- 1 shallot
- 500g fresh salad leaves
- 250g French beans
- 325g new potatoes
- 4 plum tomatoes
- 4 tomatoes
- 1 cucumber
- 22 radishes
- 2 lettuces
- 350g fresh peas
- 500g broad beans
- 8 spring onions
- 1.7kg potatoes
- 100g button mushrooms

FRUIT

- 4 lemons
- 50g raspberries
- 50g blackberries
- 50g blueberries

FRESH HERBS

- flat-leaf parsley
- basil
- chives
- chervil
- thyme
- rosemary

FRIDGE ITEMS

- 100g haloumi cheese
- 225g ricotta cheese
- 250g mascarpone cheese
- 200ml milk
- 300g frozen peas
- 140g chopped pancetta
- 200g crème fraîche
- 1.7 litres chicken stock
- 3 slices cooked ham
- 200g Parmesan cheese
- 425ml double cream
- 150ml whipping cream
- 14 eggs
- 2 packs butter

KITCHEN CUPBOARD ITEMS

- 125g black olives
- tomato purée
- 400g tin plum tomatoes
- 500g basmati rice
- 450g Arborio rice
- 400ml dry white wine
- 1 tin chickpeas
- red wine vinegar
- extra virgin olive oil
- olive oil
- Dijon mustard
- fast-action dried yeast
- 400g caster sugar
- 225g plain flour
- 200g strong white bread flour
- brandy
- 100ml Amaretto liqueur
- salt

SPICES

- coriander seeds
- black pepper
- paprika
- whole nutmeg
- caraway seeds

Chicken and tomatoes + rice

This dish has a Spanish theme full of brazen flavours, which means you don't have to pay too much attention to it's composition, which is great for a Monday evening.

Chicken and tomatoes

2 tablespoons olive oil
1kg chicken pieces on the bone, skin removed (drumsticks and thighs)
1 onion, finely chopped
1 tablespoon coriander seeds, ground in a pestle and mortar
150ml dry white wine
400g tin plum tomatoes
200ml water
1 sprig thyme
1 green pepper, cored and finely chopped
1 dessertspoon tomato purée
100g black olives
salt and pepper

- Heat the olive oil in a large, heavy-bottomed saucepan.
- Brown the chicken pieces all over, a few at a time, setting them aside once they are done.
- Keep the saucepan on a low heat, add the onion and sauté it for 10 minutes until soft.
- Sprinkle on the ground coriander.
- Return the chicken to the pan.
- Increase the heat to high and pour on the wine.
- Boil rapidly for 1 minute.
- Add the tomatoes, water, thyme, green pepper, tomato purée and black olives and bring back to a simmer.
- Season with salt and pepper.
- Reduce the heat, cover and simmer on the hob for 40 minutes.

Rice

500g basmati rice
750ml water
salt

- Put the rice in a saucepan with the water and a pinch of salt.
- Place it on a high heat and as soon as it comes to the boil, cover the saucepan with a lid and turn the heat right down to very low. Leave it for 15 minutes, giving it one stir only during the cooking time.
- Take it off the heat and leave it covered for a further 10 minutes before removing the lid.

Prawn risotto

It was learning to make a risotto that first stirred my interest in cooking. A risotto doesn't cook itself; it relies upon your efforts to ensure that it is a success. I think risottos cause problems for some people in the kitchen because no exact cooking time can be given. Your taste and sight let you know when the rice is ready.

1.5 litres chicken or vegetable stock, well seasoned
salt and pepper
50g butter
1 tablespoon olive oil
1 stick celery, finely chopped
1 onion, finely diced
450g Arborio rice
250ml dry white wine
300g cooked prawns
2 tablespoons mascarpone cheese
3 tablespoons flat-leaf parsley, chopped
optional Parmesan cheese for serving

- Heat the stock in a large saucepan and season it with salt and pepper.
- Gently heat the butter and olive oil in another large pan.
- Add the celery and onion to the butter and oil and sauté for 3–5 minutes until soft.
- Then add the rice and stir round making sure it is coated it in the butter and olive oil.
- Add the wine a little at a time, ensuring that each addition is absorbed before adding the next.
- Now start to add the hot stock a ladle or two at a time, allowing the rice to absorb it, but don't let the rice get too dry between each addition.
- When the rice is done add the prawns and let them warm through.
- Stir in the mascarpone cheese and chopped parsley and check the seasoning.
- Serve immediately.
- Italians wouldn't serve Parmesan cheese with a seafood risotto. This is a matter or choice.

Roast chicken, pancetta and haloumi salad

A chicken salad sounds rather 1970s but this salad is a wonderful concoction of fresh flavours, perfect for an early summer's evening meal. When I make this dish, I buy a beautiful French-style poulet d'or, which tends to acquire a more golden colour when roasted.

1 x 2.5kg chicken
olive oil
salt and pepper
300g fresh salad leaves
100g watercress
1 tin chickpeas, drained
½ cucumber, thinly sliced
100g haloumi cheese, thinly sliced
70g pancetta, chopped into small pieces
For the dressing
1 shallot, finely chopped
1 tablespoon crème fraîche
150ml whipping cream
1 teaspoon Dijon mustard
salt and pepper

- Preheat the oven to 200°C/400°F/gas 6.
- Place the chicken in a roasting tin.
- Drizzle the bird with olive oil, season with salt and pepper and roast for 1 hour 30 minutes.

To make the dressing

- Place the shallot in a small bowl.
- Spoon the crème fraîche into the bowl and pour on the cream.
- Stir in the mustard and season with a little salt and pepper.

To prepare the salad

- Place the salad leaves and watercress in a serving bowl with the chickpeas and cucumber.
- When the chicken is cooked and has rested for 20 minutes, carve as much of it as you want, cutting it into reasonably small pieces. Arrange these pieces on top of the salad already assembled in the serving dish.
- Fry the haloumi slices and pancetta in a frying pan in a little olive oil until the haloumi turns a rich golden brown.
- Tip the cheese and pancetta over the top of the salad, pour on the dressing and serve.

Pea, ricotta and herb tart
+ summer salad

This tart is a wonderful, light, summery dish that banishes memories of cold winter evenings. By this time in June if we are lucky, the weather is warmer, and people do not feel like eating the heavy, meaty comfort food they so often crave in the winter. This tart also makes use of the fresh garden peas that are available this time of year. If you can't get hold of them, however, use frozen peas.

For the pastry

200g strong white bread flour
salt
½ packet fast-action dried yeast
1 egg
3 tablespoons olive oil

For the filling

225g ricotta
2 eggs
200ml milk
4 tablespoons Parmesan cheese, grated
4 spring onions, thinly sliced
3 tablespoons chopped mixed herbs such as chives, chervil, thyme and parsley
salt and pepper
350g fresh peas, cooked

To make the pastry

- Mix the flour with a pinch of salt and stir in the yeast.
- Make a well in the centre and break in the egg.
- Add the oil and gradually work it and the egg into the flour.
- Then add enough water to form a soft dough.
- Turn the dough out onto a floured surface and knead for 5 minutes until smooth and elastic. Cover the bowl and leave to rise for 1 hour.

To make the filling

- Grease a 25cm tart tin.
- In a bowl beat the ricotta with the eggs and gradually mix in the milk.
- Stir in 3 tablespoons of Parmesan and add the spring onions, herbs, salt and pepper.
- Place a baking sheet in the oven and heat the oven to 190°C/375°F/gas 5.
- Punch down the prepared dough and knead again briefly.
- Line the tart tin with the dough. The rim of the tart case should be slightly thicker than the rest so that it rises above the edge of the tin as it cooks.
- Now scatter the cooked peas over the dough and pour the ricotta mixture on top.
- Sprinkle the remaining tablespoon of Parmesan cheese over the top.
- Place the tart on top of the hot baking sheet in the oven and cook for 30 minutes. The tart edges and top will be golden brown but there will still be a wobble to the ricotta filling.
- Serve hot or cold.

Summer salad

1 lettuce
4 tomatoes, sliced
½ cucumber, sliced
12 radishes, trimmed and halved

For the dressing

3 dessertspoons extra virgin olive oil
1 dessertspoon red wine vinegar
salt and pepper

- Mix the dressing in a small bowl.
- Place the salad in a serving dish and pour the dressing over when ready to serve.

Salmon salade Niçoise

This dish is a twist on the usual tuna Niçoise, using the fresh new flavours of early summer. Make the dressing first.

250g French beans, cooked
325g new potatoes, cooked until tender
200g fresh salad leaves
4 plum tomatoes, quartered (if you can't get plums use an alternative)
10 radishes, sliced
6 'just hard' boiled eggs, quartered
25 black olives
1 tablespoon fresh basil leaves, torn
400g salmon fillet, cut into 2cm wide strips
flour for dusting
salt and pepper
olive oil

For the dressing

1½ tablespoons of red wine vinegar
6 tablespoons extra virgin olive oil
1 teaspoon Dijon mustard
2 teaspoons fresh basil, shredded
salt and pepper

To make the dressing

- Combine the dressing ingredients in a small bowl.

To make the salad

- While the beans and potatoes are still warm, coat them in a little of the dressing and set aside.
- Arrange the salad leaves in a large serving bowl, along with the tomatoes, radishes and eggs.
- Add the beans and potatoes and the rest of the dressing.
- Toss everything to combine.
- Garnish with the olives and basil.
- Dust the salmon fillets with a little flour and season with salt and pepper.
- Brush the fillets with a little olive oil.
- Heat a large, heavy-bottomed frying pan until hot.
- Put the salmon fillets in the pan and fry them for 1 minute on each side.
- Place the cooked salmon fillets on top of the rest of the salad and serve with bread.

Fried lamb chops + peas and broad beans à la Française + roasted rosemary potatoes

Peas à la Française are delicious and even tastier with the addition of seasonal broad beans. They go very well with the lamb chops. Prepare the potatoes first.

Fried lamb chops

8–10 lamb chops
salt and pepper

- Heat a large, heavy frying pan until hot. You will not need any oil.
- Season the lamb chops with salt and pepper and fry them for 4 minutes on each side.
- Add a little more seasoning and serve.

Peas and beans à la Française

30g butter
5 lettuce leaves, washed and shredded
300g frozen or fresh peas
300g broad beans
4 spring onions, sliced
70g chopped pancetta
salt and pepper
1 tablespoon crème fraîche

- Heat the butter in a medium-sized saucepan.
- Add the lettuce, peas, beans, spring onions and pancetta and stir.
- Add 1 tablespoon of warm water.
- Season with pepper but no salt at this stage, as it will make the broad beans tough.
- Cover the saucepan and cook on a very low heat for 10 minutes.
- Season with salt, some more pepper and stir in the crème fraîche.

Roasted rosemary potatoes

1kg potatoes, peeled and quartered
salt and pepper
2 sprigs rosemary
2 tablespoons olive oil

- Preheat the oven to 200°C/400°F/gas 6.
- Parboil the potatoes for 4 minutes in salted water.
- Drain and place them in a roasting tin along with the rosemary.
- Drizzle with olive oil and roast for 45 minutes until golden brown.
- Season with more salt and pepper.

Turkey breasts with ham and cheese + sautéed potatoes + buttered broad beans

This is based on an Elizabeth David recipe. I don't tend to like poultry with ham and cheese. Once I had cooked this, though, I was pleasantly surprised. Bear in mind that to make really good sautéed potatoes, they need to be cooked thoroughly before you sauté them.

Turkey breasts with ham and cheese

6 turkey breasts
salt and pepper
a little flour for dusting
30g butter
100g button mushrooms, halved
3 tablespoons olive oil
3 slices cooked ham, cut in half to make 6 pieces
3 tablespoons Parmesan cheese, grated
200ml of chicken stock (a cube will do)

- Preheat the oven to 150°C/300°F/gas 2.
- Cover each turkey breast with tin foil and give them a good bash with a rolling pin on a wooden board to flatten them.
- Season with salt and pepper, dust lightly with seasoned flour and set aside.
- Heat the butter in a frying pan, fry the mushrooms until golden brown and set aside.
- Then add the olive oil to the same pan and heat it through.
- Add two of the turkey breasts and fry for 4 minutes on each side, adjusting the cooking time accordingly for thicker ones. When the turkey breasts are nicely browned, place them in an ovenproof dish.
- Next, lay a piece of ham on top of each breast with a spoonful of mushrooms and half a tablespoon of the Parmesan cheese.
- Spoon 1 tablespoon of chicken stock over each turkey breast.
- Finally, place the ovenproof dish in the oven for 10 minutes until the cheese has melted.

Sautéed potatoes

700g potatoes, peeled and quartered
salt and pepper
3 tablespoons olive oil
½ teaspoon paprika

- Cook the potatoes in boiling salted water until they are tender.
- Drain them well.
- Heat the olive oil in a heavy-bottomed frying or sauté pan. Once the oil is hot, chop the potatoes haphazardly straight into the frying pan. Once all in the pan give them a stir and then leave them on a medium heat, moving them occasionally.
- Once the potatoes are browned enough, lower the heat and leave them, turning them very occasionally to make sure they are not burning.
- When ready to serve sprinkle them with the salt, pepper and paprika.

Buttered broad beans

200g broad beans
a knob of butter
salt and pepper

- Place the beans in a pan of unsalted boiling water. Never use salted water, as this causes the beans to become tough while cooking.
- Boil them for 4 minutes, drain well and serve them with a tiny knob of butter and a generous grinding of salt and pepper.

Lemon posset
+ baked summer fruits

Lemon posset is very rich so you will only need a small amount. The creamy lemon goes very well with the baked summer fruits.

Lemon posset

425ml double cream
grated zest 2 lemons
125g caster sugar
110ml fresh lemon juice

- Place the cream, lemon zest and caster sugar in a saucepan and bring to the boil.
- Reduce the heat and simmer for 3 minutes.
- Remove from the heat and whisk the lemon juice into the cream mixture.
- Strain the mixture through a sieve and pour it into 6 small pots or glasses.
- Chill in the fridge for an hour or so.
- In the meantime, prepare the summer fruits.

Baked summer fruits

50g raspberries
50g blackberries
50g blueberries
100ml Amaretto liqueur
100ml water
2 tablespoons caster sugar

- Preheat the oven to 200°C/400°F/gas 6.
- Place the fruit in an ovenproof dish.
- Pour the liqueur and water over the fruit and sprinkle with the sugar.
- Bake for 20 minutes.
- Allow the fruit to cool and then serve spooned on top of the possets.

Seed cake

My mother used to make this seed cake when we were little. I think the recipe originally came from *The Constance Spry Cookery Book*, which was the first cookery book my father bought for my mother in the 1960s.

225g butter, softened
225g caster sugar
5 eggs
225g plain flour, sifted
½ teaspoon grated nutmeg
1 teaspoon caraway seeds
1 tablespoon brandy

- Preheat the oven to 180°C/350°F/gas 4 and grease and line a 23cm cake tin.
- Beat the butter and sugar together for 5 minutes, using an electric beater, until you have a creamy white consistency.
- Separate the eggs, retaining both the yolks and the whites.
- Add one yolk at a time to the butter and sugar, along with a tablespoon of the flour, beating well between each addition.
- Whisk the egg whites in a clean bowl until they stand in soft peaks.
- Add the nutmeg, caraway seeds and fold in the egg whites and the remaining flour.
- Then stir in the brandy and spoon the mixture into the cake tin.
- Bake for 1 hour.
- Allow the cake to cool in the tin before turning it out.

Week 4

Monday p326	Chicken fricassée + buttered rice with diced courgettes
Tuesday p328	Lamb and peas + boiled potatoes
Wednesday p329	Chicken breast stuffed with pesto + grated potatoes + buttered spinach
Thursday p330	Succotash
Friday p331	Cheese and potato tart + summer salad
Saturday p332	Rigatoni with spring vegetables
Sunday p333	Baked ham with mustard sauce + new potatoes with walnuts + green salad
Sunday pudding p334	Honey cake + fruit salad and greek yoghurt
Extra tasty treat p335	Summer fruit with white chocolate sauce

Shopping list

MEAT

- ☐ 1kg chicken breasts, boneless and skinless
- ☐ 6 chicken breasts with skin
- ☐ 1kg diced leg of lamb
- ☐ 1.2kg gammon joint, unsmoked

VEGETABLES

- ☐ 250g spinach leaves
- ☐ 6 onions
- ☐ 1 red onion
- ☐ 2 carrots
- ☐ 225g courgettes
- ☐ 500g garden peas
- ☐ 1 garlic bulb
- ☐ 6 tomatoes
- ☐ 950g new potatoes
- ☐ 1.25kg potatoes
- ☐ 1 bunch of celery
- ☐ 2 lettuces
- ☐ 1 cucumber
- ☐ 12 radishes
- ☐ 1 green pepper

FRUIT

- ☐ 400g black seedless grapes
- ☐ 400g white seedless grapes
- ☐ 2 satsumas
- ☐ 2 lemons
- ☐ 1 orange
- ☐ 2 punnets strawberries
- ☐ 2 punnets raspberries
- ☐ small punnet blueberries

FRESH HERBS

- ☐ thyme
- ☐ flat-leaf parsley
- ☐ chives
- ☐ oregano
- ☐ basil
- ☐ mint

FRIDGE ITEMS

- ☐ 200ml whipping cream
- ☐ 70g chopped pancetta
- ☐ 100g hard cheese (mixture of Gruyère, Cheddar or Parmesan)
- ☐ 225g Parmesan cheese
- ☐ 1 litre of milk
- ☐ 2 packs butter
- ☐ 5 eggs
- ☐ 1 tub Greek yoghurt
- ☐ 300ml double cream

KITCHEN CUPBOARD ITEMS

- ☐ brandy
- ☐ 400g basmati rice
- ☐ 100ml dry white wine
- ☐ salt
- ☐ 50g pine nuts
- ☐ 1 white loaf for breadcrumbs
- ☐ 340g tin sweetcorn
- ☐ 200g tinned butter beans
- ☐ vegetable stock cubes
- ☐ dried mustard powder
- ☐ 400g rigatoni pasta
- ☐ capers
- ☐ salted anchovies
- ☐ Dijon mustard
- ☐ extra virgin olive oil
- ☐ olive oil
- ☐ red wine vinegar
- ☐ balsamic vinegar
- ☐ 100g hazelnuts
- ☐ 40g walnut pieces
- ☐ 85g soft brown sugar
- ☐ clear honey
- ☐ 375g plain flour
- ☐ baking powder
- ☐ 100g white chocolate
- ☐ 50g caster sugar

SPICES

- ☐ whole nutmeg
- ☐ black pepper
- ☐ 12 cloves
- ☐ coriander seeds
- ☐ cumin seeds
- ☐ fennel seeds
- ☐ fenugreek

Chicken fricassée
+ buttered rice with diced courgettes

This dish went out of fashion long ago, which is a shame because it is quick and easy to make and also very tasty.

Chicken fricassée

70g butter
1kg chicken breasts, boneless and skinless, chopped into 2cm square pieces
1 large or 2 medium onions, peeled and finely chopped
salt and pepper
¼ teaspoon curry powder*
100ml brandy
200ml whipping cream
1 tablespoon flat-leaf parsley, finely chopped

- Gently heat the butter in a large saucepan.
- Add the chicken and cook it on a low heat in the butter for 5 minutes, without letting it brown.
- Remove the chicken and set aside.
- Stir the onions into the butter and fry very gently for 5 minutes. Do not let them brown.
- Return the chicken to the pan and season with salt, pepper and curry powder.
- Increase the heat and pour on the brandy.
- Cook rapidly for 5 minutes, letting the liquid all but disappear.
- Reduce the heat and pour on the cream. Simmer gently for 5 minutes.
- Check the seasoning.
- Scatter with parsley and serve.

Buttered rice with diced courgettes

400g basmati rice
600ml water
½ teaspoon salt
30g butter
200g courgettes, diced

- Place the rice, water and salt in a saucepan.
- Bring to a good boil.
- Cover and reduce the heat to very low. Cook for 15 minutes.
- Remove from the heat and leave covered for 10 minutes.
- Heat the butter in a sauté pan.
- Add the courgettes and sauté for 2 minutes.
- Tip these along with the butter onto the rice and season with pepper.

To make your own curry powder:
1 tablespoon coriander seeds
1 dessertspoon cumin seeds
1 teaspoon fennel seeds
½ teaspoon fenugreek

- *Place the coriander seeds into a small, heavy-bottomed pan and heat through for 30 seconds.*
- *Add the other ingredients and toast until you smell the lovely aroma of the spices.*
- *Transfer the spices to a coffee grinder, a small processor or grind them in a pestle and mortar.*

Lamb and peas
+ boiled potatoes

This lamb cooks beautifully, whatever you do to it and one of the bonuses of using peas in a stew like this is the lovely fresh colour they add to it.

Lamb and peas

50ml olive oil
1kg diced leg of lamb
1 large onion, finely chopped
100ml dry white wine
400g fresh peas
100ml water
salt and pepper
2 tablespoons flat-leaf parsley, chopped

- Heat 2 tablespoons of olive oil in a large saucepan.
- Add the meat and onions and brown on a medium heat for 10 minutes.
- Pour in the wine and cook uncovered for 10 minutes on a medium heat.
- Then add the rest of the olive oil and cook on a gentle simmer, covered, for 10 minutes.
- Add the peas and water and simmer for a further 10 minutes, covered.
- Season with salt and pepper and add the parsley just before serving.

Boiled potatoes

750g potatoes, peeled and quartered
salt
butter
black pepper

- Put the potatoes in a saucepan of salted water.
- Bring to the boil and reduce the heat to a simmer.
- Simmer the potatoes until tender to the tip of a sharp knife.
- Serve with a dab of butter and a few grindings of black pepper.

Chicken breast stuffed with pesto + grated potatoes + buttered spinach

The idea for this lovely summer recipe comes from Jill Dupleix's *Simple Food*, which is full of brilliant ideas for quick but beautifully cooked food. If your children won't eat spinach, give them a different vegetable and cook the spinach for the adults.

Chicken breast stuffed with pesto

For the pesto

2 handfuls pine nuts
2 cloves garlic
6 good handfuls fresh basil leaves
4 tablespoons Parmesan cheese, grated
extra virgin olive oil
salt and pepper

For the chicken

6 chicken breasts with skin
3 tablespoons pesto
3 tablespoons white breadcrumbs
2 tablespoons olive oil
1 tablespoon lemon juice
salt and pepper

To make the pesto

- Place the pine nuts in a small, heavy-bottomed pan and toast them until slightly browned.
- Set aside to cool.
- Whizz the garlic and basil leaves in a food processor or chop finely by hand.
- Add the pine nuts and give these a whizz.
- Then stir in the Parmesan cheese and a good glug of olive oil to make a wet, paste-like consistency. If the mixture is too thin, add a little more oil.
- Season with salt and pepper to taste.

To cook the chicken

- Heat the oven to 200°C/400°F/gas 6.
- Combine the pesto and breadcrumbs in a bowl. Add a little olive oil if it is too dry.
- Work your fingers under the skin of the chicken breasts, keeping it attached at one end. Stuff the pesto under the skin to cover the breast.
- Heat the olive oil in a frying pan and sear the skin side of each breast until golden brown. This should take less than a minute for each one.
- Place the chicken breasts skin side up on a baking tray and drizzle with the juices from the frying pan, the lemon juice, salt and pepper.
- Bake for 20 minutes.

Grated potatoes

500g potatoes, peeled and grated, with any excess water squeezed out
1 onion, thinly sliced
2 tablespoons Parmesan cheese, grated
leaves from 2 sprigs thyme, finely chopped
3 tablespoons olive oil

- Place the grated potato in a bowl.
- Add the onion, cheese and thyme and mix.
- Heat the oil in a frying pan until hot.
- Fry tablespoons of the mixture for 3 minutes on each side until golden brown.

Buttered spinach

250g spinach leaves
salt
knob of butter
nutmeg
black pepper

- Place the spinach in a large saucepan with a tablespoon of water and a sprinkling of sea salt.
- Cover and place the saucepan on a low heat.
- Gradually wilt the spinach for 10 minutes, until the leaves are a glossy dark green.
- Then remove the lid and stir to get rid of any excess water. Drain any extra off if necessary.
- Add a knob of butter, a tiny grating of nutmeg

Succotash

I came across this recipe quite by chance in an old cookery book, when I was looking for something simple to make for my husband. He loves pulses and soups and this soup is so easy, as it uses canned butter beans and tinned sweetcorn.

45g butter
2 cloves garlic, peeled and crushed
1 large onion, finely chopped
2 sticks celery, sliced
340g tin sweetcorn, drained
200g tinned butter beans, drained
1 sprig thyme
450ml milk
450ml vegetable stock (a stock cube will do)
salt and pepper
10 fresh basil leaves

- Heat the butter in a saucepan over a low heat and add the garlic, onion and celery. Gently sauté for 10 minutes until softened.
- Add the sweetcorn, butter beans, thyme, milk, and stock and simmer, covered, for 10 minutes.
- Season to taste and scatter the ripped basil leaves over the top just before serving with crusty bread.

Cheese and potato tart + summer salad

Once you have mastered the technique of pastry making, the world of the 'savoury tart' opens up before you. Tarts make a very pleasant summer supper.

Cheese and potato tart

For the pastry

225g plain flour

150g butter, chilled and cubed

salt

1 egg yolk

2 tablespoons cold water

For the filling

1 tablespoon olive oil

1 onion, finely chopped

70g chopped pancetta

250g new potatoes, cooked until tender and sliced to the thickness of a pound coin

100g hard cheese, grated (mix of Gruyère, Cheddar or Parmesan)

2 tablespoons flat-leaf parsley and chives mixed, chopped

2 eggs

double cream

salt and pepper

½ teaspoon dried mustard powder

To make the pastry

- Put the flour and butter in the bowl of a food processor and incorporate them so that the resulting mixture looks like fine breadcrumbs.
- Add a pinch of salt.
- Mix the egg yolk with the cold water in a small bowl and then add this liquid to the flour and fat.
- Turn on the food processor and mix until a dough just begins to form. Turn the mixture onto a floured work surface and combine thoroughly, with a light hand, until you have a smooth dough.
- Wrap the dough in cling-film and chill in the fridge for 20 minutes.

To make the tart

- Preheat the oven to 200°C/400°F/gas 6 and grease a 24cm diameter, 3½cm deep flan tin.
- Roll out the pastry on a lightly floured surface and line the flan tin with it. Place a sheet of baking parchment over the pastry case and then pour on some baking beans. Place the flan tin on a baking sheet and bake for 15 minutes.
- Take the flan out of the oven and remove the parchment and baking beans. Return the flan to the oven for a further 5 minutes.
- Remove the flan tin from the oven and reduce the oven temperature to 190°C/375°F/gas 5.

To fill the tart

- Warm the olive oil in a frying pan.
- Sauté the onion and pancetta for 5 minutes on a low heat until soft but not brown.
- Spread the pancetta and onion evenly over the base of the flan tin.
- Next, lay the potatoes on top and sprinkle over the cheese and finely chopped herbs.
- Break the eggs into a measuring jug, add enough double cream to make the liquid up to 500ml and whisk.
- Season well with salt, pepper and mustard powder and pour into the flan case.
- Bake for 30 minutes.

Summer salad

1 lettuce

4 tomatoes, sliced

½ cucumber, sliced

12 radishes, trimmed and halved

For the dressing

3 dessertspoons extra virgin olive oil

1 dessertspoon red wine vinegar

salt and pepper

- Mix the dressing in a small bowl.
- Place the salad in a serving dish and pour the dressing over when ready to serve.

Rigatoni with spring vegetables

The rich Mediterranean flavours of this pasta sauce herald the arrival of summer in the kitchen.

3 tablespoons olive oil
1 red onion, finely diced
1 stick celery, diced
2 carrots, peeled and diced
1 courgette, diced
100g fresh peas
1 clove garlic, peeled and finely chopped
400g rigatoni pasta
2 tomatoes, diced
1 tablespoon fresh oregano, chopped
1 tablespoon fresh basil, chopped
1 dessertspoon capers, rinsed
3 salted anchovies, finely chopped
salt and pepper
2 tablespoons double cream
Parmesan cheese, grated for serving

- Heat the olive oil in a saucepan.
- Gently sauté the onion, celery, carrots, courgette, peas and garlic for 10 minutes on a low heat.
- Meanwhile, boil the water for the pasta and cook the rigatoni according to the packet instructions.
- Add the tomatoes to the other vegetables and cook, covered, for 5 minutes.
- Then add the herbs, capers,and anchovies and season to taste.
- Stir in the cream and then pour the sauce over the cooked pasta.
- Serve with the grated Parmesan sprinkled over the top.

Baked ham with mustard sauce + new potatoes with walnuts + green salad

It is pretty straightforward to cook gammon well. It is also easy to carve and there are various sauces that complement it, making it a versatile dish.

Baked ham with mustard sauce

For the baked ham

1.2kg gammon joint, unsmoked
12 cloves
2 tablespoons runny honey

For the mustard sauce

40g butter
1½ tablespoons plain flour
550ml milk
salt and pepper
1 dessertspoon Dijon mustard
2 tablespoons Parmesan cheese, grated
3 tablespoons fresh mint, chopped

To cook the ham

- Place the gammon joint in a large saucepan of water and bring to the boil.
- Reduce to a simmer, cover, and cook for 50 minutes.
- Preheat the oven to 200°C/400°F/gas 6.
- Remove the gammon from the water and place the joint in a roasting tin.
- Remove the thick layer of skin from the gammon with a sharp knife, leaving some of the fat.
- Stud the fatty area with cloves and brush with honey.
- Roast for 30 minutes.
- While the joint is cooking, baste it with the honey once or twice.
- Remove from the oven and let the joint rest for 20 minutes.
- Remove the cloves before carving and serve with mustard sauce.

To make the sauce

- Melt the butter on a low heat in a small pan.
- Add the flour and stir for 1 minute.
- Remove from the heat and stir in the milk.
- Return to the heat and bring the sauce to a gentle simmer.
- Reduce the heat to very low to avoid burning and cook the sauce for 10 minutes.
- Season with salt and pepper.
- Remove from the heat and add the mustard, cheese and chopped mint.

New potatoes with walnuts

700g new potatoes
salt
2 tablespoons olive oil
black pepper
40g walnut pieces
1 stick celery, finely sliced

- Boil the potatoes in salted water for 20 minutes until tender.
- Drain and toss the potatoes in olive oil and season with salt and pepper.
- Add the walnuts and celery pieces and serve with the ham and green salad.

Green salad

1 lettuce washed
½ cucumber, sliced
1 green pepper, finely diced

For the dressing

2 tablespoons extra virgin olive oil
½ tablespoon balsamic vinegar
salt and pepper

- Place the salad ingredients in a serving bowl.
- Combine the dressing ingredients and drizzle over the salad when ready to serve.

Honey cake
+ fruit salad and greek yoghurt

People often feel let down when offered fruit salad as a dessert, which is a shame. It is hardly a winner in many people's eyes when competing with such delights as sticky toffee pudding or chocolate cake. We have helped to relegate fruit salad to the lower divisions in the dessert leagues by assuming that a few chopped bananas and apples thrown into a serving bowl will suffice. This fruit salad has a clean, citrus taste that goes very well with the honey cake, which, in turn, complements the addition of Greek yoghurt.

Honey cake

100g hazelnuts
140g butter
85g soft brown sugar
5 tablespoons clear honey
2 eggs, beaten
125g plain flour
1 teaspoon baking powder

- Preheat the oven to 170°C/325°F/gas 3.
- Grease a small loaf tin (23cm long and 7cm deep) and line the bottom of the tin with greaseproof paper.
- Grind the hazelnuts to a fine powder in a food processor or blender and set aside.
- Place the butter, sugar and honey in a saucepan and gently heat it so that the butter melts.
- Remove the saucepan from the heat and when the mixture has cooled slightly, add the eggs.
- Fold in the flour, baking powder and hazelnuts and pour the mixture into the loaf tin.
- Bake for 30 minutes.
- When cooled slightly, turn out onto a rack.
- Serve cut in slices.

Fruit salad

400g black seedless grapes, halved
400g white seedless grapes, kept whole
2 satsumas, peeled
grated zest 1 lemon
1 tablespoon caster sugar
juice 1 orange
Greek yoghurt for serving

- Place the grapes in a serving bowl.
- Separate the segments of the satsumas and add these to the grapes.
- Sprinkle on the grated lemon zest, sugar and orange juice and serve with the cake and Greek yoghurt.

Summer fruit with white chocolate sauce

This is a great pudding to encourage children to eat the delicious fresh berries that are in season at this time of year.

6 servings of strawberries and raspberries, mixed
handful blueberries
100g white chocolate
100ml double cream

- Place the cream and chocolate in a glass bowl over a saucepan of barely simmering water.
- Keep the sauce over the water for 30 minutes, stirring occasionally.
- Pour the warm sauce over the fruit and serve.

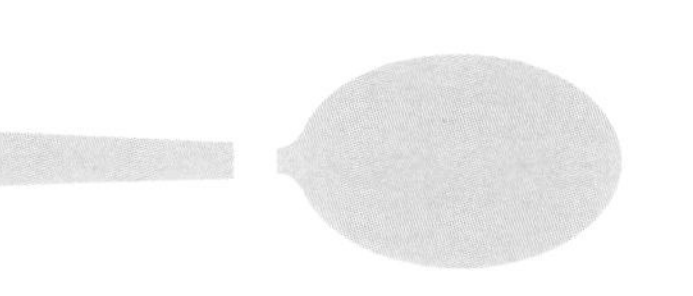

Week 1

Monday p338	Chicken breasts with tarragon + coleslaw + mashed potato
Tuesday p339	Spaghetti with creamy pepper, courgette and tomato sauce
Wednesday p340	Grilled spiced chicken legs + mozzarella, tomato and basil salad + boiled rice
Thursday p342	Smoked haddock cakes + gorgonzola and onion salad + baked potatoes
Friday p343	Ham and rice salad + egg mayonnaise
Saturday p344	Focaccia with tomatoes, avocados and mozzarella
Sunday p345	Hungarian lamb stew + macaroni
Sunday pudding p346	Nectarine and almond tart
Extra tasty treat p347	Chocolate coffee cakes

Shopping list

MEAT

- ☐ 6 chicken breast fillets, skinless
- ☐ 1kg lamb neck fillet
- ☐ 6 chicken legs

FISH

- ☐ 850g undyed smoked haddock

VEGETABLES

- ☐ 1 small white cabbage
- ☐ 3 carrots
- ☐ 1 garlic bulb
- ☐ 1 bunch celery
- ☐ 1 Romaine lettuce
- ☐ ½ cucumber
- ☐ 4 spring onions
- ☐ 50g green beans
- ☐ 2 avocados
- ☐ 2 onions
- ☐ 2 shallots
- ☐ 13 tomatoes
- ☐ 12 baking potatoes
- ☐ 1kg potatoes
- ☐ fresh ginger
- ☐ 150g red pepper
- ☐ 100g courgettes

FRUIT

- ☐ 5 or 6 fresh nectarines

FRESH HERBS

- ☐ tarragon
- ☐ flat-leaf parsley leaves
- ☐ chives
- ☐ rosemary
- ☐ basil leaves
- ☐ thyme

FRIDGE ITEMS

- ☐ 50g Parmesan cheese
- ☐ 300ml light vegetable or chicken stock
- ☐ 100g Gorgonzola cheese
- ☐ 50g frozen petits pois
- ☐ 70g pancetta
- ☐ 100g cooked ham
- ☐ 200ml crème fraîche
- ☐ 4 tubs buffalo mozzarella
- ☐ 3 packs butter
- ☐ 18 eggs
- ☐ 575ml milk
- ☐ 150g mascarpone cheese

KITCHEN CUPBOARD ITEMS

- ☐ 1 bottle dry white wine
- ☐ 1 bottle red wine
- ☐ mayonnaise
- ☐ 2 x 400g tins chopped tomatoes
- ☐ 500g macaroni
- ☐ 500g spaghetti
- ☐ tomato ketchup
- ☐ anchovy fillets
- ☐ Worcestershire sauce
- ☐ 50g pistachio nuts
- ☐ 900g basmati rice
- ☐ salt
- ☐ Dijon mustard
- ☐ groundnut oil
- ☐ light olive oil
- ☐ extra virgin olive oil
- ☐ olive oil
- ☐ balsamic vinegar
- ☐ white wine vinegar
- ☐ fast-action dried yeast
- ☐ 500g white bread flour
- ☐ 100g ground almonds
- ☐ 250g plain flour
- ☐ 225g self-raising flour
- ☐ instant coffee
- ☐ cocoa powder
- ☐ baking powder
- ☐ 250g caster sugar
- ☐ 350g icing sugar
- ☐ 100g milk chocolate
- ☐ 50g granulated sugar
- ☐ 1 or 2 focaccias (see p.344)

SPICES

- ☐ black peppercorns
- ☐ paprika
- ☐ coriander seeds
- ☐ cardamom pods
- ☐ turmeric
- ☐ cloves

Chicken breasts with tarragon + coleslaw + mashed potato

This coleslaw recipe bears no resemblance to the shop-bought item. It is so much nicer and is the perfect accompaniment to the chicken and mashed potato. If you don't have time to make your own mayonnaise, use the bought stuff.

Chicken breasts with tarragon sauce

1 tablespoon olive oil
40g butter
6 chicken breast fillets, skinless
salt and pepper
200ml dry white wine
2 tablespoons fresh tarragon, finely chopped

- Preheat the oven to 200°C/400°F/gas 6.
- Heat the oil and 20g of the butter in a heavy-bottomed frying pan on a medium to high heat.
- Place two of the chicken breasts in the pan. They should start sizzling straight away.
- Season the side of the chicken breast facing upwards and don't move them for 2 minutes. The fillets should be golden brown before you turn them over.
- Then, turn the chicken over and cook the other side for 1 minute only.
- If the meat gets too brown it will acquire a tough texture. Set the breasts aside in an ovenproof serving dish.
- Do the same with the other breasts, two at a time. Don't be tempted to save time by putting all the chicken breasts in the pan at the same time – this will just reduce the temperature and you will risk overcooking them.
- Once all the chicken is cooked, keep the pan hot and add the wine. Stir it round to deglaze the pan and form the basis of the sauce.
- Add the chopped tarragon and let the wine bubble away for about 30 seconds.
- Next, add the rest of the butter and keep stirring for about 30 seconds more, check the seasoning and then pour the sauce over the chicken breasts in the serving dish.
- Place the dish in the oven and cook the chicken for 5 minutes.

Coleslaw

1 small white cabbage
3 carrots
1 shallot
salt and pepper
2 tablespoons mayonnaise

- Shred the cabbage as thinly as possible and place in a serving bowl.
- Peel the carrots and grate them on the large side of the grater.
- Peel and finely slice the shallot and add this and the carrots to the cabbage.
- Season with salt and pepper, add the mayonnaise and mix well.

Mashed potato

1kg potatoes, peeled and quartered
salt and black pepper
200ml warmed milk
40g butter

- Place the potatoes in cold, salted water and bring to the boil.
- Turn the heat down to a robust simmer on a medium heat.
- Once the potatoes are soft but not mushy, drain them and put them through a potato ricer.
- Return the mashed potato to the saucepan and place over a low heat.
- Add the milk and butter and gently stir in.
- Remove from the heat and serve.

Spaghetti with creamy pepper, courgette and tomato sauce

Courgettes used to have a reputation for being rather a disappointing vegetable, mainly because they used to be grown to marrow-size and were watery and lacking in flavour. The petite courgettes you find in the shops now have a lovely, subtle flavour and are hugely versatile. If you've ever tried 'zucchini fritti' – deep-fried courgettes dipped in flour and batter – you know how delicious they can be. Here, they add a Meditteranean flavour to this pasta sauce.

3 tablespoons olive oil
1 shallot, peeled and finely chopped
150g red pepper, very finely chopped
100g courgettes, very finely chopped
1 clove garlic, peeled and finely chopped
leaves from 1 sprig fresh rosemary, finely chopped
4 tablespoons red wine
2 x 400g tins chopped tomatoes
salt and pepper
150g mascarpone cheese
500g spaghetti
Parmesan cheese, grated for serving

- Place the olive oil in a saucepan with the shallot, pepper, courgettes, garlic and rosemary and fry gently for 10 minutes until everything is very soft.
- Increase the heat, add the wine and let it simmer gently for 5 minutes.
- Add the tomatoes, season with salt and pepper and simmer, covered, for 30 minutes.
- Add the mascarpone cheese and stir well to combine. Keep on a very gentle simmer.
- While the sauce is simmering, cook the spaghetti in boiling, salted water until *al dente* and drain.
- Serve the sauce with the spaghetti and sprinkle the Parmesan cheese on top.

Grilled spiced chicken legs + mozzarella, tomato and basil salad + boiled rice

Grilling is a great way to cook chicken. You can control the heat well enough to ensure it gets cooked through properly without over-browning the outside, so the chicken ends up with crisp, golden skin.

Spiced grilled chicken legs

3 teaspoons coriander seeds
12 cardamom pods
30g fresh ginger
2 cloves
salt and pepper
30g butter
1 tablespoon olive oil
6 chicken legs with skin

For the sauce

20g butter
1 tablespoon olive oil
1 onion, finely chopped
¼ teaspoon turmeric
1cm piece fresh ginger, peeled and finely chopped
salt and pepper
200ml crème fraîche

- First, toast the coriander seeds in a small frying pan until you see the seeds browning and you can smell a strong aroma. Take care not to burn them.
- Pound the cardamom pods in a mortar with a pestle and remove the outer husks, which will come away from the seeds.
- Next, add the coriander seeds, ginger, cloves, salt and pepper to the cardamom seeds and pound them in the pestle and mortar until you have a rough, dry paste.
- Add the butter and oil and mix well.
- Pull back the skin from the chicken legs and smear lumps of the paste under the skin, next to the chicken flesh.
- Place the chicken legs in a bowl and chill in the fridge for 1 hour.
- Preheat the grill.

To make the sauce

- Heat the butter and oil in a frying pan.
- Add the onion and cook for 5 minutes on a medium heat until soft.
- Stir in the turmeric, ginger, salt and pepper and cook for 5 minutes, stirring occasionally.
- Then add the crème fraîche and set aside while you cook the chicken.
- Place the chicken legs on the wire rack of the grill pan and grill for 4 minutes.
- Turn them over and grill them for a further 4 minutes.
- Remove the wire rack and place the legs inside the grill pan.
- Lower the heat of the grill.
- Season the legs with salt and pepper and grill for another 4 minutes.
- Baste the legs in the juices, turn them again and grill for another 4 minutes.
- They should be ready now, but test them by inserting a skewer and if the juices run clear they are cooked.
- Serve with the sauce, boiled rice and the salad below.

Mozzarella, tomato and basil salad

1 tub buffalo mozzarella
4 tomatoes, thinly sliced
10 basil leaves, roughly torn

For the dressing

2 tablespoons extra virgin olive oil
salt and pepper

- Slice the mozzarella and arrange it on a serving plate with the tomato and basil.
- Mix together the oil and seasoning and pour over the salad just before serving.

Boiled rice

500g basmati rice
750ml water
salt

- Put the rice in a saucepan with the water and a pinch of salt.
- Place the rice on a high heat and as soon as it comes to the boil, cover the saucepan with a lid and turn the heat right down to very low. Leave it for 15 minutes, giving it one stir only during the cooking time.
- Then take the pan off the heat and leave it covered for a further 10 minutes, before removing the lid.

Smoked haddock cakes + gorgonzola and onion salad + baked potatoes

Everyone likes fish cakes and using a smoked fish ensures a good flavour. This recipe makes approximately 12 cakes.

Smoked haddock cakes

850g undyed smoked haddock
300ml milk
300ml water
4 tablespoons tomato ketchup
5 anchovy fillets, rinsed and finely chopped
pepper
1 tablespoon Worcestershire sauce
1 egg, beaten
30g butter and 1 tablespoon olive oil for frying
a little flour for dusting

- Place the fish in a meat tray, skin side up.
- Pour over the milk and water and bring to the boil on the hob.
- Cover the tray with tin foil, reduce the heat and simmer gently for 5 minutes.
- Then take the fish out of the tray and put on a plate, removing the skin and any stray bones.
- Put the fish in a bowl and mash it gently with a fork.
- Add the tomato ketchup, anchovies, pepper and Worcestershire sauce.
- Then mix in the beaten egg to combine all the ingredients and chill in the fridge for 20 minutes or so.
- Preheat the oven to 120°C/250°F/gas ½.
- Remove the fish mixture from the fridge and form it into 12 small cakes. Dip each cake in some flour, for a light dusting.
- Heat the butter and olive oil in a frying pan and then fry each fishcake for 3 minutes on each side.
- Place the cooked fish cakes in the oven to keep warm while you cook the rest.

Gorgonzola and onion salad

1 Romaine lettuce, washed and chopped
½ cucumber, sliced
4 spring onions, chopped
100g Gorgonzola cheese, cut into small cubes
50g pistachio nuts
For the dressing
1 tablespoon olive oil
2 teaspoons balsamic vinegar
salt and pepper

- Assemble the salad in a serving bowl, mix the dressing ingredients together well and pour over the dressing when ready to serve.

Baked potatoes

6 baking potatoes
butter for serving
salt and pepper

- Preheat the oven to 220°C/425°F/gas 7.
- Pierce the potato skins with a sharp knife and bake them for 1 hour 30 minutes.
- Split each potato and serve with butter, salt and pepper.

Ham and rice salad
+ egg mayonnaise

One of my favourite meals when we were little was rice salad. It was not the buffet table staple it is now.

Ham and rice salad

400ml basmati rice
600ml water
salt
50g petits pois, cooked
50g green beans, cooked
100g cooked ham
4 medium tomatoes, chopped
1 tablespoon flat-leaf parsley, chopped
1 tablespoon chives, snipped
70g pancetta
For the dressing
3 tablespoons extra virgin olive oil
1 dessertspoon white wine vinegar
salt and pepper
2 teaspoons Dijon mustard

- Put the rice in a saucepan with the water and salt.
- Place the rice on a high heat and as soon as it comes to the boil, cover the saucepan with a lid and turn the heat right down to very low. Leave it for 15 minutes, giving it one stir only during the cooking time.
- Then take it off the heat and leave it covered for a further 10 minutes before removing the lid.
- Add the cooked peas, beans, ham, tomatoes and herbs to the rice.
- Fry the pancetta and then cut it up into the rice.
- Mix the dressing ingredients in a small bowl and pour over the salad while the rice is still warm.

Egg mayonnaise

6 eggs, hard-boiled and halved
For the mayonnaise
2 egg yolks
1 tablespoon white wine vinegar
1 teaspoon Dijon mustard
salt
100ml groundnut oil
200ml light olive oil (important to use the light variety)

- Whisk the egg yolks with the white wine vinegar, mustard and a pinch of salt in a bowl.
- Mix the oils together in a small jug and start adding, a drop at a time, to the eggs, whisking constantly. If you add the oil more quickly than this, the mixture will curdle. Make sure you have thoroughly combined each addition of oil before adding the next. The mixture will start to thicken gradually. At this stage, add the oil mixture at a quicker pace.
- If the mayonnaise is very thick once all the oil has been added, spoon in a couple of tablespoons of cold water and mix.
- Serve the eggs with the mayonnaise and the ham and rice salad.

Focaccia with tomatoes, avocados and mozzarella

This a lovely, fresh summertime meal, and very healthy. If you don't have time to make the focaccia, use a bought one. Alternatively, you could use ciabatta bread if you prefer.

1 or 2 shop-bought focaccias or 1 focaccia following the recipe below
extra virgin olive oil
3 buffalo mozzarella cheeses, thinly sliced
2 avocados, peeled, de-stoned and sliced
4–5 ripe tomatoes, sliced
salt and pepper
good handful basil leaves

- Split the focaccia as though you were making a sandwich.
- Drizzle each slice with olive oil and pile with mozzarella, avocado and tomatoes.
- Season with salt and pepper and another drizzle of olive oil and scatter the torn basil leaves over the top.

Focaccia

1 sachet fast-action dried yeast
280ml warm water
3 tablespoons olive oil
1 heaped teaspoon salt
2 tablespoons fresh rosemary leaves, chopped
500g white bread flour

- Mix the yeast with a little of the water in a large mixing bowl and leave to stand for 5 minutes.
- Add the oil, the remaining water, salt, rosemary and 250g of the flour.
- Combine to a sticky dough and turn out onto a floured surface.
- Keep adding flour from the remaining 250g as you knead the dough, until you have a smooth silky dough. This takes about 10 minutes. You may not use all of the flour.
- Place the dough back in the mixing bowl with a teaspoon of olive oil. Turn the dough to coat it with the oil.
- Cover with a tea towel and leave it to rise for 1 hour.
- Knock back by punching the air out of it and roll into a rectangle.
- Press into a greased roasting or baking tin, cover and let it rise for another hour.
- Preheat the oven to 220°C/425°F/gas 7.
- Press your fingertips into the dough to make dimpled impressions at intervals on the top of the bread dough.
- Place rosemary sprigs into the dimples in the dough and drizzle with olive oil.
- Sprinkle with sea salt and bake for 20–25 minutes until golden.

Hungarian lamb stew + macaroni

This stew is similar to goulash, although it doesn't contain tomatoes. It goes very well with the macaroni.

Hungarian lamb stew

1 tablespoon olive oil
25g butter
1 large onion, chopped finely
2 sticks celery, finely chopped
1 teaspoon sugar
1kg lamb neck fillet, chopped into 2cm thick slices
1 teaspoon paprika
1 teaspoon salt
black pepper
1 tablespoon flour
300ml light vegetable or chicken stock
a few sprigs fresh thyme

- Heat the olive oil with the butter in a large saucepan.
- Add the onions and the celery, sprinkle on the sugar and sauté for 10 minutes on a low heat.
- Remove the onions and celery from the saucepan and set aside.
- Keep the saucepan on the heat and brown the lamb in batches, adding a little more olive oil if necessary.
- Set each batch of browned lamb aside while you proceed with the next.
- Return all the meat to the pan.
- Sprinkle on the paprika, salt, pepper and flour and stir to incorporate.
- Next, add the onions and celery to the pan with the meat.
- Pour over the stock, add the thyme and bring to a gentle simmer.
- Cover and cook for 1 hour.
- Serve with the macaroni below.

Macaroni

500g macaroni
salt
25g butter
2 tablespoons flat-leaf parsley, finely chopped

- Cook the macaroni in boiling salted water following the packet instructions.
- Drain the macaroni and place it in a serving bowl with the butter and parsley.

Nectarine and almond tart

Nectarines encapsulate the feeling of high summer, especially when they are perfectly ripe. This recipe requires you to halve the nectarines but if you find that when you try to do so they won't come apart, cut what you can from the nectarines without wasting too much. The nectarines get pushed down into the filling so the appearance of the tart will not be spoiled.

For the sweet pastry

180g butter
75g icing sugar
2 egg yolks
225g plain flour

For the filling

5 or 6 fresh nectarines, halved with stones removed
100g ground almonds
100g icing sugar
3 eggs

To make the pastry

- Mix the butter, icing sugar, egg yolks and flour together in a food processor, until the mixture starts to combine.
- Turn the mixture out onto a floured surface and form into a ball.
- Wrap it in cling-film and chill in the fridge for about 30 minutes.

To make the tart

- Preheat the oven to 200°C/400°F/gas 6.
- Grease and line a 20cm tart tin with baking parchments.
- Roll out the pastry and line the tart tin with it.
- Prick the base of the pastry with a fork. Line the case with a sheet of baking parchment and then pour some baking beans on top of the paper.
- Place the pastry case in the oven to bake for 10 minutes.
- Remove the beans and baking parchment and return the tart case to the oven for 5 minutes.
- Reduce the oven temperature to 180°C/350°F/gas 4.
- To make the filling, beat the eggs with an electric hand mixer until pale and the thickness of double cream.
- Fold in the ground almonds, sift in the icing sugar and fold this in as well.
- Spoon the mixture into the pastry case.
- Place the nectarine halves cut side down into the almond mixture and bake for 30 minutes.
- Serve with cream.

Chocolate coffee cakes

These are a good tea-time treat as they can be thrown together without too much fuss or time.

For the cakes

2 tablespoons of instant coffee dissolved in 2 tablespoons of water
1 tablespoon cocoa powder
225g butter, softened
225g caster sugar
4 eggs
225g self-raising flour
1 level teaspoon baking powder

For the icing

100g milk chocolate
50g butter
3 tablespoons milk
175g icing sugar, sieved

To make the cakes

- Preheat the oven to 180°C/350°F/gas 4.
- Grease and line a shallow rectangular tin measuring approximately 25 x 20cms. Don't worry if the tin doesn't measure this exactly but it should be there or thereabouts.
- In a large bowl blend together the cake ingredients, mixing just until they are thoroughly combined.
- Spoon the mixture into the prepared tin and cook for 35 minutes.
- Leave to cool in the tin.

To make the icing

- Melt the chocolate and butter together in a glass bowl over a saucepan of barely simmering water.
- Add the milk and then add the icing sugar off the heat. Once the icing has cooled and the cake is also cool, spread the icing over the top.
- Cut the cake into about 16–20 squares, depending on how big you like them.

Week 2

Shopping list

MEAT

- ☐ 750g piece of beef fillet
- ☐ 1kg chicken thigh fillets

FISH

- ☐ 500g cooked prawns
- ☐ 3 whole Dover sole
- ☐ 600g monkfish tail fillets

VEGETABLES

- ☐ 12 spring onions
- ☐ 1 large lettuce
- ☐ 16 plum tomatoes
- ☐ 6–8 radishes
- ☐ 1.2kg new potatoes
- ☐ 700g potatoes
- ☐ 4 onions
- ☐ fresh ginger
- ☐ 2 green chillies
- ☐ 1 cucumber
- ☐ 4 shallots
- ☐ 1 garlic bulb
- ☐ 650g green beans

FRUIT

- ☐ 2 apricots
- ☐ 5 lemons
- ☐ 1 lime
- ☐ 8 ripe peaches
- ☐ 100g summer berries
- ☐ 2 oranges
- ☐ 200g soft fruit

FRESH HERBS

- ☐ basil
- ☐ bay leaves
- ☐ flat-leaf parsley
- ☐ coriander
- ☐ mint
- ☐ chives

FRIDGE ITEMS

- ☐ 200g Caerphilly cheese
- ☐ 250g ricotta cheese
- ☐ 1 tub natural yoghurt
- ☐ 70g chopped pancetta
- ☐ 150ml double cream
- ☐ 25g Parmesan cheese
- ☐ 1 carton whipping cream
- ☐ 13 eggs
- ☐ 2 packs butter

KITCHEN CUPBOARD ITEMS

- ☐ salt
- ☐ 500g Arborio rice
- ☐ 350g caster sugar
- ☐ 75g ground almonds
- ☐ 100g dried apricots
- ☐ pitted black olives
- ☐ capers
- ☐ 1 loaf white bread for breadcrumbs
- ☐ Dijon mustard
- ☐ 50g walnuts
- ☐ balsamic vinegar
- ☐ extra virgin olive oil
- ☐ vegetable oil
- ☐ olive oil
- ☐ mayonnaise
- ☐ 1 bottle red wine
- ☐ 1 bottle dry white wine
- ☐ tomato purée
- ☐ 400g strong white bread flour
- ☐ 100g wholemeal or malthouse flour
- ☐ fast-action dried yeast
- ☐ 200g red lentils
- ☐ 400g tin chopped tomatoes
- ☐ 400ml coconut milk
- ☐ 25g brown sugar
- ☐ 25g desiccated coconut
- ☐ 1kg basmati rice
- ☐ 2 teaspoons tamarind paste
- ☐ 50g cashew nuts
- ☐ horseradish sauce
- ☐ Amaretto liqueur
- ☐ vanilla pod
- ☐ 100g plain flour
- ☐ granulated sugar
- ☐ 25g icing sugar

SPICES

- ☐ dried oregano
- ☐ paprika
- ☐ fennel seeds
- ☐ cardamom pods
- ☐ black peppercorns
- ☐ chilli flakes
- ☐ saffron strands
- ☐ coriander seeds
- ☐ cumin seeds
- ☐ fenugreek
- ☐ cayenne pepper
- ☐ black mustard seeds
- ☐ asafoetida powder
- ☐ turmeric
- ☐ curry leaves
- ☐ cinnamon sticks
- ☐ mustard seeds

Sicilian risotto

This is a simple summer risotto with a very fresh flavour – just the right kind of light meal when the weather is warm.

50g butter
1 onion, finely chopped
1 clove garlic, peeled and finely chopped
500g Arborio rice
250ml dry white wine
1.5–2 litres salted simmering water
2 tablespoons pitted black olives, roughly chopped
6 plum tomatoes, skinned, seeded and chopped
1 tablespoon capers, rinsed and chopped
grated zest 1 lemon
large pinch dried oregano
2 tablespoons extra virgin olive oil
handful basil leaves, torn
salt and pepper

- Warm the butter in a large saucepan.
- Add the onion and the garlic and sauté for 5 minutes until soft.
- Add the rice, stirring to coat it thoroughly in the butter. Fry for 1 minute, stirring continuously.
- Pour on the wine and stir to incorporate it into the rice.
- Once the wine has disappeared, start to add the salted water two ladlefuls at a time.
- Don't let each addition become completely absorbed before adding the next two. I tend to keep the rice quite wet between each addition as it cooks more evenly this way.
- After 20 minutes of adding the water as above, add the olives, tomatoes, capers, lemon zest and dried oregano.
- Taste the rice to see if it is cooked. If so, add the extra virgin olive oil and basil and adjust the seasoning if necessary.

Cheese croquettes
+ potato and walnut salad + tomato salad

These are wonderfully light little cheese delights that, together with the salads, make a healthy meat-free meal.

Cheese croquettes

200g Caerphilly cheese, grated
250g ricotta cheese
50g white breadcrumbs
12 spring onions, finely chopped
2 tablespoons fresh basil, chopped
2 teaspoons Dijon mustard
salt and pepper
2 eggs, beaten
3 tablespoons olive oil
To coat the croquettes
50g white breadcrumbs

- Place the cheeses, breadcrumbs, spring onions, basil and mustard in a mixing bowl.
- Season with salt and pepper.
- Stir in the beaten egg and form into 10 croquettes.
- Roll each one in the remaining 50g of breadcrumbs.
- Chill in the fridge for 30 minutes.
- Heat the olive oil in a frying pan and brown each croquette all over.

Potato and walnut salad

500g new potatoes, peeled and halved
salt and black pepper
50g walnuts, roughly chopped
1 clove garlic, peeled and finely chopped
pinch of paprika
2 shallots, finely chopped
2 tablespoons flat-leaf parsley, chopped
juice 1 lemon
2 tablespoons extra virgin olive oil

- Boil the potatoes in salted water until tender.
- Place the potatoes in a serving bowl with the walnuts, garlic, paprika, shallots and parsley and dress with the lemon juice and olive oil. Season with pepper.

Tomato salad

6 tomatoes, sliced
2 tablespoons extra virgin olive oil
¼ tablespoon balsamic vinegar
salt and pepper

- Lay the tomatoes on a serving plate.
- Dress with the oil, vinegar, salt and pepper.

Grilled Dover sole
+ new potatoes + green beans

Dover sole has a lovely delicate flavour and the best way to serve it is simply, with a little butter, lemon juice and no fuss.

Grilled Dover sole

3 whole Dover sole
40g butter, melted
salt and pepper
1 fresh lemon

- Preheat the grill and cover the grill rack with tin foil.
- Place the fish on the tin foil and brush the top with some of the melted butter.
- Sprinkle with salt and pepper.
- Each side will take approximately 4 minutes to grill. When you turn the fish over, remember to brush the other side with melted butter and season with salt and pepper.
- Once cooked, split each fish into two fillets. This is easily done by cutting into the fish with a sharp knife and prising the flesh away from the bone. It comes away very easily when it is cooked.
- Then squeeze some lemon juice over each fillet and serve immediately.

New potatoes

700g new potatoes
salt
butter
mint leaves, roughly chopped

- Wash the potatoes and cook them in salted water for 15–20 minutes until tender. It is a matter of personal taste whether you prefer new potatoes with their skins on or not. It is probably easier to remove the skins after you have cooked the potatoes if they are very small and then toss them in the butter and mint leaves once you have removed the skins.

Green beans

250g green beans, topped and tailed
salt and pepper

- Bring a saucepan of water with a pinch of salt to the boil.
- Once you have a rolling boil, add the beans and boil for 5 minutes.
- Drain well and serve with a knob of butter and freshly ground black pepper.

Egg and prawn Coronation salad + onion rolls

This is a take on Coronation chicken. At the time of writing, we are experiencing the hottest summer on record in England. It is a testing time for cooks, as a hot kitchen is not the place to spend much time and the family do not seem to have a great appetite for meat. This is a good recipe on both counts. If you can't face making the bread then buy some. If you can, make it first and if you are making your own mayonnaise (see page 343), do that next.

Egg and prawn Coronation salad

1 tablespoon olive oil
1 onion, finely diced
1 dessertspoon curry powder*
1 teaspoon tomato purée
2 fresh apricots, liquidized with 1 tablespoon water
100ml red wine
75ml water
1 bay leaf
salt
1 teaspoon sugar
1 slice of lemon
juice ½ lemon
6 tablespoons mayonnaise (shop-bought will do)
500g cooked prawns
1 large lettuce, washed
4 plum tomatoes, sliced
6–8 radishes, sliced
½ cucumber, sliced
bunch chives, snipped finely
1 tablespoon flat-leaf parsley, chopped
6 hard-boiled eggs, shelled and quartered
1 tablespoon extra virgin olive oil
salt and pepper

- Heat the oil in a sauté pan.
- Add the onion and cook gently for 5 minutes.
- Add the curry powder and cook for 1 minute.
- Next, add the tomato purée, apricot purée, wine, water and bay leaf.
- Bring to a simmer and add a good pinch of salt, the sugar, lemon slice and lemon juice.
- Simmer with the pan uncovered for 5 minutes.
- Strain through a sieve and leave to cool.
- Spoon the mayonnaise into the cooled mixture and stir until smooth.
- Add the prawns to the mixture and mix gently.
- Place the lettuce, tomatoes, radishes and cucumber in a large salad serving bowl, along with the herbs and eggs. Drizzle over the olive oil and season with salt and pepper.
- Spoon the prawns and mayonnaise over the top.

continues

**** To make your own curry powder:***
1 tablespoon coriander seeds
1 dessertspoon cumin seeds
1 teaspoon fennel seeds
½ teaspoon fenugreek

- *Place the coriander seeds into a small, heavy-bottomed pan and heat through for 30 seconds.*
- *Add the other ingredients and toast until you smell the lovely aroma of the spices.*
- *Transfer the spices to a coffee grinder, a small processor, or grind them in a pestle and mortar.*

Onion rolls

25g butter
1 onion, finely diced
½ teaspoon sugar
400g strong white bread flour
100g wholemeal or malthouse flour
2 teaspoons salt
1 sachet fast-action dried yeast
300ml tepid water
1 egg, beaten to glaze

- Heat the butter in a sauté pan.
- Add the onion and sugar and sauté on a low heat for 5 minutes.
- Place the flours and salt into a large mixing bowl.
- Mix the yeast with a little of the 300ml of water and pour this into the flours and salt.
- Add the onions and the rest of the water and mix well to combine.
- Turn out onto a floured surface and knead for 10 minutes.
- Place back in the bowl and cover with a clean tea towel.
- Leave to rise for 1 hour.
- Knock back by punching the air out of it and divide into 12–14 pieces.
- Shape into rolls.
- Place on a greased baking tray, cover and leave to rise for 30 minutes.
- Meanwhile, heat the oven to 220°C/425°F/gas 7.
- Brush the rolls with the glaze just before you place them in the oven to bake for 20 minutes.
- Cool on a rack and serve the rolls with the Coronation salad.

Curried monkfish + saffron rice

Monkfish has become expensive recently. If it is out of your price range, substitute another white fish such as haddock or pollack, both of which are good. Plain poppadums also go nicely with this meal.

Curried monkfish

200g red lentils
500ml water
2 cloves garlic, peeled and finely chopped
2.5cm piece fresh ginger, peeled and finely chopped
1 teaspoon cumin seeds
seeds from 5 cardamom pods
½ teaspoon black peppercorns
¼ teaspoon chilli flakes
¼ teaspoon turmeric
1 tablespoon vegetable oil
1 onion, finely chopped
600g monkfish tail fillets, sliced across into 5cm pieces
200g tinned chopped tomatoes
200ml coconut milk
1 teaspoon brown sugar
1 teaspoon salt
1 tablespoon fresh mint, finely chopped
1 tablespoon fresh coriander, finely chopped

- Put the red lentils in a saucepan with the water, bring them to a slow simmer and cook for about 45 minutes until they are tender and have lost their bite. Don't season them at this stage. You may need to add a little more water while they cook. Once cooked, set aside.
- Next, place the garlic and ginger in 100ml of water and set aside.
- Place a small frying pan on a medium heat and toast the cumin, cardamom seeds, peppercorns and chilli flakes until they start to smoke and you can smell their aroma.
- Put the toasted spices in a pestle and mortar and grind to a very fine powder. Add the turmeric and set aside.
- Heat the vegetable oil in another frying pan and then add the onion and fry it for 5 minutes, until it has softened and the onion has started to become tinged with brown.
- Then add the garlic, ginger and water and cook for 1 minute.
- Next, stir in the toasted spices.
- Now add the monkfish pieces and stir round, coating the fish in the spices.
- Add the tomatoes, coconut milk, cooked lentils and sugar and simmer for 5 minutes.
- Season with salt and when ready to serve, stir in the coriander and mint.

Saffron rice

1 teaspoon saffron strands
500g basmati rice
750ml water
½ teaspoon salt
grated zest 1 lemon
2 teaspoons black mustard seeds

- Place the saffron strands in a small bowl with one tablespoon of boiled warm water.
- Put the rice in a saucepan and add the 750ml of water, saffron strands and their liquid, salt, lemon zest and mustard seeds.
- Bring the rice to a good rolling boil. Cover the saucepan with a close-fitting lid and reduce the heat to low for 15 minutes.
- After 15 minutes remove the rice from the heat but leave the lid on the saucepan for another 10 minutes, as the rice will finish cooking in the steam.
- Serve with the monkfish and lentils and some plain poppadums.

Grilled chicken + pilaf rice + cucumber salad

You can grill this chicken under a conventional grill or on a barbecue. The robust flavours of the spices make the chicken very tasty and contrast well with the delicious cooling cucumber salad.

Grilled chicken

1 teaspoon coriander seeds
1 teaspoon cumin seeds
½ teaspoon fenugreek
1 teaspoon mustard seeds
6 curry leaves
1 dessertspoon desiccated coconut
¼ teaspoon turmeric
1 teaspoon salt
¼ teaspoon cayenne pepper
5 tablespoons natural yoghurt
handful mint leaves, chopped
1 green chilli, deseeded and finely chopped
1kg chicken thigh fillets, skin removed

- Take a small frying pan and place it on a high heat.
- Add the coriander seeds and toast for 1 minute.
- Add the cumin seeds and fenugreek and toast for a few seconds more.
- Next add the mustard seeds, curry leaves and desiccated coconut and keep the pan on the heat until the coconut starts to brown.
- Transfer the spices to a pestle and mortar and add the turmeric, salt and cayenne pepper.
- Grind to a coarse powder and set aside.
- In a mixing bowl, place the yoghurt with the chopped mint and chilli.
- Scoop the ground spices into the yoghurt mixture and stir to combine.
- Add the chicken pieces, coating them all over with the spiced yoghurt mixture and leave these to marinate for at least 1 hour.
- Preheat the grill and place the chicken pieces under, turning each piece as it browns. I find that they take about 20 minutes to cook.

Pilaf rice

400g basmati rice
600ml water
½ teaspoon salt
2 tablespoons vegetable oil
½ teaspoon black mustard seeds
2 pinches asafoetida powder
1 green chilli, deseeded and chopped
¼ teaspoon turmeric
6 curry leaves
2 teaspoons tamarind paste
a few cashew nuts to garnish

- Place the rice in a saucepan of salted water.
- Bring to a good rolling boil, cover the saucepan with a close-fitting lid and reduce the heat to low for 15 minutes.
- After 15 minutes remove the rice from the heat but leave the lid on the saucepan for another 10 minutes, as the rice will finish cooking in the steam.
- Heat the oil in a frying pan or sauté pan large enough to hold the rice.
- When hot put the mustard seeds into the oil.
- Once they have started to pop, add the asafoetida powder and stir-fry on a medium heat for a few seconds.
- Add the green chilli and turmeric and fry for 1 minute.
- Now add the curry leaves and stir-fry for a few seconds.
- Next add the rice, breaking it up with a wooden spoon as you go.
- Add the tamarind paste and stir again for few seconds.
- Garnish with a handful of cashew nuts.

Cucumber salad

½ cucumber, finely sliced
1 shallot, peeled and thinly sliced
salt and pepper
½ tablespoon lime juice
1 tablespoon coconut milk

- Place the cucumber slices and shallots in a serving bowl.
- Season with salt and pepper.
- Add the lime juice and coconut milk and toss to coat the cucmber and shallots evenly.

Beef fillet in a horseradish cream sauce + roast potatoes + Parmesan green beans

Even though the weather is warmer at this time of year it doesn't stop my family wanting, and enjoying, roast potatoes. Beef fillet is a relatively expensive cut of meat but quite good value for money, as there is no waste so you can get away with buying a small piece.

Beef fillet in a horseradish cream sauce

750g piece of beef fillet
salt and pepper
1 tablespoon olive oil

For the sauce

2 tablespoons olive oil
1 shallot, finely chopped
1 clove garlic, finely chopped
70g chopped pancetta
50ml dry white wine
150ml double cream
1 small bunch fresh chives, snipped
1 tablespoon horseradish sauce
salt and pepper

To prepare the beef

- Preheat the oven to 200°C/400°F/gas 6.
- Season the beef fillet all over with salt and pepper.
- On the hob heat the olive oil in a roasting tin.
- Add the beef fillet and brown it all over.
- Cover the fillet with greaseproof paper and put the tin in the oven to roast; give it 10 minutes for a nice rare pink fillet, but longer if you prefer it well cooked.
- When it comes out of the oven, leave it to rest for 10 minutes or so.

To make the sauce

- Warm the olive oil in a frying pan.
- Add the shallot, garlic and pancetta and sauté gently until the pancetta starts to brown slightly and the shallot has softened.
- Add the wine and simmer for 1 minute.
- Add the cream and let this bubble gently for 1 minute.
- Stir in the chives and horseradish and season with salt and pepper.

Roast potatoes

700g potatoes, peeled and parboiled
salt
2 tablespoons olive oil

- Preheat the oven to 220°C/425°F/gas 7.
- Parboil the potatoes in salted water for about 4 minutes.
- Drain them and place in a roasting tin.
- Drizzle with the olive oil and roast for 45–60 minutes until golden brown.

Parmesan green beans

400g green beans
salt and black pepper
olive oil
1 tablespoon grated Parmesan cheese

- Cook the green beans in salted water as normal.
- When cooked transfer to a small pan on a low heat with the olive oil and Parmesan and stir round to coat for a minute or two.
- Season with pepper and serve.

Baked vanilla peaches

Peaches are equally delicious eaten cooked as they are fresh.

100ml Amaretto liqueur
100ml water
100g caster sugar
1 vanilla pod, split lengthways
2cm piece of cinnamon stick
8 ripe peaches, halved and destoned
2 or 3 handfuls summer berries
whipping cream for serving

- Preheat the oven to 200°C/400°F/gas 6.
- Pour the liqueur, water and sugar into a small saucepan, along with the vanilla pod and cinnamon stick.
- Bring to a simmer and cook for 1 minute.
- Place the peaches and berries in an ovenproof dish and pour the liqueur mixture over the fruit.
- Bake for 30 minutes.
- Serve with whipped cream.

Apricot and orange cake

This is an Italian-style cake full of the flavours of summer. It works either as a teatime treat with a cup of tea, or as a dessert with some fresh fruit and cream.

250g butter, softened
250g caster sugar
4 eggs
grated zest 1 orange
75g ground almonds
100g plain flour, sieved
100g dried apricots, finely chopped
juice ½ orange
icing sugar for dusting
cream and soft fruit for serving

- Preheat the oven to 180°C/350°F/gas 4.
- Grease and line a 23cm cake tin.
- Beat the butter and sugar together with an electric mixer, until light and fluffy.
- Add the eggs one at a time, combining each one thoroughly before adding the next.
- Add the orange zest along with half the ground almonds and flour.
- Mix in slowly.
- Add the rest of the flour and almonds, the apricots and orange juice and fold in gently with a wooden spoon.
- Spoon the mixture into the cake tin and bake for 35 minutes or until a skewer inserted into the middle of the cake comes out clean.
- Dust with icing sugar.
- Serve with cream and soft fruit.

Week 3

Monday p364	Chicken curry + green bean sambol + boiled rice
Tuesday p366	Spaghetti with prawn and tomato sauce
Wednesday p367	Goat's cheese, mint and broad bean tart + salad
Thursday p368	Eggs Benedict + buttered spinach
Friday p369	Bistro salad
Saturday p370	Burgers + chips + green salad
Sunday p371	Roast poussins + potatoes and petits pois
Sunday pudding p372	Apricot frangipane tart
Extra tasty treat p373	Lemon almond cookies

Shopping list

MEAT

- ☐ 1.5kg chicken pieces on the bone
- ☐ 10 pork sausages
- ☐ 300g minced beef
- ☐ 250g minced pork
- ☐ 3 poussins

FISH

- ☐ 400g raw tiger or king prawns

VEGETABLES

- ☐ 2 tomatoes
- ☐ fresh ginger
- ☐ 500g green beans
- ☐ 2 green chillies
- ☐ 1 garlic bulb
- ☐ 1 red chilli
- ☐ 100g very young broad beans or, if unavailable, peas
- ☐ 2 Romaine lettuces
- ☐ 500g spinach leaves
- ☐ 200g salad leaves
- ☐ 5 shallots
- ☐ 1 red onion
- ☐ 1 onion
- ☐ 500g potatoes
- ☐ 1 cucumber
- ☐ 1 green pepper
- ☐ 7 spring onions
- ☐ 1.6kg new potatoes

FRUIT

- ☐ 10 ripe apricots
- ☐ 2 lemons

FRESH HERBS

- ☐ basil
- ☐ mint
- ☐ flat-leaf parsley leaves
- ☐ chives

FRIDGE ITEMS

- ☐ 180g goat's cheese
- ☐ 170g sliced pancetta
- ☐ 170g chopped pancetta
- ☐ 50g Parmesan cheese
- ☐ 550ml chicken stock
- ☐ 500g frozen petits pois
- ☐ 200g creme fraîche
- ☐ 4 packs butter
- ☐ 21 eggs
- ☐ 500ml double cream

KITCHEN CUPBOARD ITEMS

- ☐ 100g cashew nuts
- ☐ Dijon mustard
- ☐ extra virgin olive oil
- ☐ white wine vinegar
- ☐ olive oil
- ☐ balsamic vinegar
- ☐ 1 jar cornichons
- ☐ vegetable oil
- ☐ 200ml coconut milk
- ☐ 100g desiccated coconut
- ☐ 550g basmati rice
- ☐ 1 bottle dry white wine
- ☐ 2 x 400g tins chopped tomatoes
- ☐ 400g spaghetti
- ☐ salt
- ☐ 4 muffins
- ☐ 75g icing sugar
- ☐ 50g amaretti biscuits
- ☐ 275g caster sugar
- ☐ 850g plain flour
- ☐ 365g ground almonds

SPICES

- ☐ coriander seeds
- ☐ cumin seeds
- ☐ fenugreek seeds
- ☐ cinnamon sticks
- ☐ cardamom pods
- ☐ turmeric
- ☐ whole nutmeg
- ☐ black peppercorns
- ☐ paprika

Chicken curry
+ green bean sambol + boiled rice

This is a typical Sri Lankan curry meal. The Sri Lankans eat a lot of vegetable curries which are far removed from the taste and flavour of Indian curries.

Chicken curry

1.5kg chicken pieces, on the bone, skin removed

For the spice marinade

1 tablespoon coriander seeds
2 teaspoons cumin seeds
½ teaspoon fenugreek seeds
3 tablespoons cashew nuts
1 tablespoon basmati rice, uncooked
2 tablespoons desiccated coconut
2cm piece cinnamon stick
seeds from 3 cardamom pods
1 tablespoon garlic, crushed

For the sauce

2 tablespoons vegetable oil
1 green chilli, deseeded and finely chopped
2 shallots, thinly sliced
1cm fresh ginger, finely chopped
1½ teaspoons salt
2 small tomatoes, chopped
200ml coconut milk
100ml water

To prepare the marinade

- Take a heavy frying pan and heat it up on the hob.
- Add the coriander seeds and toast until they are lightly browned and set aside.
- Except for the cinnamon, cardamom seed and garlic, do the same with each of the other marinade ingredients, toasting each one separately until lightly browned.
- Place all of the toasted ingredients into a food processor and grind them to a fine powder.
- Add the cinnamon and cardamom seeds and grind these in as well.
- Then add the garlic and one tablespoon water and mix in.
- Place the chicken pieces in a large bowl and spoon the marinade over them, rubbing in the spice paste with your fingers.
- Set aside for at least 20 minutes.

To prepare the sauce

- Heat the vegetable oil in a large saucepan.
- Throw in the chilli, shallots and ginger and fry on a low heat for 3 minutes.
- Add the chicken and salt and brown the chicken lightly all over.
- Next, add the tomatoes and cook for 2 minutes.
- Finally, add the coconut milk and water and bring to the boil.
- Reduce the heat and cover.
- Simmer gently for 40 minutes.

Green bean sambol

500g green beans
1 finely red onion, chopped
1 green chilli, deseeded and finely chopped
¼ teaspoon turmeric
1 teaspoon salt
50g desiccated coconut

- Place the beans in a food processor and chop them finely.
- Then put the beans into a large pan with all the other ingredients.
- Heat the mixture through on a high heat stirring all the time.
- Reduce the heat, cover and cook for 10 minutes.
- Serve with the chicken curry.

Boiled rice

500g basmati rice
750ml water
salt

- Put the rice in a saucepan with the water and a pinch of salt.
- Place the rice on a high heat and as soon as it comes to the boil, cover the saucepan with a lid and turn the heat right down to very low. Leave it for 15 minutes, giving it one stir only during the cooking time.
- Then take the pan off the heat and leave it covered for a further 10 minutes, before removing the lid.

Spaghetti with prawn and tomato sauce

Prawns and tomato sauce are not ingredients we normally associate with each other but they work well in this dish.

4 tablespoons olive oil
2 garlic cloves, peeled and finely chopped
1 red chilli, deseeded and finely chopped
5 tablespoons dry white wine
2 x 400g tins chopped tomatoes
salt and pepper
1 teaspoon sugar
400g raw tiger or king prawns, shelled and cleaned
2 handfuls basil leaves, roughly torn
2 tablespoons flat-leaf parsley, roughly chopped
400g spaghetti

- Warm the olive oil in a medium saucepan.
- Add the garlic and chilli.
- Gently fry for a few seconds, stirring all the time so as not to burn the garlic.
- Add the wine and cook, stirring for 2 minutes.
- Add the tinned tomatoes and bring to a simmer.
- Season well with salt and pepper and add the sugar. Reduce to the gentlest of simmers for about 45 minutes.
- Add the prawns and cook until they lose their pinkness; this should take about 1 minute or even less.
- Scatter in the torn basil leaves and parsley and remove from the heat.
- Meanwhile cook the spaghetti in plenty of boiling salted water and serve with the sauce.

Goat's cheese, mint and broad bean tart + salad

Broad beans are easy to obtain in July and go superbly with the cheese and mint.

Goat's cheese, mint and broad bean tart

For the pastry

225g plain flour
150g butter
salt
1 egg yolk
2 tablespoons cold water

For the filling

1 tablespoon olive oil
70g sliced pancetta, chopped
1 onion, finely diced
100g very young broad beans or, if unavailable, peas, cooked
180g goat's cheese, thinly sliced
2 eggs
double cream
salt and pepper
1 handful fresh mint leaves, finely chopped

To make the pastry

- Put the flour and butter in a food processor, or a bowl, if you are combining by hand, and incorporate so that the mixture resembles fine breadcrumbs.
- Add a pinch of salt.
- Mix the egg yolk with the cold water in a small bowl and add them to the pastry mixture.
- Combine the mixture quickly into a dough.
- Turn the dough out onto a lightly floured work surface and combine thoroughly until you have a smooth dough.
- Wrap the dough in cling-film and chill in the fridge for 30 minutes.

To make the tart

- Preheat the oven to 180°C/350°F/gas 4.
- Grease a 30cm diameter tart tin.
- Heat the olive oil in a sauté pan.
- Gently sauté the pancetta and onion on a medium heat for 3 minutes.
- Roll out the pastry and line the tart tin.
- Scatter the sautéed pancetta and onion over the bottom of the case.
- Next scatter over the cooked broad beans.
- Lay the sliced goat's cheese out in circles on top of the pancetta, onion and broad beans. Don't overlap the cheese.
- Crack the eggs into a measuring jug and pour in enough double cream to make up 250ml of liquid.
- Season with salt and pepper.
- Pour this mixture into the pastry case and scatter over the mint.
- Bake for 25–30 minutes.

Salad

1 Romaine lettuce, washed and chopped
½ cucumber, sliced
4 spring onions, chopped

For the dressing

1 tablespoon olive oil
2 teaspoons balsamic vinegar
salt and pepper

- Assemble the salad in a serving bowl and pour over the dressing when ready to serve.

Eggs Benedict + buttered spinach

My children and husband love eggs Benedict. They are very easy to make, and the hollandaise sauce only takes a few minutes in a food processor. I add spinach to the dish to make it more substantial. I also use duck eggs when I can get them, but ordinary hens' eggs will do just as well.

Eggs Benedict

8 eggs
salt and pepper
4 muffins
100g sliced pancetta
For the hollandaise sauce
110g unsalted butter
2 egg yolks
salt and pepper
squeeze of fresh lemon juice

To make the hollandaise sauce

- Melt the butter gently over a medium heat, but don't let it brown.
- Put the egg yolks, salt, pepper and lemon juice in a food processor and whizz until smooth.
- Keep the food processor going on a slow speed and start trickling in the melted butter. Don't add more than a trickle or it will curdle.
- Stop adding the butter once you reach the cloudy sediment in the bottom of the saucepan. Adjust the seasoning, if necessary.
- If you are not serving the sauce immediately, set it in a bowl over a pan of hot water to keep warm. You will not be able to heat it up again, as it will curdle.

To complete the eggs Benedict

- Half fill a frying pan with water and bring it to a simmer. This water is to poach the eggs in.
- Preheat the grill and split the muffins in two ready for toasting.
- Place the pancetta in a small frying pan and start to fry it very gently without adding any oil.
- The water should now be ready for the eggs. Poach 4 eggs at a time for 1–2 minutes. You poach the eggs by cracking them into the simmering water. With a spoon try and scoop the egg round the yolk, so the poached egg is nice and compact. When ready, take them out with a slotted spoon and set aside. They will still be warm by the time the other 4 eggs have cooked.
- Toast the muffins and finish cooking the pancetta.
- Serve the eggs Benedict by placing a muffin on each plate. If you are having spinach, follow the recipe below and place a spoonful on top of the toasted muffin and then place the egg on top. Pour over a spoon or 3 of the hollandaise sauce. Garnish each egg with a piece of pancetta.

Buttered spinach

500g spinach leaves
salt
a knob of butter
nutmeg
black pepper

- Place the spinach in a large saucepan with a tablespoon of water and a sprinkling of sea salt.
- Cover and place the saucepan on a low heat.
- Gradually wilt the spinach for 10 minutes, until all the leaves are a glossy dark green.
- Then remove the lid and stir round for a few seconds to get rid of any excess water. If there is still too much, drain the extra off.
- Add a knob of butter, a tiny grating of nutmeg and a good grinding of black pepper.

Bistro salad

This is a substantial summer salad full of fresh flavours tempered only by the presence of the sausages. Children like this salad.

1 tablespoon olive oil
10 pork sausages
For the dressing
750g new potatoes, peeled
salt and pepper
2 tablespoons white wine vinegar
1 teaspoon Dijon mustard
4 tablespoons extra virgin olive oil
1 large shallot, finely chopped
3 tablespoons flat-leaf parsley, chopped
200g salad leaves
12 or so cornichons

- Heat the olive oil in a frying pan.
- Gently brown the sausages all over.
- Add 2 tablespoons of water, turn the heat to low and cook the sausages for 20 minutes.
- Cook the potatoes in plenty of salted water and simmer them until just tender.
- Slice the potatoes thickly and set aside.
- Next prepare the dressing by mixing the vinegar with the mustard in a small bowl.
- Season well with salt and pepper.
- Pour the extra virgin olive oil onto the vinegar mixture a little at a time whisking continuously.
- Add the shallot to the dressing.
- Pour the dressing over the warm potatoes and then sprinkle over the parsley.
- Cut the sausages into diagonal pieces and arrange them in a large serving dish that will also hold the potatoes, salad leaves and cornichons.
- Serve with French bread.

Burgers
+ chips + green salad

Beef burgers acquired a bad name some years ago, thanks to the cheap processed brands sold in most supermarkets. I love burgers if they are good quality, as do my family. They need to be made from high-quality meat and ideally served in a homemade bread roll. If you haven't time for this, use a muffin rather than a bought burger bun, as these tend to go soggy. Ciabatta also works well.

Burgers

300g minced beef
250g minced pork
2 shallots, finely diced
1 bunch chives, finely snipped
2 heaped tablespoons Parmesan cheese, freshly grated
100g chopped pancetta
1 egg, beaten
1 teaspoon salt
freshly ground black pepper
olive oil for frying
toasted bread for serving

- Put all the ingredients in a mixing bowl and combine thoroughly.
- Season well with salt and pepper.
- Form the mixture into six burgers, weighing approximately 100g each.
- Put some flour on a plate and gently pat the burger on both sides into the flour.
- Heat one tablespoon of olive oil in a heavy-bottomed frying pan and, when hot, put in 3 burgers at a time.
- Cook each one for about 5 minutes on each side, on a medium heat. As these burgers contain minced pork you want them to be well cooked. They should be nice and brown on each side when they are ready.
- An optional extra that works well in my house is cheese and extra bacon, which you can do at this stage. I put the cheese on top of the burger in the pan whilst I am cooking it on the other side, and it has usually melted by the time the burger is cooked.
- Gently toast the bread you are going to serve the burger in and enjoy!

Chips

500g potatoes
1 tablespoon olive oil
1 teaspoon paprika

- Preheat oven to 220°C/425°F/gas 7.
- Don't peel the potatoes. Cut them in half lengthways and then in half lengthways again.
- Parboil the potatoes in boiling, salted water for 5 minutes.
- Drain well and place the potatoes on a baking sheet. Drizzle over the olive oil.
- Sprinkle the paprika over the potatoes and bake them for 40 minutes.
- Sprinkle with sea salt on serving.

Green salad

1 lettuce, washed
½ cucumber, sliced
1 green pepper, finely diced
For the dressing
2 tablespoons extra virgin olive oil
½ tablespoon balsamic vinegar
salt and pepper

- Combine the salad in a serving bowl.
- Combine the dressing ingredients and drizzle over the salad when ready to serve.

Roast poussins
+ potatoes and petits pois

I find simple meals much more satisfying than hugely complicated ones, as I feel that I have achieved something good for relatively little effort. The preparation of this meal is very straightforward. One poussin should stretch to two people. It is also a good idea to carve the poussins in two, away from the table prior to serving, as it's a little fiddly and messy.

Roast poussins

2 tablespoons olive oil
3 poussins
salt and pepper

- Preheat the oven to 190°C/375°F/gas 5.
- Take a large saucepan and heat the olive oil in it.
- Brown the poussins one at a time all over. Spend no more than 5 minutes on each one.
- Season each poussin with salt and pepper and place them in a meat tin. Keep the saucepan with the oil and juices to cook the potatoes and peas in later.
- Roast the poussins for 35 minutes.

Potatoes and petits pois

3 spring onions, chopped
70g cubed pancetta
800g new potatoes, peeled and quartered
550ml chicken stock
salt and pepper
500g fresh or frozen petits pois
2 tablespoons crème fraîche

- Reheat the oil and juices from the poussin in the saucepan, on a moderate heat on the hob.
- Sauté the spring onions and the pancetta for 3 minutes.
- Add the potatoes and stir them round to coat them in the oil.
- Pour the stock in and bring it to a simmer.
- Season with salt and pepper.
- Cover and simmer for 10 minutes.
- Add the petits pois.
- Bring back to a simmer and cook, covered, for a further 5 minutes or so until the potatoes and peas are nicely tender.
- Stir in the creme fraîche.
- Check the seasoning and add more salt and pepper if necessary.
- You can reheat this dish when you are ready to eat.

Apricot frangipane tart

I have a huge liking for cooked, fresh apricots. Their full flavour bursts forth when they are warmed by cooking.

For the sweet pastry
180g butter
75g icing sugar
2 egg yolks
225g plain flour
For the filling
240g ground almonds
50g amaretti biscuits, crushed
150g caster sugar
200g butter, softened
3 eggs
100g plain flour
10 ripe apricots
cream for serving

To make the pastry

- Place the butter, icing sugar, egg yolks and flour together in a food processor. Mix briefly until a dough starts to form.
- Turn out onto a floured work surface and form into a ball.
- Wrap in cling-film and chill in the fridge for 30 minutes.

To make the tart

- Preheat the oven to 180°C/350°F/gas 4 and place a baking tray in the oven.
- Grease a 24cm tart tin.
- Roll out the pastry and line the tin.
- Place the ground almonds, amaretti biscuits, sugar and butter in a food processor and process until smooth and pale.
- Add the eggs one by one, processing between each addition until combined.
- Finally beat in the flour.
- Spoon the mixture into the pastry case.
- Halve the apricots and de-stone them.
- Place them cut side down into the cake mixture and bake the tart in the oven for approximately 45–50 minutes.
- Serve with cream or crème fraîche.

Lemon almond cookies

Cookies do not take a long time to prepare and bake. They contain no preservatives and far less sugar than factory processed biscuits and so do make a good snack for children when they come in from school. This recipe makes approximately 30 biscuits, which will keep well for a few days in an airtight container.

250g butter, softened
125g caster sugar
2 egg yolks
grated zest 1 lemon
250g plain flour
125g ground almonds

- Preheat the oven to 180°C/350°F/gas 4.
- Cream the butter and sugar with an electric or hand-held mixer.
- Beat in the egg yolks and lemon zest. Don't worry if the mixture curdles.
- Add the flour and ground almonds and mix briefly.
- Turn the mixture out onto a floured surface and quickly form into a ball of dough.
- Pinch off and roll walnut-sized balls of the dough and place these on greased baking trays. They can be placed reasonably close together as they will not spread too much, but you won't get them all on one baking tray. If you do only possess one baking tray, then cook them in batches as they only take 10 minutes to bake.
- Take a fork and a cup of cold water.
- Dip the fork in the water and press it down gently on each biscuit. If the fork starts to stick to the dough dip it in the water again.
- Bake the biscuits for 10 minutes.
- Allow them to cool slightly and then transfer them carefully to a cooling rack.

Week 4

Monday p376	Chicken, spinach and coriander rice
Tuesday p377	Prawn and crème fraîche tart + new potatoes + tomato salad
Wednesday p378	Tomato and macaroni soufflé + green salad
Thursday p379	Mediterranean fish casserole
Friday p380	Grilled spiced mackerel + tomato salad + cheese and onion bread
Saturday p382	Fried plaice + minty broad beans and peas with Parmesan + sautéed potatoes
Sunday p383	Orvietan chicken + roast potatoes + green salad
Sunday pudding p384	Blackcurrant pie
Extra tasty treat p385	Fruity flapjacks

Shopping list

MEAT

- ☐ 8 chicken thighs
- ☐ 2 x 1.5kg organic chickens

FISH

- ☐ 250g cooked prawns
- ☐ 1kg cod fillets
- ☐ 6 mackerel fillets
- ☐ 6 plaice fillets

VEGETABLES

- ☐ 100g spinach leaves
- ☐ 2 carrots
- ☐ 1 red pepper
- ☐ 1 onion
- ☐ 25 spring onions
- ☐ 400g baby broad beans
- ☐ 450g peas
- ☐ 1 garlic bulb
- ☐ 1 fennel bulb
- ☐ 1.7kg potatoes
- ☐ 700g new potatoes
- ☐ 1 cucumber
- ☐ 2 lettuces
- ☐ 12 plum tomatoes

FRUIT

- ☐ 2 lemon
- ☐ 900g blackcurrants

FRESH HERBS

- ☐ coriander
- ☐ chives
- ☐ thyme
- ☐ oregano
- ☐ basil
- ☐ mint
- ☐ rosemary

FRIDGE ITEMS

- ☐ 200g crème fraîche
- ☐ 100g Parmesan cheese
- ☐ 40g Gruyère cheese
- ☐ 225g mature Cheddar
- ☐ 600ml semi skimmed milk
- ☐ 3 packs butter
- ☐ 9 eggs
- ☐ 1 carton double cream

KITCHEN CUPBOARD ITEMS

- ☐ 400g basmati rice
- ☐ 600g plain flour
- ☐ Dijon mustard
- ☐ red wine vinegar
- ☐ 100g macaroni
- ☐ extra virgin olive oil
- ☐ olive oil
- ☐ balsamic vinegar
- ☐ white wine vinegar
- ☐ 2 x 400g tins chopped tomatoes
- ☐ 650g white bread flour
- ☐ mustard powder
- ☐ fast-action dried yeast
- ☐ 300g polenta flour
- ☐ 150ml dry white wine
- ☐ pitted black olives
- ☐ cornflour
- ☐ 150g porridge oats
- ☐ 275g caster sugar
- ☐ baking powder
- ☐ 50g raisins
- ☐ French bread
- ☐ salt

SPICES

- ☐ black peppercorns
- ☐ fennel seeds
- ☐ paprika
- ☐ turmeric
- ☐ curry leaves
- ☐ cumin seeds
- ☐ coriander seeds
- ☐ cayenne pepper
- ☐ cinnamon sticks
- ☐ fenugreek
- ☐ ground cinnamon

Chicken, spinach and coriander rice

This chicken dish is fast, tasty and a good way of introducing spinach to the family.

100g spinach leaves
20g fresh coriander
125ml water
2 tablespoons olive oil
8 chicken thighs, skin removed
salt and pepper
1 clove garlic, peeled and finely chopped
2 carrots, peeled and diced
50g peas
½ red pepper, diced
¼ teaspoon cayenne pepper
400g basmati rice

- Place the spinach leaves, coriander and water in a food processor, purée and set aside.
- Heat the olive oil in a large saucepan.
- Brown the chicken pieces all over for 5 minutes, seasoning them with salt and pepper as they brown. Cover the chicken and cook on a low heat for 15 minutes. Remove the chicken from the pan and set aside.
- Keep the pan on the hob and increase the heat to medium.
- Add the garlic, carrots, peas and red pepper and sauté for 5 minutes, stirring occasionally.
- Place the spinach and coriander purée into the pan, along with the browned chicken pieces.
- Season well with salt, pepper and the cayenne pepper.
- Add the rice to the pan and stir round, coating the rice in all the juices.
- Pour 600ml of water into the pan.
- Bring the dish to a good boil, cover the saucepan, reduce the heat to low and cook for 15 minutes.
- Remove the pan from the heat and keep it covered for 10 minutes.
- Check the seasoning and serve.

Prawn and crème fraîche tart + new potatoes + tomato salad

We don't eat prawns very often in our family, usually using them as an addition to a tart, as here, or a salad, in small quantities.

Prawn and crème fraîche tart

For the pastry

225g plain flour

salt

150g butter

1 egg yolk

2 tablespoons cold water

For the filling

20g butter

8 spring onions, chopped

2 eggs

5 tablespoons crème fraîche

salt and pepper

75g Cheddar cheese, grated

20g chives, snipped

250g cooked prawns

- Put the flour, a pinch of salt and the butter in a food processor, or in a bowl if you are combining by hand, and incorporate so that the mixture looks like fine breadcrumbs.
- Mix the egg yolk with the cold water in a small bowl and add to the pastry mixture.
- As the mixture begins to form a dough, turn it out onto a lightly floured work surface and combine thoroughly until you have a firm dough.
- Wrap the dough in cling-film and chill in the fridge for 30 minutes.
- Grease a 30cm flan tin.
- Preheat the oven to 190°C/375°F/gas 5.
- Warm the butter in a sauté pan and gently cook the spring onions in the butter for 2 minutes.
- Crack the eggs into a bowl and add the crème fraîche.
- Season well with salt and pepper and whisk to combine.
- Sprinkle in the cheese and add the snipped chives.
- Roll out the pastry and line the flan tin with it.
- Place the spring onions and prawns on the bottom of the pastry case.
- Pour on the crème fraîche and cheese mixture.
- Bake on a baking tray for 30 minutes.

New potatoes

700g new potatoes, peeled

1 tablespoon Dijon mustard

3 tablespoons red wine vinegar

1 teaspoon fennel seeds

½ teaspoon paprika

100ml extra virgin olive oil

salt and pepper

- Simmer the potatoes in salted water for 15–20 minutes until tender.
- Mix the mustard and vinegar together in a small bowl.
- Add the fennel seeds and paprika.
- Drizzle on the olive oil, whisking the mixture with a fork as you go, so that the mixture thickens.
- Season with salt and pepper.
- Pour the dressing over the warm potatoes.

Tomato salad

6 tomatoes

2 tablespoons extra virgin olive oil

¼ tablespoon balsamic vinegar

salt and pepper

- Slice the tomatoes and lay them on a serving plate.
- Dress with the oil, vinegar, salt and pepper.

Tomato and macaroni soufflé + green salad

This recipe is based on a recipe found in *The Constance Spry Cookery Book*, which was first published in 1956 and republished again recently. My mother donated her original copy to my kitchen a few years ago and it is a treasured possession.

Tomato and macaroni soufflé

100g macaroni, cooked in plenty of salted water
2 ripe plum tomatoes, thinly sliced
2 sprigs fresh thyme leaves
40g butter
40g flour
400ml milk
salt and pepper
100g Parmesan cheese, grated
3 eggs

- Preheat the oven to 180°C/350°F/gas 4.
- Butter a soufflé dish of approximately 20cm in diameter.
- Mix together the cooked macaroni, tomatoes and thyme in a bowl and set aside.
- Melt the butter in a small saucepan.
- Add the flour, stirring to combine.
- Remove from the hob and add the milk gradually, stirring all the time.
- Return the pan to the heat and bring the sauce to a simmer, stirring all the time.
- When the sauce has thickened, remove from the heat and season with salt and pepper.
- Add 50g of the Parmesan cheese.
- Separate the eggs keeping both the whites and the yolks. Add the yolks to the sauce, one at a time, thoroughly combining each one before you add the next.
- Whisk the egg whites in a separate bowl until stiff and then fold them into the sauce.
- Spoon a third of the sauce into the bottom of the soufflé dish.
- Add half the macaroni and tomato mix and half the remaining cheese.
- Cover with half the remaining sauce.
- Add the rest of the macaroni mix and then the rest of the sauce.
- Scatter the remaining cheese over the top.
- Season with salt and pepper.
- Bake for 30 minutes.

Green salad

½ cucumber, sliced
1 lettuce, washed
6 or 7 spring onions, sliced
To dress
2 tablespoons extra virgin olive oil
½ tablespoon balsamic vinegar
salt and pepper

- Combine the salad ingredients in a serving bowl and dress just before serving.

Mediterranean fish casserole

Everyone enjoyed this dish when I first made it including the children. It's a straightforward meal with a light, fresh taste.

3 tablespoons olive oil
1 tablespoon white wine vinegar
1 onion, finely diced
1 clove garlic, peeled and finely chopped
salt and pepper
1kg cod fillets
2 x 400g tins chopped tomatoes
3 or 4 sprigs fresh oregano
40g Gruyère cheese, grated
French bread for serving

- Preheat the oven to 200°C/400°F/gas 6.
- Take an ovenproof dish with a lid.
- Pour the oil and vinegar into the bottom of the dish along with the onion and garlic.
- Season with salt and pepper and mix.
- Lay the fish fillets in the dish and spoon the oil and vinegar mixture over them.
- Leave for 15 minutes.
- Pour over the tinned tomatoes and season well with salt and pepper.
- Sprinkle over the oregano leaves.
- Place in the oven for 35 minutes.
- As you take the dish from the oven, just before serving, sprinkle with the grated Gruyère.
- Serve with French bread.

Grilled spiced mackerel
+ tomato salad + cheese-and-onion bread

These cheese-and-onion rolls are heaven on earth, but I understand that making bread after a long day at work is a tall order. Buy bread if you have not got time to make your own. It won't stop you enjoying this delicious but simple meal which is so appropriate at this time of year.

Grilled spiced mackerel

6 mackerel fillets
squeeze of fresh lemon juice
For the spice
½ teaspoon turmeric
6 curry leaves
1 teaspoon cumin seeds
1 teaspoon coriander seeds
1 teaspoon salt
¼ teaspoon cayenne pepper
1cm piece cinnamon stick
½ teaspoon fenugreek

- Make sure all the pin bones have been removed from the fish fillets. The easiest way to do this is to run your finger along the line of symmetry on the fleshy side of the fish and use tweezers to remove the bones.
- Grind up all the spice ingredients in a pestle and mortar.
- Preheat the grill to high.
- Slash the mackerel fillets and rub the spice mixture into the fish where you have made the cuts.
- Grill each fillet for 2 minutes on the skin side. Flip the fillets over and grill for another 2 minutes on the other side.
- Place the fillets on a serving dish, squeeze fresh lemon juice over them and serve.

Tomato salad

4 plum tomatoes, sliced
2 tablespoons extra virgin olive oil
salt and pepper
handful torn basil leaves

- Place the tomatoes on a serving dish.
- Drizzle over the olive oil and season with the salt and pepper.
- Scatter over the torn basil leaves.

Cheese-and-onion rolls

650g white bread flour
2 teaspoons salt
1 teaspoon mustard powder
150g mature Cheddar, grated
40g spring onions, finely chopped
1 sachet fast-action dried yeast
200ml tepid semi-skimmed milk
200ml tepid water
a little milk and grated cheese

- Put the flour, salt, mustard, Cheddar and onions in a large mixing bowl.
- Mix the yeast with the milk and add the water.
- Gradually work the liquid into the flour mixture.
- Turn out onto a floured surface and knead for 10 minutes, until smooth, or for 5 minutes if you are using a food mixer with a dough hook.
- Return the dough to the bowl, cover with a tea towel and leave to rise for 1 hour 30 minutes.
- Divide the dough into 12–13 pieces (each piece should weigh about 75g), shape each piece into a roll and place on a greased baking sheet.
- Brush each roll with milk and sprinkle each one with a little grated cheese.
- Cover with the tea towel and leave to rise for a further 30 minutes.
- Preheat the oven to 220°C/425°F/gas 7.
- Bake for 17 minutes.

Fried plaice + minty broad beans and peas with Parmesan + sautéed potatoes

This plaice takes no time to cook and the polenta gives it a nice crunchy coating that children love. You might even get them to eat the broad beans by disguising them with mint and Parmesan. The sautéed potatoes complete the dish.

Fried plaice fillets

300g polenta flour
salt and pepper
40g butter for frying
6 plaice fillets
lemon for serving

- Put the polenta flour on a large plate and season it well with salt and pepper.
- Coat each plaice fillet on both sides in the polenta.
- Heat the butter in a frying pan and fry each fillet for 2 minutes on each side.
- Season with more salt and pepper.
- Serve the fish with a wedge of lemon.

Minty broad beans and peas with Parmesan

400g baby broad beans
400g peas
salt and pepper
1 tablespoon extra virgin olive oil
2 sprigs of mint
a few shavings of Parmesan cheese

- Boil a saucepan of unsalted water.
- Add the broad beans and peas and simmer for 2–5 minutes, depending on the size of the peas and beans.
- Drain well and season with salt, pepper and the olive oil.
- Sprinkle with the torn mint leaves and the shavings of Parmesan cheese.

Sautéed potatoes

700g potatoes, peeled and quartered
salt and pepper
2–3 tablespoons olive oil

- Boil the potatoes in plenty of salted water for about 20 minutes until tender.
- Cut the cooked potatoes into small cubes.
- Heat the olive oil in a large frying pan and add the potatoes.
- Sauté until golden brown and season with more salt and some pepper.

Orvietan chicken
+ roast potatoes + green salad

This chicken dish is based on a recipe in Mary Contini's book *Dear Francesca*, but she used poussin instead of chicken. It's a wonderfully tasty, summery dish that is easy to make. I suggest here that you serve the dish with extra roast potatoes as the quantity used in the stuffing will not be enough for 6 people.

Orvietan chicken

olive oil
2 cloves garlic, bashed
1 fennel bulb, trimmed and finely chopped
3 large potatoes, peeled and diced into 1cm dice
1 tablespoon pitted black olives
salt and pepper
2 x 1.5kg organic chickens
2 sprigs of rosemary
150ml dry white wine

- Preheat the oven to 180°C/350°F/gas 4.
- Warm the olive oil in a large frying pan.
- Gently sauté the garlic for a few seconds.
- Add the fennel and the potato and sauté for 10 minutes.
- Add the olives, season well with salt and pepper and stir for 30 seconds
- Remove from the heat.
- Stuff the neck of each chicken with the potato, olive and fennel mixture. Don't worry if there is some left over; place this around the chickens in the roasting tin.
- Insert a rosemary sprig in each stuffed neck cavity.
- Drizzle the skin of each chicken with olive oil and season with salt and pepper.
- Place the chickens in a roasting tin, along with any excess stuffing and roast them for 1 hour.
- Next, remove the stuffing out of each neck cavity and leave it in the bottom of the tin.
- Pour the white wine into the roasting tin.
- Increase the oven temperature to 200°C/400°F/gas 6 and roast the chickens for a further 20 minutes.
- Remove from the oven and let the birds rest for 20 minutes before carving.
- Pour the juices into a jug and serve with the stuffing and carved chickens.

Roast potatoes

700g potatoes, peeled
salt
2 tablespoons olive oil

- Preheat the oven to 220°C/425°F/gas 7.
- Parboil the potatoes in salted water for about 4 minutes.
- Drain and place them in a roasting tin.
- Drizzle with the olive oil and roast for 45–60 minutes until golden brown.

Green salad

½ cucumber, sliced
1 lettuce, washed
6 or 7 spring onions, sliced
To dress
2 tablespoons extra virgin olive oil
½ tablespoon balsamic vinegar
salt and pepper

- Combine the salad ingredients in a serving bowl and dress just before serving.

Blackcurrant pie

I love blackcurrant pie with cream, despite the tartness of the fruit. Blackcurrants are difficult to get hold of at any other time of the year, so do make the most of them.

For the pastry
225g plain flour
150g butter
salt
1 tablespoon caster sugar
1 egg yolk
2 tablespoons cold water
For the filling
900g blackcurrants
1 tablespoon cornflour
2 tablespoons caster sugar
cream for serving

To make the pastry

- Put the flour and butter in a food processor, or in a bowl if you are combining by hand, and incorporate so that the mixture looks like fine breadcrumbs.
- Add a pinch of salt and the sugar.
- Mix the egg yolk with the cold water in a small bowl and then add them to the pastry mixture.
- Mix until the ingredients are just combined.
- Turn the dough out onto a lightly floured work surface and combine thoroughly until you have a firm dough.
- Wrap the dough in cling-film and chill in the fridge for 30 minutes.

To make the pie

- Grease a 23–24cm pie tin.
- Preheat the oven to 200°C/400°F/gas 6.
- Line the bottom of the pie tin with half the pastry.
- Pile in the fruit.
- Sprinkle over the cornflour and sugar.
- Cover the top of the pie with the remainder of the pastry.
- Sprinkle a little caster sugar over the top of the pie and bake for 30 minutes until golden brown.
- Serve with cream.

Fruity flapjacks

Despite the sugar and syrup, these flapjacks are a healthy treat. Children don't need sugar but food is about enjoyment as well as sustenance and nutrition, and children do like to eat sweet things occasionally. Homemade cakes and biscuits should not be seen as a problem and are far healthier than bought ones. Flapjacks are so simple to make, there is absolutely no excuse for buying them from the supermarket.

150g butter
2 tablespoons golden syrup
150g rolled porridge oats
200g caster sugar
2 eggs
1 tablespoon flour
1 teaspoon baking powder
1 teaspoon ground cinnamon
50g raisins

- Preheat the oven to 180°C/350°F/gas 4.
- Melt the butter in a saucepan.
- Add the rest of the ingredients and mix well with a wooden spoon.
- Pour into a square, shallow cake tin measuring approximately 23cm.
- Bake for 30 minutes.
- Leave to cool in the tin before serving.

Week 5

Monday p388	Grilled pork chops à la charcutière + sautéed potatoes + creamy spinach
Tuesday p390	Tuna fish curry + spiced grated carrots + boiled rice
Wednesday p391	Sausages + potato and watercress salad + carrots and peas
Thursday p392	Baked cod on potatoes + sautéed Mediterranean vegetables
Friday p393	Double-cheese omelettes with chives + green salad
Saturday p394	Spaghetti with pesto and summer vegetables
Sunday p395	Italian roast pork and roast potatoes + cannellini beans
Sunday pudding p396	Meringues with summer fruits
Extra tasty treat p397	Fruit fudge layer cake

Shopping list

MEAT

- ☐ 6 pork chops
- ☐ 12 sausages
- ☐ 1kg boned loin of pork

FISH

- ☐ 700g fresh tuna fillets
- ☐ 700g cod fillets

VEGETABLES

- ☐ 6 shallots
- ☐ 3 kg potatoes
- ☐ 250g spinach leaves
- ☐ fresh ginger
- ☐ 1 garlic bulb
- ☐ 2 green chillies
- ☐ 1 onion
- ☐ 1kg new potatoes
- ☐ 13 spring onions
- ☐ 100g watercress
- ☐ 400g fresh peas
- ☐ 350g carrots
- ☐ 1 red onion
- ☐ 4 small and 2 medium courgettes
- ☐ 1 fennel bulb
- ☐ 1 red pepper
- ☐ 150g cherry tomatoes
- ☐ 1 lettuce
- ☐ ½ cucumber
- ☐ 1 green pepper
- ☐ 100g small fresh broad beans

FRUIT

- ☐ 1 lemon
- ☐ 225g strawberries
- ☐ 225g raspberries
- ☐ 100g blueberries

FRESH HERBS

- ☐ flat-leaf parsley
- ☐ coriander
- ☐ thyme
- ☐ rosemary
- ☐ 2 packs basil
- ☐ chives
- ☐ sage

FRIDGE ITEMS

- ☐ 2 packs butter
- ☐ 200ml single cream
- ☐ 550ml double cream
- ☐ 100ml natural yoghurt
- ☐ 600ml chicken stock
- ☐ 200g feta cheese
- ☐ 240g cream cheese
- ☐ 18 eggs
- ☐ 175g Parmesan cheese

KITCHEN CUPBOARD ITEMS

- ☐ salt
- ☐ extra virgin olive oil
- ☐ vegetable oil
- ☐ olive oil
- ☐ Dijon mustard
- ☐ coarse grain mustard
- ☐ white wine vinegar
- ☐ capers
- ☐ balsamic vinegar
- ☐ 400g spaghetti
- ☐ 75g pine nuts
- ☐ 2 x 400g tins chopped tomatoes
- ☐ 2 x 400g tins cannellini beans
- ☐ 325g caster sugar
- ☐ vanilla extract
- ☐ 25g light brown sugar
- ☐ 125g vanilla fudge
- ☐ 175g self-raising flour
- ☐ 25g plain flour
- ☐ 1 bottle dry white wine
- ☐ vegetable stock cubes
- ☐ cornichons
- ☐ 50g desiccated coconut
- ☐ tamarind paste
- ☐ 500g basmati rice

SPICES

- ☐ whole nutmeg
- ☐ black peppercorns
- ☐ ground coriander
- ☐ black mustard seeds
- ☐ curry leaves
- ☐ turmeric
- ☐ cloves

Grilled pork chops à la charcutière + sautéed potatoes + creamy spinach

Seeking some inspriration for a pork chop recipe that was a little different from the usual way I serve them, I happened upon this recipe in Jane Grigson's *Food with the Famous*. The book is a gem of a read about the history of numerous dishes that have appeared at one time on the tables of the rich and famous. I have changed the recipe slightly.

Grilled pork chops à la charcutière

6 pork chops
salt and pepper
a little olive oil

For the sauce

25g butter
4 shallots, finely chopped
1 tablespoon plain flour
50ml dry white wine
50ml white wine vinegar
500ml vegetable stock (a cube will do)
125g tinned chopped tomatoes
1 teaspoon sugar
10 cornichons, sliced widthways
2 tablespoons flat-leaf parsley, finely chopped

- Season the chops with salt and pepper.
- Brush both sides of each chop with a little olive oil and set aside.

To make the sauce

- Heat the butter in a saucepan.
- Add the shallots and gently fry them for 5 minutes until soft.
- Stir in the flour and gradually add the wine, white wine vinegar and stock, stirring all the time to combine the ingredients smoothly.
- Simmer gently for 10 minutes, uncovered.
- Add the tomatoes and the sugar and continue to simmer uncovered for 20 minutes.
- Add the cornichons and parsley and set the sauce aside.

To grill the chops

- Heat the grill until hot and grill the chops for 5 minutes on each side.
- Season again with salt and pepper and serve with the sauce and the vegetables below.

Sautéed potatoes

1 kg potatoes, peeled and quartered
2 tablespoons olive oil
salt and pepper

- Boil the potatoes in salted water until tender.
- Drain well and cut them into 3cm chunks.
- Heat the oil in a large sauté pan, add the potatoes and sauté them on a medium heat for 20 minutes until golden brown all over.

Creamy spinach

250g spinach leaves
salt and black pepper
200ml single cream
nutmeg

- Place the spinach in a large saucepan with a tablespoon of water and a sprinkling of sea salt.
- Cover and place the saucepan on a medium heat. Gradually wilt the spinach for 10 minutes, until all the leaves are a glossy dark green.
- As soon as the leaves have wilted, remove the lid and stir around for a few seconds to get rid of any excess water. If there is still too much, drain the extra water off.
- Add the cream, a tiny grating of nutmeg and a good grinding of pepper.

Tuna fish curry
+ spiced grated carrots + boiled rice

These recipes are typical Sri Lankan ones and make a delicious meal. Once you have organized the spices, they are very quick to assemble.

Tuna fish curry

700g fresh tuna fillets
1 tablespoon vegetable oil
2 teaspoons black mustard seeds
10 curry leaves
250ml water
4 teaspoons tamarind paste
1 teaspoon salt

For the curry paste

3 tablespoons fresh ginger, finely chopped
4 cloves garlic, finely chopped
2 shallots, chopped
1 green chilli, deseeded and chopped
2 tablespoons desiccated coconut, mixed with 2 tablespoons cold water
1 tablespoon fresh coriander, chopped
1 teaspoon ground coriander
¼ teaspoon turmeric

- Cut the tuna fish fillets into 4cm pieces.

To prepare the curry paste

- Place the ginger, garlic, shallots, chilli, coconut and fresh coriander in a mini food processor or pestle and mortar and grind or process to a coarse paste.
- Stir in the coriander and turmeric and set aside.

To cook the fish

- Heat the oil in a saucepan.
- Add the mustard seeds and as soon as they pop add the curry leaves and the curry paste.
- Lower the heat and cook, stirring occasionally, for 2 minutes.
- Add the water and tamarind paste and bring to a simmer.
- Add the salt and fish and simmer for 1 minute, as tuna becomes tough if cooked for too long.

Spiced grated carrots

2 tablespoons vegetable oil
1 teaspoon black mustard seeds
1 onion, finely chopped
¼ teaspoon turmeric
2cm piece of fresh ginger, finely chopped
1 clove garlic, finely chopped
1 green chilli, deseeded and finely chopped
10 curry leaves
4 medium carrots, coarsely grated
½ teaspoon salt
black pepper
100ml natural yoghurt

- Heat the oil in a saucepan.
- Add the mustard seeds and when they pop add the onion and turmeric and stir for 1 minute.
- Add the ginger, garlic, chilli and curry leaves and fry for 3 minutes.
- Add the carrots and season with salt and pepper.
- Fry for 3 minutes, stirring occasionally.
- Remove from the heat so it doesn't curdle and stir in the yoghurt.
- Serve with the fish and rice.

Boiled rice

500g basmati rice
750ml water
pinch of salt

- Put the rice in a saucepan of salted water.
- Place the rice on a high heat and as soon as it comes to the boil, cover the saucepan with a lid and turn the heat right down to very low. Leave it for 15 minutes, giving it one stir only during the cooking time.
- Then take it off the heat and leave it covered for a further 10 minutes, before removing the lid.

Sausages + potato and watercress salad + carrots and peas

At this time of year when the vegetable patch goes into overdrive, I tend to use as many of the vegetables that are ready. You may not, however, want both the vegetable dishes as you may find that just one of them is filling enough.

Sausages

12 or so sausages depending upon your family's appetite
a drizzle of olive oil

- Fry the sausages in a little olive oil in a frying pan on a medium heat to brown them all over.
- Turn the heat down to cook them through.
- It takes about 12–15 minutes to cook a sausage.

Potato and watercress salad

600g new potatoes
7 spring onions, peeled and finely chopped
salt and black pepper
100g watercress
1 tablespoon extra virgin olive oil

For the dressing

½ teaspoon Dijon mustard
½ teaspoon coarse grain mustard
salt and pepper
½ tablespoon fresh thyme leaves
1 tablespoon white wine vinegar
3 tablespoons extra virgin olive oil

- Boil the potatoes in salted water for 15–20 minutes until tender.
- Drain them well, cut them into thick slices and return them to the saucepan with the spring onions.

To make the dressing

- Place the mustards, salt, pepper, thyme and vinegar in a small bowl.
- Measure out 3 tablespoons of extra virgin olive oil into a jug and gradually, in a slow steady stream, add the oil to the mustard mixture, whisking constantly. The dressing will thicken slightly.
- Toss the hot potatoes and spring onion in the salad dressing, seasoning with extra pepper if necessary.
- In a serving bowl arrange the watercress and drizzle over 1 tablespoon of olive oil.
- Spoon the potatoes and onions on top and serve.

Carrots and peas

300g fresh peas
300g carrots, peeled and thinly sliced
30g butter
salt and pepper

- Place the vegetables in a small saucepan with the butter.
- As the butter melts reduce the heat, cover and sweat the peas and carrots for 5 minutes until tender, stirring them occasionally.
- Season with salt and pepper and serve.

Baked cod on potatoes
+ sautéed Mediterranean vegetables

You can use pollack instead of cod for this recipe if you prefer.

Baked cod on potatoes

1kg potatoes, peeled and cut into long thin quarters
1 red onion, sliced
600ml chicken stock
salt and pepper
2 sprigs rosemary
700g cod fillets
juice ½ lemon

- Preheat the oven to 200°C/400°F/gas 6.
- Place the potatoes and onion in a roasting tin and pour the stock over them.
- Season with salt and pepper and lay the rosemary sprigs on top.
- Bake for 30 minutes.
- Turn the potatoes over and bake for a further 30 minutes.
- Lay the cod fillets on top of the potatoes, season and bake for a further 10 minutes.
- Squeeze some lemon juice over the cooked fish and serve.

Sautéed Mediterranean vegetables

2 tablespoons olive oil
4 small courgettes, diced into 1cm cubes
½ fennel bulb, diced into 1cm pieces
1 red pepper, diced into 1cm cubes
150g cherry tomatoes, quartered
200g feta cheese, diced
1 dessertspoon capers, rinsed
handful basil leaves, torn
salt and pepper

- Warm the olive oil in a large sauté pan.
- Add the courgettes, fennel and red pepper and sauté gently for 5 minutes.
- Place in a serving bowl with the tomatoes, feta, capers and basil.
- Season with salt and pepper.

Double-cheese omelettes with chives + green salad

These omelettes are fantastic. For six people you will need to cook the omelettes in three batches, as each omelette serves two people, but they don't take long to cook. Serve with bread and butter and salad, which I think are the best things to eat with omelettes.

Double-cheese omelette with chives

30g chives, chopped
240g cream cheese
12 eggs
100g Parmesan cheese, grated
salt and pepper
knob of butter for each omelette

- Mix the chives with the cream cheese and set aside.
- Beat four eggs in a bowl with a third of the Parmesan cheese and some salt and pepper.
- Heat a knob of butter in a frying pan over a high heat and as it starts to foam, pour the beaten eggs into the pan.
- Move the egg around by tilting the pan, so the egg coats the whole pan. As the edges start to set pull the edges of the egg towards you and tilt the pan so that uncooked egg replaces the cooked egg.
- When all that remains is a little unset egg in the centre of the omelette, remove the pan from the heat.
- Add a third of the cream cheese and chives to the centre of the omelette and flip over the edges to enclose.
- Cut in half and serve while you cook the other two omelettes.
- Serve with salad and bread and butter.

Green salad

1 lettuce, washed
½ cucumber, sliced
1 green pepper, finely diced
For the dressing
2 tablespoons extra virgin olive oil
½ tablespoon balsamic vinegar
salt and pepper

- Combine the salad in a serving bowl.
- Combine the dressing ingredients and drizzle over the salad when ready to serve.

Spaghetti with pesto and summer vegetables

This recipe makes use of most of the great vegetables that summer has to offer.

400g spaghetti
2 tablespoons olive oil
2 medium courgettes or 4 small ones, thinly sliced
6 spring onions, sliced
100g fresh peas, cooked
100g small fresh broad beans, cooked
400g new potatoes, cooked, peeled and sliced into thick pieces
salt and pepper
extra virgin olive oil and Parmesan for serving

For the pesto

80g fresh basil
8 tablespoons extra virgin olive oil
3 tablespoons pine nuts
2 cloves garlic, peeled
salt
50g Parmesan cheese, grated
30g butter, softened

To make the pesto

- In a food processor process the basil, olive oil, pine nuts, garlic and a generous pinch of salt to an even, creamy consistency. Turn into a bowl.
- With a wooden spoon mix in the cheese and butter.

To prepare the summer vegetables

- Start to heat the salted water ready for the spaghetti.
- In a sauté pan heat the olive oil.
- Add the courgette and spring onion and sauté gently for 3 minutes.
- Add the other cooked vegetables to warm through and season with salt and pepper.
- Remove from the heat.
- Stir the pesto into the cooked vegetables.
- Once the spaghetti is cooked, combine the pasta with the pesto and vegetables.
- Spoon over another tablespoon of extra virgin olive oil and serve with more Parmesan.

Italian roast pork and roast potatoes + cannellini beans

The idea of roast pork may not appeal to you during the summer months, but this is roasted in the Italian way and is a meal often eaten in the summer in Tuscany. You could always include a green salad as well to make it a more summery dish. I don't bother trying to get a crispy crackling with this pork dish, so I remove the thick outer rind from the meat prior to cooking.

Italian roast pork and roasted potatoes

1kg potatoes, peeled and quartered
1kg boned loin of pork
leaves from two sprigs rosemary, finely chopped
2 cloves garlic, peeled and finely chopped
salt and pepper
2 tablespoon olive oil
2 cloves

- Preheat the oven to 180°C/350°F/gas 4.
- Parboil the potatoes in boiling, salted water for 5 minutes.
- Drain and set aside.
- Remove the thick rind from the pork, leaving as much fat as you can.
- Mix the rosemary and garlic together with a good amount of salt and pepper.
- Score the skin of the pork with a sharp knife and rub with the olive oil.
- Scatter the rosemary, garlic, salt and pepper onto the skin.
- Stud the pork with the 2 cloves.
- Place the meat and potatoes in a roasting tin and roast them for 1 hour.
- After this, increase the oven temperature to 220°C/425°F/gas 7 and roast for 10 minutes.
- Remove the meat from the tray and leave to rest for 10 minutes.
- Return the potatoes to a slightly cooler oven while the meat rests.
- Carve the meat and serve with the roast potatoes and the beans below.

Cannellini beans

4 tablespoons olive oil
2 cloves garlic, unpeeled but bashed with a rolling pin
1 sprig sage
400g tin chopped tomatoes
2 x 400g tins cannellini beans, drained
salt and pepper

- Heat the olive oil in a medium-sized saucepan.
- Put the garlic cloves and sage in the pan and sauté for 1 minute.
- Add the tomatoes and simmer for 20 minutes.
- Then add the beans and simmer gently for 30 minutes.
- Season with salt and pepper.

Meringues with summer fruits

This is a classic summer dish. Meringues have a reputation for being difficult to make but they are actually very easy. You must, however, use an electric mixer to get the egg whites stiff and not have a hint of grease on the whisk or in the bowl in which you are whisking the whites. If you are doubtful about this, then rub a lemon half over the whisk and the bowl before you start.

For the meringues

3 egg whites

175g caster sugar

¼ teaspoon vanilla extract

For the summer fruit

150g strawberries

150g raspberries

100g blueberries

For serving

250ml double cream

- Preheat the oven to 130°C/260°F/gas ¾.
- Cover a baking sheet with a sheet of baking parchment.
- Place the egg whites in a bowl and whisk until they form peaks when you remove the whisk.
- Add a tablespoon of sugar at a time, whisking between each addition, until all the sugar is used and you have a glossy white mass of meringue that forms stiff peaks.
- Dollop tablespoons of the mixture onto the greaseproof paper and bake for 50 minutes, until the meringues have crisp outsides but marshmallow insides.
- Serve with the fruit and cream.

TIP

If you have egg whites in the fridge and you can't remember how many you have, weigh them instead. 1 egg white weighs about 25g.

Fruit fudge layer cake

This is a lovely cake and one that is quite easy to make. The idea for the cake came from Linda Collisters *Easy Cakes*. I have used soft fruit instead of the bananas she suggests, as it would be a crime not to use soft fruit when it is relatively cheap and plentiful. Also note that the cake is in 3 layers and each cake is quite thin, so don't panic when you see only a sparse amount of cake mixture in each cake tin.

For the cake

175g butter, softened
150g caster sugar
25g light brown sugar
3 eggs
175g self-raising flour
½ teaspoon vanilla extract
1 tablespoon milk

For the filling and the icing

300ml double cream
125g vanilla fudge
150g soft fruit such as raspberries, blackberries and strawberries

- Grease 3 x 20cm diameter cake tins.
- Preheat the oven to 180°C/350°F/gas 4.
- Put the butter, caster sugar, brown sugar, eggs, flour, vanilla and milk into a large mixing bowl.
- Beat with an electric mixer until smooth.
- Divide the mixture between the 3 cake tins and bake for 20 minutes.
- Remove the cakes and, when they have cooled slightly, turn them out onto a wire rack.
- Whip the cream and grate the fudge into it, stirring it in gently.
- Spread some of the fudge cream onto the first cake.
- Spoon in some fruit and sandwich with one of the cakes.
- Do the same with the next layer, and then the same with the top.
- You may not want fruit on the top, but I think it looks good.
- Store the cake in the fridge.

Week 1

Monday p400	Spiced chicken + boiled rice
Tuesday p401	Goat's cheese and tomato tart + green salad
Wednesday p402	Vegetable curry + boiled rice
Thursday p403	Fillet steak with brandy + baked onion and celery + runner beans + roast potatoes
Friday p404	Macaroni and sausage + roast tomato and rocket salad
Saturday p405	Grilled trout with herb sauce + sautéed potatoes + tomato salad
Sunday p406	Roast leg of lamb with onions + roast potatoes + runner beans and carrots
Sunday pudding p408	Blackcurrant fool + shortbread biscuits
Extra tasty treat p409	Peanut and chocolate chip cookies

Shopping list

MEAT

- ☐ 1kg chicken pieces, on the bone
- ☐ 6 pieces beef fillet
- ☐ 8 pork sausages or equivalent weight in sausage meat
- ☐ 2.5kg leg of lamb

FISH

- ☐ 6 fresh river trout

VEGETABLES

- ☐ 200g swede
- ☐ ½ cucumber
- ☐ 1 lettuce
- ☐ 9 spring onions
- ☐ 250g courgettes
- ☐ 150g green beans
- ☐ 150g fresh peas
- ☐ 550g carrots
- ☐ fresh ginger
- ☐ 1 bunch celery
- ☐ 5 onions
- ☐ 16 plum tomatoes
- ☐ 2 red onions
- ☐ 100g rocket leaves
- ☐ 250g spinach
- ☐ 1 garlic bulb
- ☐ 200g shallots
- ☐ 3.5kg potatoes
- ☐ 700g runner beans

FRUIT

- ☐ 3 lemons
- ☐ 1 orange
- ☐ 600g blackcurrants

FRESH HERBS

- ☐ basil
- ☐ coriander
- ☐ sage
- ☐ tarragon
- ☐ flat-leaf parsley
- ☐ thyme
- ☐ rosemary

FRIDGE ITEMS

- ☐ 200g frozen petits pois
- ☐ 250g Camembert-style goat's cheese
- ☐ 4 slices pancetta
- ☐ 30g chopped pancetta
- ☐ 100g Parmesan cheese
- ☐ 500ml full-fat milk
- ☐ 200g Gruyère cheese
- ☐ 100g Cheddar cheese
- ☐ 800ml double cream
- ☐ 3 packs butter
- ☐ 9 eggs

KITCHEN CUPBOARD ITEMS

- ☐ 2 tins coconut milk
- ☐ Dijon mustard
- ☐ balsamic vinegar
- ☐ vegetable oil
- ☐ extra virgin olive oil
- ☐ olive oil
- ☐ 50g cashew nuts
- ☐ mango chutney
- ☐ poppadums
- ☐ 1kg basmati rice
- ☐ 150ml brandy
- ☐ redcurrant jelly
- ☐ goose fat
- ☐ 500g macaroni
- ☐ capers
- ☐ anchovy fillets
- ☐ 1 loaf white bread
- ☐ 1 bottle Italian red wine
- ☐ elderflower cordial
- ☐ 1 vanilla pod
- ☐ cornflour
- ☐ salt
- ☐ 125g ground rice
- ☐ 375g caster sugar
- ☐ 200g crunchy peanut butter
- ☐ 1kg plain flour
- ☐ baking powder
- ☐ 100g chocolate chips

SPICES

- ☐ fennel seeds
- ☐ fenugreek
- ☐ mustard seeds
- ☐ curry leaves
- ☐ turmeric
- ☐ cayenne pepper
- ☐ whole nutmeg
- ☐ cumin seeds
- ☐ coriander seeds
- ☐ black peppercorns

Spiced chicken
+ boiled rice

This appetising dish is very easy to make. If you already have some chicken and vegetables to hand, you can have it on the table in a flash. I first made it when we had just got back from holiday and the children were demanding food.

Spiced chicken

1 tablespoon vegetable oil
1 red onion, finely chopped
1kg chicken pieces, on the bone, skin removed
200g potatoes, peeled and quartered
200g swede, peeled and cut into 3cm cubes
4 carrots, peeled and thickly sliced
200g frozen petits pois
1 tablespoon curry powder*
1 tin coconut milk
salt

- Warm the vegetable oil in a large saucepan.
- Fry the onion on a medium heat for 10 minutes.
- Add the vegetables and chicken pieces and stir to coat everything in the oil and onions.
- Sprinkle on the curry powder and stir round for a few seconds.
- Pour on the coconut milk and enough water to bring the liquid up to just below the level of the meat and vegetables.
- Season with salt.
- Cover and simmer gently for 40 minutes.

Boiled rice

500g basmati rice
750ml water
salt

- Put the rice in a saucepan with the water and a pinch of salt.
- Place the rice on a high heat and as soon as it comes to the boil, cover the saucepan with a lid and turn the heat right down to very low. Leave it for 15 minutes, giving it one stir only during the cooking time.
- Then take the pan off the heat and leave it covered for a further 10 minutes, before removing the lid.

To make your own curry powder:

1 tablespoon coriander seeds
1 dessertspoon cumin seeds
1 teaspoon fennel seeds
½ teaspoon fenugreek

- *Place the coriander seeds into a small, heavy-bottomed pan and heat through for 30 seconds.*
- *Add the other ingredients and toast until you smell the lovely aroma of the spices.*
- *Transfer the spices to a coffee grinder, a small processor, or grind them in a pestle and mortar.*

Goat's cheese and tomato tart + green salad

Goat's cheese and tomato are a great partnership in a tart.

For the pastry

225g plain flour
150g butter, chilled and cubed
1 tablespoon Parmesan cheese, finely grated
salt
1 egg yolk
2 tablespoons cold water

For the tart

100ml extra virgin olive oil
1 dessertspoon thyme leaves, chopped
1 dessertspoon basil leaves, chopped
1 dessertspoon rosemary leaves, chopped
1 clove garlic, crushed
salt and pepper
1 tablespoon Dijon mustard
100g Gruyère cheese, grated
4 plum tomatoes, sliced
250g Camembert-style goat's cheese, thinly sliced

To make the pastry

- Combine the flour and butter in a food processor until they resemble fine breadcrumbs.
- Add the Parmesan cheese and a pinch of salt and mix in quickly.
- Mix the egg yolk with the water and pour onto the flour and butter mixture. Give the mixture a quick blast in the food processor and then turn it out onto a floured surface and form it into a ball of dough.
- Cover with cling-film and chill in the fridge for 30 minutes.

To make the tart

- Preheat the oven to 190°C/375°F/gas 5 and place a baking sheet inside the oven.
- Grease a 30cm tart tin.
- In a small bowl combine the olive oil with the herbs, garlic, salt and pepper and set aside.
- Roll out the pastry and line the tart tin with it.
- Spread the mustard evenly over the base of the pastry case.
- Sprinkle the grated Gruyère cheese over this.
- Cover the cheese with alternate overlapping slices of goat's cheese and sliced tomatoes.
- Drizzle the herb oil over the top and bake for 35 minutes.

Green salad

½ cucumber, sliced
1 lettuce, washed
5 spring onions, sliced

To dress

2 tablespoons extra virgin olive oil
½ tablespoon balsamic vinegar
salt and pepper

- Combine the salad ingredients in a serving bowl and dress just before serving.

Vegetable curry
+ boiled rice

This colourful curry makes good use of seasonal vegetables. Serve it with rice and poppadums and even the children won't notice that it is meat-free.

Vegetable curry

1kg mixed summer vegetables, such as potatoes, courgettes, green beans, peas and carrots
1 tablespoon vegetable oil
1 clove garlic, peeled and finely chopped
1 onion, finely chopped
1cm fresh ginger, peeled and finely chopped
5 curry leaves
1 teaspoon coriander seeds
¼ teaspoon turmeric
¼ teaspoon cayenne pepper
100ml water
150ml coconut milk
1 teaspoon olive oil
50g cashew nuts
½ teaspoon mustard seeds
1 tablespoon fresh coriander, chopped
mango chutney and poppadums for serving

- Cook the vegetables in salted water until tender, then set them aside.
- Heat the oil in a large saucepan.
- Add the garlic, onion, ginger and curry leaves and sauté them for 3 minutes.
- Grind the coriander seeds in a pestle and mortar until you have a reasonably fine powder.
- Add the ground coriander, turmeric and cayenne to the onion mixture in the pan and stir for 30 seconds.
- Next, add the cooked vegetables and sauté for 2 minutes.
- Pour in the water and coconut milk and bring to a simmer.
- Remove from the heat and check the seasoning.
- In a small frying pan heat 1 teaspoon of olive oil and gently fry the cashew nuts and mustard seeds.
- Garnish the vegetables with the nuts, seeds and fresh coriander.
- Serve with boiled rice, poppadums and mango chutney.

Boiled rice

500g basmati rice
750ml water
salt

- Put the rice in a saucepan with the water and a pinch of salt.
- Place it on a high heat and as soon as it comes to the boil, cover the saucepan with a lid and turn the heat right down to very low. Leave it for 15 minutes, giving it one stir only during the cooking time.
- Then take the pan off the heat and leave it covered for a further 10 minutes, before removing the lid.

Fillet steak with brandy + baked onion and celery + runner beans + roast potatoes

Prepare the onion dish, the potatoes and beans first, then cook the steaks just before everyone is ready to eat.

Fillet steak with brandy

6 pieces of beef fillet
black pepper
30g butter
salt
150ml brandy
2 teaspoons redcurrant jelly
3 tablespoons double cream

- Season the steaks with pepper on each side.
- Heat the butter in a large frying pan and once it is foaming add the pieces of beef.
- Fry the steaks for 2 minutes on each side, or less if you prefer your steak rare.
- Remove from the pan and season with salt.
- Add the brandy, stirring for a few seconds until the fierce sizzling stops.
- Add the redcurrant jelly and stir to combine.
- Pour in the cream and stir.
- Then pour over the steaks and serve.

Baked onion and celery

2 tablespoons olive oil
2 sticks celery, diced
4 medium onions, peeled and cut into large chunks
1 clove garlic, peeled and finely chopped
4 slices pancetta
1 sprig rosemary, leaves removed and finely chopped
salt and pepper
200ml double cream
2 tablespoons Parmesan cheese, grated

- Preheat the oven to 200°C/400°F/gas 6.
- Heat the olive oil in a frying pan and add the celery and onion.
- Fry gently for 5 minutes and then add the garlic, pancetta and rosemary.
- Fry for a further 5 minutes, keeping the heat low.
- Season with salt and pepper.
- Add the cream and remove from the heat.
- Spoon this into a small gratin dish and sprinkle the cheese over the top.
- Bake for 30 minutes.

Runner beans

400g runner beans, prepared and sliced
salt and pepper
butter for serving

- Prepare the beans by topping and tailing them and then cutting a thin sliver off the side of each bean. There are no rules on how to slice the beans. I hold the bean upwards and cut at an angle from the top downwards, shaving an angled slice off. This is the best description I can give to anyone who never saw their mother preparing runner beans. Place the prepared beans into boiling water.
- Cook them for 4 to 7 minutes, depending on how young and tender the beans are. Runner beans have to be well cooked to be enjoyable.
- Drain well and serve with salt, pepper and a little butter.

Roast potatoes

1kg potatoes, peeled and quartered
1 dessertspoon goose fat or 2 tablespoons olive oil
salt

- Preheat the oven to 220°C/425°F/gas 7.
- Parboil the potatoes in salted water for 4 minutes.
- Drain and place them in a roasting tin.
- Drizzle with the goose fat or olive oil and roast for 45–60 minutes until golden brown.

Macaroni and sausage
+ roast tomato and rocket salad

Macaroni is a much underused and underrated pasta. It usually pops up as macaroni cheese, which is a lovely dish, but I feel macaroni does have slightly more potential than this.

Macaroni and sausage

8 pork sausages or the equivalent weight in sausage meat
1 tablespoon olive oil
6 fresh sage leaves, finely chopped
1 sprig rosemary, finely chopped
2 cloves garlic, peeled and chopped
500g macaroni
salt

For the Béchamel sauce

30g butter
30g flour
500ml full-fat milk
salt and pepper
nutmeg
100g Gruyère cheese, grated
100g Cheddar cheese, grated

- Preheat the oven to 200°C/400°F/gas 6.
- Unless using sausage meat, split the skin of the sausages and squeeze out the contents.
- Warm the oil in a heavy saucepan.
- Fry the sausage meat, herbs and garlic until the sausage meat starts to turn brown. Do this on a medium heat to avoid burning the garlic.

For the Béchamel

- Melt the butter gently in a small saucepan and then add the flour.
- Stir until the two ingredients combine and a 'roux' forms.
- Remove the saucepan from the heat and gradually pour on the milk, stirring continuously.
- Return to the heat and bring to a simmer, again stirring continuously, to avoid lumps forming.
- Reduce to a very low heat and cook for 10 minutes.
- Season with a pinch each of salt, pepper and nutmeg.
- Stir in the cheeses and set aside.
- Cook the macaroni in a large saucepan in plenty of salted water, following the packet instructions.
- Combine the macaroni with the sausage and pour the cheese sauce over the top.
- Bake for 30 minutes.

Roast tomato and rocket salad

6 plum tomatoes, halved
1 red onion, finely sliced
1 tablespoon olive oil
¼ teaspoon cumin seeds
¼ teaspoon coriander seeds
salt
100g rocket leaves
extra virgin olive oil

- Preheat the oven to 190°C/375°F/gas 5.
- Place the tomatoes and onion in a roasting tin with the olive oil and roast for 20 minutes.
- Roast the cumin and coriander seeds in a small frying pan on the hob over a medium heat, until you can smell their toasty aroma.
- Grind the spices roughly with a good pinch of salt in a pestle and mortar.
- Sprinkle the spices and salt over the tomatoes and onions as they come out of the oven.
- Place the tomatoes and onions in a serving dish with the rocket leaves.
- Dress the salad with a tablespoon of extra virgin olive oil and serve with the macaroni.

Grilled trout with herb sauce + sautéed potatoes + tomato salad

This herb sauce goes very well with the grilled trout which is in season during the month of August.

Grilled trout with herb sauce

6 fresh river trout, gutted with heads and fins removed
olive oil
salt and pepper
lemon juice for serving

For the herb sauce

1 tablespoon capers, rinsed and drained
salt and pepper
3 anchovy fillets, rinsed
1 teaspoon tarragon leaves
handful flat-leaf parsley
250g spinach, cooked and drained
60g white bread, soaked in warm water and thoroughly squeezed to remove the water
yolks 3 hard-boiled eggs
100ml extra virgin olive oil
1 teaspoon lemon juice

To make the herb sauce

- Blitz all the ingredients, except the olive oil and lemon juice, in a food processor until smooth.
- Trickle in the olive oil gradually, pulsing between each addition.
- Add the lemon juice.

To grill the fish

- Preheat the grill.
- Slash each trout two or three times on each side with a sharp knife.
- Brush each side of each fish with olive oil and season with salt and pepper.
- Place the fish under the hot grill for 4 minutes and then turn over and do the same.
- Squeeze each fish with lemon juice and serve with the sauce.

Sautéed potatoes

1 kg potatoes, peeled and cut into chunks of about 3cm
salt
2 tablespoons olive oil
black pepper

- Boil the potatoes in salted water until tender.
- Drain them well.
- Heat the oil in a large sauté pan, add the potatoes and sauté them on a medium heat for 20 minutes until golden brown all over.
- Season just before serving.

Tomato salad

6 plum tomatoes
2 tablespoons extra virgin olive oil
¼ tablespoon balsamic vinegar
salt and pepper

- Slice the tomatoes and lay them on a serving plate.
- Dress with the oil, vinegar, salt and pepper.

Roast leg of lamb with onions + roast potatoes + runner beans and carrots

There is no way to avoid runner beans and carrots at this time of year, and who would want to? They accompany this lamb dish. If you can marinate the lamb overnight then do so, but it's not vital. The lamb is cooked beyond the pink stage in this recipe, but I like this sometimes.

Roast leg of lamb with onions

2.5kg leg of lamb
30g chopped pancetta
3 garlic cloves, peeled and cut into slivers
salt and pepper
3 tablespoons olive oil
leaves from a sprig of thyme and rosemary, finely chopped
300ml Italian red wine
200g shallots, peeled but kept whole
1 teaspoon sugar
juice 1 lemon
juice 1 orange

- Place the lamb joint in a roasting tin.
- Make a few deep slits in the leg of lamb.
- Push pieces of pancetta and garlic into the slits together.
- Rub the lamb with salt, pepper and olive oil.
- Then scatter the herbs over the joint and leave to marinate for 1–2 hours.
- Preheat the oven to 180°C/350°F/gas 4.
- Pour the wine over the joint and roast for 2 hours, basting every 30 minutes or so.
- After the lamb has cooked for 1 hour add the shallots to the tin, and return to the oven for another hour.
- Remove the roasting tin from the oven and take the joint and shallots out of the tin. You can now prepare the sauce.
- Place the roasting tin on the hob and start to heat up the cooking juices.
- Add the sugar, and the orange and lemon juice.
- Taste and adjust the seasoning as necessary. The sauce is now ready.
- Serve the sauce with the lamb and the vegetables below.

Roast potatoes

1kg potatoes, peeled and quartered
1 dessertspoon goose fat or 2 tablespoons olive oil
salt

- Preheat the oven to 220°C/425°F/gas 7.
- Parboil the potatoes in salted water for 4 minutes.
- Drain well and place them in a roasting tin.
- Spoon on the goose fat or olive oil and roast for 45–60 minutes until golden brown.

Runner beans and carrots

300g runner beans
300g carrots, peeled and sliced thinly
salt
black pepper
butter for serving
a little flat-leaf parsley, chopped

For the runner beans

- Prepare the beans by topping and tailing them and then cutting a thin sliver off the side of each bean. There are no rules on how to slice the beans. I hold the bean upwards and cut at an angle from the top downwards, shaving an angled slice off. This is the best description I can give to anyone who never saw their mother preparing runner beans.
- Place the prepared beans into boiling water.
- Cook them for 4 to 7 minutes, depending on how young and tender the beans are. Runner beans have to be well cooked to be enjoyable.

- Place the prepared beans into boiling water.
- Cook them for 4 to 7 minutes, depending on how young and tender the beans are. Runner beans have to be well cooked to be enjoyable.

For the carrots

- Simmer the carrots in boiling salted water for 5 minutes.
- Drain and serve the carrots with the runner beans, some butter, pepper and a little chopped parsley.

TIP

Cooking with one oven: *Most people only have one oven so put your potatoes and shallots round the lamb while it cooks and when you take the meat out to rest pop the potatoes back into the oven in another tin so you have the meat tin for the gravy.*

Blackcurrant fool + shortbread biscuits

If you have a terribly sweet tooth then this dessert is probably not for you, although the shortbread does provide a certain sweetness. Blackcurrants are tart and there is no point trying to make them something they are not by hurling sugar at them. I think this dessert is a welcome taste on a hot summer's day. If you can't get fresh blackcurrants, frozen will do. The shortbread recipe is based on the one my mother used when we were children, and which she obtained from Muriel Downes' *Cake Making in Pictures*. I still have her copy of this book, which is falling apart but contains memories of my childhood in so many of its pages.

Blackcurrant fool

600g blackcurrants
6 tablespoons elderflower cordial
2 tablespoon caster sugar
568ml double cream
1 vanilla pod
3 egg yolks
1 tablespoon caster sugar
1 teaspoon cornflour

- Place the blackcurrants in a pan with the cordial and 2 tablespoons of sugar.
- Bring to the boil, reduce the heat and simmer for 10 minutes.
- Purée the blackcurrants in a blender, pass them through a sieve and then set aside to cool.
- In another saucepan, heat the cream with the vanilla pod to just before boiling point.
- In a small bowl mix the egg yolks, 1 tablespoon of sugar and the cornflour to a smooth paste.
- Remove the vanilla pod from the cream. (You can store this and use it another time.)
- Pour the cream into the egg yolk mixture, whisking as you do so.
- Now pour the entire mixture into a saucepan and cook over a gentle heat until the custard thickens. This happens relatively quickly.
- Remove from the heat and mix the custard with the blackcurrant sauce.
- Place in a bowl in the fridge to cool.
- If you want to eat the fool frozen, you can put it in the freezer.

Shortbread biscuits

240g butter, softened very slightly
125g caster sugar
240g plain flour
salt
125g ground rice

- Preheat oven to 170°C/325°F/gas 3.
- Beat the butter in a mixer until soft and creamy.
- Stir in the sugar, flour, salt and ground rice.
- Work until you have a dough similar to pastry.
- Divide the mixture into two and roll each half out to a thickness of about 1.5cm.
- Place each round on a baking sheet and bake for about 15 minutes until it is a very pale brown.
- Allow to cool, cut into fingers and serve with the blackcurrant fool.

Peanut and chocolate chip cookies

These biscuits are very straightforward and the children love them with a glass of cold milk. This recipe makes about 32 biscuits. They keep very well in an airtight container.

100g butter, softened
175g caster sugar
200g crunchy peanut butter
2 eggs
250g plain flour
1 teaspoon baking powder
100g chocolate chips

- Preheat the oven to 180°C/350°F/gas 4.
- Cream the butter and sugar in a food processor or food mixer.
- Add the peanut butter and combine.
- Add the eggs, flour, baking powder and chocolate chips and mix to combine into a dough.
- Shape into balls the size of walnuts and place on a greased baking tray, 3cm apart.
- Take a glass of water and a fork.
- Wet the fork and flatten down each biscuit slightly, but not too much.
- When the fork starts to stick, wet it again in the water.
- Bake for 12 minutes and cool on a rack.

Week 2

Monday p412	Soy-seared seabass + French country salad
Tuesday p413	Penne rigate with sausage
Wednesday p414	Summer vegetable risotto
Thursday p415	Smoked haddock Benedict with pancetta and creamy leeks on toast
Friday p417	Chicken with pancetta and capers + smashed potatoes + roasted courgettes
Saturday p418	Beef fillet in red wine + new potatoes + green salad
Sunday p419	Grilled lamb cutlets + roast courgettes + tomato and mint salad
Sunday pudding p420	Raspberry tart
Extra tasty treat p421	Dried fruit and walnut loaf

Shopping list

MEAT

- ☐ 600g sausage meat or equivalent weight in sausages
- ☐ 3 large chicken breasts
- ☐ 5 pieces beef fillet
- ☐ 10–12 lamb cutlets

FISH

- ☐ 6 portions sea bass fillet
- ☐ 700g smoked undyed haddock

VEGETABLES

- ☐ fresh ginger
- ☐ 200g French beans
- ☐ 1 red onion
- ☐ 1 garlic bulb
- ☐ 1 bunch celery
- ☐ 100g peas
- ☐ 100g carrots
- ☐ 100g broad beans
- ☐ 4 leeks
- ☐ 6 shallots
- ☐ 2kg new potatoes
- ☐ 200g young spinach leaves
- ☐ 200g watercress
- ☐ 1.2kg courgettes
- ☐ 4 plum tomatoes

FRUIT

- ☐ 4 lemons
- ☐ 500g fresh raspberries

FRESH HERBS

- ☐ flat-leaf parsley
- ☐ basil
- ☐ rosemary
- ☐ thyme
- ☐ mint

FRIDGE ITEMS

- ☐ 1.75 litres chicken stock
- ☐ 200ml crème fraîche
- ☐ 150g Parmesan cheese
- ☐ 140g sliced pancetta
- ☐ 100g chopped pancetta
- ☐ 200ml beef stock
- ☐ 250ml double cream
- ☐ 3 packs butter
- ☐ 12 eggs
- ☐ 700ml milk

KITCHEN CUPBOARD ITEMS

- ☐ light soy sauce
- ☐ fish sauce
- ☐ 400g tin haricot beans
- ☐ 50g pitted black olives
- ☐ 500g penne rigate
- ☐ 400g Arborio rice
- ☐ 1 loaf white bread
- ☐ tinned anchovy fillets
- ☐ capers
- ☐ tomato purée
- ☐ 1 bottle red wine
- ☐ 1 bottle dry white wine
- ☐ balsamic vinegar
- ☐ red wine vinegar
- ☐ white wine vinegar
- ☐ extra virgin olive oil
- ☐ vegetable oil
- ☐ sesame oil
- ☐ salt
- ☐ Dijon mustard
- ☐ 1 small jar raspberry jam
- ☐ 75g ground almonds
- ☐ 125g icing sugar
- ☐ 100g caster sugar
- ☐ 600g plain flour
- ☐ 100g walnuts
- ☐ 250g dried figs
- ☐ 250g soft, dried apricots
- ☐ baking powder
- ☐ olive oil

SPICES

- ☐ cloves
- ☐ black peppercorns
- ☐ whole nutmeg
- ☐ ground cinammon
- ☐ ground ginger

Soy-seared sea bass + French country salad

This is a lovely, light summer supper. If you want to make it more filling, serve with bread. Prepare the salad first, then the soy-sauce mixture for the fish, and sear the sea bass last of all.

Soy-seared sea bass

4 tablespoons light soy sauce
2 teaspoons fish sauce
4cm piece fresh ginger, grated
3 teaspoons sesame oil
6 portions sea bass fillet
vegetable oil

- Mix together the soy sauce, fish sauce, ginger and sesame oil in a small bowl.
- Heat a frying or griddle pan on the hob until hot.
- Brush the skin side of the sea bass with a little vegetable oil and place half the portions in the frying pan, skin side down for 1–2 minutes, depending on the thickness of the fillets. Thin fillets will only take 1 minute to cook each side, while thick fillets will take a little longer.
- Remove the pan from the heat and spoon over half the soy sauce mixture.
- Do the same with the remaining fillets.

French country salad

500g new potatoes, boiled until tender
200g French beans, cooked
1 small red onion, very finely chopped
50g pitted black olives
2 tablespoons flat-leaf parsley, finely chopped
400g tin haricot beans, drained
1 tablespoon capers, rinsed
For the dressing
4 tablespoons extra virgin olive oil
2 tablespoons lemon juice
salt and pepper

- Once cooked, remove the skins from the potatoes if you prefer them without, and then chop them into 2cm dice.
- Chop the French beans into 3cm pieces.
- Combine these and the rest of the ingredients in a serving bowl and set aside while you prepare the dressing in a small jug.
- Just before serving, drizzle the dressing over the salad.

Penne rigate with sausage

Although this is a quick meal to prepare, it's still very satisfying.

150g butter
2 shallots, finely chopped
2 cloves garlic, peeled and finely chopped
600g sausage meat or the equivalent weight in sausages with the meat squeezed out
400ml dry white wine
1 sprig rosemary, finely chopped
pinch freshly ground nutmeg
pinch ground cloves
pepper
500g penne rigate
Parmesan cheese, freshly grated for serving

- Warm the butter in a sauté pan and gently fry the shallot and garlic for 5 minutes.
- Add the sausage meat and cook, uncovered, until the meat starts to turn brown.
- Add the wine and rosemary and cook gently, uncovered, for 10 minutes.
- Add the spices, season with pepper and stir round. You shouldn't need to add any salt.
- Meanwhile, cook the pasta according to the packet instructions.
- Drain the pasta well, stir in the sausage mixture and serve with the cheese sprinkled on top.

Summer vegetable risotto

There is something very satisfying about using vegetables that are in season. This dish is full of summer flavours and perfect for an evening meal.

25g butter
1 stick celery, finely chopped
2 shallots, peeled and finely chopped
400g Arborio rice
1.75 litres chicken stock
350g mixed summer vegetables such as:
 courgettes, sliced
 peas
 carrots, peeled and sliced thinly
 broad beans
salt and pepper
10 basil leaves
25g Parmesan cheese, grated
25g butter for serving

- Warm the first portion of butter in a large pan.
- Add the celery and shallots and sauté for 4 minutes until soft.
- Add the rice and fry for 3 minutes, stirring constantly.
- Meanwhile, heat the stock until it is simmering.
- Add the vegetables to the stock, keeping the stock on a gentle simmer.
- Simmer the vegetables for 5 minutes, by which time they should all be tender.
- Remove them from the stock and set aside.
- Season the stock with salt and pepper.
- Start to add the stock to the rice a ladleful at a time.
- The rice should be on a medium heat. Stir it round after each addition and once you see the stock becoming incorporated, but while the rice is still wet, add another couple of ladles of stock. Keep adding the stock using this method until the risotto is cooked.
- A risotto takes approximately 25 minutes to cook properly.
- Fold the vegetables and basil into the rice.
- Adjust the seasoning if necessary.
- Stir in the cheese and butter and serve immediately.

Smoked haddock Benedict with pancetta and creamy leeks on toast

This dish sounds quite complicated but you can prepare the Hollandaise and leeks in advance. Do note, however, that you shouldn't try and reheat the Hollandaise sauce, as it will curdle. Incidentally, if for any reason you can't get smoked haddock, smoked cod will work just as well.

500ml milk
250ml water
700g smoked undyed haddock
6 slices pancetta
6 slices toast

For the poached eggs

1 teaspoon white wine vinegar
6 eggs

For the Hollandaise sauce

110g unsalted butter
2 egg yolks
salt and pepper
squeeze fresh lemon juice

For the creamy leeks

4 leeks
salt
200ml crème fraîche
black pepper

To cook the fish

- Pour the milk and water into a meat or vegetable roasting tin.
- Place the tray on the hob and bring the liquid to a simmer.
- Place the fish in the milk and water and poach it for 4 minutes.

continues

To poach the eggs

- Take a large sauté pan and fill it with 3cm of water.
- Add the white wine vinegar and get the water simmering. A simmer is all that is necesary to poach eggs and will stop the egg white breaking up too much.
- Crack the eggs into the water carefully. I would suggest cooking 3 at a time.
- Poach the eggs for 1 minute and then remove them. You can pop them back into the warm water just before you are ready to serve.

To make the Hollandaise sauce

- Melt the butter over a medium heat. Don't let it brown.
- Put the egg yolks, salt, pepper and lemon juice in a food processor and whizz until smooth.
- Keep the food processor going on a slow speed and start trickling in the butter. Don't add more than a trickle or it will curdle.
- Stop adding the butter once you reach the cloudy sediment at the bottom of the saucepan.
- Adjust the seasoning if necessary.
- If you are not serving the sauce immediately, set it in a bowl over a pan of hot water to keep warm. You will not be able to heat it up again as it will curdle.

To make the creamy leeks

- Prepare the leeks by cutting them lengthways, stopping about 1cm from the bottom of the leek so it's still in one piece. Wash them under the tap, fanning each leek out as you wash them, to get rid of any grit between the leaves of the leek.
- Slice the leeks as thinly as possible and place them in a sauté pan with a sprinkling of salt.
- Gently sauté the leeks on a medium heat for 3 minutes, until they are soft but not brown.
- Stir in the crème fraîche and remove the leeks from the heat.
- Season with black pepper.

To assemble the smoked haddock Benedict

- Fry the pancetta and toast the bread and then assemble each serving individually by placing the toast on the plate, topping it with a spoon or so of leeks. Place the fish on top of the leeks, followed by an egg. Spoon some Hollandaise sauce over and then top with a slice of fried pancetta.

TIP

Hollandaise sauce: *If you use a food processor to make this sauce it takes a few minutes only.*

Chicken with pancetta and capers + smashed potatoes + roasted courgettes

This recipe works best with thinly sliced chicken breasts, so buy 3 large breasts and slice them in half so that they are half as thick. If the breasts are small buy 6 and give them a good bash to thin them out.

Chicken with pancetta and capers

1 sprig rosemary
4 bottled or tinned anchovy fillets
1 garlic clove
1 tablespoon salted capers, rinsed
3 tablespoons olive oil
3 large chicken breasts, sliced in half or 6 small breasts
salt and pepper
1 tablespoon lemon juice
100g chopped pancetta

- Remove the leaves from the sprig of rosemary and chop them finely with the anchovies, garlic and capers and set aside.
- Warm a serving dish in the oven.
- Heat the olive oil in a frying pan and cook the breasts, 3 at a time, for 1 minute on each side until golden brown. While the breasts are cooking, generously season them with salt and pepper and half the lemon juice.
- Remove the breasts from the pan, place in the warmed serving dish and cover with tin foil. Cook the remaining 3 chicken breasts in the same way.
- Turn the anchovy mixture into the pan with the pancetta and cook until the pancetta is golden brown. Scatter this mixture over the chicken and serve immediately.

Smashed potatoes

800g new potatoes, scrubbed
salt and black pepper
extra virgin olive oil

- Cook the potatoes in boiling salted water for 20 minutes until tender. This timing depends on the size of your potatoes, but they need to be tender so you can smash them up with a fork.
- Once cooked, add a good drizzle of the olive oil and a good grinding of pepper and break the potatoes up with a fork. Serve.

Roasted courgettes

500g courgettes, sliced into discs the thickness of a pound coin
salt and pepper
olive oil
1 tablespoon Parmesan cheese, freshly grated

- Preheat the oven to 200°C/400°F/gas 6.
- Lay the courgettes on a large baking tray and generously season them with salt and pepper and a drizzle of olive oil.
- Place them in the oven and cook for 20 minutes until browned.
- Sprinkle with Parmesan cheese and serve.

Beef fillet in red wine
+ new potatoes + green salad

This is a French-style meal. It is easy to make, as beef fillet takes just a moment to cook. Fillet is expensive so sharing one piece of fillet between two younger children makes it more affordable. Prepare the potatoes and salad first, but dress the salad just before serving.

Beef fillet in red wine

1 tablespoon olive oil
50g butter
5 pieces beef fillet
salt and pepper
70g sliced pancetta, chopped into pieces
2 shallots, finely sliced
250ml red wine
200ml beef stock (a cube will do)
1 tablespoon tomato purée
leaves from 1 sprig thyme
1 knob butter

- Heat the olive oil and butter in a sauté pan.
- Once the butter starts to foam, place the fillets in the pan. They will cook better if you fry them in two batches. The cooking time depends upon the thickness of the fillets and how you like your meat cooked, but a starting guide would be 2 minutes each side for thick fillets cooked rare, but slightly less for thinner slices.
- Season each side of each fillet with salt and pepper as you cook them and set aside to keep warm while you prepare the sauce, which only takes a few minutes.
- Keep the pan on the heat and add the pancetta pieces and shallot to brown for 1 minute.
- Turn the heat to high, add the wine and boil for 1 minute.
- Add the stock, tomato purée and thyme and simmer for 1 minute.
- Whisk in the knob of butter until incorporated.
- Check the seasoning.
- Return the pieces of fillet to the pan, warm through and serve with the potatoes and salad.

New potatoes

700g new potatoes
salt
a little butter
pepper

- Boil the potatoes in salted water for 20 minutes, until tender.
- Drain and peel them, if you like them peeled.
- Toss the potatoes in the butter and season with black pepper.

Green salad

200g young spinach leaves
200g watercress
For the dressing
2 tablespoons extra virgin olive oil
½ tablespoon balsamic vinegar
salt and pepper

- Put the spinach leaves and watercress in a serving dish.
- Mix up the dressing and spoon it over the leaves just before serving.

Grilled lamb cutlets + roast courgettes + tomato and mint salad

Grilled lamb cutlets are fast food as far as I am concerned. There is no need to eat microwave meals when you can produce healthy, nutritious food so quickly. Prepare the salad while the oven is warming up and then start roasting the courgettes before grilling the cutlets.

Grilled lamb cutlets

10–12 lamb cutlets, depending on your children's appetites
salt and pepper

- Preheat the grill.
- Lay a sheet of tin foil in the bottom of the grill pan to save on washing up.
- Put the cutlets under the hot grill for 5 minutes.
- Turn them over and grill for another 5 minutes.
- Season the cutlets with salt and pepper and serve immediately.

Roast courgettes

6–8 courgettes, sliced lengthways in strips to a thickness of a pound coin
1 tablespoon olive oil
salt and pepper

- Preheat the oven to 200°C/400°F/gas 6.
- Lay the courgettes in a single layer on a baking sheet.
- Drizzle over the olive oil and season well with salt and pepper.
- Roast for about 20 minutes until they turn golden brown and are slightly crisp at the edges.

Tomato and mint salad

4 plum tomatoes, sliced
2 sprigs fresh mint, finely chopped
For the dressing
1 tablespoon red wine vinegar
salt and black pepper
1 teaspoon Dijon mustard
4 tablespoons extra virgin olive oil

- Lay the tomatoes on a serving plate and sprinkle over the mint leaves.
- In a small bowl mix the dressing by firstly pouring in the red wine vinegar along with the salt and mustard.
- Slowly drizzle in the olive oil, whisking continuously so that the dressing emulsifies.
- Pour this over the tomatoes when you are ready to serve them and then season the whole dish with a good grinding of black pepper.

Raspberry tart

This raspberry tart is truly delicious. Raspberries are in abundance at this time of year so make use of them. My one fussy child was converted to raspberries after tasting this tart for the first time.

For the pastry
250g plain flour
salt
½ teaspoon ground cinnamon
150g cold butter, cut into cubes
125g icing sugar
grated zest 1 lemon
75g ground almonds
1 egg and 1 egg yolk, beaten together
For the raspberry filling
500g fresh raspberries
2 tablespoons caster sugar
For the glaze
1 small jar raspberry jam
cream for serving

- Preheat the oven to 180°C/350°F/gas 4.
- Grease a 23cm tart tin.

To make the pastry
- Place the flour, a pinch of salt, the cinnamon, butter, icing sugar, lemon zest and ground almonds in a food processor.
- Blitz until the mixture looks like breadcrumbs.
- Tip into a bowl and add the eggs gradually until you have a manageable dough.
- Turn out on to a floured surface and bring together quickly.
- Shape the dough into a ball, flatten it slightly, wrap it in cling-film and chill in the fridge for 30 minutes.

To make the raspberry filling
- Place the raspberries and sugar into another saucepan and bring to a simmer.
- Turn up the heat and boil for 4 minutes.
- Leave to cool in the pan.

To assemble the tart
- Roll out the pastry to twice the thickness of a pound coin.
- Line the tart tin with the pastry, retaining any leftover pastry.
- Pour the raspberry mixture into the pastry case.
- With the leftover pastry make strips to lay over the top of the tart in a lattice.
- Bake for 40 minutes.

To make the glaze
- Tip the raspberry jam into a small saucepan and warm through.
- Pour through a sieve into a small bowl and set aside.
- Once the tart is completely cool brush the top of the tart with the raspberry jam glaze using it all, so that you have a really thick coating.
- Serve with cream.

Dried fruit and walnut loaf

This recipe is a slight twist on the usual date and walnut loaf. Serve it cut in thick slices spread with butter. It tastes even better after a day or two.

50g butter, softened
50g caster sugar
2 eggs
350g plain flour
salt
100g walnuts, roughly chopped
250g dried figs, roughly chopped
250g soft, dried apricots, roughly chopped
1 teaspoon baking powder
½ teaspoon ground cinnamon
½ teaspoon ground ginger
200ml milk

- Preheat the oven to 180°C/350°F/gas 4.
- Grease a loaf tin and line the bottom with a rectangle of parchment paper.
- Cream the butter and sugar together using a hand-held mixer, until fluffy and pale.
- Beat an egg into the butter and sugar with a tablespoon of flour.
- Beat in the other egg with another tablespoon of flour and then fold in the remaining flour, a pinch of salt, the nuts, dried fruit, baking powder and ground spices.
- Stir in the milk and then spoon the mixture into the loaf tin.
- Bake for 1 hour and 10 minutes.
- Turn the cake out of the tin once it has cooled slightly and place it on a wire rack to cool completely.

Week 3

Monday p424	Chicken and peanut wraps + red onion and avocado salad
Tuesday p425	Tomato, pasta and basil soup
Wednesday p426	Hake with roast-pepper mayonnaise + sautéed potatoes + roasted courgettes
Thursday p427	Tomato and mustard tart + aubergine + beetroot + green bean salad
Friday p429	Turkey burgers + new potato, tomato and pea salad
Saturday p430	Creamed salmon gratin + peas and green beans
Sunday p431	Braised leg of lamb + buttered new potatoes
Sunday pudding p432	Mini fruit puddings
Extra tasty treat p433	Iced walnut cake

Shopping list

MEAT

- ☐ 4 chicken breasts, boneless and skinless
- ☐ 750g minced turkey
- ☐ 100g sausage meat
- ☐ 1.2kg (approx) boned leg of lamb

FISH

- ☐ 6 pieces hake fillet

VEGETABLES

- ☐ 1 red onion
- ☐ 1 avocado
- ☐ 1 Romaine or Cos lettuce
- ☐ 1 cucumber
- ☐ 6 courgettes
- ☐ 13 plum tomatoes
- ☐ 1 aubergine
- ☐ 6–10 beetroot
- ☐ 1 garlic bulb
- ☐ 800g French beans
- ☐ 200g cherry tomatoes
- ☐ 100g shallots
- ☐ 1.4kg potatoes
- ☐ 300g fresh garden peas
- ☐ 2 onions
- ☐ 225g leeks
- ☐ 225g carrots
- ☐ 225g parsnips
- ☐ 1.4kg new potatoes

FRUIT

- ☐ 250g mixed soft fruits e.g. blackcurrants, redcurrants, strawberries and raspberries
- ☐ 2 lemons

FRESH HERBS

- ☐ coriander
- ☐ basil
- ☐ chives
- ☐ mint
- ☐ oregano
- ☐ rosemary
- ☐ bay leaves

FRIDGE ITEMS

- ☐ 125g Parmesan cheese
- ☐ 300g frozen peas
- ☐ 50g Gruyère cheese
- ☐ 3 packs butter
- ☐ 750ml double cream
- ☐ 11 eggs
- ☐ 350ml milk
- ☐ 70g sliced pancetta

KITCHEN CUPBOARD ITEMS

- ☐ mustard powder
- ☐ 1 jar peanut butter
- ☐ 1 tin coconut milk
- ☐ 10–12 tortilla wraps
- ☐ 170g small tubular pasta
- ☐ 1 jar roasted red peppers
- ☐ Dijon mustard
- ☐ salt
- ☐ 6–8 muffins
- ☐ Worcestershire sauce
- ☐ vegetable oil
- ☐ extra virgin olive oil
- ☐ olive oil
- ☐ groundnut oil
- ☐ light olive oil
- ☐ white wine vinegar
- ☐ balsamic vinegar
- ☐ 2 x 180g tins of red salmon
- ☐ 1 bottle white wine
- ☐ 300g self-raising flour
- ☐ 400g tin peeled Italian plum tomatoes
- ☐ 600g plain flour
- ☐ baking powder
- ☐ 325g caster sugar
- ☐ 150g walnut pieces
- ☐ vanilla extract
- ☐ 210g icing sugar

SPICES

- ☐ coriander seeds
- ☐ cumin seeds
- ☐ black peppercorns

Chicken and peanut wraps
+ red onion and avocado salad

Tortilla wraps can provide a range of different meals that are quick and easy and are very popular with children.

Chicken and peanut wraps

For the peanut sauce

3 shallots
3 garlic cloves
3 stalks fresh coriander
1 tablespoon vegetable oil
1 teaspoon coriander seeds, ground
1 teaspoon cumin seeds, ground
salt and pepper
4 tablespoons peanut butter
8 tablespoons coconut milk

For the chicken

1 tablespoon olive oil
20g butter
4 chicken breasts, boneless and skinless

For the wraps

10–12 tortilla wraps
1 Romaine or Cos lettuce, shredded
½ cucumber, cut into thin batons

To make the peanut sauce

- Using a food processor or liquidizer mince the shallots, garlic and fresh coriander together.
- Heat the vegetable oil in a frying pan and add the minced garlic mixture and the ground coriander and cumin.
- Fry for 2 minutes on a low heat.
- Season with a little salt and pepper.
- Add the peanut butter and coconut milk and stir.
- Bring to a simmer and remove from the heat.

To cook the chicken

- Heat the olive oil and butter in a frying pan.
- Put the chicken breasts in the pan and brown them on each side for 1 minute.
- Reduce the heat to low. Place old butter papers or baking parchment over the breasts and cook them like this for 10 minutes.
- Once cooked, cut the chicken up into small pieces with a sharp knife.

To construct the wraps

- Spread each wrap with some of the peanut sauce and then spoon some chicken onto one half along with some shredded lettuce and cucumber.
- Roll the tortilla up and cut each one on the slant.

Red onion and avocado salad

1 red onion, diced
1 avocado, peeled and chopped
4 tomatoes, chopped
½ cucumber, diced

For the dressing

1 tablespoon extra virgin olive oil
squeeze of fresh lemon juice
salt and pepper

- Assemble the salad in a bowl and then spoon over the dressing.

Tomato, pasta and basil soup

This is a substantial tomato soup. It's really an Italian soup and should only be made when you can get good, tasty, ripe tomatoes. I try and compensate for the fact that you don't get such tasty tomatoes in England, even in the summer, by adding a tin of peeled plum tomatoes, but if you are confident that your tomatoes are good enough, just use fresh ones. Don't think that you shouldn't eat soups in the summer. If they are made with seasonal ingredients they are generally appropriate for this time of year.

5 tablespoons olive oil
2 cloves garlic, peeled and finely chopped
1 onion, thinly sliced
5 ripe plum tomatoes, peeled and coarsely chopped
400g tin peeled Italian plum tomatoes
10 or so fresh basil leaves, torn
salt and pepper
2 teaspoons sugar
170g small tubular pasta
Parmesan cheese, freshly grated

- Heat the olive oil in a large saucepan and when warmed through add the garlic, onion, fresh tomatoes, tinned tomatoes and half the basil.
- Cook on a medium heat for 10 minutes, stirring frequently.
- Add 1.75 litres of water and season with salt, pepper and sugar.
- Bring the soup to a simmer and then cook it very gently, uncovered, for 20 minutes.
- After 20 minutes, raise the heat and add the pasta. Cook the soup for as long as the directions on the pasta packet indicate, less 1 minute.
- When ready, add the rest of the torn basil leaves and serve with the Parmesan cheese.
- Remember that every time you reheat this soup the pasta will cook some more. Don't allow it to become too soft.

Hake with roast-pepper mayonnaise + sautéed potatoes + roasted courgettes

It is nearly the end of the courgette season so enjoy them while you can. Hake is a beautifully flavoursome fish and it is simple to cook. Prepare all the vegetables and the mayonnaise first, as the fish takes just a few minutes to grill.

Hake with roast-pepper mayonnaise

For the fish

6 pieces hake fillet
salt and pepper

For the roast pepper mayonnaise

3 slices bottled roasted red peppers
2 egg yolks
1 teaspoon Dijon mustard
200ml groundnut oil
100ml light olive oil
salt

To make the roast-pepper mayonnaise

- Mash up the slices of pepper with a fork and set aside.
- Mix the egg yolks with the mustard in a medium mixing bowl.
- Combine the oils in a pouring jug and gradually start to add the oil, drop by drop, to the yolk mixture, whisking as you go. Once half the oil has been incorporated at a trickle you can increase the pace of each addition, but go steady and make sure each addition of oil is combined before the next one is added.
- Add the mashed peppers, season with salt and set aside.

To grill the fish

- Preheat the grill and line the grill pan with aluminium foil.
- Place the hake on the grill rack and grill for 2–3 minutes on each side.

Sautéed potatoes

1 kg potatoes, peeled and cut into chunks of about 3cm
2 tablespoons olive oil
salt and pepper

- Boil the potatoes in salted water until tender.
- Drain them well.
- Heat the oil in a large sauté pan, add the potatoes and sauté them on a medium heat for 20 minutes until golden brown all over.

Roasted courgettes

6 courgettes, sliced lengthways
salt and pepper
olive oil

- Preheat the oven to 200°C/400°F/gas 6.
- Lay the courgettes on a large baking tray and season them generously with salt, pepper and a drizzle of olive oil.
- Place the tray in the oven and cook for 20 minutes until browned.

Tomato and mustard tart
+ aubergine + beetroot + bean salad

This meal contains some beautifully fresh flavours and is perfect for mid summer.

Tomato and mustard tart

For the pastry

275g plain flour

175g butter

salt

25g Parmesan cheese, grated

1 egg yolk

2 tablespoons water

For the filling

4 plum tomatoes, sliced widthways

300ml double cream

3 eggs

100g Parmesan cheese

salt and pepper

1 teaspoon mustard powder

To make the pastry

- Put the flour and butter in a food processor, or in a bowl if you are combining by hand, and incorporate so that the mixture looks like fine breadcrumbs.
- Add a pinch of salt and the cheese and mix briefly.
- Mix the egg yolk with the cold water in a small bowl, and then add it to the bread-crumbed flour and fat.

continues

- Combine and, as a ball of dough starts to form, turn it out onto a lightly floured work surface.
- With a light hand, gently knead the pastry dough until its appearance is smooth.
- Wrap in cling-film and chill in the fridge for at least 20 minutes.

To make the tart

- Grease a 30cm flan tin.
- Preheat the oven to 200°C/400°F/gas 6.
- Roll out the pastry and line the flan tin with it.
- Cover the pastry with greaseproof paper and on top of the paper scatter some baking beans.
- Bake the pastry case for 10 minutes.
- Remove the greaseproof paper and beans and return the pastry case to the oven for 5 minutes.
- Take the pastry case from the oven and reduce the oven temperature to 180°C/350°F/gas 4.
- Lay the sliced tomatoes on the bottom of the pastry case.
- Mix the rest of the filling ingredients together in a bowl and then pour them into the pastry case on top of the tomatoes.
- Bake for 20 minutes.

Aubergine

1 aubergine, sliced widthways into 5mm thick slices
salt and pepper
1 tablespoon olive oil
10 fresh basil leaves, shredded
1 tablespoon extra virgin olive oil

- Preheat the oven to 200°C/400°F/gas 6.
- Place the aubergine in a colander, sprinkle over a teaspoon of salt and leave for 30 minutes
- Using some kitchen paper dry off the slices of aubergine and then brush each slice with olive oil and lay on a baking sheet.
- Place the aubergine in the oven for 15 minutes.
- Remove the aubergine from the oven and dress it with the extra virgin olive oil, salt, pepper and basil leaves.

Beetroot

6–10 beetroot (depending on how large an appetite your family has)
1 sprig rosemary
1 clove garlic, mashed
2 tablespoons olive oil
1 dessertspoon balsamic vinegar
salt and pepper

- Preheat the oven to 200°C/400°F/gas 6.
- Prepare the beetroot by cutting the leaf stems down to as close to the top of the beetroot as you can without cutting into the beetroot.
- Scrub the beetroots to remove any remaining mud and then place them on a large square of aluminium foil along with the rosemary, garlic, oil and vinegar.
- Season well with salt and pepper.
- Make a parcel of the beetroot by folding up the edges of the foil to make a little packet and then place this on a baking sheet.
- Bake for 1 hour, although a little longer will do no harm.

Bean salad

500g French beans, prepared for cooking
salt and black pepper
2 tablespoons extra virgin olive oil

- Boil the beans in salted water for 7 minutes.
- Drain well and then dress them in the oil, with a good grinding of black pepper.

Turkey burgers
+ new potato, tomato and pea salad

I know turkey burgers conjure up images of processed golden crumb-covered burgers, but I can assure you that these are a different thing altogether. Turkey meat is reasonably healthy as it is low in fat compared to some other meats. This recipe makes approximately 8 burgers.

Turkey burgers

750g minced turkey
2 tablespoons chives, snipped
1 shallot, finely chopped
70g sliced pancetta, finely chopped
100g sausage meat
2 tablespoons Worcestershire sauce
salt and pepper
flour for dusting
2 tablespoons olive oil
6–8 muffins

- Place the turkey, chives, shallot, pancetta, sausage meat and Worcestershire sauce in a bowl, seasoning the mixture well with salt and pepper.
- Form the mixture into burger patties, weighing approximately 100g each.
- Heat the olive oil in a frying pan.
- Dip each burger in some flour. Fry the burgers in the olive oil for 1 minute on each side. Reduce the heat to low for 5 minutes so that the burger cooks all the way through.
- Split the muffins and place a burger inside each one.

New potato, tomato and pea salad

700g new potatoes, peeled or unpeeled depending on how you like them
200g cherry tomatoes, halved
300g frozen peas, cooked

For the dressing
4 tablespoons extra virgin olive oil
1 tablespoon white wine vinegar
30g fresh mint, finely chopped
salt and pepper

- Cook the new potatoes in boiling salted water until tender. This takes approximately 15 minutes from point of boiling, but obviously the exact time depends on the size of the potatoes.
- In the meantime, prepare the dressing by combining the oil and vinegar with the mint, salt and pepper.
- Place the potatoes in a serving bowl along with the tomatoes and peas and pour over the dressing while the potatoes are still warm.

Creamed salmon gratin
+ peas and green beans

This dish is easy to make but quite rich, so you won't want a huge helping. The peas and beans will temper the richness slightly.

Creamed salmon gratin

2 x 180g tins of red salmon
50g butter
25g shallots, finely chopped
30g flour
200ml milk
50ml white wine
2 tablespoons double cream
½ teaspoon oregano, chopped
salt and pepper
3 hard-boiled eggs, sliced
4 large cooked potatoes, sliced to a thickness of 5mm
50g Gruyère cheese, grated

- Preheat the oven to 200°C/400°F/gas 6.
- Separate the salmon from the liquid and set both aside.
- Heat the butter in a sauté pan and cook the shallots in the butter on a medium heat for 5 minutes until soft but not browned.
- Stir in the flour and cook for 2 minutes on a low heat.
- Whisk in the milk, wine and the liquid from the salmon tins.
- Simmer gently for 10 minutes, stirring frequently.
- Add the cream and oregano.
- Then gently stir in the salmon and season with salt and pepper.
- Spoon the creamy salmon mixture into a greased gratin dish.
- Scatter on the eggs and over the top of these lay the potato slices.
- Sprinkle the cheese over the potatoes.
- Bake for 18 minutes.

Peas and green beans

300g fresh garden peas
300g French beans
salt
2 tablespoons extra virgin olive oil
black pepper

- Cook the peas and beans in boiling salted water for about 6 minutes until tender.
- Drain the vegetables well and place them in a serving bowl.
- Pour the olive oil over the peas and beans and season with a little black pepper.

Braised leg of lamb
+ buttered new potatoes

Braising is a lovely way to cook lamb. It is slow, but the lamb just falls apart when it is cooked. It is a good Sunday recipe, as it doesn't really matter if the cooking takes a bit longer.

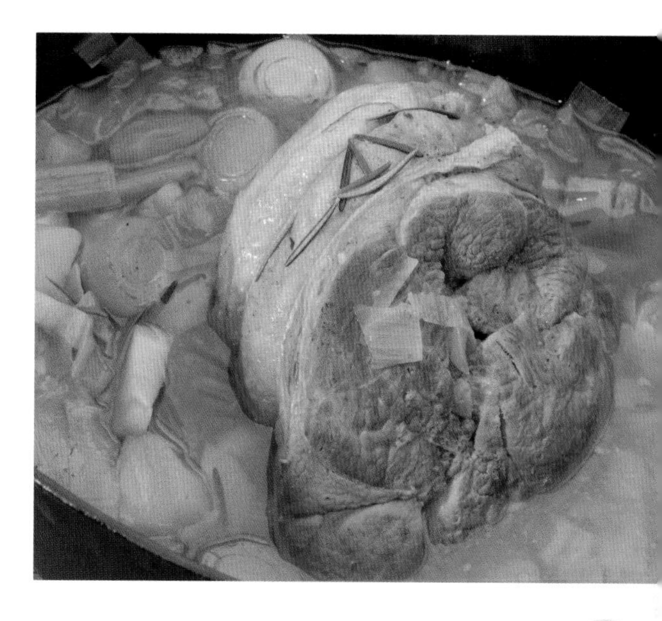

Braised leg of lamb

2 tablespoons olive oil
1.2kg (approx) boned leg of lamb
salt and pepper
1 large onion, peeled and roughly chopped
225g leeks, roughly chopped
225g carrots, peeled and roughly chopped
225g parsnips, peeled and roughly chopped
1 sprig rosemary
1 bay leaf
300ml white wine
300ml water

- Pour the olive oil into a large saucepan and heat it until hot.
- Brown the lamb joint in the oil all over and season it with salt and pepper.
- Remove the lamb from the saucepan and set aside.
- Keep the pan on the heat and add the vegetables and herbs.
- Stir the vegetables and herbs to coat them in the juices and fat.
- Season with salt and pepper and return the lamb to the pot.
- Pour on the wine and water.
- Bring to a very slow simmer, cover and cook for 2 hours on a low heat.
- Remove the meat from the pot and carve the joint into slices.
- Check the seasoning of the vegetables and serve with the lamb and the juices.

Buttered new potatoes

700g new potatoes
salt and pepper
a little butter

- Boil the potatoes in salted water for 20 minutes until tender.
- Drain and peel them if you prefer them peeled.
- Toss the potatoes in the butter and season them with salt and pepper.

Mini fruit puddings

These puddings are delicious and elegant enough for a dinner party. They make the best use of the superb fruit available during the summer months.

300g self-raising flour
salt
3 teaspoons baking powder
150g butter
75g caster sugar
grated zest 1 lemon
150ml water
250g mixed soft fruits e.g. blackcurrants, redcurrants, strawberries and raspberries
cream for serving

- Preheat the oven to 200°C/400°F/gas 6.
- Generously butter and flour 6 individual pudding moulds.
- Sift the flour, a pinch of salt and baking powder in a food processor or mixing bowl.
- Add the butter to the dry ingredients.
- Combine either by hand or in the food processor until the mixture resembles breadcrumbs.
- Stir in the sugar and lemon zest.
- Add the water a little at a time, mixing as you go, until you have a ball of dough.
- Roll out the dough on a lightly floured surface to a thickness of about 5mm, and line each mould with dough, saving a small circle for the top of each pudding.
- Fill each lined mould almost to the top with fruit, then add a dessertspoon of caster sugar and a teaspoon of water.
- Press the pastry lids firmly onto the top of each pudding.
- Cover each mould with a piece of baking parchment tied with string.
- Place the moulds in a meat tray.
- Pour enough water into the tray to reach 2cms up the side of the pudding moulds.
- Cover the whole tray with foil and place in the oven for 1 hour.
- Turn out the puddings when ready to eat and serve with cream.

Iced walnut cake

This cake is a traditional teatime treat popular in most households.

For the cake
225g plain flour
salt
1½ level teaspoons baking powder
125g butter, softened
250g caster sugar
2 eggs, beaten
150ml milk
½ teaspoon vanilla extract
150g walnut pieces
For the filling
100g butter, softened
110g icing sugar
a few drops vanilla extract
For the icing
100g icing sugar
1 tablespoon warm water

- Preheat the oven to 190°C/375°F/gas 5.
- Grease and line 2 x 21cm cake tins.
- Sieve the flour, a pinch of salt and the baking powder together in a bowl and set aside.
- Cream the butter until light and fluffy with an electric mixer.
- Gradually add the sugar, mixing all the while.
- Next, beat in the eggs.
- Fold in the sifted flour with the milk and vanilla.
- Lastly, stir in the walnuts.
- Divide the mixture between the two tins.
- Bake for 30 minutes.
- Test with a skewer and then turn the cakes out onto a cooling rack.

To make the filling
- Cream the butter until white and fluffy with an electric mixer.
- Add the icing sugar and vanilla and mix thoroughly until combined.
- Spread the filling onto one of the cakes and then sandwich the other one on top.

To make the icing
- Sieve the icing sugar into a bowl.
- Add the water and mix until you have a smooth icing. You may need to add a little more water.
- Spread the icing on top of the cake and decorate with walnut halves if desired.

AUGUST

Week 4

Monday p436	Fried-chicken sandwiches + coleslaw
Tuesday p437	Fried sea bass + bubble and squeak + diced tomato salad
Wednesday p438	Meat and potato pie + runner beans
Thursday p440	Warm new potato salad
Friday p441	Mushrooms à la crème on cheese brioche toast
Saturday p442	Courgette and pancetta risotto
Sunday p443	Grilled marinated chicken thighs + avocado orange salad + baked potatoes
Sunday pudding p444	Sautéed apples and pears + cinnamon buns
Extra tasty treat p445	Treacle bread

Shopping list

MEAT
- ☐ 5–6 chicken breasts, boneless
- ☐ 1kg stewing beef
- ☐ 400g pork steaks
- ☐ 6 chicken thighs

FISH
- ☐ 6 fillets of sea bass, skin on

VEGETABLES
- ☐ 1 garlic bulb
- ☐ 800g white cabbage
- ☐ 5 carrots
- ☐ 1 red pepper
- ☐ 1 green pepper
- ☐ 3 red onions
- ☐ 7 spring onions
- ☐ 1 bunch of celery
- ☐ 2 onions
- ☐ 1 leek
- ☐ 4 plum tomatoes
- ☐ 300g runner beans
- ☐ 600g new potatoes
- ☐ 6 baking potatoes
- ☐ 1.9kg potatoes
- ☐ 3 avocadoes
- ☐ 7 asparagus spears
- ☐ 150g mixed salad leaves
- ☐ 350g button mushrooms
- ☐ 350g white mushrooms
- ☐ 1 cucumber
- ☐ 3 courgettes

FRUIT
- ☐ 2 limes
- ☐ 1 orange
- ☐ 300g apples
- ☐ 300g pears

FRESH HERBS
- ☐ rosemary
- ☐ flat-leaf parsley
- ☐ thyme
- ☐ sage
- ☐ chives
- ☐ tarragon
- ☐ coriander

FRIDGE ITEMS
- ☐ 2 packs butter
- ☐ 100g Parmesan cheese
- ☐ 200g feta cheese
- ☐ 9 eggs
- ☐ 300g chopped pancetta
- ☐ 380ml milk
- ☐ 100g Gruyère cheese
- ☐ 220g sliced pancetta
- ☐ 350g crème fraîche
- ☐ 1.5 litres chicken stock
- ☐ 100g mascarpone cheese
- ☐ 1 small tub natural yoghurt
- ☐ whipping cream

KITCHEN CUPBOARD ITEMS
- ☐ fast-action dried yeast
- ☐ olive oil
- ☐ extra virgin olive oil
- ☐ salt
- ☐ mayonnaise
- ☐ white wine vinegar
- ☐ Dijon mustard
- ☐ balsamic vinegar
- ☐ 1 bottle red wine
- ☐ tomato purée
- ☐ 1 loaf bread
- ☐ 400g risotto rice
- ☐ 100g brown sugar
- ☐ fish sauce
- ☐ sunflower seeds
- ☐ clear honey
- ☐ 250g caster sugar
- ☐ baking powder
- ☐ 650g plain flour
- ☐ black treacle
- ☐ 800g strong white bread flour

SPICES
- ☐ pepper
- ☐ whole nutmeg
- ☐ dried oregano
- ☐ fennel seeds
- ☐ ground cinnamon
- ☐ cayenne pepper
- ☐ ground ginger

Fried-chicken sandwiches + coleslaw

This is a tasty, satisfying meal that is quick if you use bought bread. I've included a recipe for focaccia, which is great if you have time. Prepare the coleslaw first so it's ready when the chicken is done.

Fried-chicken sandwiches

For the focaccia bread

1 sachet fast-action dried yeast
280ml warm water
3 tablespoons olive oil
1 heaped teaspoon salt
2 tablespoons fresh rosemary, chopped
500g white bread flour
a few sprigs of rosemary for the top of the bread

For the fried chicken

5–6 chicken breasts, boneless and skinless
olive oil
salt and pepper

To make the bread

- Mix the yeast with a little of the water in a large mixing bowl and leave to stand for 5 minutes.
- Add the oil, the remaining water, salt, rosemary and 250g of the flour.
- Combine to a sticky dough and turn out onto a floured surface.
- Keep adding flour from the remaining 250g, as you knead the dough until you have a smooth silky dough. This takes 10 minutes. You may not need all of the flour.
- Place the dough back in the mixing bowl with a teaspoon of olive oil, and turn it to coat with oil.
- Cover the bowl and leave to rise for 1 hour.
- Knock back by punching the air out of it and roll into a rectangle, with a thickness of 2.5cm.
- Press into a greased roasting or baking tin, cover and allow to rise for another hour.
- Preheat the oven to 200°C/400°F/gas 6.
- Press your fingertips into the dough to make dimpled impressions on the top, place rosemary sprigs into the dimples and drizzle with olive oil.
- Sprinkle with salt and bake for 20–25 minutes.

To cook the chicken

- Brush the chicken breasts with olive oil.
- Heat a large frying pan and cook the chicken, three breasts at a time.
- Allow 3 minutes on each side, set aside and do the next three breasts.
- Lower the heat and return all the chicken to the pan for 5 minutes to ensure that they have been cooked through and to keep warm.
- Season with salt and pepper.
- Slice each breast into 3 pieces, put it into a piece of focaccia that you have sliced open and spoon some coleslaw on top of the chicken.

Coleslaw

4 tablespoons mayonnaise
2 cloves garlic, peeled and finely chopped
1 teaspoon Dijon mustard
pinch of sugar
1 teaspoon white wine vinegar
salt and pepper
400g white cabbage, finely shredded
3 medium carrots, grated
½ red pepper, sliced as thinly as possible
½ green pepper, sliced as thinly as possible
1 small red onion, peeled and finely diced
3 spring onions, sliced
1 stick celery, finely diced
2 tablespoons flat-leaf parsley, finely chopped

- Place the mayonnaise in a large serving bowl, add the garlic, mustard, sugar, vinegar, salt and pepper and stir to incorporate.
- Add the cabbage, carrots, peppers, red onion, spring onions, celery and parsley and gently mix into the mayonnaise mixture, so that everything is evenly coated.

Fried sea bass
+ bubble and squeak + diced tomato salad

I had this combination of sea bass with bubble and squeak in a pub. It was so good that I had to include it here. Make the bubble and squeak and tomato salad first.

Fried sea bass

6 fillets seabass, skin on
2 tablespoons olive oil
salt and pepper

- Brush the skin side of the fish with olive oil.
- Heat a heavy frying pan.
- Place the fish skin side down in the pan and fry for 1–2 minutes.
- Brush the upper side with oil and flip over, cooking for a further 1–2 minutes.
- Season with salt and pepper and serve with the bubble and squeak and a little tomato salad on the side.

Bubble and squeak

400g potatoes, peeled and quartered
salt and pepper
400g white cabbage, shredded
20g butter
1 onion, finely chopped
1 leek, thinly sliced
70g pancetta, finely chopped
a little flour for dusting
2 tablespoons olive oil

- Boil the potatoes in salted water until tender. Drain and then mash them roughly with a fork. Season and set aside.
- Boil the cabbage in a little salted water for 3 minutes until tender. Drain and set aside.
- Melt the butter in a sauté pan.
- Add the onion, leek and pancetta and cook on a medium heat for 5 minutes until the onion is soft.
- Pile all the potatoes, cabbage, onions, leeks, and pancetta into a mixing bowl. Check the seasoning and then shape the mixture into little cakes weighing approximately 100g each.
- Roll the cakes in a little flour.
- Heat the olive oil in a sauté pan and fry the bubble and squeak cakes on each side until golden brown.

Diced tomato salad

4 plum tomatoes, diced
For the dressing
1 tablespoon extra virgin olive oil
1 teaspoon balsamic vinegar
salt and pepper

- Place the tomatoes in a serving bowl.
- Spoon over the dressing and serve.

Meat and potato pie
+ runner beans

This is the Italian equivalent of a meat and potato pie. I have changed the ingredients slightly but the basis of the recipe comes from Anna Del Conte.

Meat and potato pie

5 tablespoons olive oil
20g butter
1 onion, finely chopped
1 teaspoon sugar
salt and pepper
1 sprig thyme
1 sprig rosemary
4 sage leaves, finely chopped
2 sticks celery, chopped
2 carrots, chopped
2 cloves garlic, peeled and chopped
¼ teaspoon grated nutmeg
1 teaspoon dried oregano
2 tablespoons tomato purée
1kg stewing beef, cubed
400g pork steaks, cubed
300ml red wine
180ml milk
1.5kg potatoes
60g Parmesan cheese
2 tablespoons flat-leaf parsley, finely chopped

- Warm the olive oil and butter in a large heavy sauté pan.
- Add the onion, sugar and a good pinch of salt and sauté the onion for 10 minutes on a low heat.
- Remove the leaves from the thyme and rosemary and chop finely.
- Add these herbs and the sage, celery, carrots, garlic, nutmeg and oregano to the onion.
- Season with pepper and continue to cook, on a medium heat for 10 more minutes.
- Stir in the tomato purée until everything is thoroughly combined.
- Add the meat, stirring frequently until it is slightly browned.
- Pour in the wine, bring to the boil, reduce the heat and simmer for 10 minutes.
- Add the milk and bring to the boil.
- Reduce the heat and cook, uncovered, on a bare simmer for 45 minutes.
- Check the seasoning and adjust with salt and pepper if necessary.
- Meanwhile, peel the potatoes and cut them into very thin slices with a sharp knife.
- Preheat the oven to 200°C/400°F/gas 6.
- Butter a large lasagne dish or meat tin.
- Spread half the potatoes over the bottom of the dish and season with salt and pepper.
- Spoon the meat over the potatoes and sprinkle with half of the Parmesan cheese.
- Spread the remaining potatoes as neatly as possible over the meat and top with the remaining cheese.
- Brush the potato topping with a little melted butter and cover with foil.
- Bake for 20 minutes.
- Remove the foil and bake for a further 30 minutes.
- Sprinkle the top of the pie with the parsley and serve.

Runner beans

300g runner beans
salt and pepper
butter for serving

- Prepare the beans by topping and tailing them and then cutting a thin sliver off the side of each bean. There are no rules on how to slice the beans. I hold the bean upwards and cut at an angle from the top downwards, shaving an

angled slice off. This is the best description I can give to anyone who never saw their mother preparing runner beans.

- Place the prepared beans into boiling water. Cook them for 4 to 7 minutes, depending on how young and tender the beans are. Runner beans have to be well cooked to be enjoyable.
- Once cooked, place a knob of butter in with the beans and season generously with salt and pepper.

Warm new potato salad

Children need to get used to eating salads and seeing them more as meals in themselves rather than a side dish. This salad might be more attractive to children if served with some interesting bread.

For the salad

600g new potatoes, boiled in their skins and cut into thick discs
4 spring onions, sliced
2 avocados, chopped into chunks
1 bunch flat-leaf parsley, finely chopped
1 bunch chives, snipped finely
7 asparagus spears, cooked and chopped into 2cm pieces
150g mixed salad leaves
200g feta cheese, cut into chunks
3 hard-boiled eggs, quartered
100g chopped pancetta

For the dressing

3 dessertspoons extra virgin olive oil
1 dessertspoon balsamic vinegar
salt and pepper
bread for serving

- Place the new potatoes in a large serving bowl.
- Add the spring onions, avocados, herbs, asparagus, salad leaves, cheese and eggs.
- Fry the pancetta until golden brown and scatter over the salad.
- Dress the salad and serve with bread.

Mushrooms à la crème on cheese brioche toast

If you don't think you have the time to make the cheese brioche then you can use another toasted bread. The recipe for the cheese brioche is, however, very straightforward.

For the cheese brioche

100ml tepid milk
1 sachet of fast-action dried yeast
2 eggs
1 teaspoon salt
¼ teaspoon cayenne pepper
300g strong white bread flour
50g butter, softened
100g Gruyère cheese, grated
1 egg, beaten to glaze

For the mushrooms à la crème

80g butter
350g button mushrooms, thinly sliced
350g white mushrooms, thinly sliced
150g sliced pancetta, chopped
350g crème fraîche
2 teaspoons Dijon mustard
salt and pepper
2 teaspoons tarragon, chopped
1 tablespoon parsley, chopped
1 tablespoon chives, snipped

To make the brioche

- Pour the milk into a mixing bowl.
- Sprinkle in the yeast and mix.
- Whisk in the eggs, salt and cayenne pepper until combined.
- Add the flour and mix until a dough forms.
- Turn the dough out onto a floured surface and knead for 10 minutes, or 5 minutes if using a food mixer.
- Add the softened butter and knead or mix until all the butter is combined.
- Place the dough back in the mixing bowl and cover with a clean tea towel.
- Leave to rise for 1 hour.
- Grease a 500g loaf tin and preheat the oven to 200°C/400°F/gas 6.
- Knead the Gruyère cheese into the dough and then shape the dough and place it in the loaf tin.
- Leave to rise for another hour.
- Using a pastry brush, paint the loaf with the egg glaze and bake for 35 minutes.
- Turn out of the tin when cooked and cool on a wire rack.

To make the mushrooms à la creme

- Heat the butter in a large sauté pan.
- Once foaming, add the mushrooms and sauté gently to start with.
- As the liquid from the mushrooms starts to disappear, turn the heat up slightly.
- Add the pancetta and keep sautéeing the mushrooms until they start to turn golden brown.
- This takes about 10 minutes altogether.
- Add the crème fraîche and mustard and stir on the heat for 1 minute.
- Season with salt and pepper and add the herbs.
- Toast slices of the brioche and pile up the mushrooms à la crème on the top of each piece of toast.

Courgette and pancetta risotto

Risotto is a labour of love. You can't leave it to bubble away merrily on the hob. You have to stand over it, taking the trouble to keep the rice on the move. But once you have done the preparation, the risotto takes about 25 minutes to cook. If you use the time to contemplate the day it can be quite relaxing. I think it's worth it and there are some evenings when only a risotto will do.

It has taken me many attempts to work out the method needed to cook a good risotto, so that it is perfectly *al dente*. The simple rules are to add the stock while it is simmering, don't let the rice get too dry before you make the next addition of stock, and cook any vegetables you are going to add to the risotto in the stock to improve the flavour. The last thing is to season your stock properly, rather than having to season the risotto at the end.

1.5 litres chicken stock
salt and black pepper
2 tablespoons olive oil
50g butter
1 red onion, chopped finely
200g chopped pancetta
2 cloves garlic, finely chopped
1 sprig rosemary, leaves removed and finely chopped
3 courgettes, sliced quite thinly
400g risotto rice
1 tablespoon mascarpone cheese
Parmesan cheese, grated

- Heat the well-seasoned stock in a saucepan.
- Heat the olive oil and butter in a large, heavy-bottomed saucepan.

- Add the onion and pancetta and cook until the onion is soft and the pancetta starts to look golden brown, which takes about 3 minutes.
- Add the garlic and rosemary and cook for 2 minutes, stirring occasionally.
- Now add the sliced courgettes to the stock while it is coming to a simmer.
- Pour the rice into the saucepan with the onion, pancetta, garlic and rosemary and stir it around, allowing all the grains to become coated with the oil and butter and the flavours from the other ingredients. This part of the cooking method is important and it takes about 2 minutes.
- Now start adding the hot stock and courgettes, two ladles at a time. The rice should be on a medium heat. Stir the rice round after each addition of stock and, once you see the stock becoming incorporated, but while the rice is still wet, add another couple of ladles. Keep adding the stock using this method until the risotto is cooked, usually about 25 minutes.
- Once it is cooked, add the mascarpone cheese and the Parmesan and season with pepper. You should not need more salt if the stock was properly seasoned at the beginning.

Grilled marinated chicken thighs + avocado orange salad + baked potatoes

This is a great summer lunch dish. You can cook the chicken on the barbecue or under the grill, whichever method you prefer. It may, of course, be dictated by the weather. Put the potatoes in the oven first and then get on with the chicken and salad.

Grilled marinated chicken thighs

3 plump cloves garlic, peeled
2 tablespoons coriander leaves
1½ tablespoons fish sauce
juice 1 lime
1 tablespoon brown sugar
black pepper
6 chicken thighs, skin removed
olive oil

- Place the garlic, coriander, fish sauce, lime juice, sugar and pepper in a food processor and blitz until smooth.
- Put the chicken thighs in a shallow dish, making sharp incisions in each thigh in several places.
- Rub the marinade over the chicken and set aside for 30 minutes or so.
- Preheat the grill to hot.
- Drizzle the chicken thighs with a little olive oil.
- Place the thighs under the grill and cook for 20–25 minutes, turning them occasionally, and moving them lower or higher, depending on how much they are browning.

Avocado orange salad

1 avocado, prepared and cut into chunks
1 orange, peeled of skin and pith, and cut into slivers
½ cucumber, cut into chunks
1 red onion, finely chopped
1 tablespoon coriander leaves, roughly chopped
1 tablespoon sunflower seeds

For the dressing
1 tablespoon lime juice
1 tablespoon natural yoghurt
3 tablespoons extra virgin olive oil
salt and pepper
½ teaspoon fennel seeds

- Place the prepared avocado, orange, cucumber, onion, coriander leaves and sunflower seeds in a serving bowl.
- Drizzle the yoghurt over the salad.
- Combine the other dressing ingredients and pour over the salad just before serving.

Baked potatoes

6 baking potatoes
butter for serving
salt and pepper

- Preheat the oven to 220°C/425°F/gas 7.
- Pierce the potato skins with a sharp knife and pop them in the oven for 1 hour 30 minutes.
- Split each potato and serve with butter, salt and pepper.

Sautéed apples and pears
+ cinnamon buns

The recipe for these delightful little buns makes 24, which is obviously too many for the dessert. You will have some left over for the children to eat through the week, as they keep quite well in an airtight container. Make the buns first and then prepare the apples and pears.

Sautéed apples and pears

300g apples
300g pears
25g butter
honey for drizzling
whipping cream for serving

- Peel and core the apples and pears and cut them into 2cm square chunks.
- Heat the butter in a sauté pan.
- Add the apples and pears and sauté them gently for 5 minutes, turning them occasionally until they are tinged all over with brown.
- Drizzle with honey and serve with loosely whipped cream and the buns.

Cinnamon buns

200g butter
200g caster sugar
200g plain flour, 1 teaspoon cinnamon and 1 teaspoon baking powder sifted together
3 eggs

- Preheat the oven to 180°C/350°F/gas 4.
- In a food mixer or food processor beat the butter and sugar together until white and fluffy.
- Add 1 egg at a time along with 1 tablespoon of flour and combine thoroughly.
- Fold in the remaining flour with a metal spoon.
- Lay out cake cups in a cake cup tray and spoon a dessertspoon of the mixture into each one.
- Bake for 15 minutes.

Treacle bread

This is delicious served warm from the oven with butter and honey.

450g plain flour
1½ teaspoons baking powder
½ teaspoon salt
½ teaspoon ground ginger
50g butter, chilled
50g caster sugar
2 tablespoons black treacle
approx 100ml milk
butter and honey to serve

- Lightly grease a baking sheet.
- Preheat the oven to 200°C/400°F/gas 6.
- Place the flour, baking powder, salt, ginger and butter in a mixing bowl or food processor and mix to a breadcrumb consistency.
- Add the sugar and treacle and mix in well.
- Add the milk a little at a time and combine until the mixture comes together into a dough.
- Knead lightly until smooth.
- Cut the dough in half.
- Roll out each piece to a circle about 1.5cm thick.
- Place the circles of dough on the baking tray and bake for 15 minutes.
- Reduce the heat to 180°C/350°F/gas 4 and bake for a further 5 minutes.
- Serve with butter and honey.

SEPTEMBER

Week 1

Monday p448	Chicken biryani + tomato, cucumber and red onion salad
Tuesday p449	Courgette and tomato soup + stuffed focaccia
Wednesday p450	Gratin of potatoes, ham, onions and eggs + green salad
Thursday p451	Pasta with mushroom sauce
Friday p452	Turkey and ham pie + cabbage
Saturday p454	Russian fish pie + runner beans
Sunday p455	Pork chops + rosemary roasted potatoes + fennel with pancetta and red onions
Sunday pudding p456	Plum pie
Extra tasty treat p457	Iced lemon cake

Shopping list

MEAT

- ☐ 1.5kg chicken thigh fillets, skin removed
- ☐ 4 turkey steaks
- ☐ 6 pork chops

FISH

- ☐ 500g white fish
- ☐ 100g cooked prawns

VEGETABLES

- ☐ fresh ginger
- ☐ 1 green chili
- ☐ 650g tomatoes
- ☐ 1kg courgettes
- ☐ 650g onions
- ☐ 1 lettuce
- ☐ 3 spring onions
- ☐ 2 cucumbers
- ☐ 700g mixed mushrooms
- ☐ 1 garlic bulb
- ☐ 100g button mushrooms
- ☐ 1 white cabbage
- ☐ 300g runner beans
- ☐ 2kg potatoes
- ☐ 2 red onions
- ☐ 1 fennel bulb

FRUIT

- ☐ 1 lime
- ☐ 8 plums
- ☐ 4 lemons

FRESH HERBS

- ☐ coriander
- ☐ basil
- ☐ chives
- ☐ bay leaves
- ☐ 2 packs flat-leaf parsley
- ☐ rosemary
- ☐ thyme

FRIDGE ITEMS

- ☐ 2 litres chicken stock
- ☐ 800ml milk
- ☐ 150g Parmesan cheese
- ☐ 175g Gruyère cheese
- ☐ 450g cooked ham
- ☐ 7 slices salami
- ☐ 1 pack ready-rolled puff pastry
- ☐ 270g chopped pancetta
- ☐ 16 eggs
- ☐ 3 packs butter
- ☐ 520ml double cream
- ☐ 500ml whipping cream
- ☐ 200ml natural yoghurt
- ☐ 250g mascarpone cheese

KITCHEN CUPBOARD ITEMS

- ☐ 600g basmati rice
- ☐ vegetable oil
- ☐ olive oil
- ☐ extra virgin olive oil
- ☐ balsamic vinegar
- ☐ salt
- ☐ fast-action dried yeast
- ☐ 500g strong white bread flour
- ☐ 1kg plain flour
- ☐ 115g self-raising flour
- ☐ 650g passata
- ☐ 500g fusilli pasta
- ☐ dried porcini mushrooms
- ☐ dark soy sauce
- ☐ chicken stock cubes
- ☐ cornichons
- ☐ 165g caster sugar
- ☐ cornflour
- ☐ 50g ground almonds
- ☐ baking powder
- ☐ 60g icing sugar

SPICES

- ☐ black peppercorns
- ☐ ground coriander
- ☐ turmeric
- ☐ cayenne pepper
- ☐ cumin seeds
- ☐ coriander seeds
- ☐ fennel seeds
- ☐ fenugreek
- ☐ caraway seeds

Chicken biryani
+ tomato, cucumber and red onion salad

Biryani is a popular dish in England. It has a rich curry flavour that hits your taste buds full on.

Chicken biryani

1.5kg chicken thigh fillets, skin removed
3 garlic cloves, peeled and crushed
2cm piece fresh ginger, peeled and finely chopped
3 teaspoons ground coriander
pinch of cayenne pepper
¼ teaspoon turmeric
1 tablespoon curry powder*
2 teaspoons salt
200ml natural yoghurt
2 tablespoons vegetable oil
400g onion, diced
600g basmati rice
500ml water

- Chop the chicken into 2cm pieces and place it in a large bowl.
- Add the garlic, ginger, coriander, cayenne, turmeric, curry powder and 1 teaspoon of salt.
- Mix well and then pour in the yoghurt.
- Place in a cool place to marinate for 1 hour.
- Preheat the oven to 170°C/325°F/gas 3.
- Warm the vegetable oil in a large casserole dish and fry the onion for 10 minutes until it starts to turn golden brown.
- Add the rice and stir it around to coat it in the oil.
- Spoon the chicken onto the rice and onions, keeping the rice on the bottom of the saucepan with the onions.
- Season with another teaspoon of salt.
- Add the water and bring to a simmer on the hob.
- As soon as it simmers, cover the casserole with a sheet of tin foil and then seal with the lid.
- Place in the oven for 45 minutes.
- Remove from the oven and stir round.
- Return to the oven for another 45 minutes.

**** To make your own curry powder:***
1 tablespoon coriander seeds
1 dessertspoon cumin seeds
1 teaspoon fennel seeds
½ teaspoon fenugreek

- *Place the coriander seeds into a small, heavy-bottomed pan and heat through for 30 seconds.*
- *Add the other ingredients and toast until you smell the lovely aroma of the spices.*
- *Transfer the spices to a coffee grinder, a small processor or grind them in a pestle and mortar.*

Tomato, cucumber and red onion salad

3 tomatoes, diced
1 cucumber, diced
1 red onion, peeled and diced
1 green chilli, deseeded and finely chopped
salt
2 teaspoons cumin seeds, toasted and ground
pinch of cayenne pepper
2 tablespoons lime or lemon juice
1 tablespoon coriander leaves, chopped

- Combine the tomatoes, cucumber, onion and chilli in a serving dish.
- Season with a pinch of salt, the cumin and cayenne pepper.
- Add the lime/lemon juice and coriander leaves.

Courgette and tomato soup + stuffed focaccia

September tends to be the time of year when you run out of ideas about what to do with courgettes, especially if you grow them. They are still relatively cheap in the shops as well, so make the most of them. Try this stuffed focaccia as it tastes superb and is not complicated to make.

Courgette and tomato soup

600g tomatoes
5 tablespoons olive oil
1 large onion, finely chopped
1kg courgettes, sliced into 5mm-thick discs
2 litres chicken stock
650g passata
salt and pepper
10 basil leaves, torn

- Prepare the tomatoes by placing them in a large glass bowl and covering them with just-boiled water from the kettle.
- Leave for 2 minutes and then remove the skins.
- Remove the pips and the core of the tomatoes, then roughly chop the remainder and set aside.
- Pour the olive oil into a large saucepan and warm it on a moderate heat.
- Add the onion and cook gently for 6 minutes until soft, but not browned.
- Add the courgettes and stir into the onion, cooking gently for 6 minutes.
- Add the stock and the tomatoes, cover and simmer gently for 25 minutes.
- Add the passata, cover and cook for a further 10 minutes.
- If your children prefer a smooth soup, blitz it with a hand blender or in a food processor.
- Season with salt, pepper and basil leaves.

Stuffed focaccia

300ml water
1 sachet fast-action dried yeast
500g strong white bread flour
1½ teaspoons salt
3 tablespoons olive oil
For the stuffing
4 tablespoons mascarpone cheese
handful basil leaves, torn
7 slices salami, chopped
3 tablespoons Parmesan cheese, grated
olive oil
salt

- Pour 200ml of the water in a small bowl. Sprinkle on the yeast and leave for 3 minutes.
- Mix the flour and salt together in a large bowl.
- Stir in the olive oil, the yeasty water and the remaining 100ml of water, and mix to a dough.
- Turn the dough onto a floured surface and knead for 10 minutes by hand or for 5 minutes in a food mixer with a dough hook.
- Place the dough back in the mixing bowl and leave to rise for 1 hour 30 minutes.
- Knock back and divide into 2 equal pieces.
- Roll out each piece into a circle approximately 33cm in diameter, using some extra flour and a rolling pin.
- Place one circle on a greased baking tray and spread the mascarpone cheese on top of it.
- Scatter the basil, salami and Parmesan on top and then lay the other circle of dough over this, like a sandwich.
- Cover and leave to rise for 30 minutes.
- Preheat the oven to 200°C/400°F/gas 6.
- Drizzle olive oil over the top of the dough and scatter some sea salt on top.
- Bake for 30 minutes.
- Flip the focaccia over and bake for 5 minutes on the other side.

Gratin of potatoes, ham, onions and eggs + green salad

This dish is great because you prepare everything in advance and then, when you are ready, pop it into the oven. As the dish is fairly rich, I suggest serving it with a simple green salad

Gratin of potatoes, ham, onions and eggs

50g butter
2 tablespoons olive oil
200g onions, finely chopped
200g cooked ham, finely chopped
8 eggs
1 clove garlic, peeled and crushed
2 tablespoons flat-leaf parsley, finely chopped
2 tablespoons chives, snipped
175g Gruyère cheese, grated
4 tablespoons double cream
4 tablespoons milk
pepper and salt
500g potatoes, peeled and grated with liquid squeezed out

- Preheat the oven to 190°C/375°F/gas 5.
- Heat the butter and oil gently in a sauté pan.
- Add the onions and cook them slowly for 5 minutes, until tender.
- Increase the heat and add the ham, cooking it for 1 minute.
- In a bowl beat the eggs with the garlic, herbs, cheese, cream and milk.
- Season with salt and pepper.
- Add the ham and onions to the egg mixture and then the potatoes, mixing well.
- Grease a gratin dish and spoon the mixture into the dish.
- Bake for 25–30 minutes until the top is a lovely golden brown.

Green salad

1 lettuce, prepared for serving
3 spring onions, sliced
1 cucumber, sliced
For the dressing
2 tablespoons extra virgin olive oil
½ tablespoon balsamic vinegar
salt and pepper

- Place the salad ingredients in a serving dish and drizzle the dressing over the top when ready to serve.

Pasta with mushroom sauce

I love mushroom pasta. It is a simple but divine combination.

30g butter
1 tablespoon olive oil
700g mixed mushrooms, depending on what is available, finely sliced
1 handful dried porcini mushrooms, soaked in warm water
1 clove garlic, peeled and finely chopped
200g chopped pancetta
1 large bunch flat-leaf parsley, chopped
salt and pepper
5 tablespoons double cream
500g fusilli pasta
Parmesan cheese, grated for serving

- Heat the butter and oil in a large sauté pan.
- Add the fresh mushrooms and sauté on a medium-high heat for 4 minutes.
- Add the dried porcini mushrooms with the liquor in which they soaked and cook for a further 5 minutes, until the moisture has disappeared.
- Throw in the garlic and pancetta and cook for 2–3 minutes, until the pancetta starts to turn a golden brown.
- Sprinkle on the parsley and season with salt and pepper.
- Pour on the cream and cook for another few seconds.
- Cook the pasta according to the packet instructions.
- Spoon the sauce over the pasta and serve with Parmesan cheese.

Turkey and ham pie + cabbage

Turkey is not just for Christmas. This hearty pie, with ham and mushrooms, is just right for early autumn when the days begin to get a little colder.

Turkey and ham pie

For the pastry

300g plain flour
180g butter
salt
2 egg yolks
2 tablespoons cold tap water

For the filling

400ml chicken stock (use a stock cube)
4 turkey steaks, cut into 2cm cubes
1 tablespoon olive oil
30g butter
1 onion, diced
100g button mushrooms, halved
2 tablespoons plain flour
3 tablespoons dark soy sauce
450g potatoes, peeled and cooked and cut into 3cm chunks
250g cooked ham, chopped into bite-sized pieces
2 tablespoons flat-leaf parsley, chopped
salt and pepper

To make the pastry

- Put the flour and butter in a food processor, or in a bowl if you are combining by hand, and incorporate them so that the resulting mixture looks like fine breadcrumbs.
- Add a pinch of salt.
- Mix the egg yolks with the cold water in a small bowl and then add to the breadcrumb mixture.
- Whizz the pastry in the food processor if using, or mix by hand if not, and then turn out onto a floured work surface and combine thoroughly until you have firm dough. Wrap the dough in cling-film and chill in the fridge for 30 minutes.

To make the filling

- Preheat the oven to 180°C/350°F/gas 4 and place a baking sheet in the oven.
- Heat the chicken stock in a medium-sized saucepan and when it is gently simmering, add the turkey pieces to the stock.
- Cover and simmer for 2 minutes.
- Remove the turkey from the stock and set both the stock and the turkey aside.
- In a saucepan heat the olive oil and butter and gently sauté the onion and mushrooms for about 5 minutes.
- Add the tablespoon of flour and stir in.
- Remove from the heat and add the soy sauce a tablespoon at a time, stirring to incorporate before adding another.
- Once the soy sauce is incorporated return the pan to the heat, add the chicken stock and bring to a simmer.
- Add the turkey, cooked potatoes, ham and parsley and check the seasoning. You should only need pepper.

To assemble the pie

- Grease a pie dish with a diameter of between 25 and 28cm.
- Cut the pastry into two pieces, bearing in mind that you need slightly more pastry for the bottom of the pie than the top.
- Roll out one piece of the pastry and line the pie dish with it.
- Spoon in the filling and then pour in as much gravy as you can without it overflowing.
- Reserve the rest of the gravy.
- Roll out the remaining pastry and cover the pie.
- Make two slits in the top of the pie and brush the pastry with an egg yolk mixed with a teaspoon of water.
- Place in the oven on the hot baking sheet and cook for 30 minutes.
- Serve with the rest of the gravy, which you can reheat, and the cabbage below.

Cabbage

1 white cabbage, cored and sliced into 1cm strips
50ml water
15g butter
½ teaspoon caraway seeds
salt and pepper

- Place the cabbage in a saucepan with the water and butter.
- Cook the cabbage on a low heat, covered, for 5 minutes.
- Sprinkle the caraway seeds into the pan and continue to cook for another 5 minutes.
- Season with salt and pepper and serve.

Russian fish pie
+ runner beans

This tasty fish pie recipe came from a very old cookery book by Elizabeth Craig, written in the 1930s. Even at that time she was espousing the importance of a balanced diet.

Russian fish pie

For the filling

500g white fish
1 bay leaf
milk
7 cornichons, finely chopped
100g cooked prawns
3 hard-boiled eggs, sliced
salt and pepper

For the white sauce

20g butter
20g flour
300ml milk – use the milk from cooking the fish and make up the difference with some extra if necessary
salt and pepper
handful flat-leaf parsley, chopped
3 tablespoons double cream
1 pack ready-rolled puff pastry

To cook the fish

- Preheat the oven to 200°C/400°F/gas 6.
- Place the fish and bay leaf in a pan with a lid. Cover the fish with milk and let it simmer very gently for 4 minutes.
- Drain the fish, reserving the milk, flake it into a gratin dish and set aside.

To make the white sauce

- Heat the butter in a small saucepan.
- Add the flour and stir to incorporate.
- Remove the saucepan from the heat and then add the milk a little at a time to avoid lumps forming in the sauce.
- Once fully incorporated, return the pan to the heat and bring the sauce to a simmer.
- Season with salt and pepper.
- Reduce the heat to low and cook for 10 minutes, stirring occasionally.
- Add the chopped parsley and cream.
- Spoon the sauce over the flaked fish in the gratin dish.
- Add the chopped cornichons and prawns.
- Then lay the eggs on top.
- Roll out the pastry and place this on top of the dish.
- Brush the pastry with a beaten egg and bake for 30 minutes.

Runner beans

300g runner beans
butter for serving
salt and pepper

- Prepare the beans by topping and tailing them and then cutting a thin sliver off the side of each bean. There are no rules on how to slice the beans. I hold the bean upwards and cut at an angle from the top downwards, shaving an angled slice off. This is the best description I can give to anyone who never saw their mother preparing runner beans.
- Place the prepared beans into boiling water.
- Cook them for 4 to 7 minutes, depending on how young and tender the beans are. Runner beans have to be well cooked to be enjoyable.
- Drain well and serve with some salt, pepper and a little butter.

Pork chops + rosemary roasted potatoes + fennel with pancetta and red onions

This meal has an Italian flavour to it, as the Italians do like to fry their pork chops. The fennel recipe makes a nice change to the way fennel is often prepared. Get the potatoes on the go first, then prepare the fennel and leave the pork chops to last.

Pork chops

6 pork chops
salt and pepper
juice 1 lemon

- Place a frying pan on a high heat.
- Without using any fat, fry the pork chops for 3 minutes on each side.
- Season with salt and pepper and a squeeze of lemon juice.

Rosemary roasted potatoes

1kg potatoes, peeled and quartered
salt
3 sprigs rosemary
2 tablespoons olive oil

- Preheat the oven to 220°C/425°F/gas 7.
- Parboil the potatoes in salted water for 4 minutes.
- Drain well and place them in a roasting tin with the rosemary.
- Drizzle with the olive oil and roast for 45 minutes until golden brown.

Fennel with pancetta and red onions

20g butter
1 red onion, thinly sliced
1 fennel bulb, thinly sliced
70g chopped pancetta
salt and pepper
1 sprig thyme
1 teaspoon balsamic vinegar

- Warm the butter in a sauté pan.
- Sauté the onion and fennel for 10 minutes until they start to turn brown.
- Add the pancetta and sauté for a further 3 minutes.
- Season with salt and pepper.
- Add the thyme and balsamic vinegar and cook for a further 2 minutes.

Plum pie

At this time of year plums are bountiful so use them when you can.

For the pastry
275g plain flour
175g butter, chilled and cubed
1 dessertspoon caster sugar
1 egg yolk
2 tablespoons cold water
For the filling
30g butter, softened
2 tablespoons ground almonds
1 tablespoon caster sugar
8 plums, halved and destoned
1 tablespoon cornflour
caster sugar
whipping cream for serving

To make the pastry
- Combine the flour and butter in a food processor until they resemble fine breadcrumbs.
- Add the sugar.
- Mix the egg yolk with the water and pour onto the flour and butter.
- Give the mixture a quick blast in the food processor and then turn out onto a floured surface and form into a ball.
- Cover with cling-film and chill in the fridge for 30 minutes.

To make the pie
- Grease a pie tin.
- Preheat the oven to 200°C/400°F/gas 6.
- Place a baking sheet in the oven.
- In a small bowl combine the butter with the almonds and sugar.
- Form the butter and almond mixture into small balls with your fingertips and insert the small balls into the space in each plum half left by the removal of the stones.
- Roll out half the pastry and line the base of the pie tin with it.
- Arrange the stuffed plum halves on the base of the pie. You can pile them up, once you have filled the base.
- Sprinkle the cornflour over the top.
- Roll out the other half of the pastry and lay this over the plums.
- Seal the pie by pinching the edges of the pastry together with your fingertips.
- Sprinkle a little caster sugar over the top of the pastry, place on the hot baking tray and bake for 40 minutes until golden brown.

Iced lemon cake

This is a lemon drizzle cake baked in a loaf tin. It's easy to make and is wonderfully light.

For the cake
115g self-raising flour
1 teaspoon baking powder
2 eggs
115g caster sugar
65ml double cream
grated zest 1 lemon
1 tablespoon lemon juice
45g butter, melted
For the icing
60g icing sugar
3 teaspoons lemon juice

- Grease a 500g loaf tin with butter and line the bottom with a piece of greaseproof paper.
- Preheat the oven to 170°C/325°F/gas 3.
- Sift together the flour and baking powder and set aside.
- In a bowl beat the eggs with the sugar quickly, and with a light hand.
- Add the cream and beat to combine.
- Add the lemon zest and 1 tablespoon of lemon juice and mix this in.
- Fold in the sifted flour, baking powder and the melted butter.
- Pour into the loaf tin and bake for 45 minutes.
- Test with a skewer and if it comes out clean the cake is ready.
- Cool and turn out onto a wire rack.

To make the icing
- Sift the icing sugar into a bowl and add the lemon juice.
- Mix with a wooden spoon and drizzle the icing over the cooled cake.

Week 2

Monday p460	Moghlai chicken + stir-fried courgettes with garlic + boiled rice
Tuesday p461	Cheese and butter risotto with sausage
Wednesday p462	Smoked salmon and courgette tart + salad
Thursday p463	Cabbage and ham soup
Friday p464	Lamb tagine + couscous with chickpeas
Saturday p465	Fried breaded cod with tartare sauce + roasted chipped potatoes + peas
Sunday p466	Roasted casserole chicken + tomato salad
Sunday pudding p467	Pear tart
Extra tasty treat p468	Ginger sandwich cake

Shopping list

MEAT

- ☐ 1.5kg chicken pieces
- ☐ 4 medium-sized sausages
- ☐ 700g joint smoked gammon
- ☐ 1kg leg of lamb, cubed
- ☐ 2.3kg–2.5kg whole chicken

FISH

- ☐ 900g cod fillet

VEGETABLES

- ☐ 500g courgettes
- ☐ 1 Romaine lettuce
- ☐ 1 cucumber
- ☐ 2 spring onions
- ☐ 2 shallots
- ☐ 15 baby onions
- ☐ 2.1kg potatoes
- ☐ 500g cabbage
- ☐ 1 garlic bulb
- ☐ 100g carrots
- ☐ 1 bunch of celery
- ☐ 1kg fresh peas
- ☐ 4 onions
- ☐ 8 tomatoes

FRUIT

- ☐ 4 pears
- ☐ 2 lemons
- ☐ 1 orange

FRESH HERBS

- ☐ basil
- ☐ sage
- ☐ thyme
- ☐ chives
- ☐ flat-leaf parsley
- ☐ mint
- ☐ rosemary
- ☐ bay leaves

FRIDGE ITEMS

- ☐ 150g smoked salmon
- ☐ 75g Parmesan cheese
- ☐ 1.5ml chicken stock
- ☐ 250g frozen peas
- ☐ 140g chopped pancetta
- ☐ 800ml double cream
- ☐ 9 eggs
- ☐ 4 packs butter
- ☐ 250ml plain yoghurt

KITCHEN CUPBOARD ITEMS

- ☐ 25g blanched slivered almonds
- ☐ 25g sultanas
- ☐ 500g basmati rice
- ☐ 500g risotto rice
- ☐ balsamic vinegar
- ☐ 400g tin cannellini beans
- ☐ 400g tin chickpeas
- ☐ 250g couscous
- ☐ 2 loaves white bread for breadcrumbs/ toast
- ☐ white wine vinegar
- ☐ Dijon mustard
- ☐ salt
- ☐ extra virgin olive oil
- ☐ light olive oil
- ☐ groundnut oil
- ☐ vegetable oil
- ☐ olive oil
- ☐ 12 green olives
- ☐ capers
- ☐ pickled cornichons
- ☐ 75g icing sugar
- ☐ 100g brioche
- ☐ 50g raisins
- ☐ 50g ground almonds
- ☐ 80g soft brown sugar
- ☐ 625g plain flour
- ☐ 55g caster sugar
- ☐ 55g black treacle
- ☐ bicarbonate of soda

SPICES

- ☐ cumin seeds
- ☐ chilli powder
- ☐ cardamom pods
- ☐ cloves
- ☐ cinnamon sticks
- ☐ black peppercorns
- ☐ chilli flakes
- ☐ ground cinnamon
- ☐ mixed spice
- ☐ ground ginger

Moghlai chicken + stir-fried courgettes with garlic + boiled rice

This is more of an Indian style curry dish, using yoghurt as the basis of the sauce.

Chicken moghlai

1.5kg chicken pieces, on the bone, skin removed (thighs and drumsticks are ideal)
salt and pepper
1 tablespoon vegetable oil
50g butter
7 whole cardamom pods
8 whole cloves
5cm cinnamon stick
2 bay leaves
25g blanched slivered almonds
25g sultanas
250ml plain yoghurt
5ml ground cumin seeds
¼ teaspoon chilli powder

- Preheat the oven to 200°C/400°F/gas 6.
- Sprinkle the chicken pieces with salt and pepper.
- Heat the oil and butter in a large frying pan over a medium heat.
- When hot, add the cardamom pods, cloves, cinnamon, bay leaves and chicken pieces, 4 at a time. Brown the chicken all over.
- As you brown the chicken pieces, remove them and set aside while you do the rest. Once all the chicken is browned, place it in a large saucepan and set aside.
- Keep the frying pan on a medium heat and add the almonds. Stir them around and as soon as they start to brown add the sultanas. Stir for a few seconds and then tip the contents of the frying pan over the chicken pieces.
- Mix together the yoghurt, cumin, chilli and a good sprinkle of salt and pepper. Pour this mixture over the chicken and cover with a lid.
- Bake for 1 hour, turning the chicken pieces over about half way through.

Stir-fried courgettes with garlic

300g courgettes
1 tablespoon vegetable oil
2 cloves garlic, peeled and finely chopped
salt and pepper
juice ½ lemon

- Cut the courgettes into batons about 5cm long and 1cm wide.
- Heat the oil in a large frying pan.
- Add the garlic and courgettes and stir fry for about 3 minutes.
- Season with salt, pepper and a squeeze of fresh lemon juice.

Boiled rice

500g basmati rice
750ml water
salt

- Put the rice in a saucepan with the water and a pinch of salt.
- Place on a high heat and as soon as it comes to the boil cover the saucepan with a lid and turn the heat right down to very low. Leave it for 15 minutes, giving it one stir only during the cooking time.
- Take it off the heat and leave it covered for a further 10 minutes, before removing the lid.

Cheese and butter risotto with sausage

This is a full-flavoured risotto that the whole family will enjoy. My mother used to make risotto for us when we were children, back in the 1970s before its huge popularity as a dish. She was influenced by the writing of Elizabeth David and tried to create the tastes and aromas of Mediterranean life in her Basingstoke kitchen.

50g butter
1 onion, finely chopped
1 sprig rosemary, leaves removed and finely chopped
500g risotto rice
1.5ml chicken stock, well seasoned with salt and pepper
25g extra butter for serving
3 tablespoons Parmesan cheese, grated
salt and pepper
4 medium-sized sausages

- Place the butter in a large saucepan and heat it until it starts to foam.
- Add the onion and rosemary and sauté gently for 5 minutes.
- Add the rice and stir to coat in the butter.
- Let the rice fry gently for 1 minute, stirring constantly. Do not let it brown.
- In the meantime, heat the stock to simmering in a separate saucepan.
- Add 2 ladlefuls of stock to the rice and stir.
- Don't let all the liquid disappear completely before adding more hot stock. The key to a good risotto is not to let the rice stick to the pan while it is cooking, so you need to keep stirring almost continuously.
- Keep adding stock until the rice is tender on the outside but retains a bite on the inside. A risotto takes about 20–25 minutes to cook.
- Meanwhile, fry the sausages on the hob in a frying pan.
- Add the extra butter and cheese to the risotto and stir in to combine.
- Adjust the seasoning if necessary.
- Roughly chop up the sausages, stir them into the risotto and serve.

Smoked salmon and courgette tart + salad

There are still British courgettes in the shops in September, and this is an ideal way to use them. Smoked salmon is a low maintenance ingredient, that gives a lot of flavour with little effort.

Smoked salmon and courgette tart

For the pastry
225g plain flour
150g butter
salt
1 egg yolk
2 tablespoons cold water

For the filling
200g courgettes, sliced into thin discs
salt
2 tablespoons olive oil
1 shallot, finely chopped
2 eggs
150–300ml double cream, depending on the size and depth of the tart tin
black pepper
150g smoked salmon
handful basil leaves, torn

To make the pastry

- Put the flour and butter in the bowl of a food processor and incorporate them so that the resulting mixture looks like fine breadcrumbs.
- Add a pinch of salt.
- Mix the egg yolk with the cold water in a small bowl and add this liquid to the flour and fat.
- Mix in the food processor until a dough just begins to form. Turn the mixture onto a floured work surface and combine thoroughly, with a light hand, until you have a smooth dough. Wrap the dough in cling-film and chill in the fridge for 20 minutes.

To make the flan

- Preheat the oven to 200°C/400°F/gas 6 and grease a 24cm diameter, 3½cm deep flan tin.
- Roll out the pastry on a lightly floured surface and line the flan tin with it. Place a sheet of baking parchment over the pastry case and pour on some baking beans. Place the flan tin on a baking sheet and bake for 15 minutes.
- Take the flan out of the oven and remove the parchment and baking beans. Return the flan to the oven for a further 5 minutes.
- Remove the flan tin from the oven and reduce the oven temperature to 190°C/375°F/gas 5.

To make the filling

- Place the sliced courgettes in a colander. Salt them to draw out the excess water and leave for about 20 minutes. Pat dry with kitchen paper.
- Warm the olive oil in a frying pan and add the courgettes and shallot.
- Sauté over a low heat for 5 minutes.
- Whisk together the eggs and cream and season with black pepper.
- Place the salmon on the bottom of the pastry case, spoon on the courgettes, shallots and basil leaves and pour over as much of the cream mixture as you can fit in.
- Place the tart tin on a baking sheet and bake for 30 minutes.

Salad

1 Romaine lettuce, washed and chopped
½ cucumber, sliced
2 spring onions, chopped

For the dressing
1 tablespoon olive oil
2 teaspoons balsamic vinegar
salt and pepper

- Assemble the salad ingredients in a serving bowl and dress just before serving.

Cabbage and ham soup

This is an easy, hearty soup to make and is definitely a meal in itself. You will need a large saucepan for this soup.

700g joint smoked gammon
3 litres water
400g potatoes, peeled and quartered
500g cabbage, roughly chopped
small bunch parsley and 1 bay leaf, tied together with string
3 sage leaves, finely chopped
2 thyme sprigs, finely chopped
2 cloves garlic, peeled and finely chopped
2 medium onions, finely chopped
100g carrots, roughly chopped
400g tin cannellini beans, drained
2 sticks celery, finely chopped
salt and pepper
hot buttered toast to serve

- Place the gammon joint in the saucepan with the water and all the other ingredients.
- Bring to the boil and then simmer for 1 hour 30 minutes, partially covered.
- Remove the joint of ham and chop it into bite-sized cubes.
- Return the ham to the pot and check the seasoning. You should find that the soup is salty enough, but you might need to add some pepper.
- Serve with buttered toast.

Lamb tagine
+ couscous with chickpeas

This is a Moroccan stew that is very simple to make and perfect to eat as the summer slips away.

Lamb tagine

1kg leg of lamb, cubed
2 tablespoons vegetable oil
1 onion, finely chopped
1 teaspoon ground ginger
1 pinch chilli flakes
salt and pepper
1kg fresh peas
2 tomatoes, chopped
12 green olives

- Put the meat in a large saucepan with the oil, onion, ginger and chilli flakes.
- Season with salt and pepper.
- Pour over enough water to barely cover the meat and then cook, covered, on the hob for 1 hour until the meat is tender.
- Add the peas, tomatoes and olives and cook uncovered for 10 minutes.
- Serve with the couscous below.

Couscous with chickpeas

250g couscous, prepared following the packet instructions
salt
40g butter
400g tin chickpeas, drained
2 tablespoons flat-leaf parsley, finely chopped

- Place the warm couscous in a serving bowl.
- Season with salt.
- Add the butter, chickpeas and parsley.
- Mix well and serve.

Fried breaded cod with tartare sauce + roasted chipped potatoes + peas

Homemade tartare sauce is a different item altogether from the vinegary gloop served in plastic packets in lots of fish and chip restaurants. I hesitate about cooking cod due to its depleted supply so, whenever I can, I buy pollack or coley instead, which cook in a similar fashion to cod.

Fried breaded cod with tartare sauce

For the breaded cod

900g cod fillet, skin removed
flour for dusting
1 beaten egg
12 tablespoons white breadcrumbs
3 tablespoons olive oil

For the tartare sauce

2 egg yolks
1 tablespoon white wine vinegar
1teaspoon Dijon mustard
salt
150ml light olive oil
150ml groundnut oil
1 shallot, finely chopped
½ tablespoon fresh chives, snipped finely
½ tablespoon flat-leaf parsley, chopped finely
1 tablespoon capers, chopped
1 tablespoon cornichons, chopped

To prepare the fish

- Cut the cod fillet into six pieces, dividing it according to individual requirements.
- Dust the pieces in flour, dip in the beaten egg and then in the breadcrumbs.
- Heat the oil in a frying pan. When hot add the fish and fry for 3 minutes on each side, until the pieces are golden brown.

To make the tartare sauce

- In a small bowl whisk the egg yolks with the white wine vinegar, mustard and a little salt.
- Combine the oils together in a jug and start adding them, literally a drop at a time to the egg yolk mixture, whisking continuously. Make sure each addition is incorporated before adding the next. Once you have added about 100ml of oil you can start adding it at a quicker pace, but be careful not to add it too quickly as the sauce will curdle.
- If the sauce does curdle, place another egg yolk in a separate bowl and slowly add the curdled sauce to it, whisking continuously
- Once you have made the sauce, add the shallot, herbs, capers and cornichons to it, and set aside.

Roasted chipped potatoes

1 kg potatoes
2 dessertspoons olive oil
salt and pepper

- Preheat the oven to 220°C/425°F/gas 7.
- Peel the potatoes and cut them lengthways into quarters.
- Place them in a pan of salted water and bring to the boil.
- Reduce the heat and let them simmer for 5 minutes.
- Drain them well, place them in a roasting tin and drizzle the olive oil over them.
- Roast for 45 minutes.
- Sprinkle a dusting of sea salt on the potatoes when you are ready to serve them.

Peas

250g frozen peas
salt
sprig of mint

- Boil the peas in salted water, along with the mint, for 5 minutes.
- Drain and serve.

Roasted casserole chicken + tomato salad

This makes a nice change from the usual roast chicken, and any meal that can be prepared and then placed in a pot to cook undisturbed is a winner as far as I am concerned. The chicken used in this recipe is rather large as it has to feed six people.

Roasted casserole chicken

50g butter
140g chopped pancetta
2.3kg–2.5kg whole chicken
700g potatoes, peeled and halved
15 baby onions, peeled and kept whole
bouquet garni of 1 bay leaf, 1 sprig thyme and 1 sprig rosemary
salt and pepper

- Preheat the oven to 160°C/320°F/gas 2½.
- Warm 25g of the butter in a large casserole pan.
- Add the chopped pancetta and sauté it for 2 minutes until it starts to turn brown.
- Remove the pancetta from the pot and set aside.
- Place the chicken in the casserole and brown the breast.
- As the breast browns turn the chicken slightly onto its side and brown. Do the same with the chicken all over.
- Remove the chicken and set aside.
- Place the casserole back on the hob and add another 25g of butter to the existing fat.
- Heat through, then add the potatoes and onions and stir to coat them in the fat for 2 minutes.
- Add the bouquet garni and then return the chicken to the pan, breast side up, along with the pancetta.
- Season with a teaspoon of salt and some freshly ground black pepper.
- Cover the chicken with some tin foil or a piece of butter paper.
- Get the whole pot sizzling and then transfer it to the oven and cook for 2 hours. Check the juices of the chicken after 1 hour and 45 minutes and if they run clear when the thigh of the chicken is pricked with a fork, the chicken is cooked.
- Serve with the tomato salad below.

Tomato salad

6 tomatoes, sliced
2 tablespoons extra virgin olive oil
¼ tablespoon balsamic vinegar
salt and pepper

- Lay the tomatoes on a serving plate.
- Dress with the oil and vinegar, and season with salt and pepper.

Pear tart

This tart started out as an experiment and the result was a pleasant surprise. Although I cook every day and would describe myself as a competent cook, I always approach experiments with some trepidation. Having 4 children and a husband to feed means that experiments that go wrong are time-costly and wasteful of ingredients.

For the sweet pastry

180g butter

75g icing sugar

2 egg yolks

225g plain flour

For the pear filling

4 pears, peeled, cored and grated

finely grated zest 1 lemon and 1 orange

2 x 40g soft brown sugar

pinch cinnamon

100g brioche crumbs

50g raisins

50g ground almonds

100ml double cream

cream for serving

- Preheat the oven to 200°C/400°F/gas 6.
- Grease a 20cm tart tin.

To make the pastry

- Mix the butter, icing sugar, egg yolks and flour together in a food processor until the mixture starts to combine.
- Turn out onto a floured surface and form into a ball.
- Wrap in cling-film and chill in the fridge for 30 minutes.
- When ready, roll out the pastry and line the tart tin with it.
- Lay a sheet of baking parchment on top of the pastry case and pour some baking beans on top of the paper.
- Bake for 15 minutes and then remove the pastry case from the oven and discard the paper and baking beans.
- Reduce the oven temperature to 180°C/350°F/gas 4.

To make the filling

- Drain any excess juice from the pears by squeezing them in your hands in a colander.
- Place the pears in a mixing bowl with the lemon and orange zest, the first lot of brown sugar, cinnamon, brioche crumbs, raisins and almonds.
- Mix together and spoon into the pastry case.
- Sprinkle over the second lot of brown sugar and pour over the cream.
- Bake for 40 minutes.
- Serve with more cream.

Ginger sandwich cake

This cake does not keep for long as it is filled with fresh cream, so is best eaten on the day you make it.

For the sponge
175g plain flour
salt
½ teaspoon ground ginger
¼ teaspoon cinnamon
¼ teaspoon mixed spice
115g butter, softened
55g caster sugar
55g black treacle, warmed
1 egg, beaten
2 tablespoons hot water with ½ teaspoon bicarbonate of soda, dissolved
For the filling
150ml cream, whipped and flavoured with a little chopped preserved ginger

- Grease 2 x 18cm sandwich tins.
- Preheat the oven to 180°C/350°F/gas 4.
- Sift the flour, spices and a pinch of salt into a bowl.
- In another bowl, cream the butter and sugar together until light and fluffy.
- Beat in the warmed treacle.
- Add the beaten egg and beat into the mixture.
- Fold in the flour and spices.
- Stir in the hot water and bicarbonate of soda.
- Spoon the mixture into the sandwich tins and bake for 20 minutes.
- Turn out and cool on a wire rack.
- When cold, fill with the cream and ginger filling.

SEPTEMBER

Week 3

Monday p472	Chicken with white wine sauce in flaky pastry + runner beans
Tuesday p473	American diner special
Wednesday p474	Fried chicken + potato, bacon and celery salad
Thursday p475	Sautéed pork chops + grilled cheesy potato + baked beetroot
Friday p476	Fried salmon fillets + herbed potatoes with cucumber
Saturday p477	Cream of spinach soup with pancetta herb croutons
Sunday p478	Roast beef + Yorkshire pudding + vegetables
Sunday pudding p480	Autumn fruit cobbler
Extra tasty treat p481	Apple cake

Shopping list

MEAT

- ☐ 300g sausage meat
- ☐ 8 chicken breasts, boneless
- ☐ 6 pork chops
- ☐ 2kg rib of beef on the bone

FISH

- ☐ 6 salmon fillets

VEGETABLES

- ☐ 400g runner beans
- ☐ 2 tomatoes
- ☐ 1 Cos lettuce, or other crispy type
- ☐ 1 red onion
- ☐ 2 green peppers
- ☐ 1 bunch celery
- ☐ 6–10 beetroot
- ☐ 400g parsnips
- ☐ 350g carrots
- ☐ 4 leeks
- ☐ 3.5kg potatoes
- ☐ 1 garlic bulb
- ☐ 1 cucumber
- ☐ 3 onions
- ☐ 400g spinach leaves
- ☐ 200g courgettes

FRUIT

- ☐ 1 lime
- ☐ 450g blackberries
- ☐ 150g blackcurrants
- ☐ 200g dessert apples
- ☐ 225g cooking apples

FRESH HERBS

- ☐ flat-leaf parsley
- ☐ dill
- ☐ tarragon
- ☐ thyme
- ☐ chives
- ☐ rosemary

FRIDGE ITEMS

- ☐ 350g crème fraîche
- ☐ 2 packs ready-rolled puff pastry
- ☐ 150ml whipping cream
- ☐ 2.2 litres chicken stock
- ☐ 200g frozen peas
- ☐ 650ml milk
- ☐ 100g Parmesan cheese
- ☐ 200g Cheddar cheese
- ☐ 500ml double cream
- ☐ 100ml single cream
- ☐ 3 packs butter
- ☐ 19 eggs
- ☐ 170g sliced pancetta

KITCHEN CUPBOARD ITEMS

- ☐ 1 bottle dry white wine
- ☐ red wine vinegar
- ☐ Dijon mustard
- ☐ extra virgin olive oil
- ☐ balsamic vinegar
- ☐ olive oil
- ☐ 1 loaf white bread
- ☐ salt
- ☐ 75g soft brown sugar
- ☐ 200g demerara sugar
- ☐ 50g caster sugar
- ☐ 780g plain flour
- ☐ baking powder
- ☐ chicken stock cubes

SPICES

- ☐ black peppercorns
- ☐ paprika
- ☐ dried oregano
- ☐ whole nutmeg
- ☐ ground cinnamon

Chicken with white wine sauce in flaky pastry + runner beans

The combination of white wine and tarragon goes really well with chicken.

Chicken with white wine sauce in flaky pastry

50g butter
2 sticks celery, chopped
1 onion, chopped
5 chicken breasts, cut into 2cm chunks
200ml dry white wine
2 tablespoons flour
200ml chicken stock (a stock cube will do)
150g crème fraîche
1 teaspoon Dijon mustard
3 medium potatoes, cooked and cut into 2cm chunks
2 carrots, sliced into discs and cooked
3 tablespoons flat-leaf parsley, chopped
5 leaves tarragon, finely chopped
salt and pepper
2 packs ready-rolled puff pastry
1 beaten egg to seal

- Preheat the oven to 200°C/400°F/gas 6.
- On a medium heat, warm the butter in a sauté pan.
- Add the celery and onion and cook gently for 5 minutes.
- Add the chicken pieces and cook these until they have lost their outer pinkness, but take care not to overcook them.
- Pour in the wine and cook for 30 seconds.
- Then add the flour and stir to coat all the ingredients.
- Next, add the chicken stock, crème fraîche, mustard, potatoes, carrots and herbs. Season with plenty of pepper and a little salt.
- Remove the pan from the heat.
- The mixture will be too runny to put on the pastry as it is, so spoon off some of the sauce and set aside.
- Cut the pastry into rectangles of 30cm x 12cm.
- Lay the pastry rectangles on a baking sheet and spoon the chicken mixture onto one half of each rectangle. Brush round the edge of the pastry with the beaten egg and fold over to seal.
- Bake for 25 minutes. When you are ready to serve, heat the rest of the sauce, cut a cross into the top of each pastry parcel and pour the sauce into the hole. It will spill out but this is fine.

Runner beans

400g runner beans, prepared and sliced
salt and pepper
butter for serving

For the runner beans

- Prepare the beans by topping and tailing them and then cutting a thin sliver off the side of each bean. There are no rules on how to slice the beans. I hold the bean upwards and cut at an angle from the top downwards, shaving an angled slice off. This is the best description I can give to anyone who never saw their mother preparing runner beans.
- Place the prepared beans into boiling water.
- Cook them for 4 to 7 minutes, depending on how young and tender the beans are. Runner beans have to be well cooked to be enjoyable.
- Drain well and serve with some salt, pepper and a little butter.

American diner special

This is the sort of meal one would get in an American diner. It has no pretensions but is a simple midweek meal.

30g butter
1 large onion, finely chopped
1 green pepper, finely chopped
300g sausage meat
300g cooked potato, cubed
2 small tomatoes, finely chopped
12 eggs
salt and pepper
2 tablespoons Parmesan cheese, grated
2 tablespoons flat-leaf parsley, finely chopped
bread and butter for serving

- Heat the butter in a saucepan.
- Add the onion, pepper and sausage meat and fry gently for 10 minutes, until the onion and pepper have softened and the sausage meat has started to brown.
- Add the potato and the tomatoes and cook for 2 minutes.
- In a bowl mix the eggs together and season well with salt and pepper.
- Take another saucepan and heat a small knob of butter.
- Pour in the eggs and cook slowly until they are just starting to combine and turn into scrambled eggs.
- Then, fold in the onion and potato mixture and cook for a few seconds longer.
- Sprinkle with cheese and parsley and serve with white bread and butter.

Fried chicken
+ potato, bacon and celery salad

The fried chicken in this recipe is really very tasty. The cooking method ensures the chicken remains tender.

Fried chicken

6 tablespoons flour
good teaspoon salt
lots of black pepper
2 teaspoons paprika
3 boneless chicken breasts, cut lengthways to about 2.5cm wide, like goujons
3 tablespoons olive oil

- Place the flour, salt, pepper and paprika in a bowl and combine.
- Get a bowl of cold water and dip each strip of chicken into the water. Then dip it into the seasoned flour,
- Heat the olive oil in a large frying pan on a medium heat and fry the chicken goujons for 1 minute on each side.
- Fry all the strips like this and then sprinkle them with a little more salt and serve with the salad.

Potato, bacon and celery salad

1 Cos lettuce, or other crispy type
4 medium potatoes, peeled and cooked until tender
½ medium red onion, finely sliced
1 green pepper, finely diced
2 sticks celery, thinly sliced
3 hard-boiled eggs
6 slices pancetta
2 tablespoons flat-leaf parsley, chopped
For the dressing
½ tablespoon red wine vinegar
1 teaspoon Dijon mustard
salt and pepper
3 tablespoons extra virgin olive oil
2 tablespoons whipping cream

- Prepare the lettuce and place it in a large serving dish.
- Slice the potatoes and arrange these on top of the lettuce.
- Sprinkle the red onion, green pepper and celery over the potatoes.
- Then, slice the eggs and lay these on top.
- Fry the pancetta until brown, chop it up and add this to the dish.
- Scatter over the parsley.
- To prepare the dressing, mix together the vinegar, mustard, salt and pepper in a small bowl.
- Whisking with a fork, add the olive oil in a slow drizzle. The dressing will thicken slightly.
- Once you have cooked the chicken, drizzle the dressing over the salad and then spoon on the whipping cream and toss the salad gently.

Sautéed pork chops
+ grilled cheesy potato + baked beetroot

These pork chops make a tasty and satisfying midweek meal that doesn't take too much effort. The beetroot and cheesy potato complement the chops well.

Sautéed pork chops

60g butter
6 pork chops
2 cloves garlic, peeled and halved
150ml white wine
salt and pepper

- Preheat the oven to 180°C/350°F/gas 4.
- Heat 30g of the butter in a large casserole on the hob.
- Brown the pork chops in the hot butter for 2 minutes on each side. Do 2 chops at a time.
- Set the browned pork chops aside.
- Drain the fat from the pan and add the remaining 30g of butter to the casserole.
- Add the garlic, return the chops to the casserole on a medium heat and, once you hear the meat sizzling, transfer the pan to the oven for about 20 minutes.
- Remove from the oven.
- Arrange the chops on a serving plate and place the casserole on the hob again.
- Turn the heat to high and get the juices in the pan bubbling.
- Pour in the white wine and bubble for 2 minutes.
- Season with salt and pepper and then pour over the chops.

Grilled cheesy potato

1kg potatoes, peeled and boiled until tender for mashing
salt and pepper
200g Cheddar cheese, grated
30g chives, finely snipped
30g butter
250ml milk
1 egg

- Mash the potatoes in a bowl.
- Add the other ingredients and mix in.
- Grease an ovenproof dish and spoon in the potato mixture.
- Place under a hot grill for 10–15 minutes until brown on top.

Baked beetroot

6–10 beetroot (depending on your family's appetite)
good pinch of salt
pepper
1 sprig rosemary
2 tablespoons olive oil
1 dessertspoon balsamic vinegar
1 clove garlic, mashed

- Preheat the oven to 200°C/400°F/gas 6.
- Prepare the beetroot by cutting the leaf stems down to as close to the top of the beetroot as you can without cutting into the beetroot.
- Scrub the beetroots.
- Place them on a large square of aluminium foil with the rosemary, garlic, oil and vinegar and season with salt and pepper.
- Make a parcel of the foil and place it on a baking sheet.
- Bake for 1 hour, although a little longer will do no harm.

Fried salmon fillets
+ herbed potatoes with cucumber

Salmon appeals to the whole family and is very healthy. One of the best accompaniments to salmon is dill.

Fried salmon fillets

1 or 2 fronds dill, finely chopped
grated zest 1 lime
black pepper
2 tablespoons extra virgin olive oil
6 salmon fillets

- Mix the dill, lime zest, pepper and olive oil together in a small bowl to combine well and set aside.
- Heat a heavy frying pan until hot.
- Place the salmon fillets, 3 at a time, skin side down in the pan for 2 minutes. Don't try to move the fillet during this time.
- Turn the fillet over and fry for about 2 minutes longer. The cooking time depends on the thickness of the fillets.
- Drizzle the dill oil over the salmon fillets and serve with the potatoes and cucumber.

Herbed potatoes with cucumber

700g potatoes, peeled and quartered
salt
2 tablespoons extra virgin olive oil
1 clove garlic, peeled and finely chopped
4 leaves tarragon, finely chopped
2 sprigs thyme, finely chopped
15g chives, finely snipped
1 cucumber, thinly sliced
black pepper

- Boil the potatoes in salted water for about 20 minutes until they are fluffing at the edges.
- Drain well and dress the potatoes while still warm with the olive oil, garlic and herbs.
- Place in a serving dish with the sliced cucumber.
- Check the seasoning and adjust if necessary.

Cream of spinach soup with pancetta herb croutons

This soup is a beautiful colour and can be the perfect way to persuade children to eat spinach. The crunchy croutons are fun.

For the soup

50g butter

1 onion, finely chopped

400g spinach leaves

200g courgettes, chopped roughly

200g frozen peas

1 teaspoon sugar

2 litres chicken stock

100ml single cream

nutmeg

salt and pepper

For the pancetta herb croutons

2 tablespoons olive oil

3 x 1.5cm thick slices white bread, cut into 1cm cubes

100g sliced pancetta, cut into 1cm strips

½ teaspoon dried oregano

To make the soup

- Heat the butter in a large saucepan.
- Gently fry the onion for 5 minutes.
- Add the spinach, courgettes, peas and sugar.
- Cover the saucepan and let the vegetables cook for 10 minutes on a low heat.
- Add the chicken stock and bring to the boil.
- Reduce the heat to a simmer and cook, covered, for 35 minutes.
- Using a hand-held blender, whizz the soup until is it smooth.
- Stir in the cream and season with a good grating of nutmeg, salt and pepper.

To make the croutons

- Heat the olive oil in a frying pan.
- When hot, add the bread and pancetta and fry until golden brown.
- You can then turn the temperature down and keep frying them gently so that they become nice and crispy.
- Sprinkle with the dried oregano and serve scattered over the soup.

Roast beef
+ Yorkshire pudding + vegetables

Roast beef with all the trimmings is a real feast and if you don't have it very often, you can splash out on a really good joint. I use a rib joint on the bone for this meal. The way I tackle a roast lunch is to prepare all the vegetables first and cook them when the meat is nearly ready.

Roast beef

2kg rib of beef on the bone
old roasting fat or olive oil
salt and pepper

- Heat the oven to 220°C/425°F/gas 7
- Place the joint in a roasting tin.
- Smear the joint with olive oil and sprinkle salt and pepper over it.
- This weight of joint will take 1 hour 20 minutes to cook altogether, so blast the joint in a hot oven of 220°C/425°F/gas 7 for 20 minutes and then finish it off for 1 hour at 160°C/320°F/gas 2½. This will give you a medium-cooked joint. Increase the time for well-cooked meat.

Yorkshire pudding

120g plain flour
salt and pepper
1 large egg
200ml milk
2 tablespoons vegetable oil

- Place the flour and seasoning into a mixing bowl.
- Make a well in the bottom of the bowl and add the egg and a little of the milk.
- Mix to a smooth paste and then add the rest of the milk.
- Leave this batter to rest for 20 minutes.
- Place the oil in a meat tin or a yorkshire-pudding tin.
- When the meat has come out of the oven and you have increased the oven temperature to 220°C/425°F/gas 7 for the potatoes, place the oiled tray in the oven to heat.
- After 10 minutes the oil should start to smoke.
- Remove the tin from the oven and quickly pour in the pudding batter.
- Return to the oven for 20 minutes.

Potatoes and parsnips

1kg potatoes, peeled, halved and rinsed in cold water
400g parsnips, peeled and halved
2 tablespoons olive oil
salt

- Parboil the potatoes and parsnips for 4 minutes in salted water. When they are cooked, remember to strain them into a pan so you can use the vegetable water to add to the gravy.
- Give them a shake in the pan to crumble their edges a little, then set aside until the joint of beef comes out of the oven.
- Drizzle them with olive oil, sprinkle some salt on top and roast for 1 hour.

Carrots

300g carrots, peeled and cut into 1cm thick, 5cm long batons
butter
pepper
handful flat-leaf parsley, chopped

- Bring some of the used vegetable water to the boil and add the carrots.
- Simmer for 5 minutes.
- Drain well and serve with a little butter, pepper and chopped parsley.

Leeks

4 leeks
salt
200ml crème fraîche
black pepper
1 tablespoon Parmesan cheese, grated

- Prepare the leeks by cutting them lengthways, stopping about 1cm from the bottom of the leek so it is still in one piece.
- Wash them under the tap, fanning each leek out as you wash them, to get rid of any grit between the leaves of the leek.
- Next, slice the leeks as thinly as possible and then place them in a sauté pan with a sprinkling of salt.
- Gently start to cook the leeks on a medium heat, stirring continuously for about 2 minutes.
- Then stir in the crème fraîche.
- Spoon the leeks into an ovenproof serving dish.
- Season with pepper and sprinkle over the Parmesan cheese.
- Just before lunch is ready, pop the leeks into the oven to warm through.

Gravy

- Once the joint comes out of the oven it is time to start the gravy.
- Place the joint on a warm plate to rest.
- Take the roasting tin and put it on the hob.
- Sprinkle a tablespoon of flour into the tin and scrape round with a wooden spoon so that all the fat gets absorbed into the flour.
- Add the vegetable water you have reserved and bring to the boil.
- Simmer very gently for 10 minutes.
- If the gravy is a bit weak, add a stock cube.
- Reheat when lunch is ready to serve.

TIP

Cooking with one oven: *Most people only have one oven so put your potatoes and parsnips round the joint while it cooks and when you take the meat out to rest pop the potatoes back into the oven in another tin so you have the meat tin for the gravy.*

Autumn fruit cobbler

Fruit cobbler is a traditional English pudding. It can be quite heavy but the addition of cream to the topping ingredients here ensures a nice lightness.

For the filling
450g blackberries
150g blackcurrants
200g apple, peeled, cored and cut into chunks
25g butter, cut into cubes
3 tablespoons soft brown sugar
For the cobbler topping
100g butter, chilled
225g plain flour
1 teaspoon baking powder
2 tablespoons caster sugar
170ml double cream
cream for serving

- Preheat the oven to 200°C/400°F/gas 6.
- Place the fruit in a baking dish.
- Dot the butter on top and sprinkle over the sugar.

To make the topping

- Rub the butter into the flour, either by hand or using a food processor until it resembles breadcrumbs, as for pastry.
- Add the baking powder and sugar.
- Quickly stir in the cream to form a rough dough.
- Form the dough into 7 biscuits and place these on top of the fruit.
- Sprinkle a tablespoon of caster sugar evenly over the top of the dough biscuits and bake for 40 minutes.
- Serve hot with cream.

Apple cake

At this time of year when apples are in such abundance, it seems a crime not to make use of them. There are many variations of apple cake, but this has got to be one of the best. This is my husband's favourite apple cake. It doesn't keep for more than a few days.

225g cooking apples, peeled, cored and cut into 1.5cm dice
175g demerara sugar
½ teaspoon ground cinnamon
150g butter, cubed
225g plain flour
2 teaspoons baking powder
2 tablespoons milk
1 egg
1 tablespoon demerara sugar

- Grease and line a 18cm square cake tin.
- Preheat the oven to 180°C/350°F/gas 4.
- In a bowl combine the apples with the sugar and cinnamon.
- In another bowl rub together the butter, flour and baking powder until the mixture resembles fine breadcrumbs.
- Add the apples, sugar and cinammon to the breadcrumbed flour and butter and combine.
- Then add the milk and egg and mix in well.
- The mixture is quite heavy and thick, but this is fine, as the apples will release their juices while they are cooking.
- Spoon the mixture into the cake tin.
- Sprinkle the top with a tablespoon of demerara sugar and bake for 1 hour 15 minutes.
- Cool and turn out onto a wire rack.
- This cake is nicest served warm.

Week 4

Monday p484	Potato cumin cakes with curry mayonnaise + courgette and tomato salad
Tuesday p486	Orecchiette with tomato sauce
Wednesday p487	Hake in puff pastry + green beans
Thursday p488	Toad in the hole + corn on the cob
Friday p489	Eggs en cocotte
Saturday p490	Chicken chasseur + cabbage + baked potatoes
Sunday p491	Roast duck + roast vegetables
Sunday pudding p492	Apple tart + cinnamon ice cream
Extra tasty treat p493	Chocolate toffee bars

Shopping list

MEAT

- ☐ 8 or 9 sausages
- ☐ 1.5kg chicken pieces
- ☐ 8 chipolata sausages
- ☐ 6 sausages
- ☐ 2 x 2kg free-range ducks

FISH

- ☐ 600g hake fillet, skinned

VEGETABLES

- ☐ 6 spring onions
- ☐ 5 courgettes
- ☐ 3 tomatoes
- ☐ 1 red onion
- ☐ 2.2kg potatoes
- ☐ 2 onions
- ☐ 250g green beans
- ☐ 1 garlic bulb
- ☐ 6 corn cobs
- ☐ 1 bunch celery
- ☐ 250g chestnut mushrooms
- ☐ 1 white cabbage
- ☐ 6 baking potatoes
- ☐ 1 aubergine
- ☐ 4 shallots
- ☐ 10 cherry tomatoes
- ☐ 200g butternut squash

FRUIT

- ☐ 450g cooking apples
- ☐ 450g eating apples

FRESH HERBS

- ☐ coriander
- ☐ basil
- ☐ flat-leaf parsley
- ☐ 2 packs chives
- ☐ bay leaves
- ☐ sage

FRIDGE ITEMS

- ☐ 18 eggs
- ☐ 300g mascarpone cheese
- ☐ 2 packs butter
- ☐ 2 packs ready-rolled puff pastry
- ☐ 850ml milk
- ☐ 268ml double cream
- ☐ 1 tub of vanilla ice cream

KITCHEN CUPBOARD ITEMS

- ☐ 2 loaves white bread
- ☐ salt
- ☐ Dijon mustard
- ☐ olive oil
- ☐ light olive oil
- ☐ groundnut oil
- ☐ extra virgin olive oil
- ☐ vegetable oil
- ☐ white wine vinegar
- ☐ 100g sun-dried tomatoes
- ☐ anchovy fillets
- ☐ capers
- ☐ 40g pitted black olives
- ☐ 400g tin chopped Italian tomatoes
- ☐ 500–600g Orecchiette pasta
- ☐ 200ml cider
- ☐ chicken stock cubes
- ☐ tomato purée
- ☐ 540g plain flour
- ☐ 250g caster sugar
- ☐ 100g soft brown sugar
- ☐ 50g porridge oats
- ☐ 75g plain chocolate
- ☐ 1 vanilla pod

SPICES

- ☐ black peppercorns
- ☐ ground cumin
- ☐ coriander seeds
- ☐ cumin seeds
- ☐ fennel seeds
- ☐ fenugreek
- ☐ chilli flakes
- ☐ caraway seeds
- ☐ ground cinnamon

Potato cumin cakes with curry mayonnaise + courgette and tomato salad

These tasty little potato cakes go really well with the salad, whose ingredients mark the end of summer. Prepare the mayonnaise first, as it takes longest to make. If you don't have time, use bought mayonnaise. The salad gives you the last lovely taste of courgettes and tomatoes as their season comes to an end.

Potato cumin cakes with curry mayonnaise

For the curry mayonnaise

2 egg yolks
1 tablespoon white wine vinegar
1 teaspoon Dijon mustard
salt
100ml groundnut oil
200ml light olive oil
1 teaspoon curry powder*

For the potato cumin cakes

750g potatoes, boiled and skinned
3–4 tablespoons olive oil
6 spring onions, sliced
2 teaspoons ground cumin
2 tablespoons fresh coriander, chopped
salt and pepper
1 dessertspoon curry powder*
8 tablespoons white breadcrumbs
1 egg, beaten

To make the mayonnaise

- Whisk the egg yolks in a bowl with the white wine vinegar, mustard and a pinch of salt.
- Mix the oils together in a small jug and start adding to the eggs, literally a drop at a time, whisking constantly. If you add them more quickly than this the mixture will curdle. Make sure you have thoroughly combined each addition of oil before adding the next. Gradually the mixture will start to thicken and at this stage you can add the oils at a quicker pace.
- Once all the oil has been added, sprinkle on the curry powder.
- Serve with the potato cakes.

To make the potato cumin cakes

- Mash the potatoes.
- Heat one tablespoon of olive oil in a frying pan and gently sauté the spring onions for 2 minutes.
- Add the cumin and stir to coat the spring onions.
- Now tip the spring onions into the mashed potato with the coriander, salt and pepper.
- If you have time, chill this mixture in the fridge for 30 minutes or so.
- Then, form the mixture into 8 round cakes and set aside.
- Sprinkle the curry powder into the breadcrumbs.
- Dip the cakes in the beaten egg and then cover them in breadcrumbs.
- Heat the rest of the oil in a frying pan and cook the cakes until golden brown on each side.
- Drain them on kitchen paper and serve.

**** To make your own curry powder:***

1 tablespoon coriander seeds
1 dessertspoon cumin seeds
1 teaspoon fennel seeds
½ teaspoon fenugreek

- *Place the coriander seeds into a small, heavy-bottomed pan and heat through for 30 seconds.*
- *Add the other ingredients and toast until you smell the lovely aroma of the spices.*
- *Transfer the spices to a coffee grinder, a small processor or grind them in a pestle and mortar.*

Courgette and tomato salad

1 tablespoon olive oil
3 courgettes, diced into bite-sized pieces (2 yellow ones and 1 green one if you can get them)
3 tomatoes, chopped into bite-sized pieces
1 red onion, finely diced
salt and pepper
basil leaves, torn

- Warm the olive oil in a small frying pan and add the courgettes.
- Gently sauté them for 3 minutes only. They should still have a crunch.
- Place the courgettes in a serving bowl with the tomatoes and red onion.
- Season and scatter on the basil.

Orecchiette with tomato sauce

This 'ear-shaped' pasta goes particularly well with a simple tomato sauce.

100g sun-dried tomatoes
4 anchovy fillets, rinsed
3 tablespoons fresh basil, chopped
3 tablespoons flat-leaf parsley, chopped
2 teaspoons capers
small pinch chilli flakes
40g pitted black olives
9 tablespoons extra virgin olive oil
250ml water
400g tin chopped Italian tomatoes
salt and pepper
2 tablespoons mascarpone cheese
500–600g Orecchiette pasta cooked according to the packet instructions

- Soak the sun-dried tomatoes in warm water for 30 minutes.
- Drain the tomatoes and put them in a food processor with the anchovies, basil, parsley, capers, chilli flakes, olives, olive oil, water and tinned tomatoes.
- Process until smooth.
- Pour the mixture into a saucepan and bring it to a simmer.
- Cook gently for 10 minutes.
- Season with salt and pepper.
- Remove from the heat and stir in the mascarpone cheese.
- Meanwhile, cook the pasta according to the packet instructions. Drain well and serve with the sauce.

Hake in puff pastry + green beans

Hake is a nice meaty fish that keeps its shape and goes well in this recipe.

Hake in puff pastry

750g potatoes, peeled and diced
25g butter
1 onion, diced
600g hake fillet, skinned and diced
200g mascarpone cheese
1 dessertspoon curry powder*
1 tablespoon fresh coriander, chopped
salt and pepper
2 packs ready-rolled puff pastry
1 egg mixed with 2 tablespoons of water for the glaze

- Preheat the oven to 190°C/375°F/gas 5.
- Place the potatoes in a saucepan of boiling salted water.
- Bring back to a simmer and cook the potatoes for 2 minutes, until they have just started to soften. Don't allow them to disintegrate.
- Warm the butter in a large sauté pan and add the onions and cooked potatoes.
- Sauté on a medium heat for about 5 minutes until the potatoes are tender.
- Add the fish and gently combine with the potatoes and onions.
- Immediately add the mascarpone, curry powder and coriander and stir to combine.
- Season with salt and pepper.
- Remove from the heat.
- Lay out the rolled puff pastry. Roll each sheet out so that they are a little bit thinner, and cut 3 x 20cm circles from each sheet.
- Pile 2–3 tablespoons of the fish and potato mixture onto one side of each pastry circle.
- Brush the edges of the circle with the egg and water and fold the pastry over to form a pasty.
- Do the same with all 6 circles and then brush them all with more of the egg glaze.
- Chill in the fridge for 30 minutes.
- Brush them again with more egg glaze and bake them in the oven for 25 minutes.

***To make your own curry powder:**
1 tablespoon coriander seeds
1 dessertspoon cumin seeds
1 teaspoon fennel seeds
½ teaspoon fenugreek

- *Place the coriander seeds into a small, heavy-bottomed pan and heat through for 30 seconds.*
- *Add the other ingredients and toast until you smell the lovely aroma of the spices.*
- *Transfer the spices to a coffee grinder, a small processor or grind them in a pestle and mortar.*

Green beans

250g green beans, topped and tailed if necessary
a little salt and pepper

- Boil a saucepan of salted water.
- Once you have a rolling boil, add the beans and boil for 5 minutes.
- Drain well and serve with a knob of butter and freshly ground black pepper.

Toad in the hole
+ corn on the cob

Toad in the hole is often thought of as a children's dish, but if done properly it can appeal to adults as well. To make a good toad in the hole you need to make decent batter and use good-quality sausages.

Toad in the hole

8 or 9 sausages (depending on how many your family can eat)

For the batter

240g plain flour

pinch of salt

2 large eggs

600ml milk

handful parsley and chives, chopped

2 tablespoons vegetable oil

- Preheat the oven to 220°C/425°F/gas 7.
- If you have an electric mixer put all the batter ingredients, minus the herbs, into a mixing bowl and whizz until smooth. If you are mixing by hand, put the flour and salt into a bowl and gradually add the wet ingredients.
- Sprinkle on the herbs.
- Once combined, set aside and let the batter rest for at least 30 minutes.
- Pour the oil into a meat tin.
- Add the sausages and place in the oven for 10 minutes. The sausages will start to brown during this time.
- Remove the tin from the oven and carefully pour the batter on top of the sausages.
- Then, return the tin to the oven and cook for 20 minutes.

Corn on the cob

6 corn cobs

butter for serving

black pepper

- Place the cobs into boiling water and simmer for 8 minutes.
- Serve with butter and black pepper.

Eggs en cocotte

These baked eggs are great for a quick supper. They do not make a very heavy meal so you may want to serve a salad alongside, or some cheese and crackers afterwards. I tend to do two eggs per adult and older children, and one egg each for the younger children. Take care not to overcook the eggs.

butter for coating ramekin dishes
10 tablespoons double cream
10 teaspoons snipped chives
10 eggs
salt and pepper
hot buttered toast for serving

- Preheat the oven to 190°C/375°F/gas 5.
- Butter ten ramekin dishes.
- Pour one tablespoon of cream into each ramekin, then sprinkle a teaspoon of chives into each one.
- Take a large frying pan and pour 2cms of water into it.
- Place the ramekins into the frying pan and put the pan on the hob to heat the cream.
- Leave on the heat for 5 minutes until the cream is hot.
- Remove the pan from the heat and place the ramekins on a baking sheet.
- Break 1 egg into each ramekin and then place them in the oven to bake for 8 minutes, until the eggs are almost cooked through. There will still be a slight wobble to them, as they will keep cooking for a while after they have come out of the oven, and the beauty of these eggs is spoiled if they are overcooked.
- While the eggs are cooking in the oven, prepare the hot buttered toast.

Chicken chasseur + cabbage + baked potatoes

Chicken chasseur is the perfect dish to serve as the dark evenings descend. It is relatively hassle-free and very satisfying accompanied by baked potatoes.

Chicken chasseur

50g butter
1.5kg jointed chicken pieces, skin removed
8 chipolata sausages
1 onion, peeled and finely chopped
1 stick celery, finely chopped
250g chestnut mushrooms, chopped
1 scant tablespoon plain flour
200ml cider
400ml chicken stock (a cube will do)
1 heaped teaspoon tomato purée
salt and pepper
1 bouquet garni, made up of 1 bay leaf, 1 sprig parsley, 1 sprig rosemary

- Preheat the oven to 180°C/350°F/gas 4.
- Warm the butter in a large casserole with a lid that can go either on the hob or in the oven.
- Once the butter starts to foam, add the chicken pieces and brown them all over. This should take about 5 minutes on a high heat.
- Remove the chicken pieces and set aside.
- Add the chipolatas to the butter, brown them all over and set aside with the chicken.
- Next add the onion, celery and mushrooms and sauté gently for 10 minutes until lightly browned.
- Sprinkle over the flour and stir in.
- Add the cider, stock and tomato purée.
- Return the chicken and chipolatas to the pan.
- Season with salt and pepper and add the bouquet garni.
- Bring to a simmer, cover and place in the oven for 35 minutes.

Cabbage

1 white cabbage, cored and sliced into 1cm strips
50ml water
15g butter
½ teaspoon caraway seeds
salt and pepper

- Place the cabbage in a saucepan with the water and butter.
- Cook the cabbage on a low heat, covered, for 5 minutes.
- Sprinkle on the caraway seeds and continue to cook, covered, for another 5 minutes.
- Season with salt and pepper and serve.

Baked potatoes

6 baking potatoes
butter for serving
salt and pepper

- Preheat the oven to 220°C/425°F/gas 7.
- Pierce the potatoes with a sharp knife and bake them for 1 hour 30 minutes.
- When cooked, split each one and serve with butter, salt and pepper.

TIP

Cooking with one oven: *If you only have one oven get the potatoes cooking first until almost ready and then lower the temperature to cook the chicken so that everything is ready together.*

Roast duck
+ roast vegetables

Roast duck is truly delicious if cooked properly. It's a very fatty bird, so you need to drain the fat off at various points during the cooking time. In order to feed six people you will need two birds, so this is a special occasion meal, given the cost of duck. If you don't want to splash out on two ducks, then bulk out on the vegetables. You can also prepare some broccoli for those reluctant to eat more 'exotic' vegetables such as aubergine.

Roast duck

6 sausages
salt and pepper
6 sage leaves, finely chopped
1 large crisp eating apple, peeled, cored and chopped into large chunks
2 x 2kg free-range ducks
1 tablespoon flour
1 chicken stock cube
400ml water

- Preheat the oven to 220°C/425°F/gas 7.
- Squeeze the sausage meat out of the sausages and fry in a sauté pan until golden brown.
- Season with salt and pepper and add the herbs and the apples, stirring gently for 1 minute.
- Once cool, spoon this stuffing mixture into the duck neck cavities.
- Dry the skin of the duck with kitchen paper.
- Pierce the duck skin all over with a sharp knife.
- Season each duck with salt and pepper and place them in a meat tin.
- Roast for 20 minutes, then reduce the oven temperature to 180°C/350°F/gas 4 and cook for a further hour and 10 minutes, draining off the duck fat at regular intervals. Keep the fat and use it for roasting the vegetables.
- Once cooked, remove the ducks from the meat tin.
- Take away the bulk of the fat and spoon out any burnt pieces.
- Place the meat tin on a medium heat on the hob.
- Add a tablespoon of flour to the remaining juices and stir to incorporate the fat into the flour.
- Then add a stock cube, incorporating it using the back of a wooden spoon.
- Add the water and stir round.
- Bring to a simmer and cook for 10 minutes on a very low heat.
- Serve with the duck and vegetables.

Roast vegetables

1 aubergine, cut into 2cm cubes
2 small courgettes, cut into 2cm cubes
4 shallots, peeled and halved
2 cloves garlic, peeled
10 cherry tomatoes
700g potatoes peeled, quartered and parboiled for 4 minutes
200g butternut squash, peeled and cut into 4cm cubes
salt and pepper
4 sage leaves, finely chopped

- Preheat the oven to 200°C/400°F/gas 6.
- Prepare the vegetables and place them in a roasting tin.
- Season with salt, pepper and the sage leaves.
- It is tempting to cook the vegetables around the duck, but I think they get too greasy this way so as you drain off some of the duck fat, retain it in a bowl and spoon a couple of tablespoons of it over the vegetables.
- Roast for 45 minutes, turning the vegetables occasionally.

TIP

Cooking with one oven: *If you only have one oven cook the vegetables for one hour and 10 minutes at 180°C required for the duck.*

Apple tart
+ cinnamon ice cream

This classic apple tart is delicious served with the cinnamon ice cream or simply with double cream.

To make the pastry

- Beat the sugar and butter together in a food processor until smoothly combined.
- Incorporate the egg.
- Add the flour and a pinch of salt and once you have a dough starting to form, turn the mixture out onto a lightly floured surface and form it into a ball.
- Wrap the pastry in cling-film and chill in the fridge for 30 minutes.

To make the tart

- Preheat the oven to 200°C/400°F/gas 6.
- Grease a 28cm shallow tart tin.
- Roll out the pastry and line the tart tin with it.
- Place the tart case in the fridge to chill while you prepare the apples.
- Place the cooking apples in a saucepan with 110g of sugar and the vanilla pod.
- Cover the saucepan and cook the apples on a medium heat until they have collapsed and become almost puréed.
- Set aside to cool.
- Fill the pastry case with the puréed apples and arrange the eating apples over the top. Brush the apples with melted butter and place in the oven for 35 minutes.

Apple tart

For the pastry

125g butter, softened
90g caster sugar
1 egg
250g plain flour
salt

For the filling

450g cooking apples, peeled, cored and chopped
160g caster sugar
1 vanilla pod
400g eating apples, peeled and sliced to about 3mm
30g butter, melted

Cinnamon ice cream

- Take a tub of ice cream from the freezer and when soft enough, fold in half a teaspoon of ground cinnamon. Return it to the freezer until you are ready to serve with the tart.

Chocolate toffee bars

I can't recall how these little bars of sweet delight came about, but my children love to eat them. I used to do weekly cookery classes at the local primary school and got the children to make these on one occasion. They definitely provided more pleasure, both in their production and consumption, than any shop-bought chocolate bar would have done.

100g butter
100g soft brown sugar
1 egg yolk
50g plain flour
50g porridge oats
For the topping
75g plain chocolate
25g butter

- Preheat the oven to 190°C/375°F/gas 5.
- Grease a Swiss roll tin measuring 17cm x 27cm.
- In a bowl beat together the butter and sugar, using an electric whisk, until light and fluffy.
- Mix in the egg yolk.
- Add the flour and oats and mix well.
- Press the mixture into the greased tin and bake for 20 minutes until lightly browned.
- Remove from the oven and allow to cool slightly in the tin.

To make the topping

- Place the chocolate and butter in a glass bowl over a saucepan of barely simmering water, until they have melted.
- Spread the chocolate sauce over the cake.
- Cut into slices and leave in the tin to cool completely before serving.

Week 1

Monday p496	Sausages + mashed potato + onion gravy
Tuesday p497	Tomato soup + cheese muffins
Wednesday p498	Fusilli pasta with pancetta, mushroom and cream sauce
Thursday p499	Red pork curry with green beans + jasmine rice
Friday p500	Lamb cutlets + couscous
Saturday p501	Butternut squash, cream and bacon tart + green salad
Sunday p502	Stuffed roast chicken + roast potatoes + carrots + gratin of leeks + gravy
Sunday pudding p504	Plum and almond tarte tatin
Extra tasty treat p505	Apple brownie + cream

Shopping list

MEAT

- ☐ 18 sausages
- ☐ 10–12 lamb cutlets
- ☐ 800g pork shoulder
- ☐ 2 x 2kg whole chickens

VEGETABLES

- ☐ 2.25kg potatoes
- ☐ 4 red onions
- ☐ 1.1kg fresh tomatoes
- ☐ 3 onions
- ☐ 1 bunch celery
- ☐ 1 garlic bulb
- ☐ 250g chestnut mushrooms
- ☐ 150g green beans
- ☐ 1 cucumber
- ☐ 1 butternut squash
- ☐ fresh ginger
- ☐ 3 leeks
- ☐ 300g carrots
- ☐ 2 spring onions
- ☐ 1 Romaine lettuce

FRUIT

- ☐ 1 lemon
- ☐ 1 lime
- ☐ 7 or 8 round purple plums
- ☐ 450g cooking apples

HERBS

- ☐ thyme
- ☐ chives
- ☐ flat-leaf parsley
- ☐ 1 lemon grass stalk
- ☐ coriander
- ☐ mint
- ☐ sage
- ☐ rosemary

FRIDGE ITEMS

- ☐ 3 packs butter
- ☐ 1 small tub crème fraîche
- ☐ 250g Parmesan cheese
- ☐ 180g mature Cheddar cheese
- ☐ 600ml milk
- ☐ 9 eggs
- ☐ 300g sliced pancetta
- ☐ 220ml single cream
- ☐ 300ml double cream
- ☐ 1.2 litres fresh chicken stock

KITCHEN CUPBOARD ITEMS

- ☐ salt
- ☐ wholegrain mustard
- ☐ olive oil
- ☐ balsamic vinegar
- ☐ chicken stock cubes
- ☐ 450g plain flour
- ☐ 450g self-raising flour
- ☐ bicarbonate of soda
- ☐ 400g fusilli pasta
- ☐ vegetable oil
- ☐ 175g soft brown sugar
- ☐ 400ml tin coconut milk
- ☐ 100ml coconut cream
- ☐ fish sauce
- ☐ 400g jasmine rice
- ☐ 250g couscous
- ☐ 240g tin chickpeas
- ☐ sun-dried tomatoes
- ☐ jar roasted peppers
- ☐ pine nuts
- ☐ 1 small loaf white bread for breadcrumbs
- ☐ goose fat
- ☐ 200g marzipan
- ☐ 85g caster sugar
- ☐ vanilla essence
- ☐ 85g sultanas
- ☐ 55g walnuts

SPICES

- ☐ black peppercorns
- ☐ cloves
- ☐ cumin seeds
- ☐ coriander seeds
- ☐ ground nutmeg

Sausages
+ mashed potato + onion gravy

Sausage, mash and onion gravy is a national favourite. Buy good sausages, free range or organic if possible. Cheap sausages don't contain enough pork to have much nutritional value. I use a potato ricer to make mashed potato, as I have found it is the best way of removing all the lumps and much quicker than a masher. I also resist the temptation of cutting the potatoes into small cubes prior to cooking them. It may help the potatoes cook more quickly, but I don't think you get such a good flavour.

Sausages

9 or 10 sausages depending on the appetite of your children

- Fry the sausages in a frying pan on a medium heat to brown them all over.
- Then turn the heat down to cook them through. It takes about 12–15 minutes to cook a sausage.

Mashed potato

1kg potatoes, peeled and quartered
40g butter
salt and pepper
200ml warmed milk
1 dessertspoon crème fraîche
1 dessertspoon wholegrain mustard

- Place the potatoes in cold, salted water and bring to the boil.
- Turn the heat down to a robust simmer on a medium heat.
- Once the potatoes are soft but not mushy, drain them and put them through a potato ricer.
- Return the mashed potato to the saucepan and place over a low heat.
- Add the milk and butter and gently stir in.
- Remove from the heat.
- Stir in the crème fraîche and mustard.

Onion gravy

3 medium red onions, peeled and finely sliced
1 tablespoon olive oil
5 tablespoons balsamic vinegar
60g butter
2 chicken stock cubes

- Fry the onions gently in a pan with the olive oil for 15 minutes until soft.
- Then turn up the heat for a few minutes to brown them slightly.
- Add the balsamic vinegar and boil it until the majority of the liquid has disappeared.
- Turn the heat down and add the butter and stock cubes.
- Add 565ml of water and stir well.
- Let the gravy simmer, uncovered, for 15 minutes.
- Serve with the sausages and mash.

Tomato soup + cheese muffins

This recipe makes 12 muffins and is very easy. They don't stay fresh for long, but they freeze very well, so eat them quickly and freeze the ones you don't use.

Tomato soup

1kg fresh tomatoes
1 tablespoon olive oil
1 large onion, chopped
1 stick celery, chopped
1 clove garlic, peeled and finely chopped
1 dessertspoon plain flour
1.2 litres chicken stock (stock cubes will do)
1 sprig thyme
1 teaspoon sugar
salt and pepper

- Place the tomatoes in a large bowl, cover them with boiling water and leave for 1 minute.
- Remove the skin from the tomatoes and chop them up roughly, removing any hard cores.
- Heat the oil in a large saucepan.
- Add the onion, celery and garlic and cook on a low heat for about 10 minutes until they are soft.
- Stir in the flour and add the stock a little at a time to avoid getting lumps.
- Add the tomatoes, thyme and sugar and cook, covered, for 35 minutes.
- Remove from the heat.
- If you prefer smooth tomato soup, whizz it with a hand-held blender until the lumps have gone.
- Once smooth, adjust the seasoning if necessary and stir in a knob of butter just before serving.

Cheese muffins

350g self-raising flour
½ teaspoon bicarbonate of soda
salt
1 tablespoon chives, snipped
50g Parmesan cheese, grated
180g mature Cheddar cheese, grated
300ml milk, soured with 2 teaspoons lemon juice
2 eggs, lightly beaten
100g butter, melted

- Preheat the oven to 190°C/375°F/gas 5.
- Grease a 12-cup muffin tin. If you grease each mould with butter and then flour each mould the muffins won't stick.
- Place the flour, bicarbonate of soda, a pinch of salt, chives and cheeses in a mixing bowl.
- In another bowl or jug whisk together the milk, eggs and butter and then pour these onto the dry ingredients and stir to combine. Take care not to overmix, as this will spoil the texture of the muffins.
- Spoon the mixture into the 12 moulds.
- Sprinkle with some extra Cheddar and bake for 25–30 minutes.
- Allow to cool in the tin and then turn them out.

Fusilli pasta with pancetta, mushroom and cream sauce

This is a quick and easy supper that tastes great. Children and mushrooms is an unlikely combination but if you cook the mushrooms until they are a lovely toffee brown they go down quite well.

2 tablespoons olive oil
30g butter
250g chestnut mushrooms, sliced to a 3mm thickness
3 cloves garlic, peeled and finely chopped
200g sliced pancetta, chopped
220ml single cream
1 tablespoon flat-leaf parsley, chopped
400g fusilli pasta
salt
black pepper
4 tablespoons Parmesan cheese, freshly grated

- Heat the olive oil and butter in a frying pan on a medium heat.
- Add the mushrooms and cook for 5 minutes, stirring occasionally.
- Once the mushrooms are golden brown, add the garlic and cook for 1 minute, stirring the whole time to make sure the garlic doesn't burn.
- Add the pancetta and cook for 2 minutes until the pancetta starts to brown.
- Remove from the heat and add the cream and parsley.
- Meanwhile, cook the pasta in boiling salted water, following the packet instructions. Check it 1 minute before the end of the cooking time so it doesn't overcook.
- Drain the pasta thoroughly.
- Pour the mushroom sauce over the pasta.
- Season with plenty of black pepper and a good sprinkling of Parmesan cheese.

Red pork curry with green beans + jasmine rice

This curry recipe is good because there is so much in the one pot; the meat, beans and potatoes. It's really the Asian version of the European stew.

Red pork curry with green beans

5 cloves
1 teaspoon cumin seeds
1½ teaspoons coriander seeds
1 teaspoon salt
black pepper
½ teaspoon ground nutmeg
1 red onion, quartered
3 cloves garlic, peeled and chopped
20g fresh coriander
2.5cm piece fresh ginger, roughly chopped
½ piece lemon grass stalk, outer leaves removed and roughly chopped
grated zest and juice 1 lime
3 tablespoons vegetable oil
800g pork shoulder, chopped into 2.5cm cubes
1 tablespoon brown sugar
2 tablespoons fish sauce
400g tin coconut milk
100ml coconut cream
150g green beans
250g pototoes, peeled and chopped into quarters

- Take a small frying pan and gently toast the cloves, cumin and coriander for 1 minute until you can smell the toasty aroma of the spices.
- Place the spices in a pestle and mortar with the salt, pepper and nutmeg and grind to as fine a powder as you can.
- Place the onion, garlic, coriander, ginger, lemon grass, lime zest and juice in the bowl of a food processor, whizz to a fairly smooth paste and set aside.
- Pour the oil into a large saucepan and heat it through.
- Brown the pork in batches in the hot oil, setting each browned batch aside as you go.
- To the hot oil add the coriander and onion paste from the food processor, and fry it for 1 minute.
- Return the pork to the saucepan and stir to coat the pork in the paste.
- Then sprinkle on the spices, sugar and fish sauce.
- Cook, stirring for 2 minutes.
- Next, pour on the coconut milk and cream and bring to a simmer.
- Add the green beans and potatoes and cook, covered, on a gentle simmer for 45 minutes until the pork is tender.
- Serve with the jasmine rice.

Jasmine rice

400g jasmine rice
600ml water
½ teaspoon salt

- Place the rice, water and salt in a saucepan and bring to the boil.
- Turn the heat down low, cover the saucepan, and cook for 15 minutes.
- Remove from the heat, but leave covered for 10 minutes before serving.

Lamb cutlets

+ couscous

Lamb cutlets and couscous have become a pretty popular combination. You can vary the couscous by changing the ingredients rather like you would do with a salad.

Lamb cutlets

10–12 lamb cutlets (depending on the eating appetites of your children)
salt and pepper

- Trim the coarse strip of fat from the side of each cutlet. You can do this with your fingers or with the aid of a sharp knife.
- Season each side of each lamb cutlet with salt and pepper.
- Heat a griddle or frying pan until hot.
- Fry four cutlets at a time.
- Cook them for about 5 minutes altogether, so they get 2 minutes on one side and 3 minutes on the other. This will give a pink finish to the meat.
- Place the cooked cutlets under aluminium foil to keep warm.
- You might need to season the cooked cutlets with more salt.

Couscous

250g couscous
4 tablespoons olive oil
400ml boiling water
240g tin chickpeas, drained
2 tomatoes, roughly chopped
4 sun-dried tomatoes, chopped into small pieces
3 slices roasted pepper from a jar, roughly chopped
¼ cucumber, cut into bite-sized cubes
20g fresh mint, finely chopped
salt and pepper

- Place the couscous in a mixing bowl.
- Pour over the boiling water and add one tablespoon of olive oil.
- Cover with a plate or cling-film, and set aside for 5 minutes.
- Separate the couscous with a fork and add the remaining ingredients, not forgetting the rest of the olive oil.
- Season generously.

Butternut squash, cream and bacon tart + green salad

Make the most of the beautiful squash available in the shops at this time of year. They are reasonably priced and full of goodness.

Butternut squash, cream and bacon tart

For the pastry

225g plain flour

150g cold butter, cut into chunks

salt

2 tablespoons Parmesan cheese, finely grated

1 egg yolk

2 tablespoons cold water

For the filling

200g butternut squash, peeled and cut into 2cm chunks

2 tablespoons olive oil

salt and pepper

1 sprig thyme

100g pancetta, chopped

1 egg

1 egg yolk

300ml double cream

1 tablespoon pine nuts

To make the pastry

- Put the flour and butter in a food processor, or a bowl if you are combining by hand, and whizz so that the mixture looks like fine breadcrumbs.
- Add a pinch of salt and the cheese and stir.
- Mix the egg yolk with the cold water, and then add these to the bread-crumbed flour and fat.
- Combine the wet and dry ingredients and, as a dough starts to form, turn it out onto a lightly floured work surface.
- With a light hand, gently knead the pastry dough until it is smooth.
- Wrap it in cling-film and chill it in the fridge for at least 20 minutes.

To make the filling

- Grease a 30cm tart tin.
- Preheat the oven to 200°C/400°F/gas 6.
- Drizzle 1 tablespoon of olive oil over the squash and season with salt and pepper.
- Sprinkle the thyme leaves over the squash.
- Bake the squash for 20 minutes until soft but not mushy.
- Place a baking tray in the oven once the butternut squash has finished cooking.
- Roll out the pastry and line the tart tin with it.
- Cover the pastry case with a sheet of baking parchment and spread some baking beans on top of the parchment.
- Place the pastry case on top of the baking tray in the oven and bake for 10 minutes.
- Then remove the parchment and baking beans and cook for a further 5 minutes.
- Reduce the oven temperature to 190°C/375°F/gas 5.
- Meanwhile, fry the pancetta with the remaining tablespoon of olive oil.
- Spoon the pancetta and the butternut squash on to the baked pastry case.
- In a small bowl mix together the eggs and cream and season well with salt and pepper.
- Pour the cream and egg mixture carefully into the pastry case over the pancetta and squash.
- Scatter over the pine nuts.
- Bake for 25 minutes.

Green salad

1 Romaine lettuce, washed and chopped

½ cucumber, sliced

2 spring onions, chopped

1 tablespoon olive oil

2 teaspoons balsamic vinegar

salt and pepper

- Place the salad ingredients in a serving bowl and pour the dressing on when ready to serve.

Stuffed roast chicken + roast potatoes + carrots + gratin of leeks + gravy

For 6 people I usually buy 2 organic chickens weighing about 2 kg each. This stops the children fighting over the breast meat and leaves enough for sandwiches and a good batch of stock. I also make sure I buy organic chickens as they taste better. I cook my chickens for 20 minutes per 500g at 190°C/375°F/gas 5 and if I am cooking two birds at once I add another 10 minutes. You will find that at the end of this cooking time the legs may not be quite cooked but the breast will be perfect. I think it is impossible to cook the breast perfectly and get the legs done as well, so once the birds have rested for 20 minutes I remove the legs and return them to the oven while the potatoes finish cooking. If you can't be bothered with this, cook the birds for 20 minutes per 500g and add another 30 minutes at the end.

Stuffed roast chicken

2 x 2kg whole chickens
olive oil
salt and pepper
For the stuffing
1 onion, finely chopped
150g white breadcrumbs
1 pack free-range sausages
10 sage leaves, finely chopped
1 tablespoon hot water from the kettle
1 egg
30g butter
salt and pepper

- Preheat the oven to 190°C/375°F/gas 5.
- Place the onion in a bowl with the breadcrumbs.
- Pierce the sausages and squeeze out the sausage meat into the bowl with the onion and breadcrumbs.
- Add the sage leaves, water, egg and butter and season well.
- Mix with a wooden spoon until the mixture is combined and holds together quite loosely.
- I always stuff chickens between the skin and the breast. To do this, you gently start wriggling your fingers under the skin, releasing it from the breast. It might be a good idea to remove any rings you are wearing as these often tear the skin of the bird and then the stuffing leaks through. If this does happen don't despair, just seal the hole with a cocktail stick, folding the skin over as you do this so that the hole is closed. Once you have released the skin as far up as you can get, take a lump of stuffing in your hand and push it under the skin.
- Push all the stuffing in like this and then tuck in the loose skin under the wings.
- Place the chickens in a high-sided roasting tin.
- Drizzle about 1 dessertspoon of olive oil onto the breast of each chicken and season them with sea salt and pepper.
- Roast them for 1 hour 30 minutes.

Roast potatoes

1kg potatoes, peeled, quartered and rinsed in cold water
1 dessertspoon goose fat or 2 tablespoons olive oil
salt

- Preheat the oven to 220°C/425°F/gas 7.
- Place the potatoes in a saucepan of salted water.
- Bring them to the boil and keep them on a gentle simmer for 5 minutes.
- Drain them and then return them to the saucepan and, with the lid on, give them a good shake.
- Put the fat into a roasting tin and pop it into the oven for 5 minutes to get it nice and hot.

- Once this is done, carefully add the potatoes to the tin, rolling each one around in the fat.
- Roast them for 50–60 minutes until they are beautifully golden and crispy.

Carrots

knob of butter
300g carrots, peeled and cut into slanted discs
1 sprig rosemary
salt and pepper

- Put the butter in a saucepan and add the carrots and sprig of rosemary.
- Cover the saucepan and cook the carrots on a gentle heat, stirring occasionally, for about 15 minutes.
- Season with salt and pepper.

Gratin of leeks

3 leeks
1 tablespoon crème fraîche
1 tablespoon Parmesan cheese, grated
salt and pepper

- To prepare the leeks, slice them lengthways down the middle, leaving a centimetre uncut so the leek is not severed in two.
- Rinse the leeks under the tap, fanning out the leaves as you do so to clean the dirt and grit out.
- Then slice them widthways thinly, to a thickness of about 5mm.
- Put the leeks in a heavy-bottomed frying or sauté pan.
- While they are cooking sprinkle a little salt and pepper on them.
- Cook them until they are soft, which takes about 2–3 minutes only.
- Add the crème fraîche and stir in gently.
- Add the Parmesan and transfer the leeks to a gratin dish.
- When you are about to serve the meal, place the leeks under a hot grill to brown slightly.

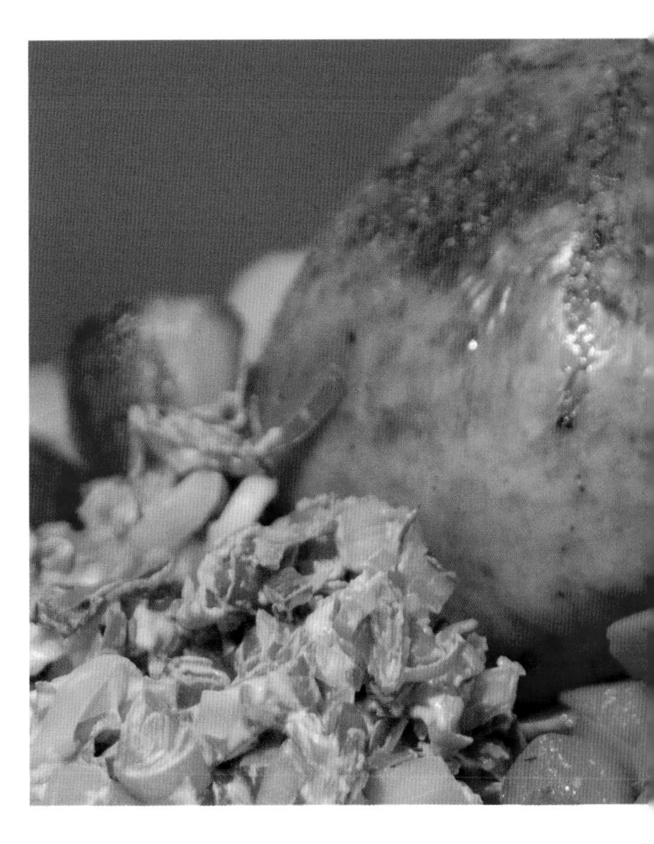

Gravy

- Once the chickens are cooked and you have set them aside to rest, begin making the gravy.
- Place the roasting tin on the hob and turn the heat to medium.
- Sprinkle a dessertspoon of flour into the tin and with a wooden spoon scrape all the juices, bits, and flour together into a paste.
- Turn the heat up high and add either fresh stock to make up the liquid, or put a stock cube in and then add water. Keep stirring to avoid lumps.
- Once the gravy has thickened, turn the heat down to very low so that the gravy cooks, but you don't lose a huge quantity to evaporation.

TIP

Cooking with one oven: *Most people only have one oven so put your potatoes round the chicken while it cooks and when you take the meat out to rest pop the potatoes back into the oven in another tin so you have the meat tin for the gravy.*

Plum and almond tarte tatin

This is my version of apple tarte tatin, with the added almond flavour. It's definitely a dish that celebrates the glory of nature's autumn harvest.

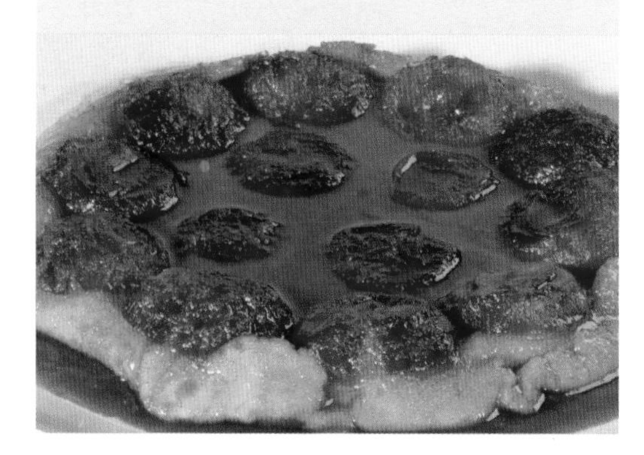

For the pastry
180g plain flour
salt
85g butter, chilled
1 egg yolk
2 dessertspoons cold water

For the filling
7 or 8 round purple plums
85g caster sugar
40g butter
200g marzipan

To make the pastry

- Place the flour and a pinch of salt in a bowl or a food processor.
- Add the butter and combine with the flour until you have the consistency of breadcrumbs.
- Add the egg yolk and water and mix to combine until you have a rough dough.
- Turn the dough out onto a floured surface and form a smooth ball of dough.
- Wrap the dough in cling-film and chill it in the fridge for 30 minutes.

To make the tart

- Preheat the oven to 190°C/375°F/gas 5.
- Halve the plums and remove the stones.
- Put the sugar into a pan suitable for both hob and oven use – a cake tin would probably work. If you love making tarte tatins, then invest in a proper tarte tatin tin. In the meantime, you can easily improvize with the equipment you have.
- Heat the sugar gently, watching it all the time. The middle will start to brown. Don't stir the sugar, but tilt the tin to redistribute the sugar so that it slowly browns all over. Don't try to do this too quickly on a high heat as you will burn the sugar. You want the sugar to become a dark brown liquid. It's not hard to do and is very rewarding when you produce your first tarte tatin.
- Once the sugar is dark brown, remove the pan from the heat and add the butter in small pieces.
- Now place the plum halves into the sugared tin, cut side up.
- Dot a little more butter over the plums and put the tin back onto a gentle heat, until you hear the sound of the heat getting through to the tin again and the plums starting to cook, and remove from the heat once again.
- Roll out the marzipan thinly to the approximate shape of the tin containing the plums.
- Lay the marzipan on top of the plums.
- Next, roll out the pastry so it is just bigger than the tin and lay it loosely over the marzipan tucking in the pastry edges underneath, rather than cutting them away.
- Bake for 30 minutes.
- Leave to cool in the tin for about 15 minutes. Then cover the tin with a plate and invert so that you turn the tart out onto the plate.
- Be careful, as if you don't do this quickly and cleanly you will spill the juice.
- Serve with crème fraîche.

Apple brownie + cream

With apples in abundance at this time of year, this is a good teatime treat.

Apple brownie

115g self-raising flour
3 tablespoons melted butter
2 eggs
1 teaspoon vanilla essence
175g soft brown sugar
85g sultanas
55g walnuts, chopped
450g cooking apples, peeled, cored and cut into large chunks
cream for serving

- Grease an ovenproof pudding dish measuring approximately 24cm in diameter.
- Preheat the oven to 200°C/400°F/gas 6.
- Sift the flour into a mixing bowl.
- Pour in the butter and eggs and mix lightly.
- Add the rest of the ingredients and gently combine them.
- Spoon the mixture into the pudding dish and bake for 45 minutes.
- Serve with cream.

Week 2

Monday p508	Minced beef stew + baked potatoes
Tuesday p509	Salmon teriyaki + mustard cream linguine
Wednesday p510	Chicken schnitzel + tomato spaghetti
Thursday p512	Autumn vegetable soup + crunchy pitta pockets
Friday p513	Chicken fajitas + pinto beans in tomato sauce + guacamole
Saturday p514	Cheese, onion and potato pie
Sunday p515	Pork chops + roast potatoes + white beans + courgettes + tomato salad
Sunday pudding p516	Oatmeal apple crumble + cream
Extra tasty treat p517	Apple purée + buttered breadcrumbs

Shopping list

MEAT

- ☐ 800g minced beef
- ☐ 10 chicken breasts, skinless
- ☐ 6 pork chops

FISH

- ☐ 6 salmon fillets, with skin

VEGETABLES

- ☐ 7 onions
- ☐ 1 shallot
- ☐ 1 red onion
- ☐ 1 bunch celery
- ☐ 3 carrots
- ☐ 1 courgette
- ☐ 6 baking potatoes
- ☐ 1 garlic bulb
- ☐ 1 celeriac
- ☐ 1 swede
- ☐ 4 leeks
- ☐ 2.5kg potatoes
- ☐ 10–12 radishes
- ☐ 4 spring onions
- ☐ 10–12 cherry tomatoes
- ☐ 1 cucumber
- ☐ 1 red pepper
- ☐ 8 medium tomatoes
- ☐ 1 avocado

FRUIT

- ☐ 2 lemons
- ☐ 800g sharp dessert apples
- ☐ 700g cooking apples

HERBS

- ☐ chives
- ☐ flat-leaf parsley
- ☐ coriander
- ☐ rosemary

FRIDGE ITEMS

- ☐ 1 pack butter
- ☐ 75g frozen petits pois
- ☐ 225g crème fraîche
- ☐ 50g Parmesan cheese
- ☐ 1 egg
- ☐ 1.2 litres fresh chicken stock
- ☐ 100ml apple juice
- ☐ 12 slices pancetta
- ☐ 350ml milk
- ☐ 50g Stilton cheese
- ☐ 240g Cheddar cheese
- ☐ large tub double cream

KITCHEN CUPBOARD ITEMS

- ☐ beef stock cubes
- ☐ salt
- ☐ pine nuts
- ☐ groundnut oil
- ☐ 225g soft brown sugar
- ☐ 50g plain flour
- ☐ 30g walnuts pieces
- ☐ 55g porridge oats
- ☐ 2 x 400g tins chopped Italian tomatoes
- ☐ 400g tin pinto beans
- ☐ 2 x 400g tins butter beans
- ☐ Japanese rice wine
- ☐ sweet sherry
- ☐ dark soy sauce
- ☐ Worcestershire sauce
- ☐ red wine vinegar
- ☐ balsamic vinegar
- ☐ olive oil
- ☐ extra virgin olive oil
- ☐ Dijon mustard
- ☐ 250g linguine
- ☐ 350g spaghetti
- ☐ 1 loaf white bread for breadcrumbs
- ☐ 6 pitta breads
- ☐ 10–12 tortillas

SPICES

- ☐ black peppercorns
- ☐ cumin seeds
- ☐ coriander seeds
- ☐ cinnamon stick
- ☐ ground cinnamon

Minced beef stew
+ baked potatoes

Minced beef is often seen as a cheap, second-rate meal, but I think this recipe makes a great family dinner that both tastes good and is satisfying.

Minced beef stew

1 tablespoon olive oil
1 large onion, finely chopped
1 stick celery, chopped
2 medium carrots, peeled and chopped
800g minced beef
1 tablespoon plain flour
1 beef stock cube
550ml water
salt and pepper
1 courgette, diced
1 tablespoon pine nuts

- Heat the olive oil in a large saucepan.
- Add the onion, celery and carrot and cook for 10 minutes on a low heat until soft.
- Add the minced beef and stir with a wooden spoon until thoroughly browned.
- Add the flour and stir.
- Crumble in the stock cube and add the water.
- Cover and simmer gently for 1 hour.
- Season with salt and pepper.
- Add the courgette and pine nuts and cook uncovered for a further 30 minutes.

Baked potatoes

6 baking potatoes
butter for serving
salt and pepper

- Preheat the oven to 220°C/425°F/gas 7.
- Pierce the potato skins with a sharp knife and bake them for 1 hour 30 minutes.
- Split each one and serve with butter, salt and pepper.

Salmon teriyaki
+ mustard cream linguine

My children love this meal, although they are normally not so keen on salmon, but the teriyaki sauce helpfully disguises the oiliness of the fish, which is the thing that usually puts them off. You won't need as much pasta as you would normally use as the salmon makes the meal quite filling. Prepare the sauce for the linguine first and then start the salmon and pasta.

Salmon teriyaki

For the fish

6 salmon fillets, with skin

2 tablespoons groundnut oil

For the sauce

1 heaped tablespoon sugar

4 tablespoons Japanese rice wine

3 tablespoon sweet sherry

4 tablespoon dark soy sauce

- Make the sauce first by mixing the ingredients together in a small bowl and then set aside.
- Brush the skin of each salmon fillet with some of the groundnut oil.
- Heat the frying pan on the hob until hot.
- Place three fillets into the pan skin side down and cook for 2 minutes, without moving them.
- Turn the fillets over and add half the sauce.
- Cook for a further 2–3 minutes, depending on the thickness of the fillets.
- Cook the remaining three fillets in the same way using the other half of the sauce.
- Serve the salmon on top of the linguine.

Mustard cream linguine

1 tablespoon Worcestershire sauce

1 tablespoon Dijon mustard

200g crème fraîche

250g linguine

salt

75g petits pois, cooked

- Mix the Worcestershire sauce, mustard and crème fraîche in a small bowl.
- Bring a large saucepan of generously salted water to the boil.
- Once boiling, add the linguine and cook following the instructions on the packet.
- Test the pasta 1 minute before the end of the cooking time as the instructions on the packet are not always accurate.
- Toss the cooked pasta in the crème fraîche sauce and then add the cooked peas.

Chicken schnitzel + tomato spaghetti

The chicken is the star of this dish and quite filling, so you won't need a great deal of pasta to satisfy the hungry hordes.

Chicken schnitzel

12 tablespoons breadcrumbs
2 tablespoons Parmesan cheese, grated
salt and pepper
6 chicken breasts, skinless
flour for dusting
1 egg, beaten
2–3 tablespoons olive oil

- Preheat oven to 180°C/350°F/gas 4.
- Place the breadcrumbs in a small bowl.
- Add the Parmesan cheese to the breadcrumbs and season with salt and pepper.
- Place the chicken breasts one at a time between 2 sheets of tin foil and bash them with a steak mallet or a rolling pin until the thickness of the breast has been reduced by half.
- Dust each breast with some flour and then dip each one in the beaten egg.
- Coat each breast in the breadcrumbs.
- Heat 1 tablespoon of olive oil in a frying pan and when hot start cooking the chicken breasts 2 at a time.
- Turn the heat to moderate as you don't want to burn the breadcrumb coating.
- Cook each breast for 4 minutes on each side.
- You can then pop the chicken in the oven to keep warm while you cook the rest, using the remaining olive oil.
- Sprinkle each chicken breast with sea salt just before serving.
- Serve with the tomato spaghetti and some extra Parmesan cheese if you like.

Tomato spaghetti

2 tablespoons olive oil
1 medium onion, finely chopped
½ stick celery, finely chopped
1 small carrot, peeled and finely chopped
1 clove garlic, peeled and chopped
400g tin chopped Italian tomatoes
1 teaspoon sugar
salt and pepper
350g spaghetti

- Heat the olive oil in a heavy-bottomed pan.
- Add the onion, celery, carrot and garlic and cook over a low heat for 10 minutes until softened.
- Add the tomatoes and sugar.
- Bring to a simmer and then reduce the heat to very low and cook uncovered for 30 minutes.
- Season with salt and pepper.
- Meanwhile, cook the spaghetti following the packet instructions.
- Pour the sauce over the spaghetti when cooked.

Autumn vegetable soup + crunchy pitta pockets

This soup combines all the lovely autumn root vegetables that are available in October. You can use a cube for the stock as the vegetable flavours are so strong that the stock cube will just be providing background flavour.

Autumn vegetable soup

60g butter
1 celeriac, peeled and cut into chunks
½ swede, peeled and cut into chunks
1 leek, sliced
500g potatoes, peeled and cut into chunks
1 litre chicken stock
salt and pepper
2 tablespoons double cream and a scattering of chopped flat-leaf parsley for serving

- Warm the butter in a large saucepan.
- Place all the vegetables in the saucepan, cover the pan and cook them for 20 minutes.
- Add the chicken stock and cook, covered, for 30 minutes.
- Purée the vegetables in a food processor or using a hand-held blender.
- If you want the soup to be really smooth you can pass it through a sieve at this stage.
- Once smooth, check the seasoning and when you are ready to serve, warm the soup and add the cream and chopped parsley.

Crunchy pitta pockets

10–12 radishes, sliced
4 spring onions, sliced
10–12 cherry tomatoes, halved
1 stick celery, thinly sliced
½ cucumber, cut into chunks
1 bunch fresh chives, snipped finely
12 slices pancetta
6 pittas, cut in half widthways
For the dressing
1 shallot, thinly sliced into rings
2 dessertspoons red wine vinegar
3 dessertspoons double cream
salt and pepper

- Put all the salad vegetables into a serving bowl.
- Mix the dressing ingredients together in a small bowl and pour over the salad vegetables.
- Fry the pancetta slices until crispy and place in the pitta halves with a spoonful or two of the dressed salad vegetables.
- Serve with the soup.

Chicken fajitas + pinto beans in tomato sauce + guacamole

This sounds complicated but it isn't; you can prepare all the dishes in advance and then heat them up once you are ready to eat – tasty and convenient!

Chicken fajitas

1 tablespoon cumin seeds
1 tablespoon coriander seeds
1 teaspoon salt
1 teaspoon ground black pepper
1 tablespoon olive oil
1 onion, finely chopped
1 red pepper, cored and sliced
1 clove garlic, peeled and finely chopped
4 chicken breasts, cut into strips
10–12 tortillas

- Take the cumin, coriander, salt and pepper and place them in a small, heavy frying pan.
- Toast them over a low heat for 3 minutes, or until you start to smell their aroma.
- Then transfer them to a pestle and mortar, grind to a powder and set aside.
- Next, pour the olive oil into a frying pan and warm it through.
- Add the onion and pepper to the pan and gently fry them for 5 minutes.
- Add the garlic and cook for 30 seconds more.
- Sprinkle the vegetables with the ground spices.
- Turn up the heat and add the chicken, stirring it while it cooks, for 3 minutes.
- Next follow the packet instructions for heating the tortillas.
- Place everything on the table and let everyone assemble their own tortillas with the chicken, beans and guacamole.

Pinto beans in tomato sauce

1 tablespoon olive oil
1 onion, diced
1 clove garlic, peeled and finely chopped
400g tin pinto beans, drained
400g tin chopped tomatoes
salt and pepper
handful flat-leaf parsley, chopped

- Warm the olive oil in a small saucepan, add the onion and garlic and gently cook them for 4 minutes.
- Add the beans and tinned tomatoes and stir.
- Cook them on a low heat for about 40 minutes, uncovered, by which time the tomato sauce should have thickened.
- Season with salt and pepper and sprinkle over the chopped parsley.

Guacamole

1 ripe avocado, peeled and de-stoned
2 ripe tomatoes
1 red onion, finely diced
juice 1 lemon
handful fresh coriander, chopped
salt and pepper

- Place the avocado in a serving bowl and mash it roughly with a fork.
- Prepare the tomatoes by placing them in a small bowl and covering them with boiling water.
- After 1 minute remove them from the water and peel the skins off.
- Chop them roughly and add them to the mashed avocado, along with the red onion, lemon juice, coriander, salt and pepper.
- Mix well and serve.

Cheese, onion and potato pie

This is the time of year when your body starts to crave comfort food. I'm a believer that if your body craves something, it generally needs it and so this pie fits the picture perfectly for a meal on a cold, dark, autumn evening.

1 kg potatoes, peeled and cut into large chunks
1 tablespoon olive oil
60g butter
3 large onions, chopped roughly
3 leeks, washed and sliced into 1cm rounds
3 sticks celery, chopped into 1cm pieces
150ml milk
240g Cheddar cheese, grated
50g Stilton cheese
30g walnuts, chopped into small pieces
salt and pepper

- Boil the potatoes in plenty of salted water until tender.
- Meanwhile, warm the olive oil with 30g of the butter in a frying or sauté pan.
- Add the onions, leeks and celery and cook on a low heat for 20 minutes until the vegetables are lovely and soft with a slight golden tinge.
- Drain the potatoes.
- Take the saucepan in which the potatoes were cooked and pour the milk and the other half of the butter into it.
- Put the potatoes through a potato ricer, allowing them to fall from the ricer back into the saucepan.
- Gently combine the potato with the milk and the butter.
- Fold the Cheddar cheese into the potato and set aside.
- Place the onions, leeks and celery into a medium-sized ovenproof dish and crumble the Stilton cheese over them.
- Sprinkle the walnuts on top.
- Check the seasoning. You probably won't need any salt but you will need pepper.
- Cover the vegetables in the cheesy mashed potato and place under a hot grill for 5 minutes until golden brown.

Pork chops + roast potatoes + white beans + courgettes+ tomato salad

This meal was devised in an effort to use up the last of the season's courgettes and tomatoes. Prepare the vegetables first as the chops do not take long to grill.

Pork chops

6 pork chops
salt and pepper
1 lemon for serving

- Preheat the grill.
- Cover the grill pan with tin foil.
- Season the chops with salt and pepper.
- Place the chops on the grill rack and grill for 5 minutes on each side.

Roast potatoes

1kg potatoes, peeled and quartered for roasting
salt
2 tablespoons olive oil

- Preheat the oven to 220°C/425°F/gas 7.
- Parboil the potatoes in salted water for 4 minutes.
- Drain well and place them in a roasting tin.
- Drizzle with olive oil and roast for 45 minutes until golden brown.

White beans

2 x 400g tins butter beans, drained
1 tablespoon olive oil
1 sprig rosemary, leaves finely chopped
200ml fresh chicken stock
1 tablespoon crème fraîche
salt and pepper

- Place the beans in a small saucepan.
- Add a tablespoon of olive oil, the rosemary, stock and the crème fraîche and heat through on a gentle simmer for 20 minutes.
- Season to taste.

Courgettes

- Preheat the oven to 200°C/400°F/gas 6.
- Slice the courgettes lengthways.
- Lay them on a large baking tray and season them generously with salt and pepper and a drizzle of olive oil.
- Place them in the oven and roast for 20 minutes until browned.
- Sprinkle with the Parmesan cheese and serve.

Tomato salad

6 tomatoes
2 tablespoons extra virgin olive oil
¼ tablespoon balsamic vinegar
salt and pepper

- Slice the tomatoes and arrange them on a serving plate.
- Dress with the oil vinegar, salt and pepper.

Oatmeal apple crumble
+ cream

This is a good Sunday lunch pudding, which starts to make the most of the apples that are in season.

700g cooking apples, peeled, cored and thickly sliced
115g brown sugar
25g plain flour
55g porridge oats
1 teaspoon ground cinnamon
55g butter
cream for serving

- Preheat the oven to 190°C/375°F/gas 5.
- Place the apples in a buttered, ovenproof dish and sprinkle them with half the sugar.
- Sprinkle over 1 tablespoon of water.
- In a bowl, mix together the flour, oats, cinnamon and remaining sugar and rub in the butter.
- Sprinkle this mixture over the apples and place the dish in the oven for 30 minutes.
- Serve with cream.

Apple purée
+ buttered breadcrumbs

This is a dish we always used to have when we were small children.

Apple purée

800g dessert apples, peeled, cored and chopped roughly into chunks
100g soft brown sugar
100ml apple juice
4cm piece cinnamon stick
cream for serving

- Place all the ingredients in a covered saucepan on a low heat and bring to a very gentle simmer.
- Cook for 30 minutes, stirring occasionally, until all the apple pieces are tender.
- Pour the mixture into a food processor and process until smooth.

Buttered breadcrumbs

100g white breadcrumbs
50g butter

- Melt the butter in a frying pan.
- Just as it starts to foam put in the breadcrumbs and, over a medium heat, sauté the breadcrumbs for 5 minutes until golden brown.
- Make sure you stir the breadcrumbs occasionally, so they don't burn.
- Serve them sprinkled on top of the apple purée with the cream.

Week 3

Monday p520	Chicken pie + green beans
Tuesday p522	Meatballs in tomato sauce + spaghetti
Wednesday p523	Baked sea bass + roasted winter vegetables
Thursday p524	Potato bacon cakes + Greek salad
Friday p525	Lentil soup
Saturday p526	Steak Béarnaise + chipped roast potatoes + roast tomatoes with button mushrooms
Sunday p528	Stuffed chicken thighs + mashed potatoes + sautéed leeks
Sunday pudding p530	Eve's pudding
Extra tasty treat p531	Chocolate brownies

Shopping list

MEAT

- [ ] 600g chicken thighs and drumsticks
- [ ] 500g minced beef
- [ ] 500g minced pork
- [ ] 4 sirloin steaks, 200g each in weight
- [ ] 8 chicken thigh fillets

FISH

- [ ] 2 whole sea bass, with skin

VEGETABLES

- [ ] 4 large onions
- [ ] 1 bunch celery
- [ ] 7 carrots
- [ ] 500g button mushrooms
- [ ] 250g green beans
- [ ] garlic bulb
- [ ] 3.5 kg potatoes
- [ ] 1 parsnip
- [ ] 1 red pepper
- [ ] 1 yellow pepper
- [ ] 2 red onions
- [ ] 3 courgettes
- [ ] 5 leeks
- [ ] 9 spring onions
- [ ] 1 cucumber
- [ ] 8 tomatoes
- [ ] 3 shallots

FRUIT

- [ ] 600g bramley apples
- [ ] 2 lemons

FRESH HERBS

- [ ] flat-leaf parsley
- [ ] thyme
- [ ] coriander
- [ ] tarragon

FRIDGE

- [ ] 4 packs butter
- [ ] 11 eggs
- [ ] 26 slices pancetta
- [ ] 200g chopped pancetta
- [ ] 100g frozen peas
- [ ] 2 tablespoons crème fraîche
- [ ] 150g Parmesan cheese
- [ ] 1 small tub mascarpone cheese
- [ ] 250g ricotta cheese
- [ ] 75g soft goat's cheese
- [ ] 200g feta cheese
- [ ] 2 litres ham stock
- [ ] 125ml chicken stock
- [ ] 568ml milk
- [ ] 284ml double cream
- [ ] 2 packs bacon for sandwiches

KITCHEN CUPBOARD ITEMS

- [ ] 500g plain flour
- [ ] salt
- [ ] olive oil
- [ ] chicken stock cubes
- [ ] Dijon mustard
- [ ] 2 x 400g tins chopped tomatoes
- [ ] 500g spaghetti
- [ ] extra virgin olive oil
- [ ] 1 small white loaf for breadcrumbs
- [ ] 150g black olives
- [ ] dried oregano
- [ ] red wine vinegar
- [ ] 500g red lentils
- [ ] white wine vinegar
- [ ] 1 bottle dry white wine
- [ ] 120g light brown sugar
- [ ] 365g caster sugar
- [ ] 65g ground almonds
- [ ] baking powder
- [ ] vanilla extract
- [ ] 100g good-quality milk chocolate
- [ ] 100g good-quality dark chocolate
- [ ] cocoa powder
- [ ] 150g chopped walnuts
- [ ] 1kg cheap sea salt

SPICES

- [ ] black peppercorns
- [ ] paprika
- [ ] ground cinnamon
- [ ] dried oreganno

Chicken pie + green beans

Chicken pie is a great comfort meal at this time of year and usually very popular.

Chicken pie

For the pastry

225g plain flour

140g butter, chilled and cubed

salt

1 egg yolk

2 tablespoons cold water

For the filling

1 tablespoon olive oil

1 large onion, finely diced

1 stick celery, finely chopped

2 carrots, peeled and chopped into 1cm dice

100g button mushrooms

100g sliced pancetta, cut into pieces

600g chicken thighs and drumsticks, skin removed

100g frozen peas

4 medium potatoes, peeled and cut into 2cm cubes

600ml chicken stock (a cube will do)

20g butter

20g plain flour

1 teaspoon Dijon mustard

2 tablespoons crème fraîche

salt and pepper

To make the pastry

- Put the flour and butter in a food processor, or a bowl if you are combining by hand, and incorporate so that the mixture looks like fine breadcrumbs.
- Add a pinch of salt.
- Mix the egg yolk with the cold water in a small bowl, and add to the breadcrumbed mixture.
- Give this a quick whiz in the food processor, if using, and turn out onto a lightly floured work surface and combine thoroughly until you have a firm dough.
- With a light hand, gently knead the pastry dough until its appearance is smooth.
- Wrap it in cling-film and chill in the fridge for at least 20 minutes, while you prepare the filling.

To make the filling

- Preheat the oven to 200°C/400°F/gas 6.
- Heat the oil in a heavy-bottomed saucepan.
- Sauté the onion, celery, carrots and mushrooms gently for 10 minutes until soft.
- Add the pancetta and cook for 3 minutes.
- Add the chicken, peas, potatoes and stock and cook, uncovered, on a medium heat for 40 minutes.
- When the chicken is cool enough to handle remove the meat from the bones and cut it up into small pieces.
- Strain the vegetables and set the stock aside.
- In a small saucepan melt the butter and stir in the flour.
- Cook on a low heat for 2 minutes.
- Gradually add the reserved stock to the butter and flour, slowly at first to avoid lumps, and then more quickly. When you have added all the stock, let the gravy simmer on a low heat for 10 minutes.
- Add the Dijon mustard and crème fraîche to the gravy and stir to combine.
- Place the cut chicken and vegetables in a pie dish and pour over the gravy.
- Cover the top of the pie filling with the pastry, cutting a slit in the top of the pie to allow the steam to escape.
- Glaze the pie with an egg wash (1 egg mixed with 1 tablespoon water), using a pastry brush.
- Place the pie on a baking sheet in the oven and cook for 40 minutes.

Green beans

250g green beans, topped and tailed

salt

knob of butter

black pepper

- Boil a saucepan of salted water.
- Once you have a rolling boil, add the beans and simmer for 5 minutes.
- Drain well and serve with a knob of butter and freshly ground black pepper.

Meatballs in tomato sauce + spaghetti

I struggle to think of a country that doesn't have in its nation's food repertoire a dish that involves rolling ground meat of some sort into a ball and serving it in a broth or sauce. We spend a lot of time in Italy and so this recipe is the Italian version.

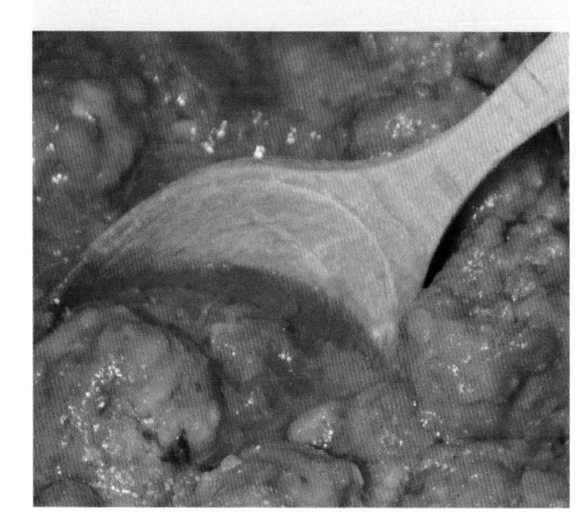

Meatballs in tomato sauce

For the meatballs

500g minced beef
500g minced pork
1 large onion, finely diced
60g Parmesan cheese, finely grated
1 bunch flat-leaf parsley, finely chopped
100g pancetta, finely chopped
salt and pepper
olive oil for frying

For the tomato sauce

1 onion, finely diced
1 carrot, finely diced
1 stick celery, finely chopped
2 cloves garlic, finely chopped
2 x 400g tins chopped tomatoes
salt and pepper
1 teaspoon sugar
1 tablespoon mascarpone cheese
2 tablespoons olive oil

To make the meatballs

- Combine the beef, pork, onion, cheese, parsley and pancetta in a large bowl and season well. To check that you have seasoned the meatballs adequately, fry a little bit of the mixture before you proceed to the next step.
- Form the mixture into balls about the size of a fresh apricot.
- Heat 2 tablespoons of olive oil in a heavy-bottomed frying pan.
- When the oil is hot add 5 or 6 meatballs, turn them regularly so that they brown all over. I use a knife and fork to do this as it tends to stop the meatballs falling apart.
- Once all the meatballs are browned set them aside while you prepare the tomato sauce.

To make the tomato sauce

- Heat the olive oil in a large, heavy-bottomed saucepan on a medium heat.
- Add the onion, carrot, celery and garlic and keep stirring so that the garlic does not burn.
- Sauté the vegetables for 10 minutes until soft.
- Add the tomatoes, sugar, and mascarpone and season with salt and pepper.
- Put the meatballs into the sauce and cook slowly for 1 hour on the hob or in the oven at a setting of 190°C/375°F/gas 5.
- Adjust the seasoning to taste.

Spaghetti

500g spaghetti
salt
Parmesan cheese, grated for serving

- Bring a saucepan of salted water to the boil.
- Cook the spaghetti according to the packet instructions and serve with the meatballs and plenty of grated Parmesan cheese.

Baked sea bass
+ roasted winter vegetables

Sea bass is a great fish to introduce to children as it is quite meaty and the bones come away from the cooked flesh of the fish very easily. Don't be put off by the amount of salt in the recipe, as it does not affect the flavour of the fish in any way.

Baked seabass

2 whole sea bass (skin left on)
1kg sea salt (use the cheapest sea salt you can find)
lemon juice
extra virgin olive oil
salt and pepper

- Preheat the oven to 200°C/400°F/gas 6.
- Take an ovenproof dish that the fish will fit snugly into and cover the bottom of the dish with 1cm of sea salt.
- Place the bass on top and then pile more salt over the fish until it is completely covered.
- Bake for 25 minutes.
- Remove the fish from the salt and serve drizzled with extra virgin olive oil, lemon juice, salt and pepper. The best way to remove the fish from the salt is to pick it up in a couple of layers of kitchen paper. It is a firm fish so it won't disintegrate when you touch it.

Roasted winter vegetables

500g potatoes, peeled and chopped into 2cm pieces
1 parsnip, peeled and chopped into 2cm pieces
1 red pepper, deseeded and sliced into 8 pieces
1 yellow pepper, deseeded and sliced into 8 pieces
1 red onion, quartered
3 courgettes, thickly sliced
1 leek, sliced into 2cm pieces
3 or 4 sprigs fresh thyme
3 whole garlic cloves, peeled
salt and pepper
olive oil

- Preheat the oven to 200°C/400°F/gas 6.
- Parboil the potatoes in salted water for 4 minutes.
- Drain and place them with the other vegetables in a large roasting tin with the thyme, garlic and plenty of salt and pepper and a good amount of olive oil.
- Roast for 45 minutes until golden brown.

Potato bacon cakes + Greek salad

Apart from the little bit of pancetta used in this recipe, the meal is meat free. It is important for a healthy diet to have at least 3 meals a week that don't feature meat as the main item.

Potato bacon cakes

1kg potatoes, peeled and quartered
250g ricotta cheese
4 tablespoons Parmesan cheese, grated
75g soft goat's cheese, crumbled
2 tablespoons fresh coriander, chopped
6 spring onions, finely chopped
100g chopped pancetta
salt and pepper
1 egg, beaten
breadcrumbs for coating
approximately 3 tablespoons olive oil for frying

- Boil the potatoes in a large saucepan of salted water for 15 minutes, until tender.
- Place all the cheeses, coriander, spring onions and pancetta in a mixing bowl.
- When the potatoes are ready mash them, using a masher or a potato ricer. I find that a potato ricer is the best as it is quick and allows the potatoes to stay nice and fluffy.
- Add the mashed potato to the other ingredients in the mixing bowl.
- Season well and add the egg.
- Combine everything together gently and form the mixture into small cakes, weighing approximately 100g each.
- Place the breadcrumbs on a plate and coat each cake with the breadcrumbs.
- Heat the olive oil in a frying pan and cook 4 potato cakes at a time.
- They will need about 7 minutes, on a medium heat, to get nicely brown all over.
- While you are frying the potato cakes, prepare the salad.

Greek salad

1 cucumber, cut in thick slices and quartered
2 tomatoes, cut into chunks
2 sticks celery, sliced
150g black olives
1 small red onion, finely sliced
handful fresh coriander, chopped
200g feta cheese, crumbled
sprinkling dried oregano
For the dressing
1 tablespoon red wine vinegar
2 tablespoons olive oil
salt and pepper

- Place all the salad ingredients in a serving bowl.
- Mix the dressing ingredients together and pour over the salad when ready to serve.

Lentil soup

Pulses should form part of your diet if your goal is to eat in a healthy and balanced way. Serve the soup with a stack of bacon sandwiches. I use pancetta instead of English bacon as I find that most English bacon gives off too much water when you cook it and also lacks flavour.

2 tablespoons olive oil
1 onion, finely diced
4 carrots, peeled and chopped
1 clove garlic, peeled and finely chopped
1 sprig fresh thyme
handful flat-leaf parsley, chopped
500g red lentils
2 litres ham stock
salt and pepper
bacon sandwiches for serving

- Gently heat the olive oil and sauté the onion, carrots and garlic for 5 minutes until soft.
- Add the sprig of thyme and parsley and stir round for 1 minute.
- Add the lentils and stir them round.
- Start to add the ham stock.
- Bring the lentils to the boil.
- As the stock becomes absorbed, add more and cook on a gentle simmer, uncovered, for 45 minutes until the lentils are soft.
- You probably won't need to season it depending on how salty the ham stock is, so taste and see.
- Serve with bacon sandwiches.

TIP

If you haven't got ham stock, use chicken stock instead.

Steak Béarnaise + chipped roast potatoes + roast tomatoes with button mushrooms

Making your own Béarnaise sauce is very satisfying and it really is nothing like the processed substitute. It also is very easy to make. I timed myself making it and it took approximately 10 minutes from start to finish. Steak is quite expensive but get the children to share one between two.

Steak Béarnaise

For the Béarnaise sauce

1 shallot, finely chopped
3 tablespoons white wine vinegar
2 egg yolks
150g soft butter, cut into cubes
salt and pepper

For the steak

4 sirloin steaks, 200g each in weight
salt and pepper
olive oil

To make the Béarnaise sauce

- Place the shallot and vinegar in a small saucepan and bring to the boil.
- Boil the vinegar for 2 minutes to reduce its volume to about 1 tablespoon.
- Strain the vinegar and dispose of the shallot.
- Fill a saucepan with 2cm of water.
- Take a glass bowl that fits snugly over the saucepan, without touching the water below.
- Bring the water to a simmer.
- Place the egg yolks in the glass bowl and mix in the reduced vinegar.
- With a little whisk start adding the butter a cube at a time, making sure it is incorporated before adding another cube.
- Keep the water simmering gently, as you don't want the sauce to curdle.
- Continue until all the butter has been used.
- You should have a thick, pale-yellow sauce.
- Check the seasoning.
- Keep the sauce over the saucepan but remove the saucepan from the heat.
- You can't reheat Béarnaise as it will curdle if you do, but I think it is best served at room temperature anyway, so this doesn't matter.

To cook the steaks

- It is best to cook sirloin steaks on a griddle pan, but if you don't have one use a heavy frying pan.
- Get the pan hot on a high heat.
- Brush both sides of the steak with oil.
- Place the steaks on the hot griddle. You will probably only manage to cook two steaks at a time. If the steaks are about 1.5cm thick then 2 minutes each side will cook them so that they are pink in the middle, but adjust this time to your taste. A thicker sirloin steak, say about 2.5cm thick, will take about 3 minutes each side.
- Season the steaks well with salt and pepper once cooked.

Chipped roast potatoes

500g potatoes
1 tablespoon olive oil
1 teaspoon paprika

- Preheat oven to 220°C/425°F/gas 7.
- Peel the potatoes and cut them into thick chips.
- Parboil the potatoes in boiling, salted water for 3 minutes.
- Drain well and place the potatoes on a baking sheet with the olive oil.
- Sprinkle the paprika over the potatoes and place them in the hot oven for 40 minutes.
- Sprinkle with sea salt on serving.

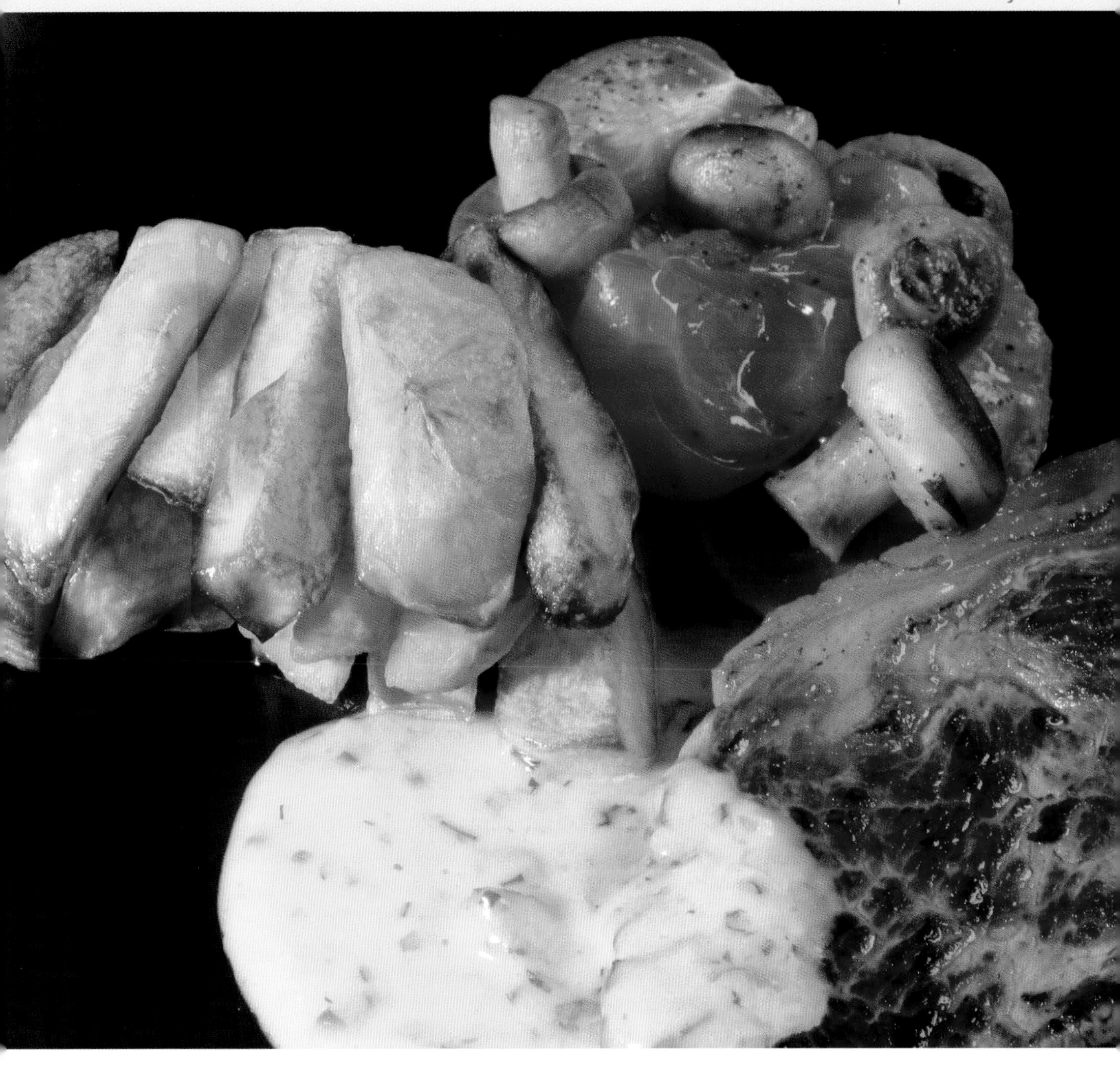

Roast tomatoes with button mushrooms

6 tomatoes, halved
1 dessertspoon olive oil
salt and pepper
40g butter
200g button mushrooms, halved
½ teaspoon tarragon, finely chopped

- Preheat the oven to 200°C/400°F/gas 6.
- Place the tomatoes in a small baking dish and drizzle with olive oil.
- Season with salt and pepper.
- Roast for 15 minutes.
- Melt the butter in a frying pan and cook the mushrooms for 5 minutes on a medium heat until golden brown.
- Season with salt and pepper.
- Toss with the tomatoes and sprinkle the chopped tarragon over the top.

Stuffed chicken thighs
+ mashed potatoes + sautéed leeks

These are slightly more fiddly than most recipes in this book, but not so much as to suppose you couldn't manage them. I have included them on a Sunday as this gives you a bit more time to deal with a more complicated meal.

Stuffed chicken thighs

2 shallots, finely chopped

1 tablespoon flat-leaf parsley, finely chopped

200g button mushrooms, finely chopped

½ teaspoon dried oregano

3 spring onions, finely chopped

salt and pepper

1 egg

8 chicken thighs, bone and skin removed
16 slices pancetta
1 tablespoon olive oil
15g butter
½ tablespoon flour
125ml dry white wine
125ml chicken stock
1 sprig thyme

- Place the shallots, parsley, mushrooms, oregano and spring onions in a small bowl.
- Season with salt and pepper.
- Mix in the egg.
- Lay the chicken thighs out on a work surface or chopping board.
- Spoon a tablespoon of the mushroom mixture onto each thigh and then roll each one up, holding them together by wrapping two slices of pancetta round each one. There will be some stuffing left but you can use this later.
- Heat the olive oil and butter in a sauté pan.
- Place the pancetta wrapped thighs in the pan and brown them all over, taking care when you turn them to prevent them falling apart.
- Remove the thighs from the pan and set aside. Keep the pan on the heat.
- Add the remaining stuffing to the pan and sauté on a medium heat for 2 minutes.
- Sprinkle on the flour and give it a stir to combine.
- Pour on the wine and stock and simmer for about 2 minutes.
- Return the chicken thighs to the pan along with the sprig of thyme.
- Check the seasoning.
- Cover the pan with a lid and cook the chicken on a gentle simmer for 20 minutes.
- Serve with the mashed potato and leeks.

Mashed potato

1kg potatoes, peeled and quartered
40g butter
salt and pepper
200ml warmed milk

- Place the potatoes in cold, salted water and bring to the boil.
- Turn the heat down to a robust simmer on a medium heat.
- Once the potatoes are soft but not mushy, drain them and put them through a ricer.
- Return the mashed potato to the saucepan and place over a low heat.
- Add the milk and butter and gently stir in.
- Remove from the heat.

Sautéed leeks

4 leeks
salt and pepper

- Prepare the leeks by cutting them lengthways, stopping about 1cm from the bottom of the leek so they are still in one piece.
- Wash them under the tap, fanning each leek out as you wash it, to get rid of any grit between the leaves.
- Slice the leeks as thinly as possible and place them in a sauté pan with a sprinkling of salt.
- Gently sauté the leeks on a medium heat for 3 minutes until they are soft. Try not to overcook them as they do not taste as nice when they turn brown.

Eve's pudding

This is an old-fashioned pudding that is becoming popular again. It is good for a Sunday lunch, providing comfort and great taste.

For the fruit filling

600g bramley apples, peeled, cored and finely sliced
120g light brown sugar
1 teaspoon cinnamon

For the sponge

210g butter, softened
165g caster sugar
3 eggs
100g plain flour
65g ground almonds
1 teaspoon baking powder
1 teaspoon vanilla extract
grated zest 1 lemon
1 tablespoon milk
cream for serving

- Preheat the oven to 180°C/350°F/gas 4.
- Grease an ovenproof dish.
- Put the apples into the ovenproof dish and sprinkle the sugar and cinnamon over them.

To make the sponge

- Cream the butter and sugar in a mixing bowl.
- Add 1 egg with 1 tablespoon of flour.
- Mix in completely.
- Add the other 2 eggs in the same way.
- Add the rest of the flour, ground almonds and baking powder and fold in using a metal spoon.
- Add the vanilla extract, lemon zest and the milk and mix in gently.
- Spoon the cake mixture over the top of the apples and place in the oven for 50 minutes.
- Serve with cream.

Chocolate brownies

Does the world need another chocolate brownie recipe? I guess not, but in my defence I would say that I have tried many recipes over the years and my children often say that the brownies are too rich or bitter, but I think this one is just right. Try not to overmix the cake mixture as this produces more of a cake-like quality, which misses the point of brownies.

100g good-quality milk chocolate
100g good-quality dark chocolate
200g butter
3 large eggs
2 teaspoons vanilla extract
200g caster sugar
200g plain flour
1 tablespoon cocoa powder
pinch of salt
150g chopped walnuts

- Preheat the oven to 180°C/350°F/gas 4.
- Grease a 4–5cm deep, 21 x 26cm wide square-shaped cake tin.
- Melt all the chocolate with the butter in a medium saucepan on a very low heat.
- Leave to cool for 10 minutes.
- Gently stir in the rest of the ingredients.
- Pour the mixture into the cake tin and bake for 20 minutes.
- Leave to cool completely in the tin and then cut into squares and serve.

Week 4

Monday p534	Cheese and onion frittata + green salad
Tuesday p535	Keralan chicken stew + cucumber raita + boiled rice
Wednesday p536	Pumpkin soup + cheese on toast
Thursday p538	Sausages + spicy sautéed potatoes + creamy mustard leeks
Friday p539	Baked potatoes with smoked haddock + cucumber and chickpea salad
Saturday p540	Breast of chicken with cream and pea risotto
Sunday p541	Paprika lamb + white beans + mint sauce
Sunday pudding p542	Treacle pudding + ginger cream
Extra tasty treat p543	Vanilla cup cakes

Shopping list

MEAT

- ☐ 1.5 kg chicken thighs and drumsticks
- ☐ 8–10 sausages
- ☐ 4 whole chicken breasts, boneless
- ☐ 1.5kg shoulder lamb

FISH

- ☐ 500g undyed smoked haddock

VEGETABLES

- ☐ 1kg onions
- ☐ 1 Romaine lettuce
- ☐ 2 cucumbers
- ☐ 2 spring onions
- ☐ fresh ginger
- ☐ 1 green chilli
- ☐ 2kg potatoes
- ☐ 6 large baking potatoes
- ☐ 5 shallots
- ☐ 1 pumpkin, weighing about 1.5 kg
- ☐ 1 garlic bulb
- ☐ 5 leeks

FRUIT

- ☐ 2 lemons

FRESH HERBS

- ☐ rosemary
- ☐ chives
- ☐ flat-leaf parsley
- ☐ thyme
- ☐ mint

FRIDGE

- ☐ 12 eggs
- ☐ 200g Parmesan cheese
- ☐ 2 packs butter
- ☐ 200ml natural yoghurt
- ☐ 4 litres chicken stock
- ☐ 700ml double cream
- ☐ 150g Gruyère cheese
- ☐ 300ml milk
- ☐ 150g Cheddar cheese
- ☐ 100g crème fraîche
- ☐ 200ml whipping cream
- ☐ 200g frozen petits pois

KITCHEN CUPBOARD ITEMS

- ☐ olive oil
- ☐ extra virgin olive oil
- ☐ balsamic vinegar
- ☐ vegetable oil
- ☐ salt
- ☐ 1 loaf brown bread
- ☐ 275g plain flour
- ☐ 2 tins coconut milk
- ☐ 225g caster sugar
- ☐ 500g basmati rice
- ☐ sunflower seeds
- ☐ Dijon mustard
- ☐ Worcestershire sauce
- ☐ 400g tin chickpeas
- ☐ Madeira wine
- ☐ 500g Arborio rice
- ☐ 2 x 400g tins cannellini beans
- ☐ red wine vinegar
- ☐ golden syrup
- ☐ black treacle
- ☐ vanilla extract
- ☐ baking powder
- ☐ 250g icing sugar
- ☐ 75g sweetened condensed milk

SPICES

- ☐ black peppercorns
- ☐ cinnamon sticks
- ☐ cloves
- ☐ cardamom pods
- ☐ dried curry leaves
- ☐ black mustard seeds
- ☐ cumin seeds
- ☐ whole nutmeg
- ☐ fennel seeds
- ☐ paprika
- ☐ ground ginger

Cheese and onion frittata + green salad

A frittata is an open Italian omelette, but unlike a French omelette, it is set, not runny. It can have various fillings, but here I have chosen cheese and onion.

Cheese and onion frittata

2 tablespoons olive oil
300g onions, thinly sliced
8 eggs
salt and pepper
150g Parmesan cheese, grated
25g butter
brown bread and butter for serving

- Heat the olive oil in a frying pan and gently cook the onions for 10 minutes, then set aside.
- Place the eggs in a bowl and beat them for 1 minute.
- Add some salt and pepper to the eggs.
- Sprinkle in the cheese.
- Add the onions.
- Preheat the grill.
- Take a heavy-bottomed skillet or frying pan and melt the butter on a medium heat.
- Once the butter starts to foam add the egg mixture and turn the heat to low.
- Once you can see that the eggs are starting to set, place the frying pan under the hot grill, until the top of the frittata has set.
- Cut into pie wedges and serve with the salad and brown bread and butter.

Green salad

For the salad
1 Romaine lettuce, washed and chopped
½ cucumber, sliced
2 spring onions, chopped
For the dressing
1 tablespoon extra virgin olive oil
2 teaspoons balsamic vinegar
salt and pepper

- Assemble the salad in a serving bowl and then pour over the dresssing.

Keralan chicken stew + cucumber raita + boiled rice

This stew, with slight modification, comes from a Madhur Jaffrey recipe. For me, she is the queen of Indian cooking.

Keralan chicken stew

3 tablespoons vegetable oil
1½ teaspoons whole black peppercorns
4cm piece cinnamon stick
10 whole cloves
8 whole cardamom pods
450g onion, thinly sliced
2cm piece fresh ginger, peeled and cut into slivers
1 tablespoon plain flour
1 whole green chilli, cut in half and de-seeded
1.5 kg chicken thighs and drumsticks, skin removed
600ml coconut milk
450g potatoes, cut into thick chips
2 teaspoons salt
1 tablespoon lemon juice
3 shallots, finely chopped
15 dried curry leaves

- Heat 2 tablespoons of vegetable oil in a large casserole saucepan on a medium heat.
- When hot add the peppercorns, cinnamon sticks, cloves and cardamom pods.
- Stir briefly and add the onion and ginger, sautéeing for 10 minutes, on a medium heat.
- Add the flour, stir and add the green chilli, the chicken pieces and coconut milk.
- Bring to a simmer, cover, reduce the heat, and cook for 10 minutes.
- Add the potatoes and salt.
- Bring to a simmer again, cover, turn the heat to low, and cook for 30 minutes.
- Stir in the lemon juice.
- Next, take a small frying pan, heat the remaining tablespoon of vegetable oil and fry the shallots until golden brown.
- Add the curry leaves and cook for 30 seconds.
- Add the shallots and curry leaves to the stew.
- If you are not serving this straight away be careful when you reheat it, as it will curdle unless you heat it very gently.

Cucumber raita

200ml natural yoghurt
salt
sugar
10cm piece cucumber, cut into 1cm cubes
1 dessertspoon vegetable oil
½ teaspoon black mustard seeds
¼ teaspoon whole cumin seeds

- Put the yoghurt in a small serving bowl with a good pinch of salt and sugar and the cucumber.
- Heat the oil in a small frying pan, on a medium heat and add the mustard and cumin seeds.
- As soon as you hear the mustard seeds pop, pour the contents over the yoghurt mixture.
- Stir and serve chilled.

Boiled rice

500g basmati rice
750ml water
salt

- Put the rice in a saucepan with the water and a pinch of salt.
- Place the rice on a high heat and as soon as it comes to the boil, cover the saucepan with a lid and turn the heat right down to very low. Leave it for 15 minutes, giving it one stir only during the cooking time.
- Then take it off the heat and leave it covered for a further 10 minutes, before removing the lid.

Pumpkin soup + cheese on toast

This is the perfect time of year to make use of pumpkin, which is quite reasonably priced when it is in season.

Pumpkin soup

1 pumpkin, weighing about 1.5kg
40g butter
2 onions, finely chopped
1 sprig rosemary
2 cloves garlic, peeled and finely chopped
3 potatoes, peeled and diced
2 litres chicken stock (a cube will do)
3 tablespoons sunflower seeds
1 teaspoon black mustard seeds
nutmeg
salt and pepper
200ml double cream
150g Gruyère cheese, freshly grated

- Preheat the oven to 200°C/400°F/gas 6.
- Quarter and de-seed the pumpkin.
- Wrap the pumpkin pieces in tin foil.
- Place them on a tray in the oven for 1 hour until the pumpkin flesh is tender.
- Using a spoon, remove the pumpkin flesh from the skin and set aside.
- Warm the butter in a large saucepan big enough to accommodate all the soup.
- Add the onion, rosemary and garlic and cook on a low heat for 10 minutes.
- Next, add the pumpkin, potato and chicken stock and cook, covered, for 35 minutes.
- While the soup is cooking, toast the sunflower seeds, mustard seeds and a grating of nutmeg in a small frying pan over a medium heat, until you can smell the aroma of the spices.
- Set aside.
- When the soup has finished cooking, remove the rosemary sprig and purée the soup with a hand-held blender.
- Season to taste.
- Stir in the cream
- Serve with the cheese, seeds and spices scattered on top.
- Accompany the soup with cheese on toast if you have a hungry family.

Cheese on toast

I am not going to patronize anyone by explaining how to make cheese on toast. You can use brown or white bread and don't think you should just stick to Cheddar cheese. Experiment with other cheese you may have lying around in your fridge. Remember to leave the cheese under the grill until it starts to go brown, as I think this makes the difference between a good cheese on toast and a wonderful cheese on toast.

Sausages + spicy sautéed potatoes + creamy mustard leeks

Sausages have acquired a bad name in the crusade against junk foods; but if you are careful about the quality of sausages you buy and you team them up with some good vegetables, then they are great as the basis for a meal.

Sausages

8–10 sausages
olive oil

- Fry the sausages in a little olive oil in a large frying pan.
- Get them brown on a reasonably high heat and then reduce the heat until they are cooked through, which should take about 20 minutes.

Spicy sautéed potatoes

1kg potatoes, peeled and cut into chunks of about 3cm
2 tablespoons olive oil
½ teaspoon fennel seeds
½ teaspoon cumin seeds
½ teaspoon black mustard seeds
salt and pepper

- Boil the potatoes in salted water until tender.
- Drain them and set them aside.
- Heat the oil in a large sauté pan and add the fennel, cumin and mustard seeds.
- Once the seeds start to pop, add the potatoes and sauté them on a medium heat for 20 minutes, until golden brown all over.
- Season with salt and pepper.

Creamy mustard leeks

5 leeks
2 tablespoons double cream
2 teaspoons Dijon mustard
salt and pepper

- Prepare the leeks by removing the outer leaves you don't want and trimming the non root end.
- Cut them lengthways down the middle, stopping about 2cms before the end so the leek is still in one piece.
- Fan the leaves of the leek out under the cold tap while you wash them, to ensure that there is no mud or grit between the leaves.
- Slice them as thinly as possible, widthways.
- Place the leeks in a big frying pan and heat through gently, cooking the leeks until soft, which takes approximately 3 minutes. You need no fat to do this; just cook the leeks in the residual water from washing them.
- When cooked, stir in the double cream and mustard, and season with salt and pepper.

Baked potatoes with smoked haddock + cucumber and chickpea salad

These stuffed baked potatoes are delicious, satisfying and easy to make.

Baked potatoes with smoked haddock

6 large baking potatoes, weighing about 20g each
500g undyed smoked haddock
250ml milk
150g Cheddar cheese, grated
100g crème fraîche
15g chives, snipped
1 dessertspoon Worcestershire sauce
salt and pepper

- Preheat your oven to 200°C/400°F/gas 6.
- Bake the potatoes for 1 hour 20 minutes.
- Meanwhile, place the fish in a large pan with a lid and pour over the milk.
- Poach on the hob on a medium heat, covered, for 3 minutes, then turn the fish over in the pan and cook for 1 further minute.
- Take the fish from the milk and place in a medium-sized bowl.
- Remove the skin and gently flake it up.
- Add the cheese to the fish along with the crème fraîche, chives and Worcestershire Sauce.
- Season to taste.
- Halve the baked potatoes lengthways and spoon the filling on top of each half.
- Place the halves of potato under a hot grill for 1 minute until bubbly and golden brown.

Cucumber and chickpea salad

1 cucumber, sliced
400g tin chickpeas, drained
2 tablespoons flat-leaf parsley, chopped
2 tablespoons extra virgin olive oil
1 dessertspoon balsamic vinegar
salt and pepper

- Put the cucumber, chickpeas and parsley in a serving dish.
- Mix the olive oil, vinegar, salt and pepper together and pour over the salad.

Breast of chicken with cream and pea risotto

I love making risottos and this one is just right for a cold autumn night. It is fragrant and goes well with the tender chicken.

For the breast of chicken with cream

4 whole chicken breasts, boneless
½ lemon
salt and pepper
30g butter
2 wrappers from butter packs or 1 sheet buttered baking parchment
100ml chicken stock
100ml Madeira wine
200ml whipping cream
2 tablespoons flat-leaf parsley, chopped
salt and pepper

For the pea risotto

1.5ml chicken stock
200g frozen petits pois
30g butter
2 shallots, finely chopped
500g Arborio rice
salt and pepper
3 tablespoons Parmesan cheese, grated

To prepare the chicken

- Preheat the oven to 200°C/400°F/gas 6.
- Rub each chicken breast with a little lemon juice and season with salt and pepper.
- Set aside while you get on with the risotto.

To make the risotto

- Heat the stock in a saucepan.
- Season the stock and add the peas, letting the stock simmer gently.
- Take a large, heavy-bottomed pan and melt the butter on a medium heat.
- Add the shallots to the butter and sauté for 5 minutes until soft.
- Add the rice to the shallots and stir to ensure that it gets coated with the butter and oil.
- Cook for 2 minutes, stirring round continuously.
- Add 2 ladlefuls of stock and peas to the rice and stir round.
- Don't let all the liquid disappear completely before adding more hot stock, as you don't want the rice to stick to the pan during cooking.
- Keep adding the stock until the rice is *al dente* (soft on the outside but a little firm in the middle). Cook the risotto for about 20–25 minutes, stirring it almost continuously.
- When the rice is almost cooked you can start to cook the chicken.

To cook the chicken

- Heat the butter in a casserole pan until foaming.
- Place the chicken breasts in the pan and roll them in the butter.
- Remove the pan from the heat and cover with the butter papers or baking parchment.
- Place the casserole pan in the oven, covered, and cook for 7 minutes.
- Remove the breasts from the casserole pan.
- Place the casserole pan on the hob.
- Get the chicken juices bubbling and add the stock and Madeira.
- Boil for 1 minute.
- Add the cream and boil for another minute.
- Add the parsley.
- Place the chicken breasts in a serving dish and pour the sauce over the top.
- Sprinkle the Parmesan cheese over the risotto and serve with the chicken.

Paprika lamb
+ white beans+ mint sauce

This is a change to the usual roast lamb one would eat for Sunday lunch. Get the lamb into the oven, then prepare the mint sauce and lastly the beans.

Paprika lamb

1.5kg shoulder of lamb
olive oil
1 tablespoon cumin seeds
1 teaspoon paprika
1 tablespoon salt

- Preheat the oven to 230°C/450°F/gas 8.
- Place the lamb joint in a roasting tin.
- Rub the olive oil into the joint.
- Grind the cumin seeds with the paprika and salt, and rub them into the lamb joint.
- Roast the lamb for 10 minutes.
- Reduce the temperature to 140°C/275°F/gas 1 and roast for another 2 hours.
- Remove from the oven to rest for 15 minutes before carving.

White beans

2 x 400g tins cannellini beans, drained
1 potato, peeled and halved
1 onion, peeled and halved
1 sprig fresh thyme
300ml chicken stock
salt and pepper

- Place the beans in a saucepan with the potato, onion, thyme and stock.
- Bring the pan to a simmer and cook gently for 40 minutes, covered.
- Remove the pan from the heat.
- Take the potatoes out of the saucepan and gently mash them with a fork.
- Return the mashed potato to the saucepan with the beans.
- Check the seasoning and serve with the lamb.

Mint sauce

2 tablespoons olive oil
1 clove garlic, peeled and finely chopped
4 tablespoons fresh mint, finely chopped
1 teaspoon cumin seeds
1 tablespoon red wine vinegar
1 teaspoon caster sugar
salt and pepper

- Gently heat the olive oil in a small saucepan.
- Add the garlic and fry for a few minutes, making sure that it does not burn.
- Add the mint and cumin seeds and fry for about 1 minute.
- Add the wine vinegar and stir round for about 30 seconds.
- Add the sugar and season with salt and pepper.

Treacle pudding + ginger cream

Treacle pudding is a quintessential English dessert. It is the perfect end to an Autumn Sunday lunch. The only thing you will feel like doing after lunch is putting your feet up in front of the television.

Treacle pudding

100g plain flour
1 teaspoon baking powder
100g butter, softened
100g caster sugar
2 eggs
2 tablespoons golden syrup
2 tablespoons black treacle
1 tablespoon milk
1 teaspoon ground ginger
extra warmed syrup for serving

- Grease a small pudding basin.
- Sift together the flour and baking powder and set aside.
- Cream the butter and sugar together in a mixing bowl using a hand-held mixer.
- Add 1 egg to the butter and sugar with 1 tablespoon of sifted flour and mix in.
- Add the next egg with a further tablespoon of sifted flour and mix in.
- Add the rest of the flour, syrup, treacle, milk and ground ginger and fold in using a metal spoon.
- Spoon the mixture into the pudding basin and cover the top of the pudding with a circle of baking parchment.
- Cover the pudding basin with more baking parchment and secure it with string.
- Take a large saucepan and fill it with a couple of centimetres of water.
- Place the pudding basin inside the saucepan, cover the saucepan and bring the water to the boil.
- Keep the water simmering around the pudding basin for 2 hours. Top up the water regularly so that it doesn't run dry.
- Remove the basin from the saucepan.
- Place a plate on top of the basin and then tip the basin over to release the pudding.
- Serve with ginger cream and more syrup if you like.

Ginger cream

400ml double cream
½ teaspoon ground ginger

- Pour the cream into a mixing bowl and whisk it until it is thickening, taking care not to overwhisk as you will end up with butter.
- Sprinkle on the ground ginger and serve with the treacle pudding.

Vanilla cup cakes

Like many people, I collect recipes from newspapers and magazines. I then mislay them and never get round to using them more than once. This book, at the very least, has given me the opportunity to record some of my favourites.

For the cakes
125g butter, very soft
125g caster sugar
2 eggs
2 teaspoons vanilla extract
150g plain flour
2 teaspoons baking powder
For the frosting
75g butter, very soft
250g icing sugar, sieved
75g sweetened condensed milk
75ml double cream

- Preheat the oven to 180°C/350°F/gas 4.
- Place the butter, sugar, eggs and vanilla into the bowl of an electric mixer.
- Beat on the highest speed for 3 minutes.
- Sift the flour and baking powder together twice and then turn them into the egg mixture.
- Beat for 30 seconds.
- Spoon the mixture into 8 muffin cups, placed in a muffin tray.
- Bake for 25 minutes until golden and firm.
- Once cool prepare the frosting.
- Beat the ingredients in a bowl until smooth and combined.
- Swirl onto the cakes.

NOVEMBER

Week 1

Monday p546	Beef stew + dauphinois potatoes
Tuesday p547	Tuna and sweetcorn bake + broccoli
Wednesday p548	Lamb and bacon patties with curry sauce + boiled rice
Thursday p550	Herbed breaded haddock + chipped roast potatoes + mushy peas
Friday p551	Spaghetti amatriciana
Saturday p552	Roast ham and egg on toast + baked beans
Sunday p553	Bean and chorizo stew
Sunday pudding p554	Pears in caramel sauce + coconut sponge
Extra tasty treat p555	Chocolate fudge cake

Shopping list

MEAT

- ☐ 1.3kg joint unsmoked gammon
- ☐ 500g minced lamb
- ☐ 1.5kg stewing steak

FISH

- ☐ 6 skinless haddock fillets, weighing approx. 150–200g each

VEGETABLES

- ☐ 7 onions
- ☐ 3.5kg potatoes
- ☐ 1 garlic bulb
- ☐ 400g broccoli
- ☐ 5 carrots
- ☐ 1 bunch celery
- ☐ 200g white cabbage
- ☐ 1 fresh chilli

FRUIT

- ☐ 6 pears
- ☐ 1 lemon

FRESH HERBS

- ☐ bay leaves
- ☐ thyme
- ☐ mint
- ☐ flat-leaf parsley
- ☐ chives
- ☐ dill
- ☐ rosemary

FRIDGE ITEMS

- ☐ 1 litre double cream
- ☐ 284ml single cream
- ☐ 150ml low-fat crème fraîche
- ☐ 650ml milk
- ☐ 3 packs butter
- ☐ 12 eggs
- ☐ 400g chopped pancetta
- ☐ 100g chorizo sausage
- ☐ 200ml chicken stock
- ☐ 250g frozen peas
- ☐ 150g Cheddar cheese
- ☐ 100g Gruyère cheese
- ☐ 50g Parmesan cheese

KITCHEN CUPBOARD ITEMS

- ☐ vanilla extract
- ☐ 175g dark chocolate
- ☐ 300g icing sugar
- ☐ golden syrup
- ☐ 200g plain flour
- ☐ 325g caster sugar
- ☐ baking powder
- ☐ bicarbonate of soda
- ☐ 40g cocoa powder
- ☐ 75g self-raising flour
- ☐ 75g desiccated coconut
- ☐ 100g soft brown sugar
- ☐ black treacle
- ☐ 3 x 400g tins haricot beans
- ☐ 400g tin borlotti beans
- ☐ 400g tin butter beans
- ☐ Worcestershire sauce
- ☐ tomato purée
- ☐ olive oil
- ☐ 2 loaves white bread
- ☐ salt
- ☐ black pepper
- ☐ 4 x 400g tins chopped tomatoes
- ☐ 475g spaghetti
- ☐ 500g basmati rice
- ☐ vegetable stock cubes
- ☐ 50g sultanas
- ☐ 500g tin yellow fin tuna
- ☐ 350g tin sweetcorn
- ☐ 600ml Guinness
- ☐ 1 bag Maltesers

SPICES

- ☐ coriander seeds
- ☐ cumin seeds
- ☐ fennel seeds
- ☐ fenugreek
- ☐ whole nutmeg
- ☐ black pepper
- ☐ dried oregano

Beef stew
+ dauphinois potatoes

This recipe is one of those that needs to be prepared well in advance of the mealtime as it is all cooked slowly. The kitchen will, however, be full of wonderful cooking smells as everyone comes in. On the subject of potatoes, I do advocate using organic ones. I once read an article written by a non-organic potato grower, who wouldn't eat the potatoes he produced commercially, because in order to guarantee a profitable yield he had to make sure that, through the use of chemicals, there were no living creatures in the ground in which he grew his crops. He consequently grew organic potatoes for his own family's consumption.

Beef stew

2 tablespoons olive oil
1.5kg stewing steak
1 onion, finely chopped
4 carrots, sliced into batons
1 stick celery, finely chopped
4 cloves garlic, peeled and kept whole
1 tablespoon plain flour
2 tablespoons tomato purée
600ml Guinness
sprig fresh thyme, bay leaf, and sprig fresh rosemary
salt and pepper

- Preheat the oven to 150°C/300°F/gas 2.
- Heat the olive oil in a heavy casserole pan that has a lid and can also be used in the oven.
- Brown the beef in batches and set aside.
- Keep the saucepan on the heat and add the onion, carrots, celery and garlic.
- Once they start to brown, sprinkle with the flour and stir.
- Add the tomato purée, stir and put the meat back into the saucepan.
- Pour in the Guinness and add the herbs.
- Bring to a simmer.
- Season and cover the saucepan with a sheet of greaseproof paper and the lid.
- Cook in the oven for 1 hour 30 minutes.

Dauphinois potatoes

1kg waxy potatoes, peeled and sliced to the thickness of a pound coin
1 clove garlic, peeled and halved
salt and pepper
100g Gruyère cheese, grated
75g butter
200ml milk
nutmeg

- Preheat the oven to 170°C/325°F/gas 3.
- Rinse the potatoes in cold water and pat them dry with kitchen paper.
- Butter an ovenproof gratin dish.
- Rub the garlic clove over the buttered dish.
- Scatter half the potatoes on the bottom of the dish and season with salt and pepper.
- Next, sprinkle over half the cheese and half the butter, cut into little pieces.
- Arrange the remaining potatoes on top and season with salt and pepper.
- Sprinkle on the remaining cheese and the rest of the butter, again in little pieces.
- Pour on the milk and sprinkle on a grating of nutmeg.
- Bake for 1 hour 30 minutes.

Tuna and sweetcorn bake + broccoli

This is a great dish to get smiles on the faces of your children and I must say that I like the excuse to eat it as well, so make enough for the whole family. I use yellow fin tuna as this is superior to the everyday variety.

Tuna and sweetcorn bake

1kg potatoes, peeled and quartered
50g butter
40g plain flour
450ml milk
500g tin yellow fin tuna, drained of its oil
350g tin sweetcorn, drained
1 tablespoon flat-leaf parsley, chopped
150g Cheddar cheese, grated
black pepper

- Put the potatoes into salted water and boil them until cooked.
- Drain them and once cool enough slice them to the thickness of a pound coin.
- Set the potatoes aside.
- Melt the butter in a medium-sized saucepan and add the flour.
- Remove the saucepan from the heat and add the milk little by lttle, to avoid lumps.
- Once the milk is incorporated, return the saucepan to a medium heat and bring to a gentle simmer.
- When the sauce starts to bubble, turn down the heat to low and let it cook very gently for about 10 minutes, stirring occasionally. This will avoid the floury taste one often experiences with badly cooked white sauces.
- Add the tuna fish, sweetcorn and parsley.
- Then add the cheese, saving a small sprinkling for the top of the dish once it is ready to go in the oven.
- Add a grinding of black pepper. It shouldn't need any salt.
- Put the mixture into a gratin dish, arrange the cooked potatoes on top and sprinkle on the spare cheese.
- Set the dish aside until you are ready to serve.
- When you are ready, place the dish under a preheated very hot grill until it browns and starts to bubble.

Broccoli

400g broccoli
salt
lemon juice
black pepper

- Trim the broccoli into florets. If the stalks are very thick trim them down a little.
- Bring a pan of slightly salted water to the boil.
- Add the broccoli florets and cook on a simmer for 3 minutes.
- Drain well and season with a squeeze of lemon juice and a grinding of black pepper.

Lamb and bacon patties with curry sauce + boiled rice

This recipe is based on one by Nigel Slater in an old *Sainsbury Magazine*. As is usual with his recipes, you can conjure up something in the kitchen which is tasty, quick and perfectly in tune with what one feels like eating. I have changed the odd thing, but the gist of it remains the same.

Lamb and bacon patties with curry sauce

For the curry sauce

1 tablespoon olive oil
1 medium onion, finely diced
2 level teaspoons curry powder*
2 tablespoons sultanas
300ml vegetable stock (a cube will do)
150ml low fat crème fraîche

For the lamb and bacon patties

500g minced lamb
70g chopped pancetta
1 small onion, finely chopped
1 garlic clove, peeled and finely chopped
1 tablespoon dill, finely chopped
2 tablespoons flat-leaf parsley, finely chopped
salt and pepper
2 tablespoons olive oil

To make the curry sauce

- Preheat the oven to 220°C/425°F/gas 7.
- Heat the olive oil in a small saucepan.
- Add the onions and sauté for 10 minutes until soft and tinged with brown.
- Stir in the curry powder and cook for 2 minutes.
- Add the sultanas and vegetable stock and bring to the boil.
- Turn down to a very gentle simmer for about 10 minutes.
- Remove from the heat and gently beat in the crème fraîche.

To make the lamb and bacon patties

- Mix the lamb, pancetta, onion, garlic and herbs together in a mixing bowl and season generously with salt and pepper.
- Divide the mixture into 8 patties and roughly shape these into rounds.
- Don't flatten them, they should remain round rather than be burger-like.
- Heat the olive oil in a frying pan and brown three patties at a time, for 2 minutes on each side.
- Then place the browned patties into an ovenproof dish.
- Pour the curry sauce over the patties, cover the dish with tin foil and cook in the oven for about 20 minutes.

To make your own curry powder:

1 tablespoon coriander seeds
1 dessertspoon cumin seeds
1 teaspoon fennel seeds
½ teaspoon fenugreek

- *Place the coriander seeds into a small, heavy-bottomed pan and heat through for 30 seconds.*
- *Add the other ingredients and toast until you smell the lovely aroma of the spices.*
- *Transfer the spices to a coffee grinder, a small processor or grind them in a pestle and mortar.*

Boiled rice

500g basmati rice
750ml water
salt

- Put the rice in a saucepan with the water and a pinch of salt.
- Place the rice on a high heat and as soon as it comes to the boil cover the saucepan with a lid and turn the heat right down to very low. Leave it for 15 minutes, giving it one stir only during the cooking time.
- Then take it off the heat and leave it covered for a further 10 minutes, before removing the lid.

Herbed breaded haddock
+ chipped roast potatoes + mushy peas

These mushy peas are just perfect with the haddock. Make the peas first and set them aside. Then prepare the potatoes and bread the fish. Cook the fish at the last moment.

Herbed breaded haddock

150g–200g white breadcrumbs
1 teaspoon thyme leaves, finely chopped
1 tablespoon flat-leaf parsley, chopped
1 tablespoon chives, finely snipped
1 heaped teaspoon dried oregano
salt and pepper
6 skinless haddock fillets, weighing approx. 150–200g each
flour for dusting
2 eggs, beaten
2 tablespoons olive oil

- Place the breadcrumbs and herbs in a bowl.
- Season well with salt and pepper.
- Dust each fish fillet with flour and then dip each one in the beaten egg.
- Next dip each one in the breadcrumb mixture, ensuring each fillet is well covered with breadcrumbs.
- When ready to cook the fish, heat the olive oil in a large frying pan.
- Fry two fillets at a time, for 2 minutes on each side and drain on kitchen paper.

Roasted chipped potatoes

1 kg potatoes
2 dessertspoons olive oil
salt and pepper

- Preheat the oven to 220°C/425°F/gas 7.
- Peel the potatoes and cut them lengthways into quarters.
- Place them in a pan of salted water and bring to the boil.
- Reduce the heat and let them simmer for 5 minutes.
- Drain them.
- Place the potatoes in a roasting tin and drizzle the olive oil over them.
- Roast for 45 minutes.
- Sprinkle a dusting of sea salt on the potatoes when you are ready to serve them.

Mushy peas

30g butter
1 onion, finely diced
60g cubed pancetta
250g frozen peas
1 fresh mint sprig
200ml chicken stock, fresh or cube
200g potatoes, peeled and diced
1 fresh thyme sprig
salt and pepper
3 tablespoons single cream

- Warm the butter in a sauté pan or medium saucepan.
- Sauté the onion and pancetta in the butter for 10 minutes until the onion is soft and golden.
- Add the peas, mint, stock, potato and thyme and season with salt and pepper.
- Bring to a simmer.
- Reduce the heat, cover the pan and cook gently until the potato is tender, which should take 10 minutes. The potato should be soft enough to purée well.
- Remove the herbs and purée the mixture very briefly in a liquidiser or using a hand-held blitzer. It shouldn't be too smooth.
- Stir in the cream and add extra stock if the mixture needs loosening slightly.
- Adjust the seasoning if necessary.

Spaghetti amatriciana

Amatriciana is a very well known tomato-based pasta sauce. It is well deserving of its renown.

1 dessertspoon olive oil
150g chopped pancetta
1 onion, finely diced
2 x 400g tins chopped Italian tomatoes
1 fresh chilli, deseeded and finely chopped
salt and pepper
475g spaghetti
Parmesan cheese, freshly grated

- Gently warm the olive oil in a heavy sauté pan.
- Add the pancetta and cook for 1 minute on a low heat.
- Add the onion and cook for 10 minutes until soft and slightly browned.
- Add the tomatoes and chilli and season with salt and pepper.
- Reduce the heat, cover and simmer gently for 40 minutes.
- Add a little water if you feel the sauce is too thick at the end of the cooking period.
- Cook the spaghetti in a large pan of well-salted boiling water.
- Drain well and top with the sauce and some grated Parmesan cheese.

Roast ham and egg on toast + baked beans

Needless to say, these are homemade baked beans. They have a smoky barbecued flavour and are great with baked ham. This is really an American-style meal. Prepare the beans while the gammon is simmering.

Roast ham and egg on toast

For the roast ham

1.3kg joint unsmoked gammon

For the eggs and toast

6 eggs

olive oil for frying

6 slices bread for toasting

To prepare the ham

- Place the gammon joint in a large saucepan and cover it with water.
- Bring it to the boil, cover and then simmer gently for 1 hour.
- Preheat the oven to 200°C/400°F/gas 6.
- Remove the layer of skin from the gammon joint and place the joint on a meat tray.
- Roast the joint for 30 minutes.
- Remove from the oven and leave to rest for 15 minutes.
- When ready to serve, slice the ham to a medium thickness.

To prepare the eggs

- Fry the eggs in the olive oil and serve each egg on top of a slice or two of ham and toast with the beans on the side.

Baked beans

1 tablespoon olive oil

1 medium onion, diced

1 bay leaf

100g chopped pancetta

3 x 400g tins haricot beans, drained

1 tablespoon Worcestershire sauce

1 tablespoon tomato purée

400g tin chopped tomatoes

2 teaspoons brown sugar

1 tablespoon black treacle

salt and pepper

- Heat the olive oil in a saucepan.
- Add the onion, bay leaf and pancetta and sauté for 5 minutes.
- Add the haricot beans and the rest of the ingredients and bring to a gentle simmer.
- Season with salt and pepper.
- Cover and simmer for 1 hour.

Bean and chorizo stew

Chorizo provides a lovely smoky flavour when it is used in stews. It is one of those ingredients that adds so much more than one usually anticipates.

3 tablespoons olive oil
1 onion, finely chopped
1 stick celery, finely chopped
1 carrot, chopped
1 sprig thyme
2 medium potatoes, peeled and cut into eighths
200g tinned tomatoes
200g white cabbage, thinly shredded
400g tin borlotti beans, drained
400g tin butter beans, drained
500ml water
salt and pepper
100g chorizo sausage, sliced
olive oil
Parmesan cheese, grated

- Heat a little olive oil in a large saucepan.
- Gently cook the onion, celery and carrot for about 5 minutes.
- Add the thyme, potatoes and tomatoes and cook for 2 minutes.
- Next add the cabbage, beans and water.
- Cook on a steady simmer, slightly covered, for 30 minutes.
- Season generously with salt and pepper.
- Fry the chorizo in a little olive oil and add it to the stew.
- Serve with grated Parmesan cheese.

Pears in caramel sauce + coconut sponge

English pears are still plentiful at this time of year so make the most of them. Here the pears go very well with the caramel sauce.

Pears in caramel sauce

6 pears, peeled, cored and quartered
50g butter
75g soft brown sugar
150ml double cream

- Preheat the oven to 200°C/400°F/gas 6.
- Place the pears in an ovenproof dish.
- Dot with butter and sprinkle with sugar.
- Bake for 15 minutes.
- Remove the pears from the oven and baste them in the juices and sugar and then return them to the oven for a further 15 minutes.
- Remove from the oven, stir in the cream and serve the pears with the slices of the sponge and whipped cream.

Coconut sponge

125g butter, softened
125g caster sugar
2 tablespoons warm water
2 eggs
75g self-raising flour
½ teaspoon baking powder
75g desiccated coconut
whipped cream for serving

- Grease and line a 1kg loaf tin.
- Preheat the oven to 180°C/350°F/gas 4.
- Cream the butter and sugar together until light and fluffy. This takes a good 5 minutes with an electric mixer.
- Add the water and stir to combine.
- Add the eggs and beat to combine. The mixture will look curdled at this point, but once you fold in the flour it will be fine.
- Fold in the flour, baking powder and coconut.
- Spoon the mixture into the loaf tin and bake for 35 minutes.
- Cool on a wire rack before turning out.

Chocolate fudge cake

This chocolate cake will not disappoint. It's quick and easy to bake. It's moist and really chocolatey.

For the cake

200g plain flour
200g caster sugar
1 teaspoon baking powder
½ teaspoon bicarbonate of soda
40g cocoa powder
175g butter, softened
2 large eggs
2 teaspoons vanilla extract
150ml double cream

For the icing

75g butter
175g dark chocolate
300g icing sugar
1 tablespoon golden syrup
125ml double cream
1 teaspoon vanilla extract
Maltesers (optional)

To make the cake

- Preheat the oven to 180°C/350°F/gas 4.
- Butter and line 2 x 20cm sandwich tins with removeable bases.
- Place all the cake ingredients into a mixing bowl and incorporate with a hand-held electric mixer until smooth.
- Then divide the mixture evenly between the 2 cake tins.
- Bake the cakes for 25–30 minutes. Test with a skewer in the centre of the cakes and if it comes out clean then they are ready.
- Remove the cakes from the tins and cool on a wire rack before icing.

To make the icing

- Melt the chocolate and butter in a glass bowl over a saucepan of barely simmering water.
- Sieve the icing sugar into another mixing bowl.
- Add the golden syrup to the chocolate and pour this chocolate mixture over the icing sugar, mixing with a wooden spoon.
- Then stir in the cream and vanilla. If the icing is too thick, add a teaspoon or so of water.
- Sandwich the 2 cakes together with the icing and then spread what is left over the top and round the sides of the cake.
- Decorate the top with Maltesers if desired.

Week 2

Monday p558	Pork curry + lentil curry + tomato salad + boiled rice
Tuesday p560	Tagliatelle with pink prawn cream sauce + green salad + garlic bread
Wednesday p561	Chicken stew + buttered brown rice
Thursday p562	Fontina-filled omelettes + roasted pepper salad
Friday p563	Baked halibut + sautéed paprika potatoes + shredded Brussels sprouts with pancetta
Saturday p564	Steak and kidney pie + carrots and parsnips + boiled potatoes
Sunday p565	Roast soy chicken + spicy roasted potatoes + sesame broccoli
Sunday pudding p566	Bread and butter pudding
Extra tasty treat p567	Christmas mincemeat

Shopping list

MEAT
- ☐ 1kg diced pork
- ☐ 1kg chicken drumsticks
- ☐ 1kg shin beef
- ☐ 250g lambs kidneys
- ☐ 2 x 1.2kg chickens

FISH
- ☐ 375g cooked king prawns
- ☐ 6 halibut steaks

VEGETABLES
- ☐ 4 onions
- ☐ 1 garlic bulb
- ☐ fresh ginger
- ☐ 2 green chillies
- ☐ 7 tomatoes
- ☐ 1 shallot
- ☐ 1 Romaine lettuce
- ☐ 1 cucumber
- ☐ 5 spring onions
- ☐ 2.9kg potatoes
- ☐ 3 peppers mixed colour
- ☐ 125g young spinach leaves
- ☐ 1 bunch celery
- ☐ 300g Brussels sprouts
- ☐ 300g carrots
- ☐ 300g parsnips
- ☐ 1 whole broccoli

FRUIT
- ☐ 2 lemons
- ☐ 500g apples
- ☐ 1 orange
- ☐ 250g mixed berries

FRESH HERBS
- ☐ flat-leaf parsley
- ☐ coriander
- ☐ thyme
- ☐ bay leaf
- ☐ rosemary

FRIDGE ITEMS
- ☐ 1 litre double cream
- ☐ 1 pack butter
- ☐ 250g frozen peas
- ☐ 12 eggs
- ☐ 50g Parmesan cheese
- ☐ 150g Fontina cheese
- ☐ 100g feta cheese
- ☐ 200g Gruyère cheese
- ☐ 70g chopped pancetta
- ☐ 100ml double cream
- ☐ 1 pack puff pastry
- ☐ 575ml whole milk

KITCHEN CUPBOARD ITEMS
- ☐ 200g red lentils
- ☐ 600ml coconut milk
- ☐ 500g basmati rice
- ☐ salt
- ☐ 1 bottle red wine
- ☐ brandy
- ☐ 1 bottle dry white wine
- ☐ olive oil
- ☐ vegetable oil
- ☐ sesame oil
- ☐ balsamic vinegar
- ☐ soy sauce
- ☐ 500g tagliatelle
- ☐ 200g pitted black olives
- ☐ 500g brown rice
- ☐ 200g tinned tomatoes
- ☐ tomato purée
- ☐ beef stock cubes
- ☐ chicken stock cubes
- ☐ Dijon mustard
- ☐ 1 loaf brown bread
- ☐ 60g glace cherries
- ☐ 250g vegetables suet
- ☐ 170g caster sugar
- ☐ 350g brown sugar
- ☐ clear honey
- ☐ 200g candied peel
- ☐ sesame seeds
- ☐ 6 or 7 croissants
- ☐ 250g currants
- ☐ 310g sultanas
- ☐ 375g raisins
- ☐ 60g whole almonds
- ☐ 1 baguette
- ☐ 50g plain flour
- ☐ 1 vanilla pod

SPICES
- ☐ black peppercorns
- ☐ curry leaves
- ☐ chilli powder
- ☐ turmeric
- ☐ ground cumin
- ☐ cardamom pods
- ☐ cloves
- ☐ cinnamon stick
- ☐ cumin seeds
- ☐ black mustard seeds
- ☐ coriander seeds
- ☐ fennel seeds
- ☐ fenugreek
- ☐ whole nutmeg
- ☐ piccante paprika
- ☐ Chinese five spice powder
- ☐ sichuan pepper
- ☐ mixed spice

Pork curry + lentil curry + tomato salad + boiled rice

This is a very tasty Sri-Lankan style curry. My mother cooked it regularly when I was growing up and I loved it.

Pork curry

1 tablespoon vegetable oil
1 medium onion, thinly sliced
3 cloves garlic, peeled and finely chopped
2cm fresh ginger, peeled and finely chopped
10 curry leaves
¼–½ teaspoon chilli powder
2 dessertspoons curry powder*
1 fresh green chilli, deseeded and quartered
¼ teaspoon turmeric
1 teaspoon ground cumin
10 cardamom pods, bruised in a pestle and mortar
5 cloves
3cm piece cinnamon stick
1 dessertspoon tomato purée
1kg pork, diced
400ml coconut milk
200ml water
salt

- Heat the oil until hot in a large, heavy-bottomed saucepan.
- Add the onion and sauté for 2 minutes on a medium heat.
- Add the garlic, ginger and curry leaves and cook for a further 2 minutes.
- Then add the chilli powder, curry powder, fresh chilli, turmeric, cumin, cardamom, cloves and cinnamon stick, stirring constantly for 1 minute.
- Add the tomato purée and stir in.
- Next add the meat and stir fry for 2 minutes.
- Pour in the coconut milk and enough water to make a reasonably thick gravy.
- Season with salt and cook on a slow simmer for 30 minutes, until the meat is tender to the bite.

Lentil curry

1 tablespoon vegetable oil
1 medium onion, finely diced
6 curry leaves
½ teaspoon cumin seeds
½ teaspoon turmeric
½ teaspoon black mustard seeds
200g red lentils
1 teaspoon salt
200ml coconut milk
600ml water

- Heat the vegetable oil in a medium saucepan.
- Add the onion, curry leaves, cumin seeds, turmeric and black mustard seeds and cook until the onion starts to turn a golden brown. This should take about 5 minutes.
- Add the lentils and water and bring to a simmer.
- Reduce the heat to the slightest simmer and cook, partially covered, for about 40 minutes.
- Try the lentils and if there is still the slightest hardness to them, cook for a few minutes longer.
- Add the coconut milk and bring back to a simmer.
- Finally, add the salt and set aside.
- Reheat when you are ready to serve.

Tomato salad

3 fresh tomatoes, chopped into pieces
squeeze of fresh lemon
salt and pepper
½ shallot, chopped finely
fine shavings fresh green chilli

- Mix all the ingredients together in a serving bowl and serve with the pork and lentils.

Boiled rice

400g basmati rice
600ml water
salt

- Cook the rice by placing it in a saucepan with the water and a small pinch of salt.

- Put the rice on a high heat and as soon as it comes to the boil, cover the saucepan with a lid and turn the heat right down to very low.
- Leave it on a low heat for 15 minutes.
- Then remove the pan from the heat, but leave it covered for a further 10 minutes.

**** To make your own curry powder:***

1 tablespoon coriander seeds
1 dessertspoon cumin seeds
1 teaspoon fennel seeds
½ teaspoon fenugreek

- *Place the coriander seeds into a small, heavy-bottomed pan and heat through for 30 seconds.*
- *Add the other ingredients and toast until you smell the lovely aroma of the spices.*
- *Transfer the spices to a coffee grinder, a small processor or grind them in a pestle and mortar.*

Tagliatelle with pink prawn cream sauce + green salad + garlic bread

This recipe originates from Marcella Hazan. I have adapted it to use cooked prawns and slightly more of them. I would not normally advocate having a salad with pasta as it is certainly not the way the Italians eat it. They would only eat pasta as a precursor to something more substantial. The everyday English way of eating is not quite like this. This pasta dish is too rich, however, to serve in large quantities, so a salad and some bread makes it more filling. Don't be put off by the amount of olive oil used, the dish in no way tastes oily.

Tagliatelle with pink prawn cream sauce

1½ tablespoons tomato purée
100ml dry white wine
6 tablespoons olive oil
2 cloves garlic, peeled and finely chopped
375g cooked king prawns
salt and pepper
100ml double cream
2 tablespoons fresh flat leaf parsley, chopped
500g tagliatelle, cooked following the packet instructions

- In a small measuring jug, mix the tomato purée and wine together and set aside.
- Heat the olive oil in a sauté pan.
- Add the garlic and cook it on a medium heat until it turns a golden brown. Be careful not to hurry this as the garlic will burn.
- Add the tomato purée and wine to the garlic and oil and cook on a gentle heat for 10 minutes.
- Add the prawns to the garlic and tomato purée mixture and warm through for 1 minute only, as the prawns are already cooked.
- Season with salt and pepper.
- Remove from the heat.
- Purée 3 tablespoons of the prawn mixture in a blender or food processor.
- Mix the puréed prawns into the whole prawns and add the cream and parsley.
- Put on a low heat and very slowly bring it to the boil.
- Pour the sauce over the cooked tagliatelle and serve with the salad below.

Green salad

For the salad
1 Romaine lettuce, washed and chopped
½ cucumber, sliced
2 spring onions, chopped
For the dresssing
1 tablespoon olive oil
2 teaspoons balsamic vinegar
salt and pepper

- Assemble the salad in a serving bowl and then pour the dresssing over the top.

Garlic bread

1 baguette
40g butter, softened
2 cloves garlic, peeled and crushed

- Preheat the oven to 200°C/400°F/gas 6.
- Make diagonal incisions into the baguette every 3cm, without cutting through the bread completely.
- Mix the garlic with the butter and fill each incision with a spreading of garlic butter.
- Wrap the baguette completely in tin foil and bake for 20 minutes.

Chicken stew + buttered brown rice

This is slightly different from your everyday stew due to the black olives and the simplicity of the other vegetables.

Chicken stew

1 tablespoon olive oil
1 medium onion, finely diced
2 cloves garlic, peeled and finely chopped
½ teaspoon turmeric
1kg chicken drumsticks, skin removed
600ml water
150g pitted black olives
4 medium potatoes, peeled and quartered
250g frozen peas
salt and pepper
1 tablespoon fresh coriander, chopped

- Heat the olive oil in a large saucepan and add the onion and garlic, cooking them on a medium heat for 5 minutes.
- Add the turmeric and stir round.
- Add the chicken drumsticks and cook for 5 minutes until the chicken is slightly browned.
- Add the water, olives, potatoes and peas.
- Season with salt and pepper.
- Bring to a simmer.
- Turn the heat down, cover and cook for 20 minutes.
- Remove the lid of the saucepan and cook for a further 20 minutes.
- Garnish with coriander and serve.

Buttered brown rice

500g brown rice
750ml water
salt
knob of butter

- Place the rice in a saucepan with the water and a small pinch of salt.
- Put the rice on a high heat and as soon as it comes to the boil, cover the saucepan with a lid and turn the heat right down to very low.
- Leave it on a low heat for 15 minutes.
- Then take the pan off the heat but leave it covered for a further 10 minutes.
- Gently fold in the butter.

Fontina-filled omelettes + roasted pepper salad

I am always rather unexcited by the thought of omelettes for dinner, until I sit down to eat them and then I feel that they are definitely worth their place in culinary history. Prepare the salad first and then make the omelettes. You will need a frying pan that fits under the grill, as these omelettes are a little different from the normal French-style omelette.

Fontina-filled omelettes

8 eggs
salt and pepper
1 tablespoon flat-leaf parsley, chopped
2 tablespoons Parmesan cheese, grated
1 tablespoons olive oil
150g Fontina cheese, grated
brown bread and butter for serving

- Beat 4 of the eggs in a glass bowl.
- Season them with salt and pepper and sprinkle in half the parsley and half the Parmesan cheese.
- Heat the olive oil in a frying pan and when hot add the egg mixture.
- Cook it through on one side but keep it runny on the top.
- Sprinkle all the grated Fontina cheese over the top of the eggs.
- Beat the reamining 4 eggs in a bowl, adding the rest of the Parmesan and parsley.
- Pour these eggs over the cooked eggs in the pan and place under a hot grill for 3 minutes.
- Serve immediately with the salad below and bread and butter.

Roasted pepper salad

3 peppers of mixed colour, each deseeded and sliced into 8 pieces
1 tablespoon olive oil
salt and pepper
125g young spinach leaves
4 tomatoes, chopped
1 tablespoon olives
100g feta cheese, cubed
½ cucumber, sliced
3 spring onions, sliced
For the dressing
3 dessertspoons olive oil
1 dessertspoon balsamic vinegar
salt and pepper

- Preheat the oven to 200°C/400°F/gas 6.
- Place the peppers on a baking tray with the olive oil. Season them with salt and pepper and roast them for 30 minutes.
- Meanwhile, prepare the rest of the salad ingredients and place them in a serving bowl.
- When the peppers are done, toss them into the bowl as well.
- Pour the dressing over the salad just as you are ready to serve.

Baked halibut + sautéed paprika potatoes + shredded Brussels sprouts with pancetta

Halibut goes very well with cheese. It's very simple and straightforward.

Baked halibut

6 halibut steaks (if you can only get fillets, reduce the cooking time to about 8 minutes)
salt and pepper
200g Gruyère cheese, grated
1 tablespoon Dijon mustard
3 tablespoons double cream

- Preheat the oven to 190°C/375°F/gas 5.
- Butter an ovenproof dish.
- Place the fish steaks in the dish and season with salt and pepper.
- Mix the cheese with the mustard and cream and spread this mixture over the fish steaks.
- Bake for 20 minutes.

Sautéed paprika potatoes

850g potatoes, peeled and chopped into chunks
salt
2 tablespoons olive oil
1 teaspoon piccante paprika

- Boil the potatoes in salted water until tender.
- Heat the olive oil in a large sauté pan.
- Put in the potatoes and sauté them for 20 minutes, moving them occasionally.
- Sprinkle on the paprika and a little more salt if necessary and serve.

Shredded Brussels sprouts with pancetta

300g Brussels sprouts, tailed, trimmed and finely shredded
70g chopped pancetta
1 tablespoon olive oil
salt and pepper

- Heat the olive oil in a sauté pan.
- Add the sprouts and stir them in the hot oil for 1 minute.
- Reduce the heat and continue to cook the sprouts until they become tender, which should take about 5 minutes.
- Then add the pancetta and sauté for 2 minutes more.
- Season with salt and pepper.

Steak and kidney pie
+ carrots and parsnips + boiled potatoes

Steak and kidney pie is an English favourite. I use shin of beef, which has a full beefy flavour and requires long, slow cooking. If you are short of time, use stewing beef, but my own view is that there is no point bothering with braising beef as it is completely tasteless.

Steak and kidney pie

3 tablespoons olive oil
1kg beef shin, cut into 3cm pieces and trimmed of any obvious pieces of fat
250g lamb's kidneys, cut into 2cm pieces
1 onion, finely chopped
1 stick celery, finely chopped
2 glasses red wine
1 heaped tablespoon plain flour
salt and pepper
1 bay leaf
1 sprig thyme
200ml tinned tomatoes
600ml beef stock (a cube is fine)
1 pack puff pastry

- Heat the olive oil in a heavy-based saucepan.
- Brown the beef in two batches, setting each browned batch aside while you do the other.
- Briefly brown the kidneys in the same oil and set aside with the browned beef.
- Keep the saucepan on the heat and sauté the onions and celery for 5 minutes until soft.
- Remove the onions and celery and set aside with the meat.
- Add the wine to the empty saucepan and, as it reduces, scrape round the saucepan with a wooden spoon to loosen all the bits of meat.
- Let the wine reduce at a simmer for 2 minutes.
- Meanwhile, sprinkle the flour over the meat and vegetables and season with salt and pepper.
- Return the meat and vegetables to the saucepan and add the herbs, tomatoes and beef stock.
- Bring to the boil and then turn down to a very gentle simmer.
- Cook for 1 hour 45 minutes, partially covered. If you are using stewing beef, cook for 1 hour.
- Stir occasionally, and if you feel you have too much liquid, remove the saucepan lid altogether.
- Preheat the oven to 220°C/425°F/gas 7.
- Pile the meat into a pie dish, cover it with a layer of puff pastry and make a hole in the top for the steam to escape.
- Place in the oven for 30 minutes until the pastry has risen and is a lovely golden colour.

Carrots and parsnips

15g butter
300g carrots, peeled and cut into 1cm slices
300g parsnips, peeled and cut into 1cm slices
100ml white wine
1 sprig rosemary
salt and pepper

- Warm the butter in a medium saucepan.
- Add the carrots and parsnips and stir them round, coating them in the butter.
- Add the wine and let it sizzle away for 2 minutes.
- Add the rosemary, cover the pan and cook the vegetables on a low heat for 20 minutes until they are tender.
- Season with salt and pepper.

Boiled potatoes

750g potatoes, peeled and quartered
salt and pepper

- Put the potatoes into a saucepan of salted water.
- Bring to the boil and reduce heat to a simmer.
- Simmer the potatoes until tender to the tip of a sharp knife.
- Serve with black pepper and a dab of butter.

Roast soy chicken
+ spicy roasted potatoes + sesame broccoli

This chicken recipe is somewhat different from the standard Sunday roast chicken. It is far from authentic Chinese fare, but uses some eastern flavours that I think make a nice change.

Roast soy chicken

1 tablespoon clear honey
1 teaspoon fresh ginger, finely chopped
1 tablespoon sesame oil
1 teaspoon ground sichuan pepper
1 tablespoon soy sauce
2 x 1.2kg chickens
salt

- Preheat the oven to 180°C/350°F/gas 4.
- In a small bowl mix together the honey, ginger, oil, sichuan pepper and soy sauce.
- Place the chickens in a meat tin and coat them with half the honey mixture.
- Sprinkle each chicken with crumbled sea salt and cover them with tin foil.
- Roast the chickens for 20 minutes.
- Remove the foil and re-coat the chickens with the remaining honey mixture.
- Increase the oven temperature to 200°C/400°F/gas 6.
- Return the chickens to the oven, uncovered, and roast for a further 40 minutes.

Spicy roasted potatoes

1kg potatoes, peeled and chopped into quarters
salt
Chinese five spice powder
1 tablespoon olive oil
2 teaspoons sesame oil

- Preheat the oven to 200°C/400°F/gas 6.
- Parboil the potatoes for 5 minutes.
- Drain well, return them to the saucepan and sprinkle them with chinese five spice powder and drizzle them with the olive and sesame oil.
- Put them in a roasting tin and roast for 40 minutes until crispy and brown.

Sesame broccoli

1 whole broccoli, trimmed and cut into florets
salt
1 teaspoon sesame seeds

- Place a saucepan of slightly salted water on the stove and bring to the boil.
- Add the broccoli and cook for 3 minutes.
- Sprinkle with the sesame seeds and serve.

Bread and butter pudding

This recipe is based on Alastair Little's panettone bread and butter pudding that appeared in his book *Keep it Simple*, which, unfortunately, has now gone out of print. I first tasted this pudding at a friend's house and could not get over how wonderful it was. I tried to get the book, not knowing it had gone out of print and then happened upon it in a second-hand bookshop. It is truly one of the best puddings you will ever eat at home, so please try it. It will need at least 3 hours to chill before serving, so make it the night before you require it or first thing in the morning.

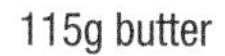

115g butter
6 or 7 croissants
55g sultanas
575ml whole milk
575ml double cream
4 eggs
170g caster sugar
1 teaspoon vanilla essence
double cream and berries to serve

- Preheat the oven to 160°C/320°F/gas 2½.
- You will need an ovenproof dish that is about 5cm deep.
- Split and butter the croissants using the sultanas as a filling. Sandwich the croissants back together.
- Cut each croissant into 3 pieces and place all the pieces into an ovenproof dish, squashing them in so they fit snugly.
- Next, whisk the milk, cream, eggs, sugar and vanilla together in a bowl.
- Pour the mixture over the croissants and leave it to soak for 30 minutes.
- Place the dish in a large meat tin.
- Pour 2cm of water into the meat tin to surround the ovenproof dish (this is called a 'bain Marie') and place the meat tin in the oven for 1 hour, until golden brown.
- Remove from the oven and serve with double cream and berries.

Christmas mincemeat

It never ceases to amaze me how quickly Christmas comes round each year. It is a good idea to get organized and make your mincemeat now as it benefits from a few days in the mixing bowl before you put it into jars. If you have never made mincemeat before, then do try this as homemade mincemeat is so much nicer than bought mincemeat and it is easy to make. Over the years, my mother and I have tried various recipes but we have always returned to this one, which was the recipe she always used when we were children. I am not sure where it originally came from.

375g raisins
500g apples, unpeeled and grated
250g currants
250g sultanas
60g almonds
rind and juice 1 lemon
rind and juice 1 orange
2 teaspoons mixed spice
60g glace cherries, chopped
250g vegetable suet
350g brown sugar
200g candied peel, chopped small
1 small nutmeg, grated
½ teaspoon salt
3 tablespoons brandy

- Place all the ingredients in a large mixing bowl and mix thoroughly.
- If you have a mincer, mince half of the mixture, placing it back in the mixing bowl with the other unminced half. If you don't have a mincer, use a food processor instead.
- Cover the mincemeat with a cloth and set aside in the kitchen.
- The mincemeat is much better if you give it a good stir every day for a week and then put it into jars. Leaving it in the bowl for a while stops the mincemeat fermenting.
- Put the mincemeat into jars, making sure that you squash it in as tightly as you can. This is to make sure that there are no trapped air pockets.
- Cover the top of the mincemeat with a small circle of greaseproof paper and secure the lid of the jar. You can keep mincemeat for at least 1–2 years.

Week 3

Monday p570	Spicy prawn and chicken pilaf + tomato, cucumber and yoghurt salad
Tuesday p571	Minestrone soup
Wednesday p572	Sausage and bean casserole + mashed potato
Thursday p573	Pasta with pesto sauce + red onion and cheese bread
Friday p574	Cottage pie + white cabbage
Saturday p575	Grilled cod + roasted chipped potatoes + mushy peas
Sunday p576	Roast beef fillet + roast potatoes + vegetables + Yorkshire pudding + gravy
Sunday pudding p578	Apple and banana crunch
Extra tasty treat p579	Christmas pudding + brandy butter

Shopping list

MEAT

- 3 small chicken breasts
- 10 pork sausages
- 1kg minced beef
- 750g fillet beef

FISH

- 300g cooked prawns
- 6 thick cod fillets

VEGETABLES

- 5 onions
- 1 garlic bulb
- fresh ginger
- 6 tomatoes
- ½ cucumber
- 1 bunch celery
- 400g carrots
- ½ Savoy cabbage
- 4.35kg potatoes
- 1 red onion
- 400g parsnips
- 1 white cabbage
- 1 shallot
- 4 leeks

FRUIT

- 5 lemons
- 675g cooking apples
- 3 bananas

FRESH HERBS

- coriander
- sage
- 2 packs basil
- thyme
- mint
- flat-leaf parsley

FRIDGE ITEMS

- 9 eggs
- 250ml natural yoghurt
- 100g chopped pancetta
- 3.7 litres chicken stock
- 450g frozen peas
- 100g Parmesan cheese
- 1 litre milk
- 2 packs butter
- 100g Pecorino cheese
- 200ml double cream
- 100ml single cream
- 200ml crème fraîche
- 250g butter *(for brandy butter: make it in Christmas week)*

KITCHEN CUPBOARD ITEMS

- olive oil
- balsamic vinegar
- 600g basmati rice
- 50g creamed coconut
- salt
- 75g cashew nuts
- 200g tin borlotti beans
- 600g tin chopped tomatoes
- 400g tin cannellini beans
- extra virgin olive oil
- pine nuts
- 500g spaghetti
- fast-action dried yeast
- 375g strong white bread flour
- 450g plain flour
- tomato purée
- beef stock cubes
- 225g soft brown sugar
- 75g walnut pieces
- 500g vegetable suet
- 500g raisins
- 250g mixed peel
- 75g caster sugar
- 1 large loaf white bread for breadcrumbs
- 500g sultanas
- 250g currants
- 110g whole almonds
- vegetable oil
- 250g icing sugar *(for brandy butter: make it in Christmas week)*
- brandy *(for brandy butter: make it in Christmas week)*

SPICES

- black peppercorns
- coriander seeds
- cumin seeds
- fennel seeds
- fenugreek
- ground cinnamon
- whole nutmeg
- mixed spice

Spicy prawn and chicken pilaf
+ tomato, cucumber and yoghurt salad

It always amazes me that a pilaf actually works. Everything looks so uncooked when you cover it and leave it for the 15 minutes or so, and then when you remove the lid of the saucepan you are hit with the sight of a perfectly cooked rice dish and the wonderful eastern smell of the pilaf.

Spicy prawn and chicken pilaf

3 tablespoons olive oil
1 onion, finely chopped
1 clove garlic, peeled and finely chopped
1cm fresh ginger, peeled and finely chopped
500g basmati rice
1 teaspoon curry powder*
50g creamed coconut, cut into 1cm pieces
1.5 litres chicken stock
3 small chicken breasts, cut into bite-sized chunks
salt and pepper
75g cashew nuts
300g cooked prawns
2 tablespoons coriander, chopped

- Heat the oil in a large saucepan with a lid.
- Add the onion, garlic and ginger and cook on a medium heat for 7 minutes.
- Stir in the rice to coat it with the oil.
- Add the curry powder and creamed coconut, stirring until dissolved.
- Pour in the stock.
- Add the chicken pieces.
- Season with a little salt and pepper.
- Cover and simmer on a low heat for 15 minutes until the liquid is absorbed and the rice is tender. Avoid removing the lid during this time.
- Meanwhile, place the cashew nuts in a small frying pan with a dessertspoon of olive oil and stir continuously until browned.
- When the rice is cooked stir in the prawns, chopped coriander and cashew nuts.
- Adjust the seasoning if necessary.

To make your own curry powder:
1 tablespoon coriander seeds
1 dessertspoon cumin seeds
1 teaspoon fennel seeds
½ teaspoon fenugreek

- *Place the coriander seeds into a small, heavy-bottomed pan and heat through for 30 seconds.*
- *Add the other ingredients and toast until you smell the lovely aroma of the spices.*
- *Transfer the spices to a coffee grinder, a small processor or grind them in a pestle and mortar.*

Tomato, cucumber and yoghurt salad

3 tomatoes, chopped
½ cucumber, chopped
250ml natural yoghurt
salt and pepper

- Place the tomato, cucumber and yoghurt in a small serving bowl and season with salt and pepper.

Minestrone soup

This is a really thick winter soup, filled with goodness. My children tend to eat the bits they like and leave those they don't, such as the cabbage.

40g chopped pancetta
1 clove garlic, finely chopped
1 onion, finely chopped
1 tablespoon flat-leaf parsley, chopped
1 stick celery, finely chopped
2 tablespoons olive oil
3 fresh tomatoes, chopped
2 carrots, chopped into small pieces
3 potatoes, peeled and chopped into 2cm chunks
200g tin borlotti beans, drained
2 litres chicken stock
½ Savoy cabbage, finely shredded
200g frozen peas
100g basmati rice
4 fresh sage leaves, roughly chopped
6 fresh basil leaves, roughly chopped
Parmesan cheese, grated to serve

- Finely re-chop the pancetta with the garlic and onion.
- Add the parsley and celery to the pancetta, garlic and onion and chop again.
- Heat the olive oil in a large saucepan, add the chopped vegetables and pancetta and cook for 5 minutes until softened.
- Add the tomato, carrots, potatoes and beans and stir around.
- Pour on the stock and cook, covered, on a slow simmer for 30 minutes.
- Add the cabbage and peas and simmer for a further 10 minutes.
- Add the rice and cook for about 18 minutes until it is tender.
- Stir in the herbs, season and serve with plenty of grated Parmesan and crusty bread.

Sausage and bean casserole + mashed potato

This is one of those meals that makes you wonder how and why people have given up cooking for their families. It is so easy and absolutely appropriate for the time of year.

Sausage and bean casserole

1 tablespoon olive oil
10 pork sausages
1 onion, finely chopped
1 stick celery, chopped
4 sage leaves, roughly chopped
600g tin chopped tomatoes
400g tin cannellini beans, drained
salt and pepper

- Heat the olive oil in a large saucepan over a medium heat.
- Fry the sausages, browning them all over.
- Add the onion, celery and sage leaves to the sausages and cook on a medium heat for 7 minutes until soft.
- Add the tomatoes and beans and bring to a gentle simmer.
- Cover and cook for 45 minutes.
- Season with salt and pepper.

Mashed potato

1kg potatoes, peeled and quartered
salt and pepper
200ml warmed milk
40g butter

- Place the potatoes in cold, salted water and bring to the boil.
- Turn the heat down to a robust simmer on a medium heat.
- Once the potatoes are soft but not mushy, drain them and put them through a potato ricer.
- Return the mashed potato to the saucepan and set on a low heat.
- Add the milk and butter and gently stir in.
- Remove from the heat and season to taste.

TIP

I use a potato ricer to make mashed potato, as I have found it's the only way of removing all the lumps and it's quicker than a masher. I also resist the temptation of cutting the potatoes into small cubes prior to cooking them as, while the potatoes cook more quickly, I don't think you get such a good flavour when they're mashed.

Pasta with pesto sauce + red onion and cheese bread

Home-made pesto is far superior to the processed kind and it is straightforward to make. I know pesto is not a wintry dish, but this recipe comes as a welcome relief from all the winter comfort food that one feels obliged to serve up at this time of year. The strong flavour of a traditional green pesto has been tempered slightly by the addition of double cream. I know that bread is time-consuming to make, but I have included this recipe as it is simple.

Pasta with pesto sauce

50g fresh basil leaves
8 tablespoons extra virgin olive oil
3 tablespoons pine nuts
2 cloves garlic, peeled and finely chopped
good pinch of salt
50g Parmesan cheese, freshly grated
2 tablespoons Pecorino cheese, freshly grated
45g butter, softened
200ml double cream
500g spaghetti

- Put a large saucepan of salted water on to boil.
- Whizz the basil, olive oil, pine nuts, garlic and salt in a food processor until creamy.
- Transfer this mixture to a bowl and stir in the cheeses, butter and cream by hand.
- Cook the spaghetti following the packet instructions.
- When ready, drain the pasta and pour the pesto sauce over it. Serve with the bread and some more grated Parmesan.

Red onion and cheese bread

For the bread
250ml warm water
1 x 7g sachet fast-action dried yeast
375g strong white bread flour
1 tablespoon olive oil
1 good teaspoon salt
For the topping
1 tablespoon olive oil
1 medium red onion, thinly sliced
1 sprig fresh thyme
1 tablespoon balsamic vinegar
50g Pecorino cheese, grated

To make the bread
- Pour 50ml of the water into a large mixing bowl and add the yeast.
- Leave for 2 minutes and then stir briefly.
- Add the flour, olive oil, salt and remaining water.
- Mix until loosely combined.
- Turn out onto a sparsely floured work surface, work to a manageable dough and continue to knead for 10 minutes.
- Return the dough to the bowl, cover with a clean tea towel and let the dough rise for 1½–2 hours.

To make the topping
- Heat the olive oil in a frying pan or saucepan.
- Add the onion and thyme sprig and cook on a gentle heat for 10 minutes until softened.
- Add the vinegar and stir round until incorporated, for about 1 minute.
- Remove the thyme sprig and set aside.

To assemble the bread
- Preheat the oven to 220°C/425°F/gas 7 and grease a baking tray.
- Once the bread has risen, turn it out onto a floured surface and, with a rolling pin, roll out the dough into a rectangle with dimensions of about 35cm x 25cm.
- Spread the red onion on to the bread and sprinkle on the Pecorino cheese.
- Cover with a tea towel and leave to rise for 30 minutes.
- Bake for 15 minutes.

Cottage pie
+ white cabbage

This is a winter warmer favourite in most families. Cottage pie is satisfying, tasty and can be prepared in advance so you can pop it in the oven when you get home.

Cottage pie

2 tablespoons olive oil
1 medium onion, finely chopped
1 carrot, peeled and chopped
1kg minced beef
1 tablespoon plain flour
1 tablespoon tomato purée
175ml beef stock (a cube will do)
salt and pepper
1kg potatoes, peeled and quartered
300ml milk
30g butter
2 tablespoons flat-leaf parsley, finely chopped

- Warm the olive oil in a large saucepan.
- Add the onion and carrot and cook on a medium heat for 10 minutes.
- Increase the heat and add the mince, stirring continuously to brown it and break it up.
- Once the meat is brown, reduce the heat and add the flour, stirring it in.
- Then add the tomato purée and stock.
- Season with a little salt and pepper.
- Bring the meat to a simmer and cook very gently for 30 minutes, covered.
- Remove the saucepan lid and cook the mince uncovered for another 30 minutes.
- Cook the potatoes by boiling them in salted water for 10–15 minutes until they are soft enough to mash.
- Drain them.
- Put the potatoes through a ricer back into the saucepan in which they were cooked. Pour in the milk, add the butter and set aside.
- Check the seasoning of the meat and adjust as necessary.
- Add the chopped parsley.
- Spoon the meat into an ovenproof dish and smooth the mashed potato over the top.
- Mark ridges on the top of the pie with a fork.
- When ready to serve, place under a hot grill for 5 minutes until browned on top.

White cabbage

1 white cabbage, thinly sliced
20g butter
salt and pepper
squeeze of fresh lemon juice

- Place the cabbage in a large saucepan with a dessertspoon of water and the butter.
- Put the lid on and cook the cabbage on a low heat, stirring occasionally, for 5 minutes.
- Season to taste with salt, freshly ground black pepper and a squeeze of lemon juice.

Grilled cod
+ roasted chipped potatoes + mushy peas

Mushy peas go wonderfully with cod. On the subject of cod, I am conscious of its diminishing quantity so try to buy Icelandic, line-caught cod, or other more plentiful white fish where possible. Prepare the peas first, then the potatoes and finally, the fish.

Grilled cod

6 thick fillets cod
salt and pepper
lemon juice

- Heat the grill until hot.
- Line the grill tray with aluminium foil. This will make less mess when you come to grill the fish.
- Season the fillets with salt and pepper and place them under the grill.
- Grill the fillets for 2 minutes and then turn them over. If the cod you have is not thick, then adjust the cooking time accordingly.
- Season the fish again and grill it for a further 2 minutes.
- Squeeze some lemon juice onto the fish and serve on top of a tablespoon or two of the mushy peas with the potatoes on the side.

Roasted chipped potatoes

1kg potatoes
2 dessertspoons olive oil
salt and pepper

- Preheat the oven to 220°C/425°F/gas 7.
- Peel the potatoes and cut them lengthways into quarters.
- Place them in a pan of salted water and bring them to the boil.
- Reduce the heat and simmer for 5 minutes.
- Drain them well.
- Place the potatoes in a roasting tin and drizzle the olive oil over them.
- Roast for 45 minutes.
- Sprinkle with sea salt and serve.

Mushy peas

1 onion, finely diced
60g chopped pancetta
30g butter
250g frozen peas
1 fresh mint sprig
200ml chicken stock, fresh or cube
200g potatoes, peeled and cut into 1cm dice
1 fresh thyme sprig
salt and pepper
3 tablespoons single cream

- Sauté the onion and pancetta in the butter on a low heat for 10 minutes.
- Add the peas, mint, stock, potatoes, thyme and salt and pepper.
- Bring to a simmer, cover and cook gently until the potato is tender. This should take about 10 minutes. The potato should be soft enough to purée well.
- Remove the herbs and purée the mixture briefly in a liquidizer or using a hand-held blitzer. The purée doesn't need to be too smooth.
- Stir in the cream and add extra stock if the mixture needs loosening.
- Adjust the seasoning if necessary.

Roast beef fillet + roast potatoes + vegetables + Yorkshire pudding + gravy

Fillet of beef is an expensive cut of meat and, while I am conscious of not suggesting food that is out of some people's price range, I have included it here because I think it is one of the most superb cuts of beef you can eat. If you feel it is rather expensive, buy a smaller piece of fillet and have plenty of vegetables and Yorkshire puddings with it. Also, you will see that the other meals this week are relatively cheap, so overall you should stay within your weekly budget. One of the most difficult things about preparing a roast lunch is to get everything ready to come to the table at the same time. The beef here takes just a short time to roast, so get it ready to go in the oven and cook it about 15 minutes before you are ready to eat and plan the accompanying dishes around this time.

Roast beef fillet

750g fillet of beef (based on 2 adults and 4 children eating)
1 shallot, finely sliced
1 sprig fresh thyme
1 tablespoon olive oil
salt and pepper

- Bring the meat to room temperature by taking it out of the fridge 30 minutes before you are going to cook it.
- Preheat the oven to 230°C/450°F/gas 8.
- Sprinkle the sliced shallot in the bottom of a roasting tin with the thyme and place the meat on top of it.
- Coat the joint in olive oil and season it with salt and pepper.
- Place the meat in the oven for about 15 minutes.
- Reduce the oven temperature to 140°C/275°F/gas 1 and roast the beef for another 10 minutes.
- When cooked, leave the meat to rest for 15 minutes before carving into slices.

Roast potatoes and parsnips

1kg potatoes, peeled, halved and rinsed in cold water
400g parsnips, peeled and halved
salt
2 tablespoons olive oil

- Preheat the oven to 220°C/425°F/gas 7.
- Parboil the potatoes and parsnips for 4 minutes in salted water. Before you drain them, remember to keep all the vegetable water to add to the gravy, so strain the potatoes and parsnips into something that will catch the water.
- Give them a shake in the pan to crumble their edges a little.
- Place the vegetables in a roasting tin with the olive oil.
- Roast the potatoes and parsnips for 1 hour 20 minutes.

Carrots

300g carrots, peeled and cut into 1cm thick, 5cm long batons
butter
salt and pepper
handful flat-leaf parsley, chopped

- Bring some of the used vegetable water to the boil and add the carrots.
- Simmer for 5 minutes and then drain.
- Serve with a little butter, salt, pepper and some parsley.

Leeks

4 leeks
salt and pepper
200ml crème fraîche
1 tablespoon Parmesan cheese, grated

- Prepare the leeks by cutting them lengthways down the middle, stopping about 1cm from the bottom of the leek so it's still in one piece.
- Wash the leeks under the tap, fanning each leek out as you wash it to get rid of any grit between the leaves.
- Slice the leeks as thinly as possible and place them in a sauté pan with a sprinkling of salt.
- Start to cook the leeks gently on a medium heat.
- Cook for 2 minutes, stirring regularly.
- Stir in the crème fraîche.
- Spoon the leeks into an ovenproof serving dish.
- Season with pepper and sprinkle over the Parmesan cheese.
- Just before lunch is ready, pop the leeks into the oven to warm through.

Yorkshire pudding

120g plain flour
salt and pepper
1 large egg
200ml milk
2 tablespoons vegetable oil

- Place the flour and seasoning into a mixing bowl.
- Make a well in the flour and add the egg and a little of the milk.
- Whisk to a smooth paste and then add the rest of the milk.
- Leave the batter to rest for 20 minutes.
- Place the oil in a meat tin or a Yorkshire-pudding tin and place the tin in the oven.
- After 10 minutes the oil should start to smoke.

- Remove the tin from the oven and quickly pour in the pudding batter.
- Return to the oven for 20 minutes until the yorkshire pudding is puffed up and golden.

Gravy

- Once the joint comes out of the oven it is time to start the gravy.
- Place the joint on a warm plate to rest.
- Take the roasting tin and put it on the hob.
- Sprinkle a tablespoon of flour into the tin and scrape round with a wooden spoon so that all the fat gets absorbed into the flour.
- Add the used vegetable water and bring it to the boil.
- Simmer very gently for 10 minutes.
- If the gravy is too weak, add a stock cube.
- Reheat when lunch is ready.

Apple and banana crunch

This recipe makes a nice change from traditional apple crumble. I don't like cooked bananas very much but I was pleasantly surprised about how well they work in this dessert.

For the filling

675g cooking apples, peeled, cored and cut into smallish chunks

3 bananas, peeled and sliced

juice 1 lemon

75g caster sugar

For the topping

100g butter

225g soft brown sugar

150g plain flour

1 teaspoon ground cinnamon

75g walnut pieces

- Preheat the oven to 180°C/350°F/gas 4.
- Mix the apple and banana together in a bowl with the lemon juice and caster sugar.
- Spoon into an ovenproof dish.

To make the topping

- Gently melt the butter in a small saucepan.
- Place the other topping ingredients in a bowl and stir the melted butter into them.
- Spoon the mixture on top of the apples and bananas.
- Bake for 1 hour and serve with cream.

Christmas pudding + brandy butter

This is another recipe that has featured in my life since I can remember. My mother says that it originally came from Mrs Beeton. The recipe makes 3 puddings. We sometimes use 2 in one year and then store the other for the next year. If you don't want to do this, halve the quantities and make a large pudding and a small one. As far as the brandy butter is concerned, you are either a fan or not, so you may prefer cream or brandy sauce. You won't want to prepare the brandy butter this far in advance, so earmark this recipe and return to it nearer the time. I have simply put it here for ease of reference.

Christmas pudding

500g vegetable suet
120g plain flour
500g raisins
250g mixed peel
1 nutmeg, grated
28g mixed spice
28g ground cinnamon
500g white breadcrumbs
500g sultanas
250g currants
110g almonds, chopped
good pinch of salt
zest 1 lemon, finely chopped
300ml milk
juice 1 lemon
8 eggs

- Put all the dry ingredients in a large mixing bowl.
- Add the milk, lemon juice and eggs one at a time, mixing as you add each egg.
- Give the pudding mix a good stir with a wooden spoon to ensure that everything is well incorporated. I use a big Kenwood mixer which takes the pain out of the mixing, but a wooden spoon is probably more gratifying.
- Grease the pudding basins well with butter.
- Spoon the pudding mixture into the basins, leaving 1cm clear at the top.
- Cover the top of the mixture with a round of greaseproof paper and then wrap each basin in a double layer of tin foil.
- Put about 4cm of water in a large lidded saucepan.
- Bring the water to the boil and pop a pudding basin inside the saucepan.
- Cover and cook on a gentle simmer for 4 hours. Check the level of the water as the pudding cooks and add more as it evaporates.
- Once cooked, remove the tin foil and greaseproof paper and replace with dry greaseproof and tin foil. This should ensure that the pudding stays fresh for as long as you need.
- On Christmas Day, or whenever you are going to eat the pudding, simmer it again for 2 hours and serve with brandy butter or brandy sauce.

Brandy butter

250g butter, softened
250g icing sugar
5 tablespoons brandy

- Cream the butter in a mixer or using a hand blender until the butter becomes white.
- Add the icing sugar gradually, beating as you go.
- Beating continuously, add the brandy a few drops at a time. Don't add it too quickly as it will curdle.
- Pile up in a dish, cover with cling-film and place in the fridge to firm up.

NOVEMBER

Week 4

Monday p582	Spaghetti carbonara + green salad
Tuesday p583	Smoked haddock with chive and mustard sauce + spinach and butter beans
Wednesday p584	Spicy tuna cakes + rice salad
Thursday p586	Chicken stew with root vegetables + mashed potato
Friday p587	Fried pork chops + sweet potatoes and shallots
Saturday p588	Roasted pepper and squash soup + cream cheese and herb sandwiches
Sunday p589	Beef stew + mashed potato
Sunday pudding p590	Baby fruit cakes + custard
Extra tasty treat p591	Sticky toffee ginger muffins

Shopping list

MEAT

- ☐ 1kg chicken pieces on the bone
- ☐ 4–6 pork chops
- ☐ 1kg shin of beef

FISH

- ☐ 6 pieces smoked haddock fillet

VEGETABLES

- ☐ 1 Romaine lettuce
- ☐ 1 cucumber
- ☐ 9 spring onions
- ☐ 200g young spinach leaves
- ☐ 1 large red onion
- ☐ 1 bunch celery
- ☐ 900g sweet potatoes
- ☐ 200g celeriac
- ☐ 300g swede
- ☐ 2.9kg potatoes
- ☐ 2.5cm fresh ginger
- ☐ 1 garlic bulb
- ☐ 1 green chilli
- ☐ 2 carrots
- ☐ 3 tomatoes
- ☐ 1 avocado
- ☐ 2 shallots
- ☐ 1 red pepper
- ☐ 1 orange pepper
- ☐ 1 yellow pepper
- ☐ 2 onions
- ☐ 1 butternut squash
- ☐ 300g button mushrooms

FRUIT

- ☐ 2 lemons
- ☐ 1 orange

FRESH HERBS

- ☐ flat-leaf parsley
- ☐ chives
- ☐ coriander
- ☐ thyme
- ☐ bay leaf
- ☐ rosemary
- ☐ sage
- ☐ mint

FRIDGE ITEMS

- ☐ 660ml double cream
- ☐ 2 packs butter
- ☐ 100g Parmesan
- ☐ 11 eggs
- ☐ 380g chopped pancetta
- ☐ 1.1 litres milk
- ☐ 200g crème fraîche
- ☐ 290ml natural yoghurt
- ☐ 100g frozen peas
- ☐ 1.5–2 litres chicken stock
- ☐ 600ml beef stock
- ☐ 284ml single cream
- ☐ 75ml orange juice
- ☐ cream cheese
- ☐ vanilla ice cream

KITCHEN CUPBOARD ITEMS

- ☐ olive oil
- ☐ 50ml dry white wine
- ☐ 500g spaghetti
- ☐ balsamic vinegar
- ☐ salt
- ☐ Dijon mustard
- ☐ 400g tin butter beans
- ☐ tomato purée
- ☐ vegetable oil
- ☐ 400g tin yellow fin tuna
- ☐ 300g basmati rice
- ☐ 200g tinned chopped tomatoes
- ☐ goose fat
- ☐ 1 bottle red wine
- ☐ 440g sultanas
- ☐ 300g currants
- ☐ 580g soft brown sugar
- ☐ bicarbonate of soda
- ☐ 150ml sunflower oil
- ☐ 150g plain flour
- ☐ 385g self-raising flour
- ☐ 140g wholemeal flour
- ☐ 50g caster sugar
- ☐ 1 vanilla pod
- ☐ 1 or 2 baguettes
- ☐ mango chutney

SPICES

- ☐ whole nutmeg
- ☐ coriander seeds
- ☐ cumin seeds
- ☐ fennel seeds
- ☐ fenugreek
- ☐ mixed spice
- ☐ ground cinnamon
- ☐ ground ginger
- ☐ black peppercorns

Spaghetti carbonara + green salad

Spaghetti carbonara is too rich to be served without a salad. In Italy it would be eaten as a starter and then followed by something to offset its richness, but in England we tend to avoid starters unless it is a special occasion or we are eating out.

Spaghetti carbonara

500g spaghetti
50g Parmesan, freshly grated
black pepper
4 eggs
60ml double cream
nutmeg, grated
1 dessertspoon olive oil
280g chopped pancetta
50ml dry white wine
1 tablespoon flat-leaf parsley, chopped

- Bring some salted water for the pasta to the boil in a large saucepan.
- Cook the pasta according to the packet instructions, but remember that it will probably be ready 1 minute before the time stated.
- Meanwhile, beat together the cheese, pepper, eggs, double cream and a little nutmeg in a bowl.
- Heat the olive oil in a large frying pan and add the pancetta.
- Cook for 2 minutes until nicely browned.
- Add the wine and simmer for 1 minute, which will reduce the volume of wine slightly.
- When the pasta is ready, drain it, retaining a tablespoon of water in the bottom of the saucepan. Place the pasta in with the pancetta and wine and pour over the retained water. Make sure the pan is off the heat.
- Next, add the egg mixture and mix it into the pasta, then sprinkle on the parsley and serve immediately.
- Remember, you can't reheat carbonara sauce as it will curdle.

Green salad

1 Romaine lettuce, washed and chopped
½ cucumber, sliced
2 spring onions, chopped
For the dressing
1 tablespoon olive oil
2 teaspoons balsamic vinegar
salt and pepper

- Place the salad ingredients in a serving bowl and pour on the dressing when ready to serve.

Smoked haddock with chive and mustard sauce + spinach and butter beans

The chive and mustard sauce is made using crème fraîche. Crème fraîche is such a versatile ingredient to have in the fridge as it can be used to accompany desserts and is also great for making sauces.

Smoked haddock with chive and mustard sauce

6 pieces smoked haddock fillet
400ml milk
200g crème fraîche
1 tablespoon chives, finely snipped
1 dessertspoon Dijon mustard
2 dessertspoons Parmesan cheese, grated
salt and pepper

- Place the fish in a frying pan and cover it with the milk.
- Bring the milk to the boil, taking care as it will boil over if you don't watch it. Poach the fish in the simmering milk; about 2 minutes for a thin fillet or 4 minutes for a thick fillet.
- Meanwhile, mix together the crème fraîche, chives and mustard in a small bowl.
- Once the fish is ready, remove it and discard the milk.
- Remove the skin from the fish, which should come away easily.
- Place the fish in a buttered, ovenproof dish and spoon the crème fraîche mixture over it.
- Season well.
- Sprinkle the Parmesan cheese over the fish.
- Place the fish under a preheated grill for 2 minutes until slightly browned on top and serve immediately.

Spinach and butter beans

200g fresh young spinach leaves
15g butter
400g tin butter beans, drained
salt and pepper
1 dessertspoon olive oil

- Place the spinach in a large sauté pan with the butter and cook on a low heat until the spinach has completely wilted.
- Add the butter beans and warm them through.
- Season with salt and pepper.
- Drizzle with olive oil and serve.

Spicy tuna cakes + rice salad

These are a spicy alternative to ordinary fishcakes. They are great served with a wedge of lemon or lime. You can prepare them well in advance and fry them as you need them.

Spicy tuna cakes

300g potatoes, peeled and cut into quarters for boiling
300g sweet potatoes, peeled and cut into chunks for boiling
1 tablespoon vegetable oil
7 spring onions, finely chopped
2.5cm fresh ginger, peeled and finely chopped
2 cloves garlic, peeled and finely chopped
1 tablespoon curry powder*
400g tin yellow fin tuna, drained
100g frozen peas, defrosted
¼ fresh green chilli, deseeded and finely chopped (optional depending on your hot and spicy tolerance)
salt and pepper
flour seasoned with salt and pepper
2 tablespoons vegetable oil for frying the fishcakes

- Boil all the potatoes in salted water until tender. The sweet potatoes will cook a fraction before the ordinary ones, so remove them first. Try to avoid letting them get mushy.
- Drain the potatoes, place them in a mixing bowl, mash them roughly with a fork and set aside.
- Heat a tablespoon of vegetable oil in a frying pan on a medium heat. Add the spring onions, ginger and garlic and fry for 2 minutes, stirring continuously to prevent the garlic burning.
- Add the curry powder and fry for a further minute.
- Turn this mixture into the bowl with the potatoes and add the tuna, peas and green chilli.
- Season well with salt and pepper. Taste the mixture to check that it has enough seasoning.
- Form the mixture into approximately 14 fishcakes weighing approximately 50g each.
- Dust each fishcake with the seasoned flour.
- Heat 2 tablespoons of vegetable oil in a frying pan and when it's hot fry the fishcakes on a medium heat until golden brown all over.
- Serve the fishcakes with the rice salad and some mango chutney.

** **To make your own curry powder:***
1 tablespoon coriander seeds
1 dessertspoon cumin seeds
1 teaspoon fennel seeds
½ teaspoon fenugreek

- *Place the coriander seeds into a small, heavy-bottomed pan and heat through for 30 seconds.*
- *Add the other ingredients and toast until you smell the lovely aroma of the spices.*
- *Transfer the spices to a coffee grinder, a small processor or grind them in a pestle and mortar.*

Rice salad

300g basmati rice
450ml water
salt
1 raw carrot, peeled and finely chopped
3 tomatoes, finely chopped
½ cucumber, finely chopped
1 avocado, finely chopped
handful fresh coriander, chopped
30g butter

- Wash the rice throughly in cold water.
- Put the washed rice in a saucepan with the water and a good pinch of salt. Place on a high heat and as soon as it comes to the boil, cover the saucepan with a lid and turn the heat right down.
- Leave it on a low heat for 15 minutes.
- Remove the pan from the heat but leave it covered for a further 10 minutes.
- While the rice is still warm, add the other ingredients including the butter and mix to combine. Serve immediately.

Chicken stew with root vegetables + mashed potato

Root vegetables are one of the gifts that English soil gives us in abundance. They bring a unique flavour and a marvellous texture to stews, so make the most of their seasonality during the winter months.

Chicken stew with root vegetables

2 tablespoons olive oil
1kg chicken pieces, on the bone, skin removed
30g butter
1 large red onion, chopped
2 sticks celery, chopped
200g sweet potato, peeled and chopped into 2cm chunks
200g celeriac, peeled and chopped into 2cm chunks
300g swede, peeled and chopped into 2cm chunks
salt and pepper
2 tablespoons tomato purée dissolved in 500ml water
1 tablespoon lemon juice

- Heat the olive oil in a large casserole pan.
- Brown the chicken pieces in the oil, then remove them and set aside.
- Keep the pan on the heat. Add the butter and once it starts to foam add the onion, celery, sweet potato and root vegetables.
- Stir them round for 2 minutes on a medium heat.
- Return the chicken to the pan.
- Season with a good teaspoon of salt and some black pepper.
- Add the tomato purée, water and lemon juice.
- Bring the stew to a gentle simmer, cover and cook for 45 minutes.

Mashed potato

1kg potatoes, peeled and quartered
200ml warmed milk
40g butter
salt and pepper

- Place the potatoes in cold, salted water and bring to the boil.
- Turn the heat down to a robust simmer on a medium heat.
- Once the potatoes are soft but not mushy, drain them and put them through a ricer.
- Return the mashed potato to the saucepan and place over a low heat.
- Gently stir in the warmed milk and butter.
- Remove from the heat and season with salt and pepper.

Fried pork chops
+ sweet potatoes and shallots

The sweetness of the potatoes here complements the pork chops rather well. Prepare the vegetables first and cook the pork chops when the vegetables are almost ready.

Fried pork chops

4-6 pork chops, depending on whether your children will manage a whole pork chop each or whether they can share one between two
salt and pepper
1 tablespoon olive oil
1 lemon

- Preheat the oven to its lowest setting.
- Season the pork chops with salt and pepper.
- Heat the olive oil in a large frying pan over a medium heat.
- Add the chops. If you are frying 6 chops, do them in batches. Reasonably thick chops take about 5 minutes on each side to cook through.
- Place the cooked chops in a warm oven while you finish the others.
- Squeeze the lemon juice over the chops and add another sprinkling of salt.
- Serve with the sweet potatoes and shallots.

Sweet potatoes and shallots

600g potatoes, peeled and quartered
400g sweet potatoes, peeled and cut to a similar size as the other potatoes
salt
2 shallots, finely sliced
1 sprig fresh thyme
2 tablespoons olive oil
black pepper

- Preheat the oven to 220°C/425°F/gas 7.
- Parboil all the potatoes in salted water for 5 minutes.
- Drain the potatoes and place them in a shallow roasting tin with the shallots and thyme.
- Pour over the olive oil and season with pepper.
- Roast for 45 minutes until golden brown.

Roasted pepper and squash soup
+ cream cheese and herb sandwiches

This soup makes good use of the peppers and squashes around at this time of year. The finished dish is a really vibrant, beautiful orangey-red colour.

Roasted pepper and squash soup

1 red, 1 orange and 1 yellow pepper, deseeded and sliced into quarters
1 tablespoon olive oil
salt and pepper
30g butter
1 onion, sliced
1 butternut squash, peeled, deseeded and chopped into 4cm chunks
200g tinned chopped tomatoes
1.5–2 litres chicken stock
3 tablespoons single cream

- Preheat the oven to 200°C/400°F/gas 6.
- Place the peppers on a vegetable tray and drizzle with olive oil.
- Season with salt and pepper.
- Roast for 20 minutes.
- When the peppers are ready, warm the butter in a large saucepan on top of the stove.
- Add the peppers, onion and squash and stir to coat in the butter.
- Reduce the heat, cover the saucepan and cook the vegetables on a low heat for 20 minutes.
- Add the tomatoes and stock and season.
- Bring to the boil, reduce the heat, cover the saucepan and simmer gently for 30 minutes.
- Remove from the heat.
- To get the soup smooth, blend it in a food processor or whizz it with a hand-held blender.
- Return the soup to the hob and warm through.
- Add the cream and check the seasoning.

Cream cheese and herb sandwiches

1 or 2 baguettes
butter
cream cheese
flat-leaf parsley, chives and mint, finely chopped

- Cut and butter the baguettes.
- Mix the herbs into the cream cheese and spread onto the buttered baguettes.

Beef stew
+ mashed potato

Shin of beef is perfect for this dish, as the meat comes into its own when cooked slowly and langorously, gently simmering in plenty of flavoursome stock for well over an hour.

Beef stew

1kg shin of beef, cut into chunks and trimmed of any obvious pieces of fat
plain flour seasoned with salt and pepper
2 tablespoons goose fat
2 tablespoons olive oil
1 large onion, diced
1 large carrot, peeled and chopped
2 sticks celery, chopped
300g button mushrooms
100g chopped pancetta
1 bouquet garni bay leaf, thyme, rosemary and sage
600ml beef stock
1 bottle red wine
salt and pepper

- Toss the chunks of beef in the seasoned flour.
- Heat the goose fat in a large casserole dish and brown the meat in the fat. It is quicker if you do the beef in batches.
- Remove the beef and set aside.
- Clean the pan.
- Add the olive oil to the pan and gently brown the onion, carrot, celery, mushrooms and pancetta for 5 minutes.
- Add the bouquet garni, beef stock and red wine and bring to a simmer.
- Return the beef to the dish and cook uncovered on a very gentle simmer for 1 hour 30 minutes.
- Season with salt and pepper and serve with mashed potato.

Mashed potato

1kg potatoes, peeled and quartered
salt
200ml warmed milk
40g butter
salt and pepper

- Place the potatoes in cold, salted water and bring to the boil.
- Turn the heat down to a robust simmer on a medium heat.
- Once the potatoes are soft but not mushy, drain them and put them through a ricer.
- Return the mashed potato to the saucepan and place over a low heat.
- Gently stir in the warmed milk and butter.
- Remove from the heat and season with salt and pepper.

TIP

To make a really good stew you should never let it boil. It should cook slowly.

Baby fruit cakes + custard

These cakes are a real dream. They are as good with custard as without, but I serve them with custard here as it makes them more like a pudding. This recipe makes 16 cakes, so if your muffin tin has space for only 12, just cook the last 4 on their own.

Baby fruit cakes

150g butter
300g sultanas
300g currants
180g soft brown sugar
1 teaspoon mixed spice
1 teaspoon ground cinnamon
1 teaspoon ground ginger
1 teaspoon bicarbonate of soda
250ml water
2 eggs, beaten
150g plain flour
150g self-raising flour

- Pre-heat the oven to 180°C/350°F/gas 4.
- Butter a muffin tin and dust the buttered moulds with a little sifting of flour.
- Take a medium-sized saucepan and add the butter, sultanas, currants, sugar, mixed spice, cinnamon, ginger, bicarbonate of soda and water.
- Slowly bring to a simmer, stirring continously.
- Remove from the heat and allow to cool for 5 minutes.
- Add the beaten eggs and combine thoroughly.
- Add the two types of flour and mix in.
- Spoon approximately equal amounts of the mixture into each muffin mould and bake for 25–30 minutes, or until a skewer inserted into the middle of a cake comes out clean.
- Cool before unmoulding.
- Serve with custard.

Custard

600ml milk and double cream mixed
2 whole eggs
2 egg yolks
2 tablespoons caster sugar
1 vanilla pod or a drop or two vanilla extract

- In a glass bowl, whisk the whole eggs, egg yolks and sugar with a hand-held whisk for 2 minutes.
- Measure the milk and cream in a measuring jug, add the vanilla pod or extract and put in the microwave on high for 2 minutes. The milk and cream should be just at boiling point but not actually boiling.
- Take a saucepan with 1cm or so of water in the bottom and bring the water to a simmer.
- Place the bowl with the eggs over the saucepan.
- Add the milk and cream to the eggs, whisking all the time to avoid lumps.
- If you used the vanilla pod, scrape the seeds into the mixture.
- Keep stirring for 10 minutes, by which time you should have a good consistency. An indication of when the custard is thick enough is that it will coat the back of a wooden spoon as you lift it out of the mixture.
- You can make custard ahead of time but avoid reheating it, as it may curdle.

Sticky toffee ginger muffins

This is a really straightforward teatime treat that is not too sweet and goes beautifully with the brown sugar sauce.

For the muffins

140g sultanas

75ml orange juice

¼ teaspoon bicarbonate of soda

285g self-raising flour

140g wholemeal flour

2 teaspoons ground ginger

1 teaspoon mixed spice

200g soft brown sugar

grated zest 1 orange

1 egg

290ml natural yoghurt

150ml sunflower oil

For the sauce

200g soft brown sugar

300ml double cream

55g butter

To make the muffins

- Preheat the oven to 200°C/400°F/gas 6.
- Grease and flour a 12-mould muffin tray.
- Place all the ingredients in a mixing bowl.
- Using a wooden spoon, stir the ingredients together gently. Don't over-mix.
- Spoon approximately equal amounts of the mixture into the muffin moulds and bake for 25 minutes.

To make the sauce

- Place all the ingredients in a small saucepan.
- Heat through and simmer for 3 minutes.
- Pour over the muffins and serve with some vanilla ice cream.

Week 1

Monday p594	Chinese chicken + broccoli stir fry + boiled rice
Tuesday p596	Chickpea and coriander cakes with fried egg and pancetta
Wednesday p597	Chicken, ham and mushroom pie + broccoli
Thursday p598	Chunky fish broth + garlic toast
Friday p599	Meatballs in tomato sauce + boiled potatoes + Brussels sprouts
Saturday p600	Risi e bisi (rice and peas)
Sunday p601	Pheasant casserole + mashed potato + carrots
Sunday pudding p603	Apple crumble flan
Extra tasty treat p604	Christmas cake

Shopping list

MEAT

- ☐ 8 chicken breasts, boneless
- ☐ 500g minced beef
- ☐ 500g minced pork
- ☐ 3 pheasants
- ☐ 6 chipolatas

FISH

- ☐ 1kg skinned white fish (a mixture of haddock, cod, monkfish and a little smoked haddock)
- ☐ 125g cooked prawns

VEGETABLES

- ☐ 3 spring onions
- ☐ 850g broccoli
- ☐ 1 garlic bulb
- ☐ 250g crimini, button or chestnut mushrooms
- ☐ 2.7kg potatoes
- ☐ 400g carrots
- ☐ 300g Brussel sprouts
- ☐ 3 shallots
- ☐ 4 onions
- ☐ 1 bunch celery

FRUIT

- ☐ 400g dessert apples
- ☐ 150g blueberries

FRESH HERBS

- ☐ coriander
- ☐ flat-leaf parsley
- ☐ thyme
- ☐ bay leaves
- ☐ rosemary

FRIDGE ITEMS

- ☐ 13 eggs
- ☐ 140g sliced pancetta
- ☐ 200g chopped pancetta
- ☐ 400g cooked ham
- ☐ 700g frozen petits pois
- ☐ 1 pack puff pastry
- ☐ 600ml double cream
- ☐ 900ml fish stock
- ☐ 100g Parmesan cheese
- ☐ 3 packs butter
- ☐ 1.8 litres chicken stock
- ☐ 200ml whole milk

KITCHEN CUPBOARD ITEMS

- ☐ cornflour
- ☐ salt
- ☐ sesame oil
- ☐ groundnut oil
- ☐ olive oil
- ☐ 75g unsalted cashew nuts
- ☐ dry sherry
- ☐ light soy sauce
- ☐ 400g basmati rice
- ☐ chicken stock cubes
- ☐ 400g tin chickpeas
- ☐ Dijon mustard
- ☐ 500ml dry white wine
- ☐ 400g tin chopped tomatoes
- ☐ 1 loaf white bread
- ☐ 200g chestnuts
- ☐ 400g risotto rice
- ☐ black treacle
- ☐ vanilla essence
- ☐ brandy
- ☐ 500g marzipan
- ☐ 118g caster sugar
- ☐ apricot jam
- ☐ 150ml gutsy red wine
- ☐ 225g light brown sugar
- ☐ 225g currants
- ☐ 325g sultanas
- ☐ 225g raisins
- ☐ 110g glacé cherries
- ☐ 110g mixed peel
- ☐ 50g ground almonds
- ☐ 50g blanched almonds
- ☐ 375g plain flour
- ☐ 40g demerara sugar

SPICES

- ☐ coriander seeds
- ☐ cumin seeds
- ☐ mixed spice
- ☐ black peppercorns
- ☐ ground cinnamon

Chinese chicken + broccoli stir fry + boiled rice

As Christmas approaches I always feel the necessity for light food and this chicken dish certainly fits the bill.

Chinese chicken

6 chicken breasts, skinless and boneless, cut into chunks
1 egg white
2 teaspoons cornflour
1 teaspoon salt
1 teaspoon sesame oil
2 teaspoons groundnut oil
75g unsalted cashew nuts
1 tablespoon dry sherry
1 tablespoon light soy sauce
3 spring onions, finely shredded

- Place the chicken chunks in a bowl with the egg white, cornflour, salt and sesame oil and put the bowl in the fridge while you heat a saucepan of water and bring it to the boil.
- Put the chicken into the boiling water and cook for 1 minute.
- Remove the chicken from the water and set aside.
- Heat a wok or frying pan until hot.
- Add the groundnut oil and then almost immediately the cashew nuts and stir fry them for 1 minute.
- Add the sherry, soy sauce and chicken and stir fry for 2 minutes.
- Garnish with spring onions and serve immediately.

Broccoli stir fry

450g broccoli
1 tablespoon groundnut oil
4 cloves garlic, peeled and crushed
salt
6 tablespoons water
2 teaspoons sesame oil

- Cut the stems off the broccoli and separate the head into single florets.
- Peel and slice the stems into smaller pieces.
- Heat a wok or frying pan over a high heat.
- When hot, add the groundnut oil, garlic and a good pinch of salt.
- Stir fry for 30 seconds.
- Add the broccoli and stir fry for 2 minutes.
- Pour in the water and cover the pan or wok.
- Keep the heat high and cook for 3 minutes.
- Uncover and add the sesame oil.
- Serve when the chicken is ready.

Boiled rice

400g basmati rice
600ml water
salt

- Cook the rice by placing it in a saucepan with the water and a small pinch of salt.
- Put the rice on a high heat and as soon as it comes to the boil, cover the saucepan with a lid and turn the heat right down to very low.
- Leave it on a low heat for 15 minutes.
- Then remove the pan from the heat, but leave it covered for a further 10 minutes.

Chickpea and coriander cakes with fried egg and pancetta

This is an easy, healthy meal that takes no time at all to prepare. If you fancy being completely meat-free, then just omit the pancetta.

400g tin chickpeas, drained
1 onion, finely chopped
2 tablespoons fresh coriander, finely chopped
1 tablespoon flat-leaf parsley, finely chopped
salt and pepper
1 teaspoon coriander seeds
1 teaspoon cumin seeds
1 egg, beaten
1 tablespoon olive oil
400g potatoes, boiled and roughly mashed
olive oil for frying
To serve with
6–12 slices pancetta
6 eggs

- Place the chickpeas, onion, fresh coriander and parsley in a food processor and blend until everything is finely chopped.
- Season well with salt and pepper.
- Place the coriander and cumin seeds in a small pan and toast them for a few minutes until they start to smoke and you can smell their aroma.
- Grind the coriander and cumin, using a pestle and mortar, as finely as possible.
- Stir the spices into the chickpea mixture with the beaten egg, olive oil and potatoes.
- Form the mixture into little patties.
- Heat 2 tablespoons of olive oil in a frying pan and fry the patties on both sides until golden.
- Keep the patties warm while you fry the pancetta and eggs.

Chicken, ham and mushroom pie + broccoli

A classic chicken and ham pie with a puff pastry crust and a creamy filling is hard to beat on a wintry evening.

Chicken, ham and mushroom pie

1 tablespoon olive oil
2 cloves garlic, peeled and finely chopped
1 onion, finely chopped
1 tablespoon thyme leaves
250g crimini, button or chestnut mushrooms, halved
10g butter
250ml chicken stock
2 chicken breasts, chopped into 2cm pieces
400g cooked ham, cut into 1cm pieces
200g peas, cooked – if petits pois, defrosted will do
salt and pepper
1 pack puff pastry
For the sauce
25g butter
25g flour
250ml chicken stock from above
3 tablespoons double cream
1 dessertspoon light soy sauce
1 teaspoon Dijon mustard
1 tablespoon flat-leaf parsley, chopped

- Preheat the oven to 200°C/400°F/gas 6.
- Heat the olive oil in a frying or sauté pan.
- Add the garlic, onion and thyme and sauté for 5 minutes until the onion is soft.
- Add the mushrooms and butter and cook on a medium heat for a further 5 minutes.
- Bring the chicken stock to a simmer in a small saucepan.
- Add the chicken pieces and poach for 3 minutes.
- Strain the chicken and retain the stock.
- Roughly chop the chicken into smaller pieces.
- Add the ham, chicken and peas to the mushroom mixture.
- Season with salt and pepper.

To make the sauce

- Heat the butter in a small saucepan.
- Add the flour and cook on a very low heat for 1 minute.
- Take the saucepan off the heat and add the stock a little at a time.
- When all the stock has been added, bring the sauce to a simmer and stir while it thickens.
- Add the cream, soy sauce, mustard and parsley.
- Pour the sauce over the chicken, mushroom and ham and then spoon the pie filling into a large pie dish and cover with the puff pastry.
- Brush the pastry with beaten egg.
- Bake for 30 minutes.

Broccoli

400g broccoli
salt

- Trim the broccoli into florets. If the stalks are very thick, trim them down a little.
- Bring a pan of slightly salted water to the boil.
- Add the broccoli florets and cook on a simmer for 3 minutes.

Chunky fish broth
+ garlic toast

Fish soups are often complicated but this one is very simple. Prepare the garlic toast while the soup is cooking.

Chunky fish broth

500ml dry white wine
900ml fish stock
3 cloves garlic, peeled and slivered
550g potatoes, peeled and cut into chunks
400g tin chopped tomatoes
2 bay leaves
salt
a few parsley stalks
1kg skinned white fish (a mixture of haddock, cod, monkfish and a little smoked haddock is ideal)
5 tablespoons olive oil
125g cooked prawns

- Place the wine, fish stock, garlic, potatoes, tomatoes, bay leaves, salt and parsley stalks into a large saucepan.
- Bring to a simmer and cook for 20 minutes.
- Cut the fish into chunks of about 5cm by 2cm, and put them and the olive oil into the soup.
- Simmer for 4 minutes.
- Turn off the heat and add the cooked prawns.
- Serve in soup bowls with the garlic toast.

Garlic toast

6 slices toast
olive oil
2 cloves garlic, peeled but left whole

- While the toast is warm drizzle with olive oil and rub each piece with a garlic clove.
- Serve while warm.

Meatballs in tomato sauce + boiled potatoes + Brussels sprouts

Meatballs feature a few times in this book in different guises. They are one of my favourite comfort foods.

Meatballs in tomato sauce

500g minced beef
500g minced pork
1 large onion, finely diced
60g Parmesan cheese, finely grated
1 bunch flat-leaf parsley, finely chopped
100g chopped pancetta, finely chopped
salt and pepper
olive oil for frying

- Combine the beef, pork, onion, cheese, parsley and pancetta in a large bowl.
- Season well. To check that you have seasoned the meatballs adequately, fry and taste a little bit of the mixture before you proceed to the next step.
- Form rounds of the mixture into balls the size of a fresh apricot.
- Heat 2 tablespoons of olive oil in a heavy-bottomed frying pan.
- When the oil is hot add five or six meatballs to the pan.
- Turn them over so that they brown all over. I use a knife and fork to do this as it tends to stop the meatballs from breaking up.
- Add more oil if you need it.
- Once all the meatballs are browned, set aside.

Boiled potatoes

750g potatoes, peeled and quartered
salt
a little butter and black pepper for serving

- Put the potatoes in a saucepan of salted water.
- Bring to the boil and reduce the heat to a simmer.
- Simmer the potatoes until tender to the tip of a sharp knife.
- Serve with a dab of butter and a few grindings of black pepper.

Brussels sprouts

300g Brussels sprouts, trimmed
salt and pepper
knob of butter

- Bring a pan of slightly salted water to the boil.
- Add the sprouts and cook for 5 minutes.
- Drain well and serve with butter and a grinding of black pepper.

Risi e bisi (rice and peas)

This is a simple risotto but its success depends upon a good stock and good risotto rice. A stock cube will not do, in my opinion, so do try to make some chicken stock when you have a roast chicken and then freeze it for this occasion. If you cannot contemplate making your own stock, then the fresh stock sold in supermarkets would be better than a stock cube.

1.5 litres fresh chicken stock
salt and pepper
50g butter
2 tablespoons olive oil
1 onion, chopped finely
70g sliced pancetta, chopped
1 stick celery, finely chopped
400g risotto rice
500g frozen petits pois
Parmesan cheese, freshly grated
handful flat-leaf parsley, chopped

- Place the chicken stock in a saucepan and bring it to a gentle simmer.
- Season it with salt and pepper.
- Heat the butter and olive oil in a large sauté pan or saucepan.
- Add the onion, pancetta and celery and cook gently until softened. This will take approximately 5 minutes.
- Add the rice and stir round to ensure that it is coated with the butter and oil.
- Cook for 2 minutes, stirring almost constantly.
- Add the peas to the simmering stock.
- Add 2 ladlefuls of stock and peas to the rice and stir round.
- Don't let all the liquid disappear before adding more hot stock.
- Keep adding the stock until the rice is tender on the outside but has a slight bite in the centre of the grain. A risotto takes about 20–25 minutes to cook, and you need to keep stirring almost continuously.
- Remove the risotto from the heat and add a couple of tablespoons of Parmesan and the chopped parsley.
- Serve immediately.

Pheasant casserole
+ mashed potato + carrots

I have to confess that I am pretty lousy at cooking game and, until we lived in the country, it was not something I would contemplate doing. Now, given the drive towards, and the sense, in eating seasonally, I feel that not to give it a try would be missing the point. It is locally produced more often than not, pretty much organic, and is in plentiful supply at this time of year. A friend of mine prepares pheasant for me when I need them but you can ask your butcher or supplier to do the same. You can cook a whole pheasant or just the breasts on the bone, which I have done here.

Pheasant casserole

25g butter
6 pheasant breasts on the bone
6 chipolatas
3 shallots, peeled and halved, or if small kept whole
100g chopped pancetta
200g pre-prepared, cooked chestnuts
150ml gutsy red wine
300ml chicken stock
bouquet garni with sprig rosemary, some thyme, and a bay leaf

- Preheat the oven to 170°C/325°F/gas 3.
- Heat the butter in a large casserole pan.
- Add the pheasant breasts one at a time, and brown them all over. This takes approximately 1 minute for each breast.

continues

- Remove the breasts and set them aside.
- Keep the pan on the heat and add the chipolatas, shallots, pancetta and chestnuts. Cook them until they start to brown.
- Turn the heat to high. Add the wine and cook for 2 minutes.
- Reduce the heat. Add the stock and the bouquet garni and stir.
- Return the breasts to the pan.
- Season well, cover the casserole pan and place in the oven for 35 minutes.
- To serve, take each breast out of the pan and thinly slice the meat. Serve the meat on top of the mashed potato with plenty of gravy from the casserole.

TIP

If you pierce the breasts with a skewer and the juices run pink, they may need a few minutes longer. Take care, however, as what puts many people off pheasant is that it becomes stringy and chewy when it is even slightly overcooked.

Mashed potato

1kg potatoes, peeled and quartered
40g butter
salt and pepper
200ml warmed milk

- Place the potatoes in cold, salted water and bring to the boil.
- Turn the heat down to a robust simmer on a medium heat.
- Once the potatoes are soft but not mushy, drain them and put them through the ricer.
- Return the mashed potato to the saucepan and place over a low heat.
- Add the milk and butter and gently stir in.
- Remove from the heat.

TIP

I use a potato ricer to make mashed potato, as I have found it is the only way of removing all the lumps and it is much quicker than a masher. I also resist the temptation of cutting the potatoes into small cubes, prior to cooking them, as, while the potatoes may cook more quickly, I do not think one gets such a good flavour.

Carrots

400g carrots, peeled and sliced into pound-coin-thick discs
15g butter
salt and pepper

- Place the carrots and butter, in a small saucepan, on the stove at a medium heat.
- Cover the saucepan with a lid and gently cook the carrots for 10–15 minutes, stirring them occasionally, until soft.
- Season with salt and pepper.

Apple crumble flan

This is a cross between apple crumble and apple tart. Serve it with custard or cream.

For the pastry
90g caster sugar
125g butter, softened
1 egg
250g plain flour
salt

For the filling
30g butter
400g dessert apples, peeled, cored and diced
2 tablespoons brandy
100g sultanas
150g blueberries
3 tablespoons double cream

For the topping
40g butter
75g plain flour
½ teaspoon ground cinnamon
40g demerara sugar
2 tablespoons ground almonds
cream for serving

To make the pastry

- Beat the sugar and butter together in a food processor until smoothly combined.
- Incorporate the egg.
- Add the flour and a pinch of salt and once you have a dough starting to form, turn the mixture out onto a lightly floured surface and form it into a ball.
- Wrap the pastry in cling-film and chill in the fridge for 30 minutes.

To make the filling

- Preheat the oven to 190°C/375°F/gas 5.
- Grease a 20cm flan tin.
- Heat the butter (the 30g amount from the filling ingredients), in a sauté pan.
- Add the apples and stir to coat in the fat.
- Cook on a medium heat for 2 minutes.
- Add the brandy and cook for 2 minutes more.
- Remove from the heat and spoon on the cream.
- Add the blueberries and sultanas, stir to combine and set aside.

To make the flan

- Prepare the flan by rolling out the pastry and lining the flan tin.
- Place a sheet of baking parchment on top of the pastry case and pour on some baking beans, in order to 'blind bake' the pastry case.
- Place the flan tin on a baking sheet and bake for 15 minutes.
- Remove the flan from the oven, spoon the filling into the flan case and then prepare the topping.

To make the topping

- Rub the butter into the flour and add the cinnamon.
- Stir in the demerera sugar and ground almonds.
- Sprinkle over the top of the apple filling and bake for 35 minutes.
- Serve with cream.

Christmas cake

I have been making this Christmas cake for some years now. It is not a dark brown fruit cake but slightly lighter, which suits my preference. I usually just decorate the cake with marzipan, garnished with a sprig of holly, but you can put frosting on the top if you wish.

For the cake

1 x 20cm round cake tin
225g currants
225g sultanas
225g raisins
110g glace cherries
110g mixed peel, chopped
50g blanched almonds, chopped
275g plain flour
1 teaspoon mixed spice
225g butter, softened
225g light brown sugar
4 large eggs
1 tablespoon black treacle
½ teaspoon vanilla essence
salt
2 tablespoons brandy or milk

For the glaze

28g caster sugar
2 rounded tablespoons apricot jam
500g marzipan

For the frosting

2 egg whites
600g white icing sugar

To make the cake

- Grease and line the cake tin with baking parchment.
- Preheat the oven to 150°C/300°F/gas 2.
- Place the currants, sultanas and raisins in a bowl and cover with boiling water.
- Stir the fruit, strain through a colander and pat dry with a clean tea towel.
- Pour some warm water over the glacé cherries, stir and drain.
- Quarter the cherries and place with the other fruit.
- Add the chopped almonds and mixed peel.
- Sieve together the flour, mixed spice and add a good pinch of salt. Set aside.
- In a large mixing bowl, cream together the butter and sugar until light and fluffy.
- In a separate bowl mix together the treacle, eggs and vanilla essence.
- Beat ⅙ of the treacle and egg mixture into the butter and sugar, with a spoon of flour.
- Repeat until all the egg mixture is incorporated.
- Fold in half of the remaining flour with a metal spoon.
- Then fold in the remaining flour, fruit, and brandy or milk.
- Spoon the mixture into the prepared tin.
- Create a slight dip in the top of the cake and, using a pastry brush, paint the surface of the cake with cold water.
- Set the tin on a baking tray with a wad of folded baking parchment underneath.
- Fix a double thickness of baking parchment (the depth of the tin and a bit more) around the cake tin with string.
- Bake the cake for 1 hour 30 minutes, then reduce the heat to 140°C/275°F/gas 1 and bake for a further 2 hours 30 minutes. Test with a skewer, which should come out clean.
- Leave the cake to cool in the tin for 24 hours.

To make the glaze

- Place the sugar and 1 tablespoon of water in a small saucepan and stir over a low heat until the sugar has dissolved.
- Stir in the jam and bring to the boil.
- Reduce the heat and simmer gently for 2 minutes.
- Remove from heat.
- Brush the top and sides of the cake with the glaze using a pastry brush.
- Dust a worktop with caster sugar and roll out the marzipan until it is large enough to cover the top and the sides of the cake.
- Lay the cake upside down on top of the rolled marzipan and bring up the sides, pressing it into place.

To make the frosting

- Beat the whites of two eggs for 30 seconds just until they start to bubble.
- Sift 300g of white icing sugar into the egg white and mix in with a wooden spoon. Sift in another 300g of icing sugar and mix in with a wooden spoon. If it becomes too stiff add a couple of teaspoons of warm water.
- Spread onto the cake with a knife.

TIP

This cake will last for a couple of months at least, if stored in a dry, airtight container.

Week 2

Monday p608	Fried chicken + tomato pilaf + tomato and cucumber salad
Tuesday p609	Smoked haddock chowder
Wednesday p610	Pancetta and avocado salad + baked potatoes
Thursday p611	Cheese and sweetcorn flan + baked potatoes + green salad
Friday p613	Sausages and warm lentil salad
Saturday p614	Lasagne + green salad
Sunday p616	Chicken with tarragon + roast potatoes + cauliflower cheese + watercress salad
Sunday pudding p618	Winter and dried fruit compote + custard
Extra tasty treat p619	Chicken liver paté

Shopping list

MEAT
- ☐ 6 chicken breasts, boneless
- ☐ 8–10 sausages
- ☐ 500g minced beef
- ☐ 500g minced pork
- ☐ 2 x 1.5kg chickens
- ☐ 225g chicken livers

FISH
- ☐ 500g smoked haddock (preferably undyed)

VEGETABLES
- ☐ 10 tomatoes
- ☐ 2½ cucumbers
- ☐ 1 shallot
- ☐ 1 garlic bulb
- ☐ 1 bunch celery
- ☐ 1.35kg potatoes
- ☐ 3 avocados
- ☐ 10 spring onions
- ☐ 170g watercress
- ☐ 100g young spinach leaves
- ☐ 12 baking potatoes
- ☐ 200g onions
- ☐ 2 Romaine lettuces
- ☐ 7 cherry tomatoes
- ☐ 1 red onion
- ☐ 1 carrot
- ☐ 1 cauliflower

FRUIT
- ☐ 2 lemons
- ☐ 1 quince
- ☐ 1 apple
- ☐ 1 pear

FRESH HERBS
- ☐ flat-leaf parsley
- ☐ bay leaves
- ☐ thyme
- ☐ coriander
- ☐ tarragon

FRIDGE ITEMS
- ☐ 3 packs butter
- ☐ 2 litres whole milk
- ☐ 100g chopped pancetta
- ☐ 170g sliced pancetta
- ☐ 300g Cheddar cheese
- ☐ 10 eggs
- ☐ 450ml double cream
- ☐ 50ml crème fraîche
- ☐ 200g Gruyère
- ☐ 200g Parmesan
- ☐ 300g frozen peas
- ☐ 10ml apple juice

KITCHEN CUPBOARD ITEMS
- ☐ olive oil
- ☐ vegetable oil
- ☐ salt
- ☐ 650ml dry white wine
- ☐ pumpkin seeds
- ☐ 1 loaf bread
- ☐ extra virgin olive oil
- ☐ balsamic vinegar
- ☐ 500g basmati rice
- ☐ 300g plain flour
- ☐ 285g tin sweetcorn
- ☐ 300g puy lentils
- ☐ 3 x 400g tins chopped Italian tomatoes
- ☐ chicken stock cubes
- ☐ Dijon mustard
- ☐ 100g prunes
- ☐ 100g dried apricots
- ☐ 100g sultanas
- ☐ 50g soft brown sugar
- ☐ 1 vanilla pod
- ☐ 150g caster sugar
- ☐ brandy
- ☐ 1 box lasagne
- ☐ granulated sugar
- ☐ tomato purée

SPICES
- ☐ black peppercorns
- ☐ paprika
- ☐ mixed spice
- ☐ whole nutmeg
- ☐ cloves
- ☐ cinnamon sticks

Fried chicken + tomato pilaf + tomato and cucumber salad

Any meal that uses chicken breast is going to be a quick meal to make. The pilaf is great as you pile everything into the saucepan, leave it and then come back to it when ready to eat.

Fried chicken

2 tablespoons olive oil
50g butter
6 chicken breasts, skinless, cut into 1cm thick strips acrossways
3 tablespoons flat-leaf parsley, chopped
salt and pepper
1 lemon for squeezing over the chicken

- Heat the oil and butter in a frying pan and sauté the chicken pieces in batches for 5 minutes per batch.
- Sprinkle the chicken with parsley.
- Season with salt and pepper and a squeeze of fresh lemon juice.

Tomato pilaf

3 tablespoons vegetable oil
1 onion, finely diced
1 clove garlic, peeled and finely chopped
500g basmati rice
600g tinned tomatoes
1 chicken stock cube
salt and pepper
2 teaspoons sugar
300g frozen peas
150g butter

- Heat the oil in a large saucepan.
- Add the onion and garlic and fry for 5 minutes.
- Then add the rice and fry for 2 minutes, stirring it as it fries.
- Pour the tinned tomatoes into a measuring jug and make up to 1 litre with boiling water.
- Add the stock cube to the water and tomatoes and stir to dissolve.
- Pour the liquid onto the rice.
- Season with salt, pepper and the sugar.
- Add the frozen peas.
- Bring to a good simmer. Reduce the heat, cover and cook for about 20 minutes until the rice is tender and the liquid has been absorbed.
- Stir once during the cooking time to redistribute the rice and keep an eye on it in case it dries out too quickly, in which case add some more water.
- When the rice is cooked, fold in the butter and season again if necessary.

Tomato and cucumber salad

4 tomatoes, finely sliced
½ cucumber, finely sliced
squeeze of fresh lemon juice
salt and pepper

- Combine the tomatoes and cucumber in a serving dish.
- Squeeze on the lemon juice and season with salt and pepper.

Smoked haddock chowder

Chowder has become very popular recently. I first ate it in California where, on the coast, it appears on most menus. It is simple and nutritious and is reasonably popular with children.

500ml milk
1 bay leaf
500g smoked haddock (preferably undyed)
2 tablespoons olive oil
1 shallot, peeled and finely chopped
2 cloves garlic, peeled and finely chopped
2 sticks celery, finely chopped
1 tablespoon plain flour
200ml dry white wine
300ml water
350g potatoes, peeled and chopped into 2cm chunks
1 teaspoon salt
100g chopped pancetta
handful flat-leaf parsley, chopped
black pepper
bread for serving

- Heat the milk with the bay leaf until it is simmering gently.
- Add the fish and poach for 3 minutes, or 4 minutes for really thick fillets.
- Remove the fish from the milk, retaining the milk.
- If the fish has its skin, remove it and set the fish aside.
- Heat the olive oil in a large saucepan and add the shallot, garlic and celery.
- Sauté gently for 5 minutes.
- Add the flour and stir to combine.
- Now add the wine and cook, stirring continuously, for 3 minutes.
- Pour in the water, the retained milk and the potatoes and bring to a simmer.
- Season with salt and simmer uncovered for 15 minutes until the potatoes are soft.
- Add the cooked haddock to the soup.
- Fry the pancetta in a small frying pan until it is brown and crispy. Add this to the soup, along with the chopped parsley.
- Season to taste and serve with bread.

Pancetta and avocado salad + baked potatoes

This looks rather unimaginative but I find my body often craves the clean, fresh flavours of a salad to give it a rest from meat. Serve the salad with big baked potatoes filled with butter and cheese. Put the potatoes in the oven 1 hour 30 minutes before you are ready to serve.

Pancetta and avocado salad

2 avocados, peeled, destoned and sliced
6 tomatoes, quartered
½ cucumber, sliced
2 handfuls pumpkin seeds
3 spring onions, peeled and sliced
2 tablespoons flat-leaf parsley, chopped
70g watercress
100g young spinach leaves
100g sliced pancetta, chopped

For the dressing

3 tablespoons extra virgin olive oil
1 tablespoon balsamic vinegar
salt and pepper

- Prepare the salad by placing the avocados, tomatoes, cucumber, pumpkin seeds, spring onions, parsley, watercress and spinach in a serving bowl.
- Fry the pancetta in a small frying pan until crispy and add it to the salad.
- In a small bowl mix the olive oil and vinegar together.
- Season with salt and pepper and pour the dressing over the salad when you are ready to serve.

Baked potatoes

6 baking potatoes
butter for serving
Cheddar cheese, grated for serving
salt and pepper

- Preheat the oven to 220°C/425°F/gas 7.
- Pierce the potato skins with a sharp knife and bake them for 1 hour 30 minutes.
- Split each one and serve with butter, cheese, salt and pepper.

Cheese and sweetcorn flan + baked potatoes + green salad

This is simple tasty fare. If you want a completely meat-free meal then omit the pancetta. This recipe is also a great way of using up any hard cheese that is lying around in the fridge. The green salad is a foil to the richness of the flan.

Cheese and sweetcorn flan

For the pastry

225g plain flour

140g butter, chilled and cubed

salt

1 egg yolk

2 tablespoons cold water

For the filling

1 tablespoon olive oil

70g sliced pancetta, chopped

150g onion, chopped

285g tin sweetcorn, drained

150ml double cream

50ml crème fraîche

2 eggs

a little milk

salt and pepper

½ teaspoon paprika

150g cheese (Cheddar, Caerphilly, Parmesan or a mixture of these or any other cheese with a good strong flavour), grated

- Preheat the oven to 200°C/400°F/gas 6.
- Grease a 24cm diameter flan tin.

To make the pastry case

- Place the flour and butter in a food processor, or in a bowl if you are combining by hand and incorporate so the mixture resembles fine breadcrumbs.
- Add a pinch of salt.
- Mix the egg yolk with the cold water in a small bowl and add it to the flour and fat.
- Give this a quick whizz in the food processor, turn the mixture out onto a floured work surface and combine thoroughly by hand until you have a firm dough.
- Wrap the pastry dough in cling-film and then chill in the fridge for at least 30 minutes.
- When the dough has chilled roll out the pastry on a lightly floured surface and line the flan tin with it. Bake the pastry case blind, which means baking it before you put the filling in. To do this, lay a sheet of greaseproof paper on the bottom of the flan tin and place some baking beans on top.
- Place the pastry case in the oven for 15 minutes.
- Remove the greaseproof paper and baking beans and cook for a further 5 minutes.
- Reduce the oven temperature to 190°C/375°F/gas 5.

To make the filling

- Warm the olive oil in a frying pan and cook the pancetta and onion in the oil on a medium heat for 5 minutes until both are tinged with brown.
- Add the sweetcorn to the onions and pancetta and remove the frying pan from the heat.
- Measure the cream and crème fraîche in a jug.
- Add the eggs to the cream and beat to combine the mixture.
- Add milk to bring the volume of the mixture up to 400ml.
- Season the mixture with salt, pepper and paprika.
- Spread the sweetcorn, pancetta and onion into the cooked pastry case, sprinkle on the grated cheese and pour over the liquid.
- Place the flan tin with the filled pastry case on top of a baking sheet and bake for 35 minutes.

continues

Baked potatoes

6 baking potatoes
butter for serving
salt and pepper

- Preheat the oven to 220°C/425°F/gas 7.
- Pierce the potato skins with a sharp knife and bake them for 1 hour 30 minutes.
- Split each one and serve with butter, salt and a grinding of black pepper.

Green salad

1 Romaine lettuce, washed and chopped
½ cucumber, sliced
2 spring onions, chopped

For the dressing

1 tablespoon olive oil
2 teaspoons balsamic vinegar
salt and pepper

- Assemble the salad in a serving bowl and just before serving pour the dressing over the top.

TIP

Cooking with one oven: *Put the potatoes in the oven at 220°C while you prepare the flan. Reduce the heat to 200°C when you are ready to bake the pastry case blind. Reduce further to 190°C when the filled flan goes in. If the potatoes aren't cooked when the flan is ready turn up the oven again.*

Sausages and warm lentil salad

In the run up to Christmas it is sensible to have quite a simple menu that isn't too rich. This meal is perfect as the nuttiness of the lentils complements the richness of the sausages and pulses are an important part of a balanced diet.

Sausages

8–10 sausages
drizzle of olive oil

- Preheat the oven to 180°C/350°F/gas 4.
- Place the sausages on a foil-covered oven tray and drizzle with a little olive oil.
- Bake in the oven, turning the sausages occasionally, for approximately 45 minutes.

Warm lentil salad

300g puy lentils
2 litres water
1 bay leaf
1 sprig fresh thyme
3 eggs, hard-boiled and quartered
4 tablespoons flat-leaf parsley, finely chopped
2 tablespoons coriander, chopped
7 cherry tomatoes, halved
½ cucumber, diced
1 small red onion, finely diced
100g Gruyère, chopped into 1cm cubes
150ml extra virgin olive oil
good seasoning salt and pepper

- Place the lentils in a saucepan with the water, bay leaf and thyme.
- Bring to the boil and simmer, partially covered, for 20 minutes.
- Drain the lentils and place them in a serving dish with the other ingredients.
- If you are not serving the salad straight away, keep the lentils in the saucepan and warm them through at the last moment just before you dress the salad.

Lasagne
+ green salad

Lasagne has acquired a bad reputation over the last few years. I have often been disappointed with a reheated lasagne that I have had in a restaurant. Lasagne needs to be served straight from the oven and does not benefit from reheating. It also needs to be made with a homemade Béchamel sauce and the meat sauce needs to bubble away for 2 hours at least before the lasagne is assembled. I have, therefore, been realistic and made this a weekend meal. Nobody who works has time to make a proper lasagne from scratch when they come home in the evening.

Lasagne

For the meat sauce

2 tablespoons olive oil
1 onion, finely chopped
2 sticks celery, finely chopped
2 cloves garlic, peeled and finely chopped
1 carrot, peeled and finely chopped
500g minced beef
500g minced pork
salt and pepper
1 bay leaf and 1 sprig fresh thyme
250ml whole milk
250ml white wine
2 x 400g tins chopped Italian tomatoes
1 tablespoon tomato purée

For the Béchamel sauce

1 onion, peeled and studded with 4 cloves
1 bay leaf
900ml whole milk
50g butter
2 tablespoons flour
nutmeg
salt and pepper

Other items for the lasagne

1 box dried lasagne sheets – the type that doesn't need pre-cooking is preferable
3 or 4 good handfuls Parmesan cheese, grated

To cook the meat sauce

- Warm the olive oil in a large saucepan and add the onion, celery, garlic and carrot.
- Cook on a medium heat for 5 minutes until soft.
- Put the meat in the saucepan with the vegetables and turn the heat up to high.
- Stir the meat until it has all lost its pinkness.
- Add a teaspoon of salt and a good grinding of black pepper.
- Add the bay leaf, thyme and milk.
- Simmer on a medium heat for 10 minutes until most of the milk has been absorbed.
- Pour in the wine and simmer for 5 minutes.
- Add the tomatoes and tomato purée and simmer on a very low heat for 2 hours, uncovered.
- Check the seasoning.

To cook the bechamel sauce

- Place the onion and bay leaf in a small saucepan with the milk and bring it slowly to the boil.
- As the milk comes to the boil, remove the saucepan from the heat and cover it with a lid so that the milk becomes infused with the flavour of the bay leaf and the onion. Leave for 20 minutes.
- Melt the butter in a medium saucepan and when the butter is just starting to foam, add the flour and stir round until it is incorporated.
- Remove the saucepan from the heat and add the milk a little at a time to avoid lumps. If you do get lumps then give the sauce a good whisk.
- Return the sauce to the heat and bring to the boil, stirring all the time.
- When the sauce begins to boil reduce the heat to very low and let the sauce cook for 10 minutes, stirring occasionally.
- Add a grating of nutmeg and season with salt and pepper.

To assemble the lasagne

- Butter an ovenproof dish.
- Pour a layer of Béchamel onto the bottom of the dish and then add a layer of lasagne.
- Spoon enough of the meat sauce on top to cover the lasagne.
- Pour on top of this a layer of the Béchamel and then sprinkle with a good handful of grated Parmesan cheese.
- Cover with another layer of lasagne, another layer of meat sauce, the Béchamel and the Parmesan cheese and repeat until you have used up the sauces. Finish with a sprinkling of Parmesan cheese.
- Bake for 30 minutes.

Green salad

1 Romaine lettuce
½ cucumber, diced
1 avocado, diced
1 bunch coriander, finely chopped
4 spring onions, finely sliced

For the dressing

3 dessertspoons extra virgin olive oil
1 dessertspoon balsamic vinegar
salt and pepper

- Combine the salad ingredients in a serving bowl.
- Mix the dressing in a small jug or bowl.
- When you are ready to eat, spoon the dressing over the salad.

Chicken with tarragon + roast potatoes + cauliflower cheese + watercress salad

Roast chicken and tarragon is one of those special partnership of flavours that works like few others.

Chicken with tarragon

100g butter, softened
1 teaspoon fresh tarragon, finely chopped
1 clove garlic, peeled and finely chopped
salt and pepper
2 x 1.5kg chickens
olive oil
For the gravy
1 tablespoon flour
200ml white wine
500ml chicken or meat stock (a cube is fine)

- Preheat the oven to 180°C/350°F/gas 4.
- Mix the butter with the tarragon, garlic, salt and pepper in a small bowl.
- Take each chicken in turn and ease your fingers between the breast skin and meat of each, taking care not to tear the skin. Push the butter mixture under the skin and smear it over the breast meat.
- Place the birds in a roasting tin.
- Smear the outside of each chicken with olive oil and season with more salt and pepper.
- Place the chickens in the oven and roast for 1 hour 10 minutes.
- Remove the chickens from the oven and let them rest on a serving dish for about 20 minutes before carving.

To make the gravy

- Place the roasting tin on the hob over a medium heat.
- Sprinkle on 1 tablespoon of flour, and stir round thoroughly to loosen the bits from the pan and absorb the fat.
- Add the wine and simmer for 2 minutes.
- Add the stock.
- Bring to a simmer and cook, stirring occasionally, for 10 minutes.

Roast potatoes

1kg potatoes, peeled, quartered and rinsed
salt
2 tablespoons olive oil

- Preheat the oven to 220°C/425°F/gas 7.
- Parboil the potatoes in salted water for 4 minutes.
- Drain the potatoes well and place them in a roasting tin.
- Drizzle with olive oil and roast for 45–60 minutes until golden brown.

Cauliflower cheese

1 cauliflower, weighing approximately 1kg
50g butter
30g flour
500ml milk
1 teaspoon Dijon mustard
100g Gruyère cheese, grated
salt and pepper
50g Cheddar cheese, grated

- Prepare the cauliflower by removing the outer green leaves and cutting the white part into florets. You don't have to make them too small.
- Place the cauliflower in a large saucepan of salted water and bring to the boil.
- Reduce the heat, cook on a steady simmer for 6 minutes, then drain and place in a gratin dish.
- Meanwhile, melt the butter in a small saucepan over a gentle heat.
- Add the flour and stir round on the heat for 30 seconds.
- Remove the saucepan from the heat and add the milk gradually, stirring continuously to avoid lumps.

- Return the saucepan to the heat and continue stirring until the sauce comes to the boil. Reduce the heat and simmer on a very low heat for 10 minutes.
- Remove from the heat.
- Add the Dijon mustard and stir in the Gruyère cheese.
- Season with salt and pepper.
- Pour the sauce over the cauliflower in the gratin dish and set aside.
- Just before you are ready to serve, preheat the grill and sprinkle the Cheddar cheese over the top of the cauliflower.
- Place under the hot grill until bubbling and brown on top.

Watercress salad

70–100g watercress depending upon how popular it is in your household

For the dressing

6 teaspoons extra virgin olive oil

2 teaspoons balsamic vinegar

salt and pepper

- Place the watercress in a serving bowl.
- In a small bowl mix together the olive oil, vinegar, salt and pepper and then pour it over the watercress when you are ready to eat.

TIP

Cooking with one oven: *If you only have one oven cook the potatoes for one hour and 10 minutes at 180°C required for the chicken.*

Winter and dried fruit compote + custard

During the winter months make use of the small amount of English fruit available and supplement with some dried fruit.

Winter and dried fruit compote

1 quince, peeled, cored and cut into 2cm pieces
1 apple, peeled, cored and cut into 2cm pieces
1 pear, peeled, cored and cut into 2cm pieces
100g prunes
100g dried apricots
100g sultanas
10ml apple juice
50g soft brown sugar
1 vanilla pod
5cm piece cinnamon stick

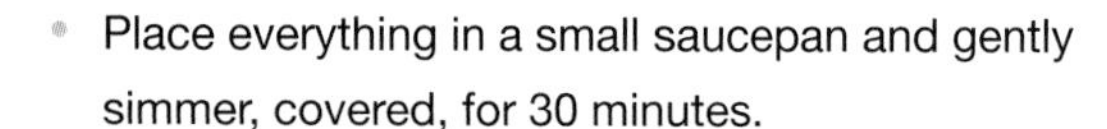

- Place everything in a small saucepan and gently simmer, covered, for 30 minutes.
- Remove the vanilla pod and serve with custard.

Custard

600ml milk and double cream mixed
2 whole eggs
2 egg yolks
2 tablespoons caster sugar
1 vanilla pod or a drop or two vanilla extract

- Place the whole eggs, yolks, and sugar in a glass bowl and hand whisk for 2 minutes.
- Measure the milk and cream in a measuring jug, add the vanilla pod or the extract and microwave on high for 2 minutes. The milk and cream should be just at boiling point, but not actually boiling.
- Place the glass bowl that contains the eggs and sugar over a saucepan containing a centimetre or two of water. Turn the stove to a medium heat to get the water simmering.
- Add the milk and cream to the eggs and sugar, whisking all the time to avoid lumps.
- If you used a vanilla pod, scrape out the seeds into the mixture.
- Keep stirring for 10 minutes, by which time you should have a good consistency. An indication of when the custard is thick enough is that it will coat the back of a wooden spoon as you lift it out of the mixture.
- You can make custard ahead of time, but avoid reheating it, as it may curdle.

Chicken liver paté

No Christmas period is complete without some paté appearing at one of the meals. My mother used to make this chicken liver paté, which we would have with bread or warm toast.

25g butter
½ small onion
1 clove garlic, peeled and finely chopped
225g chicken livers, trimmed with scissors to remove any gristly pieces
2 tablespoons brandy
50g butter, softened
1 teaspoon Dijon mustard
pinch mixed spice
salt and pepper

- Warm the butter in a sauté pan.
- Add the onion and garlic and fry gently for 3 minutes.
- Add the chicken livers and fry gently for 5 minutes.
- Remove the onion, garlic and chicken livers from the pan and set aside.
- Return the sauté pan to the heat.
- Pour the brandy into the pan and stir it round to clean the pan.
- Pour the brandy into a food processor or blender along with the chicken livers, onion and garlic, and the butter, mustard and mixed spice.
- Blend to a smooth paste, then season with salt and pepper.
- Serve with warm toast.

Week 3

Shopping list

MEAT

- ☐ 6 chicken breasts
- ☐ 500g minced beef
- ☐ 500g minced pork
- ☐ 2 sausages
- ☐ 1 turkey
- ☐ 500g sausage meat

FISH

- ☐ 400g fresh cod fillet
- ☐ 300g smoked cod fillet

VEGETABLES

- ☐ 5 spring onions
- ☐ 2 shallots
- ☐ 2 garlic bulbs
- ☐ 1 green chilli
- ☐ 9 onions
- ☐ 2 Romaine lettuces
- ☐ ½ cucumber
- ☐ 1.5kg potatoes
- ☐ 250g red onion
- ☐ 200g carrots
- ☐ 1 bunch celery
- ☐ 200g rocket leaves
- ☐ 6 baking potatoes

For Christmas Day:

- ☐ potatoes
- ☐ parsnips
- ☐ leeks
- ☐ carrots
- ☐ Brussel sprouts

☐ FRUIT

- ☐ 2 lemons
- ☐ 200g fresh raspberries
- ☐ 1 banana

FRESH HERBS

- ☐ coriander
- ☐ basil
- ☐ thyme
- ☐ sage
- ☐ bay leaves
- ☐ flat-leaf parsley

FRIDGE ITEMS

- ☐ 16 eggs
- ☐ 125g Parmesan cheese
- ☐ 200g buffalo mozarella
- ☐ 2 packs butter
- ☐ 1.9 litres chicken stock
- ☐ 300g sliced pancetta
- ☐ 200g crème fraîche
- ☐ 500g frozen peas
- ☐ 550ml whole milk
- ☐ 1 litre double cream

KITCHEN CUPBOARD ITEMS

- ☐ 1 or 2 jars mincemeat (see page 567)
- ☐ 400g medium egg noodles
- ☐ 400ml coconut milk
- ☐ dark soy sauce
- ☐ olive oil
- ☐ sesame oil
- ☐ groundnut oil
- ☐ light olive oil
- ☐ balsamic vinegar
- ☐ salt
- ☐ 4 x 400g tins chopped tomatoes
- ☐ 450g split yellow peas
- ☐ 280g caster sugar
- ☐ 350g penne
- ☐ 2 large loaves white bread for breadcrumbs
- ☐ 500g basmati rice
- ☐ Dijon mustard
- ☐ anchovy fillets
- ☐ 200ml dry white wine
- ☐ tomato purée
- ☐ 110g red lentils
- ☐ raspberry jam
- ☐ crunchy peanut butter
- ☐ dry sherry
- ☐ 350g plain flour
- ☐ vanilla extract
- ☐ 750g cooked chestnuts
- ☐ goose fat

☐ SPICES

- ☐ cumin seeds
- ☐ coriander seeds
- ☐ black peppercorns
- ☐ cumin seeds
- ☐ cloves
- ☐ fennel seeds

Coconut chicken and noodles in peanut sauce

Pre-Christmas lunch I try to steer clear of very English cooking as I feel that one gets so much of this during the festivities. This dish has a slight Thai feel to it.

6 chicken breasts, skinless
400g medium egg noodles
2–3 spring onions, trimmed and chopped into 5mm pieces

For the marinade

2 shallots, peeled and roughly chopped
3 cloves garlic, peeled and roughly chopped
1 green chilli, deseeded and roughly chopped
1 handful fresh coriander, roughly chopped
200ml coconut milk
good pinch sea salt

For the peanut sauce

200ml coconut milk
1 tablespoon sesame oil
2 tablespoons crunchy peanut butter
1 tablespoon dark soy sauce
2 tablespoons water

- Place all the marinade ingredients in a liquidizer and blend them until smooth.
- Pour the marinade over the chicken breasts and place them in the fridge for 1 hour.
- Mix the peanut sauce ingredients together in a bowl and set aside.
- Preheat the grill until hot.
- Place the chicken breasts under the grill with a generous spoon of the marinade over them.
- Grill the breasts for 10 minutes on each side, spooning over more marinade as they cook.
- Boil the noodles in water according to the packet instructions. When they are cooked, drain and spoon the peanut sauce over them.
  If the sauce is too thick loosen it with a little boiled water from the kettle.
- Once the chicken breasts are cooked, sprinkle with sea salt on each side.
- Slice each chicken breast, then place each one on a bed of noodles and sprinkle some spring onions on top.

Baked penne
+ green salad

My only caveat here is to make sure you use buffalo mozzarella as opposed to the more ordinary mozzarella, which tends to get stringy as it cools when you remove it from the oven.

Baked penne

3 tablespoons olive oil
1 onion, finely chopped
4 cloves garlic, peeled and finely chopped
2 x 400g tins chopped tomatoes
1 teaspoon caster sugar
salt and pepper
6 basil leaves, torn
350g penne
3 eggs, hard-boiled and roughly chopped
2 sausages, fried and chopped up
75g Parmesan cheese, grated
200g buffalo mozzarella, shredded roughly and placed in a small bowl with 1 tablespoon olive oil

- Preheat oven to 180°C/350°F/gas 4.
- Heat the olive oil in a large saucepan and gently fry the onion and garlic for 10 minutes.
- Add the tinned tomatoes, caster sugar, salt and pepper.
- Cook, covered, for 15 minutes.
- Add the basil leaves and cook uncovered for a further 5 minutes.
- Cook the penne according to the packet instructions.
- Mix the cooked penne with 3 tablespoons of the tomato sauce.
- Butter an ovenproof dish and spread half the penne over the bottom of it.
- Scatter half the egg and half the sausage over the penne, plus two good handfuls of Parmesan cheese.
- Cover this with a layer of mozzarella.
- Spread another 3–4 tablespoons of tomato sauce over the mozzarella, leaving enough sauce to use on the top of the dish.
- Repeat with the other half of the penne, the rest of the egg and sausage and another two good handfuls of Parmesan cheese.
- Cover with another layer of mozzarella and finish off with the rest of the tomato sauce and grated Parmesan cheese.
- Bake for 30 minutes.

Green salad

1 Romaine lettuce, washed and chopped
½ cucumber, sliced
2 spring onions, chopped
For the dressing
1 tablespoon olive oil
2 teaspoons balsamic vinegar
salt and pepper

- Assemble the salad in a serving bowl.
- Mix the dressing in a small bowl and when you are ready to eat pour it over the salad.

Meatballs in broth
+ boiled rice

There are a few meatball recipes in this book, but this is slightly different from the traditional Italian kind as a result of the spices used. The list of ingredients looks quite daunting, but the recipe is actually very straightforward.

Meatballs in broth

For the meatballs

1 teaspoon cumin seeds
1 teaspoon coriander seeds
500g minced beef
500g minced pork
2 cloves garlic, peeled and crushed
1 teaspoon salt
black pepper
10 tablespoons white breadcrumbs
olive oil for frying

For the broth

1 teaspoon cumin seeds
2 tablespoons olive oil
1 onion, finely chopped
2 carrots, peeled and chopped
1 clove garlic, peeled and finely chopped
1 stick celery, chopped
1 litre chicken stock
2 x 400g tins chopped tomatoes
salt and pepper

To make the meatballs

- Toast the cumin and coriander on a high heat in a small frying pan. Do not burn them.
- Remove them from the heat as soon as they start to smoke and you can smell their aroma.
- Grind the toasted seeds as finely as you can in a pestle and mortar.
- Place the ground spices in a large mixing bowl with the minced meats, garlic, salt, pepper and breadcrumbs.
- Thoroughly mix all the ingredients so that everything is combined evenly.
- Form the mixture into 2cm diameter balls, about the size of walnuts.
- Heat the olive oil in a frying pan and fry the meatballs in batches, moving them carefully with a knife and fork so they brown all over.
- Set them aside while you complete the rest.

To make the broth

- Toast the cumin seeds and grind them as you did for the meatballs. Set aside.
- Heat the olive oil in a large saucepan.
- Add the onion, carrot, garlic and celery and cook gently on a low heat for 10 minutes until soft.
- Pour on the stock and tinned tomatoes and bring to a simmer.
- Add the ground cumin to the stock and tomatoes.
- Season well with salt and pepper, and taste. Adjust seasoning if necessary.
- Gently add the meatballs to the stock mixture and bring to a simmer.
- Cover and cook gently for 45 minutes.

Boiled rice

400g basmati rice
600ml water
salt

- Cook the rice by placing it in a saucepan with the water and a small pinch of salt.
- Put the rice on a high heat and as soon as it comes to the boil, cover the saucepan with a lid and turn the heat down very low.
- Leave it on a low heat for 15 minutes.
- Remove the saucepan from the heat but leave it covered for a further 10 minutes.
- Serve the rice with the meatballs and broth.

Baked cod and potatoes
+ split yellow peas

To reduce the cooking time of the split peas, soak them overnight in cold water and they will only take about 25 minutes to cook. If you don't soak them, they take about an hour to cook. They go very well with the cod.

Baked cod with potatoes

1.5kg potatoes, peeled and sliced lengthways into quarters
250g red onion, thinly sliced
4 cloves garlic, peeled and kept whole
leaves from 2 or 3 sprigs fresh thyme
300ml good olive oil (not extra virgin)
juice 2 lemons
salt and pepper
400g fresh cod fillet
300g smoked cod fillet

- Preheat the oven to 200°C/400°F/gas 6.
- Put the potatoes in a roasting tin in a single layer.
- Scatter over the red onion, garlic cloves and stripped thyme leaves.
- Pour over the olive oil and lemon juice, and season well with salt and pepper.
- Place the roasting tin in the preheated oven for 1 hour.
- Turn the potatoes and then place the fish on top of them.
- Return the fish and potatoes to the oven for 10 minutes, by which time the fish should be cooked.

Split yellow peas

450g split yellow peas, pre-soaked if possible
1 tablespoon olive oil
25g butter
1 onion, finely chopped
1 clove garlic, peeled and crushed
100g carrots, peeled and finely chopped
1 stick celery, finely chopped
900ml chicken stock
salt and pepper

- Pre-soak the peas overnight as suggested above. If you don't get time to do this, increase the cooking time to 1 hour.
- Heat the olive oil and butter in a large saucepan and add the onion, garlic, carrot and celery.
- Cover the saucepan and cook the vegetables on a low heat for 10 minutes.
- Add the peas and stock and bring to the boil.
- Cover and cook for about 25 minutes on a gentle simmer.
- Season well with salt and pepper.

Roast turkey with chestnut stuffing + vegetables + bread sauce

It's that meal we love to eat, but the thought of actually producing it fills many with dread. Numerous books have tried to take us through the trials and tribulations of getting the meal to the table in an edible form. To be rational about it, the pudding is made and just needs to be steamed for a couple of hours, so the meal should be less of a chore than a normal Sunday roast lunch. I have not specified amounts or weights for the turkey and vegetables in any of the recipes, as you may have more than six people or you may just want an extra-large turkey so that you have a lot for leftovers. I have set out amounts for the bread sauce as not to do so would make life difficult. The recipe makes enough for approximately 10 people. Don't panic on Christmas Day and enlist help from your guests.

TIPS

I have set out some general tips below that you may find useful.

- *Roast the turkey at 190 °C/375 °F/gas 5.*
- *Weigh the bird once stuffed and then calculate the cooking time.*
- *For birds up to 6.5kg, roast for 30 minutes per kilo and then for every other extra half kilo add another 10 minutes.*
- *If you only have one oven, you will have to roast the potatoes and parsnips at the lower temperature and then increase the temperature once the turkey has been cooked and is resting. Ideally, you should roast them at about 220 °C/425 °F/gas 7 for 45–60 minutes, but if you are starting them at a lower temperature, roast them for longer than this.*

Turkey with chestnut stuffing

1 turkey
2 onions, thinly sliced
50g butter
salt and pepper
140g sliced pancetta
3 sprigs fresh thyme

For the chestnut stuffing

2 onions, finely chopped
75g butter
300g white breadcrumbs
500g sausage meat
15–20 sage leaves, finely chopped
2 eggs
4 tablespoons warm water
400g cooked and peeled chestnuts, roughly chopped
salt and pepper

To make the stuffing

- Combine the stuffing ingredients in a large mixing bowl and season generously.

To prepare the turkey for the oven

- Take the turkey and approach it from the rear end, i.e. the leg end. Remove any rings you may be wearing, to avoid tearing the skin.
- Gradually start to ease your fingers between the skin and breast meat, going up as far as you can.
- When you have done this, push the stuffing under the skin. Don't worry if you drop bits as you can scoop these up at the end and pop them in.
- Seal the skin down under the legs with a couple of cocktail sticks.
- Scatter the sliced onions on the bottom of the roasting tin and place the turkey on top of these.
- Coat the turkey with the butter and a good grinding of salt and pepper.
- Take the pancetta slices and lay a double layer of them over the turkey breast, tucking in the thyme sprigs at the side of the thighs.

continues

- Cover the turkey with tin foil and place it in a preheated oven (see page 626 for cooking times).
- Remove the tin foil 30 minutes before the end of the cooking time.

Roast potatoes and parsnips

potatoes
parsnips
salt
goose fat

- Wash, peel and rinse the potatoes and parsnips and cut them into the size you like for roasting. I cut parsnips into quite big chunks, as I think they roast better like this. With an average-sized parsnip, I generally cut it into three. I cut it across in the middle and then cut the fat bit in half again.
- Once the potatoes and parsnips are prepared, parboil them for about 4 minutes in salted water. Before you drain them, remember to keep all your vegetable water to add to the gravy, so strain the potatoes and parsnips into something that will catch the water.
- Give them a shake in the pan to crumble their edges a little and then set them in a roasting tin with the goose fat.
- Roast in a preheated oven but see my tip on page 626.

Creamy leeks

leeks
salt and pepper
crème fraîche

- Prepare the leeks by cutting them lengthways, stopping about 1cm from the bottom of the leek so it's still in one piece. Wash them under the tap, fanning each leek out as you wash them, to get rid of any grit between the leaves.
- Slice the leeks as thinly as possible and place them in a sauté pan with a sprinkling of salt.
- Gently sauté the leeks on a medium heat for 3 minutes, until soft. Try not to let them turn brown as they are not as nice like this.
- Stir in the crème fraîche and remove from the heat.
- Reheat the leeks when you are ready to eat.

Carrots and peas

frozen peas
carrots, peeled and thinly sliced
knob of butter

- Place the vegetables in a small saucepan with the butter.
- As the butter melts reduce the heat, cover, and sweat the peas and carrots for 10 minutes until tender, stirring them occasionally.
- Season with salt and pepper and serve.

Brussels sprouts with pancetta

Brussel sprouts, tailed and trimmed
sliced pancetta, chopped finely (if you are using 200g of Brussels use 100g of pancetta)
salt and pepper
a little butter

- Bring a pan of salted water to the boil.
- Cook the sprouts for 4 minutes.
- Drain them.
- Melt some butter in a frying pan and add the pancetta and sprouts.
- Sauté for 1 or 2 minutes until the pancetta is golden brown. Season and serve.

Bread sauce

2 cloves
1 onion, peeled and left whole
1 bay leaf
300ml milk
4 heaped tablespoons fresh white breadcrumbs
salt and pepper
20g butter
1 tablespoon double cream

- Stud the onion with cloves and place in a small saucepan with the bay leaf and milk.
- Warm on a low heat for 10 minutes.
- Remove the onion and bay leaf and stir in the breadcrumbs.
- Simmer for 3 minutes.
- Remove from the heat and add the seasoning, butter and cream.
- Reheat when you are ready to serve the turkey.

Caesar salad
+ baked potatoes + cold turkey

I think most people eat cold leftovers on Boxing Day. Nobody really wants to start cooking again after the hard slog of the day before. A big hearty salad and some baked potatoes with cold meats and chutneys is a most enjoyable meal. Don't forget that you also have the chicken liver paté, an extra Christmas pudding, mince pies and Christmas cake.

Caesar salad

For the salad

1 Romaine or Cos lettuce
200g rocket leaves
3 tablespoons olive oil for frying
3 slices white bread, cubed
10 slices pancetta, sliced into small pieces
2 tablespoons Parmesan cheese, grated

For the mayonnaise

2 egg yolks
2 teaspoons Dijon mustard
150ml groundnut oil
150ml light olive oil
salt
2 cloves garlic, peeled
4 anchovy fillets

To make the mayonnaise

- Place the egg yolks in a bowl with the mustard. Give them a good mix until combined.
- Combine the groundnut oil and olive oil in a measuring jug.
- Start adding the oil to the egg yolks and mustard, literally a drop at a time, making sure that each addition is fully incorporated before adding the next. If you add the oil too quickly, it will curdle.
- The mayonnaise will become thick. You may think it is too thick, but once it gets to this stage add a tablespoon of cold water, which instantly creates the right consistency by emulsifying the mixture.
- Add salt to taste.
- Place a little of the mayonnaise in a blender with the cloves of garlic and anchovy fillets and mix to a purée. Then add this purée to the rest of the mayonnaise.
- If you are using bought mayonnaise, just add the garlic and anchovy fillets to that.

To make the salad

- Tear the lettuce leaves into pieces and place them in a serving dish with the rocket.
- Pour the mayonnaise over the salad so that all the leaves are coated.
- Heat the olive oil in a frying pan and fry the croutons until golden. Scatter these onto the salad leaves.
- In the same frying pan, fry the pancetta pieces and add these to the salad.
- Sprinkle the cheese over the top and serve with the baked potatoes below and some cold turkey.

Baked potatoes

6 baking potatoes
butter for serving
salt and pepper

- Preheat the oven to 220°C/425°F/gas 7.
- Pierce the potato skins with a sharp knife and bake them for 1 hour 30 minutes.
- Split each one and serve with butter, salt and pepper.

Chestnut and lentil soup

This soup hits the spot for a post-Christmas meal. Serve with some sandwiches or toast and let your stomach recover from the seasonal excesses.

110g red lentils
2 litres water
1 carrot, peeled and diced
1 stick celery, diced
1 small onion, finely chopped
1 clove garlic, peeled and finely chopped
1 bay leaf
4 sprigs flat-leaf parsley
2 tablespoons olive oil
350g cooked chestnuts, chopped into small pieces
4 sprigs fresh thyme
¼ teaspoon fennel seeds, roughly ground
100ml dry white wine
1 tablespoon tomato purée
salt and pepper
1 tablespoon flat-leaf parsley, finely chopped

- Place the lentils in a saucepan with the water, carrot, celery, onion, garlic, bay leaf and parsley sprigs.
- Bring to the boil and simmer gently, uncovered, for 30 minutes until the lentils are tender.
- Meanwhile, heat the olive oil, add the chestnuts, thyme and fennel and fry for 3 minutes.
- Add the wine and tomato purée to the chestnuts and cook for 1 minute.
- When the lentils are cooked, remove the sprigs of parsley and the bay leaf. Purée half the lentils in half of the liquid. Return the purée and the remaining lentils in their liquid to the saucepan with the chestnuts. If your children are likely to baulk at the idea of chestnut pieces, simply purée the whole soup.
- Bring the soup to a simmer, taste and season with salt and pepper.
- Serve with the chopped flat-leaf parsley sprinkled over the top.

English trifle

I find that at Christmas there is a temptation to buy more food than we need and to make more food than anyone could eat. I have come to the conclusion that, unless you are doing a lot of entertaining, the Christmas pudding, cake and maybe one other dessert will suffice. A trifle is a traditional Christmas dessert that everyone enjoys.

For the trifle sponge

3 eggs

80g caster sugar

70g plain flour

salt

For the custard

4 medium egg yolks

1 teaspoon vanilla extract

75g caster sugar

300ml double cream

250ml whole milk

For the syllabub

600ml double cream

50g caster sugar

100ml dry white wine

finely grated zest 1 lemon

To assemble the trifle

raspberry jam

3 tablespoons dry sherry

200g fresh raspberries

1 banana, chopped

To make the trifle sponge

- Grease and line a round sponge cake tin of about 23cm diameter.
- Preheat the oven to 175°C/350°F/gas 4.
- Whisk the eggs and sugar in a bowl with a hand-held mixer until thick and mousse-like. This takes about 4 minutes. The mixture will lighten in colour and when you lift the whisk, ribbons will form on the top.
- Using a metal spoon, fold in the flour and a pinch of salt and spoon the mixture into the prepared tin. Cook for 20 minutes.
- Test with a skewer, which will come away clean if the cake is ready.

To make the custard

- Whisk the egg yolks in a glass bowl with the vanilla and sugar.
- Measure out the cream and milk together and heat in a microwave until just about to come to the boil.
- Whisk the cream and milk into the egg and sugar mixture.
- Place the glass bowl over a saucepan, on a medium heat, with 1–2cms of water in the bottom. Stir the custard with a wooden spoon until it thickens and coats the back of the spoon.

To make the syllabub

- Whisk the cream, sugar, wine and lemon zest together until the mixture holds in soft peaks, then set aside.

To assemble the trifle

- Split the sponge cake in two and fill it with raspberry jam.
- Rejoin the cake and cut it into approximately 4cm square chunks.
- Place these chunks into a glass serving dish.
- Pour over the sherry and then top with the berries and banana.
- Spoon the custard over the sponge and fruit and then top with the syllabub.
- Chill for a couple of hours before serving.

Mince pies

The excitement we used to feel as children when my mother started to prepare mince pies was huge, as we knew then that the Chritmas celebrations had well and truly started. Mincemeat has quite an adult flavour and it is slightly surprising how children do take to it, nonetheless. Mince pies obviously did, at one time, contain meat but gradually, over the years, the amount of meat in them lessened until we reached the 'modern day' mince pie containing only fruit.

For the pastry

250g plain flour

150g butter, chilled and cubed

salt

28g caster sugar

2 egg yolks

1 tablespoon cold water

To fill

1 jar mincemeat (see page 567)

To make the pastry

- Put the flour and butter in a food processor, or in a bowl if you are combining by hand, and incorporate so that the mixture resembles fine breadcrumbs.
- Add a pinch of salt and the sugar.
- Mix the egg yolk with the cold water in a small bowl and then add them to the breadcrumbed flour and fat.
- Give this a quick whizz in the food processor, if using, and then turn out onto a work surface and combine thoroughly until you have a firm dough.
- Once you have sufficiently kneaded the dough, wrap it in cling-film and chill it in the fridge for 30 minutes.

To assemble the pies

- Grease a fairy-cake tray.
- Preheat the oven to 200°C/400°F/gas 6.
- Roll out the pastry and, using a pastry cutter, cut out circles that fit your tray. Most cake trays have individual diameters of 6.5cm. I, therefore, use a 7.5cm cutter for the bottom of the pies and a 6.5cm cutter for the lids.
- Fill the cases with mincemeat and then cover each pie with a pastry lid.
- Bake in the oven for 15 minutes until the pies are golden brown.

Week 4

Monday p636	Salmon fishcakes + crème fraîche sauce + salad
Tuesday p637	Fried chicken + butter beans and onions
Wednesday p638	Spaghetti with spring onions and peas
Thursday p640	Garlic prawns + baked sweet potatoes with butter and ginger + salad
Friday p641	Roast ham + red cabbage + mustard mash
Saturday p642	Mushroom soup + ham sandwiches
Sunday p643	Topside stew with vegetables
Sunday pudding p644	Baked apples
Extra tasty treat p645	Crunchy oatmeal biscuits

Shopping list

MEAT

- ☐ 6 chicken breasts
- ☐ 1.5kg unsmoked gammon joint
- ☐ 2kg piece topside of beef

FISH

- ☐ 600g salmon fillet
- ☐ 600g cooked prawns

VEGETABLES

- ☐ 1.6kg potatoes
- ☐ 9 tomatoes
- ☐ 1 cucumber
- ☐ 17 spring onions
- ☐ 2 red onions
- ☐ 1 onion
- ☐ 1 bunch celery
- ☐ garlic bulb
- ☐ 6 sweet potatoes
- ☐ 1 avocado
- ☐ 5 carrots
- ☐ 1 Romaine lettuce
- ☐ 1 red cabbage
- ☐ 450g mushrooms
- ☐ fresh ginger

FRUIT

- ☐ 1 lemon
- ☐ 3 large Bramley apples
- ☐ 2 oranges

FRESH HERBS

- ☐ flat-leaf parsley
- ☐ coriander
- ☐ chives
- ☐ thyme
- ☐ bay leaf

FRIDGE ITEMS

- ☐ 500ml milk
- ☐ 4 eggs
- ☐ 250g crème fraîche
- ☐ 3 packs butter
- ☐ 125g Parmesan
- ☐ 150g sliced pancetta
- ☐ 600g frozen peas
- ☐ 1.5ml chicken stock
- ☐ 200ml single cream

KITCHEN CUPBOARD ITEMS

- ☐ Dijon mustard
- ☐ wholegrain mustard
- ☐ horseradish sauce
- ☐ capers
- ☐ olive oil
- ☐ extra virgin olive oil
- ☐ balsamic vinegar
- ☐ 2 x 400g tins butter beans
- ☐ 400g tin chopped tomatoes
- ☐ 500g spaghetti
- ☐ runny honey
- ☐ soy sauce
- ☐ maple syrup
- ☐ golden syrup
- ☐ 150g soft brown sugar
- ☐ chutney
- ☐ red wine vinegar
- ☐ salt
- ☐ 200ml white wine
- ☐ brandy
- ☐ 50g dried apricots
- ☐ 50g walnuts
- ☐ 50g sultanas
- ☐ 250g self-raising flour
- ☐ 50g porridge oats
- ☐ 75g caster sugar
- ☐ 1 small white loaf for breadcrumbs
- ☐ 1 small wholemeal loaf
- ☐ cornichons

SPICES

- ☐ mixed spice
- ☐ ground cinnamon
- ☐ black peppercorns

Salmon fishcakes
+ crème fraîche sauce + salad

I love salmon fishcakes. They have a lovely, subtle flavour and make a nice change from the stronger flavours of meat and cheese dishes. The crème fraîche sauce is very fresh-tasting and complements the fishcakes perfectly.

Salmon fishcakes

600g salmon fillet
250ml milk
400g potatoes, peeled, cut and boiled until tender
1 dessertspoon Dijon mustard
2 teaspoons horseradish sauce
salt and pepper
handful flat-leaf parsley, finely chopped
120g fresh white breadcrumbs

- Preheat the oven to 200°C/400°F/gas 6.
- Place the salmon in an ovenproof dish and pour the milk over it.
- Cover the dish with tin foil and bake the fish for 13 minutes, until just done.
- Strain and flake the fish into a bowl. Discard the milk and set the fish aside.
- Mash the cooked potato and place it in a mixing bowl with the mustard, horseradish sauce, some salt and pepper, parsley and the cooked salmon.
- Chill the mixture in the fridge for 30 minutes.
- Shape the mixture into cakes weighing approximately 100g each.
- Dip each fishcake into the white breadcrumbs and set aside.
- Heat 2 tablespoons of olive oil in a frying pan and when hot, add the fish cakes 4 at a time. Cook each one for 2 minutes on each side and until the breadcrumbs are a golden brown.
- Serve with the crème fraîche sauce, salad and some brown bread and butter.

Crème fraîche sauce

1 egg yolk
1 teaspoon Dijon mustard
200g crème fraîche
2 heaped tablespoons flat-leaf parsley, finely chopped
1 tablespoon chopped cornichons
1 dessertspoon chopped capers
salt and pepper

- Mix together the egg yolk and mustard in a small bowl and then gradually add the crème fraîche.
- Be careful not to add it all in one go as it may curdle.
- Once you have incorporated the crème fraîche, add the rest of the ingredients and season with salt and pepper.

Salad

3 tomatoes, quartered
½ cucumber, sliced
3 spring onions, sliced
½ small red onion, thinly sliced
For the dressing
2 dessertspoons olive oil
1 dessertspoon balsamic vinegar
salt and pepper

- Place the salad ingredients in a serving bowl.
- Spoon over the dressing and serve.

Fried chicken
+ butter beans and onions

This is such a quick and straightforward meal. Get the butter beans into the oven first and then cook the chicken.

Fried chicken

6 chicken breasts
50g butter
2 tablespoons olive oil
salt and pepper

- Lay the chicken breasts out flat on a chopping board and slice them so that you have 2 flat thin fillets from each of the six breasts.
- Heat the butter and oil in a frying pan and when hot, add the 2 pieces of chicken at a time and fry them gently for 2 minutes on each side.
- Season with salt and pepper.
- Place the cooked pieces on a warm dish and serve with the butter beans below.

Butter beans with onions

2 tablespoons olive oil
1 large red onion, finely sliced
1 stick celery, finely chopped
2 cloves garlic, peeled and finely chopped
2 x 400g tins butter beans, drained
400g tin chopped tomatoes
2 tablespoons fresh coriander, finely chopped
2 tablespoons Parmesan cheese, grated
salt and pepper

- Preheat the oven to 180°C/350°F/gas 4.
- Heat the olive oil in a large frying pan and gently sauté the onion, celery and garlic for 10 minutes.
- Transfer the vegetables to a medium-sized ovenproof dish.
- Add the butter beans, tomatoes and coriander.
- Sprinkle on the cheese and bake for 30 minutes.

Spaghetti with spring onions and peas

This recipe originated from the *River Cafe Cookbook Easy,* but I have made some modifications. It's delicious and easy.

500g spaghetti
150g butter
150g spring onions, trimmed and finely chopped
150g sliced pancetta, chopped
600g frozen peas
salt
2 garlic cloves, peeled and finely sliced
3 tablespoons flat-leaf parsley, chopped
olive oil
75g Parmesan, grated
black pepper

- Boil a large saucepan of salted water for the spaghetti and cook the spaghetti according to the packet instructions.
- Meanwhile, melt the butter in a large pan.
- Add the onions and pancetta to the butter and cook gently for 5 minutes.
- Add the peas, a little salt and 7 tablespoons of water.
- Cover and simmer gently until the peas are cooked, which will take about 5 minutes.
- Check the seasoning and add more salt if necessary.
- Add the garlic, parsley and 4 tablespoons of olive oil.
- Cook for 3 minutes longer.
- Add the pea mixture to the spaghetti when cooked and serve with the Parmesan and some freshly ground black pepper.

Garlic prawns + baked sweet potatoes with butter and ginger + salad

The sweetness of the potatoes here complements the garlic prawns very well. This is another simple midweek meal. Bake the potatoes an hour before serving. Fry the prawns in the last five minutes.

Garlic prawns

100g butter
3 cloves garlic
600g cooked prawns
2 tablespoons fresh coriander, finely chopped
juice 1 lemon
salt and pepper

- Melt the butter in a frying pan.
- Add the garlic and cook for 1 minute, stirring and keeping an eye on the heat so that the garlic does not brown.
- Add the prawns and stir round for 1 minute to warm through.
- Add the coriander and squeeze the lemon juice over the top.
- Season with salt and pepper.

Baked sweet potatoes with butter and ginger

6 sweet potatoes
olive oil
2cm fresh ginger, peeled and grated
3 dessertspoons runny honey
salt and pepper
butter

- Preheat the oven to 220°C/425°F/gas 7.
- Wash the potatoes and rub olive oil into the skin of each one. Wrap each potato in tin foil and bake the potatoes for 1 hour.
- Meanwhile, mix the ginger and honey in a small bowl, season with salt and pepper and set aside.
- When the potatoes are cooked, and you are ready to serve the meal, cut them in half lengthways. Fork a knob of butter into each half, drizzle with the ginger and honey mixture and season with salt and pepper.

Salad

1 avocado, chopped into small chunks
4 spring onions, finely sliced
6 tomatoes, chopped into small chunks
½ cucumber, chopped into small chunks
1 peeled raw carrot, chopped into chunks
bunch fresh chives, finely snipped
1 Romaine lettuce, torn into shreds
3 hard-boiled eggs, quartered
handful flat-leaf parsley, finely chopped
For the salad dressing
2 tablespoons extra virgin olive oil
1 tablespoon balsamic vinegar
1 teaspoon soy sauce
salt and pepper

- Place the salad ingredients into a large serving bowl.
- Mix the dressing in a small bowl and when you are ready to eat, pour it over the salad.

Roast ham
+ red cabbage + mustard mash

Red cabbage and roast ham is one of those perfect combinations. Get the gammon cooking and then start the red cabbage. Prepare the potatoes last.

Roasted ham

1.5kg unsmoked gammon joint

For the glaze

1 tablespoon maple syrup

1 dessertspoon soft brown sugar

1 dessertspoon Dijon mustard

1 dessertspoon any chutney that you have in the cupboard

- Preheat the oven to 200°C/400°F/gas 6.
- A 1.5 kg gammon will take 1 hour 30 minutes to cook, so adjust your timings accordingly if you have a smaller or larger joint.
- Place the joint in a large saucepan and cover it with water. Bring to the boil and then reduce the heat, cover, and cook for 1 hour.
- Mix the glaze ingredients together in a bowl.
- Remove the gammon from the water, place it in a meat tin and cut off the rind.
- Using a pastry brush or a wooden spoon, cover it with the glaze.
- Bake for 30 minutes.
- Leave it to rest for 20–30 minutes before you carve it.

Red cabbage

1 red cabbage, thinly sliced

40g butter

25g soft brown sugar

100ml red wine vinegar

¼ teaspoon mixed spice

a teaspoon salt

pepper

- Place all the ingredients in a large saucepan, cover and bring to a gentle simmer.
- Cook on a gentle simmer for 1 hour.
- Remove the lid and cook for a further 30 minutes, stirring occasionally.

Mustard mash

1kg potatoes, peeled and quartered

salt and black pepper

200ml warmed milk

40g butter

1 dessertspoon wholegrain mustard

1 tablespoon crème fraîche

- Place the potatoes in cold, salted water and bring to the boil. Turn the heat down to a robust simmer on a medium heat. Once the potatoes are soft but not mushy, drain them thoroughly and put them through the ricer.
- Return the mashed potato to the saucepan and place over a low heat.
- Add the milk and butter and gently stir in.
- Remove from the heat.
- Gently stir in the mustard and crème fraîche and check the seasoning.

TIP

I use a potato ricer to make mashed potato, as I have found it is the only way of removing all the lumps and it is much quicker than a masher. I also resist the temptation of cutting the potatoes into small cubes, prior to cooking them, as while the potatoes may cook more quickly, I do not think one gets such a good flavour.

Mushroom soup
+ ham sandwiches

This creamy muhsroom soup is a dream. It is often the sliminess and the look of mushrooms that put children off, but soup dispenses with this problem. Mushrooms take little time to cook so take advantage of this.

75g butter
450g mushrooms, wiped and sliced
2 sprigs fresh thyme
1 clove garlic, peeled and finely chopped
salt and pepper
1.5ml chicken stock
100g sliced wholemeal bread cut into chunks
200ml single cream
flat-leaf parsley for serving

- Place the butter in a large saucepan over a moderate heat.
- Add the mushrooms, thyme and garlic and cook for 10 minutes in the butter, stirring occasionally.
- Season with salt and pepper.
- Pour on the stock and add the bread chunks to the soup.
- Cook for 20 minutes, covered, and then blitz the soup until smooth in a food processor or with a hand-held blender.
- Pour in the cream just before serving and scatter some parsley over each serving.
- Serve with ham sandwiches made using the leftover ham from Friday.

Topside stew with vegetables

This is a one-pot meal that takes a reasonable time to cook, which is why I have included it on a Sunday. It makes a change from the usual roast.

2 tablespoons olive oil
2kg piece topside of beef
1 onion, roughly chopped
2 cloves garlic, peeled and chopped
2 sticks celery, roughly chopped
200ml white wine
100ml brandy
a bouquet garni 1 sprig rosemary, 1 sprig thyme, slice orange peel and bay leaf
salt and pepper
6 medium potatoes, peeled and chopped into quarters
4 carrots, peeled and chopped

- Heat the olive oil in a large saucepan and brown the joint of meat all over.
- Set the meat aside but keep the saucepan on the heat.
- Add the onions, garlic and celery and cook for 10 minutes until soft and slightly tinged brown.
- Add the wine, brandy and bouquet garni and return the meat joint to the pan.
- Season with salt and pepper.
- Bring the pot to a simmer.
- Cover, reduce the heat and cook for 2 hours on a very gentle simmer.
- After this time, add the potatoes and carrots and return the pot to the simmer.
- Cover again and cook for a further 20 minutes until the potatoes and carrots are soft.
- Adjust the seasoning and serve by slicing the meat, along with spoonfuls of the cooking juices and the vegetables.

Baked apples

Baked apples look majestic when they come out of the oven; beautiful greenish globes bursting with goodness. You can double this recipe and make one for each person if you like, although we tend to share one between two.

25g butter
50g dried apricots, chopped
50g walnuts, chopped
50g sultanas
1 dessertspoon brown sugar
grated zest 1 orange
½ teaspoon ground cinnamon
2 tablespoons maple syrup
3 large Bramley apples

- Preheat the oven to 180°C/350°F/gas 4.
- Gently melt the butter in a small saucepan and add the apricots, walnuts and sultanas.
- Stir for 1 minute until all the ingredients are nicely coated in butter.
- Then add the sugar, zest, cinnamon and syrup and stir in.
- Remove the saucepan from the heat.
- With an apple corer, remove a hole of about 2cm in diameter, keeping the apple whole. I tend to remove a little more than just the core, so that more filling fits in the centre.
- Spoon a third of the mixture into the centre of the apple with a little for the top.
- Wrap each apple loosely in a piece of tin foil, place in a roasting tray and bake for 40 minutes.
- Serve half an apple per person with some whipped cream.

Crunchy oatmeal biscuits

These golden circles of chewiness encapsulate for me why home-baked biscuits knock the spots off factory processed ones. As with most homemade biscuits they are a cinch to make.

250g self-raising flour
50g porridge oats
75g caster sugar
75g soft brown sugar
salt
125g butter
3 teaspoons golden syrup
2 tablespoons milk

- Grease 2 baking sheets.
- Preheat the oven to 190°C/375°F/gas 5.
- Put the flour, oats, sugars and a pinch of salt in a bowl.
- Rub in the butter.
- Mix the golden syrup and milk together and pour this onto the dry ingredients.
- Mix to a dough.
- Shape into a thick tube shape and chill in the fridge for 30 minutes or so.
- Cut the roll of dough into ½cm slices.
- Place the slices onto the baking sheets and bake for 15 minutes.
- Allow to cool slightly and then transfer them to a cooling rack.

Index

C

D

I

J

K

L

M

R

S

T

Acknowledgements

My husband Simon who has been very supportive throughout the three year period this book has taken to come to fruition. His advice, patience and counsel have been invaluable.

My four children Joseph, Emil, Emanuel and Yolanda who have been my guinea pigs with all the recipes contained in these pages, when sometimes all they wanted was spaghetti Bolognaise.

Gemma McGowan for the majority of the photographs. Her enthusiasm was very encouraging.

Sarah Diamandis for her help with the cooking during those long photography sessions.

Ann, Helen and Margaret for their energy in clearing up all my cooking chaos during the photography sessions.

Camilla and Lorraine for all their hard work and commitment.

Paul Whitfield of 2020 Photography for stepping in at the last minute with some emergency photography.

Sarah Siese for her expert advice and guidance and for keeping me enthused about the book through many trails and tribulations.

Nick Heal and Carole Melbourne for the design of the book which has turned my words and effort into something lovely to look at and easy to use.

May Corfield and Antonia Cunningham for their editorial help which has reassured me as to the quality of the book.

Any profits from the sale of the cookbook will go towards the establishment and funding of a food education trust